REALbasic
Cross-Platform
Application
Development

Mark Choate

DEVELOPER'S
LIBRARY

Sams Publishing, 800 East 96th Street, Indianapolis, Indiana 46240

REALbasic Cross-Platform Application Development

International Standard Book Number: 0-672-32813-5

Library of Congress Catalog Card Number: 2005902141

Printed in the United States of America

First Printing: April 2006

09   08   07   06   4   3   2   1

Trademarks

Warning and Disclaimer

Bulk Sales

Sams Publishing offers excellent discounts on this book when ordered in quantity for bulk purchases or special sales. For more information, please contact

U.S. Corporate and Government Sales
1-800-382-3419
corpsales@pearsontechgroup.com

For sales outside of the U.S., please contact

International Sales
international@pearsoned.com

Acquisitions Editor
Scott Meyers

Managing Editor
Charlotte Clapp

Project Editor
George E. Nedeff

Copy Editor
Barbara Hacha

Indexer
Aaron Black

Proofreader
Suzanne Thomas

Technical Editor
William H. Murray

Publishing Coordinator
Vanessa Evans

Multimedia Developer
Dan Scherf

Series Designer
Gary Adair

Page Layout
Bronkella Publishing
Michelle Mitchell

Contents at a Glance

Table of Contents

About the Author

Mark Choate is an author, educator, and consultant specializing in eBusiness and online publishing. His experience includes eight years of Internet development and content management at *The News and Observer Publishing Company*, one of the very first newspapers in the country to publish a web edition. Mark's particular area of expertise is with cross-media content management tools and XML. For two years he has used REALbasic to develop cross-platform tools for use in online publishing.

Acknowledgments

I would be remiss if I also did not mention two people to whom I am particularly indebted. Both Connor Choate and Christine Goertz Choate provided patient support while I wrote the book. They gave up more than a few weekends and vacations, and without their help I would not have been able to complete this book. They both have my heartfelt thanks and sincere appreciation.

We Want to Hear from You!

As the reader of this book, *you* are our most important critic and commentator. We value your opinion and want to know what we're doing right, what we could do better, what areas you'd like to see us publish in, and any other words of wisdom you're willing to pass our way.

You can email or write me directly to let me know what you did or didn't like about this book—as well as what we can do to make our books stronger.

Please note that I cannot help you with technical problems related to the topic of this book, and that due to the high volume of mail I receive, I might not be able to reply to every message.

When you write, please be sure to include this book's title and author as well as your name and phone or email address. I will carefully review your comments and share them with the author and editors who worked on the book.

Email: opensource@samspublishing.com
Mail: Mark Taber
            Associate Publisher
            Sams Publishing
            800 East 96th Street
            Indianapolis, IN 46240 USA

Reader Services

Visit our website and register this book at www.samspublishing.com/register for convenient access to any updates, downloads, or errata that might be available for this book.

Introduction

IN A WORLD OF OPEN SOURCE OR FREELY available programming languages and integrated development environments, you might be wondering why you would want to purchase REALbasic, a proprietary language that is closed-source and definitely not free. I think there is a very good reason to do so—because REALbasic offers some unique characteristics that cannot be found anywhere else. First of all, it's remarkably easy to use. It also compiles into native machine code for three operating systems: Windows, Macintosh, and Linux.

REALbasic is a dynamic language. REAL Software, the company that produces REALbasic, releases a new version every six months. This means that new features are being added (and old bugs are being fixed) all the time. There is so much you can do with REALbasic that it is impossible to cover it in one book, so I have tried to focus on the primary features of the language that most programmers will use. Rest assured, however, that by the time you read this, there will be more features available and still plenty more to learn about.

REALbasic also has a very active and friendly user community. If you have not done so already, it's a good idea to sign up for one of the mailing lists where users post questions and get answers from other users as well as REALbasic engineers themselves. Throughout the years, I have been an avid reader of the messages from these lists, and this book owes a debt of gratitude to everyone who has participated.

In the coming pages, you will read about what you will find in the rest of the book. Wherever possible I have used real-world examples that you can use in your own development. I have tried to present the information in such a way that it is useful to both first-time and experienced programmers.

Chapter 1, Introduction to REALbasic

Find out what's new in the latest version of REALbasic and decide if it's the right programming language for your needs.

Chapter 2, Programming with REALbasic

Learn the basics of programming in REALbasic. This chapter covers datatypes and modules, and it walks you through your first REALbasic application—a rudimentary web browser.

Chapter 3, Classes and Objects

REALbasic is an object-oriented programming language, and this chapter delves into object-oriented programming concepts and how they are implemented in REALbasic.

Chapter 4, Cross–Platform Application Development

REALbasic gives you the capability to create applications for Windows, Macintosh, and Linux operating systems. This chapter provides you with some basic information about the differences among the platforms that will help you to write quality applications on all of them.

Chapter 5, Designing a Desktop Application

Desktop applications are applications that make use of a graphical user interface. The REALbasic IDE lets you use the drag-and-drop feature to design your user interface, and this chapter shows you how.

Chapter 6, XML and Advanced Text Processing

XML, regular expressions, and styled text are discussed in this chapter.

Chapter 7, Console Programming and the Shell

You can also create programs in REALbasic that run on the command line, without a graphical user interface. You can interact with the Shell programmatically through REALbasic's Shell class, and you can also write your own console applications that can be run from within the shell on each platform.

Chapter 8, Databases

You can design a graphical front-end to your database without writing a single line of code. This chapter shows you how.

Chapter 9, Networking and Internet Programming

Read about REALbasic's networking classes and learn how to write your very own web server.

Chapter 10, Graphics

This chapter delves into REALbasic's Graphics class and shows you how to manipulate graphics and draw to the screen.

Chapter 11, Scripting and Extending REALbasic

Learn how to script Microsoft Office applications as well as how to make your REALbasic application scriptable. You'll also be given an overview on how you can extend REALbasic by using shared libraries and writing plug-ins in C++.

Appendix

Read about where you can go online to find additional information and how to get copies of the sample code referenced in the book.

Introduction to REALbasic

REALBASIC IS A MODERN, OBJECT-ORIENTED DESCENDENT of the venerable Basic programming language that I first encountered in my high school computer programming class, whose code I laboriously typed out on a dot-matrix terminal.

The original version of the language was developed in 1964. It was designed to be a good language for beginning programmers to learn, which is the very reason I learned to use it. In fact, the name "Basic" means Beginners All-purpose Symbolic Instruction Code.

Microsoft released its first version of the language in the mid-1970s. New life was breathed into the language in 1991, when Microsoft released Visual Basic 1.0 (the latest iteration of Visual Basic is known as Visual Basic .NET, or Visual Basic 7.0, which was first released in 2001). Visual Basic was a modern version of Basic that made it much easier to develop programs with graphical user interfaces. Because it is a highly accessible language that's easy to learn and capable of enabling programmers to develop applications quickly, programmers have flocked to it, and now Visual Basic has a huge base of users.

REAL Software, Inc., the company responsible for REALbasic, was founded in 1996. REALbasic first came to prominence when it was released in 1998 as a tool for rapid application development on the Macintosh platform. Although AppleScript was an easy-to-use language for scripting applications, it was not usable at that time as a tool for developing applications. As a result, REALbasic established itself as the perfect entry-level application development environment for the Macintosh.

The language has its roots in the Macintosh environment, but the plan from the beginning was to develop a cross-platform development environment. In 1999, REALbasic Professional Edition for Macintosh shipped. For the first time, it included the capability to compile Windows applications.

The next real step forward came in 2003, when REAL Software added a Windows version of the IDE with the release of REALbasic 5.0. The 5.0 release was an important one for REALbasic and also included the addition of new features that made it a much more viable programming language for serious application developers. It included the capability to write command-line applications and support for XML (which was a feature surprisingly late in arriving). Although you had been able to compile Windows apps since 1999, this was the first time you could develop them in Windows. Version 5.5, released in 2004, added the capability to compile Linux apps.

What's New in REALbasic 2005

An easier question to answer would be what *isn't* new in REALbasic 2005. With the release of this version, the integrated development environment (IDE) has been totally overhauled and much improved, especially if you have used the Windows version of REALbasic 5.5 which, well, let's just let bygones be bygones.

With the 2005 release, REAL Software offers integrated development environments for Macintosh, Windows, and Linux. The IDE was written in REALbasic, which means that the interface is now consistent across platforms. Although you could create cross-platform apps with REALbasic prior to this, the actual IDE was quite different between the Windows and Macintosh versions. If you are a Windows developer who tried RB 5.0 and was disappointed with it, you should give RB 2005 a chance. Your experience will be totally different.

The IDE makes it extremely easy to develop applications with graphical user interfaces (in fact, until RB 5.0, apps with GUIs were all you could create). It provides easy access to databases and it's possible to write a client app that browses a database without writing a single line of code.

There are two versions of REALbasic—Standard and Professional. The difference between the two is that with the Professional Edition, you can compile your application in all three platforms, whereas in the Standard Edition, you can compile the application only for the host environment. Although it's officially capable of compiling on Linux, I've had success running it on FreeBSD, one of the Unix variants.

Deciding if REALbasic Is Right for You

In my opinion, the single most compelling reason to use REALbasic instead of something like Visual Basic is that you can compile REALbasic applications to run natively on Windows, Macintosh, and Linux machines. Whereas older versions of Basic were interpreted, REALbasic is compiled. It also makes use of the native operating system whenever possible so that Macintosh programs act like most other Macintosh programs and most Windows programs act like other Windows programs.

There are a lot of languages to choose from—some closed-source and others open-source. For example, there is that other cross-platform programming language, Java, for which there are high-quality and free IDEs.

The advantage of programming in a modern Basic variant is twofold. First, an awful lot of us have programmed in Basic before, so the learning curve won't be too steep. Second, Basic is called Basic because it's supposed to be, well, basic. In other words, even if you've never heard of Basic before, Basic is a good choice because it is easy to learn.

REALbasic has taken a big leap in maturity in recent years, both as a cross-platform development solution and as a serious tool for programmers, so don't let the word "basic" fool you. You can write very complex programs with it. Although the best of REALbasic is the cross-platform application development potential, it also lets you pop the hood and get deep into the underlying system and do whatever you want. This book will focus on the cross-platform aspects of REALbasic, but I will give you enough information to get you started in the more single-platform topics. If you're a VB developer, you'll be familiar with Declares; if you code in C++, you'll be interested in hearing about writing plug-ins for REALbasic.

Strengths and Weaknesses

I'm not the type to gush. I'm not an ideological platform freak or a disciple for some clever and deliciously quirky scripting language somewhere. All languages are good in their own way. Some are better than others at particular tasks. In a lot of situations, which language you use doesn't matter at all. Scrimping on allocating space in your brain to learn yet another language is a perfectly acceptable reason to avoid learning a new language. After all, learning is a good thing, but so is spending time with your children.

REALbasic is not a replacement for Java, especially for large-scale enterprise applications. It if sits on the server, stick with Java. If your project needs a responsive cross-platform graphical user interface, REALbasic may be the perfect solution.

Although REALbasic is relatively easy to program with, it's also not a scripting language. It's definitely a programming language. In particular, it's statically typed and compiled. This means that there are some quick and dirty scripting tasks that are better done in Python (or Perl or Ruby).

As for me, I don't like typing, so I am not particularly pleased with any extra typing I might have to do. I really don't like brackets of the sort used by JavaScript and Java, although they are admittedly useful in certain circumstances. For this reason, I prefer Python for scripting and REALbasic for developing client applications. When developing content management solutions, I use Java and Apache Cocoon on the server.

If you're learning to program and you need to pick a language to learn in, I can think of no better language than REALbasic. Java is a lot easier to learn if you already know Basic. Python is good, but it lacks an IDE with the polish of REALbasic; therefore, it is not as easy to develop GUI applications in Python as it is with REALbasic. There's nothing like being able to design a user interface to provide a novice programmer with enough psychological gratification and sense of accomplishment to give them the energy to overcome the obstacles and challenges that are such an integral part of the programming challenge.

Who Should Read This Book

If you are standing in the bookstore sipping a latte, flipping through this book and trying to decide whether to buy it, there's a good chance you'll fall into one of the following groups:

- Novice programmers who want to get their feet wet programming in REALbasic.

  You may be someone who has never written a line of programming code before. You could also be a former AppleScript scripter nursing repetitive stress injuries from having to type so many sentences of grammatically correct, but horrifically wordy, English-like code in order to set the value of the first word of the first paragraph of the document in the front-most window of application such-and-such to value something-or-other.

- Experienced REALbasic programmers who want an updated reference on the new features found in REALbasic 2005.

  A lot has changed with recent releases. You need a reference to guide you through all the new features and to help you negotiate the challenges of cross-platform development.

- Visual Basic programmers who want to learn about REALbasic and how to port applications from Visual Basic to REALbasic.

  If you fall into this category, you may have an existing Visual Basic project you want to port to REALbasic so that it can run on Macintosh and Linux machines. You also may be looking for an alternative to Visual Basic 6.0 rather than "upgrading" to the latest .NET Microsoft twiddling.

- Other experienced programmers who are thinking about making the move to REALbasic.

  There are even a few Java developers malingering in the shadows of the bookstore who, while deeply loving the ever-proper, thoroughly stable and dependable Java, still long for something a little easier, a little quicker, maybe even something with a little more gloss on the old user interface.

I'm sure there's even one or two Linux developers who are frothing at the mouth at the chance to have a commercially supported rapid application development tool so that they can quickly create new Linux apps. In fact I think REALbasic could be the very best thing that ever happened to Linux. The release of REALbasic 2005 could represent the leading edge of an explosion of Linux apps that will bring the open-source operating system into the mainstream.

What You Can Expect

I intend for this book to be helpful to both novice and experienced programmers alike. For the novice, I'll provide enough background information about programming to get you started. Although this isn't an introduction-to-programming book per se, I will certainly keep your interests in mind. For the experienced developer, I will compare and contrast REALbasic with Java and Visual Basic when it's enlightening to do so, and I will highlight any cross-platform "gotchas" you might encounter.

Cross-platform application development carries with it some added complexities that need to be explored—some features work in only one of the platforms or work somewhat differently in each platform. It is also likely that many readers will not have access to all three operating systems on their desktop for thorough cross-platform testing throughout the development environment. As a result, I will provide as much information as possible about the nuances of cross-platform development with REALbasic and help you avoid lengthy and tedious bug-fixing in an effort to compile the program on all three platforms.

Although REALbasic is flexible enough to let the programmer have direct access to the underlying operating systems, of necessity, this is done differently with each respective operating system. In many cases, the REALbasic developer will have relatively deep experience in one platform, but much less understanding of the others. I will provide basic information on how to use these tools to extend REALbasic, but space and time limitations mean that I can provide only limited information about the underlying operating systems and libraries that are available to you. In other words, this is a book about programming cross-platform applications in REALbasic. It is not a book about programming Macintosh, Windows, and Linux operating systems.

The first part of the book is devoted to the language itself and the development environment. The second part delves into more advanced topics involving the library of classes and controls available to programmers. Because REALbasic is extensible with plug-ins, there are several commercially available plug-ins for REALbasic that add valuable functionality. I will also highlight the most useful of these third-party tools so that you can evaluate them for your own particular programming needs.

2

Programming with REALbasic

REALBASIC IS A LINE-ORIENTED, STATICALLY TYPED, object-oriented, and event-driven programming language with single inheritance. Whew. That just about sums it up. If you know what this chapter's first sentence means, then much of this chapter will be a review of familiar concepts. If you have no idea what I'm talking about, read on.

If you are new to programming in general, or to object-oriented programming in particular, you should read this entire chapter. It will introduce you to the basic concepts and terminology you need to know to make sense of the rest of the book. In addition to those introductory concepts, this section covers REALbasic's intrinsic data types, built-in functions, and the steps required to create your own modules and classes.

There's sort of a chicken-and-egg problem when writing about programming languages, especially REALbasic. To get started, you need to learn some basics about the IDE, but to learn the basics about the IDE, you'll need to understand some fundamental programming concepts.

In an effort to overcome this obstacle, I'll provide a brief introduction to the IDE in the next section.

Defining a Computer Program

The computer itself speaks in a language of numbers—ones and zeros. I still find it remarkable all the things that we can do with ones and zeros. For a computer to work with these ones and zeros, it needs to be able to represent them, so it must have a place to store and then find these ones and zeros when it needs them. Then the computer can perform a calculation on them. It can add them together or subtract them or do some combination and come up with more ones and zeros. Ones and zeros are meaningful and they represent meaningful things. In some cases they represent numbers, whereas in other cases they represent letters and words. Basically, we can say that computers can store information and perform calculations on (or process) information.

In a procedural programming language, these two distinct activities are clearly separated. Constants and variables store data and subroutines, and functions perform some kind of calculation on the data. In object-oriented programming, this distinction becomes a little more muddy because a class represents a collection of constants, variables, subroutines, and functions. Whereas constants can refer only to values (known as scalar references), variables can be one of two types: a scalar, which refers to a value, or the variable can be a reference to an object. (An object is an instance of a class; I'll explain this in more detail soon.)

When we say that REALbasic is an object-oriented language, what do we mean? A programmer may tell you that it means that REALbasic isn't a procedural or imperative programming language, and she would be absolutely right. Of course, you might be saying, "So…what does that mean?" The difference between object-oriented programming and procedural programming is twofold. In part, it's a different way of organizing the information and instructions that are used to process it. Procedural programming is a kind of programming that organizes the instructions into modules. It is very much focused on the instructions. Object-oriented programming organizes the instructions and the information into things called classes. These classes describe the instructions and the information that go together to get these tasks done.

REALbasic takes a practical approach to all of this and it incorporates procedural-type programming and object-oriented elements. In its attitude and the terminology used, it's all object-oriented.

REALBasic Terminology

Terminology used to describe programming languages varies by language. Although similar concepts exist in all object-oriented languages, they don't all share the same set of features and from time to time refer to things using different terminology or the same terminology with a slightly different meaning. REALbasic is no different. Before getting started, I want to provide a quick preview of the terminology I will be discussing throughout the rest of the chapter.

Programming code in REALbasic is organized and presented in a hierarchy. When you create an application in REALbasic, you start with a project. All the programming code that you write for the application is stored in this file. A project consists of a collection of modules and classes.

- Project
    - Module
        - Constants
        - Properties
        - Methods
            - Subroutine
                - Programming code

- Function
    - Programming code
- Class
    - Constants
    - Properties
    - Events
        - Programming code
    - Menu handlers
        - Programming code
    - Methods
        - Subroutine
            - Programming code
        - Function
            - Programming code

In this list, you can see that a project is made up of modules and classes. Modules and classes represent two different approaches to programming: procedural and object-oriented. Although REALbasic is a modern, truly object-oriented programming language, it retains elements of procedural programming features when it makes sense in order to make the process of writing an application simpler and more streamlined.

REALbasic uses what is traditionally thought of as object-oriented terminology to describe modules. If we were purists, we would not say that modules have properties or methods. Instead, we would refer to them as global variables or subroutines and functions. Regardless, the folks at REALbasic have opted to use object-oriented terminology for all aspects of the language, so that's what I will do as well.

Classes and modules are made up of things such as **constants, properties,** and **methods,** and I will refer to them generically as **members.** A particular method implemented in a class is a member of that class, as is a property that has been declared for that class.

I said earlier that programs can either hold data or process data. Data can be held in memory as a constant or a property. Methods are where the data gets processed.

All the programming code you write will be written in a method. Methods come in two flavors: functions and subroutines. Functions and subroutines are composed of a series of statements, which serve as instructions to the program that tell it the kind of calculations to perform on data.

In addition to methods, classes implement events and menu handlers, which are basically methods with some special characteristics that will be discussed in the section on object-oriented programming.

The approach I take in this chapter is to start from the ground up. The first section covers the basic building blocks of a computer program, including things such as variables, constants, and methods. It concludes with an example of how to create a module in REALbasic. The second section will build on that basic information and provide a more complete discussion of object-oriented programming and how it is implemented in REALbasic.

Quick Start: A Simple Web Browser

For you to get a sense of how REALbasic works and how powerful it can be, I want to quickly step you through your first REALbasic application. I am averse to "Hello, World" examples, so I've come up with a better idea. Your first REALbasic application will be a web browser. Don't fret. It really is that easy.

When you launch REALbasic, it will launch a new untitled project by default (see Figure 2.1). In the Project tab of the main window, you'll see three items listed: **App, Window1,** and **MenuBar1,** as shown in Figure 2.1. These are three classes that are part of every REALbasic application.

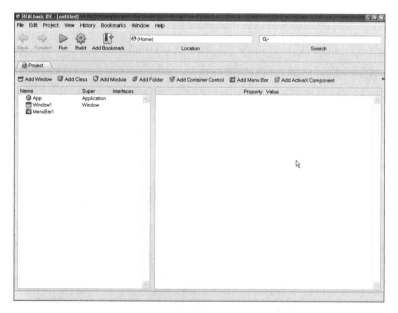

Figure 2.1   The default "Untitled" project Window.

Right now, don't worry too much about what a class is. We'll come back to that later in this chapter and discuss the details of classes and the other object-oriented aspects of REALbasic programming. What's important to understand now is that a class represents a group of code that performs a specific task. The **Window1** class is the programming code that manages the primary window in the application. **MenuBar1** handles the menu bar and the **App** class is the basic class that serves as the basis for your application.

Select `Window1` with your mouse. You will see the **Properties pane** on the right side of the main window become populated with information (see Figure 2.2). The **Properties pane** allows you to manipulate the properties of the **Window1** class. Later, you'll be creating your own classes and doing more complex manipulations, but for now, we'll use what we've got.

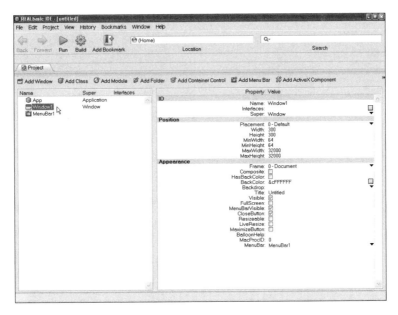

Figure 2.2   The Window1 class selected in the REALbasic IDE.

Controls

To create your web browser, double-click Window1. A new tab will appear called Window1 (see Figure 2.3). This tab will be the front-most tab and you will see the pane that is used for editing windows. There are two Edit Modes you can use in the **Window1 Tab**: one for editing the layout of the Window and another for editing the code. You can switch between modes by pressing Option=Tab, or clicking the Edit Mode button in the toolbar for Window1. By default we'll be in the **Window Editor's Layout Mode**. You'll know you're there if the panel is divided into three columns. The column on the far left has a list of controls with names like **BevelButton**, **Canvas**, and so on. In the middle, you'll see a visual representation of Window1 and to the right you'll see the **Properties pane**.

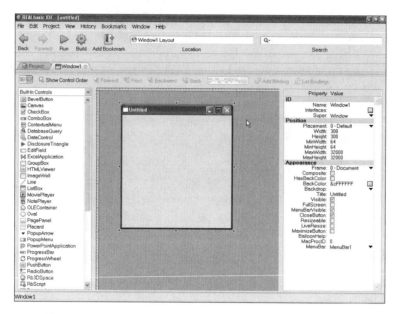

Figure 2.3   Window1 ready for editing in the Edit Layout Mode.

If by chance you are not in the **Window Editor**, you can press Alt+Tab on Windows/Linux or Option+Tab on a Macintosh and you will toggle to **Layout Mode in the Window Editor**.

Before doing anything else, click the window. When it is selected, look at the **Properties pane**. It is two columns; in the left is the property and to the right is the value of the property.

In the area labeled **Appearance**, make sure that the following **CheckBoxes** are checked: **Visible**, **MenubarVisible**, **CloseButton**, **Resizable,** and **Maximize Button**. By setting these properties, this will make it possible for you to resize the window of your new web browser.

Now that you have a window, you need to place controls on it so that you can actually do something. Controls are user-interface elements that users interact with. For this project, we will need three controls. All three of them will be found in the **Controls pane** in the left column.

The first thing to do is find the **PushButton** control in the list, which is in alphabetical order. Click it and drag it to the window. Just drop it anywhere for now.

You now have a button on your Window with a caption that reads Untitled. To give it a better caption, look in the **Properties pane** and find the **Caption** property in the **Appearance** section. Click where it says **Untitled,** and the **EditField** will become highlighted. Type in the word "Go!" or whatever word you want to use and press Return.

Your button should now say "Go!" You'll want the button positioned in the upper-right corner of the window, so select it and drag it up and to the right. Keep dragging it until you see green guidelines. You should reach a point where there is a horizontal guide on the top of the button and a vertical guide to the right of the button. These guidelines help you to position your controls consistently, according to design guidelines established by the operating system. It's a good idea to use them and follow their advice.

Now that we have a **PushButton** on the window, we'll need an **EditField**. Find the **EditField** in the list of controls and drag it onto the window just like the button. Drag it to the upper-left corner. As you do so, the horizontal guideline will appear that will ensure that the **EditField** is positioned at the same level as the **PushButton** and that everything looks nice. There's no caption to change for the **EditField**, so we're done with it for now.

Now, find the **HTMLViewer** control in the list of controls and drag it to the window. Drop it in the center. Notice that every time a control is selected, it is highlighted, and little white boxes appear in the corners and in the middle of the sides. You can use these selection boxes to make the control bigger by dragging them around. The guides will help you here, too. When it is as big as the guides say it should be, turn to the **Properties pane**. You will see four **CheckBoxes** in the **Position** section of the **Properties pane**. Check all of them: **LockLeft, LockTop, LockRight,** and **LockBottom**. This tells REALbasic that the **HTMLViewer** should get larger as the window gets larger. Recall that earlier when we were examining the window, we made sure that it was expandable and had a **Maximize** button.

So far, so good. Now for some code.

Double-click the **PushButton** labeled "Go!" and you will be switched to the **Code Editor**. In the left column you'll see the **Code Editor's Browser** with a list of all kinds of things. You should see an item called **PushButton1,** and right beneath it is the word **Action**, which should be highlighted.

Events

This is the **Action event** of the **PushButton,** and we're going to instruct the **PushButton** on what it is supposed to do when someone clicks it. REALbasic is an event-driven language. This means that much of what your REALbasic program does is in response to a user's interaction with your application. In this case, when a user clicks the **PushButton**, we want to tell the **HTMLViewer** to load the web page whose address we have typed into the **EditField**. When a user clicks the button, it causes the **Action event** to be executed.

Do it by typing the following code into the editor to the right of the browser:

```
HTMLViewer1.LoadURL EditField1.text
```

You have just told the **HTMLViewer1** control to execute the method called `LoadURL`. `EditField1.Text` is a parameter that you pass to **HTMLViewer1** to let it know which page to load. In this case, it takes the content of the **EditField1** control and uses that as the URL (web address) of the page to load.

Whereas `HTMLViewer1.LoadURL` refers to a method, `EditField1.text` refers to something else, called a property. **EditField1** is an instance of the class **EditField**, and `EditField1.text` is a property of the class instance. Later on in this chapter I'll cover methods and properties in more detail, but for now let it suffice to say that a method is an instruction to a computer to perform some task, and a property represents a value of some sort. In this case, `EditField1.Text` represents the value of the text that the user will type into **EditField1** when the application is running.

More information on methods will be covered later in this chapter in the section titled "Methods."

Run Your Application

Now double-check your spelling, and when you are satisfied that everything is in order, look for the green arrow at the top labeled Run and click it.

After a few seconds, your application will be up and running. Click the **EditField**, and then type in a URL for your favorite website. Be sure to include the "http" portion. If you can't think of one, type in **http://realsoftware.com/**. Then click the "Go!" button and wait a few seconds. Assuming you are connected to the Internet, you soon should see the front page of REAL Software's website where the **HTMLViewer** is. Be patient; it may take a few seconds depending on how fast your connection is.

After it's loaded, click a link and see where it takes you.

Voila! You've created a web browser.

If it doesn't work as planned, that's okay. Take a look and make sure that you have typed everything exactly the way I said to type it in. If the program is generating an error, a small window will pop up describing the error. Possible errors might include clicking the "Go!" button when the **EditField** contains no text, or your program may generate an error if you try to run it and you are not connected to the Internet.

Now that you've had a taste of how easy it is to write a REALbasic program, it's time to look at some of the details of the REALbasic programming language and how to create classes and modules of your own.

Procedural Programming in REALbasic

REALbasic is an object-oriented programming language, but as I said earlier, REALbasic takes a practical approach to object-oriented programming and retains procedural programming elements. In this section, I will start with the language elements of REALbasic that are more procedural and will defer until the next chapter a discussion of REALbasic's object-oriented features.

Statements and Declarations and Comments

A method is made up of a series of declarations, expressions, and statements that make up your application's programming code. These serve as the building blocks for functions and subroutines, and this is where we will start in our review of the REALbasic programming language. Throughout this section I will use snippets of code to serve as examples. One thing you will see quite often are comments that I include in the sample code to explain what's happening at a particular point or to let you know what the value of a particular variable should be. A comment is some text included by the programmer that is ignored by the program and intended to document a portion of code. A comment in REALbasic can take on one of two forms:

```
' A line starting with an apostrophe is a comment
// As is a line starting with two forward slashes
```

When writing any kind of program, it's a good idea to make liberal use of comments throughout your code. This will help you (or someone else in the future) understand what your code is doing.

Expressions: Operands and Operators

Operators and functions are related to each other. In fact, in mathematics an operator is a kind of function. The technical definition of a function is that it takes an input and returns an output according to a set of rules. In computer programming, the definitions of both functions and operators are a little more squishy, but it helps to understand their mathematical heritage.

Operators are used in expressions. An expression is a combination of one or more operands, plus one or more operators that are used to calculate a new value.

Here is an example of an expression:

```
2 + 2
```

In this example, the operator is the plus sign (+) and the operands are both 2. You should be able to see that the answer to this equation is 4. The number 4 is the value returned by this particular expression.

Like a function, you can think of the operands that make up an expression as the inputs to a function. The operators are the rules that tell the computer how to calculate the new value based on the input given.

The REALbasic programming language has a variety of operators. You will likely be familiar with most of them already, including +, -, *, /, and ^ for addition, subtraction, multiplication, division, and power, respectively. There are two others, mod and integer division (\), which I will discuss shortly.

Variables and Literals

There are two ways represent the operands of an expression in REALbasic. When I write

```
2 + 2
```

I am using what is called a *literal*. In this case, the literal value for the integer is 2. (In these examples, all the literals I am using are numbers, but you can use characters, too, as long as you use quotes around them. See the section titled "Strings" later on in this chapter for more information.)

If I wanted to solve the preceding expression on a piece of paper, I would write it out like this:

```
2 + 2 = 4
```

However, I can't do this when writing a program, because I presumably do not know the answer to the expression prior to having the program calculate the answer (why else would I express it as an expression?). When you use an expression in programming, you are making a calculation and you need to find a place to store the value that is returned from the expression.

In this example, we need to figure out what to do with the answer to the expression 2+2. You do this by declaring a variable, which is a letter or sequence of characters that represent a value of some sort. When I declare a variable, I have to declare what type of variable it is. In this case, the number 2 is an integer, so I will declare the variable as the intrinsic data type integer. In REALbasic, data types are declared using the `Dim` statement.

```
Dim a as Integer
a = 2 + 2
```

In programming terms, this is known as an assignment. I am assigning the result (or answer) from the expression to the variable a. Assignment doesn't work exclusively with expressions. For example, you can assign the value of one variable to that of another variable.

```
Dim a as Integer
Dim b as Integer
a = 2 + 2
b = a
```

Now, both the variable a and the variable b represent the value 4. You can also do something like this:

```
Dim a as Integer
Dim b as Integer
Dim c as Integer
a = 2 + 2 // a = 4
b = 3 - 1 // b = 2
c = a + b // a + b = 6
```

There is potential for confusion, however. Consider the following:

```
Dim a as Integer
Dim b as Integer
Dim c as Integer
Dim d as Integer
a = 2 // a = 2
b = 2 + 3 - 1 // b = 4
c = a * b  // c = 8
d = 2*2+3-1 // d = 6
```

Why is the answer for c equal to 8, whereas the answer for d is equal to 6, when it looks like they used the same numbers? The reason is that the expression used to calculate the value for d calculates the answer in a slightly different order than that used by c. For c, 2+3–1 is calculated first, giving an answer of 4. Then, the value of a is multiplied by 4, giving the answer 8. When d was calculated, 2*2 was calculated first, giving the answer of 4. Then, 4 was added to 3, giving an answer of 7. Finally, 1 is subtracted from 7, leaving an answer of 6.

The order in which operands are calculated is determined by the operators and the order of precedence. Basically, things are multiplied first, then divided, then added, and then subtracted. If you want to have control over the order this happens, you can use parentheses. To get the expression used to calculate d to arrive at the same answer as that given for c, you would write it this way:

```
d = 2*(2+3-1)
```

The parentheses tells the program to calculate 2+3–1 first, and then multiply the answer by 2.

Expressions are used in a few ways when writing a software application, but I think the most common is to use an expression to assign a value to a variable of a given type. There are also cases when an expression can replace a literal or a variable when used as a parameter passed to a method.

Intrinsic Data Types

When we looked at expressions, we saw that they were composed of operators and operands. I said that operands could be either literals or variables and that if you used a variable for the operand, you would have to first declare the type of the variable before you used it.

REALbasic is a statically typed programming language. This means that every variable has to be declared before it can be used. Some programming languages, especially those used for scripting, are dynamically typed. In those languages you can refer to variables that you have not declared and the type that variable represents isn't determined until the program is running.

If you are a Visual Basic programmer, REALbasic behaves like Visual Basic does when OPTION EXPLICIT has been set.

The following table lists the intrinsic data types available in REALbasic, along with information about the range of values each can hold.

Table 2.1 **Data Types**

Data Type	Range of Values
Boolean	True/False
Integer	Values between plus/minus 2,147,483,648 (4 bytes)
Single	Real number, with a decimal value, -1.175494 e-38 to 3.402823 e+38 (4 bytes)
Double	Sometimes called double precision real number, a value between 2.2250738585072013 e-308 and 1.7976931348623157 e+308 (8 bytes)
String	A string of character values, encoded in UTF-8
Color	(3 bytes)

Declaration

To use a variable in your program, you must first declare the variable. In REALbasic, you can declare a variable with the Dim statement (short for Dimension). When you declare a variable, you are telling REALbasic to set aside memory for it and what kind of information the variable represents.
For example:

```
Dim i as Integer
Dim s as String
```

If you have several variables to declare, REALbasic also lets you declare them all at once, as long as they are of the same type:

```
Dim a,b,c,d as Integer
```

Data types are important because they tell REALbasic how to interpret the value of any data stored at a particular address. All a computer knows about are numbers and at the lowest levels, the computer only knows about two numbers: 0 and 1.

For example, suppose you've declared a variable and set the value to 97. How your program will interpret the number 97 is entirely dependent on what data type the variable is. If the data type is an integer, it will treat the value as an integer. If the data type is a string, it will treat the value as the lowercase letter a.

Dim is also not the only way to declare or use variables. There are some cases where you declare the use of variables (or variable-like constants) using REALbasic's graphical user interface. In other words, when you create a module and establish properties for that module, you are effectively declaring variables, even though you are not using the Dim statement.

Variables and Constants

Behind the scenes, a variable represents an address where a value is stored in memory. It's kind of like the sales clerk at the convenience store down the street. Every morning I get up and drive down to the same street address to get a cup of coffee, but every day there's someone new behind the counter. Same address, different person.

When you create a variable, you are telling REALbasic to use the value that is stored at that particular address. If you know the value is never going to change for the duration of the variable's lifespan, then you can declare it as a constant. Unlike the convenience store example, a constant means that every time you go to a given address, you'll find the same person. Same address, same person. I suppose that makes a constant more like a tombstone or the nightly news.

The primary reason or justification for making the differentiation between variables and constants is that your program can handle constants more efficiently than it handles variables.

Scope

Variables and constants always have a certain scope. Scope refers to when and how a variable or property can be accessed and the lifetime of that variable or property.

Local Variables and Constants

Sometimes you need to use a variable inside a method as a temporary container of information. In this case, that variable is meaningful only within that method. As soon as the method is finished executing, the variable is discarded. These are usually referred to as local variables. There can also be local constants, declared and used within a method, and the same rules apply.

Global Variables (Module Properties) and Module Constants

Variables that are associated with a module are called properties (in other programming languages, they would be called global variables), and properties of a module exist as long as the module exists. Part of what makes a module a module is that it exists in memory and is accessible whenever your program is running. As you will see in the following chapters, this is not the case with classes.

A variable's scope can be further narrowed by specifying whether it is `Public`, `Protected`, or `Private`, which sets limits on which objects can have access to the property (methods have scope, too).

`Public` means that any other object can call the method or access the property. `Protected` means that only objects that share the same class as the object to whom this property is associated can access it. `Private` means it's restricted exclusively to the object itself, and subclasses cannot access it directly.

Scalar Variables and Reference Variables

There are two types of variables: scalar and object. A scalar variable represent a particular value or a certain type. REALbasic has a set of intrinsic data types that you will use when declaring scalar variables.

For the time being, I will be discussing only scalar variables. A reference variable is a reference to an object, and references work differently from scalar variables. When dealing with scalar variables, there are two things we need to know. The first is the value the variable represents and the second is the data type of the variable.

In the IDE, modules use the same basic terminology as classes do. Modules have properties, methods, and constants. It's important to understand that a module property really isn't the same name as a class property. When you create a class, the properties are associated with the class and serve as a descriptive value that is unique to any given class instance. Properties in modules are really more akin to global variables, and that is the way that you will use them.

Arithmetic with Integers, Singles, and Doubles

A computer is called a computer because it computes things. At a very basic level, computers can add, subtract, multiply, and divide numbers. The following section reviews REALbasic's approach to arithmetic.

Integer

In REALbasic, an integer requires 4 bytes of space to represent it. Recall that an integer is a whole number (no decimals), and it can be positive or negative in value. Because REALbasic uses 4 bytes of memory, that means the range of numbers an integer can represent is between plus or minus 2,147,483,648.

Singles and Doubles

Singles and doubles are floating-point numbers, which means they are numbers that can accept a decimal value. A Single uses four bytes; a Double uses eight.

A single can be within the range of 1.175494 e-38 and 3.402823 e+38. A single loses precision after about 6 decimal places.

A double can be within the range of 2.2250738585072013 e-308 and 1.7976931348623157 e+308. A double loses precision about 16 decimal places.

Number Literals

Even though you do not have to declare a literal, a literal still has a type, which REALbasic deduces for you. For example:

```
Dim i As Integer
i = 3/1.5 //i=2
```

Because you declared i as an integer, REALbasic knows it's an integer, but what about the literals 3 and 1.5? REALbasic knows what they are, too. 3 is an integer and 1.5 is a floating-point number (either a short or a double).

Coercion

Using data types properly can be tricky and can lead to unforeseen problems if you do not handle them correctly. The problems come into play when using operators with values of different types, so it's important to understand that even literals have types. Here's a simple example of mixing data types:

```
Dim i as Integer
Dim d as Double

d = 1.8
i = d // i = 1
```

In this example, i is declared as an integer, whereas d is declared as a double. Because integers by definition don't have decimal points, REALbasic drops everything after the decimal point. This is called coercion or typecasting. Note that it doesn't round up to the nearest value or anything like that. It just chops it off as if it never existed. You can try the same thing using literals and get the same results:

```
Dim i as Integer

i = 1.8 // i = 1
```

Because i is an integer and 1.8 is not an integer, everything to the right of the decimal point is dropped again. The floating-point value 1.8 is being "coerced" into being an integer.

Another situation exists when you perform a calculation on two operands of one type whose answer is of a different type. Consider the following:

```
Dim m as Integer
Dim n as Single

m = 3/2  // m = 1
n = 3/2  // n = 1.5
```

In this case, the integer 3 is divided by the integer 2, but the answer is 1.5, which is not an integer. When I assign the value of the expression to a variable that has been declared as an integer, the value is 1. However, if I assign the value to a single or a double, as I did with the variable n, the correct answer appears.

Because I've already told you that if you assign a single or double literal to an integer, REALbasic just drops everything to the right of the decimal point when assigning the value to the integer, you might find this example a little confusing:

```
Dim m as Integer
Dim n as Double
Dim o as Integer

m = 3/1.4 // m = 2
n = 3/1.4 // n = 2.142857
```

You might be tempted to assume that REALbasic drops the .4 from 1.4 and then divides 3 by 1, but that would give you an answer of 3 instead of 2, and that's clearly not happening because the answer is 2. Instead, REALbasic calculates the answer as a double, and then it drops off everything to the right of the decimal when assigning the value to the integer variable m. In this example, it gets the answer of 2.142857 and then assigns the value of two to the variable m. In other words, it does not drop the decimal values until after it calculates the expression.

As it happens, another operator that is used for integer division converts the values of the operands to integer prior to performing the division. The operator is \ and you can see how it leads to a different answer in the following example:

```
Dim m as Integer

o = 3\1.4 // o = 3
```

The value for o is 3 because 1.4 is cast to an integer prior to dividing it into 3.

Another potential problem arises when you try set the value of an integer to a number that is outside the legal range for an integer. Remember that an integer can be a number in between plus or minus 2,147,483,648. One important thing to understand is that between means between. In other words, a legal value for an integer is greater than −2,147,483,648 and less than 2,147,483,648. It cannot be equal to −2,147,483,648 or 2,147,483,648

In this example, everything happens as expected:

```
Dim d as Double
d = 2147483647.0 + 1 // d = 2,147,483,648
```

Now look at what happens if you assign the value to an integer:

```
Dim i as Integer
i = 2147483647.0 + 1 // i = -2,147,483,648
```

When you assign the value to a double, the answer is positive, but when you assign it to an integer, the answer is negative. What? The reason is that when you assign a number to an integer which is outside the legal range, it simply starts over again and starts counting from the lowest boundary. Here's what happens as the number assigned to the integer gets higher:

```
Dim i as Integer
i = 2147483647.0 + 1 // i = -2,147,483,648
i = i + 1 // i = -2,147,483,647
i = i + 1 // i = -2,147,483,646
i = i + 1 // i = -2,147,483,645
```

As you can see, it is now counting up from the lower bounds of the range. Interestingly enough, this doesn't happen when assigning a value to a single that is out of range. The single ignores the higher values, treating anything above the legal range as infinity (Inf). For example:

```
Dim s as Single
Dim s2 as Single
Dim d as Double
s = 3.402823e+38 // s = 3.402823e+38
s2 = 3.402823e+39 //      s2 = inf
d = 3.402823e+39 // d = 3.402823e+39
```

Anything out of range for a single returns Inf, for infinity. Recall that anything multiplied by infinity equals infinity, and that's just how the value works. If you assign the same value to a double, you get a double back, which means that the same literal (in this case 3.402823e+39) will be treated as infinity if the variable is a single, but as the proper value if the variable is a double. If you assign a number to a double outside of a double's range, it will also return infinity.

Floating point numbers are also not as accurate as an integer. For example, if you were to examine the decimal value of s from the previous example, you would get the following digits:

```
340,282,306,073,709,652,000,000,000,000,000,000,000
```

Mod Operator

Mod returns the remainder derived as a result of the division of two integers. The most common use of Mod is to determine whether a number is an even or an odd number. Because anything divided by two is considered an even number, all you need to do to check for this is the following:

```
Dim aNumber, result as Integer
result = aNumber Mod 2
```

Note that Mod operates only on integers. If either of the two values used with Mod are floating-point numbers, they are cast as integers, which means everything to the right of the decimal point is dropped.

Boolean and Comparison Operators

In addition to arithmetic operators, REALbasic also provides a number of operators to be used when comparing values.

```
=, <, <=, >, >=, <>
```

These are the familiar equal, less than, less than or equal to, greater than, greater than or equal to, and not equal to operators from your grade school arithmetic. When you compare two things and ask whether they are equal, or if one is greater than the other one, the answer you expect is either "Yes, they are equal," or "No, they're not." Whenever you need a yes or no answer, the data type to use is REALbasic's boolean.

Boolean

A variable that has been declared as a boolean can have one of two values: `True` or `False`. `True` and `False` are reserved words in REALbasic and you do not need to quote them when referring to them in your programming code. Here's an example of how you would declare a variable as a boolean and assign a value:

```
Dim b as Boolean
b = True
```

Comparison Operators

When using comparison operators, you can often get some constructs that look a little bit odd at first:

```
Dim b as Boolean
Dim m as Integer
Dim n as Integer

m = 1
n = 1

b = (m = n)
```

This is confusing because of the presence of two equal signs. Even though the same operator is being use in two different places, they are being used in two entirely different ways. This is the first example of operator overloading I've addressed in the book. Overloading is an important concept in object-oriented programming. It means that you do two or more different things with the operator depending on the context. The context is determined by the values (or operands) that are provided. Later in this section you will see how to do your own customized operator overloading.

In the previous example, REALbasic handles the expression in parentheses first. Because both m and n are integers, REALbasic treats this as the equal comparison operator and tests to see if the value for m is the same as the value for n. In this example, the values are, in fact, the same, so the Boolean value True is returned. The equal sign that comes right after b is the assignment operator, and it is used to apply the value from the right side of the operator to the variable on the left side. REALbasic is often smart enough to figure this out without any help from parentheses, but it's always a good idea to use them because it avoids ambiguity, both to the REALbasic compiler and to any human beings who may happen upon your code at some future date.

You use the other comparison operators the same way:

```
Dim b as Boolean

b = (4<5) // true
b = (4<4)  // false
b = (4<=4) // true
```

You can also mix and match expressions, but you still have to pay attention to operator precedence:

```
Dim b as Boolean
Dim i as Integer

b = 1<(1+4)*3-12 // true, 5 * 3 - 12 = 3
b = 1<1+4*3-12 // false, 1 + 12 - 12 = 1
```

You cannot mix comparison operators, however, regardless of what you do.

```
Dim b as Boolean

b= 1<2<3
```

This causes strange errors. In this case, the compiler raised an error that said it was expecting an integer. When I changed b to an integer, the error said that it was expecting a boolean. This was a pretty clear sign to me that the compiler had no idea what to do with it.

Boolean Operators

There are times, however, when you do need to make more than one comparison at the same time. Do not despair, for REALbasic has provided a solution, the boolean operators And, Or, and Not.

Boolean operators are used to compare boolean values. It's also the basis of boolean logic, which you use all the time, except you don't call it boolean logic. You might say to yourself, "If the department store has these jeans in my size and they are not too expensive, I'll buy them." Where's the Boolean logic? I'll rephrase the sentence in a way to make it more clear: "If it is true that the store has jeans in my size and if it is true that they are not too expensive, then it is true that I will buy them."

This kind of statement is also called a conditional because the truth of whether you will buy the jeans is based on the condition that the store has your size and that the jeans are not expensive. Now, for fun, let's turn this into some REALbasic code:

```
Dim mySize as Integer
Dim myMoney as Double
Dim storeSize as Integer
Dim storePrice as Double
Dim hasMySize as Boolean
```

```
Dim isAffordable as Boolean
Dim shouldPurchase as Boolean

mySize = 38
storeSize = 38
myMoney = 49.50
StorePrice = 45.00

hasMySize = (mySize = storeSize)
isAffordable = (storePrice <= myMoney)
shouldPurchase = hasMySize And isAffordable // shouldPurchase = True
```

In this rather long-winded example, I first compared my size with the store's size to see if they were equal. (I'm making the simplifying assumption that the store only has one size in stock.) After that, I checked to see if the price offered by the store was less than or equal to the amount of money that I had. I then used the boolean operator And to see if both hasMySize and isAffordable were True. Because they were both True, shouldPurchase is True as well.

That, by the way, is the definition of And. It takes a Boolean value on either side, and if both of those values are True, And returns True; otherwise, it returns False. Contrast And with Or, which returns True as long as only one of the values is True (but also if both are True).

```
Dim mySize as Integer
Dim myMoney as Double
Dim storeSize as Integer
Dim storePrice as Double
Dim hasMySize as Boolean
Dim isAffordable as Boolean
Dim shouldPurchase as Boolean

mySize = 38
storeSize = 38
myMoney = 49.50
StorePrice = 45.00

hasMySize = (mySize = storeSize)
isAffordable = (storePrice <= myMoney)
shouldPurchase = hasMySize Or isAffordable // shouldPurchase = True
```

The only difference in this example is the use of Or, but the answer is the same, True, because at least one of the operands is True.

In addition to And and Or, there is the Not operator, which returns the opposite of any boolean expression. If the value was True, it's now False. If it was False, it's now True. When you use Not, it's just like opposite day.

```
Dim b as Boolean

b = Not(1<4) // b = False
b = Not(1 > 4) // b = True
```

Like everything else, it can be combined with other expressions, like so:

```
Dim b as Boolean
Dim c as Boolean
b = Not(1<4) Or (5=(10/2)) // True
c = Not((1<4) Or (5=(10/2))) // False
```

Do you see why b is True and c is False? The only difference is the additional parentheses in the second expression. In the first expression, 1 is less than 4, which is true. Not negates it, which makes the left side of Or evaluate to False. On the right side of the Or, 5 does equal 10 divided by 2. After both sides of the Or are evaluated, you have False Or True, which evaluates to True.

In the second expression used to assign a value to c, Not's negation is not applied until after the rest of the expression is evaluated. Because 1 is less than 4, the left side is True, and because 5 equals 10 divided by 2, the right side is True as well. Because True Or True returns True, the Not operator negates it and assigns False to c.

Strings

A string is a sequence of characters. Chances are you will be doing a lot of work with strings as you write your REALbasic applications. You've seen how operators work with numbers such as integers and doubles, but you may be surprised to find that operators work on strings, too.

The same arithmetic operators used with numbers work on strings, but in a way that makes sense for strings. So, if I have two strings, one holds the value "a" and the other holds the value "b", here's what happens when I add them together:

```
Dim a,b,c as String
a = "a"
b = "b"

c = a + b
```

When I add two strings together, they are *concatenated*, which is a fancy way of saying they are joined together. In this case, c now equals ab. Now, let's try something else out:

```
Dim a,b,c as String
a = "1"
b = "2"

c = a + b
```

In this example, a and b are both strings, but they refer to the character "1" and the character "2". Because the variables are of the data type string, REALbasic treats it just like any other string and assigns c the value of 12.

Joining strings with the + operator is convenient, but consider yourself warned: it's a VERY slow operation, and there are many cases when there are other approaches for joining strings that are more effective (see the section "Arrays").

You can also use comparison operators on strings as well.

When you compare strings, the comparisons are not case sensitive.

```
Dim s, t as String
Dim b,c as Boolean

s = "Dog"
t = "dog"

b = (s = t) // b is True
c = (s <> t) // c is False
```

Strings can also be empty. You can assign an empty string to a string variable, like so:

```
a = ""
```

You can test for an empty string by saying:

```
Dim b as Boolean
Dim a as String
a = "a string"
b = (a <> "") // b is True
```

In addition to these operators, REALbasic provides a group of built-in functions that are used with strings. These are reviewed later on in this section.

Color

Colors are represented in REALbasic by a data type that takes up three bytes, one byte each for the colors red, green, and blue. There is a special literal format for colors, which uses hexadecimal numbers to represent each of the three colors. In decimal terms, each value ranges from 0 to 255, which is 00 to FF in hexadecimal notation. This is similar to the way that colors are represented in HTML. Here's an example that shows the literal value for the color black and the color white:

```
&c000000 // black
&cFFFFFF // white
```

Literals

There is more than one way to express a number as a literal. You can also write numbers in binary, hexadecimal, and octal format. The next example shows how to represent the value 65 in hexadecimal, octal, or binary format:

```
Dim x,y,z as Integers

x = &h41
y = &o101
z = &b1000001
// x,y and z all equal 65
```

Visual Basic Data Types

If you are porting from Visual Basic to REALbasic, you will have noticed that REALbasic has a smaller set of Data types than Visual Basic does. However, because of REALbasic's object orientation, there are usually different (and often better) ways of accomplishing the same thing.

Visual Basic provides these specific Data types not available in REALbasic:

Byte (1 byte)

The best way to work with a byte-sized piece of data is with a **MemoryBlock**, which is a flexible class offered by REALbasic that will let you work with and manipulate data in just about any way you see fit. Because it is a class, see the **MemoryBlock** section in Chapter 3, "Classes and Objects."

Char (2 bytes)

Char represents a single character. You can either use a REALbasic string that happens to be one character long, or you can use a 2-byte **MemoryBlock** in its place.

Long Integer (8 bytes) and Decimal (12 bytes)

Both Long and Decimal represent larger numbers than is currently directly supported by REALbasic. You can easily create 8-byte **MemoryBlocks** and 12-byte **MemoryBlocks** for holding data of that size, but if you're planning on doing any math, you'll have to code that yourself.

Date (8 bytes)

Date is a Data type in Visual Basic, but it's a class in REALbasic. See the **Date** class in Chapter 3.

User-Defined (Structure)

Finally, there is a User-defined type, which is used like a structure in C. You can model this almost directly with the **MemoryBlock** class, but a better choice in most cases is to create a class instead. A structure is a collection of bytes; you, the programmer, define the meaning of the data in those bytes. So, for example, if you have an 8-byte User-defined structure that describes a person, you could say that the first byte represents the person's age, the next two bytes represent the weight, and so on.

As you will see, classes have properties that are often values just like those I described. You can create a class that has a property that represents a person's age, weight, and so on. The advantage of using a class is that it is generally easier to access the value of the property. Although I'm getting a little ahead of myself, suffice it to say that you can access the property with this kind of syntax:

```
ClassName.PropertyName
```

There may be times when a **MemoryBlock** is a more efficient approach, but you can expect it to be a little more difficult to work with.

Methods

REALbasic uses the term *Method* to describe any function or subroutine, whether it is in a module or a class. In other programming languages, method is used exclusively to describe functions or subroutines associated with a class. Although module methods and class (or object) methods are very similar, they are called in slightly different ways depending on whether the method is defined in a module or a class.

When you "call" a method, you are instructing the program to execute the function or procedure in question. Methods are defined in a module or a class, but they can only be called from objects that are instances of the class.

Unlike other programming languages (Java, for instance) REALbasic doesn't have class methods that can be called without instantiating the class. (See Chapter 3 for more information about class instantiation. This fact may change in future versions of REALbasic.) A module can be used as an alternative because modules are also not instantiated.

Functions

I think of functions as questions. When using a function, I am asking a question and expect to get an answer back. With a subroutine, I'm simply telling the computer what to do and really not interested in hearing back from it. Subroutines are sometimes said to have side effects. This means that they perform some tasks, so the state of the program changes in some way (for instance, they save data to a file). It's called a side effect because it happens as a consequence of the instruction, but the instruction itself isn't the center of attention.

Most of the examples I used with operators can be re-expressed using functions. As an example, consider the following function (don't worry about where this function gets created just yet):

```
Function Add(Num1 as Integer, Num2 as Integer) As Integer
// code
End
```

Add is the name of the function. Inside the parentheses are the parameters Num1 and Num2. These serve the same role that operands do when working with operators. They are the values the function will use to calculate a new value. The data type of the value to be returned follows the parameters. In this case, the return type will be an integer, just like the parameters are.

Sometimes functions can accept optional parameters. When that is the case, I'll enclose that parameter in brackets ([]) to identify it.

```
Function Add([OptionalParam as String], Num1 as Integer, Num2 as Integer) as
➥Integer
  // code
End
```

I can use this function just like I used the + operator.

```
Dim answer as Integer
answer = Add(1,2) // answer is 3
```

When used in code, a function in REALbasic always uses parentheses to wrap the parameters. As you will see, this is in contrast to the standard practice with subroutines, in which you do not use parentheses (although REALbasic lets you use them if you choose).

Subroutines

You have already seen a subroutine in use in the quick start, where you built a simple web browser.

The signature for this subroutine is

```
Sub LoadURL(anURL as String)
```

Sub designates the fact that this is a subroutine. LoadURL is the name of the subroutine and the parameter, anURL, is defined in the parentheses. Note, there is no return value for subroutines. In practice, we wrote this line of code to execute the subroutine:

```
HTMLViewer1.LoadURL EditField1.text
```

In this particular instance, LoadURL is a method of the class HTMLViewer. The parameter bears a little explaining. Text is a property of the class **EditField**, and its type is string. The signature says that this subroutine takes a string as its only parameter. (The name anURL doesn't really mean anything; it's a placeholder.) EditField1.text is the particular string that's passed in this example.

Arrays

Up until now, I've talked about variables that represent a single value, but there are times when you have a list of values and it would be helpful to be able to refer to them as a single unit. This is when Arrays come in handy.

There are one-dimensional Arrays and multidimensional Arrays. I'll talk about one-dimensional Arrays first.

Declaring Arrays

Like any other variable, you have to declare Arrays before you use them. When you are declaring one-dimensional Arrays, you do not have to specify how many elements are going to be in the list, but you can. Here are three examples of how you declare an Array.

```
Dim anArray(-1)
Dim anArray()
Dim anArray(0)
```

In the first two examples, I have declared "null" Arrays, or Arrays with nothing in them. They are both equivalent. You might be wondering why I used -1 to declare a null Array rather than 0; that's because when you refer to positions in an Array, you start counting with the number 0, not the number 1. This means that in the third example, I declared an Array with 1 item, not 0. So the first item in an Array is numbered 0, the second item is numbered 1, and so on.

If I declare an Array for four items, I can assign values to those items as follows:

```
Dim x as Integer
Dim anArray(3) as String
Dim aString as String
anArray 0 = "First item"
anArray 1 = "Second item"
anArray 2 = "Third item"
anArray 3 = "Fourth item"
```

Note that to declare an array of four items, I do not place the number 4 in the parentheses of the Dim statement. Instead, I use 3 because this number represent the value of the upper bound of the Array, not the number of elements in the Array. The number of elements in a one-dimensional Array is equal to the number of the upper bound of the array plus one. (See the section "Ubound.")

Using the preceding example, if I want to assign the value of the second item in the Array to the variable aString, I do this:

```
aString = anArray 1
```

ReDim

After you have declared an array, and even after you have populated the array with elements, you are able to resize the array with ReDim. It works just like Dim does, except that you can do it anywhere in the body of a method. If the array already has items in it, ReDim preserves the value of those that are within the range of the new values.

Ubound

If you want to find out the index of the last item in an Array, you can use the Ubound function. Ubound comes from "upper bound," which was mentioned earlier. Ubound is not an `Array` function. It's one of a list of global functions provided by REALbasic that are always accessible. `Ubound` takes an `Array` as a parameter and returns an integer that represents the upper bound of the `Array`.

```
Dim x as Integer
Dim anArray(3) as String
x = Ubound(anArray)
```

The value assigned to x is 3. Again, this does not mean that there are three items in the `Array`—there are actually four items. What it means is that the index of the last item is 3.

You can also use `Ubound` to get a reference to the last element in `Array`.

```
Dim aString as String
Dim anArray(1) as String
anArray(0) = "One"
anArray(1) = "Two"
aString = anArray(Ubound(anArray)) // aString = "Two"
```

`Ubound` can also be used for multidimensional arrays as well. You have to specify the dimension whose upper bound you want. See "Multi-Dimensional Arrays" for an example.

Insert, Append, and Remove

When you have a one-dimensional null `Array`, you can't use the assignment method from the earlier example because the actual memory has not been allocated for individual items. In other words, `anArray(0)` doesn't exist yet. One way to assign values to a null `Array` is with the `Append` method. This can be used on any one-dimensional `Array` as a means of adding one more item. It is one of three `Array` subroutines along with `Insert` and `Remove`. The following replicated the `Array` from the previous example.

```
Dim x as Integer
Dim anArray(-1) as String
anArray.Append "First Item"
anArray.Append "Second Item"
anArray.Append "Third Item"
anArray.Append "Fourth Item"
```

You can use the `Remove` subroutine to delete any element of the `Array` by passing it the position to remove. Add the following code to remove the second item in the list:

```
anArray.Remove 1 // "Second Item" is deleted
```

If you change your mind and want to add it back, use `Insert`.

```
anArray.Insert 1
```

Note that these are called as subroutines of the `Array`, which is different than `Ubound`, which is a global function that is used with `Arrays`. This is also a good illustration of the difference between subroutines and functions. Subroutines do not return a value, and the parameters are usually not inside of parentheses. Functions do return values and the parameters are always enclosed in parentheses.

Pop

Pop is related to Ubound and allows you to use an Array like a stack. A stack is a list of values. In stack terminology, you push a value onto the stack and then you pop it off. You use append to push a value onto the stack. You use Pop to remove the last value of the stack and return a reference to it. Stacks allow you to manage Last-in/First-out (LIFO) lists, which are a common programming technique.

```
Dim anArray(-1) as String
Dim aString as String
Dim x as Integer

anArray.append("Dog")
anArray.append("Cat")
anArray.append("Pheasant")

aString = anArray.Pop // aString  = "Pheasant"
x = Ubound(anArray) // x = 1 because "Pheasant" has been popped
```

IndexOf

IndexOf is an Array function that returns the position of a particular value in the array. IndexOf can work on arrays of different types as long as the type used by the indexValue is the same type as the Array itself.

```
anArray.IndexOf(indexValue as [?], [StartPosition as Integer]) as Integer
```

IndexOf is used to search for a value in an Array. It's usually used with an Array of objects rather than scalar values, and it can also be used in combination with the Sort method to sort a list of objects. You pass a value to be searched for and the function returns the position in the array where that term appears. If the value doesn't exist in the Array, −1 is returned.

```
Dim anArray(-1) as String
Dim Position as Integer

anArray = Array("Dog", "Cat", "Pig")
Position = anArray.IndexOf("Cat") // Position = 1
Position = anArray.IndexOf("Pigeon") // Position = -1
```

You can also start your search anywhere in the Array by passing the StartPosition parameter. This might be useful if you are trying to find the same value, but in more than one position in the array.

```
Dim anArray(-1) as String
Dim Pos1 as Integer
Dim Pos2 as Integer

anArray = Array("Dog", "Cat", "Pig", "Snake", "Cat", "Lizard")
Pos1 = anArray.IndexOf("Cat") // Pos1 = 1
Pos2 = anArray.IndexOf("Pigeon",Pos1+1) // Pos2 = 4
```

Note that I added 1 to the value of Pos1 as the starting position for the second IndexOf function, otherwise it would return the same value for Pos2 that it returned for Pos1.

The Array Function

A third way of assigning values to an Array is with the Array function. This works only with one-dimensional Arrays (just like Append). You provide a list of values as parameters to the Array function, and it returns an Array containing those values. When you use the Array function with a non-null Array, the original Array is overwritten. If you declare the Array with four items, use the Array function with a list of three items; the resulting Array will have three items:

```
Dim anArray(3) as String
Dim aString, bString as String
anArray = Array("One", "Two", "Three")
aString = anArray(0) // aString = "One"
bString = anArray(2) // bString = "three"
```

Assignment by Reference

You can also assign the value of one Array to another. When I defined data types and variables, I said that the variable represents a value of a particular data type and that when you reference the variable, you are referencing the value. The value of the variable is stored at some address in your computer's memory, so when the computer retrieves the value, it first has to find the address and then return the value stored at that address. All this works quietly behind the scenes with intrinsic data types. When you assign the value of one variable to another (when the variable represents a data type), the second variable is separate and distinct from the first. For example, consider the following assignments.

```
Dim a,b as Integer
a = 5
b = a
a = 7
```

In the first assignment, I set the value of the variable a to 5. Then I set the value of variable b to 5 as well. I then modify a so that its value is now 7. After having done this, the value of b is still 5. Now consider the following example:

```
Dim anArray(-1) as String
Dim bArray(-1) as String

Dim aString as String
anArray = Array("One", "Two", "Three", "Four")
// bArray 'points' to anArray; it is not a copy
bArray = anArray
anArray.append "Five"
aString = join(bArray)// equals "One Two Three Four Five"
```

In this example, I declare two Arrays. I populate the first Array with four elements and then assign bArray the value of AnArray. Afterwards, I append another element to anArray. At this point, I convert the values of bArray into a string. If Arrays worked like a normal data type, we would expect bArray to have four elements, which is how many elements anArray had when bArray was assigned the value of anArray. But it doesn't work that way. When you convert bArray to a string, you find that it includes the "Five" element, too, just like anArray does. How can this be?

The reason is that when you say "bArray = anArray" you're not actually setting the value of bArray like you set the value of a data type. Remember that an Array is a series of elements or a group of variables, rather than just one variable. This means that the variable anArray and bArray don't represent a value per se. Instead, they point to a location in memory where the list of values is stored. When you write "bArray = anArray" you are saying that bArray points to the same location in memory that anArray does.

Contrast that behavior with this:

```
Dim anArray(-1) as String
Dim bArray(-1) as String
Dim aString as String
anArray = Array("One", "Two", "Three", "Four")
bArray = Array("Cat", "Dog", "Pigeon", "Rat")
// bArray 'points' to anArray; it is not a copy
bArray(0) = anArray(0)
anArray.append "Five"
aString = join(bArray) // "One Dog Pigeon Rat"
```

Now what do you expect will happen? When you display the list of bArray's values in a string, this is the list you will get: "One Dog Pigeon Rat". When referring to a specific element in an Array, it's like referring to a variable that represents the value of a data type. It works just like normal assignment does with data types. There's a word for this. The Arrays I've used in the example are references to a value, and not the value itself. As you will see in upcoming chapters, all objects are references, so they exhibit this same behavior. There are also times when you can get a data type variable to act like an object in this sense, using a parameter keyword ByRef, which is discussed in more detail in the section on object-oriented programming.

Multidimensional Arrays

Thus far, you've seen one-dimensional `Arrays`, but `Arrays` can actually have up to 20 dimensions. It is probably most common to see a two-dimensional `Array` that presents the equivalent of a grid of values. The first dimension represents the number of rows in the grid and the second dimension represents the number of columns.

```
Dim anArray(2,1) as String

anArray(0,0) = "First row, first column"
anArray(0,1) = "First row, second column"
anArray(1,0) = "Second row, first column"
anArray(1,1) = "Second row, second column"
anArray(2,0) = "Third row, first column"
anArray(2,1) = "Third row, second column"
```

You can also use `Ubound` with multidimensional `Arrays`, as long as you specify the dimension whose upper bound you want to know. The first dimension is referenced by the integer 1, and so on.

```
Dim x,y as Integer
x = Ubound(anArray, 1) // x = 2
y = Ubound(anArray, 2) // y = 1
```

As I said, you can have up to 20 dimensions in your `Array`. Of course, thinking about the array in terms of rows and columns goes out the door.

```
Dim anArray(2,1,1) as String

anArray(0,0,0) = "Some value"
anArray(0,0,1) = "A different value"
anArray(0,1,0) = "A different dimension"
// etc.
```

Sort and Shuffle

The `Sort` function sorts the values in an `Array` in ascending order. It works only with one dimensional arrays that are strings, integers, singles, and doubles.

```
anArray.Sort
```

`Shuffle` does the opposite and mixes up the elements in the `Array`:

```
anArray.Shuffle
```

Split and Join

`Split` and `Join` are from a set of functions that operate on strings that are always available in REALbasic.

`Split` works on a string and converts it into an `Array`, based on a delimiter that is passed to it. By default, the delimiter is a space. Also, like many functions of this sort that operate on strings, there are two ways of using the `Split` function:

```
Split(aString as String, [aDelimiter as String]) As String()
```

```
aString.Split([aDelimiter as String]) As String()
```

With `Join`, you can combine an `Array` of strings into a single string while inserting a delimiter between each element in the `Array`. Like `Split`, if the delimiter is not specific, a space is used.

```
Join(anArray() as String, [aDelimiter as String])
```

```
Dim anArray(-1) as String
Dim aLongString as String
Dim count as integer
Dim combined as String

aLongString = "this*is*a*sentence"
anArray = Split(aLongString, "*")
count = Ubound(anArray) + 1
```

You can also split a string with an empty delimiter (""), which will create an `Array` of characters.

```
anArray=Split("I am happy.", "")
```

`anArray(0)` is "I", `anArray(1)` is " ", and `anArray(2)` is "a", and so on.

```
combined = join(anArray, " ")
```

Using Arrays with Methods

`Arrays` can also be used as parameters in methods and as the return value of functions. There are two ways to pass `Arrays` as parameters:

```
Sub TestSub(anArray() as String)
```

Or

```
Sub TestSub(ParamArray as String)
```

Using either of these techniques when creating a method will enable you to pass an `Array` as a parameter. Note that when you pass the `Array` as a parameter, you do not need to use parentheses of any sort. Just pass the name of the `Array`.

```
Dim anArray(-1) as String

anArray.Append("One")
TestSub(anArray)
```

To get a function to return an array, the return value has to designate the data type of the return value, as is normally the case, followed by an empty set of parentheses:

```
Function TestFunc(aString as String) as String()
```

Then, when you call this function, the value returned is an `Array`:

```
Dim anArray(-1) as String

anArray = TestFunc("Some text")
```

Flow Control—Conditionals

We use conditional statements in every day life all the time. Things like, "if you don't clean up your room, you're grounded." Or, "If you loved me, you would." There are always at least two parts to it. The first is the statement of the condition, the "if you…" part. The second is the statement that describes what happens if the condition is met.

If…Then

`If…Then` is a simple statement and a real workhorse. It works like this:

```
If 1 > 2 Then
    // do something interesting
End If
```

If…Then…Else

`If…Then…Else` is the enhanced version of `If…Then`. Parents sometimes use an abbreviated form of this conditional, the old "clean up your room, or else." While leaving off the rest of the sentence does lend dramatic intensity when chiding your child, it has little effect when programming. The `If…Then…Else` statement provides a response whether the expression evaluates to `True` or `False`.

```
If 1 > 2 Then
    // do something interesting
Else
    // do something even more interesting
End If
```

If…Then…Elseif…Then

The addition of `Elseif` to the vocabulary means that you can write as many conditional statements as you care to type. As soon as one of the conditions evaluates to `True`, the code exits the statement. The optional `Else` serves as the catch-all, handling "all other" situations.

```
If 1 > 2 Then
   // do something interesting
Elseif 2 = (1 + 1)
   // do something even more interesting
Else
   // do something for all the conditions you haven't thought of
End If
```

Select Case

Writing out long lists of If…Elseifs can be tedious. There's a lot of typing to be done and it can be hard to read. REALbasic provides the Select…Case statement as a much more efficient and manageable alternative. As the name implies, Select is designed to provide a list of conditions to be evaluated, called Cases. The code in the first Case to evaluate to True is executed; then the program resumes operations after the end of the statement. This means only one of the conditions is acted upon, even if there are more than one condition that would evaluate to True.

```
Dim I as Integer
Dim b as Boolean
i = 2
Select Case i
Case 1
  b = False
Case 2
  b = True
Case 3
  b = False
Else
  b = False
End Select
```

In this example, you see the basic syntax of the Select statement. It always starts with Select Case followed by a variable or expression. When it is a variable, like it is in the previous example, you are testing for the value of the variable i. The following Case statements represent the alternative actions to be taken, depending on what the value of i is. In this case, i equals two, so the program first evaluates Case 1, which can be read as "In the case that i is equal to one." It doesn't equal one, so the next Case is evaluated. Because i does, in fact, equal two, the program executes the code that follows, setting the value of b to True. After that code is executed, all other processing of the Select statement ends.

Because the Select statement stops as soon as it finds a Case that evaluates to True, it will stop checking Cases at the first instance and will ignore the following cases, regardless of their status.

```
Select Case True

Case (1 > 0)
  // True
Case (2 > 0)
  // True
Case (3 < 0)
  //False
End Select
```

In this example, a series of three expressions are being evaluated to see if they are True. The first two Cases are True—one is greater than zero, and two is also greater than zero. The program will evaluate the first Case, execute the code for that Case, and then skip the rest to pick up processing after the end of the Select statement.

This can be used to your advantage, as long as you have the expressions evaluated in the proper order. The following example uses a Select statement to simplify the process of testing whether a value falls within a range.

```
Dim x as Integer
Dim s as String
x = 5
// x > 4 and x <= 5
Select Case True
Case x > 7
  s = "x is greater than 7"
Case x > 6
  s = "x is greater than 6"
Case x > 5
  s = "x is greater than 5"
Case x > 4
  s = "x is greater than 4" // 5 is greater than 4
Case x > 3
  s = "x is greater than 3"
Case x > 2
  s = "x is greater than 2"
Case x > 1
  s = "x is greater than 1"
Else
  s = "x is less than or equal to 1"
End Select
```

This is the equivalent to the following:

```
Dim x as Integer
Dim s as String
x = 5
// x > 4 and x <= 5
Select Case True
```

```
case x > 7
  s = "x is greater than 7"
case (x > 6) and (x <= 7)
  s = "x is greater than 6"
case (x > 5) and (x <= 6)
  s = "x is greater than 5"
case (x > 4) and (x <= 5)
  s = "x is greater than 4"// 5 is greater than 4
case (x > 3) and (x <= 4)
  s = "x is greater than 3"
case (x > 2) and (x <= 3)
  s = "x is greater than 2"
case (x > 1) and (x <= 2)
  s = "x is greater than 1"
else
  s = "x is less than or equal to 1"
end Select
```

In both cases, the value for s is "x is greater than 4". In this example, you are really testing to see if x is greater than 4 and less than or equal to 5, but by taking advantage of the way the Case statement works, you are able to write it in a much more streamlined way.

Flow Control—Loops

The previous section discussed one form of flow control—conditionals. It's called flow control because the code that gets executed after the conditional is dependent on what the conditional evaluates to: either True or False. It's like a switch on a train track where a single track splits into two separate tracks. The position of the switch determines which track the train will take. There's another kind of flow control that involves doing the same task one or more times in sequence. In this case, the program loops and repeats a certain series of steps, based upon some condition.

Do...Loop

The simplest loop of all is the Do...Loop, which kind of reads like a sentence: "Do loop." Because no other information is passed, REALbasic just starts to loop and will loop indefinitely unless you exit from the loop in some way. As you loop and perform your calculations, after you have met the condition you want, you use Exit to exit the loop.

```
Dim x as Integer
Dim anArray as Integer
x = 0
Do
  x = x + 1
  If x = 50 Then
```

```
      Exit
    End If
    anArray.append(x)
  Loop
```

The last number in the array is 49.

Do...Loop Until

As in the previous example, you most often loop until some kind of truth condition is met, so there are two variants of the Do...Loop statement, which take into consideration this truth test: the Do Until...Loop statement and the Do...Loop Until statement. Do Until does the truth test at the beginning of each cycle of the loop, whereas the Do...Loop Until does the test at the end. You can almost always use whichever you choose, but there are some times when it makes more sense to use one over the other.

```
Dim x As Integer
Dim anArray(-1) as Integer
x = 51

Do
  x = x * 2
  anArray.append(x)
Loop Until x > 50
```

There is only one item added to the Array, and the value is 102.

Do Until...Loop

Now, do the same loop, but use Do Until...Loop instead.

```
Dim x As Integer
Dim anArray(-1) as Integer

x = 51

// No values will appear in the ListBox1 because the value of x is tested at the
beginning of the loop
Do Until x > 50
  x = x * 2
  anArray.append(x)
Loop
```

No values appear in the Array. This is the key difference between the two and why you have to pay attention when using them; where the test is made makes a big difference in the outcome.

For Each...Next

For Each...Next iterates through each element in an `Array`. Declare a variable of the same type as the `Array` and use it as a temporary holder for each item in the `Array`:

```
Dim anArray(-1) As String
Dim newArray(-1) As String
Dim s As String

anArray = Array("one", "two", "three", "four")

For Each s in anArray
  newArray.append(s)
Next
```

This creates an exact copy of the first `Array`. It returns four rows, one for each item in the array. When using this construct, you do not need to concern yourself with how many items are in the `Array`, nor do you have to keep track of any numbers.

For...Next...Step

There are times, however, when you need to loop through something that is not an `Array` and for which you cannot use the previous construct. One example is if you wanted to identify where in a string a particular character appears. There are built-in functions to help you do this in REALbasic, but I'll show you how to do it with a `For...Next` loop.

```
Dim aString as String
Dim anArray(-1) as String
Dim x,y as Integer
Dim result as integer

aString = "abcdefg"
anArray = split(aString, "")
y = Ubound(anArray)
For x = 0 to y
If anArray(x) = "c" then
  result = x + 1 // result is 3
  Exit
End if
Next
```

There are a few things to point out in this example. The first is that I add 1 to the value of x when assigning the result. This is because arrays are zero based, but that is typically not how we identify the position of characters in a string in everyday life (nor in the not-everyday life of REALbasic, either, when working with **EditField** controls). Because c is the third character of the alphabet, I add one to the value of x.

Second, I have used Exit to terminate the loop early. If I know there is only one value I'm searching for, or if my goal is to find only the first value, then it does me little good to continue to iterate all the way to the bitter end. Exit solves that problem.

Moving Up and Down: To and DownTo

```
Dim anArray(-1) as String
Dim newArray(-1) as String
Dim s as String
Dim x, y as Integer
Dim result as String

anArray = Array("one", "two", "three", "four")



y = Ubound(anArray)

For x = 0 To y
  newArray.append anArray(x)
Next


For x = y Downto 0
  newArray.append anArray(x)
Next
result = Join(newArray, " ")
// result = "one two three four four three two one"
```

Adds eight lines altogether, from one to four and then from four back down to one.

Skipping Rows: Step

By default, For...Next loops increment or decrement in steps of one, but it doesn't have to be that way. In fact, even though the previous examples have all used integers, you are not required to use integers and can just as easily use doubles. Step determines how much you increment the value represented by the variable x in these examples.

For example, if you wanted to read every other item in an Array, you would write it like this:

```
Dim anArray(-1) as Integer
Dim x,y as Integer
Dim sum as Integer

sum = 0
anArray = Array(1,2,3,4,5,6)

y = Ubound(anArray) // equals 5
```

```
For x = 0 To y Step 2
    sum = sum + anArray(x)
Next
```

In this example, you iterate through six numbers, incrementing the value for x by 2 each time. The first time you go through the loop, x is equal to zero. The value for anArray(0) is 1, so the variable sum is equal to 1. When it loops through the second time, x is now 2 and the value for anArray(2) is 3, and this value is added to the sum variable, and so on through anArray(4) until the value for sum equals 9. The last item in the array is not accessed because when 2 is added to 4, the value is 6, which is outside the bounds of the array.

While...Wend

While...Wend works very much like Do...Loop. The expression is evaluated at the start of each loop with a slight difference. Do...Loop will execute a loop UNTIL an expression evaluates to True, which means that as soon as it is True, execution of the loop stops. While...Wend loops while a condition is True. Much like Do...Loop, you have to pay attention to when the expression will evaluate to True.

```
Dim myArray(-1) as String
Dim newArray(-1) as String

Dim x, y as Integer

myArray = array("one", "two", "three", "four")


y = ubound(MyArray)

x = 0
// This While...Wend statement works
While (x <= y)

  newArray.append MyArray(x)
  x = x + 1

Wend

x = 0
// This While...Wend throws an error
While (x <= y)
  x = x + 1

  newArray.append MyArray(x)
```

```
  Wend

Exception err
  ListBox1.addRow str(x)
```

It's best to look at this output directly.

```
newArray(0) = one
newArray(1) = two
newArray(2) = three
newArray(3) = four
newArray(4) = two
newArray(5) = three
newArray(6) = four
newArray(7) = 4
```

As you can see, when the value of x is incremented before the Append method is called; the loop displays the values as expected. When the value of x is incremented after the Append method is called, the loop starts with two, then throws an error on the last loop.

It is important to pay attention to when and where the test expression is evaluated.

Using Loops

When a loop executes in REALbasic, it takes over your application and the user is not able to interact with the user interface at all. For short loops, this isn't even noticeable to the user, but longer loops can make the interface slow and jerky. The way to solve this is to put long loops into a thread, which is discussed in more detail in Chapter 5, "Designing a Desktop Application."

Nesting Loops

All these loops can be nested. Again, this is best shown in an example:

```
Dim m,n,x,y as Integer
n = 10
y = 10

for x = 0 to y
  for m = 0 to n
    If m = 5 Then
       Exit
    End If
  next
  // program starts here after Exit is called
next
```

The `Exit` statement causes looping to stop prior to meeting any of the conditions you've established for the loop. The program starts executing right after the loop in which the `Exit` statement was called. If you have a loop nested inside another loop and you call `Exit` inside the nested loop, the program will continue execution within the outer loop.

Variants

A `Variant` is a special kind of data type. In fact, it's really a class, in contrast to a data type, but in the effort to make things easier for you, you use a `Variant` just like you use a data type when it comes to declaring it.

What's special about a `Variant` is that it is a data type that can hold any kind of data. It doesn't care if it's a string, an integer, or even an object. After you have declared the `Variant`, it can accept any data type.

```
Dim v as Variant
Dim i as Integer
Dim s as String

i = 1
s = "One"

v = i

MsgBox v.StringValue

v = s

MsgBox v.StringValue
```

As you can see in this example, the same `Variant` accepted assignment of data that was an integer and a string. It also provides a method `StringValue` that returns the value of the `Variant` expressed as a string (which is one of those things that makes it really more of a class than a data type).

A `Variant` has the following properties that are used to access the data the `Variant` represents as different types. Remember that because a `Variant` can be any type, you'll need to do some things when working with them.

Variants and Operators

`Variants` can be used in place of data types in many cases. If a method calls for an integer as a parameter, you can pass a `Variant` instead. `Variants` also work with operators, but you have to be careful. Because operators can be overloaded, you need to make certain that the operator will work the way you think it will.

```
Dim v as Variant
Dim w as Variant
Dim i as Integer
Dim j as Integer

v = 2
w = "3"

i = v * w // i = 6
j = v + w // j = 23
```

In this example, I started with two Variants, v and w. v was assigned the value of an integer and w was assigned the value of a string. When I multiplied v times w, I got the value of 6, which is what I would expect when multiplying the two times three. When I add the Variants v and w, I do not get the answer five. Instead, I get the value 23.

The reason for this is that the + operator is overloaded for strings. When REALbasic encounters that operator with two Variants, it has to choose whether to use the + operator for adding two integers or the + operator for concatenating two strings. Because * is not overloaded for strings and there is no ambiguity, REALbasic uses the integer value for both Variants. In the case of the + operator, REALbasic defaults to treating them like strings and concatenates 2 and "3" to make 23. It then coerces the string 23 into an integer.

Properties

Variants all have the following properties, which allow you to access the value of the Variant in whichever data type you choose:

```
aVariant.BooleanValue As Boolean
aVariant.ColorValue As Color
aVariant.DateValue As Date
aVariant.DoubleValue As Double
aVariant.IntegerValue As Integer
aVariant.ObjectValue As Object
aVariant.StringValue As String
```

Not every variant value can be expressed in all the options you have for expressing them. For example, if you create this Variant:

```
Dim v as Variant
Dim o as Object
v = 1
o = v.ObjectValue
```

There really is no ObjectValue for v, because the Variant v represents an integer and an integer is one of REALbasic's intrinsic data types. If you test to see if the object is Nil, you'll see that it is not Nil, but you can't do anything with it. Before accessing a property such as `ObjectValue`, you would probably want to check to see what type the underlying object or data type is prior to accessing one of these properties directly. You can do this with the `VarType` global function, or the `Variant` function `Type`.

`DateValue` returns a `Date` object. See the discussion of the `Date` class to see how the different values of a `Variant` are returned when the underlying object is a `Date`. The reason a `Variant` returns a `Date` is for the sake of compatibility with Visual Basic, which has a `Date` intrinsic data type.

Methods

The following methods are available to `Variants` as well.

```
aVariant.Equals(aVariant as Variant) as Boolean
```

This method tests to see if one `Variant` is equal to another. "Equality" is a little different when talking about `Variants`. Consider the following example.

```
Dim v as Variant
Dim w as Variant
Dim b as Boolean


v = 2
w = "2"
b = v.Equals(w) // b equals True
```

Even though v and w started off as different types (an integer and a string), they are still viewed as equal by a `Variant` because their `IntegerValue` and `StringValue` are the same.

```
aVariant.Hash() as Integer
```

According to the documentation, `Hash` returns an integer that is guaranteed to be unique for integers and colors. It is also guaranteed to be unique for objects that are in existence. From my experience, it also generates unique values for strings and floating-point values.

```
Dim v as Variant
Dim w as Variant
Dim x,y as Integer
Dim b as Boolean


v = 2
w = "2"
x = v.hash() // x = 13074
y= w.hash() // y = 50
b = (x=y) // b is false
```

As you can see from this example, if we use the same `Variants` from the previous example that evaluate to `True` when using the `Equals` function, we get different values for their hashes. You can use the hash value to assess equality in a slightly different way than you can with the `Equals` function. In this case, because v starts off as an integer and w starts off as a string, a different hash value is generated. When you test for the equality of the hash, you will find that they are not equal.

```
aVariant.isNull() as Boolean
```

If a `Variant` has been declared, but has had no value assigned to it, the `isNull` function will return `True`. Otherwise, it's `False`.

```
aVariant.IsNumeric() as Boolean
```

This tests to see whether the value stored by the `Variant` can be expressed as a number, regardless of whether it was originally a string.

```
Dim v as Variant
Dim w as Variant
Dim b,c as Boolean

v = 2
w = "2"
b = v.isNumeric() // b is True
c = w.isNumeric() // c is True
```

In both cases, v and w, `isNumeric` returns `True`.

```
aVariant.Type() as Integer
```

Returns the integer value that represents the `Variant` type. See the section "VarType" for details about what the integers mean. This function is sensitive to the type of the original value the `Variant` was set to.

```
Dim v as Variant
Dim w as Variant
Dim x,y as Integer

v = 2
w = "2"
x = v.type() // x is 2, which means Integer
y = w.typoe() // y is 8, meaning String
```

VarType

There is a global function, `VarType`, that you can use to determine what kind of data is contained in a `Variant`. You pass a `Variant` as parameter to the `VarType` function, and it returns an integer that will tell you what type the data is, as follows:

0	Nil
2	Integer
5	Double or Single
7	Date (An object, not a Data type, but is included for Visual Basic compatibility. Recall that VB treats dates as data types.)
8	String
9	Object (In very early versions of REALbasic, 13 was returned for an Object.)
11	Boolean
16	Color

Consider the following example:

```
Dim result as Integer
Dim v as Variant
Dim i as Integer
i = 1
v = i

result = VarType(v)
```

In this case, `result` equals 2.

```
Dim result as Integer
Dim v as Variant
Dim s as String

s = "One"
v = s

result = VarType(v)
```

And in this case, `result` equals 8.

When to Use Variants

When I first started writing this section, I had to dig around a lot of old code of mine to see if I had ever used one. I had, in fact, used them on a few, limited occasions.

The problem, as I understood it then, is twofold. First, because `Variants` can hold data of any type and return it as any type, there's a lot of overhead required to manage this process. This makes `Variants` slower than using the actual type. The second problem is that if your program is well designed, you should always know what kind of data to expect. If you are effectively using the object-oriented features of REALbasic, you really won't ever need them because classes, subclasses, and interfaces provide you with some of the same flexibility as a `Variant`, but in a way that is more manageable over time.

Does that mean you should never use `Variant`s? No, not at all. There are many situations where you will need to get a string representation of an integer, for example. The most common reason is that you have an integer and you want to display it in your program, and this requires that you convert it to a string first to display it.

There are a couple of ways to do this. The first is with the `Str` function, which we discussed in the "String" section. `Variant`s offer a second way of doing it.

```
Dim v as Variant
v = 100
EditField1.text = v.StringValue
```

Here you can see that by using a `Variant` instead of an integer, it's a fairly straightforward process to accomplish that. Here's how the same thing looks using the `Str` Function:

```
Dim i as Integer
i = 100
EditField1.text = Str(i)
```

Because I wasn't really a big fan of `Variant`s, I decided to do some tests using integers to see just how much slower the code that used `Variant`s was, and this is what I found:

- Assigning an integer value to a variable declared as a `Variant` is, indeed, much slower than assigning an integer value to a variable declared as an integer.

- Converting an integer to a string is much slower using `Str()` than it is using `Variant`'s `StringValue()`.

- `Str()` is so much slower than `StringValue()` that if you have an integer that needs to be viewed as a string (usually this is to show it in an **EditField** on screen), it makes sense to use a `Variant` because when you look at it from the perspective of both assignment and conversion, `Variant`s are faster. In other words, this:

  ```
  Dim v as Variant
  Dim s as String
  v = 100
  s = v.StringValue()
  ```

  is faster than this:

  ```
  Dim i as Integer
  Dim s as String
  i = 100
  s = Str(i)
  ```

When coercing a single integer, the speed difference isn't enough to notice, but nevertheless, a `Variant` *is* faster. Go figure.

Modules

Technically speaking, modules aren't object-oriented, but they are included in REALbasic because there are times when the formalisms of object-oriented programming make easy things a little harder or more tedious to do. If you're a Java programmer, you should note that as I write this, REALbasic does not have the equivalent of class methods, but modules can serve the same purpose, by making methods, properties, and constants available without having to instantiate a class.

In addition to allowing you to create your own modules, REALbasic provides some modules "free of charge," making them available to your application at all times. I want to examine one built-in module in particular to start, and then follow that up with an example of how to create a custom module.

Built-in Modules

REALbasic supplies several built-in modules, most of which I will write about in future chapters. However, one built-in module is worth discussing now. The module is called REALbasic. You really don't need to know much about this module other than it exists. The biggest impact to you, the developer, is that there are a variety of functions that are always available to you, and these functions are part of the REALbasic module. Because they are global in scope, you do not even have to refer to the REALbasic module. All you need to refer to is the function itself.

One feature of modules that differs from that of classes is that modules are always available to your application. Unlike classes (as you will see) you do not need to instantiate modules or do anything like that. If you create a module for an application, the methods and constants and properties you create will be available from the moment the program starts to the moment it stops running.

This is exactly how the REALbasic module works. It exposes a long list of functions (methods) whose scope is public and which you can call at any time.

These functions fall into two categories. One group provides various mathematical abilities, and the other group deals with strings.

Built-in Math Functions

REALbasic provides a set of built-in math functions that sometimes perform the same function as one of the operators, and some that provide additional functionality.

Trigonometry

```
REALbasic.Sin(aValue as Double) as Double
REALbasic.Asin(aValue as Double) as Double
REALbasic.Tan(aValue as Double) as Double
REALbasic.Atan(aValue as Double) as Double
REALbasic.Cos(aValue as Double) as Double
REALbasic.Acos(aValue as Double) as Double
```

REALbasic's trigonometry functions accept a double as the parameter and return the answer in terms of radians (double data type). This works like Visual Basic functions of the same name, with no surprises. To convert from radians to degrees, multiply radians times 180/PI.

Log, Exp

```
REALbasic.Exp(aValue as Double) as Double
REALbasic.Log(aValue as Double) as Double
```

Log returns the natural logarithm of a number, and Exp returns *e* raised to the power passed in the parameter (e is approximately equal to 2.71828).

isNumeric

```
REALbasic.isNumeric(anyVariable) as Boolean
```

You can pass any object or value to isNumeric to ascertain whether it represents a numeric value. Pass an object and the answer will be False, but you can also pass strings, integers, singles, and doubles and get an answer back. If you pass an integer, the answer is always True. If you pass a string, it tests to see if the string can be converted into a numeric value. This means that isNumeric will return True for a string like "505" but not for a string like "five". It also works with scientific notation.

Abs, Sign

```
REALbasic.Abs(aValue as Double) as Double
```

The Abs function takes any number as a parameter and returns the absolute value of that number. Recall that the absolute value of a number is the original number, minus its sign. It works with integers, singles, and doubles.

```
REALbasic.Sign(aValue as Double) as Integer
```

The Sign function tells you the sign of a number, whether it is positive or negative or zero.

Negative	-1
Zero	0
Positive	1

Max and Min

```
REALbasic.Max(aValue as Double, bValue as Double) as Double
REALbasic.Min(aValue as Double, bValue as Double) as Double
```

Max and Min return the highest or lowest value of a pair of numbers, respectively.

Round (Not to Be Confused with Rnd, Which Generates a Random Number)

```
REALbasic.Round(aValue as Double) as Double
```

The data type returned by the `Round()` function is always a double, even though rounding a number means, by definition, that the answer is going to be an integer. Despite the fact that it's a double, you can safely supply a variable with an integer Data type to be assigned the result of the function.

`Round` rounds numbers in the traditional way. If the decimal is .5 or higher, it rounds up; otherwise, it rounds down.

Ceil

```
REALbasic.Ceil(aValue as Double) as Double
REALbasic.Floor(aValue as Double) as Double
```

`Ceil` rounds up to the next highest integer, regardless of the value to the right of the decimal point. Therefore, 1.1 and 1.6 would both be rounded up to the value of 2.

`Floor` operates in the opposite way, rounding down regardless of the value to the right of the decimal point.

Val, CDbl

```
REALbasic.Val(aValue as String) as Double
```

Both `Val` and `CDbl` take a string as an argument and return the numeric value. The only difference between `Val` and `CDbl` is that `CDbl` takes into consideration the locale and will return the right value for strings that use characters other than . as a decimal. For example, in France a comma is used rather than a period to indicate a decimal.

```
Dim aNum as Integer
aNum = Val("200") // aNum equals 200
```

Pow, Sqrt

```
REALbasic.Pow(aValue as Double, aPower as Double) as Double
REALbasic.Sqrt(aValue as Double) as Double
```

The `Pow` function is the equivalent of the ^ operator. It takes an number and raises it to the power passed in the `aPower` parameter.

```
Dim result as Double
Dim root as Double
result = Pow(2, 2) // result = 4
root = Sqrt(result) // root = 2
```

Bin, Hex, Oct

```
REALbasic.Bin(aValue as Integer) As String
REALbasic.Hex(aValue as Integer) As String
REALbasic.Oct(aValue as Integer) As String
```

If aValue is equal to 65 (which happens to be the ASCII value of the letter A, also referred to as the decimal value), the results of these functions would be as follows:

```
Dim s As String
Dim i As Integer

i = 65
s = Hex(i) // s equals "41"
s = Oct(i) // s equals "101"
s = Bin(i) // s equals  "1000001"
```

Built-in String Functions

A string is a series of characters. Because the only thing a computer can deal with are numbers, the computer stores strings as numbers. The way that these numbers are mapped to refer to strings is called the string's encoding. ASCII was once a common form of encoding and it uses one byte for each string. The problem is that it limits the number of characters you can represent (256 or so). For English-speaking people, that's just fine, but it's too constraining for speakers of other languages. For years, Macintosh and Windows used different approaches to solve the encoding problem, which made it absurdly complicated to deal with text and to exchange it between the two platforms. It wasn't a problem only for Macs and Windows machines—Unix-like systems had the same problem, so the industry resolved it by establishing a new standard (or collection of standards) called Unicode. Unicode comes in different varieties: UTF-8, UTF-16, and UTF-32.

The default encoding for REALbasic is UTF-8. UTF-8 is a little smarter than the other two formats because it only uses the number of bytes that are necessary to represent a character. It represents the ASCII character set exactly like the ASCII character set does, using 1 byte. If you are using ASCII-only characters, you'll have no problems with UTF-8.

The old Macintosh default format was called MacRoman. In Windows, it was Latin-1. Both shared the common ASCII characters, but the numbers they used to represent character values higher than 127 were different.

In UTF-8, those non-ASCII values are all treated the same and are represented by 2 (or more) bytes. This means that in some cases, the number of characters in a string is the same value as the number of bytes in the string, but in other cases, it's not. This is an important distinction to understand when dealing with the global functions REALbasic provides for manipulating strings, because the encoding of the string itself sometimes impacts your approach. Another complicating factor when dealing with strings is that letters come in different cases. REALbasic is not case sensitive, which means that by default, it doesn't care about whether you use A or a. It's all the same to REALbasic. In this way, REALbasic is shielding you from some of the underlying complexity of dealing with strings. Even though REALbasic doesn't care whether you use A or a, the number the computer uses to represent the uppercase A is different from the one used to represent the lowercase a.

Although REALbasic doesn't care, you sometimes care, so REALbasic provides you with ways to search or manipulate strings in case-sensitive ways, too.

I have already reviewed comparison operators and how they work with strings. The problem, or limitation, with operators are that they are not case sensitive and you have no way of changing that. Although they may be convenient to type, they may not always be appropriate. To address this, the following functions provide the same functionality as the operators, plus some, including the capability to make comparisons that are case sensitive.

Most of these functions have two versions. When there are two versions, the second version's name always ends with a B to signify binary, which means that it treats the string as binary data rather than as text.

What this means, in practice, is that the standard or normal version of this function treats the string like text, which mean that each letter is counted once; REALbasic doesn't differentiate between uppercase and lowercase letters. When treated as binary, REALbasic pays attention to the actual binary values. The practical implication in most cases is that it makes the function case sensitive. A secondary side-effect of case sensitivity is that it doesn't differentiate between characters encoded in 1 byte versus those encoded to 2 or 4 bytes.

I'll point out the different results as I review each function.

The functions are also callable as global functions, like the math functions in the previous section, but you can also call them as if they were functions of string. This is one of those inconsistencies implemented in REALbasic for convenience, but which has the potential for creating confusion in someone trying to understand the difference between a data type and an object. Normally, a scalar data type, like a string, would not and could not have methods, but strings, like `Variants`, do have methods you can call.

Again, these should all be very familiar to Visual Basic programmers.

StrComp

```
REALbasic.StrComp(aString as String, bString as String, Mode as Integer) as
Integer
```

```
aString.StrComp(bString as String, Mode as Integer) as Integer
```

`StrComp` compares two strings to see if they are equal. Now, having said that most of these functions that operate on strings have two versions, I start off with one which has only one. You do, however, have control over case sensitivity be setting the mode of the function.

```
Dim aString as String
Dim bString as String
Dim mode as Integer
Dim result as Integer
```

```
mode = 1
aString = "Aaron"
bString = "aaron"

result = StrComp(aString,bString, mode)
```

In this example, result is equal to 0 because we used a mode of 1, which is the mode used when you do not care about case (it's also called the lexicographic mode). Using the same example, but setting mode equal to 0 will cause the result to be -1. The uppercase A has an ASCII value of 65, which is lower than the ASCII value of a" which is 97. Uppercase values are always lower than lowercase values.

When you used the arithmetic operators on strings, a Boolean value was returned, but when using StrComp, an integer is returned and the answer can be one of three values.

Here are the equivalent responses for each type. Assuming the value in the left column is true, the value in the right column indicates the value returned by StrComp.

a<b   -1

a=b   0

a>b   1

a<=b   -1, 0

a>=b   0, 1

The point of this is to remind you that StrComp doesn't offer exactly the same set of features as the operators do. If you want to establish that a string is less than or equal to a value, StrComp will return either -1, or 0.

InStr, InStrB

```
REALbasic.InStr([startPosition as Integer], sourceString as String, searchString
as String) As Integer

aString.InStr([startPosition as Integer], searchString as String) as Integer
```

Sometimes you need to find out if a character or a series of characters exist inside a string, and the InStr function can help you do this.

InStr is used to find a substring—to see if a string of characters exists within another string.

```
result = InStr(sourceString, searchString)
```

InStrB searches binary data, not strings. This is important when using Unicode, because some strings are represented by multiple bytes. If you are searching Unicode text and you are using InStrB, you will get the byte position of where the value was found, and not the character position.

Here's an example of the impact this has when searching for a character in a string that contains the Unicode character "©".

```
Dim s as String
Dim position as Integer

S = "© Copyright"

position = InStr(s, "C") // position equals 3
position = InStrB(s, "C") // position equals 4
```

When searching with the normal InStr, the function returns a position of 3, because "C" is the third character in the string. However, when using InStrB, the value returned is 4 because "©" takes up 2 bytes rather than 1 byte. Remember that we are using UTF-8 in these examples because that is the default encoding in REALbasic. If the string were encoded in UTF-16, where all characters are encoded in two bytes, the answer would be 6.

Earlier, I showed an example of how to search for the position of a character within an array of characters. The functionality of that example mimics the functionality of InStr. One reason you would use InStr would be to test to see if a character was included in another string. Now the string could be anything you want—it doesn't actually have to be a word or anything like that.

The following example searches through an array of characters to find the first punctuation mark. In this case, I am using InStr to test to see if one character belongs to a set of characters which, in this case, are characters used in punctuation.

```
Dim punct as String
Dim paragraph as String
Dim isPunct as Integer
Dim position as Integer
Dim chars(-1) as String
Dim x,y as Integer

punct= ".,?!;:[]{}()"
paragraph="This is a paragraph. It has two sentences!"
chars = Split(paragraph, "")

y = Ubound(chars)
For x = 0 to y
 isPunct = InStr(punct, chars(x))
If isPunct > 0 then
position = x // position equals 19
Exit
End If
Next
```

Using the same basic concept, you can use a combination of Arrays and InStr to split a sentence or paragraph into words.

```
Dim chars(-1) as String
Dim char_buffer(-1) as String
Dim word_buffer(-1) as String

Dim sentence as String
Dim whitespace as String
Dim pos as Integer
Dim x,y as Integer

whitespace = "   " + chr(10) + chr(13)
sentence = "There are four words."

chars = Array(sentence, "")
y = Ubound(chars)

For x = 0 to y
  pos = whitespace.InStr(chars(x))
  If pos > 0 Then
    word_buffer.append(join(char_buffer, ""))
    ReDim char_buffer(-1)
  Else
    char_buffer.append(chars(x))
  End if
Next
```

When this is run, the `word_buffer` Array has four elements, as follows:

```
word_buffer(0) = "There"
word_buffer(1) = "are"
word_buffer(2) = "four"
word_buffer(3) = "words."
```

You should notice that it leaves the period at the end of "words.", but it would be a simple matter of including punctuation characters in the list of characters to test for. This process is often called tokenizing, and it can be useful in a lot of situations.

Mid

```
REALbasic.Mid(sourceString as String, StartPos as Integer) as String
REALbasic.Mid(sourceString as String, StartPos as Integer, Length as Integer) as
➥String

REALbasic.MidB(sourceString as String, StartPos as Integer) as String
REALbasic.MidB(sourceString as String, StartPos as Integer, Length as Integer) as
➥String
```

`Mid` and `MidB` are used to copy a portion of one string into another. You specify the string from which to copy, the position from which to start copying, and, if applicable, the length of text to be copied. If the length value is omitted, it copies the entire string from the start position onward. The first character is numbered 1.

```
Dim aString as String
Dim result as String

aString = "Cow."
result = Mid(aString, 2, 2) //result equals "ow"
```

Left

```
result = Left(sourceString, Length)
result = LeftB(sourceString, Length)

result = aString.Left(Length)
result = aString.LeftB(Length)
```

Left, like Mid, finds a string within a string. Unlike Mid, the start position for Left is always the start of the string, and you have to define the length of the substring.

Right

```
result = Right(sourceString, Length)
result = RightB(sourceString, Length)

result = aString.Right(Length)
result = aString.RightB(Length)
```

Use Right to copy a substring of a specific length, starting from the right side of the string.

Asc

```
REALbasic.Asc(aCharacter as String) as Integer
REALbasic.AscB(aCharacter as String) as Integer
```

The following example compares the results of using Asc and AscB on three different characters. The first is a character from the ASCII character set, the lowercase "a", the others are characters used in UTF-8, the default encoding for REALbasic strings.

```
Dim aString, bString, cString as String
Dim result as Integer

aString = "a"
bString = "©"
cString = " "

result = aString.Asc // result = 97
result = aString.AscB // result = 97
result = bString.Asc // result = 169
```

```
result = bString.AscB // result = 194
result = cString.Asc // result = 8364
result = cString.AscB // result = 226
```

The answer for "a" is the same whether you are using Asc or AscB because "a" is an ASCII character and can be represented in 7 bits. The "©" character has a different value depending on whether you use Asc or AscB. Even though it can be represented in one byte, the reason it is different from the raw ASCII value is that it uses all 8 bits in the byte, whereas ASCII characters only use 7. The character " " requires two bytes to represent it. Asc returns the code point for the character, whereas AscB just returns the first byte.

Chr

```
REALbasic.Chr(aCodePoint as Integer) as String
REALbasic.ChrB(aCodePoint as Integer) as String
```

Chr takes a code point and returns a character as a string. It's the inverse of Asc.

```
Dim aString as String
aString = Chr(97) //aString equals "a"
```

Len

```
REALbasic.Len(aString)as Integer
REALbasic.LenB(aString)as Integer
```

Len counts the length of a string in terms of characters. LenB returns the length of a string in terms of bytes. For non-ASCII characters, this means that Len and LenB return different values.

```
Dim aString, bString, cString as String
Dim result as Integer

aString = "a"
bString = "©"
cString = " "
result = aString.Len() // result = 1
result = aString.LenB() // result = 1
result = bString.Len() // result = 1
result = bString.LenB() // result = 2
result = cString.Len() // result = 1
result = cString.LenB() // result = 3
```

In this example, you can see that using Len for the © returns a value of 1, whereas LenB returns a value of 2. Note that you can also use the global function for Len and LenB as follows:

```
result = Len(bString) // result = 1
result = LenB(bString) // result = 2
```

Str, CStr

```
REALbasic.Str(aNumber as Double) as String
REALbasic.Cstr(aNumber as Double) as String
```

Str and CStr return a string representation of a number. CStr is locale aware and will properly observe regional variations in the display of numbers. Both return the numbers in regular decimal format until the number grows too large, then it switches to scientific notation. The point the change occurs varies for integers and floating-point numbers. The following numbers are the first numbers that will be returned in scientific notation.

Integers: 1,000,001

Singles/Doubles: 1,000,000.0

```
Dim i,j as Integer
Dim s,t as String

i = 1000000
j = 1000001

s = Str(i) // s = "1000000"
t = Str(j) // s = "1.000001e+6"
```

Format

```
REALbasic.Format(sourceString as String, format as String) as String
```

In many cases, the strings returned by Str and CStr will be good enough, but if you need to have the strings formatted in a particular way, you should use Format. It is extremely flexible.

Placeholder	Description
#	Display a digit if present. If the digit is not present, nothing is displayed. If you use the format string ##### for the number 3, only the number 3 will show up.
0	Displays a digit if present, 0 if not present. This can be used to force a floating-point number to display a fixed number of places after the decimal point. Contrast this with #. If you use 00000 for the number 3, then 00003 will be displayed.
.	Displays the decimal point. Therefore, #.00 always displays the number with two numbers to the right of the decimal point. The number 100 is displayed 100.00.
,	Displays the thousands separator. Best used in conjunction with #. If you are expecting values from 0 to 1,000,000, use #,###,### for the format string because # doesn't display if there is not a digit for it.

Placeholder Description

%	Displays the number as a percentage, meaning it is multiplied by 100 and followed by the % character (with no space in between).
(	Displays open paren.
)	Displays close paren.
+	Displays the sign of the number, showing + if the number is positive and - if the number is negative.
-	Displays a - when a number is negative, and nothing when a number is positive.
e	Displays the number using scientific notation. You place it immediately following the number, not before it. Used in conjunction with # and ., which specify how many decimal places to show. It defaults to +, but you have the option of using e+ for clarity. It is required for negative.
\{character}	The escape character \ causes the following character to be displayed as is. Use it to place a dollar sign in front of currency: \$##.00.

The formatting string can consist of three different formatting patterns, separated by a semicolon. The first item applies to positive numbers, the second to negative numbers, and the third to the number zero.

Here are some examples of common formats:

Drop the values after the decimal point:

```
Dim d as Double
Dim s as String
d = 100.1

s = Format(d, "#") // s = "100"
```

Avoid using scientific notation (in contrast to using Str):

```
Dim i as Integer
Dim s,t as String
i = 1000001

s = Format(i, "#.###") // s = "1000001."
t = Str(i) // t = "1.000001e+6"
```

Control how scientific notation is displayed:

```
Dim d as Integer
Dim s,t as String
d = 134000

s = Format(d, "#.##e+") // s = "1.34e+5"
t = Format(d, "#.#e+") // s = "1.3e+5"
```

Display currency in a way that always shows the number of cents:

```
Dim d as Double
Dim s as String
d = 100
s = Format(d, "\$#.00") // s = "$100.00"
```

Display currency so that negative values are surrounded by parentheses (somewhat like the accounting format in Microsoft Excel):

```
Dim d as Double
Dim s as String
d = -1003
s = Format(d, "\$#,###.00;\$(#,###.00)") // s = "$(1,003.00)"
```

Display a 10-digit telephone number properly:

```
Dim d as Double
Dim s as String
d = 8005551212
s = Format(d, "(###)\ ###\-####") // s = "(800) 555-1212"
```

Note that spaces are ignored unless you escape them with \, just like any other character. Also, if you pass this format a number that is longer than 10 digits, Format displays those numbers within the parentheses. Using the preceding example, if I equaled "80055512120", the value for s would be "(8005) 551-2120". This is true whether you use "#" or "0" (and both work for this, by the way).

Trim, RTrim, LTrim

```
REALbasic.Trim(sourceString as String) as String
REALbasic.RTrim(sourceString as String) as String
REALbasic.LTrim(sourceString as String) as String
```

Trims whitespace on strings. Trim removes whitespace on both sides of the string. RTrim and LTrim trim only the right or left side of the string, respectively. Whitespace characters are include spaces, tabs, and end-of-line characters.

```
Dim aString as String
Dim newString as String
aString = "  myString  "

newString = Trim(aString) // newString = "myString"
newString = RTrim(aString)// newString = "  myString"
newString = LTrim(aString) //  newString = "myString  "
```

UpperCase, LowerCase, TitleCase

```
REALbasic.UpperCase(sourceString as String) as String
REALbasic.LowerCase(sourceString as String) as String
REALbasic.TitleCase(sourceString as String) as String
```

UpperCase and LowerCase convert a string to all lowercase or uppercase characters, respectively. TitleCase capitalizes the first letter of each word in a string. Computer programmers are often under the impression that it is proper to capitalize the first letter of each word in a string when representing a title, but that's not the case, so don't use this to capitalize the title of the English term paper you have to turn in because English teachers don't see it that way. Not every word in a title gets capitalized, so use it at your own discretion.

CountFields

```
REALbasic.CountFields(sourceString as String, delimiter as String) as Integer
REALbasic.CountFieldsB(sourceString as String, delimiter as String) as Integer
```

CountFields divides up a string into fields based on a certain delimiter. CountFieldsB treats the delimiter as binary data, which is most commonly useful when considering case when determining the delimiter (for example, when you want to split the string on "a" and not "A").

```
Dim i as Integer
i = CountFields("a*b", "*") // i = 2
```

It also counts empty (null) fields.

```
Dim i as Integer
i = CountFields("a*b*", "*") // i = 3
```

NthField

CountFields is almost always used in conjunction with NthField. NthField returns a string based on the field position of the string.

```
Dim s as String
s = NthField("a*b", "*", 2) // s = "b"
```

Much of the functionality of the CountFields/NthField functions can now be better managed with the Split, Join, and Array functions used with Arrays (see the section "Arrays").

The reason I usually avoid CountFields and NthField for this kind of activity is that arrays make it easier to iterate through a string with many fields, and it also seems to be a little more efficient. Compare the two techniques:

```
Dim s as String
Dim anArray() as String
anArray = Split("Some really long string", " ")

For Each s in anArray
    // do something with s;
Next
```

Creating the StringParser Module

In the following sections I am going to step through the process of creating a new module. For this example I want to build on some of the string processing examples I have already used and package them in a module.

The module will provide two functions for parsing (or tokenizing) a string. In the InStr example, I split a string up into words. In this new module I will create functions that can split a string up into words as well as sentences.

The first step in this process is to create a new project in the IDE and add a new module. I'll show you how to do that momentarily.

Create a New Project

In the original example, I used InStr to split up a string into an Array of sentences. Now I want to take that example and create a module that is more flexible and that can split up a string into an Array of words.

```
Dim punct as String
Dim paragraph as String
Dim isPunct as Integer
Dim position as Integer
Dim chars(-1) as String
Dim x,y as Integer

punct= ".,?!;:[]{}()"
paragraph="This is a paragraph. It has two sentences!"
chars = Split(paragraph, "")

y = Ubound(chars)
For x = 0 to y
 isPunct = InStr(punct, chars(x))
 If isPunct > 0 then
   position = x // position equals 19
   Exit
 End If
Next
```

In the original example, I had a local variable, punct, which was a string that held all of the punctuation characters. Because the punctuation characters will not ever change, it makes more sense for punct to be a constant, which will be the first step. The other advantage of using a constant is that we need to make the function that tokenizes the string more generic so that it can also be used to split a string into words as well. After punct is out of the method and into a constant, it will be easy to create other constants, too, that contain sets of characters to split the string with.

Creating a Module

Throughout the rest of this chapter, I will step you through the process of creating a module.

If the IDE is already open, select **New Project** from the **File** menu. A window will pop up so that you can select the kind of project. Select **Desktop Application** and click **OK**. If the IDE is not already open, launch it and it will open to a new desktop application project by default.

After you have the new project in place, you can create a module in the IDE by clicking the **Add Module** icon in the **Project Tab**. Whenever a new module is added, it is given the name **Module1** by default (if **Module1** already exists, it will be called **Module2**, and so on). To change that name, select the module in the **Project Editor** on the left side of the **window**. When you have done this, the **Properties pane** to the right will list the properties for this particular module; the only module property available is the module name. You should click the name in the **Property pane**. The IDE will automatically select the entire word for you. At this point, type in a more descriptive name, such as `StringParser`. You can either press Return or click somewhere else in the IDE and the new name is automatically updated. You will then see your new module in the **Project pane**, as shown in Figure 2.4.

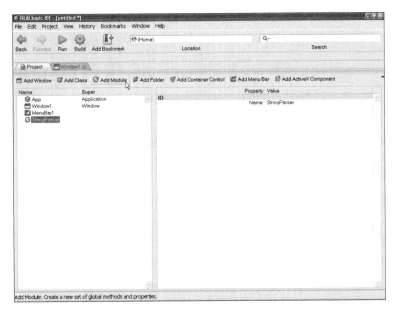

Figure 2.4   Project window showing the StringParser module.

Double-click the **StringParser** module in the **Project Item pane** and a new **StringParser Tab** will appear revealing an empty module.

The StringParser tab will have a **Module Toolbar** at the top, with the rest of the area divided into two regions. To the left will be a list of constants, methods, and properties that have been declared for this module, and to the right will be the **Code Editor**. You can add one of four things to a module: a new constant, a new method, a new property, or a new note. The purpose of a note is purely for documentation. The only programmatic features that you can add to a module are constants, methods, and properties. For starters, we'll have a constant and some methods.

Access Scope

All module members have an access scope and now that we are creating a module, we need to cover the topic in a little more depth. In the sections on developing classes, I will talk about scope in much more detail because it's an important part of object-oriented programming and the idea of encapsulation, and it also has a slightly different meaning when dealing with classes. Access scope in modules works differently than it does in classes. Module members must be designated one of the following three:

Global

Global scope means that the constant, method, or property can be accessed anywhere in your program at any time by using the member's name, and without reference to the module itself. Shortly, I will add a new constant called `kPunctuation`. This means that I can get the value of that constant at any time by referring to the name of the constant, like so:

```
aVar = kPunctuation
```

You can name a constant anything you'd like, as long as it contains legal characters. However, it's a good idea to use a naming convention when naming them so that you can more readily tell constants from other variables in your code. Some people use all uppercase letters, but I find that hard to type and harder to read. Another common approach is to begin the name of the constant with the letter k, followed by the name of the constant. The first letter after the k is capitalized.

Protected

A `protected` member means that it can be accessed anywhere, but only in reference to the module name. That means we would have to modify the previous statement to look something like this:

```
aVar = StringParser.kPunctuation
```

Although the constant can still be accessed from anywhere in your programming code, you will have to prepend the module name before calling it.

My advice would be to avoid `Global` scope if at all possible because of the potential for namespace collisions. In other words, if you create a module with a long list of global constants and properties, you run the risk that some time in the future you will import a module that also uses one of the same names for a global constant or property and this will make the compiler unhappy. Even though you have to do some extra typing when the scope is set to `Protected`, it reduces the chances of having a collision.

This is the closest thing to the use of namespaces that REALbasic currently has (something I consider to be its biggest weakness to date—and something which will likely be corrected in the future).

Private

A `Private` member can be accessed only by a member of the same module. If I were to make the kPunctuation constant `Private`, the only time I could access the value of that constant would be from within a method defined in the module itself and not elsewhere. This would not likely be used with a constant. The only time it would really make sense would be with a method or a property. I'll show you an example of why this is useful when we create the methods for our new module.

Constants

Now that the module has been created, it's time to add some members to it. The first thing to add is the constant kPunctuation. Because it might be useful for other parts of my application to read the value of kPunctuation, there's no need to make it `Private`. I avoid `Public` scope in modules as much as possible because it leaves open the possibility of potential namespace collision. That leaves us with a scope of `Protected` for our new constant.

When you create a constant in the IDE, you are provided fields to enter the data so you do not have to declare it in the same way that you declare a local variable. There is a field for the constant name and for the default value of the constant. If you only enter the default value for the constant, that is the default value that will be associated with that constant whenever it is accessed from any location.

However, there is also a **ListBox** beneath the editing area that allows you to enter values that are specific to particular platforms or locations. Important: these values override whatever value you have established for the constant in the primary editing area. In particular, if you establish add a new value that is for **Any** platform and the **Default** language, this value is the value that will appear when accessed, and not the original value entered in the primary editing area. In fact, those parameters mimic how the value in the primary editing area is used. Use the **ListBox** to provide platform or location-specific values, and the primary area for more general or universal values.

All text that is used in your application for communicating with the user should be stored as a constant in a module. This means that if you decide to distribute your application in France, you can easily add a French translation of your messages that will be localized for French users. It also ensures consistency in your interface. It's easy for slightly different phrases to be used in different parts of your application, which can create a perception of sloppiness and poor quality.

For now, we will be using only the punctuation characters common to the English language, so we will use those as a default. If, at some later time, we decide we need to add additional characters for other languages, we can simply come back and add them here.

Name the constant kPunctuation in the **Constant Name** field, and type in
., ?! () [] into the **Default Value** field. To the right of the **Constant Name** are three buttons. Select the button in the middle, with a yellow triangle. This sets the scope to Private. Below the **Default Value** Field, check to see that the string button is selected because the data type of our constant will be a string (it should be selected by default).

There you have it. Your module now has a constant as shown in Figure 2.5.

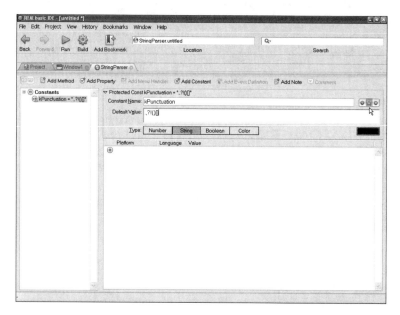

Figure 2.5   The kPunctuation constant added to your StringParser module.

Properties

Although I won't be adding a property to the module at this time, remember that module properties have scope, much like class properties have. Global module properties are accessible by all parts of your application. If your application has preferences, making those preferences available through global module properties can be convenient.

Protected module properties are available everywhere as well. The difference is that you have to use the module name when accessing the property.

Private module properties are available only to methods of the module.

Adding a Method

The next step in the process of creating our module is to add the methods that will be used to generate the tokenized string. The way the method will work is that it will take a string as a parameter and then return the string tokenized into an `Array`. Because it will return a value, we will be creating a function. The next question is to decide what the scope of the function should be. In this particular example, you can probably approach this a few ways and do just fine, but what I will do is create one function that is the generic function used to tokenize all the strings. It will take the string to be tokenized as a parameter, as well as a string that represents the characters to split with string with. If we are tokenizing the string into sentences, the `kPunctuation` constant will be the string we pass here.

I want to set the scope of this method to `Private` so that only methods defined in this module will be able to access it. In a moment, I will also create a method that is private in scope that will be used specifically for tokenizing strings into sentences.

Because my first method is `Private`, I don't need to worry about any naming conflicts, so I will name the method `Split`, because that is descriptive. Note that there's already a global function named `Split`, so I would possibly have problems if I set the scope of this method to be `Public`. `Protected` would avoid problems as well, but for now I'll stick with `Private`. The reason I say possibly have problems is because methods can exist with the same name as long as their signatures are different—meaning as long as they take a different set of parameters. This is an example of polymorphism and is explained in more detail in the object-oriented programming section.

Adding the "Split" Method

To add a method in the IDE, first get back to the **Properties** tab and then double-click the **StringParser** module. Now, instead of adding a property, select **Add Method**.

When you are adding a method, the interface is similar to that used when adding a constant. There is a field for entering the method name, the parameters that will be passed to the method and the return type. If the method is to be a function, enter something into the return type field; otherwise, leave it blank. There are also the same three buttons next to the name that allow you to set the scope of the method.

Type `Split` into the method name field and select the `Private` button, which is a red circle with a horizontal line in the center. For parameters, type in the following:

```
aString as String, DelimiterList as String
```

In the return type field, type

```
String()
```

You don't need to name the variable in the return type field, you just need to specify the type. In this case, we will return a string `Array`, so we type in `String()`. If the value were just a simple string, we would only have to type in string.

You have now created the signature for the method. Right above the method name field, you should see

```
Private Function Split(aString as String, DelimiterList as String) as String()
```

Our added method at this point is shown in Figure 2.6.

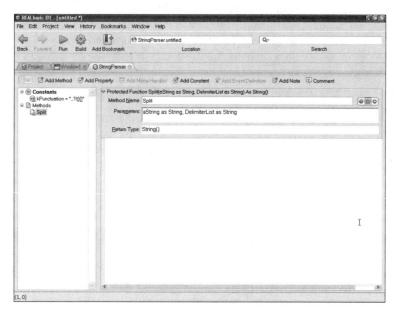

Figure 2.6   The Split method is added to StringParser,
but it still lacks the code to do its work.

Now, in the lower portion of the Editor you can write the code for this method, which follows:

```
Dim chars(-1) as String
  Dim char_buffer(-1) as String
  Dim word_buffer(-1) as String
  Dim x,y as Integer
  Dim pos as Integer
  Dim prev as Integer
  Dim tmp as String

  // Use the complete name for the global Split function
  // to avoid naming conflicts
  chars = REALbasic.Split(aString, "")
  y = ubound(chars)

  prev = 0
```

```
  for x = 0 to y
    pos = DelimiterList.inStr(chars(x))
    // If inStr returns a value greater than 0, then this character is a white
➡space
    if pos > 0 then
      word_buffer.append(join(char_buffer,""))
      prev = x+1
      redim char_buffer(-1)
    else
      char_buffer.append(chars(x))
    end if
  next

  // get the final word
  word_buffer.append(join(char_buffer,""))

  return word_buffer

exception err
  break
```

In addition to Split, I will add another method called SplitSentences. This method will be Protected and will call the Private Split method. Following the steps outlined above, create the following method in the IDE:

```
Protected Function splitSentences(aString as String) As String()
  return StringParser.split(aString, StringParser.kPunctuation)
End Function
```

Now, anytime you want to take a string and split it up into individual sentences, just call the splitSentences function, like so:

```
Dim anArray(-1) as String
Dim s1, s2 as String

anArray = StringParser.splitSentences("This is a sentence. So is this.")
s1 = anArray(0) // s1 equals "This is a sentence"
s2 = anArray(1)// s2 equals " So is this"
```

I will also add a splitWords method that works just like splitSentences except that it splits the strings on whitespace rather than on punctuation. I need to create another constant, kWhiteSpace, that is a string containing space, tab, newline, and carriage return characters. Then I create the splitWords method, like so:

```
Protected Function splitSentences(aString as String) As String()
  return StringParser.split(aString, StringParser.kWhiteSpace)
End Function
```

Now that we have a `splitWords` method, we do even more. Just for fun, let's create a method that will capitalize a sentence in a way that will win the approval of English teachers everywhere (or will at least be better than the built-in `TitleCase` method). I'll use the set of guidelines I found in my dusty and possibly out-of-date AP Stylebook, which says that words of four letters or more should be capitalized, while words fewer than four letters long should not be capitalized unless they are the first or last word in the title. A good copyeditor will tell you that the rules are actually a little more complicated than that, but this is sufficient for my purposes.

I will make this function `Public`, so that it can be accessed in the same way that the regular `TitleCase` function is accessed.

```
Function TitleCaseAP(sourceString as String) as String
Dim word as String
Dim words(-1) as String
Dim x,y as Integer

words = StringParser.splitWords(sourceString)
y = Ubound(words)

For x = 0 to y
 word = words(x)
 If Len(word) >= 4 Then
    words(x) = UpperCase(word)
 Else
    If (x=0) Or (x=y) Then
     words(x) = UpperCase(word)
    Else
     words(x) = LowerCase(word)
    End If
 End If
Next
Return Join(words, " ")
```

There you have it. The one shortcoming is that it does not account for titles with colons or semicolons which, when encountered, cause the previous word to be capitalized as if it were the end of the sentence and the following word as if it were the beginning of one. If you recall, the `splitWords()` function doesn't strip out punctuation characters, so it would be easy to add a test for words that are fewer than four characters long. The test would be to check to see if the word ended with a colon or a semicolon. If it did, you can capitalize the word. You would also need to account for capitalizing the following word, too. The easiest (but not the most efficient way) would be to test the current word and the previous word to see if it ended with a colon or a semicolon, but that means you are testing the same word twice. A better way would be to declare a variable and set its value so that you would know if the current word directly followed a colon or semicolon. You could declare a variable as an integer, name it `previousColon`, and set its initial value to -1. When you encounter a colon or semicolon, set the value of previousColon to the value of x. During each loop (before testing the new word to see if it ends with a colon), check the value of previousColon and whether it is equal to x minus 1. If it is, then you know this word should be capitalized as well.

Summary

This chapter introduced you to several important elements in the REALbasic programming language. With this knowledge in hand, it would be possible to create an application in REALbasic, but there are some important topics to cover yet before you can unleash the full functionality of the language. REALbasic is an object-oriented language, and I have not yet discussed those features at length. The next chapter includes an introduction to object-oriented programming and discusses how it is implemented in REALbasic.

3

Classes and Objects

The Class Hierarchy

A former colleague used to say that he had "developed this new technology" whenever somebody in his department wrote a few lines of VBScript for the website. He is not the first person to use overly fanciful language to describe programming exploits. It happens all the time. Object-oriented programming is a particularly jargon-rich field of study, laden with ill-formed metaphors and polysyllabic titles. There was a time when object-oriented programming (OOP) advocates would say that OOP was easier to learn than more traditional styles of programming. I don't know if that is true; I suppose the fact that I have deferred the discussion of the object-oriented features until the third chapter of this book is some indication of how I feel about this subject.

One of the biggest challenges facing a novice programmer is the reality that knowing how to program and knowing how to program well are two different things. Learning a programming language is cut and dried (albeit a bit tedious at times). Learn the syntax and you've learned the language. It's very much a science. Doing it well, however, is much more like an art—something that is learned over time and something that you get a "feel for" that is often difficult to explain simply and clearly. In this chapter, I hope to provide an overview of object-oriented concepts and how they are implemented in REALbasic, and give some insight into strategies for executing your object-oriented programming effectively.

Cities are full of buildings, and each building has a particular street address, which can tell you how to find the building if you are looking for it. Computers have addresses, too, but instead of identifying buildings, these addresses point to locations in memory. Variables, properties, functions, and subroutines all reside at a particular address, too, when they are being used by your program.

When you declare a variable, you assign a type to the variable. To date, most of the variables in the examples have been one of REALbasic's intrinsic data types. When a variable is used in this way—pointing to an intrinsic data type—it's said to be a scalar variable. The variable represents the value that's stored at a particular location in memory.

Variables can also be used to represent objects. When they do, they aren't scalar variables anymore because an object doesn't represent a value in the way that an intrinsic data type does. The variable is said to be a reference to the object; it points to the location in memory where this object resides. An object is a collection of different things and can be made up of properties and various methods. In this respect it is like a module, but it differs from a module in some very important ways.

Suppose we have an object with two different properties, one called FirstName and the other called SecondName, both of which are Strings. Let's also say that we have a variable called Person that points to this object. Referring to the object itself doesn't refer to any particular value, because the object has multiple properties. This means that to access a particular property of an object, you need to refer to the object itself, plus the property. You do this using the familiar dot notation, like so:

```
Person.FirstName
```

This should look familiar because it's the way you refer to protected properties and methods of modules. The biggest difference is that you always have to refer to an object's members this way, even if the property is public.

Now knowing that an object is a collection of values is only a small part of the story. What makes objects powerful is that they are members of classes. To create an object, you must first create a class.

To explain what classes are conceptually, I'll return to the building and street address analogy. If you pull up to any address, you'll find a building. If you were to come visit me, you could drive until you reached my address; pull in the driveway and you'd be at my house. My house is a building, but it's a different kind of building than you might find down the street a bit where there is a grocery store and a gas station. Furthermore, my house is just one example of a particular type of house. Houses come in all styles—some are ranches and others are Cape Cod or Tudor styles.

Whether you are talking about houses or grocery stores or gas stations, every building has some things in common—a roof and some walls, for example. I live in a single-family residential neighborhood, so every building on my street is a house. The fact that it is a house means that in addition to a roof and some walls (which all buildings have), it also has at least one bedroom, a bathroom, and a kitchen, because buildings that happen to be houses all have those features.

If I were to try to systemize my understanding of buildings, I might start by classifying buildings into the different types of buildings and showing how they are related. A good way to do this is by organizing buildings into a conceptual hierarchy, like the one outlined in Figure 3.1.

Every node on this tree represents a type of building or, to use object-oriented terminology, a class of building. At the top of the hierarchy is the base class, and it has two subclasses—residential and commercial. You can say that the building class is the superclass of the residential and commercial classes. In addition to the super/subclass terminology, you also hear people refer informally to them as parent classes and child classes.

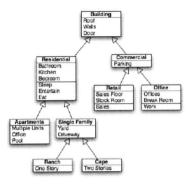

Figure 3.1   Different styles of houses can be organized in a hierarchy.

One way that we make these classifications is based on physical attributes of the buildings themselves—things such as walls and doors. At the same time, we also consider the kind of activity that takes place in them.

This isn't the only way to classify buildings. You might come up with a different hierarchy that's equally valid. For example, you might decide that the most important differentiating factor isn't whether a building is residential or commercial, but how many stories the building has. You might start off with building, and then branch to one-story buildings and multistory buildings, and go on from there.

Even the buildings themselves can be subdivided into smaller units. A house doesn't just sit empty. People live in them and do things. The house is organized into rooms and these rooms are designed for certain activities. In one room you cook, in another you watch TV, and so on. Some rooms have storage areas, such as closets and cupboards, and others have tools, such as stoves and refrigerators and washing machines.

The hierarchy shows classes of buildings, not particular buildings themselves. A description of a house is not any particular house; it's a description of what houses that are members of that class have in common. One way to think of classes is to think of them as a blueprint, or a design, for a building. You can build many houses using the same blueprint. If a class is analogous to a blueprint, an object is analogous to a particular house.

After you've driven to my house and you're standing in the driveway looking at it, you are looking at one particular instance of a house. There are other houses in the neighborhood that were built from the same plan, but they are filled with different people, doing different things.

One thing you may have noticed when I classified buildings and organized them into a hierarchy is that I didn't list all the features of each class of building at each level. At the top level, I said buildings have roofs, walls, and doors. At the second level of the hierarchy, I didn't repeat that they have roofs, walls, and doors because I wrote down only what was new and unique about the next group. The assumption is that the subclass has all the attributes of the superclass, plus some additional attributes that differentiate it from the superclass. To put it another way, the subclass inherits the features of the superclass.

Inheritance is a big deal, and it's just about the coolest part of object-oriented programming. In practical terms, this means that when you write your program, you organize your code into classes. The advantage of this kind of inheritance from a programmer's perspective is that it keeps you from having to rewrite as much code. The subclass inherits all the functionality of the superclass, so that means you don't have to write new methods in the subclass that replicate the basic functionality of the parent.

And this leads to the challenging part. It's up to you to decide how to organize your classes. You can do it any way you like, but you need to do it in a way that makes sense and in a way that maximizes code reuse (from inheritance). Knowing how to write the code that creates a class is only half the battle. Knowing what goes into the class is the hard part. There is no single solution; the answer is really dependent on the kind of program you are going to write. You have to figure out what makes the most sense for your application.

Again, I'll return to the house analogy. Inside my house, the downstairs is divided into six rooms: a living room, a dining room, a kitchen, a bedroom, a bathroom, and a laundry room. In the kitchen are cupboards. Some are full of food and others are filled with plates and dishes. There is a refrigerator, stove, and so on. Likewise, in the laundry room you'll find laundry detergent, and then there is the usual stuff that goes into a living and a dining room.

This makes sense—the reason I put the laundry detergent in the laundry room with the washing machine is because it's convenient and makes sense. Likewise, I put my clothes in my closet so that I can find them in the morning and get dressed.

That's exactly how object-oriented programming works, too. A class in object-oriented programming groups together information and instructions for what to do with the information. It's a place to store information of a particular kind, and a set of instructions for what to do with it. When you are creating classes, you have to decide what kind of information makes sense to be associated with what kind of tasks.

Although objects are capable of having properties, constants, and methods, they are not required to have them. A chair, for example, is an object. By definition, a chair doesn't do anything. It can only have things done to it. It can be sat upon. It can be held in place by gravity. It can be broken and it can be painted red. But it can't scoot itself up to the table, or teeter precariously on two legs, unless a child is in the chair to do the teetering. An object from the programming perspective can be dull and boring like a chair. It can be a thing, a set of values, or, as they are called in REALbasic and other languages, it can have properties.

An object can be nothing more than a set of properties. In this respect, an object is very similar to a struct or User Defined Type familiar to Visual Basic programmers. It can also have methods, constants, events, and menu handlers, all of which will be covered in due time.

There are some basic concepts to discuss first, and the best way to discuss them is to illustrate them by creating a class or two and looking at what we are doing. In particular, I want to discuss some important OOP concepts: inheritance, encapsulation, and polymorphism. Much like calling a new script a new technology, these words create a certain mysterious aura that make everything sound much more complicated than it is. Hopefully, after you've read this chapter you'll have enough mastery of REALbasic's flavor of object-oriented programming to use it with confidence.

Creating a New Class

A new class is created just like a new module. Open up a new project in REALbasic and click the **Add Class** button and a new class will be added, as shown in Figure 3.2. However, **App**, **Window1**, and **Menubar1** are classes, too. They are provided by REALbasic automatically, but everything you can do with this class we are about to create, you can do with them as well. These three classes will be covered in much more detail in the next two chapters.

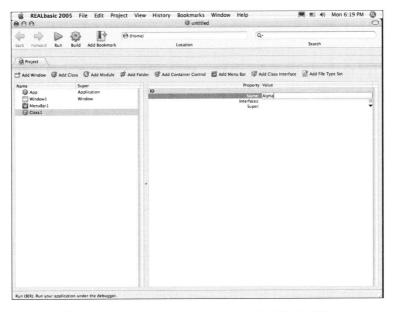

Figure 3.2   Creating a new class in the REALbasic IDE.

After you create this new class, select it, and change the name to `Alpha` in the **Properties pane** on the right side of the window. Double-click the **Alpha** class in the Project Editor to bring up the Alpha tab, as shown in Figure 3.3.

When you've done this, you'll see that you have additional buttons on the Code Editor toolbar. In addition to the familiar **Add Method**, **Add Property**, and **Add Constant**, you'll see **Add Menu Handler** and **Add Event Definition**. **Menu Handlers** and **Event Definitions** are special kinds of methods that I'll cover later.

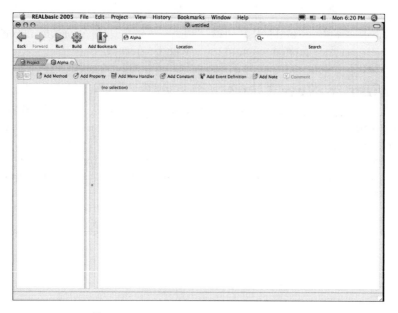

Figure 3.3   Editing code for the Alpha class.

The **Alpha** class won't do anything really useful. The purpose is to implement some methods and properties in such a way that you can see the different way that classes implement and use them. The first method to add is the getName method:

```
Function getName() as String
  Return "Alpha"
End Function
```

As you can see, this method returns the string "Alpha" when it is called.

Declaration and Instantiation

When you build a house, you start with the blueprints, but it's not a house until you build the walls, roof, and so on, and eventually people move in. I said earlier that a class is like a blueprint. Because the Alpha class is a blueprint, it needs to be built in order to be used. This is called *instantiation,* or creating an instance of the Alpha class. An instance of a class is called an *object.*

This is one area where classes differ from modules. You do not have to instantiate a module to have access to the methods and properties of the module. Instantiating an object is a two-part process. First, the object must be declared, just like variables are declared. The only difference is that the type of this variable is going to be the class name rather than one of REALbasic's intrinsic data types. The second step is the actual instantiation, the part where the "house is built." When you build a house, you need boards and nails. When you declare an object, you are setting aside space for the constants, properties, and methods of the class, and when you instantiate an object, you are filling up the space set aside with the constants, properties, and methods of the class. Again, it's like building a house—first the rooms are made, and then people move in to live in them.

```
Dim a as Alpha
Dim s as String
a = New Alpha()
s = a.getName() // s equals "Alpha"
```

The variable is declared with a `Dim` statement, and it is instantiated using the `New` operator. After the class is instantiated and assigned to the variable a, you can use dot notation to access the members of the class, much like you can access the members of a module. In this example, the method `getName()` is called and the value returned is assigned to the string s.

Always eager to provide help to those like me who have an aversion to extra typing, the engineers at REALbasic have provided a handy shortcut that combines these two steps into one (this works with data types, too).

```
Dim a as New Alpha()
Dim s as String
s = a.getName() //s equals "Alpha"
```

Constructors and Destructors

When operators were introduced, I said that they were basically functions. They are given input in the form of operands; the operator causes a calculation to be performed, and the results are returned. Because New is an operator, that must mean that it's a function, too. As you can see from this example, the value returned by the `New` operator is an instance of `Alpha`, which is assigned to the variable a. The reason I followed `Alpha` with parentheses when instantiating a is so that it will be more clear that it is acting as a function. You are, in fact, invoking a function when you use the `New` operator. Your ability to refer to the class name alone, without explicitly typing out the method, is a matter of convenience.

REALbasic (and other object-oriented languages) gives this method a unique name: `Constructor`. It is the `Constructor` method that is being called when you use the `New` operator. In many cases, the default `Constructor` is all you need—all it does is instantiate the object, setting aside space for properties and things like that, but not setting their value. You can add to this by implementing your own `Constructor`.

Right now, our `Alpha` class returns the string `"Alpha"` when we call the function `getName()`. Suppose that we want to be able to decide what value this function will return when we instantiate the object. The way to do this is to create a property, which will hold the value that the getName() function will return, and we will add a new Constructor method that will allow us to pass the string we want returned when we first instantiate the object.

The first step is to create the property, like you did when creating a module. Set the access scope of this property to Private and give it the name "Name", and a data type of string.

Next, add the method called "Constructor" (Constructors are always public). Do not specify a return value. Implement it as a subroutine (it knows automatically to return an instance of the class it's a member of).

```
Sub Constructor(aName as String)
  me.Name = aName
End
```

Finally, we need to update our getName() method.

```
Function getName() as String
    return me.Name
End
```

You have now implemented a new Constructor that takes a string as a parameter and assigns the value of that string to the property Name. Now, if you try to instantiate this class like you did before, you'll get an error. For you to instantiate it, you need to pass a string to the Constructor.

```
Dim a as Alpha
Dim s as String
a = New Alpha("Blue")
s = a.getName() // s = "Blue"
```

New in REALbasic 2005, you can set the values of properties implicitly when the class is instantiated, rather than explicitly as I did in this example. This is done by filling in the values in the Code Editor as shown in Figure 3.4.

In earlier versions of REALbasic, the Constructor method was named after the name of the class itself. So in this case, you can name the constructor "Alpha" and it would be called when the class is instantiated.

There is also a Destructor method that's called when the object is being purged from memory. It can be declared by calling it Destructor or by using the object name preceded by the tilde (~) character. For the **Alpha** class, you would name it "~Alpha". The default is to use the terms Constructor and **Destructor**, and I would recommend sticking with that—I only share the other method in case you encounter it in preexisting code.

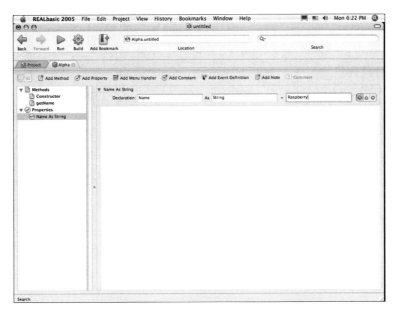

Figure 3.4   Set values for class properties in the Code Editor.

Garbage Collection

One thing you may have noticed is that I haven't had to say anything about how to manage the computer's memory in REALbasic. In programming languages such as C, much of the work you do centers on allocating memory for data and making sure that memory is freed up when you are done with it. In REALbasic, you don't have to worry about this very much because REALbasic uses a process called *garbage collection*, which means that it automatically purges objects from memory when appropriate. The operative phrase here is "when appropriate."

Garbage collection uses a process called *reference counting* to keep track of objects. Variables that refer to objects don't behave like scalar variables do. Although you may have two scalar variables whose value is "5", it does not mean that these two scalar values are references to the same location in memory. Objects, on the other hand, can easily have more than one variable serve as a reference to their location.

Reference counting refers to keeping track of how many variables (local variables and properties) reference a particular object. As long as at least one reference to an object exists, the object stays resident in memory. After the last reference goes away, the object is dumped. This is when the **Destructor** method is called.

In most cases you won't have to worry about memory, but there are some situations where references inadvertently do not go away. This can sometimes result in a situation where new objects are being instantiated while old objects are still hanging around in memory, which means that your program will consume larger and larger amounts of memory as the application runs. This is called a *memory leak*, and memory leaks are bad.

The trouble usually starts when you have two objects that each refer to each other. Because object **A** has a reference to object **B** and object **B** has a reference to object **A**, neither object is ever going to be garbage collected. The way around this is to implement a method for object **A** that explicitly sets the reference to object **B** to Nil. Do the same thing with object **B**. Now when object **A** is destroyed, the reference to object **B** is safely removed (or, more accurately, the reference count to object **B** is decremented).

Inheritance

Now you have a class that implements one method, and you know how to instantiate that class. One of the most powerful features of object-oriented programming is that you organize your classes into conceptual hierarchies, just like you can organize buildings into a conceptual hierarchy. One class can subclass another and when it does this, it inherits the members of the class from which it does the inheriting.

Although you are no doubt familiar with the idea of inheritance, object-oriented inheritance works a little differently than genetic inheritance does. First of all, people have two parents. I'm a mix of my dad and my mom; 50% of my gene pool comes from mom and 50% from dad. (I've often said that I have the distinct pleasure of having inherited all of my parents' worst qualities. In a remarkable reversal of fortune, my daughter has managed to inherit only the finest traits from her parents, mostly from her mom). REALbasic takes a simpler view of inheritance. There's only one parent, which is the superclass. In REALbasic, at the top of the family tree is the root class; **Object** and all other classes are subclasses of it.

In the object-oriented world, the child is called a subclass and the parent is referred to as the superclass. When you create a subclass in REALbasic, it automatically inherits all the methods and properties of the parent class. There is absolutely no difference other than their name.

Creating a subclass that doesn't do anything differently from the superclass is more or less a pointless exercise. The reason for creating a subclass is that you want to reuse the code you've written for the superclass, and then either add new capabilities or change the way certain things are done.

A child inherits all the features of the parent, but it can also add some new ones. In practice, this means that the subclass has all the methods, constants, and properties of the parent class (with a few exceptions), but it can also implement its own methods, constants, and properties. In this respect, at least, object-oriented inheritance isn't all that much different from the way parent-child relationships work with humans. That's why I always had to set the time on the VCR when I was growing up. My parents didn't know how to do it, but I did. In addition to the methods passed along by the parent, the child can have its own set of methods.

To create a subclass of **Alpha** in REALbasic, create a class as if it is a new class. Let's name it **Beta**, which can be done by typing the name into the **Properties pane**. There are two other properties listed in the pane that we have not discussed yet. After Name comes Interfaces, which I cover later, followed by Super. Setting the value of Super is how you designate this object's superclass, as shown in Figure 3.5. Type in **Alpha**, and you now have an official subclass of **Alpha**. It is identical in every way, except that it's called **Beta** instead of **Alpha**.

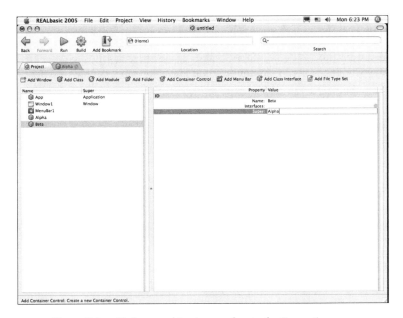

Figure 3.5   Define an object's superclass in the Properties pane.

```
Dim a as Alpha
Dim b as Alpha
a = New Alpha("Woohoo!")
b = New Beta("Woohoo!")
```

At this point, the only difference between a and b is their type (or class).

Object Operators

Now it's time to introduce some more operators that are used with classes. I've already introduced New. Two others are Isa and Is.

Isa is used to determine whether an object belongs to a class:

```
Dim t,u as Boolean
t = (a Isa Alpha) // t is True
u = (b Isa Alpha) // u is True
t = (a Isa Beta) // t is False
u = (b Isa Beta) // u is True
```

This is an example of the most basic feature of inheritance. A subclass is a member of the superclass, but the superclass is not a member of the subclass.

The related Is operator tests to see if one object is the same object as another one.

```
Dim t as Boolean
t = (a Is b) // t is False
```

Note that even though a and b both have the same values, they are different objects because they were both instantiated independently. Here's an example of when this test would return True:

```
Dim a,b as Alpha
Dim t as Boolean
a = new Alpha("Woohoo!")
b = a
t = (a is b) // t is True
```

Because b is a reference to a, it is considered the same object. In other words, both a and b point to the same location in memory. They do not simply share an equivalent value; they are, in fact, the very same object.

Adding and Overriding Methods

So far, I've created **Beta**, a subclass of **Alpha**, but that is all. Except for the type, there's really no difference between them. If you wanted to, you could add new methods to **Beta** that would be available only to **Beta** and not **Alpha**. This is easy enough to do—just add methods to **Beta** as you would to any class or module.

A more interesting thing you may consider doing is overriding an existing method.

Again, there is a shade of resemblance between object-oriented inheritance and human inheritance. Once in a while (as children are wont to do), the child decides to do something that the parent already does, but in a different way. For example, my father and I both go to church, but he goes to a Baptist church and I go to a Catholic one. In object-oriented circles, this is called overriding.

The way to override one of **Alpha's** methods in **Beta** is to implement a method with the exact (and I mean *exact*) signature as a method that is found in **Alpha**. Because **Alpha** implements only one method, getName() (well, two if you count the Constructor, which can also be overridden), we'll override getName() in **Beta**.

```
Function getName() as String
  Return "Beta says: " + me.Name
End Function
```

Now let's see how this works in practice.

```
Dim a as Alpha
Dim b as Beta
Dim s,t as String
a = New Alpha("Golly!")
b = New Beta("Golly!")
s = a.getName() // s = "Golly!"
t = b.getName() // b = "Beta says: Golly!"
```

Calling the Overridden Method

Normally, when you override a method, you want the new method to replace the overridden method, but there are also times when you want the new method to merely add a few steps to the parent method. You can do this by calling "super" on the method.

When deciding which method to call, REALbasic starts at the lowest level of the class hierarchy and looks to see whether the method is implemented there. If it is not, REALbasic checks the parent class, and so on, until it finds an implementation of the method. Because of this approach, as soon as it finds an implementation of the method, it stops looking and never touches any implementation further up the hierarchy.

Overloading

Overloading and overriding are two words that look alike, sound alike, and refer to similar things with markedly different behavior. That's a recipe for confusion if ever there was one. When you are creating classes and subclassing them, you will be making use of both overloading and overriding.

Overloading is associated with the idea of Polymorphism (who comes up with these words?). All that Polymorphism means is that you can have multiple versions of the same method that are distinguished according to the parameters that are passed to them.

Note that REALbasic does not pay any attention to the return value offered by a method when overloading methods. This means you can't do something like this:

```
Function myFunction(aString as String) as Integer
Function myFunction(aString as String) as String
```

and expect to be able to do this:

```
Dim i as Integer
Dim s as String
i = myFunction("Hello")
s = myFunction("Hello")
```

The only thing that counts are the arguments.

Now, when I instantiate the **Alpha** or **Beta** classes, I pass a string to the Constructor, and this is the value that the getName() method returns. Let's say for the moment that there are times when I want getName() to return a different value. One way to do it is to change the value of the property, but because that property is Private, it requires some extra steps, so we'll hold off on that approach for now.

Another way to do it would be to overload the getName() method, which means implementing another version of getName() with a different signature. Remember, a method signature refers to the collection of parameters that it takes. Because the original getName() doesn't take any parameters, we will implement a new version of getName() that takes a string as a parameter. For this example, implement the new method in **Beta**.

```
Function getName(aNewName as String) as String
    Return aNewName
End Function
```

Now let's see this overloaded method in practice.

```
Dim a as Alpha
Dim b as Beta
Dim s,t, u as String
a = New Alpha("Good morning.")
b = New Beta("Good night.")
s = b.getName() // s = "Good night."
t = b.getName("Hello.") // t = "Hello."
u = a.getName("Goodbye.") // Error!
// Won't compile because Alpha doesn't implement this method.
```

As you can see, REALbasic knows which version of getName() to call for the **Beta** class based solely on the parameters passed. In the first example, because nothing is passed, it returns the value of the property Name. When a string is passed, it returns the value of the string. Out of curiosity, I tried to pass a string to the **Alpha** implementation of getName(), and the compiler fell into all kinds of histrionics because **Alpha** doesn't implement a method called getName() that expects a string as a parameter. Remember, **Beta** is a subclass of **Alpha**. **Alpha's** methods are available to **Beta**, but **Beta's** aren't available to **Alpha**.

Casting

I alluded to the fact that a subclass is a member of the parent class, but the parent class is not a member of the subclass. This makes perfect sense, but it can at times make for some confusion, especially when dealing with overridden and overloaded methods.

I want to return to the **Alpha** and **Beta** classes from the previous examples and add a method to each one; this will illustrate the potential confusion (at least, it was confusing to me).

Alpha will add the following:

```
Sub TestMethod(a as Alpha)
```

Beta will add the following:

```
Sub TestMethod(b as Beta)
```

First, take a look at the following example:

```
Dim a as Alpha
Dim b as Beta
Dim s as String
a = New Beta("What's this?")
```

What is a? Is it an **Alpha** or a **Beta**? One way to tell would be to invoke the `getName()` method and see what is returned. If you recall, I overloaded the `getName()` method so that it accepted a string as a parameter.

```
s = a.getName("My String") // Error!
```

If you try to call the **Beta** method you'll get an error. That's because as far as REALbasic is concerned, a represents an **Alpha**. However, because you instantiated it as a **Beta**, you do have access to **Beta's** methods. You can do this by casting the a as a **Beta**.

```
s = Beta(a).getName("My String") // s equals "My String"
```

Reference the class to which you are casting the object, followed by the object surrounded in parentheses, and now you will get access to the methods of **Beta**.

Note that the following will not work:

```
Dim a as Alpha
Dim b as Beta
Dim s as String
a = New Alpha("What's this?")
s = Beta(a).getName("A String") // Error
```

The reason is that a is an **Alpha**, not a **Beta**. Recall that the superclass is not a member of the subclass.

```
Dim a as Alpha
Dim bool as Boolean
a = New Alpha("What's this?")
bool = (a Isa Beta) // bool is False
```

Oddities

When you subclass a class that has overloaded methods, if the subclass overloads methods, the superclass doesn't know about them. So if you instantiate the subclass but assign it to a variable as the superclass, the overloaded method can't be called from it (this contrasts with how overridden methods are handled, because you can call an overridden method in the same way and get the subclass implementation of it).

I'll provide an example of one way that really confused me for a few days until I realized what I was doing wrong.

An overloaded method is one that takes different arguments (but has the same name). An overridden method has the same signature (takes the same arguments), but is implemented differently. This applies to inheritance between a class and a subclass. An overloaded method is overloaded in the same class, and overridden method is overridden in a subclass.

Start with two classes, **Parent** and **Child**. Set the parent of the **Child** class to **Parent**. For both classes, implement a method called WhoAmI and one called GetName() as follows:

Parent:

```
Sub WhoAmI(aParent as Parent)
  MsgBox "Parent.WhoAmI(aParent as Parent) /" + _   "Parameter:
➡" + aParent.getName()
End Sub
Function getName() as String
  Return "Parent"
End Function
```

Child:

```
Sub WhoAmI(aChild as Child)
  MsgBox "Child.WhoAmI(aChild as Child) /" + _ "Parameter: " + aChild.getName()
End Sub
Function getName() as String
  Return "Child"
End Function
```

The MsgBox subroutine will cause a small **Window** to appear, displaying the string passed to it.

Next, take a look at the following code. The text that would appear in the MsgBox is listed in a comment next to the method.

```
Dim p as Parent
Dim c as Child
Dim o as Parent

p = New Parent
c = New Child
o = New Child

p.WhoAmI p // "Parent.WhoAmI : Parent.getName"
p.WhoAmI c // "Parent.WhoAmI : Child.getName"

c.WhoAmI p // "Parent.WhoAmI : Parent.getName"
c.WhoAmI c // "Child.WhoAmI : Child.getName"
```

```
o.WhoAmI p // "Parent.WhoAmI : Parent.getName"
o.WhoAmI c // "Parent.WhoAmI : Child.getName"
o.WhoAmI o // "Parent.WhoAmI : Child.getName"

Child(o).WhoAmI p // "Parent.WhoAmI : Parent.getName"
Child(o).WhoAmI c // "Child.WhoAmI : Child.getName"
Child(o).WhoAmI o // "Parent.WhoAmI : Child.getName"
```

The left side of the response shows which class implemented the `WhoAmI` method that was just called, and the right side of the response shows which class implemented the `getName()` that was called on the object passed as an argument to the `WhoAmI` method.

The first two examples show the **Parent** object p calling the `WhoAmI` method. In the first example, a **Parent** object is passed as the argument for `WhoAmI` and in the second example, a **Child** instance is passed as the argument. Both examples act as you would expect them to. The p object always uses the methods implemented in the **Parent** class and the c object uses a method implemented in the **Child** class.

The next group of examples are the same as the first two, with one important difference: A **Child** instance is calling `WhoAmI` instead of a **Parent** instance. There's something strange about the results, however:

```
c.WhoAmI p // "Parent.WhoAmI : Parent.getName"
c.WhoAmI c // "Child.WhoAmI : Child.getName"
```

If c is a **Child** object, why do the results show that c called the **Parent** class implementation of the `WhoAmI` method? Why does it call the **Child** class implementation of `WhoAmI` in the second example?

The answer is that `Child.WhoAmI()` does not override `Parent.WhoAmI()`. It overloads it. Remember that to override a method, the signatures have to be the same. When **Child** implements `WhoAmI`, the parameter is defined as a **Child** object, but when **Parent** implements it, the parameter is defined as a **Parent**. REALbasic decides which version of the overloaded method to call based on the signature. What is tricky here is that it is easy to forget that `WhoAmI` is overloaded only in the **Child** class, not in the **Parent** class, so when a **Parent** object is passed as an argument, REALbasic uses the **Parent** class implementation of `WhoAmI`. However, the c object has access to the methods of the **Parent** class because it is a subclass of the **Parent** class.

The rest of the examples work on the object o, which is in a unique situation. It was declared to be a variable in the **Parent** class, but when it was instantiated, it was instantiated as a **Child** and this makes for some interesting results. The first three sets of responses all show that o is calling the **Parent** class version of the `WhoAmI` method:

```
o.WhoAmI p // "Parent.WhoAmI : Parent.getName"
o.WhoAmI c // "Parent.WhoAmI : Child.getName"
o.WhoAmI o // "Parent.WhoAmI : Child.getName"
```

The `getName()` method is where things get interesting. As expected, when the argument is an instance of the **Parent** class, the `Parent.getName()` method is executed; likewise, if it is a member of the **Child** class. But when you pass o as the argument to

WhoAmI, o calls the **Child** implementation of getName(), rather than the **Parent** implementation.

This seems odd because when o calls WhoAmI, it calls the **Parent** class method, but when it calls getName(), it calls the **Child** class method. Because o was declared as a member of the **Parent** class, it is cast as a member of the **Parent** class, even though you used the **Child** class Constructor. In fact, when you cast o as a **Child**, you get an entirely different set of results:

```
Child(o).WhoAmI p // "Parent.WhoAmI : Parent.getName"
Child(o).WhoAmI c // "Child.WhoAmI : Child.getName"
Child(o).WhoAmI o // "Parent.WhoAmI : Child.getName"
Child(o).WhoAmI child(o)  // "Child.WhoAmI : Child.getName"
```

In the first of this quartet, you get the expected answer because p is a **Parent** instance, and that means that regardless of whether o is a **Child** or a **Parent**, REALbasic will call the **Parent** class implementation of WhoAmI. In the second example of this group, after o is cast as a **Child**, it behaves as expected, calling the **Child** class version of WhoAmI.

However, when o is passed as the argument to WhoAmI, it doesn't matter that o has been cast as a **Child**, it again calls the Parent.WhoAmI method. On the other hand, if you also cast the o object passed in the argument as a **Child** as well, things again are as they should be. So the question is why does this happen:

```
Child(o).WhoAmI o // "Parent.WhoAmI : Child.getName"
```

The implementation of WhoAmI that is used is determined by the type of the object passed in the parameter. The implementation of getName() is not determined by any parameter because it doesn't require a parameter. You can also do the following and get the same result:

```
Child(o).WhoAmI parent(o) // "Parent.WhoAmI : Child.getName"
```

The getName method is overridden, not overloaded. Because o was instantiated as a **Child** object, it will always call the **Child** implementation of getName. WhoAmI is overloaded, not overridden, and it is overloaded only in the **Child** class and not the **Parent** class.

Encapsulation

The idea of encapsulation is that an object does a lot of things privately that no one else needs to know about.

The **Public** methods of an object provide an interface to the outside world. It exposes the methods that can be called by other objects in your program. These typically aren't all the methods that compose the object because the object itself has lots of little details to attend to.

It's kind of like the drive-up window at a fast-food restaurant. When I pull up, the first thing I encounter is the menu that tells me what I can order; then there's the staticky speaker that I talk into to place my order. After ordering, I proceed to the first window to pay, then go to the second window to pick up my food, and then drive off.

A fast-food restaurant is encapsulated. It provides a means for me to place an order and pick it up, but I don't really have any idea what's going on inside, except that I know that when I place an order, it triggers a sequence of events inside the restaurant that results in food being handed over to me at the second window.

There's a fast-food restaurant near my house that I go to all the time. I do the same thing every time I go, and even order the same food (I'm a creature of habit). Even though my experience with the restaurant doesn't change, for all I know, they could have hired a consultant last week who showed them a new way to make hamburgers that was more cost efficient and would save them lots of money. I don't know about it and don't really need to know about it. As long as the steps I take to order the food are the same and the hamburger I order tastes the same, I really don't care.

Sometimes encapsulation is described in a slightly different way. These developers say that encapsulation means that an object should know how to do all the important things required to do its job. So if you create a class that represents a square, the class should also be able to display that square in a window or print that square on a sheet of paper. Although it's true that the class should group together related properties and methods that function as a unit, you shouldn't infer that the class needs to know about and be able to do everything related to it. If you follow that logic to the bitter end, all your programs will just be one gigantic class, and that defeats the purpose.

In practice, people often organize their classes quite differently. Some objects you use in your program will have only properties and no methods at all, which means that they don't know anything about themselves other than the data they represent. That's not a violation of the principle of encapsulation.

The fast-food restaurant I frequent doesn't slaughter its own cattle, grind it up in the back room, and cook my patties all the in same place. They hire someone to provide the ground-up meat. They "outsource." Classes and objects outsource, too. Often, a class is just a collection of other classes.

We'll dispense with the concepts for a moment. There's a practical side to object-oriented programming, too. Your goal is to create a program that maximizes code reuse, so you don't spend your life doing the same thing over and over. You also want a program that is easy to change in the future so that if something goes wrong, it's easy to figure out what it is that goes wrong. These factors are as important, and maybe more so, as the conceptual purity of your object model.

For example, I have a program that I use to write books and create websites. In fact, I'm using it right now. The "documents" I create will end up in print and sometimes online in different formats. Some of the documents are retrieved off of the file systems, others are pulled from Subversion, others are opened up using an HTTP request over the web.

If I took the encapsulation advice offered by some, I would have methods in my document class for opening files from the file system, from Subversion or through the web within the document class. However, because I know that I may be adding additional sources of data in the future, in different formats, which means I would have to go back and continue to add to this class, making it bigger and more complex over time, I created a group of classes. One group represents the data in the documents, another group handles getting the data from different sources, and a third group handles writing the documents out into different formats. If I have a new data source, I just subclass my `Provider` class and override the `open` method. I don't have to change the document class.

Access Scope: Public, Private, Protected

In practice, encapsulation is practiced by setting the scope of methods and properties. You've already encountered the idea of scope in the section on modules, but it takes on much greater importance when you're working with classes.

The whole point of encapsulation is that you want your objects to have a little modesty; not everything has to be hanging out in public for the whole world to see. The reason this is a good idea when programming is the same reason you don't want to do it personally. When things are exposed, other people have access to things they should not have access to and can thereby cause mischief. You might get sunburned or pregnant. Encapsulation, like modesty, is a virtue.

You only want to expose those parts of you that others have any business dealing with. Keep everything else safely tucked away.

When it comes to deciding how much of yourself you expose to others, or what others are allowed to do to or with you, it really depends on who that other person is.

Have you ever noticed that it's okay for you to make fun of your mom or dad or sister, but it's not okay if one of your friends does? What's considered acceptable behavior changes according to whether you're one of the family or not one of the family. Being a member of the family is a privileged position.

There are also some things that only certain members of the family are able to do, like drink beer out of the refrigerator. The kids and their friends don't get to do it because that's dad's beer and nobody is going to touch it.

This is how encapsulation works. If a method is `protected`, it's a method that you're keeping "in the family." Subclasses can call the method, but unrelated classes cannot. A method can also be designated as `private`, which is like Dad's beer stash. Only dad and no one else, not even his firstborn, can drink his beer. It's dad's private beer supply. A `private` method can be called only by the method that implements it, and no other classes, superclasses, or subclasses can touch it.

Recall that we have dealt with access scope before, when working with modules. The way that access scope is handled in modules is slightly different, with an emphasis on avoiding namespace collisions.

With classes, these terms have the following meaning:

- Public—Any other object or module can access this class member.
- Protected—Only members of this class or subclasses of this class can access this member.
- Private—Only this class can access this member; subclass members cannot.

Setting Properties with Methods

One thing that advocates of pure object-oriented programming often recommend is that you should avoid setting properties directly. Instead, you should use a method (sometimes called getter and setter methods).

It should be noted that there is a slight performance hit from using getter and setter methods because there's an extra step involved. I doubt that it is enough to make a substantial difference in most applications, but if you really want to convince yourself that it's okay to set your properties directly, I suppose that's about as good a reason as I can find.

The rationale behind this is our friend encapsulation. Being able to set properties directly is sort of like walking into the kitchen of the fast-food restaurant and making your own hamburger. It's not really safe to do that. In programming terms it's because the underlying mechanism that establishes the value for the property might change, or a subclass might want to set the value of the property in a different way. You obviously can't override the setting of properties.

Generally speaking, I think it's good advice to avoid directly accessing properties. That doesn't mean that it's bad to do otherwise. It's just that I've found, in practice, that the classes that use getter and setter methods tend to be easier to maintain over time. Your mileage may vary, as they say.

Default and Optional Parameters

Optional parameters are really just shortcuts to overloading methods. There are two ways to indicate that a parameter is optional. The obvious way is to use the `Optional` keyword, like so:

```
aMethod(aString as String, Optional anInteger as Integer)
```

The second way is to establish a default value for one of the parameters. Another way to accomplish what I just did in the previous example is this:

```
aMethod(aString as String, anInteger as Integer = 100)
```

Really, the `Optional` keyword just sets a default value of "0" to the `anInteger` variable, so the only real difference is that you get to set an arbitrary default value when using the second approach.

Declaring Variables Static and Const

When declaring variables within a method, they are treated by default like local variables that come in scope when the method starts and go out of scope when the method has completed executing. There are two variants of local variables that are also available.

Const

If you declare a variable within a method using `Const` instead of `Dim`, you are declaring a constant. The difference between this kind of constant and the other kind that I have written about is that these are local constants and so are active only for the duration of the method:

```
Const a = 100
```

This constant is local to the method, but it can be declared anywhere within the method.

Static

`Static` variables are new to REALbasic 2005. As such I haven't used them extensively in real-life, but they are an interesting addition. A static variable is like a local variable that's declared in a method except for one thing: It retains its value between invocations of that method.

```
Static a as Integer
```

Revisiting the StringParser Module

In the previous chapter, I created a `StringParser` module that did two things: it would take a string and split it up into sentences and it would take a string and split it up into words. Although a module works just fine, I think it would be worthwhile to take that same code and rethink it in terms of classes and objects.

Turning the module into a class is fairly straightforward. You can follow the same original steps to get started; the only difference is that you should click **New Class** rather than **New Module** in the editor and name it **Parser**. The differences come into play with the methods. Because one of the goals of object-oriented design is to maximize code reuse, it's instructive to think about this problem in terms of code reuse. You also want to think about it in terms of making it easy to work with. With the module, we had two different methods we could call, and they both called the same private method.

Right away, this creates an opportunity because the two methods are already sharing code—the `private Split` method.

Because I want to maximize code reuse, I'll dispense with the constant and use properties instead. The first step is to create a string property that will hold the string that will be used to split up the other string. There's no need for any other object to access this property directly, so I'll set its scope to Protected. If I set the scope to Private, subclasses of the base class will not be able to access it, and I want them to be able to do that.

```
Parser.Delimiter as String
```

In the module, the two primary functions returned an Array. I could do the same with this class, but that's actually a little more awkward because when I call those functions, I have to declare an Array to assign the value that's returned from them. If I were to do the same with a class, I would have to declare the Array plus the class instance, which strikes me as extra work. Instead, I can create the Array as a property of the class. You create an Array property just like any other data type, except that you follow the name with two parentheses. I'll call this Array Tokens.

```
Parser.Tokens() as String
```

Next I will implement the protected Split method, but with a few differences. The biggest is that I do not need to return the Array in a function. Instead, I am going to use the Tokens() Array, which is a property of the class. First, this means that the function will now be a subroutine and instead of declaring a word_buffer() Array, I'll refer to the Tokens() Array.

```
Protected Sub Split(aString as String)
  Dim chars(-1) as String
  Dim char_buffer(-1) as String
  Dim x,y as Integer
  Dim pos as Integer
  Dim prev as Integer
  Dim tmp as String

  // Use the complete name for the global Split function
  // to avoid naming conflicts
  chars = REALbasic.Split(aString, "")
  y = ubound(chars)

  prev = 0
  for x = 0 to y
    pos = me.Delimiter.inStr(chars(x))
    // If inStr returns a value greater than 0,
    // then this character is a whitespace
    if pos > 0 then
      Me.Tokens.append(join(char_buffer,""))
      prev = x+1
      reDim char_buffer(-1)
    else
      char_buffer.append(chars(x))
    end if
  next
```

```
// get the final word
Me.Tokens.append(join(char_buffer,""))

End Sub
```

One thing you may have noticed is the use of the word `Me` when referring to `Tokens`. That's because `Tokens` is a property of the **Parser** class and, as I said before, you refer to an object by the object's name and the name of the property or method you are wanting to access. REALbasic uses the word `Me` to refer to the parent object where this method is running, and this helps to distinguish `Tokens()` as a property rather than as a local variable. REALbasic 2005 is much more finicky about this than previous versions (and rightly so, I think). Before, `Me` was mostly optional, but now it is required. We'll revisit `Me` when talking about **Windows** and **Controls**, because there is a companion to `Me`, called `Self`, that comes into play in some situations.

I also pass only the string to be parsed as a parameter, because the delimiter list value will come from the `Delimiter` property.

Now, the final two questions are how to set the value for the `Delimiter` property and how to replicate what was done previously with two different methods. I'm going to do this by subclassing Parse, rather than implementing them directly.

Create a new class and call it **SentenceParser** and set the `Super` to be **Parser**. Create a new `Constructor` that doesn't take any parameters, like so:

```
Sub Constructor()
    me.Delimiter = ".,?!()[]"
End Sub
```

Create another method called `Parse`:

```
Sub Parse(aString as String)
    me.Split(aString)
End Sub
```

Now if I want to parse a string into sentences, I do this:

```
Dim sp as SentenceParser
Dim s as String
sp = new SentenceParser()
sp.Parse("This is the first sentence. This is the second.")
s = sp.Tokens(0) // s= "This is the first sentence"
```

If I want to add the functionality of splitting the string into words, I need to create a new class, called **WordParser**, set the `Super` to **SentenceParser**, and override the Constructor:

```
Sub Constructor()
    me.Delimiter = " " + chr(13) + chr(10)
End Sub
```

And I can use this in this manner:

```
Dim wp as WordParser
Dim s as String
wp = new WordParser()
wp.Parse("This is the first sentence. This is the second.")
s = wp.Tokens(0) // s= "This"
s = wp.Tokens(Ubound(wp.Tokens)) // s = "second."
```

In this particular example, I think a strong argument could be made that it would have been just as easy to have stuck with the module. That's probably true, because this is a simple class with simple functionality. You do have the advantage, however, of having an easy way to add functionality by subclassing these classes, and each one uses the same basic interface, so it's relatively easy to remember how to use it.

REALbasic provides a large number of predefined classes. Most of the rest of this book will be examining them. In the next section, I'll take a look at one in particular, the **Dictionary** class, and then I'll show a more realistic (and hopefully useful) example of how you can subclass the **Dictionary** class to parse a file of a different format.

The Dictionary Class

Although you will be creating your own classes, REALbasic also provides you with a large library of classes that you will use in your applications. You've been exposed to some of them already—**Windows** and **Controls**, for example.

The **Dictionary** class is a class provided by REALbasic that you'll use a lot, and it will serve as the superclass of our new **Properties** class.

A **Dictionary** is a class that contains a series of key/value pairs. It's called a **Dictionary** because it works a lot like a print dictionary works. If you're going to look up the meaning of a word in a dictionary, you first have to find the word itself. After you've found the word you can read the definition that's associated with it.

If you were to start from scratch to write your own program to do the same thing, you might be tempted to use an Array. To implement an Array that associated a key with a value, you would need to create a two-dimensional Array something like this:

```
Dim aDictArray(10,1) as String
aDictArray(0,0) = "My First Key"
aDictArray(0,1) = "My First Value"
aDictArray(1,0) = "My Second Key"
aDictArray(1,1) = "My Second Value"
aDictArray(2,0) = "My Third Key"
aDictArray(2,1) = "My Third Value"
// etc…
```

If you wanted to find the value associated with the key "My Second Key", you would need to loop through the AArray until you found the matching key.

```
For x = 0 to 10
  If aDictArray(x, 0) = "My Second Key" Then
```

```
     // The value is aDictArray(x,1)
     Exit
   End If
Next
```

Using this technique, you have to check every key until you find the matching key before you can find the associated value. This is okay if you have a small list, but it can get a little time consuming for larger lists of values. One feature of a printed dictionary that makes the search handy is that the words are all alphabetized. That means that when you go to look up a word, you don't have to start from the first page and read every word until you find the right one. If the keys in the Array are alphabetized, the search can be sped up, too.

Using the current Array, the best way to do this would be with a binary search, which isn't a whole lot different from the way you naturally find a word in the dictionary. For example, if the word you want to look up starts with an "m," you might turn to the middle of the dictionary and start your search for the word there. A binary search is actually a little more primitive than that, but it's a similar approach. To execute a binary search for "My Second Key", a binary search starts by getting the upper bound of the Array ("10", in this case) and cutting that in half. This is the position in the Array that is checked first .

```
result = StrComp(aDictArray(5,0), "My Second Key")
```

If the result of StrComp is 0, you've found the key. However, if the value returned is -1, then "My Second Key" is less than the value found at aDictArray(5,0). Because the key of aDictArray(5,0) would be "My Sixth Key", -1 is the answer we would get. So the next step is to take the value 5 and cut it in half, as well (I'll drop the remainder). This gives us 2. Now you test against aDictArray(2,0) and you still get -1, so you cut 2 in half, which gives you 1. When you test aDictArray(1,0), you find that it matches "My Second Key", so you can now find the value associated with it.

This is all well and good if you happen to have a sorted two-dimensional Array consisting of one of REALbasic's intrinsic data types. If the Array isn't sorted (and you have to jump through some hoops to get a sorted two-dimensional Array), things begin to get complicated. What happens if the key is not an intrinsic data type?

These are really the two reasons for using **Dictionaries**—you don't have to have a sorted list of keys to search on, and your keys do not have to be limited to intrinsic data types. It's still easier (and possibly more efficient) to sequentially search through an Array if the list of keys is relatively short. As the list grows larger, the more beneficial the use of a dictionary becomes.

The Properties File Format

For our new subclass, we are going to be parsing a properties file. Java developers often use properties files in their applications. The file format used by properties files is very simple, so I will use this format in my example.

The format is a list of properties and an associated value separated (or delimited) by an equal sign (=). In practice, the property names are usually written using dot notation, even though that's not necessary. Here's an example:

```
property.color=blue
property.size=1
```

The format doesn't distinguish between integers and strings or other data types, so this unknown is something that the module will need to be prepared to deal with. Because the properties file has a series of key/value pairs, a **Dictionary** is well suited to be the base class. The **Dictionary** already has members suited for dealing with data that comes in a key/value pair format, so our subclass will be able to use those properties and methods, while adding only a few to deal with the mechanics of turning a string in the properties file format into keys and values in the **Dictionary**.

Dictionary Properties

Dictionaries use hash tables to make searches for keys faster. Without getting into too much detail, you can adjust the following property at times in order to optimize performance:

```
Dictionary.BinCount as Integer
```

In most cases you'll never need to adjust this because the class automatically adjusts it as necessary, but there are times when you can improve performance. This is especially true if you know you are going to have a particularly large dictionary with lots of key/value pairs.

The following property returns the number of key/value pairs in the dictionary:

```
Dictionary.Count as Integer
```

Dictionary Methods

The following method removes all the key/value pairs from the **Dictionary**:

```
Sub Dictionary.Clear
```

This removes a particular entry, based on the key:

```
Sub Dictionary.Remove(aKey as Variant)
```

When using a **Dictionary**, you almost always access the value by way of the key. That's more or less the whole point of a **Dictionary**. You do not always know if any given key is available in the **Dictionary**, so you need to find out if the key exists first before you use it to get the associated value. Use the following method to do so:

```
Function Dictionary.HasKey(aKey as Variant) as Boolean
```

The values in a **Dictionary** are accessed through the `Value` function.

```
Function Dictionary.Value(aKey as Variant) as Variant
```

Here's an example of how to use the `Value` function:

```
Dim d as Dictionary
Dim s as String
d = new Dictionary
d.value("My key") = "My value"
If d.HasKey("My Key") Then
  s = d.value("My key") // s equals "My value"
End If
```

The **Dictionary** class also provides you with a way to get access to the keys by their index, which can be helpful in some circumstances, using the following method:

```
Function Dictionary.Key(anIndex as Integer) as Variant
```

There's no guarantee that the keys are in any particular order, but this can be used in circumstances where you want to get all the key/value pairs. Assume d is a **Dictionary** with 100 key/value pairs:

```
Dim d as Dictionary
Dim x as Integer
Dim ThisKey, ThisValue as Variant
Dim s as String

// Assign 100 haves to d…
For x = 0 to 99 //
  ThisKey = d.Key(x)
  ThisValue = d.Value(ThisKey)
  s = s  + ThisKey.StringValue + ":" + ThisValue.StringValue + Chr(13)
Next
```

This example takes all the keys and values in the **Dictionary** and places each key/value pair on a single line, separated by a colon. The ASCII value for a newline character is 13, which explains the `Chr(13)`.

The `Lookup` function is new for REALbasic 2005:

```
Function Dictionary.Lookup(aKey as Variant, defaultValue as Variant) as Variant
```

It works like the `Value` function, but instead of passing only the key, you also pass a default value to be used if the key doesn't exist in the dictionary. This saves you the nearly unbearable hassle of having to use the `HasKey()` function every time you try to get at a value in the **Dictionary**.

Here's how it works:

```
Dim d as Dictionary
Dim s as String
d = New Dictionary()
d.Value("Alpha") = "a"
d.Value("Beta") = "b"
s = d.Lookup("Delta", "d") // s equals "d"
```

In this example, the key "Delta" does not exist, so d returns the default value "d" and this value gets assigned to s.

This next example can be used in replacement of this older idiom, which is the way you had to do it before the Lookup method was added:

```
Dim d as Dictionary
Dim s as String
d = New Dictionary()
d.Value("Alpha") = "a"
d.Value("Beta") = "b"
If d.HasKey("Delta") Then
  s = d.Value("Delta")
Else
  s = "d"
End If
```

Example: Creating a Properties Class

In the following pages, I will create a new class called **Properties**, which will be a sub-class of the **Dictionary** class.

Properties.Constructor

There are three potential scenarios to consider for the Constructor. You may get the data to be parsed for the **Properties** class from a file or a string, and you also may want to be able to instantiate the class without any data so that you can add it later, either by individually setting the key/value pairs or by some other method.

To accomplish this, I'll overload the Constructor method with three versions. If I did nothing, the default Constructor would be used, which takes no parameters. However—and this is a big "however"—if I overload the Constructor class with any other Constructor, the default Constructor goes away and is not accessible. The reason is that it allows you to require that the class accept a parameter in the Constructor because you do not always want the default Constructor available.

This means that you have to reimplement the default Constructor to retain the capability to instantiate the class with no parameters, so that is what I do first:

```
Sub Constructor()
  // Do nothing
End Sub
```

The second implementation will accept a string in the parameter. Whenever this Constructor is called, the class automatically parses the file as part of the Constructor. This means that after the class is instantiated, the key/value pairs are accessible, with no further steps required.

```
Sub Constructor(myPropertyString as String)
```

```
If myPropertyString <> "" Then
  Me.parsePropertyFile(myPropertyString)
Else
  // An error as occurred
End If

End Sub
```

The following implementation accepts a `FolderItem`. It tests to make sure the `FolderItem` is readable and writeable, both of which are functions of the `FolderItem` class. If the FolderItem instance is readable and writeable, it sends the file to the overloaded `parsePropertyFile` function.

```
Sub Constructor(myPropertyFile as FolderItem)
  If myPropertyFile.exists Then

    If myPropertyFile.IsReadable and myPropertyFile.IsWriteable Then
      Me.parsePropertyFile(myPropertyFile)
    Else
      // An error has occurred
    End If

  Else
    // An error has occurred
  End If

End Sub
```

Properties.get

```
Function get(aKey as string, aDefault as string) As string
  Dim s as String
  s = Me.Lookup(aKey, aDefault)
End Function
```

The `get()` function is also overloaded to take only one string as a parameter. When this occurs, I need to test first to see whether the **Dictionary** has the key passed in the parameter, and if it doesn't, respond appropriately.

```
Function get(aKey as string) As string
  Dim s as String

  If Me.HasKey(aKey) = True Then
    s = Me.Value(aKey)
    Return
  Else
    // Handle the Error
```

```
    Return ""
  End If
End Function
```

You can accomplish the equivalent by using the **Dictionary**'s Lookup() function. Remember that nothing is stopping you from calling the Lookup() function directly from other parts of your program because it is a public method of **Dictionary**.

```
Function get(aKey as string) As string
  Dim s as String

  s = Me.Lookup(aKey, "")
End Function
```

I can also replicate the same functionality by calling the first get() function from the second:

```
Function get(aKey as string) As string
  Dim s as String

  s = Me.get(aKey, "")
End Function
```

Of the three options I have given for implementing function get(aKey) as String, the last option is preferable, in my opinion. You may be wondering why you should bother implementing the get() method at all, because you can use the native **Dictionary** methods anyway. One reason is because get() provides a simpler syntax. **Dictionaries** can use Variants for keys and values, but I really care only about strings, so get() makes the assumption that it's a string. More importantly, because of the two versions of get() that I am using, I can change the implementation in the future of how the default value is generated when no default value is given, or add tests to the code to make sure that the default value that is passed is a valid default value.

There is yet another approach to implementing get() that accomplishes the same goals, more or less: instead of overloading get(), you can override and overload Lookup() to achieve the same effect.

I'll override Lookup() first. Remember that to override a method, the signature has to be the same, which means the parameters must accept Variants. Also, the reason I said I liked using get() was that it gave me an opportunity to test for legal values first. You can do the same here, by calling the parent class's version of Lookup after you've tested the values:

```
Function Lookup(aKey as Variant, aDefaultValue as Variant) as String
  Dim key,default as String
  key = aKey.StringValue
  default = aDefaultValue.StringValue
  If default <> "" Then
    Return Dictionary.Lookup(key, default).StringValue()
  End If
End Function
```

I can also keep things simple by using an overloaded version of Lookup() that accepts only a key in the parameter and handles the default value automatically:

```
Function Lookup(aKey as Variant) as String
  Dim key,default as String
  key = aKey.StringValue
  default = aDefaultValue.StringValue
  If default <> "" Then
    Return Dictionary.Lookup(key, default).StringValue()
  End If
End Function
```

Note that in both cases, I returned a string rather than a Variant. REALbasic doesn't pay attention to the return value when determining whether a method is overloaded. This allows me to force the return of a string, even though the original Lookup() implementation returns a Variant.

Properties.set

In addition to get(), I also implemented a set() subroutine. Again, this is for simplicity's sake because I could also just call the Dictionary.Value() function directly. It also means I can test the values before assigning them, which always helps. I also use the Assigns keyword, which alters the way that the method can be called in your program. An example of how it is used follows this example:

```
Sub set(aKey as string, assigns aProperty as string)

If aKey <> "" and aProperty <> "" Then
  Me.Value(aKey) = aProperty
Else
// An error occurred
End if
End Sub
```

By using the Assigns keyword in the parameter, you can set a key/value pair using the following syntax, which mirrors the syntax used for the Value() function of **Dictionary**:

```
Dim prop as Properties
prop = New Properties()
prop.set("FirstKey") = "FirstValue"
```

Properties.parsePropertyFile

The first step to parsing the file is to split the string into individual lines. I have two functions for this—one that accepts a string and another that accepts a **FolderItem**. The string version splits the string on a newline character (ASCII value of 13) and then cycles through each line, parsing the lines individually.

```
Protected Sub parsePropertyFile(myFile as string)
  Dim my_array(-1) as String
  Dim line as String

  my_array = myFile.split(Chr(13))

  For Each line In my_array
    Me.parseLine(line)
  Next
End Sub
```

A second version of `parsePropertyFile` accepts a **FolderItem** as a parameter. **FolderItems** are discussed at length later in the book, but the code in this example is sufficiently self-explanatory that you get the general idea of what is happening. When you open a **FolderItem** as a text file, it returns a **TextInputStream**. A **TextInputStream** allows you to read it line by line by calling the `ReadLine()` function.

```
Protected Sub parsePropertyFile(myPropertyFile as folderItem)
  Dim textInput as TextInputStream
  Dim astr as string

  If myPropertyFile Is Nil Then
      // An error has occurred
    Return
  End If

  If myPropertyFile.exists Then
    Me.file = myPropertyFile
    textInput = me.file.OpenAsTextFile
    Do
      astr=textInput.ReadLine()
      Me.parseLine(astr)
    Loop Until textInput.EOF

    textInput.Close
  Else
    // An error has occurred
  End If

End Sub
```

Properties.parseLine:

Each line is parsed individually.

```
Protected Sub parseLine(my_line as string)
  Dim aKey, aValue as string
```

```
  // Split line at "=", and ignore comments
  If Left(my_line, 1) <> "#" Then
    If CountFields(my_line, "=")= 2 Then

      aValue = Trim(NthField(my_line, "=", 2))
      aKey = Trim(NthField(my_line, "=", 1))

      Me.set(aKey) = aValue

    End If

  End If // starts with "#"

End Sub
```

The first thing I test for is to see whether the line starts with a # character. In property files, a # at the beginning of a line indicates a comment, and because comments are only for human consumption, I can safely ignore them in my program.

The next step is to split the line into two values, one for the property and the other for the value. Although I could use the `split()` function, I have chosen to use the `CountFields/NthField` combination primarily because it makes it a little easier to count how many fields there are. Because each property is separated from its value by an equal sign, I will parse the line only if there are two fields in the line (which is the same thing as saying that there is only one "=" sign on the line).

The property name, or key, is in the first field, and the value is in the second field. When extracting the values using `NthField`, I trim the results, which removes whitespace on either side of the string. This accounts for situations where there are extra spaces between the "=" sign and the values themselves. As a result, both of these formats will be parsed correctly:

```
aProperty=aValue
aProperty = aValue
```

Finally, I use the `set()` method to add the key/value pair to the **Dictionary**.

Now that all the members of the class are implemented, here is an example of how you can use the class:

```
Dim prop as Properties
Dim s as String
Dim propStr as String
propStr = "First=FirstValue" + Chr(13) + "Second=SecondValue"
prop = New Properties(propStr)
s = prop.get("First") // s equals "FirstValue"
prop.set("Third") = "ThirdValue"
s = prop.get("Third") // s equals "ThirdValue"
```

Data-Oriented Classes and Visual Basic Data Types

In the previous chapter, I said that some data types in Visual Basic don't exist in REALbasic as data types. The reason is that REALbasic often has an object-oriented alternative. For example, an intrinsic data type in Visual Basic is a **Date**, but in REALbasic it's a class. In other situations, I said that similar functionality could be implemented with the **MemoryBlock** class. Now that you know about classes, I can review these two classes in more detail and complete the discussion of data types and how REALbasic compares with Visual Basic. I will also review the **Collection** class, because it is very similar to the **Dictionary** class. REALbasic recommends sticking to the **Dictionary** class for new projects and retains the **Collection** class only for compatibility with Visual Basic and earlier versions of REALbasic.

Date Class

Date is an intrinsic data type in Visual Basic, but it's a class in REALbasic. It measures time in seconds since 12:00 a.m., January 1, 1904. The total number of seconds since that time is how a particular date and time are identified, and it is stored in the `TotalSeconds` property of the **Date** class as a double.

The `Variant` type treats **Dates** in a special way to help maintain compatibility with Visual Basic. The `VarType()` function returns a 7 as the data type for dates, rather than 9, which is what is typically done with objects. Basically, all the `Variant` is doing is storing the `TotalSeconds` property as a double.

ParseDate Function

There is a `ParseDate` helper function that accepts a date formatted as a string and parses it into a `Date` object. It returns a Boolean representing success or failure in parsing the string that was passed to it. If it returns a Boolean, how then do you pass it a string and get a **Date** object back? The function signature looks like this:

```
REALbasic.ParseDate(aDate as String, aParsedDate as Date) as Boolean
```

The answer is that objects, like **Date**, are passed by reference, rather than by their value. I wrote earlier that variables that were one of REALbasic's intrinsic data types were called scalar variables. These variables refer to the value held in memory, whereas variables that referred to objects were references to the object, like a pointer to a particular section of memory. When you pass the **Date** object to the `ParseDate` function, the `ParseDate` function does its work on the **Date** object passed to it so that when it changes a value of the **Date** object, that change is reflected in the original variable that was passed to the function.

```
Dim d as Date
Dim s,t as String
Dim b as Boolean
```

```
s = "12/24/2004"
b = ParseDate(s, d) // b is True
t = d.ShortDate // t = "12/24/2004"
```

Note that all you have to do is `Declare d` as a **Date**; you do not need to instantiate it prior to passing it to the `ParseDate` function.

You can also do the same trick with scalar variables if you use the `ByRef` keyword in the function signature. There are actually two keywords here—`ByRef` and `ByVal`—and scalar variables are, by default, passed `ByVal`.

The acceptable formats of the string are the following:

```
1/1/2006
1-1-2006
1.1.2006
1Jan2006
1.Jan.2006
1 Jan. 2006
```

Date Properties

`TotalSeconds` reflects how the date and time are actually stored in a `Date` object. When you instantiate a new `Date` object, it automatically gets set to the current date and time.

```
Date.TotalSeconds as Double
```

You can also get or set different components of the time with the following properties. Changes made to these will be reflected in `TotalSeconds`:

```
Date.Second as Integer
Date.Minute as Integer
Date.Hour as Integer
Date.Day as Integer
Date.Month as Integer
Date.Year as Integer
```

The following two methods set the date or date and time using the standard SQL format used in databases. This comes in handy when dealing with databases.

```
Date.SQLDate as String
```

You can get or set the date using the format YYYY-MM-DD.

```
Date.SQLDateTime as String
```

You can get or set the date using the format YYYY-MM-DD HH:MM:SS.

These properties are all read-only and return the date or time in different formats, according to your wishes:

```
Date.LongDate as String
Date.LongTime as String
Date.ShortDate as String
Date.ShortTime as String
Date.AbbreviatedDate as String
```

The following example shows how they are used.

```
Dim d as new Date()
Dim dates() as String

d.TotalSeconds = 3204269185

dates.append "TotalSeconds: " + format(d.TotalSeconds, "#")
dates.append "Year: " + str(d.Year)
dates.append "Month: " + str(d.Month)
dates.append "Day: " + str(d.Day)
dates.append "Hour: " + str(d.Hour)
dates.append "Minute: " + str(d.Minute)
dates.append "Second: " + str(d.Second)
dates.append "--"
dates.append "SQLDateTime: " + d.SQLDateTime
dates.append "SQLDate: " + d.SQLDate
dates.append "--"
dates.append "DayOfWeek: " + str(d.DayOfWeek)
dates.append "DayOfYear: " + str(d.DayOfYear)
dates.append "WeekOfYear: " + str(d.WeekOfYear)
dates.append "--"
dates.append "LongDate: "  + d.LongDate
dates.append "LongTime: " + d.LongTime
dates.append "ShortDate: " + d.ShortDate
dates.append "ShortTime: " + d.ShortTime
dates.append "AbbreviatedDate: " + d.AbbreviatedDate

EditField1.text = join(dates, EndOfLine)
```

I executed this action using three different locale settings (which I changed on my Macintosh in System Preferences, International). The first setting was the standard (for me) setting of United States, using the Gregorian calendar. I followed that by setting my locale to France, and then Pakistan, using the Islamic civil calendar. The only properties that change according to your locale are the LongDate, LongTime, ShortDate, ShortTime, and AbbreviatedDate.

United States, Gregorian Calendar:

```
TotalSeconds: 3204269185
Year: 2005
Month: 7
Day: 15
Hour: 10
Minute: 46
Second: 25
--
SQLDateTime: 2005-07-15 10:46:25
SQLDate: 2005-07-15
--
```

```
DayOfWeek: 6
DayOfYear: 196
WeekOfYear: 29
--
LongDate: Friday, July 15, 2005
LongTime: 10:46:25 AM
ShortDate: 7/15/05
ShortTime: 10:46 AM
AbbreviatedDate: Jul 15, 2005
```

France, Gregorian Calendar:

```
LongDate: vendredi 15 juillet 2005
LongTime: 10:46:25
ShortDate: 15/07/05
ShortTime: 10:46
AbbreviatedDate: 15 juil. 05
```

Pakistan Islamic Civil Calendar:

```
LongDate: Friday 8 Jumada II 1426
LongTime: 10:46:25 AM
ShortDate: 08/06/26
ShortTime: 10:46 AM
AbbreviatedDate: 08-Jumada II-26
```

MemoryBlock Class

The **MemoryBlock** class is a catch-all class that lets you do a lot of interesting things with REALbasic. **MemoryBlocks** are generally helpful when dealing with any binary data and can replace some of the missing data types from Visual Basic. They are commonly used with Declares, which are statements in REALbasic that allow you to access functions in shared libraries.

A **MemoryBlock** is exactly what is says it is: it's a stretch of memory of a certain byte length that you can access and manipulate.

The NewMemoryBlock Function

```
REALbasic.NewMemoryBlock(size as Integer) as MemoryBlock
```

There are two ways to instantiate **MemoryBlocks** in REALbasic. The first is the old-fashioned way, using the New operator, and the second uses the global NewMemoryBlock function.

```
Dim mb as MemoryBlock
Dim mb2 as MemoryBlock
mb = New MemoryBlock(4)
mb2 = NewMemoryBlock(4)
```

You may have to look closely to see the difference between the two techniques. The second one is missing a space between New and **MemoryBlock** because it's a global function and not a `Constructor` for the **MemoryBlock** class. Whether you use the traditional way of instantiating an object or the `NewMemoryBlock` function, you need to pass an integer indicating how many bytes the **MemoryBlock** should be. The integer can be 0, but some positive number has to be passed to it (a negative number causes it to raise an **UnsupportedFormat** exception).

In this example, both **MemoryBlocks** are 4 bytes long. The fact that a **MemoryBlock** can be of an arbitrary length is what makes it so flexible. It can be anywhere from 0 bytes to however much memory your computer has available (the `NewMemoryBlock` function returns Nil if there is not enough memory to create the **MemoryBlock**).

Visual Basic has a Byte data type that takes up 1 byte. This can be replicated with **MemoryBlock** quite easily:

```
Dim bytetype as MemoryBlock
Dim i as Integer
bytetype = NewMemoryBlock(1)
bytetype.byte(0) = 1
i = bytetype.byte(0) // i equals 1
```

MemoryBlock provides a slew of functions to let you get at the individual bytes it contains. I'll review those shortly.

MemoryBlock Properties

This property refers to the order in which bytes are sequenced when representing a number:

```
MemoryBlock.LittleEndian as Boolean
```

I know that's kind of an obtuse sentence, but that's about the best I can do at the moment. As is often the case, an example will be more illuminating. Recall that an integer is made up of 4 bytes. When the computer stores or processes those 4 bytes, it expects them to be in a particular order. This makes perfect sense. The number 41 is not the same as 14, for instance. The problem is that not all operating systems use the same standard. Intel x86 platforms use one type and Macintosh uses another. (With the recent announcement that Macs are moving to Intel chips, this may be less of a problem.) Linux runs on Intel, so you can expect those applications to be the same as those compiled for Windows.

In any event, the example is this. Let's use a really big number, like 10 million. If you look at that number expressed in hexadecimal format on a Macintosh, it looks like this:

```
00 98 96 80
```

If you do it on an Intel machine, which is LittleEndian, it looks like this:

```
80 96 98 00
```

The terms *big-endian* and *little-endian* refer to where the "most significant byte" is in position. In big-endian format, the most significant byte comes first (which also happens to be the way our decimal number system works. In little-endian systems, the least significant byte comes first. According to WikiPedia, this particular nuance can also be referred to as *byte order*.

You can both read and write to this property. If you are writing a cross-platform application, you need to be aware of this if you will be sharing binary data across systems.

```
MemoryBlock.Size as Integer
```

You can read and write to this property. It refers to the size, in bytes, of this **MemoryBlock**. If you modify the Size, the **MemoryBlock** will be resized. Bear in mind that if you make it smaller than it currently is, you might lose data.

MemoryBlock Methods

All five of the following functions return a value of the given type, at the location specified by the Offset parameter:

```
Function MemoryBlock.BooleanValue(Offset as Integer) as Boolean
Function MemoryBlock.ColorValue(Offset as Integer) as Color
Function MemoryBlock.DoubleValue(Offset as Integer) as Double
Function MemoryBlock.SingleValue(Offset as Integer) as Single
Function MemoryBlock.StringValue(Offset as Integer, [Length as Integer]) as String
```

Because each of these data types has a predefined size (except for string), all you do is pass the Offset to it. If you call MemoryBlock.DoubleValue(0), the **MemoryBlock** will return a double based on the first 8 bytes of the **MemoryBlock**.

When using StringValue, you may specify the length of the string, but you do not have to. If you don't, it will just return a string from the offset position to the end of the **MemoryBlock**. The string can contain nulls and other non-normal characters, so some caution may be necessary when doing this, unless you know for certain what values you will come across.

These three functions work very much like their global function cousins LeftB, MidB, and RightB:

```
Function MemoryBlock.LeftB(Length as Integer) as MemoryBlock
Function MemoryBlock.MidB(Offset as Integer, [Length as Integer]) as MemoryBlock
Function MemoryBlock.RightB(Length as Integer) as MemoryBlock
```

They do the same thing except that instead of returning strings, they return **MemoryBlocks**.

Get or set a 1-byte integer:

```
Function MemoryBlock.Byte(Offset as Integer) as Integer
```

```
 Get or set a signed, 2-byte integer:Function MemoryBlock.Short(Offset as Integer)
as Integer
```

```
Get or set an unsigned 2-byte integer.:Function MemoryBlock.UShort(Offset as
Integer) as Integer
```

Get or set a 4-byte integer, just like REALbasic's native type.

```
Function MemoryBlock.Long(Offset as Integer) as Integer
```

These four functions, `Byte`, `Short`, `Ushort`, and `Long`, return integers based on their offset position. They return integers even though they often refer to data that requires fewer bytes to represent, because an integer is really the only thing they can return—it's the smallest numeric data type. The primary use of this is when handling `Declares`, because it allows you to pass values and access values using a broader selection of data types than those offered by REALbasic.

Also, note that when I say that one of these functions "gets or sets a 2-byte integer," I really mean an integer within the range that can be expressed by 2 bytes. An integer is an integer, and it takes up 4 bytes of memory when REALbasic gets hold of it, even if it can be stored in a **MemoryBlock** with fewer bytes.

MemoryBlock.Cstring, MemoryBlock.Pstring, MemoryBlock.Wstring, MemoryBlock.Ptr:

```
Function CString(Offset as Integer) as String
```

Returns a String terminated.

```
Function PString(Offset as Integer) as String
Function WString(Offset as Integer, [Length as Integer]) as String
Function Ptr(Offset as Integer) as MemoryBlock
```

A pointer to an address in memory. Used by Declares.

Example: Mimicking a Structure with a MemoryBlock

I'd be getting ahead of myself if I gave an example of how to use a **MemoryBlock** with a `Declare`, so I've come up with another example. One advantage to using a **MemoryBlock** (in some cases) is that you can store data in it more efficiently and can often access it faster.

To illustrate this, I've developed two classes, both of which emulate a structure. The first is a class that has only properties, and the second is a subclass of **MemoryBlock**. These two structurelike classes will hold data representing the two-character United States state abbreviation, the five-digit ZIP code, a three-digit area code, and a seven-digit phone number.

The first class is called **Struct**, and it has the following properties:

```
Struct.State as String
Struct.Zip as Integer
Struct.AreaCode as Integer
Struct.PhoneNumber as Integer
```

If I were to save these items as strings, I would need 17 bytes to represent it—one for each character. The **Struct** class already reduces that to 14 bytes because it uses Integers for the ZIP code, the area code, and the phone number, all of which can be expressed as Integers.

Implementing the **MemoryBlock** structure will be a little different because to create the **MemoryBlock**, I first have to know how many bytes to allocate for it. I could allocate 14 bytes, just like the class version, but I would be allocating more bytes than I need. For example, an area code is three digits, meaning it can be anywhere from 0 to 999. Although an Integer can represent that number, an integer takes 4 bytes and you don't need 4 bytes to represent 999; all you need are 2 bytes. The same is true for the ZIP code. The only number that requires an Integer is the phone number. This means we can shave off 4 bytes and create a **MemoryBlock** of only 10 bytes. That's a fairly significant size difference.

The next question is how do we best implement the **MemoryBlock**. I could use the `NewMemoryBlock` function and pass it a value of 10 to create an appropriate **MemoryBlock**, but that means I'd have to keep passing 10 to the function each time I wanted to create one and that seems to me to be a bit of a hassle; because I'm a little lazy by nature, I'd like to avoid that if at all possible.

The next option would be to instantiate a `New` **MemoryBlock**, but that, too, requires that I pass a parameter to the `Constructor` and I don't want to do that either. All I want is a class that I can instantiate without having to think about it. The answer is to subclass **MemoryBlock** and overload the `Constructor` with a new `Constructor` that does not take any integers as a parameter. Then, while in the `Constructor`, call the `Constructor` of the superclass. Create a subclass of **MemoryBlock** and call it **MemBlockStruct**. Create the following `Constructor`:

```
Sub MemBlockStruct.Constructor()
  MemoryBlock.Constructor(10)
End Sub
```

Now you can do this to create a 10-byte **MemoryBlock**:

```
Dim mb as MemBlockStruct
Dim sz as Integer
mb = New MemBlockStruct
sz = mb.Size // sz = 10
```

Because this is a subclass of **MemoryBlock**, you can still call the original constructor and pass any value you want to it, like so:

```
Dim mb as MemBlockStruct
Dim sz as Integer
mb = New MemBlockStruct(25)
sz = mb.Size // sz = 25
```

If you don't want that to happen, you need to override that `Constructor` and ignore the value that is passed to it:

```
Sub MemBlockStruct.Constructor(aSize as Integer)
 Me.Constructor()
End Sub
```

Note that I could have called the superclass `MemoryBlock.Constructor(10)`, like I did in the other `Constructor`, but that would mean that if at a later time I decided I wanted to add 1 or more bytes to the **MemBlockStruct** class, I would have to go back and change the value from 10 to something else in both `Constructors`. This way, should I decide to do that, I need to change only the `MemBlockStruct.Constructor()` method and no other.

I now have done enough to have two workable classes. Here is how they can be used in practice:

```
Dim ms as MemBlockStruct
Dim ss as Struct
Dim a,b,c as Integer
ss = new Struct()
ss.State = "NH"
ss.Zip = 3063 // the first character is "0", which is dropped
ss.AreaCode = 603
ss.PhoneNumber = 5551212
ms = new MemBlockStruct()
ms.StringValue(0,2) = "NH"
ms.Short(2) = 3063
ms.Short(4) = 603
ms.Long(6) = 5551212
a = ms.Short(2) // a = 3063
b = ms.Short(4) // b = 603
c = ms.Long(6) // c = 5551212
```

Accessing the values of the **MemBlockStruct** class by the offset position is a little clunky, so I can optionally take the step of creating methods for this class to make it easier. Here is an example for how the methods would look for setting the state abbreviation:

```
Function MemBlockStruct.setState(aState as String) as String
  If LenB(aState) = 2 Then
    me.StringValue(0,2) = aState
  End If
End Function

Function MemBlockStruct.getState() as String
   Return me.StringValue(0,2)
End Function
```

Collection Class

The **Collection** class is another class, similar to the **Dictionary** class. The documentation for REALbasic recommends that you use the **Dictionary** class instead, but that they have retained the collection class for reasons of compatibility with Visual Basic.

The big differences between a **Collection** and a **Dictionary** are these:

- **Collections** can only have strings as their keys.
- A **Collection** does not use a hash table like a **Dictionary** does. This means that the time required searching for a value is determined by how many key/value pairs are in the collection. The larger the collection, the longer, on average, it will take to find your value.

Collection Methods

Collection uses a slightly different terminology than **Dictionaries** do. The Add method is roughly equivalent to Value() for **Dictionaries**, in the sense that you use it to add items to the **Collection**.

```
Sub Collection.Add(Value as Variant, Key as String)
```

Much like it does with a **Dictionary**, the Count property returns the number of items in the **Collection**:

```
Function Collection.Count As Integer
```

As you would expect, you can get and remove values using the key:

```
Function Collection.Index(Key as String) as Variant
Function Collection.Remove(Key as String) as Variant
```

You can also get or remove an item by referring to it's indexed position:

```
Function Collection.Index(Index as Integer) as Variant
Function Collection.Remove(Index as Integer) as Variant
```

When getting or removing an item in a collection using the index, remember that **Collection** indexes are 1 based, not 0 based like Arrays and **Dictionaries**.

Advanced Techniques

In this section I will review some relatively more advanced programming techniques you can use to extend the functionality of your REALbasic classes.

Interfaces and Component-Oriented Programming

Interfaces are an alternative to subclassing. With subclassing, one class can be a subclass of another. Interfaces do not deal in subclasses. When talking about Interfaces, you say that a class implements a particular Interface.

Interfaces are another means by which you encapsulate your program. This is also one of those areas where the term is used differently in different programming languages. In REALbasic, an interface is used much in the same way that the term is used with Java. Other languages, such as Objective-C, refer to a similar concept as a protocol.

Nevertheless, when one class is a subclass of another, it shares all the same members with the parent class. Although the subclass may optionally reimplement or override a method from the parent class, it doesn't have to reimplement any method unless it wants to modify what that method does. The benefit to this, so the story goes, is that it enables code reuse. Simply put, you don't have to write any new methods for the subclass to get the functionality resident in the superclass.

There are some cases when you have two objects (or classes) that are related and that perform the same tasks, but they both do it in such a fundamentally different way that establishing the class/subclass relationship doesn't really buy you anything. At the same time, it's convenient to formally establish this relationship so that the different objects can be used in similar contexts. If two class share a common set of methods, it is possible to link these two classes together by saying they share a common interface. This task involves defining the interface itself and then modifying to classes to indicate that they both implement this common interface.

When this is the case, no code is shared. In the immediate sense, at least, code reuse isn't the object of this activity, but as you will see, it does make it possible to streamline the code that interacts with objects that share the same interface, which is why it can be so helpful.

When I talked about encapsulation, I used the fast-food restaurant drive-up window as an example. The fast-food restaurant I was thinking about when I wrote that example had three points of interaction for me: the first was the menu and speaker where I placed my order, the second was the first window, where I paid, and the third was the second window where I picked up my order. I said that the fast-food restaurant was encapsulated because I only had three touch points where I interacted with it, even though a whole lot happened between the time I placed my order and picked up my order.

Fast-food restaurants aren't the only places that use the drive-up window "interface." Banks use them, too. Even liquor stores in Texas do. At least they did when I lived in Texas—at that time the drinking age was 19, and as a 19-year-old living in Texas, I thought that drive-up liquor stores were a very clever idea. I know better than that now. But I digress.

The point is that fast-food restaurants, banks, and liquor stores really don't have all that much in common, other than the drive-up window. As a consumer of hamburgers, liquor, and money (for hamburgers and liquor), I go to each place for entirely different reasons, but there is an advantage to my knowing that all three locations have drive-up windows. From a practical perspective, it means that I can drive to all three locations and never have to get out of my car. As long as I am in my car, I can interact with things that have drive-up windows. I might drive to the bank for a little cash, then swing by the fast-food restaurant for a hamburger and cola, followed by a quick jaunt to the liquor store for an aperitif. Same car, same guy at all three locations.

In my own humble opinion, I think interfaces are underrated and underused in REALbasic. Whenever you read about object-oriented programming, you almost invariably read about classes and objects and inheritance and things like that. Based on my own experience, I used to try to squeeze everything into a class/subclass relationship, regardless of whether it made sense to do so, when I could more easily have implemented an interface and be left with a more flexible program. So my advice to you (painfully learned, I might add) is to give due consideration to interfaces when you are thinking about how to organize your program.

Interfaces seem to have higher visibility in the Java programming world. I really began to see and understand their usefulness when I worked with the Apache Cocoon content-management framework. At the heart of Cocoon is the Cocoon pipeline, and the pipeline represents a series of steps that a piece of content must take to be displayed in a web page, or written to a PDF file. Basically, there are three stages:

1. The content must first be generated. Perhaps it resides as a file on the local file system, or it could live somewhere out on the Web, or it could even be stored in a database or some other dynamic repository.

2. The content must then be converted or transformed into the format required for the particular task at hand. If you are using Cocoon to manage your website, you might take the source data and transform it into HTML.

3. Finally, the content must be sent to the destination—either to a web browser at some distance location or into a file of a particular format to be stored on your computer.

In all three cases, the basic task is the same, but the specific steps taken within each stage are different, depending on the situation.

Cocoon uses a component-based approach; a *component* is basically an object that implements a particular interface. In the Cocoon world of components there are Generators, Transformers, and Serializers. These are not classes—they are interface definitions that say that any object that is a Generator is expected to behave in a certain way. There is a component manager that manages these components and shepherds the content through the pipeline as it goes from component to component.

The task or activity that a Generator must do is simple. It has to accept a request for content in the form of a URL, and it returns XML. That's it. Regardless of where the content comes from—a local file, a remote file, or a database, the same basic activity gets done. All the component manager knows about the Generator is that it can ask for a file at a given URL, and it can expect a file in return in XML format.

Now, if you are a programmer and you need to supply Cocoon with content, all you have to do is write an object that implements the interfaces specified by the Generator component and plug it into the pipeline. It's as simple as that. That's the beauty of components—you can mix and match them, plug them in, and take them out.

If you were to try the same thing using classes, you'd find your life to be extremely more complicated. You'd have to start with some abstract "Generator" class that had methods for requesting data and returning data as XML. Then you'd have to write a subclass for each kind of content you might want to retrieve and then override the associated methods. But what happens if you want to use a class as a generator that doesn't subclass your "Generator" class? Because REALbasic supports only single inheritance, each class can have only one superclass, and this imposes some limits on what you can do.

Interfaces, on the other, do not have the same limitations. A class can implement any number of interfaces, as long as it has the right methods.

Interfaces in REALbasic

To demonstrate how interfaces can be put to use in REALbasic, I'll define an Interface and then modify the **Properties** class to work with this interface. The interface will also be used extensively in the following section when I talk about how to create your own customized operator overloaders in REALbasic.

Before I get started, I should say that REALbasic uses interfaces extensively with Controls in a process called Control Binding. In the chapters that follow, I will revisit interfaces and show you how REALbasic uses them to make it easier to program your user interface.

If you recall, the **Properties** class implemented earlier in the chapter was designed to be able to accept both a string or a **FolderItem** in the `Constructor`. This is good because it makes it convenient to use, but it gets a little ugly when you get inside to look at the guts of the program. The reason I don't like it is that there are also two `ParsePropertyFile` methods, one for strings and the other for FolderItems, and each one is implemented differently. I don't like this because if I want to make a change in the future, I need to make sure that the change doesn't break either method. I'd rather have to check only one.

I will repeat them here to refresh your memory:

```
Protected Sub parsePropertyFile(myFile as string)
  Dim my_array(-1) as String
  Dim line as String

  my_array = myFile.split(Chr(13))

  For Each line In my_array
    Me.parseLine(line)
  Next
End Sub
```

This first version accepts a string in the parameter and then does two things. First, it splits the string into an `Array` and then it cycles through that `Array` to parse each individual line. Next, take a look at the **FolderItem** version:

```
Protected Sub parsePropertyFile(myPropertyFile as folderItem)
  Dim textInput as TextInputStream
  Dim astr as string

  If myPropertyFile Is Nil Then
      // An error has occurred
    Return
  End If
```

```
If myPropertyFile.exists Then
  Me.file = myPropertyFile
  textInput = me.file.OpenAsTextFile
  Do
    astr=textInput.ReadLine()
    Me.parseLine(astr)
  Loop Until textInput.EOF

  textInput.Close
Else
  // An error has occurred
End If

End Sub
```

   This, too, can be divided into two basic steps. First, the file is opened and a
TextInputStream is returned, and second, a loop cycles through the **TextInputStream**
parsing each line in the file. A much better design would be to have the "looping" take
place in one method, and the other prep work take place elsewhere. To do that, we need
to find a common way to loop through these two sources of data so that they can be
handled by one method.

   The obvious and easiest-to-implement solution would be to get a string from the
TextInputStream and then pass that string to the `parsePropertyFile` method that
accepts strings. Unfortunately, that doesn't help me explain how to use interfaces, so I'm
not going to do it that way. Instead, I'm going to implement an interface called
ReadableByLine and then pass objects that implement the **ReadableByLine** interface
to a new, unified `parsePropertyFile` method.

   There are advantages to doing it this way—some of which are immediate, whereas
others are advantageous later on when you want to do something else with this class. In
fact, this interface will come in even handier in the next section when I am writing custom operators for the **Properties** class.

   To implement the class interface, you first have to decide which methods will compose the interface. To make it the most useful, you want to use ones that will be applicable to the most situations. In the previous implementation of the `parsePropertyFile`
methods, the loop that iterated over the **TextInputStream** is most promising. (Because
`Arrays` are not really classes, the techniques used to iterate over the `Array` aren't applicable.) The methods are used by the **TextInputStream** class, and the code in question is
this:

```
Do
  astr=textInput.ReadLine()
  Me.parseLine(astr)
Loop Until textInput.EOF
```

If you look up **TextInputStream** in the language reference, you'll find that there are two implementations of `Readline`, and that `EOF` is a method. Their signatures follow:

```
TextInputStream.ReadLine() as String
TextInputStream.ReadLine(Enc as TextEncoding) as String
TextInputStream.EOF() as Boolean
```

There are other methods used by **TextInputStream**, but these are the ones I used previously. The language reference also says that the **TextInputStream** implements the **Readable** class interface. (The current language reference is in a state of flux as I write this, so I can only assume it still says this, but it's possible that it may not.) If REALbasic has already defined an interface, that's worth looking into. **Readable** is also implemented by **BinaryStream**, and the interface has two implementations of a `Read` method:

```
.Read(byteCount as Integer) as String
.Read(byteCount as Integer, Enc as Encoding) as String
```

Rather than reading text line by line, it reads a certain number of bytes of data, which isn't what we need. Therefore, inspired by the **Readable** title, I'll create a **ReadableByLine** interface that can be implemented by any class that wants you to be able to read through it line by line.

You create a class interface just like you create a class or a module. In the same project that contains the **Properties** class, click the **Add Class Interface** button on the **Project toolbar**, and you'll be presented with an screen much like the one used for modules and classes. The primary difference is that all your options are grayed out except **Add Method**; that's because interfaces contain only methods.

All you do when creating an interface is define the signature of the method—you do not implement it in any way. To implement the **ReadableByLine** interface, we'll implement the `ReadLine()` and `EOF()` methods like those used by **TextInputStream**. I'll also add another called `GetString()`, the usefulness of which will become evident later.

```
.ReadLine() as String
.ReadLine(Enc as TextEncoding) as String
.EOF() as Boolean
.GetString() as String
```

The next step is to go back to the **Properties** class and make the following modifications.

Implement the following `parsePropertiesFile` method:

```
Protected Sub parsePropertyFile(readable as ReadableByLine)
Dim aString as String

  If Not (Readable Is Nil) Then
    Me.readableSource = readable
    Do
      aString=readable.readLine()
      me.parseLine(aString)
```

```
    Loop Until readable.EOF
  End if
End Sub
```

Note that in the parameter, we refer to **ReadableByLine** exactly as if it were a class and readable was an instance of the class. Any variable that is declared an "instance" of **ReadableByLine** only has access to the methods of the interface, regardless of what the underlying class of the object is (which can be anything as long as it implements the **ReadableByLine** methods).

Next, the Constructors need to get updated. Instead of supplying a **FolderItem** or a string to the parsePropertyFile method, we want to send objects that implement the **ReadableByLine** interface.

The **TextInputStream** implements those methods. After all, that's where we got them from, but this also presents a problem. Because **TextInputStream** is a built-in class, I just can't go in and say that **TextInputStream** implements the **ReadableByLine** interface. REALbasic doesn't provide a mechanism for that.

The next possibility is to create a custom subclass of the **TextInputStream** and then say that it implements the interface, but that creates a problem, too. **TextInputStream** is one of a handful of built-in classes that can't be subclassed. Every time you use **TextInputStream**, you generate it from a **FolderItem** as a consequence of calling the OpenAsTextFile method. You can instantiate it yourself, or subclass it, but you can't assign any text to it (as far as I can tell), so it's only worthwhile when you get it from a **FolderItem**.

There's a third approach, which does mean you have to create a new class, but it's a good solution for these kinds of problems. All you do is create a class that's a wrapper of the **TextInputStream** class and say that it implements the **ReadableByLine** interface. This is a common tactic and it's sometimes called the "façade design pattern" in object-oriented circles because its one object provide a false front to another.

When you create the class, name it **ReadableTextInputStream** and add **ReadableByLine** to the interfaces label in the **Properties pane**.

ReadableTextInputStream Methods

The Constructor accepts a **TextInputStream** object and assigns it to the protected InputStream property.

```
Sub Constructor(tis as TextInputStream)
  InputStream = tis
End Sub
```

The other methods call the associated method from the **TextInputStream** class. They also append the value to the SourceLines() Array, which is primarily a convenience. It also provides a way to get at the data after you have iterated through all the "ReadLines" of **TextInputStream**.

```
Function ReadLine() As String
  Dim s as String
  s = InputStream.ReadLine
  Me.SourceLines.Append(s)
  Return s
End Function
Function ReadLine(Enc as TextEncoding) As String
  Dim s as String
  s = InputStream.ReadLine(Enc)
  Me.SourceLines.Append(s)
  Return s
End Function
Function EOF() As Boolean
  Return InputStream.EOF
End Function
Function getString() As String
  Return Join(SourceLines, EndOfLine.UNIX)
End Function
```

The final `getString()` method provides a way to get a string version of the **TextInputStream**.

ReadableTextInputStream Properties

```
Protected InputStream As TextInputStream
SourceLines(-1) As String
```

Now that the **TextInputStream** problem is solved, something similar needs to be done for strings.

ReadableString Methods

The string to be read is passed to the `Constructor`. Because I will be reading the string line by line, the first step is to "normalize" the character used to signify the end of a line. The `ReplaceLineEndings` function does that for me, and I have opted to standardize on Unix line endings, which are the ASCII character 13, otherwise known as the newline character.

Then I use the familiar `Split` function to turn the string into an `Array`. Finally, I will need to be able to track my position in the `Array` when using `ReadLine` so that I will know when I come to the end. I initialize those values in the `Constructor`. `LastPosition` refers to the last item in the `Array`. The `ReadPosition` is the current item in the `Array` being accessed, and it starts at zero. It will be incremented with each call to `ReadLine` until all lines have been read.

```
Sub Constructor(aSource as String)
  Source = ReplaceLineEndings(aSource, EndOfLine.UNIX)
  SourceLines = Split(Source, EndOfLine.UNIX)
  LastPosition = Ubound(SourceLines)
  ReadPosition = 0
End Sub
```

If you recall, the Do...Loop we used to iterate through the ReadLines() of the **TextInputStream** tested to see if it had reached the end of the file after each loop. The EOF() function provides for this functionality and will return true if the ReadPosition is larger than the LastPosition.

```
Function EOF() As Boolean
  If ReadPosition > LastPosition Then
    Return True
  Else
    Return False
  End if
End Function
```

In the ReadLine() methods, the line is accessed using the ReadPosition prior to incrementing the ReadPosition. The line text is assigned to the s variable. After that, ReadPosition is incremented, then s is returned. ReadPosition is incremented after accessing the Array because the EOF test comes at the end of the loop. This is also the way we check to see if ReadPosition is greater than LastPosition, because after you have read the last line and incremented ReadPosition, it will be equal to LastPosition + 1.

```
Function ReadLine() As String
  Dim s as String
  s = SourceLines(ReadPosition)
  ReadPosition = ReadPosition + 1
  Return s
End Function
Function ReadLine(Enc as TextEncoding) As String
  // Not implemented;
  Return ReadLine()
End Function
```

Because I start with a string, the getString() method is only a matter of returning it. The Source property is assigned the passed string in the Constructor.

```
Function getString() As String
  Return Source
End Function
```

ReadableString Properties

```
ReadPosition As Integer
Encoding As TextEncoding
Source As String
SourceLines(-1) As String
LastPosition As Integer
```

Finally, the two constructors for the **Properties** class need to be modified as follows:

```
Sub Properties.Constructor(aPropertyFile as FolderItem)
  Dim readable as ReadableTextInputStream
  readable = new _ ReadableTextInputStream(myPropertyFile.OpenAsTextFile)
  parsePropertyFile readable
End Sub
```

```
Sub Properties.Constructor(myPropertyString as String)
  Dim readable As ReadableString

  readable = New ReadableString(myPropertyString)
  parsePropertyFile readable

End Sub
```

For good measure, I create a `Constructor` that accepts a **ReadableByLine** implementing object directly.

```
Sub Properties.Constructor(readable as ReadableByLine)
  parsePropertyFile readable

End Sub
```

This may seem like a lot of work to implement an interface, but it shows you a realistic example of how one might be used. Now that this groundwork is laid, it is easy to come up with additional sources of "properties." For example, you could store them in a database. A database cursor would adapt to the **ReadableByLine** interface easily, and it would take very little work to add that as a new source for key/value pairs.

In the next section it will come up again, and at that point you will be able to see how the interface provides a lot more flexibility as the class you are working on grows in functionality.

Custom Operator Overloading

The fact that you can use the + with integers and strings is an example of operator overloading that you have already encountered. Customizable operator overloading is a relatively new feature in REALbasic, and I think it's extremely powerful and fun to use. It creates a lot of flexibility for the developer, and it is a good thing. A very good thing.

To refresh your memory, an operator works like a function except that instead of arguments being passed to it, operators work with operands. There's usually an operand to the left and the right of the operator, and REALbasic determines which overloaded version of the operator to use, based upon the operand types. That's how REALbasic knows to treat 1+1 different from "One" + "Two".

Customized operator overloading is accomplished by implementing one or more of the following methods in your class. I'm going to use the **Properties** class as our operator overloading guinea pig and add a lot of new features that will allow you to do all kinds of lovely things with the class, including adding together two **Properties** objects, testing for equality between two different instances, coercing a **Properties** object into a string and so on.

The operators will also work with the **ReadableByLine** interface so that in addition to being able to add two **Properties** objects together, you can add an object that implements **ReadableByLine** to a **Properties** object, and so on.

Special Operators

Function Operator_Lookup(aMemberName as String) as Variant

`Operator_Lookup()` counts among my favorite operators to overload. I don't know why. I just think it's fun because it effectively allows you to define objects in a much more dynamic way by adding members to the object at runtime. You're not really adding members, but it gives the appearance of doing so. The `Operator_Lookup()` function overloads the "." operator, which is used when accessing a method or property of an object.

Here is an example from the **Properties** class:

```
Function Operator_Lookup(aKey as String) as String
 Return me.get(aKey)
End Function
```

By implementing this function, I can now access any key in the **Properties** class as if it were a public property or method of the **Properties** class. This is how it would work in practice:

```
Dim prop as Properties
Dim s as String
prop = New Properties()
prop.set("FirstKey") = "FirstValue"
prop.set("SecondKey") = "SecondValue"
s = prop.FirstKey // s equals "FirstValue"
```

As you can see in this example, I am able to access the "FirstKey" key using dot (".") notation. When you try to access a member that REALbasic doesn't recognize, it first turns to see if an `Operator_Lookup()` method has been implemented. If one has been implemented, it passes the member name to the `Operator_Lookup()` method and lets that function handle it any way it likes.

In the **Properties** example, it calls the `get()` function, which returns a value for the key or, if the key is not in the **Properties** object, returns an empty string. Basically, I have a **Dictionary** whose keys are accessible as if they were members of the object. If you are familiar with Python, this may sound familiar because Python objects *are* Dictionaries, and you can access all Python objects both through Python's **Dictionary** interface or as members of the Python class. I should say, however, that I would not recommend using a **Dictionary** subclass with the `Operator_Lookup()` overloaded method as a general replacement for custom objects because there is a lot of overhead when instantiating **Dictionaries**. It's a perfect solution for situations like the **Properties** class, which needs to be a **Dictionary** subclass for a lot of reasons.

Function Operator_Compare(rightSideOperand as Variant) as Double

The `Operator_Compare()` function overloads the "=" operator. It tests to see if one operand is equal to the other one. The developer gets to decide what constitutes "equal to."

This is illustrated in the following example, which was implemented in the **Properties** class. The **Properties** object is the operand on the left side of the expression, and the right side of the expression is the argument passed using the "readable as **ReadableByLine**" parameter.

One thing you should notice right away is that the right side operand isn't of the same class as the left side operand; that's okay because you get to decide how this works. I find this approach useful because I may want to compare a file with an instantiated **Properties** object to see if there are any differences between the two. It's an extra step if I have to open the file, instantiate a **Properties** object, and then compare it with the original. This approach lets me compare the values represented by two distinct but related objects.

In practice, you can return any numeric data type—an integer, a short, or a double, but the answer is evaluated much like the `StrComp()` function. In other words, the number 0 means that both operands are equal to each other. A number greater than 0 means the left-side operand is greater than the right-side operand, and a number less than 0 means the left operand is less than the right.

```
Function Operator_Compare(readable as ReadableByLine) as Integer
  // mode = lexicographic
  dim newReadable as ReadableString

  Return StrComp(me.getString, readable.getString, 1 )
Function
```

This example actually uses `StrComp()` to make the comparison between the two related objects. It compares the string provided by the **Properties** object with that provided by the **ReadableByLine** argument. The function returns the results of the `StrComp()` function.

Function Operator_Convert() as Variant

There is an `Operator_Convert()` function and an `Operator_Convert` subroutine, both of which work with the assignment operator, but in slightly different ways. Consider the following implementation:

```
Function Operator_Convert() as String
 Return Me.getString()
End Function
```

This is how it is used:

```
Dim prop as Properties
Dim s as String
prop = New Properties("a=first" + chr(13) + "b=second")
s = prop // s equals the string '"a=first" + chr(13) + "b=second"'
```

In this example, the `prop` object is assigned to a variable with a string data type. The `Operator_Convert()` function coerces the `prop` object into a string. This is functionally equivalent to called the `prop.getString()` method.

Sub Operator_Convert(rightSideOperand as Variant)

The subroutine version handles assignment as well. The difference is that whereas the function assigns the value of the object executing the method to some other variable, the subroutine assigns the value of some other variable to the object executing the method. The argument passed in the "`readable as ReadableByLine`" parameter is the object whose value is being assigned to the calling object.

```
Sub Operator_Convert(readable as ReadableByLine)
  Dim tmpReadable as ReadableByLine

  If Not (me.readableSource is Nil) Then

    Me.Clear
    tmpReadable = Me.readableSource
    Me.readableSource = Nil
    Try
      Me.parsePropertyFile(readable)
    Catch
      // If new file fails, restore old version
      me.readableSource = tmpReadable
      me.parsePropertyFile(me.readableSource)
    End

  Else
    // No pre-existing data; so read new data
    Me.parsePropertyFile(readable)
  End If

End Function
```

In this example, I assign the value of a **ReadableByLine** object to that of a **Properties** object. This means that I can use the assignment operator ("=") to instantiate a new **Properties** object.

```
Dim prop1, prop2 as Properties
Dim s1, s2 as String
Dim r as ReadableString
s1 = "a=first" + chr(13) + "b=second"
s2 = "c=third" + chr(13) + "d=fourth"
prop1 = New Properties(s1)
```

```
r = New ReadableString(s2)
prop2=r
```

In this example, `prop1` is instantiated using the `New` operator, whereas `prop2` is instantiated using simple assignment. In a sense, this functionality gives the **Properties** class something of the flavor of a data type.

Addition and Subtraction

You can also overload the "+" and "-" operators, enabling you to add objects to each other or subtract objects from each other. You have already seen an overloaded version of "+" that is used with strings. When used with strings, the "+" operator concatenates the strings. Because our **Properties** class deals with strings, you can create similar functionality for your objects. In this case, you can add two **Properties** objects together and this will concatenate the strings associated with each object and return a new object generated from the concatenated string.

Listing 3.1   Function Operator_Add(rightSideOperand as Variant) as Variant

```
Function Operator_Add(readable as ReadableByLine) as Properties
  // Since parsePropertyFile does not reset
  //the data when called, this adds more values
  //to the Property object
  Dim s as String
  Dim newProp as Properties

  s = Self.getString + EndOfLine.UNIX + readable.getString

  newProp = New Properties(s)

  return newProp
End Function
```

When you implement the `Operator_AddRight()` version, you do the same thing, but switch the order in which the strings are concatenated. In the following example, note that the string concatenation happens in the opposite order from the previous example.

Listing 3.2   Operator_AddRight(leftSideOperand as Variant) as Variant

```
Function Operator_AddRight(readable as ReadableByLine) as Properties
  Dim prop as Properties
  Dim s as String

  s = readable.getString+ EndOfLine.UNIX +  me.getString
  prop = New Properties(s)

  Return prop
End Function
```

Operator_Subtract(rightSideOperand as Variant) as Variant, Operator_SubtractRight (leftSideOperand as Variant) as Variant

The subtraction operators work in a predictable way, just like the add operators, except that the values are being subtracted. Although I did not implement this method in the **Properties** class, I can imagine it working something like this: Any key/value pair that exists in the left-side operand is deleted from that object if it also exists in the right-side operand. If I wanted to delete a group of key/value pairs from a **Properties** object, I could use a **Properties** object that contained these key/value pairs as one of the operands.

Boolean

Operator_And(rightSideOperand as Variant) as Boolean, Operator_AndRight (leftSideOperand as Variant) as Boolean, Operator_Or(rightSideOperand as Variant) as Boolean, Operator_OrRight(leftSideOperand as Variant) as Boolean

For the And operator to return True, both operands must evaluate to True as well. Here's a scenario where this might make sense: the **Properties** class (and many other classes, too) can be instantiated, but not populated by any values. If you tested to see if the operands were equal to Nil, you would be told that they are not Nil. However, it might be useful to be able to distinguish whether there are any values at all in the object. You can use the And operator to do this. Within the Operator_And method, test to see if each operand has a value. If both do, return True. If one or more does not, return False.

More Operator Overloading

There are several more operators that can be overloaded, but they do not have an application with the **Properties** class. They work much like the ones I have covered here, except that they overload negation, the Not operator, and the multiplication operators such as *, /, Mod, and so on. They are

```
Operator_Negate() as Variant
Operator_Not() as Boolean
 Operator_Modulo(rightSideOperand as Variant) as Variant
Operator_ModuloRight(leftSideOperand as Variant) as Variant
Operator_Multiply(rightSideOperand as Variant) as Variant
Operator_MultiplyRight(leftSideOperand as Variant) as Variant
Operator_Power(rightSideOperand as Variant) as Variant
Operator_PowerRight(leftSideOperand as Variant) as Variant
Operator_Divide(rightSideOperand as Variant) as Variant
Operator_DivideRight(leftSideOperand as Variant) as Variant
Operator_IntegerDivide(rightSideOperand as Variant) as Variant
Operator_IntegerDivideRight(leftSideOperand as Variant) as Variant
```

Extends

Finally, there is an additional way of extending a class that does not involve subclassing or interfaces. REALbasic allows you to implement methods in Modules and use those methods to extend or add functionality to other classes. Some classes, like the **TextInputStream** class I discussed earlier, can't really be effectively subclassed in REALbasic, and this is where using the `Extends` keyword can come in handy because it gives you an opportunity to add methods to **TextInputStream** without subclassing it.

I'll start with an example, which should make things clearer.

Unix Epoch

Unix uses a different epoch to measure time than REALbasic does. Instead of January 1, 1904 GMT, Unix measures time since January 1, 1970 GMT. The difference between these two values is 2,082,848,400 seconds. One useful addition to the Date object would be a method that converted REALbasic's measurement of time to the way that Unix measures time.

It's possible to subclass **Date**, but that only provides a partial solution because it doesn't help you with all the other instances of data objects that you encounter while programming. For example, the `FolderItem` class has **Date** properties for the file creation date and the date the file was last modified. A subclass won't help you there.

It is for this kind of problem in particular that `Extends` is made. `Extends` allows you to *extend* a class with a new method without having to subclass it. The method that will be used to extend the class must be implemented in a module, and the first parameter must be preceded by the `Extends` keyword, followed by a parameter of the class that is being extended.

The following example adds a method `UnixEpoch` that can be called as a member of the `Date` class. It returns the date as the number of seconds since January 1, 1970, rather than January 1, 1904.

```
Protected Function UnixEpoch(Extends d as Date) As Double
   Return d.TotalSeconds - 2082848400
End Function
```

Conclusion

In addition to being an object-oriented programming language, one of the most important distinguishing characteristics of REALbasic is that it is a cross-platform application development environment. You can compile applications for Windows, Macintosh, and Linux. In my experience, REALbasic is the easiest language to use for this kind of development, but it is not without its own idiosyncrasies and, despite their similarities, the three platforms vary in fundamental ways that a developer needs to be aware of. In the next chapter, I write about the cross-platform features of REALbasic and how the differences among the platforms will impact your development.

4

Cross-Platform Application Development

DESPITE HOW WELL REALBASIC HAS DONE masking developers from all the underlying considerations required to develop applications for Macintosh, Windows, and Linux, there are still some things about the different platforms that you, the developer, should be aware of.

One consistent element of REALbasic is that they take a practical approach to everything they do. They are not purists. They are pragmatic. As a consequence, their object-oriented language retains procedural programming features that often make things easier to do. Likewise, they take a practical approach to cross-platform development. This means that as a developer, you are often given access to platform-specific features, something that is a little different from the philosophy of Java, which tends to view that sort of thing as if not impure, then at least not pure. That makes perfect sense in many situations, but there are also times when it makes sense to leverage the unique aspects of the individual platforms for which the application is being developed.

Throughout REALbasic's documentation are references to platform-specific features, most commonly Macintosh features that reflect the language's Macintosh origins. If you're a Windows or a Linux developer, you might find it a little confusing. Likewise, both modern Macintosh operating systems and Linux share a common UNIX heritage, and if you are a Windows developer, you might find this confusing as well.

The most fundamental cross-platform activity is compiling your application, so I will return to the HTMLViewer example application from Chapter 2, "Programming with REALbasic," and walk through the steps required to compile that simple application for all the platforms REALbasic supports (recall that the cross-platform compilation features of REALbasic are a feature of the Professional Edition).

As I step through this example I will give a brief history of each platform and an overview of platform-specific terminology or functionality that you are likely to run into while developing your cross-platform applications.

The second aspect of REALbasic programming where you will encounter the idiosyncrasies of each platform is when dealing with folders and files. All three platforms use different file systems, and they organize their file structure in different ways. I will document each platform's file system and delve into REALbasic's **FolderItem** class and supporting functions that you will use to manipulate files and folders.

Beyond this, there are also some classes provided by REALbasic that apply only to a particular platform or that have methods or properties that apply only to a particular platform. These will be discussed in detail in the section pertaining to the class. Before I get started, I think it can be informative to take a brief look at Java's approach to cross-platform programming, pointing out the differences between the two strategies and weighing the relative strength of both approaches.

That Other Cross-Platform Language

There are certainly cross-platform solutions other than REALbasic, the most notable of which is Java. Java may make the most sense for you in some situations, but sometimes REALbasic will make the most sense. The marketing material for REALbasic 2005 confidently asserts that Java on the desktop has failed. That's overstating things just a bit, but it is true that Java has never flourished as a language used to develop client applications. Instead, Java's strength has been at the server level, where it has found its way into many enterprise applications.

A brief history of Java will help to explain the different approach that REALbasic takes, especially with respect to user-interface elements. REALbasic and Java take two fundamentally different approaches, each with its own strengths and weaknesses.

AWT

The first way to code GUIs in Java was known as AWT—something which reportedly took only a few weeks to create. AWT used native application controls for Java application controls, but the engineers made available only those controls that were available on both platforms. This led to there being only a small subset of available controls. This wasn't the biggest problem, however. What didn't work was that the controls behaved differently on different platforms. It was next to impossible (and believe me, I tried) to get one GUI application to work the same way on a Macintosh and a Windows machine.

Swing

Part of the underlying problem with AWT is that the controls on different operating systems often work in different ways. As a way around this, the next GUI solution for Java was Swing. The Swing library provided access to a set of custom-designed Java controls. This avoided the not-working-the-same problem, but created a new one. Java apps were different than native apps on each platform and people didn't like this. The apps themselves stood out like a sore thumb.

Incidentally, the Mozilla web browser bills itself as a cross-platform development solution. Although it's a web browser, you can also create apps with it. It suffers from the same problem with Swing, in that the developers chose to create user-interface elements specifically for Mozilla, which leads to a nonstandard-looking application.

SWT

There is a relatively recent alternative to AWT and Swing called SWT (for Standard Widget Toolset), and I must say that it is a much, much better solution than either AWT or Swing. SWT uses native controls as well, but does so in a way that avoids the problem with controls working differently on different platforms. All in all, SWT is quite good, but there is still a little sluggishness in the application, which comes less from the interface than it does from Java itself. Java applications are slow to start up and they consume a lot of memory.

Despite the obvious benefits of Java, most commercial applications are still compiled applications because the Java approach just doesn't seem to work that well with desktop applications.

Compiling REALbasic Applications

REALbasic takes a different approach and creates a user interface that is compiled into native machine code for each application. There is nothing like Java's Virtual Machine; REALbasic apps are apps just like any other. Although REALbasic uses native controls when possible, in some instances they have REALbasic-specific implementations (the ListBox is an example). In those cases, there can be some minor differences between REALbasic and a native app, but the interface is responsive and quick.

Despite these differences, REALbasic has gone to great lengths to shield the developer from most (but not all) of the differences between the underlying systems. However, there is no avoiding the fact that you will encounter meaningful differences in the way that certain things work on different platforms; it is absolutely essential that if you plan to deploy your application on multiple platforms, you test them accordingly.

Some of the differences can be subtle and can manifest in the way that text and binary data is handled, the order in which events are fired, and how users expect to interact with the application itself. This chapter will focus on the more generalized differences, particularly those that impact user interaction with your application. Throughout the rest of the book, I will provide platform-specific information when necessary.

There are also several platform-specific classes provided by REALbasic. My focus in this book is the cross-platform aspects of programming in REALbasic, so I will limit the amount of space I devote to those classes, unless you really need to use them to provide basic functionality on that platform. For example, I'm not going to provide an in-depth and comprehensive look at AppleScript and the AppleScript classes provided by REALbasic.

A Note About UNIXlike Systems

The word UNIX is trademarked, and to be called UNIX, an operating system must be certified. Both Macintosh OS X and Linux are said to be UNIXlike systems, a phrase whose intent is to avoid trademark issues. The goal of Linux developers is for Linux to be compatible with UNIX in practice, even if not certified as such. The code used to develop Linux was written from the ground up for that purpose, and it does not use any actual code from UNIX-related systems like FreeBSD. Although OS X was, in fact, based on FreeBSD (BSD refers to the Berkeley Software Distribution of UNIX, a version developed at U.C. Berkeley), it has not been certified. There apparently has been a little quibbling over the fact that OS X is billed as being built on UNIX even though it lacks certification. In any event, throughout this section I'll refer to both Linux and OS X as UNIXlike systems.

The RSS Reader Application

Throughout the rest of the book, most of the examples are going to be used to create an RSS Reader application from the ground up. RSS stands for Really Simple Syndication, or something like that, depending upon whom you ask. It is a simple XML format that websites use to syndicate their content. In the web world, syndication usually means letting another website display headlines and story summaries from your site on their site. A lot of people use RSS as a way to view a website's content in a more convenient way. Software applications developed for this purpose are called RSS Readers.

An RSS Reader works by maintaining a list of URLs for RSS files that you are subscribed to. At predetermined intervals, the reader gets a copy of the file and stores it locally on your computer. It converts the RSS format into HTML to read it.

In this chapter, I will show you the basic steps required to set up an application that will be compiled for Windows, Macintosh, and Linux computers. This is a good point to review some of the differences between the three platforms because the platforms you are building for impact a variety of things, including the name that you choose for your application.

Compiling Applications

In the Quick Start, where the HTMLViewer application was introduced, I ran the application by clicking the **Run** button in the IDE. This compiled the application and launched it. When you are actively developing your application, you will run it this way. When a REALbasic application is run from the IDE like this, it's in **Debug** mode, which allows you to use REALbasic's excellent debugging tools. However, after you are finished programming your application, you will want to compile it. The compiler takes the source programming code written by you, the programmer, and converts it into the binary format suitable for the target application.

To compile an application, there are a few things you need to do. Actually, you don't *have* to do anything. You could compile an empty project if you wanted to, but there are a few things you will probably want to do before you compile the application. If you are using the Professional Edition, you will need to decide which platforms to compile your application for and what you are going to call it. It is especially important to decide up front whether your application will be running on multiple platforms because that will impact how you proceed.

You probably recall that when you create a new desktop application project in REALbasic, there are a few classes that get prepopulated in the integrated development environment. These are classes that have certain special characteristics, the most important of which is that they are all instantiated automatically when the program is launched. They are as follows:

```
App
MenuBar1
Window1
```

In this chapter, I will focus on **App** (which is a subclass of the **Application** class) because it represents the actually application and the **App** object is always available to your program. Many of the properties of the **App** class refer to the platform for which the application is being compiled, so to understand what those properties mean, you must first know a little bit more about the platforms on which the application will be compiled.

The operating systems that REALbasic compiles for are similar in many ways—they all have a graphical user interface and rely on a desktop metaphor to organize files and directories into documents and folders, and in most cases, the user interaction is very similar. But there are also some important differences in the user interface, the way that windows are displayed, and how files are named, and where they get stored.

Windows

The progenitor of the modern Windows operating system is DOS, an acronym for the unimaginative moniker Disk Operating System, which Microsoft developed for use in IBM's personal computers (a precursor to DOS was known as QDOS, which reportedly means Quick and Dirty Operating System). There are DOS variants, not all of which were produced by Microsoft. The Microsoft versions are called MS-DOS, to contrast with IBM's PC-DOS and other non-Microsoft variants.

Even though DOS is ancient history, the DOS legacy is still readily identifiable in the modern Windows operating systems. Whereas Macintosh and Linux operating systems have their roots in UNIX, Windows has its roots in DOS. Although DOS was not derived from UNIX, it uses some UNIXlike concepts such as the shell, which provides a command-line interface to the underlying operating system.

The file system used by DOS is FAT (or FAT16), another one of those engaging acronyms that means File Allocation Table. The most memorable feature of this file system was that filenames were limited to eight characters, followed by a period, and a three-character extension. Although it is possible to come up with a large number of unique filenames using this system, it is almost impossible to do so in a meaningful way using descriptive names.

The first version of Windows was released in 1985 and was really just an application that ran on DOS. Windows 3.1 (released in 1992) represented a much more mature operating system, one that was capable of multitasking and using virtual memory. Windows represented Microsoft's version of a graphical user interface—one which was designed to be very similar to that of the competing Macintosh systems.

With Windows 95, Windows began to rely less on DOS for operating system services (for instance, it no longer relied on file-system services from DOS). Windows also adopted the FAT32 file system, which allowed the use of long filenames. Windows 98 followed, and the last of this line of development was Windows ME (the ME is for Millennium Edition, because it was released in 2000).

The current versions of Windows are rooted in Windows NT, which was a version of Windows developed for business users and was intended to compete in the corporate server market. It was first developed in 1993. Microsoft eventually decided to combine its operating system products into one system, so that both consumer-oriented and business-oriented systems would be built on the same underlying technology. In 2001, Windows XP represents that unified approach to operating systems. Microsoft still markets different operating systems to different end users, but all of them are built on the same basic technology. Current variants are

- Windows XP Personal Edition
- Windows XP Professional Edition
- Windows Server 2003

Macintosh

Apple computer develops both the hardware and the operating system for Macintosh computers, which means that there is a tight connection between the two.

There are two lines of development worth noting. The first is that of the processors used by the Macintosh operating system, and the second is that of the operating system itself.

When Macintosh computers were first released in 1984, they used processors from Motorola's 68K line of microprocessors. In 1995, Macintosh switched to PowerPC (PPC) processors. To provide developers a relatively painless transition, applications were compiled into binary code that could run on both 68K Macs and PPC Macs. Code compiled into this format is called PEF (or CFM).

Macintosh recently announced that it was abandoning the PPC platform in favor of Intel processors, and this represents the third round of hardware changes.

In addition to changing the underlying hardware, Apple also made a revolutionary overhaul of its operating system that was released in March, 2001, called OS X. This was the replacement for System 9, the last version of the original Mac operating system.

OS X was a completely redesigned system based on the FreeBSD/Mach-O distribution of UNIX and technology originally developed by NeXT Computing. With such a major transition in operating systems, Apple found that it needed to help developers make the transition. Now, instead of compiling applications to run on two different processors, Apple needed to produce software that could run on two different operating systems.

The answer to this problem was Carbon, a C library based on the old Macintosh Toolkit that allowed developers to write applications that would run on both System 9 and OS X. In addition to Carbon, there is Cocoa, which is an Objective-C object library used to build modern OS X applications.

Linux

Linux is a UNIXlike operating system created by Linus Torvalds. Unlike Windows and Macintosh operating systems, the source code is freely available and anyone can use it. Because it behaves like UNIX, you will find there are more similarities between the way that modern Macintosh computers work and a Linux workstation—at least in terms of the command-line environment, file system, and reliability.

Linux was originally developed for x386 machines (like Windows), but it is now capable of running on a variety of platforms. Linux applications compiled by REALbasic work only on x386 platforms, though. The requirements are that the Linux installation should run GTK 2.2 or greater and have CUPS installed, but REALbasic officially supports only Red Hat and SUSE distributions.

Even though Linux is not UNIX, there are compatibility layers that emulate Linux on UNIX machines. For example, I was able to get REALbasic CGI applications to run on FreeBSD. Contemporary distributions of FreeBSD include a Linux compatibility layer, but it is usually not turned on by default. There is more than one compatibility layer, and they are based on different Linux distributions, so the key is to use a compatibility layer based on a Linux distribution that REALbasic is compatible with. In this instance, I used a Red Hat-based compatibility layer. You can read more about compatibility layers on the FreeBSD website, http://freebsd.org/.

Technically speaking, Linux refers to the kernel and not all the other software that comes with it. One consequence is that there are different desktop environments, with slight differences among them. The two leading contenders are the KDE desktop environment and Gnome. REALbasic applications should work on both, but there may be differences.

While writing this book, I tested the sample applications on SUSE Linux 9.2, using the KDE desktop environment. I have made every effort to make sure the Linux information is comprehensive, but I should also say that I think it's a good idea to double-check your application on both KDE and Gnome, if possible. Also, at the time of writing this, the Linux implementation of REALbasic was trailing the Windows and Macintosh implementations, and the final version had yet to be released.

Configuring the Compiler

Before turning to the App class, I want to discuss REALbasic's build settings. I'm assuming you have created a new project in REALbasic and decided that the project will be a desktop application. When you first create a project, it is untitled, and you give it a name when you save it for the first time. I always save it right away and give the project a name. For the purposes of the examples I give, I'll be calling this project RSSReader.

Even though you don't need to set the build settings until you are ready to compile the application, I think it's valuable to start at that point because it identifies the platform choices you will have to make and will serve as a good place to begin discussing the differences between the apps.

In the **Project** menu, select **Build Settings,** and the window shown in Figure 4.1 will appear:

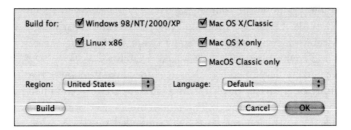

Figure 4.1   Build settings.

Because you certainly already know that REALbasic compiles for Windows, Macintosh, and Linux, you might be surprised at the number of options you have when compiling a Macintosh program. This comes as a consequence of the variety of hardware and system changes that Macs have undergone over the years.

Here is what the options available for compiling on Macintosh mean:

- Mac OS X/Classic—Carbon (PEF), executable on any PPC-based Macintosh.
- Mac OS X—Cocoa (Mach-0), will run on PPC-based Macintosh computers running OS X.
- Mac "Classic"—System 9 Only, executable on either 68K or PPC-based computers.

Here are some factors to consider when deciding which Macintosh platforms you should build for:

- The only practical reason to compile for Mac "Classic" is if you already have an application created and you have customers who use it on a System 9-Only Macintosh. These folks are few and far between and chances are they could run a Carbon version of your application as well, unless their Mac is really, really old.
- Use the Cocoa (Mach-0) build if you want to make use of some OS X specific features, such as accessing Frameworks, which are the equivalent of shared libraries.
- Otherwise, the simplest choice is to choose the Carbon build, because the largest number of Mac users will be able to use it.

- Remember that Macintosh is switching to Intel processors and REALbasic will provide support for compiling on the new processors when they are available. Some of these choices may change as a consequence, but at this point, it's too early to say how that might impact your choices.

Next Steps

Now that you understand the different formats you can compile your application to, you can turn to the **App** class. When you configure **App**'s properties, you will need to decide your application's name for each platform, how you are going to manage different versions of your application, the file types your application will access, and which icon should be used to represent it.

All this work is done with the **App** class.

The App Class

Every application you create in REALbasic, whether it's a console application or a desktop application, has a special object, **App**, which is an instance of the **App** class, a subclass of the **Application** class. If your applications are relatively simple, the **App** object could very well be the only area of your application where you have to be concerned about cross-platform issues.

I call **App** a class, but it's really kind of a magical thing that falls somewhere between a class and an object. Like a regular class, it can be subclassed. At the same time, if you do nothing it will be implicitly instantiated every time your application runs, so you never have to do that yourself. If you subclass **App**, the subclass lowest in the hierarchy is the subclass that is instantiated. For instance, if you create a class **MyApp** that is a subclass of **App**, **MyApp** will be the version that is instantiated. In REALbasic lingo, the instantiated version is the "blessed" version of **App**.

After you've launched a new project in the IDE (shown in Figure 4.2), select **App** in the **Project Editor;** you will see the list of **App**'s properties, which you can set.

App Properties Pane

The **App Properties** pane also provides you opportunities to configure your application for cross-platform development. The **ListBox** is divided into sections, and I'll address each one individually.

The ID Section

The ID properties are the same basic ID properties that every class has—Name, Interfaces, and Super. In the default **App** class, you can see that it does not implement any interfaces, but it does subclass the **Application** class. As I mentioned earlier, you can subclass **App**. The subclass of **App** that is the lowest in the hierarchy (the **App** subclass that's not a superclass of anything) is treated as the "blessed" version, and it is the one that is automatically instantiated. Regardless of which subclass is used, the values set in the **Properties** pane remain valid.

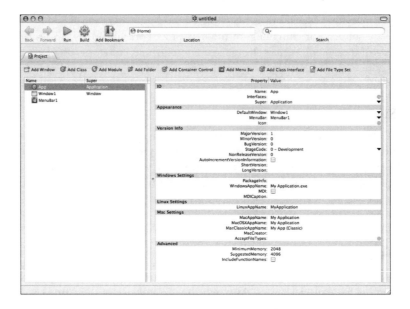

Figure 4.2   The App object.

The Appearance Section

The Appearance Section sets values for windows, menus, and icons.

Default Window

This setting determines the default window that gets automatically launched when your application starts. It defaults to **Window1**, which is the default window that REALbasic places in each project.

MenuBar

MenuBars are discussed in much greater detail in the next chapter, but this is where the default menu bar for the application is set. **MenuBars** are one area where some significant differences exist between the Macintosh platform and either Windows or Linux.

Macintosh computers have only one **MenuBar** available at a time, and it is always at the top of the window. Contrast this with standard Windows and Linux behavior where the **MenuBar** is associated with each window. You can have two or more windows open, and each one can have a different **MenuBar** assigned. This is not the case with Macs.

By default, this value is set to **MenuBar1**, which is the magically instantiated **MenuBar** that is created whenever you create a new REALbasic project.

Icons

Applications normally have a group of icons associated with them. One is for the application itself, and potentially others are associated with files created by the application. The **App** object provides a simple interface for associating an icon with the application—one that lets you avoid the details of doing this on the native platforms (all of which handle this differently).

In the **App Properties** pane, click **Icon** in the **Appearance Section** and the `Edit Icon` window will appear. On the left side is the list of **Icon Variations**, which list the standard sizes and the different color depths to be used for them. The largest icons are 128×128 pixels, and the smallest are 16×16 pixels. With the exception of the 128×128 pixel icon, all others come in two color depths—millions of colors and 256 colors. When you prepare a REALbasic application for cross-compilation, you will need to have an icon for each size established. If you don't, REALbasic will use the default application icon on each platform.

To the right of the **Icon Variations ListBox** are three boxes, labeled Image, Mask, and Preview. In the following example, I have selected the 128×128 size icon, and I have simply cut and pasted an image I created in a graphics program. Immediately, the **Preview** box is filled in, refer to Figure 4.3.

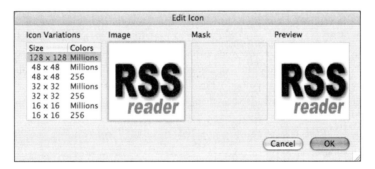

Figure 4.3   Create an icon for your application.

As you can see in the previous example, the background in the **Preview** box is white, just like the image that was pasted into the Image box. This means that every time you see this icon, it will have a white background—on the desktop, in different folders, and so on. To have a transparent background, you need to use a mask.

When I created this icon, I used Canvas; it has a convenient feature that lets me automatically generate a mask for an image. Using the same graphic as the starting point, I had Canvas export the mask, which left two images that I pasted into the **Icon Editor**. In the Image box is an image with a white background (note that it looks a little different from the original pasted one), and in the Mask box is an image that also has a white background, but in the Previous box you can see the icon with a transparent background.

Think of it like a mask you wear for Halloween. If you put a mask on, your face is covered, but your eyes can be seen. The Mask image in the **Icon Editor**, the white part is the "mask" and the black part are the "holes" that you can see through. The mask is laid over the original image; the parts that are masked are transparent, and the parts that "show through" are seen, see Figure 4.4.

Figure 4.4   Make the icon background transparent.

After you have your icon properly masked, you need to cut and paste the icon into the other sizes. The following example shows the same icon in 256 colors and 48×48 size. The reason REALbasic gives you the option of creating different sizes instead of doing it automatically for you is that sometimes automatic scaling doesn't look good, especially if you use an icon with a lot of colors or complex shading patterns. To create an icon that looks good at all sizes, you may need to create distinct versions in various sizes before copying them into REALbasic as shown in Figure 4.5.

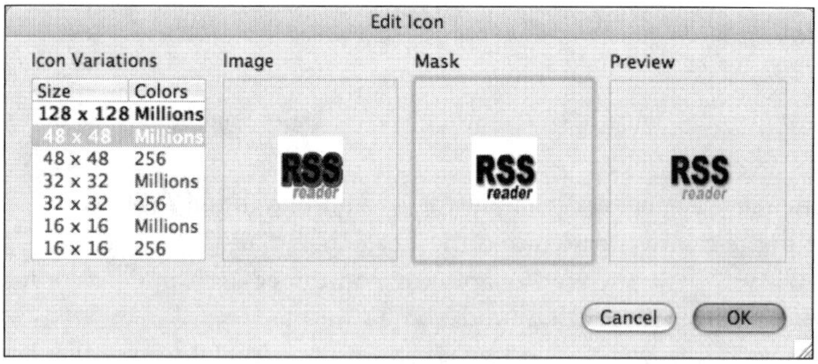

Figure 4.5   Copy and paste to create different-sized icons.

The Version Info Section

The **Version Info** section lets you document the particular stage of development your application is in. How you want to use it is largely up to you, but some of this data is made available to the system and accessible by the user, so you want to make sure you fill it out.

Although there is no "standard" way to version an application, some ways are more standard than others. A common practice is to use three digits separated by a period, like so:

```
1.2.3
```

The first digit is the `App.MajorVersion` number, the second is the `App.MinorVersion` number, and the last of the numbers is referred to as the `App.BugNumber`. `MajorVersion` and `MinorVersion` are constrained to values between 0 and 255.

In addition to these three numbers, you can also identify the `App.StageCode` value. There are class constants that can be used for the `StageCode` values (and, yes, as of RB 2005 r2, the misspelling of Development is required):

```
App.Developement = 0
App.Alpha = 1
App.Beta = 2
App.Final = 3
```

Alpha means the application is in the early stages of development; it may be unstable and is probably not suitable for daily use. A Beta version is further along and is much more stable; it is at the stage of bug fixes and is not subject to major changes prior to the final release. Final is, of course, ready for production.

Finally, there is the `App.NonRelease` version, which refers to the current stage of development. So, altogether, a number like this:

```
0.1.1.4
```

Means the following: A `MajorVersion` of 0 means that you have not released a major version. Projects that are in Alpha or Beta usually use a `MajorVersion` number of 0 to signify the fact. The `MinorVersion` is 1, which is followed by the `StageCode` of 1, which indicates that this is an Alpha version of your application. This happens to be the fourth version of your Alpha. When you decide you've reached the Beta stage, the `App.NonRelease` version will start over again at 0.

Generally speaking, incrementing the `MajorVersion` indicates a big change in functionality. A `MinorVersion` increment indicates a relatively smaller update in features, and the `BugVersion` represents releases that coincide with bug fixes and things like that.

`ShortVersion`, `LongVersion`, and `PackageInfo` are text strings used to represent the name of your application. You can have a short and long version of the name. `PackageInfo` is additional text that can be used however you like. On Macintosh computers, what you enter in `PackageInfo` is used in the Info.plist file, in the CFGetBundleInfo element.

The Windows Settings Section

Windows Settings is the first of the platform-specific properties that you can set.

WindowsAppName

Here you place your application name. All Windows applications end with a .exe extension. This tells the operating system that this is an executable file. Also of great importance is that the name of each platform's version of your app should be different. This is because the applications will be compiled in the same directory and you do not want to overwrite them.

Bear in mind that this represents the filename of your application, not what the application should be called. You can use spaces in the name, if you'd like, but in general I'd suggest using a short, simple, and to-the-point name for the file.

MDI and MDI Caption

MDI stands for Multiple-Document Interface, and this is a Windows-only feature that even the Windows design guidelines say you should avoid. As shown in Figure 4.6, an MDI application has a single containing window, and all other windows that get open in your application are constrained to live within that area.

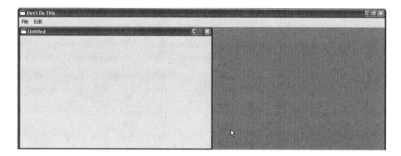

Figure 4.6   MDI window.

The Windows development site says that the reason to avoid MDI applications is that new users find them confusing. A better reason to avoid them is the reason offered by Apple. If you are a designer working on a Macintosh computer, there's a good chance that you are going to have multiple applications open with multiple documents open. You will probably also be cutting and pasting from a document from one application into a document of another application. The MDI interface makes this awkward, at best, to do—it is application oriented rather than window oriented. When you create an MDI application, you are placing limits on how your user can use the application, and that's not such a good idea.

Macintosh Settings

The Macintosh Settings area contains configuration options for both Carbon and Mach-O builds of Macintosh applications.

MacAppName

This is the name for the Carbon version of your application. You do not have to end the name with a particular extension. Any name will do (although I will talk about some constraints on filenames in the upcoming section on files).

MacOSXAppName

The OS X version of your application name will end with .app, but you do not have to enter it here—it will be done for you automatically. The name used for an OS X name differs from that used for Windows and the Carbon version because it doesn't refer to a file, even though the Macintosh user interface treats it like a file. This name points to a folder that contains folders and files related to your application, which is called a *bundle* in Macintosh terminology. I'll return to this later.

MacClassAppName

The name for your "Classic" Mac application. It has to be limited to 31 characters or fewer, but it can include spaces.

MacCreator

All Macintosh applications have a creator code, which is a series of four letters. These codes have to be registered with Apple to use them, and it provides a unique identifier that the system uses to identify an application and files created by that application. Although Apple seems to be moving away from this approach, you will need it to successfully build your application in REALbasic and link your application icons and files created by your application to the application itself.

AcceptFileTypes

Macintosh applications let you drag and drop a file onto the application as a method of opening the file (it can be used to do anything you want, but that's what it is most commonly used for). You can list the names of the accepted file types here. However, to do that, you need to know how to define file types, and that is discussed later in this chapter.

The Linux Settings Section

Linux settings are simple enough: the application name. Linux requires no special extensions on its applications. Because it is a UNIXlike environment, the operating system knows that it is an application if the Executable permission is set to true for either the owner, the group, or the world. File permission settings will be discussed later in this chapter.

The Advanced Section

The advanced settings are new to REALbasic. The first two allow you to determine a minimum amount of memory for your application to use, as well as a suggested amount of memory for your application to use. The general rule is that the more memory your application has available to it, the faster it will run, but there is one big caveat: You don't want to allocate so much that you use so much of your computer's memory that it has to begin relying on virtual memory, which involves saving data to a file and reading out again, which will slow down your application terribly.

I do not know of any general rule or guidelines about how best to set these values, because it depends on a lot things.

The last of the advanced options is `IncludeFunctionNames`, which determines whether the English (or whatever language you speak) function names you use are compiled into your application. If you select yes, others can peek and see how you've named your functions. This may or may not be interesting information to them, and you may or may not want them to have it.

In addition to the properties available in the **Properties pane**, the **App** object has a full range of events and methods as well. I will revisit the **App** object in the next chapter.

Files and Directory Organization

Because one of the properties you are asked to identify refers to the kind of file types your application will be handling, this is a good point to introduce how REALbasic handles documents and folders and discuss the cross-platform implications of it all.

The way in which the folders and files are organized in each platform vary greatly. Each platform has standards for where applications, documents, preference files, and so on should be stored. Additionally, each platform uses a different file system with different requirements.

In this section I will review the **FolderItem** class and how it interacts with the underlying operating system; then I'll cover how each operating system organizes its files.

Table 4.1 documents the file systems in use on the three platforms:

Table 4.1   **Windows, Macintosh, and Linux File Systems**

File System	Characteristics	Operating System
FAT16	8.3 filenames	DOS
FAT32	Long filenames (255 character limit)	Windows 95
NTFS	Long filenames (255 character limit)	Windows NT
HFS	31 Character Limit	"Classic" Mac
HFS Plus	255 Character Limit	OS X

NTFS and HFS Plus are the two default file systems on Windows and Macintosh OS X, respectively. Windows application files end in .exe; Macintosh application files end in .app. You do not necessarily have to use extensions on other files, but REALbasic uses file extensions to detect file types, so my advice is to use them. The extension is also no longer limited to three characters. When compiling for Carbon, filenames are limited to 31 characters.

FolderItem Class

A **FolderItem** is a reference to both folders and files. Depending on which platform you first learned about computers, you may use the term directory instead of folders; I happen to use the two terms interchangeably.

Although folders and files may seem like entirely different things to you, they have a lot in common—hence, a single class to represent both.

Referencing a FolderItem: Paths and URLs

Folders and files are organized into hierarchical trees. At the root of the tree is the volume—typically a hard drive or some other storage device—and this volume can contain folders or files of different types. All three platforms organize their folders and files in a different way. Figures 4.7, 4.8 and 4.9 show the basic structure for each platform:

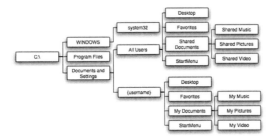

Figure 4.7   Windows XP file structure.

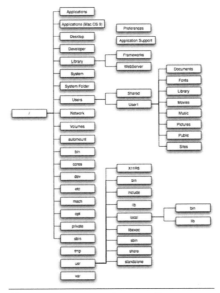

Figure 4.8   Macintosh OS X file structure.

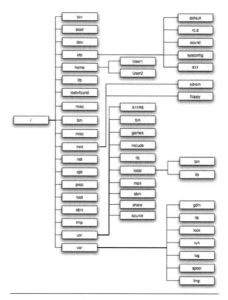

Figure 4.9   Linux file structure.

Momentarily I will show you how all these folders are supposed to be used, but for now, it's important to see that all three are organized into trees. You refer to a specific folder or file by its path. The path is the path you have to take from the root folder to get to the individual file. Referring to the Linux structure shown in Figure 4.9, consider the following path:

```
/usr/var/tmp/temp.file
```

The path starts at the root folder, which on UNIXlike systems is represented by a forward slash. If you were navigating this file structure in a graphical user interface, you would next find the usr folder and click it. Inside /, you'd look for var and click it, and so on, until you got to temp.file.

The / is the path separator. Each platform uses a different separator to separate the elements in the path.

Paths that show the entire path from the root of the volume are called absolute paths, but you can sometimes use a shortcut, called a relative path, to identify a file relative to another file.

Using the same Linux path from the preceding example, suppose I am in the var folder and want to refer to the temp.file relative to the var folder. I would write the path like this:

```
tmp/temp.file
```

You should notice that the path does not start with a forward slash (/). This indicates that it is a relative path and not an absolute path. It also starts with the child of the item being used as the point of reference.

This is important: on Linux, filenames and paths are case sensitive. That means the following paths refer to different files:

```
/usr/var/tmp/TEMP.file
```

Neither Windows nor Macintosh paths are case sensitive.

The same concepts apply to Windows as well, but with a different separator and a different way of referring to the root directory. Here is an absolute path to a similar file in Windows:

```
C:\WINDOWS\TEMP\temp.file
```

In Windows, the drive is represented by a letter, followed by a colon. This is customizable, but the primary volume is usually C:. The separator is a backslash (\) instead of a forward slash (/). An example of a relative path follows:

```
TEMP\temp.file
```

In this example, the path is relative to the WINDOWS folder. Also, remember that paths are not case sensitive on Windows, so I could just as easily do this:

```
temp\temp.file
```

And I would be referring to the same file.

Since OS X, Macintosh uses a UNIXlike approach to paths, but REALbasic throws a curve ball at you. It actually makes sense why they do this, but it can be confusing at first. Prior to OS X, Macintosh used the colon (:) as the file separator; it worked like the Linux path with the exception that it used a : rather than a /. Because REALbasic will compile on pre-OS X Macintosh computers, the native reference to Macintosh paths is the old-fashioned : rather than the current /.

Absolute Paths

```
FolderItem.AbsolutePath as String
```

This returns the absolute path in the native format of each platform.

```
FolderItem.URLPath as String
FolderItem.ShellPath as String
```

For Windows, the **FolderItem**.`ShellPath` uses the short filename, which means that it must comply with the original DOS filename constraints. Each **FolderItem** must have a name of eight or fewer characters, and, at most, a three-character extension. Short filenames are automatically generated by taking the first six letters of the filename and appending a tilde (~) followed by a number. If there are no other files with the same first six letters, the number is 1. The number gets incremented if a file with the same first six letters exists. Directories (or folders) don't have extensions. If it's a file, the extension is truncated to three characters.

```
C:\Program Files\Microsoft Office\
```

can be truncated to

```
C:\PROGRA~1\MICROS~1
```

Remember that the paths are not case sensitive, but it is common to see the short name rendered in all uppercase, as was the practice when using DOS.

Although you commonly use URLs to locate remote files using the HTTP protocol, it can also be used to locate files on the file system as well. The URL path from the previous example is:

```
FILE:///Program%20Files/Microsoft%20Office/
```

The HTTP portion has been replaced with FILE to show that it's a file on the local file system. The URL has also been encoded, which means that the spaces have been removed. Finally, a URL always uses the UNIXlike practice of using forward slashes for the separator and not backslashes, even when using a Windows machine. This makes the URLPath property a truly cross-platform way of referring to the path of a **FolderItem**.

Getting a FolderItem

There are three ways to get a reference to a **FolderItem**. The first is with the New operator, and the other two use global functions GetFolderItem() and GetTrueFolderItem(). The New operator works as follows:

```
Dim f as FolderItem
f = New FolderItem("file.txt")
```

When you instantiate a **FolderItem** in this manner, you can pass it either an absolute or a relative path. In this example, I passed a relative path and when you do that, the folder in which the application resides is the folder that the path is relative to. Therefore, this **FolderItem** is a reference to a file called "file.txt" in my REALbasic application folder.

I can also pass an absolute path, but regardless of whether it is absolute or relative, I either have to use the application-specific absolute path or add an additional argument that signifies which form of path reference I am going to use.

The options are

```
FolderItem.PathTypeAbsolute
FolderItem.PathTypeShell
FolderItem.PathTypeURL
```

Note that if you use the class constant PathTypeURL as the format for your path, you won't have to worry as much about which platform your application is running on.

In addition to instantiating a **FolderItem**, REALbasic offers two global functions that make getting a reference to a **FolderItem** easy:

```
REALbasic.GetFolderItem(aPath as String, [aPathType as Integer]) as FolderItem
REALbasic.GetTrueFolderItem(aPath as String,
➥[aPathType as Integer]) as FolderItem
```

You can use these functions anywhere, anytime, and you can pass it a path and an optional argument specifying which path format to use, just like you do when using the `New` operator. The only difference between the two is that `GetFolderItem()` resolves aliases and returns a reference to the file the alias points to, whereas `GetTrueFolderItem()` returns a reference to the alias itself, without resolving it. This is an important distinction because you can royally screw things up—for example, you want to delete the alias, while preserving the original file. To do this, you need to use `GetTrueFolderItem()`, like so:

```
Dim f as FolderItem
f = GetTrueFolderItem("someAlias.txt")
f.Delete
```

Otherwise, if you did the same thing, using the same path, with the only difference being that you used `GetFolderItem()` instead, you would have deleted the original file, and not the alias.

Relative Paths

There are many situations when it makes the most sense to use relative paths to refer to a folder or file; for example, it is more than likely that absolute paths are not cross-platform compatible. It also makes your application more flexible because you can move the root directory without changing any path reference other than the one that refers to the root directory itself. This is especially true if you are saving a reference to a path for use at a later time, such as saving path information in a preferences file that will be opened later.

There are also some platform-specific quirky reasons for avoiding absolute paths. Macintosh computers have the unusual capability to have more than one volume mounted with the same name. This is an issue only when using the Carbon, colon-delimited format for the absolute path.

REALbasic provides a way to store relative paths using the `FolderItem.GetSaveInfo()` method. It does not return a simple string representation of the relative path, however. REALbasic uses a string of binary data to represent the relative path, and at least one reason for doing this is that you can leverage some unique Macintosh qualities. If you use the data returned from the `GetSaveInfo()` method to open a file at a later date, Macintosh will find the file, even if it has moved, because of how Macs handle aliases.

```
FolderITem.GetSaveInfo(RelativeTo as FolderItem,
➥SaveInfoMode as Integer) as String
FolderItem.GetRelative(aSaveInfoPath as String) as FolderItem
```

These two **FolderItem** functions are used in tandem. `GetSaveInfo()` produces the binary data that references the file, and `GetRelative` returns a file, based on the `SaveInfo` data that is passed to it. I'll use a somewhat artificial example to show you how this can be used:

```
Dim f,g, h as FolderItem
Dim s as String

f = GetFolderItem("C:\Apps")
g = f.Child("myApp").Child("myPrefs.txt")
s = g.GetSaveInfo(f, FolderItem.SaveInfoRelativeMode)
h = f.GetRelative(s)

MsgBox h.AbsolutePath // displays "C:\Apps\MyApp\myPrefs.txt"
```

In this example, I have a reference to an Apps folder in the variable f, along with a reference to a document called `myPrefs.txt`, which is in the **myApp** folder, which happens to be a child of the original Apps folder; this is variable g. I want to save the location of g relative to the f folder, so I call

```
s = g.GetSaveInfo(f, FolderItem.SaveInfoRelativeMode)
```

The value returned to s represents data that REALbasic will use to find g relative to f at some future time. If you were saving this in a preference file, you would first need to encode s in a format that can be saved as text while preserving the underlying data. A good way to do this is to encode it in Base64.

In the example, for the sake of convenience, I don't save it. I just use the string to get another reference to the file, which I get by calling this method:

```
h = f.GetRelative(s)
```

Although you will generally use `GetSaveInfo()` to get a relative path, you can also pass a class constant to `GetSaveInfo()` which causes it to store absolute path data. You still get a reference to the folder using `GetRelative()`, but this ensures that the absolute path data is used. This means that if the folder you are using as the base reference has moved, an error will be generated because the file cannot be found in the original absolute path.

```
FolderItem.SaveInfoDefaultMode
FolderItem.SaveInfoRelativeMode
FolderItem.SaveInfoAbsoluteMode
```

How Folders and Files Are Organized

Each platform has a systematic way of organizing files that defines where system software, applications, and documents are stored. REALbasic simplifies the task of keeping track of the location of your files on different platforms in two ways. First, there is a group of global functions that return references to special folders, such as the preferences folders, for example. In REALbasic 2005, they have updated this functionality with the `SpecialFolders` function, which is always available and which returns references to a large number of special folders, each depending on which platform the user is on.

The available functions are as follows:

```
REALbasic.PreferencesFolder as FolderItem
REALbasic.ApplicationSupportFolder as FolderItem
REALbasic.DesktopFolder as FolderItem
REALbasic.FontsFolder as FolderItem
REALbasic.StartupItemsFolder as FolderItem
REALbasic.SystemFolder as FolderItem
REALbasic.TemporaryFolder as FolderItem
REALbasic.TrashFolder as FolderItem
```

The following functions are available, but have been deprecated as of REALbasic 2005:

```
REALbasic.AppleMenuFolder as FolderItem
REALbasic.ExtensionsFolder as FolderItem
REALbasic.ControlPanelsFolder as FolderItem
```

These functions work as expected. To get a reference to the preferences folder, do this:

```
Dim f as FolderItem
f = PreferencesFolder
```

The `SpecialFolder()` function is a more flexible approach. Pass the name of a special folder and it will return a reference to it if the folder exists, Nil if it doesn't.

```
REALbasic.SpecialFolder(aFolderName as String) as FolderItem
```

Because each platform uses a different set of special folders, I will document each platform separately.

Table 4.2   **Macintosh File Special Folders**

.AppleMenu	Nil
.ApplicationData	Mac HD:Users:{username}:Library:Application Support:
.Applications	Mac HD:Applications:
.Bin	Mac HD:bin:
.ControlPanels	Nil
.Cookies	Nil
.Desktop	Mac HD:Users:{username}:Desktop:
.Documents	Mac HD:Users:{username}:Documents:
.Etc	Mac HD:private:etc:
.Extensions	Nil
.Favorites	Mac HD:Users:{username}:Library:Favorites:

Table 4.2 **Continued**

.Fonts	Mac HD:System:Library:Fonts:
.History	Mac HD:Users:{username}:Sites:
.Home	Mac HD:Users:
.InternetCache	Mac HD:Library:Caches:
.Library	Mac HD:Library:
.Mount	Mac HD:Volumes:
.Music	Mac HD:Users:{username}:Music:
.NetworkPlaces	Nil
.Pictures	Mac HD:Users:{username}:Pictures:
.Preferences	Mac HD:Users:{username}:Library:Preferences:
.Printers	Mac HD:System:Library:Printers:
RecentItems	Mac HD:Users:{username}:Library:Recent Documents:
SBin	Mac HD:sbin:
SendTo	Nil
SharedApplicationData	Mac HD:Library:Application Support:
SharedApplications	Nil
SharedDesktop	Nil
SharedDocuments	Mac HD:Users:Shared:
SharedFavorites	Nil
SharedPreferences	MacHD:Library:Preferences:
SharedStartupItems	Nil
SharedTemplates	Nil
ShutdownItems	Nil
StartupItems	Nil
System	Mac HD:System:
Templates	Nil
Temporary	Mac HD:private:var:tmp:folders.501:TemporaryItems:
Trash	Mac HD:Users:{username}:.Trash:
UserBin	Mac HD:usr:bin:
UserHome	Mac HD:Users:{username}:
UserLibrary	Nil
UserSBin	Mac HD:usr:sbin:
Var	Mac HD:private:var:
VarLog	Mac HD:private:var:log:
Windows	Nil

Table 4.3 **Windows XP Special Folders**

AppleMenu	C:\Documents and Settings\{username}\Start Menu\Programs\
ApplicationData	C:\Documents and Settings\{username}\Application Data\
Applications	C:\Program Files\
Bin	Nil
ControlPanels	Nil
Cookies	C:\Documents and Settings\{username}\Cookies\
Desktop	C:\Documents and Settings\{username}\Desktop\
Documents	C:\Documents and Settings\{username}\My Documents\
Etc	Nil
Extensions	C:\WINDOWS\system32\
Favorites	C:\Documents and Settings\{username}\Favorites\
Fonts	C:\WINDOWS\Fonts\
History	C:\Documents and Settings\{username}\Local Settings\History\
Home	Nil
InternetCache	C:\Documents and Settings\{username}\Local Settings\Temporary Internet Files\
Library	Nil
Mount	Nil
Music	C:\Documents and Settings\{username}\My Documents\My Music\
NetworkPlaces	C:\Documents and Settings\{username}\NetHood\
Pictures	C:\Documents and Settings\{username}\My Documents\My Pictures\
Preferences	C:\Documents and Settings\{username}\Application Data\
Printers	C:\Documents and Settings\{username}\PrintHood\
RecentItems	C:\Documents and Settings\{username}\Recent\
SBin	Nil
SendTo	C:\Documents and Settings\{username}\SendTo\
SharedApplicationData	C:\Documents and Settings\All Users\Application Data\
SharedApplications	C:\Program Files\Common Files\
SharedDesktop	C:\Documents and Settings\All Users\Desktop\
SharedDocuments	C:\Documents and Settings\All Users\Documents\
SharedFavorites	C:\Documents and Settings\All Users\Favorites\
SharedPreferences	C:\Documents and Settings\All Users\Application Data\
SharedStartupItems	C:\Documents and Settings\All Users\Start Menu\Programs\Startup\
SharedTemplates	C:\Documents and Settings\All Users\Templates\
ShutdownItems	Nil
StartupItems	C:\Documents and Settings\{username}\Start Menu\Programs\Startup\
System	C:\WINDOWS\system32\

Table 4.3 **Continued**

Templates	C:\Documents and Settings\{username}\Templates\
Temporary	C:\Documents and Settings\{username}\Local Settings\Temp\
Trash	C:\Documents and Settings\{username}\Desktop\Recycle Bin\
UserBin	Nil
UserHome	Nil
UserLibrary	Nil
UserSBin	Nil
Var	Nil
VarLog	Nil
Windows	C:\WINDOWS\

Table 4.4 **Linux Special Folders**

AppleMenu	Nil
ApplicationData	Nil
Applications	Nil
Bin	/bin/
ControlPanels	Nil
Cookies	Nil
Desktop	Nil
Documents	Nil
Etc	/etc/
Extensions	Nil
Favorites	Nil
Fonts	Nil
History	Nil
Home	/home/
InternetCache	Nil
Library	/lib/
Mount	/mnt/
Music	Nil
NetworkPlaces	Nil
Pictures	Nil
Preferences	Nil
Printers	Nil
RecentItems	Nil
SBin	/sbin/
SendTo	Nil

Table 4.4 **Continued**

SharedApplicationData	Nil
SharedApplications	Nil
SharedDesktop	Nil
SharedDocuments	Nil
SharedFavorites	Nil
SharedPreferences	Nil
SharedStartupItems	Nil
SharedTemplates	Nil
ShutdownItems	Nil
StartupItems	Nil
System	Nil
Templates	Nil
Temporary	Nil
Trash	Nil
UserBin	/usr/bin/
UserHome	/home/{username}/
UserLibrary	/usr/lib/
UserSBin	/usr/sbin/
Var	/var/
VarLog	/var/log/
Windows	Nil

Where Files Go

All three platforms organize the directory structure so that it is easy to distinguish
between files that are for the use of an individual user and files that are on the file system for everyone to use.

User Directories

For all three platforms, every user has his or her own home directory, which can be
found in the following locations:

Macintosh:

```
/Users/{username}
```

Windows:

```
C:\Documents and Settings\{username}
```

Linux:

```
/home/{username}
```

Applications

Applications are placed into specialized folders as follows:

Macintosh:

There are two Applications folders. The first is for applications usable by anyone logged in to the computer. The second is for the use of the user within whose home directory the Applications folder resides:

```
/Applications
   /Users/{username }/Applications
```

On computers that have both OS X and System 9 installed, there is a special folder for System 9 applications:

```
/Applications (Mac OS 9)
```

Windows:

```
C:\Program Files
```

Linux:

Application files usually are installed in bin directories, but there are several locations where you will find a bin directory in Linux, and each one has a particular purpose. The SpecialFolders class returns values for `Bin`, `UserBin`, `Sbin`, and `UserSBin`.

The only applications that should go in `/sbin` and `/usr/sbin` are applications that are for the use of system administrators. Basic commands that are used by all users go in `/bin` and `/usr/bin`. Neither of these locations are appropriate for you to install your REALbasic application. The programs that reside here are generally command-line programs that users execute in the shell.

If you have a command-line application to install that you want to be available to everyone on the system, the alternative is `/usr/local/bin`. This is where programs reside that are installed locally. You should install them here so that they will not be overwritten when a new version of the system software is installed. In most cases, your REALbasic applications should be stored in `/home/{username}/bin`.

```
/home/{username}/bin
```

Documents

Documents are stored in the following locations:

Macintosh:

```
/Users/{username}/Documents
```

According to Macintosh design guidelines, the documents directory should be used only for files created by the user; your program should not create anything automatically in this directory. (Your program can create directories there, but only at the user's discretion.) All other support files, which may include templates, graphics, data files, and so on that your application needs, but which are not created by the user, should go in the Application Support directory.

Windows:

```
C:\Documents and Settings\{username}\My Documents
```

Linux:

```
/home/{username}/
```

Preferences

There is no single, cross-platform way to handle preferences. What this means in practice is that you will probably have to come up with a cross-platform way to handle preferences if you want to avoid writing separate code for each platform.

Preference files are files that contain information that is saved between running your application and is usually tied to the user of the application, so that when two people use the same application, the preferences themselves are different.

REALbasic provides a method for accessing what it calls the preferences folder.

```
Dim Prefs as FolderItem
Prefs = PreferencesFolder
```

Here are the paths to the folders that REALbasic returns on each platform:
Macintosh:

```
/Users/{username}/Library/Preferences
```

One advantage of sticking with the Plist format is that you can use the command-line application Defaults to manipulate the preferences for your application without actually having to do so within your application. This can be helpful during debugging if you want to clear preferences or set them to some default value between iterations.
Windows:

```
C:\Documents and Settings\{username}\Application Data
```

On Windows, there is no specific standard for handling user preferences. Although REALbasic returns the Application Data directory from `PreferencesFolder()`, many Windows applications use the Registry to store preferences. The Registry is a Windows-only item and REALbasic provides access to it through the **RegistryItem** class. For more information about the Registry, see the "Windows Registry" section later on in this chapter.

With respect to the current topic at hand, there may be some advantages to using the Registry for user preferences, but it creates a problem when programming in a cross-platform environment. Ultimately, this is the reason that the `PreferencesFolder()` function returns the folder it does. I recommend using this folder to store user preferences as well.

Unlike Apple's Plist format, there is no specific file format for Windows preferences. If you are using Plists for your Macintosh application, it may make sense to use the same file for Windows (and Linux for that matter). Java often makes use of properties files that use a very simple format of key/value pairs. Because I use REALbasic to write clients for Java-based content-management systems, I have a class that can read and write Java properties files. I often use this format when appropriate for preferences. The downside is that they are not suitable for any kind of hierarchical data, so when that is needed, a custom XML format is used. I also tend to stick with the Macintosh naming convention for files because it ensures that I won't overwrite any other files inadvertently, and it makes them easy to identify.

Linux:

```
/home/{username}
```

Linux and related systems usually store preferences files in the user's home directory, inside a directory whose name starts with a period. On all platforms, a file whose name starts with a period is invisible in the user interface. This is helpful with preferences files because you do not want users inadvertently overwriting them or manually adjusting them in most cases.

Again, within that directory you can store just about anything you want.

Configuration Files

It's also important to note that a preference file is different from a configuration file. Configuration files typically apply to the application itself and are not user specific. An example is a web server such as Apache. It has a configuration file called `httpd.conf` that stores systemwide configuration information. This kind of data is often stored in the etc directory on UNIX.

Macintosh:

```
/Library/Application Data
```

Windows:

On Windows, the Registry is likely the best place for this because it can accommodate and differentiate between user-specific and systemwide data. However, the following directory can work as well:

```
C:\Documents and Settings\All Users\Application Data
```

Linux:

Configuration files usually end in .conf and are available in the /etc Directory.

The files in the etc directories are static and do not change. No executable files can be installed here. The primary use of etc directories is for configuration files. User-specific configuration files should go in `/home/{username}/etc`. Otherwise, they should be installed in the appropriate etc directory. For example, if your application resides in `/usr/local/bin`, your configuration files should be in `/usr/local/etc`.

Log Files

Log files are stored in the following locations:

Macintosh:

Log files are stored in

```
/var/log
```

In Applications, Utilities is an application called Console that will enable you to view log files (a similar program called Event Viewer is available in Windows). It can be used to view any file that ends with the `.log` extension, but by default it reads the system and application logs and can be very helpful when debugging REALbasic applications.

Windows:

Many log files are scattered in the `C:\WINDOWS` folder. Some log files end in `.log` or `.Evt`; `.Evt` files are called Event logs and can be accessed in Control Panel, Administrative Tools, Event Viewer.

Linux:

```
/var/log
```

The var directories are used to store data that changes—the "var" is short for "variable." Because the data that is stored here is variable, the user under whose name the application is running must have write access to it. The kinds of variable data that go here are logs and caches.

File Types

Macintosh uses a system of four-character codes to designate application types and file types. It is my understanding that they are migrating away from this in favor of other means of linking a file extension to a particular application, but it is still in use and you can make use of it in your application.

You can register an app type with Apple at the following address:

```
http://developer.apple.com/datatype/
```

Case matters. I registered an application type and was surprised that I didn't run into any problems finding one still available. Apparently there are enough variants to satisfy everyone.

Mac also checks file extensions, and this can lead to some confusing behavior if you are not used to it. For example, you can have two different files with the same extension, both of which store text, but when you double-click the file, a different application launches to open the file. This is because the system determines which application to use based on the application code.

The file type, too, can be designated in a four-character code. You are most likely to run into this when working with the **FileTypes** class and the **FolderItem** class.

File Type Sets

The RSS Reader application will be working with RSS files, so the appropriate file types need to be established for it. There are several competing implementations for RSS, so I will create two file types.

In the **Project Tab,** click **Add FileType Set,** and a **FileTypes** icon will appear in the **Project Editor**. Select the item and name it **RSSTypes**. If you double-click the **FileType** icon, the **RSSTypes tab** will appear. In the upper-left side of this tab is an **Add File Type** button, which you should click to make the **ListBox** below it editable.

When you refer to file types in your code, you will refer to each individual type as if it were a member of the **FileType** set. (The **FileType** set is not a class, but you treat it as such.) Because this set is named **RSSTypes**, you would use that name, followed by the name of the type itself that is designated in the **RSSTypes** tab, refer to Figure 4.10:

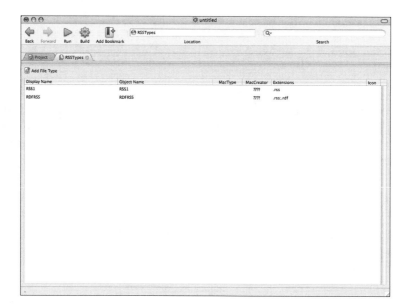

Figure 4.10   FileType sets.

In this example, I created two types, one called RSS1 and the other called RDFRSS, to reflect the different RSS formats. I give each one a Display Name and an Object Name. In most cases, you should use the same name. The Object Name is the name you use when referring to it in code:

```
RSSTypes.RSS1
RSSTypes.RDFRSS
```

When you set the value for which file types Macintosh applications will accept on drops, you will be presented with a choice based on the file types you have established, as shown in Figure 4.11.

All you need to do is select the check box beside the types that your application will accept and click the OK button.

Figure 4.11   Macintosh application Accept File Type configuration.

Volume and VolumeCount Functions

```
Volume(anIndex as Integer) as FolderItem
VolumeCount as Integer
```

Volumes are mounted drives on your computer. This includes local hard drives as well as mounted network drives, DVDs, and so on. The hard drive on which the operating system software resides is always `Volume(0)`. Because your computer can have more than one drive mounted at a time, REALbasic provides the `VolumeCount` function to let you know how many you have. You get a reference to a volume by calling the `Volume()` function with the index position of the desired volume passed as an argument.

Because each platform uses a different way to describe a path to a folder, it's usually best to use REALbasic's cross-platform way to do it.

```
Volume(0).Child("Program Files").Child("Microsoft Office")
```

is equivalent to

```
C:\Program Files\Microsoft Office
```

Navigating the Directory Tree

Rather than using paths, REALbasic provides a group of methods that allow you to navigate the directory tree using `Child` and `Parent` properties.

```
FolderItem.Child(aName as String) as Folderitem
FolderItem.Item(anIndex as Integer) as FolderItem
FolderItem.TrueChild(aName as String) as FolderItem
FolderItem.TrueItem(anIndex as Integer) as FolderItem
FolderItem.Directory as Boolean
FolderItem.Parent as FolderItem
FolderItem.Count as Integer
```

Here is an example of how you can navigate the directory tree programmatically using recursion. This subroutine starts with a base folder and compiles a list of paths for all the descendent folders:

```
Function getList(aParent as FolderItem, aList() as String)
Dim x,y as Integer
y = aParent.Count
For x = 1 to y
  aList.Append(aParent.Item(x).AbsolutePath)
  If aParent.Item(x).Directory = True Then
    getList(aParent.Item(x), aList)
  End If
Next
End Function
```

There are two important observations to make. The first is that the `FolderItem.Item()` method is an example of a 1-based index. Unlike `Arrays`, which start at 0, the first child **FolderItem** encountered is referenced using the number 1. Second, you may have noticed that I do not return a value. `Arrays` are passed by reference, so it doesn't need to return a value. `aList()` is a reference to the original `Array`, and each item added is added to the original `Array`.

File Properties

`Parent` refers to the directory that contains the **FolderItem**.

```
FolderItem.Parent as FolderItem
```

If you need to know when the file was created, or the last time it was modified by someone, you can check the following two properties:

```
FolderItem.CreationDate as Date
FolderItem.ModificationDate as Date
```

The `Length` property indicates how large the file is in bytes:

```
FolderItem.Length as Integer
```

The following properties refer to different aspects of a file's name:

```
FolderItem.Name as String
FolderItem.DisplayName as String
FolderItem.ExtensionVisible as Boolean
```

The `Name` property refers to the actual name of the file, which includes the file extension. `DisplayName` is the name that the user sees in the user interface and may or may not include the extension, depending on how the computer is configured. The `ExtensionVisible` will let you know what the configuration is with respect to extension visibility. You should always use `DisplayName` for the name shown to the user, but when referring to the file in your code or in the path, you must use `Name`.

The property will return the file type, according to the platform the application is running on:

```
FolderItem.Type as String
```

Windows and Linux rely on the extension to determine the file type, but things are a little less clear on a Macintosh. There are some Mac-specific properties that impact this. Originally, Macintosh computers didn't use file extensions at all—a lot of Mac aficionados looked down on file extensions as being a little archaic and not user friendly. To identify a file's type, they used a four-character code to represent it. For example, TEXT is the four-character code for a text file. In addition to a `MacType`, there is also a `Creator` code which is four characters long. The `Creator` associated with a file is what determines the application that opens when that file is double-clicked.

Now, Apple is moving away from creator codes and type codes and even uses file extensions. For those of you who are interested, they will be moving to a new system for identifying file types called Uniform Type Identifiers (UTI), and you can read about it here:

```
http://developer.apple.com/macosx/uniformtypeidentifiers.html
```

The **FolderItem** class also has properties that let you read the type and creator codes for Macintosh files. You encountered a reference to these in the **FileTypes** section:

```
FolderItem.MacCreator as String
FolderItem.MacType as String
```

Here is a small sampling of some common types. I added single quotes so that you could see space characters (see the example for PDF), but they are not part of the four-character type code:

Table 4.5 **Common File Types**

Gif	'GIFf'
PDF	'PDF '
Text	'TEXT'
Unicode Text	'utxt'
Movie	'MooV'

Whether you call it a trash can or a recycling bin, the cute little receptacle that our platforms all have is really just a folder like any other folder, and you can get a reference to it as a property of any **FolderItem**. You can also get references to the temporary folder and the desktop folder.

```
FolderItem.TrashFolder as FolderItem
FolderItem.SharedTrashFolder as FolderItem
FolderItem.TemporaryFolder as FolderItem
FolderItem.DesktopFolder as FolderItem
```

These are not the only ways to find out about these kinds of folders. REALbasic also has a SpecialFolders class that will give you access to a large range of special folders on each platform; it will be discussed in subsequent sections.

Permissions and File Access

One overriding difference between the two UNIXlike operating systems and Windows is that UNIX was designed from the ground up to be a multiuser operating system. Users on UNIXlike systems are organized into groups, and these groups are used to determine access permissions. As a consequence, all files and folders have an owner, and all files and folders belong to a group.

Permissions are categorized according to the user trying to do something to it. The user can be one of three things: the owner, a member of the same group as the file, or anybody else. This "anybody else" is usually referred to as the "world." In other words, if anybody has permission to read a file, you can say that it is "world-writeable." In REALbasic-speak, "anybody else" is referred to as "Other," which is fine, except that saying things like "other-writeable" doesn't quite sound right.

There are a few ways to find out what kind of permissions are available on any given file. The **FolderItem** class has a group of properties that you can check, and there is also a **Permissions** class.

Properties

The following properties are part of the **FolderItem** class.

```
FolderItem.Exists as Boolean
```

Although strictly not a permission, checking to see whether a file exists does seem to be a related idea. The `FolderItem.Exists` property returns a Boolean, and it lets you check to see if a **FolderItem** exists.

```
Dim f as FolderItem
Dim tis as TextInputStream
f = New FolderItem("myFile.txt")
If f.Exists Then
  // Do Something
Else
  tis = f.CreateAsTextFile
End If
```

In this example, a **FolderItem** is instantiated and called "`myFile.txt`". Instantiating a **FolderItem** is not the same thing as creating a **FolderItem**. This is a good thing, because if you did create a **FolderItem** simply by instantiating a **FolderItem** class, you would run the risk of overwriting existing files. When you pass a filename or relative path to the **FolderItem** Constructor, it uses the application directory as the point of reference. In this example, I test to see whether the file exists after I instantiate it. If it does not exist, I create it as a text file.

I am also able to test to see whether the file is an alias:

```
FolderItem.Alias as Boolean
```

Finally, I am able to check to see what kind of access I have to the files:

```
FolderItem.isReadable as Boolean
FolderItem.isWriteable as Boolean
FolderItem.Locked as Boolean
FolderItem.Visible as Boolean
FolderItem.Permissions as Integer
FolderItem.Owner as String
FolderItem.Group as String
```

To understand the meanings of these **FolderItem** members, it's best to turn to the **Permissions** class to see how REALbasic handles permissions.

Permissions Class

The concept of permissions comes from the UNIX world and applies only to Linux and Macintosh. It's important because permissions "problems" can be the cause of any number of hassles, so it's good to get it right from the beginning.

First things first, there are a few concepts to know. Every file or directory has an owner, which is a user on the computer. Sometimes the owner is a real person, and other times it's a user account used for a particular purpose. The best example of this is root, which is the root user. The root user is all powerful and can read, write, or execute anything it wants to. You do not normally stay logged in as root for extended periods of time because it's a little risky.

Users also belong to Groups. A user's ability to read, write, or execute a file is set according to whether the user is the owner, and the group the user belongs to. Permissions can also be set so that anybody can access it; the following functions refer to this as "Other", so when you see the word "Other", read it as "Everybody". A file that is readable by everybody is also sometimes called world readable, in contrast to owner readable or group readable.

```
Permissions.OwnerRead as Boolean
Permissions.OwnerWrite as Boolean
Permissions.OwnerExecute as Boolean
Permissions.GroupRead as Boolean
Permissions.GroupWrite as Boolean
Permissions.GroupExecute as Boolean
```

```
Permissions.OtherExecute as Boolean
Permissions.OtherRead as Boolean
Permissions.OtherWrite as Boolean

Permissions.StickyBit as Boolean
Permissions.UIDBit as Boolean
Permissions.GIDBit as Boolean
```

The **FolderItem.Permissions** class returns an integer, and this integer signifies the permissions available for the owner, the group, and everyone else. It does this by using a little bit of octal trickery. The basic permissions are these:

- 4 Read Permissions
- 2 Write Permissions
- 1 Execute Permissions

If you want the owner to both read and write to a file, you add 4+2, and you get the number 6. If you want the owner to be able to read, write, and execute the file, the number used is 4+2+1, or 7.

You calculate this number for the owner, the group, and everybody else and list them in that order, so that if you had a file that everyone could read, write, or execute under all circumstances, you'd set the permissions to 777. If you want only the owner to be able to read it and write to it, but not execute it (let's say it's a text file), but no one else should be able to do anything, you'd set permissions to 700.

Your REALbasic application runs as the user who launched the program. This means that you could run your application on a computer without any problems, and someone else can run the same application on the same computer and find it unusable.

- 3 Write and Execute (1 + 2)
- 5 Read and Execute (4 + 1)
- 6 Read and Write (4 + 2)
- 7 Read, Write and Execute

Moving, Copying, and Deleting Files

The `CopyFileTo()`, `MoveFileTo()`, and `Delete()` methods let you perform some basic file operations such as copying, moving, and deleting files. The destination folder passed as an argument must be a folder and not a file, because the source folder will be copied or moved to inside the destination folder.

```
FolderItem.CopyFileTo(destinationFolder as FolderItem)
FolderItem.MoveFileTo(destinationFolder as FolderItem)
FolderItem.Delete
```

All of these methods share a common limitation: if the source **FolderItem** is a folder rather than a file, it must be empty before you copy, move, or delete it. Later on in this chapter, I provide an example that shows how to work around this limitation.

Whenever you use one of these methods, you should check the `LastErrorCode` property to see if any errors were generated:

```
FolderItem.LastErrorCode as Integer
```

This is a highly un-object-oriented way of handling errors, but it is a perfectly workable solution. The following table describes the potential errors.

Table 4.6 `LastErrorCode` **Property Generated Errors**

Constant	Value	Description
FolderItem.NoError		The last action taken was successful and no errors were generated.
FolderItemDestDoesNotExistError	100	When copying and moving a file, you must specify the destination directory into which the files will be copied or moved. This error will appear when that directory is nonexistent.
FolderItem.FileNotFound	101	Because a FolderItem reference can exist for a file or directory that does not actually exist, you might sometime find yourself trying to access a property of a FolderItem that is only valid for an actual file—like the CreationDate, for example. Doing so results in a FileNotFound error.
FolderItem.AccessDenied	102	In almost all cases, this is a permissions problem and the username the program is running under does not have adequate permissions to read the referenced file.
FolderItem.NotEnoughMemory	103	Simple enough: the file is too big for the amount of memory your computer has available.
FolderItem.FileInUse	104	The file has been opened by another application.
FolderItem.InvalidName	105	The name of this file is invalid. Bear in mind that valid or invalid filenames can differ according to the platform the application is running in.

In addition to moving, copying, and deleting files with the **FolderItem**, there's one more thing you can do with them that is of interest—you can launch applications:

```
FolderItem.Launch(Args as String, [Activate as Boolean])
```

All platforms have applications that are the default applications that are executed when a file with a given extension is clicked. For instance, if I double-click a file that ends with `.html` on my Windows computer, Internet Explorer is launched. If I do the same thing on my Macintosh, Safari opens up. The `FolderItem.Launch()` method provides a way to effectively do the same thing as double-clicking a file. To read an HTML file in Internet Explorer, I would do the following:

```
Dim f as FolderItem
f = GetFolderItem("index.html")
f.Launch()
```

If all I wanted to do was to do was launch an application, I would do this:

```
Dim f as FolderItem
f = GetFolderItem("myApp.exe ")
f.Launch()
```

If I had arguments to pass, I could send them in the `Launch()` method. I also can optionally tell it to activate the application in question, which means I get to choose whether it launches in the foreground, in front of the current application, or behind the current application. The default value is `True`.

Extending FolderItem

As I said earlier, there are some severe limitations to how you can use the `CopyTo()` and `MoveTo()` functions. In a nutshell, you can't copy or move a folder if it has files and folders inside of it, which means that you have to manually move each file from one location to the next. This is a good opportunity to extend the **FolderItem** to give it the capability to move entire directory trees from one location to the next.

Although **FolderItem**s can be subclassed, it's rarely much use to do so. The reason is that you often access them through the `GetTrueFolderItem()` function, or something similar that returns a reference to a **FolderItem**, rather than situations where you instantiate the **FolderItem** itself. What this means to us is that subclassing **FolderItem** and extending it in that way is not a very viable option.

The ideal solution, as it turns out, is creating a new method or two in a module and using the `Extends` keyword to associate it with a **FolderItem**. The following example is for a method called `DeepCopyTo()`, which will copy a folder and all its contents into a new directory. It's based on an example that appeared in an earlier edition of the Language Reference that comes with REALbasic, but that wasn't available in the current release of REALbasic as I wrote this.

```
Sub DeepCopyTo(Extends source as FolderItem, destination as FolderItem)
  Dim newFolder as FolderItem

  If destination.Exists And destination.IsWriteable Then
    If source.Directory Then //it's a folder
      newFolder=destination.Child(source.name)
      newFolder.createAsFolder
      For i=1 To source.count //go through each item
        If source.Item(i).directory then
          //it's a folder
          source.Item(i).DeepCopyTo newFolder
          //recursively call this
          //routine passing it the folder
        Else
          source.Item(i).CopyFileTo newFolder
          //it's a file so copy it
        End If
```

```
      Next
    Else //it's not a folder
      source.CopyFileTo destination
    End If
  Else
    MsgBox "DeepCopyTo Failed for " + source.URLPath
  End If

End Sub
```

In any application that includes the module that implements this method, you will now be able to call the `DeepCopyTo()` method to copy entire trees. The method starts off by checking to see that the destination directory actually exists, and that it is writeable, too. Because you cannot copy a directory that has any child elements, you have to create a new directory with the same name in the new location.

After the new directory is created, the method then loops through each child **FolderItem** of the source **FolderItem**. With each child, it tests to see if it is a directory or a file. If it's a file, it calls the `CopyFileTo()` method and then moves on to the next child.

If it's a directory, however, it does something interesting. It calls the `DeepCopyTo()` method on the child item. It has to do this because it cannot use the `CopyFileTo()` method. This is a technique called *recursion,* and there are a lot of situations where it can be particularly effective. In this case, you have no idea how deep the directory tree is, so coding the method in this way lets you effectively move a directory tree of any depth. (Up to a point—there is a limit to how many recursions a programming language can take, and if you inadvertently put yourself into an infinite recursive loop, your program will eventually crash.)

A similar method could be developed for moving directories. You would replace the `CopyFileTo()` references with `MoveFileTo()` and add a means of deleting the original source directories and files.

Opening, Creating, and Saving Files

The first feature I'll add to the RSSReader is a cross-platform way to handle user preferences. On Windows, I will use the Windows Registry to store preferences, and on Macintosh, I'll subclass the **Properties** class from the previous chapter and use it as a simple mechanism for saving values. This example will illustrate how to write platform-specific code in REALbasic, as well as how to create and write files.

The new subclass must be able to read and write files from the file system. REALbasic provides methods for opening and saving a lot of different file types, which helps to address cross-platform differences. Most of them relate to saving graphic files and these are covered in Chapter 10, "Graphics." There are a two other methods worth reviewing at this stage: `FolderItem.OpenAsBinary` and `FolderItem.SaveAsBinary`. As you may have surmised, this reads and writes files in binary format.

```
FolderItem.CreateAsFolder
FolderItem.CreateTextFile as TextOutputStream
FolderItem.AppendToTextFile() as TextOutputStream
FolderItem.OpenAsTextFile as TextInputStream
FolderItem.CreateBinaryFile(aFileType as String)
FolderItem.OpenAsBinaryFile as BinaryStream
FolderItem.CreateVirtualVolume as VirtualVolume
FolderItem.OpenAsVirtualVolume as VirtualVolume
```

The preferences file for the **Preferences** class will be a text file. If you want to get a reference to the appropriate preferences folder, you can do the following:

```
Dim f as FolderItem
f = PreferencesFolder
```

Or you can use the **SpecialFolder** object:

```
Dim f as FolderItem
f = SpecialFolder("Preferences")
```

The **Properties** example from the previous chapter showed how to read a **TextInputStream** object. Here's an example of a more detailed approach that takes into account some additional features of the **FolderItem** class:

```
Dim f as FolderItem
Dim tis as TextInputStream
f = GetFolderItem("somepath.txt")
If f.Exists And Not (f.directory) Then
tis = f.OpenAsTextFile
While Not tis.EOF
MsgBox tis.ReadLine
Wend
tis.Close
Else
MsgBox "An error occurred"
End If
```

You can write a file using a very similar approach, except that you get a reference to a **TextOutputStream**. If you want to overwrite an existing file, do this:

```
Dim f as FolderItem
Dim tos as TextOutputStream
f = GetFolderItem("somepath.txt")
tos = f.OpenAsTextFile
tos.WriteLine("This is a line")
tos.Close
```

BinaryFiles use **BinaryStreams** to read and write data. **BinaryStreams** will look familiar to you because they work very much like a **MemoryBlock**, the only difference is that you read it in sequence. There is a Position property that tracks where you are in a file and automatically adjusts itself whenever you read some data. You can also set the value of the `Position` property and thereby read from anywhere in the file. Unlike reading text files, which have to be read sequentially, binary files do not. If you don't want to read a text file sequentially, just open it as a binary file and read it that way. The difference is that you won't automatically be able to read lines. Rather, you'll have to select a number of bytes to read, or read characters one by one until you encounter a new line, if line numbers make a difference to you. A lot of the parsing that I did in Chapter 2 could also be done with a binary stream.

Another file type is called a **VirtualVolume**. A **VirtualVolume** is a single file that the developer can interact with as if it were a volume. This means that you can create folders in a **VirtualVolume** and create both text and binary files as if they were real, separate files. On the computer, all that is created is one file. You would use a **VirtualVolume** if you wanted to create a file format for your application that contained both text and binary data. To be example-efficient, I'll show you how to create a **VirtualVolume** and write both a text file and a binary file to it.

In this artificial example, I create a **VirtualVolume** that saves a text file with a string of text, plus a binary file that stores a double and an integer. To create a virtual volume, do this:

```
Dim vv As VirtualVolume
Dim aFile As FolderItem
Dim newVirtualFile As FolderItem
Dim tos As TextOutputStream
Dim bs as BinaryStream
Dim d as New Date
// in my neverending quest for example-efficiency

aFile = GetFolderItem("somefile.txt")
//not a directory, but a file, turning aFile into a VirtualVolume
If aFile.Exists Then
  vv = aFile.OpenAsVirtualVolume
Else
  vv = aFile.CreateVirtualVolume
End If
If vv <> Nil Then
  newVirtualFile = vv.Root.Child("VirtualFile.txt")
  tos = newVirtualFile.CreateTextFile
  tos.Write "This is some important text."
  tos.Close

  bs = newVirtualFile.CreateBinaryFile("")
  bs.WriteDouble(d.TotalSeconds)
  bs.WriteLong(Ticks)
  bs.Close

End If
```

You can read the file like so:

```
Dim vv As VirtualVolume
Dim aFile As FolderItem
Dim vTextFile As FolderItem
Dim vBinFile as FolderItem
Dim tis As TextInputStream
Dim bs as BinaryStream
Dim d as New Date
Dim aTick as Integer

aFile = GetFolderItem("somefile.txt")
//not a directory, but a file, turning aFile into a VirtualVolume
If aFile.Exists Then
  vv = aFile.OpenAsVirtualVolume
Else
  Return
End If

If vv <> Nil Then
  vTextFile = vv.Root.Child("VirtualFile.txt")
  tis = vTextFile.OpenAsTextFile
  While Not tis.EOF
    MsgBox tis.ReadLine
  Wend
  tis.Close

  vBinFile = vv.Root.Child("BinaryData.bin")
  bs = vBinFile.OpenAsBinaryFile
  While Not bs.EOF
    d.TotalSeconds = bs.ReadDouble
    aTick = bs.ReadLong
  Wend
  bs.Close

End If
```

One thing to note is that you don't have to pay attention to where you are in the binary file as you read the data because the position is automatically adjusted. Also, there are some limits to **VirtualVolumes**. You can only save text or binary files and you cannot use paths. You must use the `Child()` methods to refer to such files because paths do not work.

Compiler Directives

As you can see, there are a lot of differences between the platforms, and despite how well REALbasic has done at making cross-platform application development easy to do, you will undoubtedly find yourself writing code for specific platforms. Fortunately, you do not have to maintain separate projects for each platform. Instead, REALbasic provides some compiler directives that allow you to tell the compiler which lines of code should be compiled for which platform.

Compile directives can be used in any part of your code, and they are always wrapped in a special kind of If…Then statement, one that starts with a # character. Here's an example:

```
#if TargetWin32 then
// Do something unique to Windows
#elseif TargetMacOS then
// Do something Mac-like
#else
// Do it for Linux
#endif
```

I have a real-life example of how you would use this later on in this chapter. This ends up being extremely helpful because you are able to leverage some of the unique qualities of each platform and provide a more platform-specific feel to the application than you would otherwise. Several compiler directives can be used, offering you fine-grained control over managing your code:

```
TargetMacOS
TargetCarbon
TargetMacOSClassic
TargetMachO
TargetWin32
TargetLinux
```

The previous targets all correspond to the build settings that I already covered. The directives TargetCarbon and TargetMacOSClassic are mutually exclusive subsets of TargetMacOS. See the example for System.EnvironmentVariable() later in this chapter for an example of how you can use this to further narrow down which version of the system you are running on. In addition to those targets, you can also target desktop applications that run with a graphical user interface:

```
TargetHasGui
```

You can also test to see if your target is a big-endian platform or a little-endian platform:

```
TargetBigEndian
TargetLittleEndian
```

If you are a REALbasic old-timer, you should know that these targets have been deprecated:

```
TargetPPC (Deprecated)
Target68K  (Deprecated)
```

Finally, one last directive is this:

```
DebugBuild
```

It allows you to embed code in your application that runs only when you are running it in debug mode, which is when you run it from the IDE instead of running it after you've compiled the application. This allows you to write debugging code that automatically gets stripped out of the finished application so that the real app doesn't suffer any performance hit from the debugging code.

User Interface Differences

The desktop metaphor has taken over the world. You'll find it everywhere you look—on Macintosh (which popularized the notion), Windows, and Linux. Much like high school students, who all want to dress like their friends but each in their own special way, computer operating system designers want to create operating systems that are familiar to users of other platforms. That's probably a good thing, even if a little lacking in imagination. At the same time, there's only so far they're willing to go with this, so here and there they also insert little improvements, modifications, or allegedly better ways of doing things.

For example, Macintosh and Linux have trash, whereas Microsoft has a Recycle Bin. (From time to time Mac aficionados accuse Microsoft of recycling Apple's innovations, so the name may be appropriate.)

Each platform has a way of navigating through folders. It's the software that lets you drag files around, copy them, put them in the trash, and double-click them to open them up. They all use different names.

For Macs, it's the Finder, and for Windows it's Windows Explorer. There is more than one competing system for Linux—the two leading ones are Konqueror (KDE) and Nautilus (Gnome).

Desktops

The following figures show a sample of each desktop. Another one of those things that they all do, but in a different way is the taskbar/dock/pane thing, which is usually something across the bottom of the screen (by default) that provides easy access to programs you use often, among other things. On Windows, it's called the taskbar. An example of the Windows desktop is shown in Figure 4.12. On the left side of the taskbar is the Start menu, which is where you can launch applications, and at the far right is the notification area. At a minimum, you're notified of what time it is.

The Macintosh desktop (see Figure 4.13) has a MenuBar across the top, giving users access to Finder functions, and it has a taskbar-like Dock across the bottom. The AppleMenu on the far left of the MenuBar contains options for setting preferences, shutting down applications, and switching users. To the far right is the time display. Volumes are mounted directly on the desktop, unlike Windows.

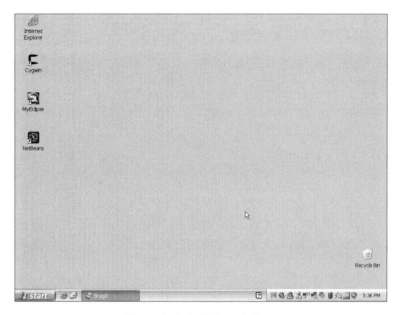

Figure 4.12   Windows desktop.

Figure 4.13   Macintosh desktop.

The Linux desktop (see Figure 4.14) is an interesting hybrid of the two, although definitely more Windows-like than Macintosh-like. KDE and Gnome are similar, but different enough that you would need to look at each one to do anything special.

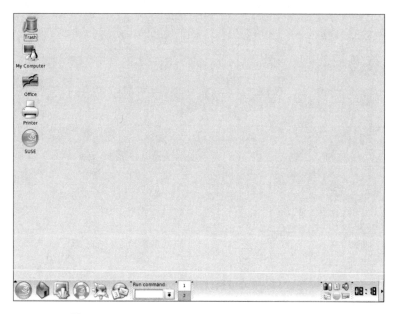

Figure 4.14   A screenshot of the KDE Linux desktop.

Because the Linux build is relatively new, REALbasic has fewer Linux-specific classes than it does for Windows and Macintosh. As you'll see in the next sections, REALbasic does provide limited access to the Windows taskbar and the Macintosh Dock. I'll show you a few brief examples of how to use them.

Windows: Taskbar

The Windows Task bar is shown in Figure 4.15.

Figure 4.15   Windows XP taskbar.

- Start menu—This is where the user starts applications, accesses the Control Panel, logs in and out, and shuts down the computer.
- Quick Launch toolbar—Icons that allow applications to be launched with a single click are in this location. This is user customizable.
- Taskbar buttons—There is a button for each window that is open without a parent, which means that there is a button for each open application and document window (but not for things like alert boxes and other related windows). If there is not enough room to show all the open windows, the taskbar groups open windows by type.

- Status (Notification) area—Applications can put icons in the status area to notify the user about events or other important information. The actual functionality of these buttons isn't regulated, so there is not much in the way of standard behavior. This area also displays the current date and time.

TrayItem Class

The **TrayItem** class is not a control, per se, but it is often treated like one. Controls and control-like classes will be discussed in full in the next chapter. In the meantime, just know that a **TrayItem** shows up in the notification area. You can assign a **TrayItem** an icon, and the user can click or double-click that icon and your application will respond accordingly.

Macintosh: Dock

The Dock plays a similar role that the taskbar does for Windows, but with some important differences.

The Dock does not have the equivalent of a Start menu. Instead, the menu bar at the top of the screen (and available with every application, unless hidden) has a menu item designated with an image of an Apple (called the Apple menu, of course). Here the user can access systemwide preferences, stop and restart applications, force quit hung applications, and related tasks. The clock is also available on the menu bar, at the far right edge, which is also where the user can search the hard drive.

The Dock itself is customizable. It combines the functionality of the Quick Launch toolbar and the taskbar. The user can drag applications and files onto the Dock, where they will stay, and which can be launched or opened by clicking them. A black arrow is shown for every open application, in contrast to creating a button in a different part of the screen, as is done with the Windows taskbar.

A **DockItem** object is available in two locations while your application runs—the App object and any window:

```
App.DockItem as DockItem
Window.DockItem as DockItem
```

The **DockItem** object has one property, which is a graphic that represents the icon that appears in the dock:

```
Dockitem.Graphics as Graphic
```

Two methods allow you to reset the icon to the original form, or to update the icon immediately:

```
Dockitem.ResetIcon
Dockitem.UpdateNow
```

The **Graphics** class may be new to you, but one of the features it provides is being able to automatically draw certain items onto an existing graphic. This example leverages that capability and draws a Stop icon on the application icon that appears in the Dock.

See Figure 4.16 for an example of the output before the icon is drawn; Figure 4.17 shows an example of what it looks like after it's drawn.

```
#If TargetMacOS Then

Dim di as DockItem
di = app.DockItem

di.Graphics.DrawStopIcon(15,16)
di.UpdateNow

#Endif
```

Figure 4.16   Dock showing default application icon.

Figure 4.17   Dock showing the default application icon with the Stop sign.

As you can see, it's very easy to do. Usually, the icon in the Dock is supposed to convey some kind of meaningful information. For example, the Mail application that comes as a default on OS X places a red oval circle in the upper-right corner of the icon that shows how many new mail messages you have.

Linux: Pane (KDE and Gnome)

The Linux environments use an approach that is closer to Windows than the Macintosh Dock. Both KDE and Gnome use different approaches to the Pane, and at the time of this writing, REALbasic did not provide any special classes to manipulate the Pane.

Keyboard

The **Keyboard** object is used to test to see if certain keys are being held down. The keys in question are usually used in combination with another key to interact in some special way with the application. Menu shortcuts are a prime example; on a Macintosh you can quit an application by holding down the Command and Q keys at the same time. On a Windows PC, you hold down the Control and X keys to accomplish the same thing.

The following table identifies some common tasks and the keys used to accomplish them on the different platforms.

Table 4.7   **Common Keyboard Shortcut Commands**

	Macintosh	**Windows/Linux**
Copy	Command+C	Control+C
Cut	Command+X	Control+X
Paste	Command+V	Control+V
Undo	Command+Z	Control+Z
New	Command+N	Control+N
Open	Command+O	Control+O
Save	Command+S	Control+S
Select All		Control+A
Print	Command+P	Control+P
Cancel current action	Esc	Esc

Table 4.8   **Macintosh-Specific Keyboard Commands**

Macintosh Shortcuts

Activate most recently used app	Command+Tab
Activate the least recently used app	Command+Shift+Tab
Show/hide Dock	Command+Option+D
Hide Active app	Command+H
Hide all but the active app	Command+Option+H
Log out	Command+Shift+Q
Log out/no confirmation	Command+Shift+Option+Control+Q
Toggle Spotlight search field	Command+spacebar
Force Quit dialog	Command+Option+Esc
Toggle VoiceOver	Command+F5
Toggle full keyboard navigation	Control+F1
Toggle keyboard navigation in windows	Control+F7
Tile open windows	F9
Tile open windows in current app	F10
Hide/show all windows	F11
Toggle Dashboard	F12

Table 4.9 **Windows-Specific Keyboard Commands**

Windows Shortcuts

Contextual Help	F1
Activate Context-sensitive help mode	Shift+F1
Shortcut menu	Shift+F10
Spacebar	Select
Toggle menu bar mode	Alt
Show next primary window or app	Alt+Tab
Show next window	Alt+Esc
Show shortcut for window	Alt+spacebar
Show properties for current selection	Alt+Enter
Close active window	Alt+F4
Switch to next window	Alt+F6
Copy active window image to the Clipboard	Alt+Print Screen
Copy desktop image to the Clipboard	Print Screen
Get the taskbar Start button	Control+Esc
Officially, reserved for system use; used to quit applications that aren't responding.	Control+Alt+Delete
Show Start button menu	Windows key
Show Help Topics	Windows+ F1
Activate next app	Windows+Tab
Explore computer	Windows+E
Find a file	Windows+F
Minimize all	Windows+M
Undo minimize	Shift+Windows+M

Linux has keyboard shortcuts, as well, but there isn't the same level of standardization, and many of them apply to the console rather than GUI apps. Generally speaking, Linux tends to mirror Windows so you can use that as a guide.

By default, Macintosh computer mice have only one button. To emulate a two-button mouse, the user holds down the Control key while clicking the mouse.

The **Keyboard** object has the following properties, which enable you to test to see which keys are being pressed. There are two versions for each key—a regular one and an asynchronous one. The asynchronous property is used to find out what key is being held down at that particular moment, and it is usually called from a **Timer**. The other version tests to see whether the key was being held down when the current method or event handler was called.

```
Keyboard.AltKey as Boolean
Keyboard.AsyncAltKey as Boolean
Keyboard.ControlKey as Boolean
```

```
Keyboard.AsyncControlKey as Boolean
Keyboard.ShiftKey as Boolean
Keyboard.AsyncShiftKey as Boolean
Keyboard.MenuShortcutKey as Boolean
Keyboard.AsyncMenuShortcutKey as Boolean
Keyboard.AlternateMenuShortCutKey as Boolean
Keyboard.AsyncAlternateMenuShortCutKey as Boolean
Keyboard.OSKey as Boolean
Keyboard.AsyncOSKey as Boolean
```

Because the platforms use different names for what is effectively the same key (Macintosh calls it Option, whereas Windows calls it Alt), REALbasic refers only to a generic name for the key (which is the name used by Windows). The following table shows the equivalent keys on a Macintosh.

Table 4.10   Macintosh/Windows/Linux Key Command Translations

	Macintosh	Windows/Linux
AltKey	Option	Alt
ControlKey	Command	Control
ShiftKey	Shift	Shift
OSKey	Command	Key with Window
MenuShortCutKey	Command	Control
AlternateMenuShortcutKey	Option	Shift

At one time, REALbasic had properties for Macintosh-specific Command and Option keys, but as of REALbasic 2005, those properties have been deprecated.

The Keyboard object also has two methods for you to use. The first provides a generic way to test whether a particular key code is being pressed. However, you have to know the key code for the particular key you are interested in, which is no small task because it seems to vary quite a lot in some circumstances.

```
Keyboard.AsyncKeyDown(aKeyCode as Integer) as Boolean
```

There are some keys that have been given a name, such as the Escape key or the Shift key. The `Keyname()` method provides a way of getting the name of a key associated with a particular key code. If the key code passed is not a named key, the letter associated with the key is returned. Note that in the early releases of REALbasic 2005, there was a bug in this method that caused a rather nasty crash in certain circumstances.

```
Keyboard.Keyname(aKeyCode as Integer) as String
```

If you check REALbasic's documentation and dig around on the web, you'll find charts that map key codes to letters according to REALbasic. Each one I found is a little different, and it depends on the keyboard being used.

Menu Bar

Macintosh computers have one menu bar that stays positioned at the top of the screen at all times. Windows and most Linux distributions (as well as Java applications) associate a menu bar with each window. REALbasic shields you from most of those differences, but it's good to be aware of. The specifics of how to create **MenuItems** in REALbasic is covered in the next chapter, but there are a few things you should be aware of.

I've already written about key modifiers, but Windows has another concept called *keyboard accelerators*, which is how users interact with the Windows menu entirely through the use of the keyboard.

If you look at the constants in the **App** object, you'll see the following values:

```
kEditClear = &Delete
kFileQuit = &Exit
```

These constants are used to determine the names of **MenuItems**. When the application is running, the letters that follow the ampersand (&) are underlined. The standard File **MenuItem** looks like this:

File

The user can activate this on Windows by pressing Alt+F. The **MenuItem** opens up and all the options have one character underlined as well (each unique, of course). Continue to select **MenuItems** by the pressing the Alt key and the underlined letter to navigate through the menu.

Even though Macintosh does not have the same concept, you will need to make provisions for this if your application will be running on Windows. It's an important part of the way that Windows is made accessible to people with disabilities, so it's not something to ignore.

REALbasic provides you with views of how the menu will look on all three platforms. Macintosh computers also have some special **MenuItems,** and they are given special classes to handle them:

PrefsMenuItem Class

On Macintosh OS X, the **Preferences MenuItem** is under the **Application Menu**, which doesn't exist for Windows and Linux systems. Place the item in the menu where you want it to appear on Windows and Linux, but make it a subclass of the **PrefsMenuItem** class so that it will appear in the proper location when compiled for an OS X computer.

AppleMenuItem

The **AppleMenuItem** applies only to "Classic" Macs. You use it the same way as the **PrefsMenuItem** class except that instead of showing up in the **Application MenuItem**, the new **MenuItem** will show up under the **Apple MenuItem**.

Screen

The presence of the Dock, the taskbar and the Pane have an impact on how much of the user's screen space is available to your application. REALbasic provides a generic means of managing this issue with the **Screen** class, and the related `Screen()` and `ScreenCount()` functions.

You never access the **Screen** class directly; you always use the two functions to access it.

The `ScreenCount()` function returns the number of screens the user is using. Most of us use one, but there are many situations when a person may have two or more monitors in use. One common example is when you have a projector attached to your laptop—the laptop monitor represents one screen (screen 0) and the projector represents the other (screen 1).

After you know how many screens are available and which one you want to access, you then turn to the `Screen()` function, passing an index position to it, as in the following example:

```
Dim aScreen as Screen
aScreen = Screen(0)
```

After you have a reference to the **Screen** instance that interests you, the following properties will be accessible.

`Depth` refers to the color depth of the screen:

```
Screen.Depth as Integer
```

`Height` and `width` measure the absolute height and width of the screen in pixels:

```
Screen.Height as Integer
Screen.Width as Integer
```

`Top` and `Left` refer to the position of the current screen relative to the main screen:

```
Screen.Top as Integer
Screen.Left as Integer
```

`Top` and `Left` are applicable when more than one screen is available. When you place the position of a window in your application, the coordinates are measured in terms of the main screen, and this allows you to control where your window is viewed.

The "Available" properties refer to the screen space that is left over after you take into consideration the Dock, taskbar, or Pane:

```
Screen.AvailableTop as Integer
Screen.AvailableLeft as Integer
Screen.AvailableHeight as Integer
Screen.AvailableWidth as Integer
```

On Macintosh in particular, the available screen space can be significantly smaller than the overall screen space. You should always check the available screen space if there is any chance that the window will be larger than the available space.

System Module

The **System** module is always available to your applications. It has a variety of properties and methods that will be of use to you at some time or another, but right now I want to write about two in particular because they are both used to get important information about the native environment your application is running in. They are

```
System.EnvironmentVariable
System.Gestalt
```

Environment Variables

Windows, Macintosh OS X, and Linux computers all have the concept of environment variables (the current REALbasic document erroneously says that environment variables are available only for OS X and Linux). An environment variable is basically a variable whose value is available to any application running on the computer. They are used for a lot of things, especially with scripting. The reason I mention them here is that they provide another way to get information about the operating system your REALbasic application is running on. In particular, there are some environment variables that contain information similar to that returned by the `SpecialFolders()` function.

In addition to reading environment values, your application can set them as well. This is most commonly used when writing console applications; later on, when I cover console programming, I will show you an example of how to write a CGI program. CGI programs make heavy use of environment variables. CGI stands for common gateway interface and refers to one method that's used to create dynamic web pages. The web server invokes the script or program and passes information about the request to the CGI program in the form of environment variables. See Chapter 7, "Console Programming and the Shell," for more details.

Environment variables are accessed like this:

```
Dim s as String
s = System.EnvironmentVariable("PATH")
```

You can set the value of the variables in this manner:

```
System.EnvironmentVariable("PATH") = "/usr/bin"
```

These examples get and set the value of the "PATH", which is an environment variable that shows the folders the operating system will look in to find programs that are being executed in the shell. The "PATH" is a list of paths separated by a delimiter, and the operating system searches those paths in the order in which they are listed. I'll talk about the shell more in a later chapter, but this serves as a good example of how to manage cross-platform issues in REALbasic.

In the previous example, I completely overwrote the path when I set it equal to /usr/bin. It is probably a more common task to add another directory to the path, without overwriting the ones that are already listed. To do that, you have to append (or prepend) the new path to the other paths. Windows uses semicolons to separate paths, and Macintosh and Linux both use colons. Therefore, we have three cross-platform issues. The first is that they use different delimiters to separate the list of paths, and the second is that they use different formats for listing paths (backslashes and forward slashes). Finally, all three have different ways of organizing the paths. Let's say our application created a folder called "MyApp" at an appropriate place for that platform and that we have a shell script called "MyScript" in that folder that we want to be able to run. (Don't worry right now about how to make it run—see Chapter 7 for more information.) Here is how you would set the "PATH" variable in your REALbasic application:

```
#if TargetWin32 then
System.EnvironmentVariable("PATH") =      System.EnvironmentVariable("PATH") +
➥";C:\MyApp"
#elseif TargetLinux then
System.EnvironmentVariable("PATH") = System.EnvironmentVariable("PATH") +
➥":/usr/local/bin/MyApp"
#elseif TargetMachO then
System.EnvironmentVariable("PATH") = System.EnvironmentVariable("PATH") +
➥":/usr/local/bin/MyApp"
#endif
```

One thing I should point out in this example is that you can see that I didn't test for `TargetMacOS`. Instead, I tested for `TargetMachO`. That's because the shell does not exist on pre-OS X Macintosh computers, so knowing that it's a Macintosh is not enough information. In this case, I need to know specifically that it is running OS X and I know for sure that if it is Mach-O, it's running OS X. This isn't an entirely satisfactory solution, however, because it is possible that this could be running in a Carbon application, in which case it may be running under OS X or System 9, but I want to run it only under OS X. The trick to determining this is to test to see if you are on a Macintosh platform and then test to see that you are not running on a "Classic" Macintosh. With this in mind, the revised code looks like the following:

```
#if TargetWin32 then
System.EnvironmentVariable("PATH") =      System.EnvironmentVariable("PATH") +
➥";C:\MyApp"
#elseif TargetLinux then
System.EnvironmentVariable("PATH") = System.EnvironmentVariable("PATH") +
➥":/usr/local/bin/MyApp"
#elseif (TargetMacOS) and NOT(TargetMacOSClassic)then
System.EnvironmentVariable("PATH") = System.EnvironmentVariable("PATH") +
➥":/usr/local/bin/MyApp"
#endif
```

The following tables show some of the basic environment variables you will find on the different platforms.

Table 4.11 **Windows XP**

Variable	Sample Value
PATH	C:\WINDOWS\System32;C:\apache-ant-1.6.2\bin
APPDATA	C:\Documents and Settings\Mark Choate\Application Data
ALLUSERSPROFILE	C:\Documents and Settings\All Users
COMMONPROGRAMFILES	C:\Program Files\Common Files
COMPUTERNAME	VAIO
COMSPEC	C:\WINDOWS\system32\cmd.exe
HOMEDRIVE	C:
HOMEPATH	\Documents and Settings\Mark Choate
LOGONSERVER	\\VAIO
NUMBER_OF_PROCESSORS	1
OS	Windows_NT
PATHEXT	.COM;.EXE;.BAT;.CMD;.VBS;.VBE;.JS;.JSE;.WSF;.WSH
PROCESSOR_ARCHITECTURE	x86
PROGRAMFILES	C:\Program Files
SESSIONNAME	Console
SYSTEMDRIVE	C:
SYSTEMROOT	C:\WINDOWS
TEMP	C:\DOCUME~1\MARKCH~1\LOCALS~1\Temp
USERDOMAIN	VAIO
USERPROFILE	C:\Documents and Settings\Mark Choate
WINDIR	C:\WINDOWS

Table 4.12 **Macintosh**

Variable	Sample Value
TERM_PROGRAM	Apple_Terminal
TERM	xterm-color
SHELL	/bin/bash
TERM_PROGRAM_VERSION	133
USER	mchoate
__CF_USER_TEXT_ENCODING	0x1F5:0:0
PATH	/bin:/sbin:/usr/bin:/usr/sbin
PWD	/Users/mchoate
JAVA_HOME	/Library/Java/Home
SHLVL	1

Table 4.12 **Continued**

HOME	/Users/mchoate
LOGNAME	mchoate
SECURITYSESSIONID	11a1aef0
_	/usr/bin/env

Table 4.13 **Linux**

Variable	Sample Value
HOME	/home/mchoate
LESS_ADVANCED_PREPROCESSOR	No
OSTYPE	Linux
LS_OPTIONS	-N --color=tty -T 0
XCURSOR_THEME	Crystalwhite
WINDOWMANAGER	/usr/X11R6/bin/kde
GTK_PATH	/usr/local/lib/gtk-2.0: /opt/gnome/lib/gtk-2.0: /usr/lib/gtk-2.0
G_FILENAME_ENCODING	@locale,UTF-8, ISO-8859-15, CP1252
LESS	-M -I
MACHTYPE	i686-suse-linux
LOGNAME	mchoate
ACLOCAL_FLAGS	-I /opt/gnome/share/aclocal
PKG_CONFIG_PATH	/opt/gnome/lib/pkgconfig
LESSOPEN	lessopen.sh %s
USE_FAM	
INFOPATH	/usr/local/info: /usr/share/info: /usr/info
DISPLAY	:0.0
LESSCLOSE	lessclose.sh %s %s
G_BROKEN_FILENAMES	1
JAVA_ROOT	/usr/lib/jvm/java
COLORTERM	
_	/usr/bin/env

System.Gestalt

`System.Gestalt` is a feature from when REALbasic was a Mac-only application.

`System.Gestalt(fourCharCode as String, ByRef result as Integer) as Boolean`

In the Macintosh world, you use Gestalt to get a lot of information about the system and environment. This is actually a pre-OS X Carbon thing, but if you are interested in using it, the way it works is that you pass it a four-character code and it returns a numeric value that you will need to interpret. You can find the codes and their possible responses at the following address:

```
http://developer.apple.com/documentation/Carbon/Reference/Gestalt_Manager/gestalt_
➥refchap/chapter_1.4_section_1.html
```

You can use Gestalt to get an incredibly large amount of data about the underlying Macintosh system. The example I give lets you find out exactly which version of the Macintosh system software you are running.

```
Dim result as Integer
If System.Gestalt("sysv", result) = True Then
// do something
End if
```

Because result is passed ByRef, it is assigned the value of the answer. The answer is returned as an Integer, but the key to understanding its meaning is to remember that Macintosh uses four-character codes, which are really just another way to say that it is composed of two hexadecimal numbers. One way to get the answer you are looking for is to convert the integer to a hexadecimal number, like this:

```
Dim s as String
s = Hex(result)
```

Perhaps a better way is to test specifically for the systems you want, like so:

```
Select Case result
  Case &h1000
    // version 10.0
  Case &h1010
    // version 10.1
  Case &h1020
    // version 10.2
  Case &h1030
    // version 10.3
  Case &h1040
    // version 10.4
End Select
```

If your application is going to be saving files in binary format and opening binary files, decide which "endian" you will use as the standard and stick with it. If your application created the binary file and opened the binary file, this is sufficient. At the same time, if you are reading binary data produced by another application on a different platform, you need to be aware of what the endianness is and adjust your work accordingly.

The good news is that while I was writing this book, Apple announced the adoption of Intel chips for future Macintosh computers. This means that the endian problem will be less of a problem in the future.

Line Endings

Each platform uses a different character or string of characters to represent the end of a line of text. REALbasic offers two functions to help you work with different line endings.

EndOfLine Functions

```
REALbasic.EndOfLine() as String
```

This function returns the line ending for the current platform.

```
REALbasic.ReplaceLineEndings(aSourceString as String, aLineEnding as String)
➡as String
```

This function converts all the line ends in a string to the line ending of your choice. You typically use an EndOfLine property for the aLineEnding parameter, but you could theoretically use whatever you wanted.

EndOfLine Properties

```
REALbasic.EndOfLine.Windows as String
```

Windows uses two characters to represent a newline, a carriage return with an ASCII value of "13" followed by a line feed, with an ASCII value of "10" (I bet there are some younger readers who do not know why it is called "carriage return").

```
REALbasic.EndOfLine.Macintosh as String
```

Macintosh only uses a carriage return.

```
REALbasic.EndOfLine.Linux as String
```

Linux uses a line-feed character only.

The trick to all of this is knowing when these EndOfLine characters are used. If you are typing into an **EditField** in a REALbasic application, the line ending that is inserted every time you press Enter is going to be a carriage return, regardless of which platform you are on. However, if you open a text file on a Windows machine, there's a good chance it will use the standard carriage return plus line feed (sometimes referred to as CRLF). Likewise, if you write a file on a Windows platform, the line ending will be converted to the local standard.

Although this may seem a little odd at first, it's actually the right way to approach it. If the string was created in REALbasic, you know that the line ending is a carriage return. When you open a file, use the ReplaceLineEndings() function to convert the string that you read from the file so that it uses carriage returns for the string.

Windows Registry

The Windows Registry is a centralized database that stores settings, options, and preferences on Windows computers. REALbasic provides a class, called **RegistryItem,** to access the Registry.

The Registry organizes the data into a hierarchy. There are five basic categories of data in the Windows Registry, known as Hives for some reason (as one who has plenty of food allergies, the word "hives" has negative connotations for me). They are as follows:

HKEY_CLASSES_ROOT

This is where file extensions are mapped to applications and where ActiveX controls are registered. The file extensions are important because that is how Windows knows which application to open when you double-click a file. If you muck about in this part, you can quite maliciously set things up so that double-clicking just about any file opens up your particular application. Don't do that. As a matter of fact, it's considered good practice to check with the user before making any kind of change to the application/file-type association.

HKEY_CURRENT_USER

This represents the currently logged in user's preferences. If you are saving preferences for an application that you have created, you would want to create a **RegistryItem** at a path similar to this:

```
HKEY_CURRENT_USER\Software\MyApp\Preferences
```

HKEY_LOCAL_MACHINE

Systemwide configuration goes here. You might include data that is applicable to all users of your application. In other words, if you had some application-specific configuration data you wanted to save that did not vary by user, you'd save it here.

HKEY_USERS

This contains the underlying data from which HKEY_CURRENT_USER is derived. This is not an area that is commonly modified and I would avoid it unless I really knew what I was doing.

HKEY_CURRENT_CONFIG

This hive stores data for the current hardware profile. Much like HKEY_USERS, I wouldn't do anything here unless I absolutely knew what I was doing.

The Windows Registry is hierarchical and is organized into folders, much like the file system is. The Hives are the root folders and each subfolder can contain a series of key/value pairs. Also, just like you can refer to real files and folders using a path, you can do the same with **RegistryItems**. All **RegistryItems** have a path, and the Hive is the first element in a **RegistryItem** Path. The data in each key/value pair is also of a particular type. The types are outlined in Table 4.14.

Table 4.14   **Windows Registry Data Types**

Value Type	Windows Designation	Integer Value
Not supported		-1
String, Expandable String	REG_SZ and REG_EXPAND_SZ	0
DWORD	REG_DWORD	1
Binary String	REG_BINARY	2
String array (Or multistring)	REG_MULTI_SZ	3

Strings are just strings. Expandable strings are strings that contain variables that need to be expanded, or filled in. In Windows, environment variables are signified by being enclosed with %. Expanding the string will replace the value of the variable with its true value. This means that this:

```
%TEMP%\SomeFile.txt
```

Would be expanded to this:

```
C:\WINDOWS\TEMP\SomeFile.txt
```

You cannot assign an Expandable String to the Registry, but you can receive the value of it, already expanded.

You can receive the value of a Multi-String, but you cannot set it. The string is delimited by a character with the ASCII value of zero. You can use the standard `Split` function to convert it into an `Array`.

```
myArray = Split(someMultiString, Chr(0))
```

Binary strings and DWORDs both represent binary data. DWORDs represent numeric data, whereas binary strings can represent anything. In other words, if you wanted to store a small graphic file, you would store it as a binary string, but if you wanted to store the fact that the application has been used 100 times, you'd use a DWORD.

Later on in the chapter, I will create a **Preferences** class for the RSSReader project that uses the RegistryItem class.

RSSReader Preferences Example

Prior to compiling our new application, I want to implement a way to handle preferences in a cross-platform way. For the Windows version of the application, I'll use the Registry, and for the Macintosh version I'll use the preferences folder (for brevity's sake, I'll leave out Linux for the moment).

Exporting and Importing Items

In the following sections, I will be subclassing the **Properties** class that I shared with you in Chapter 2, "The REALbasic Programming Language." To be able to subclass it, I will need to import the Properties class into my current project. To accomplish this, you need to open the original project and select the item you would like to export. In the File menu, select Export, and the class will be exported to the file system. You can do this with any class in the **Project Editor**.

To import the **Properties** class, you can use the Import item in the File menu, or you can just drag the exported item from the file system and drop it into the **Project Editor**.

If you do this, you have made a copy of the original class and any changes you make to it in this application will not be reflected in the original application, which may be exactly what you want to happen.

Often, developers do not want that to be the case. They want to be able to share the same class among applications, but have only one copy of that class available at any given time, meaning that if they make a change in one application, the change is reflected in all applications.

In REALbasic 2005, you can make a class external, which accomplishes this task for you, but in a somewhat awkward way. If you want to have a class be an external class that is shared among different applications, you need to export the class from the original application, delete the item from the IDE in the original application, and then drag the exported class back into the IDE while holding down the Command+Option keys (Control+Alt for Windows).

You will be able to tell that it is an external class because it will be italicized in the **Project Editor** and will have a little arrow icon near the name. You should be careful when doing this because it is easy to inadvertently break your other applications if you make a change in one of them. Be sure to test the other applications regularly to make sure they work as planned.

Creating the Preferences Class

For the Macintosh version, I'll subclass the **Properties** class and use that as the format for my preferences file. To make my future programming easier, I would like to use the same interface regardless of whether I am using a Macintosh or a Windows machine. This is a perfect situation for interfaces, so the first thing I will do is create a class interface called **iPreferences**, which will be the interface I use to manage preferences regardless of which platform I am on.

The interface defines four methods, as follows:

```
Interface iPreferences
    Function get(aKey as String) As String
    End Function
    Sub set(aKey as String, assigns aValue as String)
    End Sub
    Sub setAppIdentifier(aName as String)
    End Sub
    Function getAppIdentifier() As String
    End Function
End Interface
```

The get and set functions are modeled after the get and set functions of the Properties class. I've also added to other methods, `getAppIdentifier` and `setAppIdentifier`. Regardless of the platform, I have to use a unique name to identify the application, so these methods allow me to set and get this value.

After the Interface is defined, I need to subclass the **Properties** class so that it implements the interface; then I need to implement a class for Windows that interacts with the Registry but that also implements this interface.

The **Properties** subclass is called **Preferences**, and the first thing I do is add a new constructor that takes the application name as the parameter:

```
Sub Preferences.Constructor(anApplicationRef as String)
  // expects application name like info.choate.metawrite


  dim pf as folderItem



  // Use the PreferencesFolder function
  pf = PreferencesFolder

  me.appID = anApplicationRef

  if pf<> nil then
    if pf.child(me.appID).exists then
      parsePropertyFile(pf.childme.appID))
    else
      createPreferenceFile(pf, me.appID)
    end if
  end if
End Sub
```

In this example, I use the `PreferencesFolder()` function to get a reference to the Preferences folder. The preferences folder is the root folder, not the folder I'm looking for. The next thing I do is check to see if a file exists with the same name as the application name that I passed in the constructor. If it does exist, I open and parse the file. If it doesn't exist, I have to create the preferences file for the first time.

Here is the `createPreferenceFile` method:

```
Sub Preferences.createPreferenceFile(aPrefFolder as FolderItem, anAppID as String)
  Dim tos as TextOutputStream

  tos = aPrefFolder.child(anAppID).createTextFile

  tos.writeLine("#Metawrite Preference File v.05")
  // write default data
  tos.close

  me.file = aPrefFolder.child(anAppID)

End Sub
```

Whenever you are going to write to a file, you need an instance of a **TextOutputStream**. In this case, you get a reference to that instance by calling the `CreateTextFile` method on the **FolderItem** you are creating. **TextOutputStreams** work similarly to **TextInputStreams**, but in the opposite direction. In this case, I write just one line to the file by calling `tos.WriteLine()`. After that, I close the **TextOutputStream** and the string has been written to the file. I also assign a reference to the preference file to the file property so that I can reference it later.

In addition to creating the file, I also need to be able to save data to the file. Because it makes sense to be able to save Properties files, too, it makes the most sense to implement the save method in the **Properties** class rather than the **Preferences** class:

```
Sub Properties.save
  Dim textOutput as TextOutputStream

  textOutput = me.file.CreateTextFile
  TextOutput.Write(me.getString)
  TextOutput.close


End Sub
```

When saving the file, I start with the file property and call `CreateTextFile` again. This creates a new file and erases whatever was there before. Also, like before, it returns a **TextOutputStream**. Recall that the **Properties** class is a **Dictionary** subclass and when the properties file gets parsed, the values are parsed into key/value pairs and assigned to the dictionary. When it's time to save the file, the values in the dictionary have to be converted to a string to be saved. I do this by called the `getString()` method, which I write to the **TextOutputStream**. Note that in this example, I used `Write` instead of `WriteLine`. The primary difference is that `WriteLine` ends the line with an appropriate `EndOfLine` character and will append additional lines when it is called again. Write doesn't append any `EndOfLine` characters and writes the data to the file as is. After the string is written to the file, the **TextOutputStream** is closed and the file is saved.

When I have written the **Preferences** class, I need to create a **WindowsPreferences** class that implements the **iPreferences** interface. To get a **RegistryItem** to implement the **iPreferences** interface, I have to subclass **RegistryItem** and implement the appropriate methods. The methods that I develop in turn call the underlying methods of the **RegistryItem** class.

The **WindowsPreferences** class looks like this:

```
Class WindowsPreferences
    Inherits RegistryItem
    Implements iPreferences
    Function getAppIdentifier() As String
        return me.appID
    End Function
    Sub setAppIdentifier(aName as String)
```

```
        me.appID = aName
    End Sub
    Function get(aKey as String) As String
        return me.Value(aKey).StringValue
    End Function
    Sub set(aKey as String, assigns aValue as String)
        me.Value(aKey)= aValue
    End Sub
    Sub Constructor(anAppID as String)
       If anAppID <> "" Then

       RegistryItem.RegistryItem("HKEY_CURRENT_USER\SOFTWARE\" + anAppID)
       me.setAppIdentifier(anAppID)
      Else
        //raise an error
    End If
End Sub
    appID as String
End Class
```

The first two methods get and set the appID property (the appID property is added to the **WindowsPreferences** class as well) and this works just as you would expect it to. The get and set methods are implemented as defined in the Interface, and you can see that all they do is take the key/value pair that is passed to the method and use it to call the `RegistryItem.Value` method. This is an example of creating methods purely to implement an interface.

After the interface methods are implemented, I create a new `Constructor` that takes anAppID argument in the parameter. What I want to do is take the string that represents the application and use it to build a path to create a reference to a **RegistryItem**. This is complicated, because I'm doing this from a `Constructor` of a subclass of the **RegistryItem**. In this situation, I get the string, build the path, and then call the `Constructor` of the super class.

Although you usually use the word "Constructor" to name the `constructor` method, you can also use the name of the class itself, which is why when I call `RegistryItem.RegistryItem()`, I am calling the constructor of the super class.

When I was writing this code, I was using REALbasic 2005 r2. When I first wrote it, I called `RegistryItem.Constructor("the path")`, but it created an error, so I changed the reference from `Constructor` to **RegistryItem** and it worked fine. At first I thought this was a bug, but I'm not so sure it would qualify as such; it is an example of some of the trickiness that you can encounter when overriding a method. In the **WindowsPreferences** class, the signature for the constructor is the same as the constructor for the parent **RegistryItem** class. Both constructors take a string in the parameter. As far as the compiler is concerned, it's the same signature, even though the meaning of the string is different in both cases. In **WindowsPreferences**, the string is the name of the application, whereas in **RegistryItem** the string is the path to the particular **RegistryItem**.

Calling `RegistryItem.Constructor("the path")` from within the `WindowsPreferences.Constructor("the app id")` method confuses the compiler—it's like a **Constructor** calling itself. By calling the **RegistryItem** constructor method, the compiler was able to recognize the method as the constructor of the parent class and execute it accordingly.

The rest of the constructor assigns the name of the application to the appID property.

Now we have two classes that implement the **iPreferences** interface, each intended for a different platform. The next question is what do you do with them? In this example, I create the following property of the **App** object:

```
App.Prefs as iPreferences
```

Next, I turn to the `Open()` event. The next chapter discusses events in detail, but it is sufficient right now to know that the `Open()` event is triggered when the application first opens. Any code you place in the `Open()` event gets executed right when the application starts. This is where I'll put the code that configures our cross-platform preference files:

```
App.Open() Event
  #if TargetWin32 then

    Prefs = iPreferences(new _ WindowsPreferences("info.choate.metawrite"))


  #elseif TargetMacOS then

    Prefs = iPreferences(new Preferences("info.choate.metawrite"))

  #endif

  If Prefs <> Nil Then
    Prefs.set("Name") = "Mark Choate"
    Prefs.set("Location") = "Raleigh, NC"
    #if TargetMacOS Then
      Preferences(Prefs).save
    #endif
  End If
End Event
```

I use compiler directives to determine the steps I take. If the application is running on a Windows computer, I instantiate a **WindowsPreferences** object and assign the value of that object to the `App.Prefs` property. If I were to instantiate the `Windows.Preferences` class and assign it to Prefs without first casting it to **iPreferences**, the compiler would generate an error message and tell me that it was expecting an **iPreferences**, but got a **WindowsPreferences** instead. Therefore, I have to explicitly cast it as an **iPreference** before assigning it to Pref.

If I am running on a Macintosh, I instantiate a **Preferences** object instead. Just like the **WindowsPreferences** object, I have to first cast it as an **iPreference** object before assigning it to `Prefs`.

Here's the beauty of interfaces. From here on out, my application just calls `Prefs` as is, without any concern which platform the application is running from. Both classes implement the same interface, and the other parts of your program need to know which methods to call and that is that.

In the next part of the event, I assign some values to the `Prefs` object so that when this application is run on Windows, those values are stored in the Windows Registry and on a Macintosh they are stored in a file in the users **Preferences** folder. After adding the values, I had to do one additional step and test to see if I was on the Macintosh platform to know if I needed to save the file. The Registry automatically saves the values, but my preferences class doesn't. A better place for this step would be in the `App.Close()` event, so that it would save the values only on the application closing, but I placed it here so that the values would be written to the file immediately (you can check to see the contents of the file while the application is still running).

A Final Word About Macintosh

If you are one a Windows machine and compile a Mac OS X application with the Professional Edition, you might be surprised to see that instead of an application icon you see a folder. That's because Macintosh OS X uses the concept of bundles.

Macintosh Bundles

A file isn't always just a file. There are certain cases when the user interface makes a folder look like an individual file. If you are compiling applications for OS X, you will encounter Macintosh bundles, which are a collection of folders and files that look like a file on Macs.

Prior to OS X, Macintosh used a proprietary file format to group related resources used by a file (or application). This format used two forks, a resource fork and a data fork. Although OS X has dispensed with the idea of resource forks in favor of something called *bundles*, the term *resource* is still used a lot (and is referred to in the REALbasic documentation). Figure 4.18 illustrates the folders and files that make up a bundle. These days, you can have a resource file that contains icons, strings, and pictures that you can access from REALbasic. I would strongly advise you to avoid creating any application that uses a resource file and instead either import any graphics you need into the REALbasic application itself, or access the files from the file system.

Figure 4.18   Application Bundle.

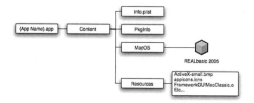

Summary

In this chapter, I wrote about cross-platform programming and the **App** object, which is one of the objects automatically created in every new **Application** project. There are two more to review, **MenuItem1** and **Window1,** and that will come in the next chapter.

Most of your interaction with **Windows** and **Controls** with be through the IDE, so this chapter will go into more detail about how the IDE works and what all of the options are. You also can't talk about **Windows** and **Controls** without talking about events. Events are much like methods, but they have some unique properties that make them a powerful tool to be used in your REALbasic application development.

5

Designing a Desktop Application

THERE ARE TWO PARTS TO REALBASIC. The first part is the language itself and the compiler. This is what turns programming code, written by a human being into machine code, to be read by your computer. The second part is the Integrated Development Environment (IDE), which is the application the developer uses to write REALbasic applications. In other programming languages, these two aspects are distinct pieces of software. In REALbasic's case, they are tightly integrated. There is no separate compiler to run, nor can you use a different editor to edit REALbasic code (that's 99% true). If you're an experienced developer, there may be times when this kind of tight integration feels constricting because you do not have as much flexibility as you do with other compilers or IDEs. At the same time, it also makes life easier because REALbasic stores all your code for each application in a single file and you don't have to worry about importing classes into source code files and managing packages like you do with Java, Python, C, and so on.

In addition to being an object-oriented programming language, REALbasic is also an event-driven programming language. Programs that are used to develop applications with graphical user interfaces (desktop applications in REALbasic parlance) often use the event-driven paradigm to manage program flow. Because the subject of this chapter is developing desktop applications, it is also a chapter about the event-driven aspects of REALbasic programming.

Up until this point, a large portion of this book has been devoted to the REALbasic programming language syntax. Understanding syntax is a necessary foundation to writing a program; it is not the only tool you need to develop effective applications. Just like a person may know the meaning of a lot of words and how to place those words into sentences, and even how to understand what others mean when they use words, it is not necessarily true that the same person can use that understanding to construct a persuasive argument on behalf of any particular cause. I can read a Shakespeare play but I cannot write one.

Part of the task at hand, then, is to help to get you started writing applications in REALbasic rather than writing lines of code. There are some standard approaches and design patterns that computer programmers have developed that can help to provide a framework you can use to write better programs. One such architecture is called Model-View-Controller (MVC) and it is often used when developing applications with graphical user interfaces.

I have used the basic elements of the Model-View-Controller architecture in the design of the RSSReader application. In this chapter, then, I will walk through the code of the RSSReader application and show you how I chose to implement MVC using REALbasic. It is my hope that this will provide you with a practical, hands-on feel for one way to approach the challenge of creating an application. It is by no means the only way, nor is it necessarily the best way, but it is certainly a good way to go about it and it can serve as a starting point for you, especially if you are new to programming.

I will also describe the few remaining language elements that make up the REALbasic programming language that I have yet to discuss, which includes Menu Handlers and Exceptions.

Integrated Development Environment

A number of new features in REALbasic 2005 are worth touching on, and there are a few features I have yet to discuss. Because this chapter makes such heavy use of the IDE, I do want to spend a moment and touch on a few points of interest.

IDE MenuItems

First off, I'd like to familiarize you with a few of the more important features of REALbasic that are accessible through various **MenuItem**s or toolbars. The IDE has changed considerably and has added a few new features that you will find very helpful. Although some people who are familiar with the old way of using REALbasic may begrudge some of the changes, I find it hard to understand why because the user interface of REALbasic 2005 is, in the vast majority of instances, exceedingly better than previous versions, especially if you are a Windows developer.

File, New Project

At the top of the list is **New Project.** Every program you write in REALbasic is called a project. A project will be saved on the file system as a single file (with a few exceptions) and will contain all the code, graphics, and so on required by your application to compile and run. By now, this is nothing new to you.

However, one of the best new features is that you can now open more than one project at a time. Prior to REALbasic2005, you couldn't do this, and there are lots of times when it is convenient to look at code in one application while you're writing code in another. Now you can even cut and paste code from one application to the next.

File, New Window

The **New Window MenuItem** duplicates the current **Window**, so you can now have two **Windows** open for the same project. Again, this is a simple, but greatly appreciated, new feature in the latest IDE.

File, Import/Export

You can import and export specific classes and modules so that you can share them among applications. Normally when you export a class, you are exporting a copy of it, so that when another application of yours imports the class and modifies it, the original is not modified. This may be exactly what you want to do, so that you can avoid breaking other programs that already work. The downside to this is that you can easily end up with lots of different versions of classes and modules that are difficult to keep track of.

External items are a solution to this. When you important a class or module into your application, the easiest way to do so is to drag it into REALbasic from the desktop. If you hold down the Command+Option (or Control+Alt for Windows) keys while doing so, you will import them as External items, which means that they are stored outside of the REALbasic project file.

When you export an item, you have the same options that you have when saving a project file: you can export it as a native REALbasic file, or you can export it in XML format. My recommendation is to use REALbasic's XML format whenever possible, for the following reasons.

When using external items, you need to be cautious because when you change code in one project, you are changing code in all the other projects that share this code, which means you can easily break something. If you export REALbasic items in the XML format, you can more easily manage those files using version control software such as CVS or Subversion. Because version control software lets you track the changes that have been made to a file, you can use it to review which changes have been made to the code in your application that have caused it to stop working. You can either fix the problem or roll back the file to the previous version.

If you choose not to use external items, one potential solution is to assign a version number to each class. You can establish a constant called Version, or a method that returns the version of this class. When you import it into your next project, be sure to increment the number if you make any changes to it. (Note that this will change the version number in all projects that use the class if you are using external items. That's okay, but you may want to have your application test for the class number first. If it's not a recognized version, you can be notified that it has been changed in a different application.)

Project Menu

Under the **Project** menu, you also have the option of encrypting the selected class. This is for those who want to distribute classes or groups of classes, but not reveal the source code.

Following the **Encrypt** item are several selections for managing the placement of controls on pages. **Controls** are layered onto a Window, so the **Arrange MenuItem** lets you manage which layers individual controls are on. **Align** helps you align your controls so that they line up properly. The **Find MenuItem** is your entry into REALbasic's powerful Find and Replace features, which I discuss separately.

View, Editor Only

Under the **View** menu are most of the new features (with respect to the IDE). The first selection says **Editor Only**. If you select this, the main toolbar and the bookmark tool-bar will disappear and you will be left with the tabs for your project. This gets some of the clutter out of the way and lets you focus more on what you are doing.

One important design feature of REALbasic's IDE is the use of **Toolbars**—there are several of them within the application, and they are all customizable. Here's a list of what's available for each toolbar.

Main Toolbar

By default, the **Main Toolbar** contains the following items: Back, Forward, Run, Build, Add Bookmark, Location, Search.

In addition, you have the option of adding the following items: New Project, Open, Save, Save As, Print, Home, Build Settings, Stop, Cut, Copy, Paste, Delete, Undo, Redo, and Language Reference.

The Editor Toolbar

The **Editor Toolbar** varies according to which tab you have selected. For example, if the **Project** tab is selected, you will have the **Project Toolbar**. These context-sensitive **Toolbars** are as follows.

- Project Toolbar
    - Default: Add Window, Add Class, Add Module, Add Folder
    - Optional: Encrypt
- Code Editor Toolbar (when editing a class)
    - Default: Edit Mode, Add Method, Add Property, Add Menu Handler, Add Constant, Add Event Definition, Add Note, Comment
- Menubar Toolbar
    - Default: View Mode, Add Menu, Add Menu Item, Add Separator, Add Submenu, Convert To Menu
    - Window Toolbar (Edit Code Mode)
    - Default: Edit Mode, Add Method, Add Property, Add Menu Handler, Add Constant, Add Event Definition, Add Note, Comment
- Window Toolbar (Edit Layout Mode)
    - Default: Edit Mode, Show Control Order, Forward, Front, Backward, Back, and Align
    - Option: Add Bind and List Binds

History

REALbasic now tracks your **History**. This works just like the history does on your web browser and helps you to go back to recently modified items. There is nothing exceptional here.

Bookmarks

This is a convenience added that allows you to bookmark sections of your project that you will return to often. This is helpful when you have multiple windows open, and so on.

Help

I am not certain that it is accurate to say that REALbasic has an improved help system. It is probably more accurate to say that at this time, REALbasic has laid the foundation for an improved help system. There are some new items under the **Help** menu to be aware of. First, if you add any plug-ins to your project, you will be able to access their documentation under this menu. There is also a new language reference which, at the time of this writing, was in the process of being rewritten. Although it has its fair share of problems, the new language reference is written in HTML, is searchable, and has the promise of being much improved. One word of warning, however: parts of it are outdated and other parts are just plain wrong. Hopefully, this book will help offset that issue, and there are also a lot of online resources that you can refer to, including a REALbasic documentation Wiki. Rather than putting URLs that might change at some point in the future into this book, I have included links to them at the following site: http://realbasicbook.com/.

Preferences

The new IDE also offers more control in the way of preferences. When you select **Preferences** from the preference menu (or **Options**), a **Window** will be displayed that looks more or less like a typical preferences window. On the left is a column of icons that represent the preferences you can change. Select one and the right side of the **Window** displays the specific values that can be updated.

Code Editor

If you select **Code Editor** (which is selected by default), you'll have the opportunity to change the default font REALbasic uses in the code editor, as well as how large the font should be displayed. There's even a handy alphabet listing below so that you can see what it will look that.

Below that is the second option that allows you to control syntax highlighting. You can adjust them to suit your own personal fancy.

You also have the option of having REALbasic apply the standard case when using Autocomplete. Autocomplete is a tool available in the code editor that tries to detect what you are typing; when it thinks it knows, an ellipsis appears (three little dots...). When that shows up, you can press the Tab key and a menu will pop up with all the options. This comes in handy when you are referring to REALbasic classes or functions and you're not sure what the name of the property or method is that you want to call. By using Autocomplete, you're provided a list from which you can choose the rest of the statement.

That's a long explanation, but the point of it was to explain what it means to apply standard case to Autocomplete. Generally speaking, REALbasic doesn't care about case. You can refer to objects in uppercase or lowercase and REALbasic will accept it regardless. What this feature does is make sure that the code is in the "Standard" case if you use Autocomplete.

REALbasic capitalizes the first letter in most classes, modules, and methods. If the name is the combination of two words, like **ListBox** or **EditField**, the first character of each word is capitalized. Names of classes have to be one word, but they often make more sense if you are more descriptive. By joining a few words together and capitalizing the first letter of each word, you make your code much more legible.

Window Editor

You can set font attributes for the **Window** Editor as well. **Controls** are the user-interface elements you see on any application, such as **PushButtons**, **EditFields**, and so on. All I will say at this point is that controls can contain other controls, and this preference item lets you decide whether to highlight the parent control and what color you'd like that highlight to be. I'd recommend keeping highlighting of the parent control on because it can sometimes be difficult to tell whether one control is embedded in another, or just overlapping it, and this can provide you with immediate feedback and save you a lot of time.

Build Process

After you have built (compiled) your application, you have the option of being shown the location of the built applications on your hard drive. The Macintosh version of the IDE refers to this as the Finder, which is equivalent to Windows Explorer on the PC.

A second option is to show multiple compile errors.

Debugger

The debugger is the tool that helps you track down errors with your application. You will need to get intimately involved with the debugger eventually. REALbasic has an excellent debugger—it is extremely easy to use. Because REALbasic allows you to compile applications for three platforms, there are times when you will want to be able to debug the Windows version of your application, even though you are writing the code on your Macintosh, or perhaps the other way around. The Professional Edition of REALbasic allows you to compile applications for all platforms, but the IDE runs only on the platform you purchased it for.

You can set up the information you need to be able to debug apps running on other computers here. See the section titled "Debugger" later in this chapter for more information.

Printing

Printing is…well…let's just say that there's not a lot you can do with the printing features of REALbasic. About the only thing you can do is decide which font to use when printing your source code.

Find and Replace

The new find and replace **Window** provides a much better way of searching through your code than in the previous edition of REALbasic.

In the default layout, a search box appears on the **Main Toolbar**. Click the magnifying glass icon to narrow your search to the entire project, the item, or the method. Item means the currently active class or module.

A more powerful interface can be found under the **Edit** menu. Go to **Edit, Find, Find and select**. A dialog box appears, with an **EditField** to enter your search criteria and, if applicable, a field to enter the replace value.

Two new features of note are that the search saves recent searches, which are accessible by clicking the **BevelButton** decorated with a stop watch icon. Next to that is the Favorites **BevelButton**, signified with a heart icon.

You can search for the whole word, match case, or use regular expressions. When matching the whole word, REALbasic will match only when a complete word matches what is searched for. In other words, if you search for the word "for," it will match only "for" and not "ford." Matching cases means that REALbasic will pay attention to uppercase or lowercase when matching words, and will treat "mark" as distinct from "Mark."

After the search term is entered, you have the option of finding the first occurrence, or of finding all occurrences. The results of the **Find All** search will appear in a **Search** tab and will be listed along with information about the type of match, the fully qualified name of the member in which the match occurred, and the match itself. At the bottom of this list is a **Replace** field, which allows you to do a search and replace against the selected matched items.

If the **Search Results** tab is already up and you search in the search field in the **Main Toolbar**, the search will default to a **Find All** search.

Suppose you have a single method that is called from several places in your code and you decide that instead of one method, you want two methods. You can search for the method name, finding all occurrences of its use, and then you can select the ones you want to change and replace the old name with the new name. In earlier versions, you had to either replace all occurrences of a phrase with the new phrase or manually cycle through each match to decide whether to perform the replace. This is particularly useful when refactoring code.

Desktop Applications: Programming Graphical User Interfaces

Desktop applications have graphical user interfaces, and these user interfaces are developed in REALbasic graphically—using drag and drop to place **Controls** onto the **Window**. There are some development tasks in REALbasic that can be accomplished only by using the graphical user interface. One of the most fundamental is dragging controls onto a **Window**. There is no programmatic way to do this; you must drag it in the **Window Layout Editor**.

In this section, I will produce the basic shell of the RSSReader application, which will be a desktop application, which means it will have a graphical user interface, or GUI. There are some defining characteristics of GUI applications, one of them being that they use an event-driven paradigm.

Event-Driven Programming

A computer program is a sequence of steps or actions that are taken in a predetermined sequence. Sometimes the particular steps that are taken are conditional upon the state of some piece of information, but the program itself identifies that information, tests it, and responds accordingly. Now, contrast that with a program designed with a graphical user interface. Much of what the program does, it does in reaction to user input. The program does not simply start, execute, and exit in one act. It starts up, does some housecleaning, and then waits for user input for deciding what to do next. The most important distinction is that an event-driven program requires external information to know what to do next.

Event-driven programs use an event loop that constantly looks for information indicating that an event has been triggered. It identifies the type of event and then executes an event handler, which is basically a method that the programmer has written to respond to the event. Bear in mind that user interaction isn't the only way to trigger an event. You can do so programmatically, and one event can trigger another event (called an event cascade), and so on.

This gets to the general concept of events, but there is a lot more to it than that. To come to a better understanding, let's consider for a moment events of other kinds—those that take place in the real world.

The Declaration of Independence begins with the phrase: "When in the course of human events...." It goes on to say (generally speaking) that when certain conditions are met, a series of new events are triggered. In this particular instance, the event being justified was the revolution, and the reason it was justified, they claimed, was because of preceding events. The revolution was triggered by what the revolutionaries claimed were injustices. So this is one concept of an event: it is "triggered" by something. It is contingent upon some state or condition that, when met, causes the event in question to be executed.

Revolutions aren't the only kind of events in the world. There are lots of different kinds of human events—things like weddings and birthdays. Many times, we let each other know about pending events by sending an invitation, which provides the basic details about the event: where it's going to be, when it's going to happen, what you need to bring, whether you should RSVP, and so on. In this respect, an event is something that takes place at a certain place, during a certain time, for a particular purpose. It is something that you know about in advance.

There are some events that take place at regular intervals, something that you can predict quite easily. Let's use as an example a high school graduation—it happens every year, like clockwork. Everybody knows that graduation is coming and they have an idea of how the ceremony will go, but a lot of planning and details must be attended to in order to pull off any particular graduation. Most importantly, when you receive an invitation to the graduation, you have to decide whether you are going to attend the graduation, what you're going to wear, and what kind of graduation present to buy.

There are other events that are not something planned in advance. This means that they are not triggered by a particular date or time, nor are they triggered by reaching an expected stage in some process. These events are triggered by something unexpected, like an accident in which someone gets hurt. In this case there isn't an invitation that gives you advance notice—you have to react right away, based on what you know about this unexpected condition.

REALbasic is an event-driven language, and an event in REALbasic works in a similar way—it is code that is executed within an object at a certain time for a particular purpose. For example, every time an application is launched, an Open event is triggered—just like every year there is a high school graduation. Your job as a developer is to decide what you are going to do in response to the event.

Another common kind of event that REALbasic developers must respond to is user interaction with the **MenuBar**. When a user selects **File, Open**, the application must respond to that request. There are some unique characteristics to how these events get handled, and the code you write for them is called a Menu Handler, to distinguish it from the more general-purpose event handlers that you will be writing in other situations.

There are also unexpected events in REALbasic, too. Suppose your application expects to find a file at a certain location, only to find that it's not there, or it finds that the contents of the file are not in the expected format. In those situations, a different kind of event is triggered—one that has its own unique rules—and it is called an exception. Because exceptions are not planned, it is next to impossible to write code at every point in your application to respond to specific errors. Rather than being triggered, exceptions are raised, which is basically a process whereby the exception goes in search of a solution. You will create your own exception types and your own exception handlers when programming in REALbasic.

An event handler is a lot like a method. Like a method, it can be like a subroutine and execute a task when triggered, or it can be like a function and return a value (a Boolean). Also, like a method, events are members of classes, but it is here that the similarities between events and methods begin to disappear, because the normal rules of inheritance and overriding do not apply with events.

Controls and Events

You will probably encounter events most often when working with **Controls**. **Controls** are user-interface elements (usually—as with everything, there are some exceptions) that respond to user interaction, which is why they are so event focused.

One of the goals of modern operating systems is to provide a consistent appearance to the end user. It is much easier to learn a new program if you have a reasonable idea about what to expect when clicking a button or selecting New from the File menu. You have many different programs, but they all share some consistent user-interface elements.

The use of events helps to make that possible. Although the interface for opening a file is the same from the user's perspective, what takes place as a result of that user interaction will vary from program to program. If your program edits text files, when the user opens a file, your program will open the file, get the text, and display it in an **EditField**. If your program uses files that are formatted as XML, it will need to open the file, parse it into an **XMLDocument** or something similar, and then display it.

Events are processed differently from overwritten methods. If a class declares an event, that class does not implement the event (unlike when a class declares a method). The event is implemented by either a subclass or a special kind of instance of parent class.

In REALbasic, you can drag a class to a **Window**, and the result will be a little icon, which you can double-click, representing the class. When you double-click, a **Window** in the IDE pops up that will allow you to implement the events declared in the class. When you drag an item to a **Window**, the item is automatically instantiated by the **Window** when the application runs (it used the default Constructor, with no arguments passed to it). When the events for that instance are called, REALbasic runs the code that was edited from the **Window**.

When you create a subclass in the IDE (not by dragging it to a **Window**), you can implement the events that were declared in the parent class. If you subclass the subclass, you will see that the event you implemented in the parent class is not available in the subclass. Unlike methods, events cannot be overridden.

One major difference between events and methods is that when an event is triggered, REALbasic starts looking for an implementation of the event from the top of the class hierarchy, not from the bottom. This means that if you implement an event in a superclass, the event is called in the superclass and it never reaches the subclass.

You can declare a new event in the subclass, which can in turn be implemented in its subclass. However, if you do this, REALbasic will still start from the top of the class hierarchy and traverse it until it finds an implementation of the event, which it will trigger, ignoring any implementations further down the tree. That is, unless you trigger the same event again from the implemented event.

App Events

If you start a new project and double-click the **App** object so that you can edit it, you will see a label called event handlers listed with the other **App** members. If the disclosure arrow is closed, click it open and you will see a list of events. If you select one, you can look in the editing area and see the signature for that event— you'll see that it looks just like a method in many respects.

Events occur at particular stages of your application and when an application first starts, a series of events are triggered. For example, when I launch an application, the following **App** events occur, in the following order:

```
App.Open
App.NewDocument
```

```
App.Activate
App.EnableMenuItems
```

The first event, `App.Open`, makes sense. It's the event that fires when the application first starts up. The `Open` event is a good place to do any of the housekeeping necessary to get your program underway—things like accessing preference files or loading data into memory.

The `App.NewDocument` event is a little more difficult to understand. Why would a `NewDocument` event be triggered when the application is just opening? You've no doubt seen some applications that when launched start up with an empty document. In fact, unless you have it configured differently, Microsoft Word launches with an empty, but new, document.

A related event, called `OpenDocument`, is triggered when the application has been opened as the consequence of a user launching the application by double-clicking a file type associated with the program.

The `Activate` event is called after the `Open` and `NewDocument` event, and it is called every time the application becomes the front-most application on the user's computer. The opposite of the `Activate` event is the `Deactivate` event, which is triggered when the application loses its front-most position.

Finally, the `EnableMenuItems` event is called. This is an event that shows up in the **App** object, in **Windows,** and in **Controls**. There are points along the way in your application when you need to change the state of your menu and make some of the **MenuItem**s active and others inactive. For example, if you have a document open, but it hasn't been changed from the original, there would be no reason for the **Save MenuItem** to be enabled until the document actually needed saving. So, for example, the `EnableMenuItems` event is triggered when a user clicks the **MenuBar**. The `EnableMenuItems` event is designed to let you manage this process so that when a menu is accessed, only the proper items are available to the user.

There are two `Close` events that are worth elaborating. `Close` is the last event to be called, and `CancelClose` comes right before it. The `CancelClose` event gives you the opportunity to check to see if users really meant to close the application. This means that generally speaking, you throw up a dialog box of some sort and ask if they really want to quit. If they happen to have any documents with unsaved data, you may prompt them to see if they want to save them. If you return `True`, the application will not close; otherwise, it will.

```
Application.CancelClose() as Boolean
Application.Close
```

AppleEvents are part of the Macintosh environment and are used to add scriptability to your application. Because it is a Macintosh-only feature, I will not dwell on it.

```
Application.HandleAppleEvent(event as AppleEvent, EventClass as String, EventID as
➥String)as Boolean
```

The final event, `UnhandledException`, is discussed later in the chapter in the section on handling errors. Suffice it to say at this point this is the event that is triggered right before your application crashes, so it's your last chance to fend it off.

```
Application.UnhandledException(error as RuntimeException) as Boolean
```

Model-View-Controller

The fact that REALbasic uses an event-driven paradigm is out of your control. You have no choice in the matter and you need to program within those constraints. You do have a choice about how you program within those constraints, and one of the most basic choices is how you go about organizing your code—both from the practical perspective of where you save your files and from the conceptual perspective of how you go about creating classes and performing tasks. I'll start first with the conceptual perspective.

The Model-View-Controller architecture (MVC) is the one that I have used with the RSSReader application. In this framework, the program is divided up into three distinct domains or areas of responsibility. The view refers to the user interface (which is why MVC is so commonly used when programming GUI applications). The view presents information to the user and accepts input from user interaction. The model is the data model for your application, the units of information that your program is manipulating. The controller mediates the interaction between the view and the model. The view responds to a user request by referring it to the controller. The controller performs any application logic required to process the request and then refers the appropriate model (an object) to the view to be presented to the user.

When you are writing your application, some code that you write will be involved in managing the user interface—things such as determining how particular controls respond to particular events. This is sometimes referred to as presentation logic. You will also be writing code that performs the logic of your application, sometimes called domain or business logic. You want to minimize instances where business logic and presentation logic appear in the same method or object, and this can be something of a challenge at times. In the RSSReader application, I keep these unique areas of responsibility distinct, and I also organize my project in such a way as to make it clear which classes belong to which particular layer.

Organizing Your Code

One way to organize your project is to make judicious use of folders. Folders in the IDE work just like folders do on your hard drive. You are able to save classes and modules into folders.

REALbasic doesn't have the concept of packages in the same way that Java does. This means that organizing your classes into folders doesn't affect the way that you call those classes. This lack of namespaces is a limitation of REALbasic that should be corrected in the future. One side effect is that it makes "namespace collisions" easier to happen. In other words, no two classes can have the same name. In languages such as Java, you can avoid this by grouping classes into packages and using that as a way to refer to the class. Not so in REALbasic.

In the RSSReader application, I have the following folders set up:

- Providers
- Preferences
- RSSItems
- Viewers
- Writers

The **Providers** and **Writers** folders hold classes responsible for the model layer. **Viewers** holds classes responsible for the view layer—namely **Window** and **Control** subclasses and supporting classes. **RSSItems** contains the **RSS** class, which is a subclass of **App** and which serves as the controller for this application.

Windows and **Controls** are responsible for two things: presenting information to the user and responding to user requests.

In this case I am developing an RSS reader, so the model will represent the RSS data. The view—the way that the data encapsulated in an **RSS** object—is presented to the user. This is done using **Windows** and **Controls**. In addition to presenting information to the user, **Windows** and **Controls** also allow the user to interact with the application and edit data, request data, or whatever happens to be appropriate for that action. The third area, the controller, manages the interactions between the model and the view, and this is managed by the RSS class. I'll use this basic approach to develop the rest of the RSS application.

At this stage, the RSSReader application is not complete, and the following represents a simplified view of the final application, primarily because I have not yet covered XML. In what follows, I will present the classes I have developed along with some explanation of the role they play. I will not spend a lot of time reviewing individual lines of code now, but will instead refer to it when writing about programming with Windows and **Controls** later in the chapter.

The RSSReader Application

There are many small applications where the formalisms of this kind of structure are not required. As you will see in the following pages, REALbasic makes it very easy to mix your application's business logic with that of its presentation logic. Sometimes that's okay. At the same time, my experience has been that your life is much easier if you keep a distinct line between presentation and business logic because of the flexibility it gives you in the future. A screenshot of the RSSReader application can be seen in Figure 5.1.

Figure 5.1   RSSReader application screenshot.

Here is a description of how the RSSReader application will work:

- The user will be able to subscribe to RSS channels by typing a URL into an **EditField** and clicking a Subscribe button.

- A complete list of subscribed-to RSS channels will be maintained and displayed in a **ListBox**. The list will be originally maintained in a text file. Later in the text, it will be reimplemented using a database.

- The application will use XSLT to convert the RSS XML files into HTML for viewing.

- A **TabPanel** will allow the user to switch between the HTML view and the plain text/XML view of the channel.

- When a channel that is listed in the **ListBox** is selected, the channel will be displayed in an **HTMLView** control on the **TabPanel.**

- The plain text will be viewed in an EditField on the **TabPanel** as well.

Preferences will be maintained so that the main application **Window** returns to the same state as it was the previous time it was opened. Next, I will review the classes that will implement this functionality.

Controller

Class RSS Inherits Application

The **App** object is supposed to represent the application itself, so I implemented the controller as a subclass of **App**, called **RSS**. There are now two related objects in the project—**App** and **RSS**—but you can safely ignore **RSS** and call **App** when you need to. REALbasic automatically uses the lowest subclass on the **App** hierarchy, so all the properties and methods I have established in **RSS** will be available.

The complete implementation follows. There are some items in it that you may not understand yet, but most of them will be discussed later on in the chapter. I want to present the class completely so that you can see how everything fits together, and I will refer back to it when necessary.

RSS Properties

The **RSS** object has five properties, three of which are interfaces. The **iPreferences** interface has been seen before; this is what gives us the capability to easily employ a cross-platform way of handling user preferences. At this stage in the application, I will not be using the **iProvider** property. Its function will be to read XML files from either the file system or through an **HTTPSocket** connection. This will be revisited when we examine REALbasic's XML classes. The **iWriter** interface is used to write data to some source, whether it's a file, a socket, or the like. At this stage, it is used to save updated versions of the **RSSFeeds** file that stores the user's subscription information. Viewer is currently a **ListBox,** but in a later version this will be updated to use a **ListBox** subclass called **mwNodeListBox** that can be used to display hierarchical data. Finally, the Feeds property represents the class that's responsible for opening and saving the RSS feed file.

```
Preferences As iPreferences
Provider As iProvider
Writer As iWriter
Viewer As ListBox
Feeds As SubscribedFeeds
```

The **RSS** class itself implements only two methods at this point—Subscribe and Delete. These methods will be called from different parts of the application, including the **MenuBar** and as a consequence of user action. The methods themselves make use of properties of the **RSS** object, which I discuss next.

Listing 5.1   **Sub RSS.Subscribe(aUrl as String)**

```
    Me.Feeds.addItem(aUrl)
```

Listing 5.2   **Sub RSS.Delete()**

```
    Me.Viewer.RemoveRow(Me.Viewer.ListIndex)
    Me.Writer.Write(Me.Feeds)
```

The following **Events** and **MenuItems** will be discussed throughout the rest of the chapter. One thing to notice at this point is how the **RSS** object uses the Open event to initialize all its properties.

Listing 5.3   **Sub RSS.Open() Handles Event**

```
        // Initalize Preferences
        #if TargetWin32 then
                Preferences = iPreferences(new
➥WindowsPreferences("info.choate.rssreader"))

                Dim myTrayItem as CustomTray
                myTrayItem = New CustomTray
                Me.AddTrayItem( myTrayItem )

        #elseif TargetMacOS then
                Preferences = iPreferences(new
➥Preferences("info.choate.rssreader"))
        #endif

        If Preferences <> Nil Then
                Preferences.set("Name") = "Mark Choate"
                Preferences.set("Location") = "Raleigh, NC"
                #if TargetMacOS Then
                        Preferences(Preferences).save
                #endif
        End If

        // Initialize Viewer
        Viewer = Window1.ListBox1
        // Initialize Feeds
        Feeds = New SubscribedFeeds()
        Feeds.registerListBox(Window1.ListBox1)
        Feeds.open
        // Initialize Writer Thread
        Writer = new tWriter
// Start running the Thread
        tWriter(Writer).Run
```

Listing 5.4   **Sub RSS.EnableMenuItems() Handles Event**

```
        If Window1.EditField1.Text <> "" Then
                FilekSubscribe.Enabled = True
        Else
                FilekSubscribe.Enabled = False
        End If

        If Viewer.ListIndex > -1 Then
                EditClear.Enabled = True
        Else
                EditClear.Enabled = False
        End If
```

Listing 5.5   **Sub RSS.CancelClose() as Boolean Handles Event**

```
Dim res as Integer
res = MsgBox("Are you sure you want to quit?", 17, "Quit RSSReader")
If res = 2 Then
  Return True
End if
```

Listing 5.6   **MenuHandler Function RSS.EditClear() As Boolean**

```
    // Call RSS.Delete method
    Delete
```

Listing 5.7   **MenuHandler Function RSS.FilekSubscribe() As Boolean**

```
    // Call RSS.Subscribe method
    Subscribe(Window1.EditField1.Text)
```

iPreferences Interface

The **iPreferences** interface is the first of several interfaces the RSSReader uses. **iPreferences** specifies a generic way of setting and accessing preference data so that the interface is the same, whether the Windows Registry is being used, or a preferences file is being used on Macintosh or Linux. Preferences are considered part of the controller—it's how the controller maintains state between user interactions. The data that is saved does not represent the actual data model.

```
Function get(aKey as String) As String
End Function

Sub set(aKey as String, assigns aValue as String)
End Sub

Sub setAppIdentifier(aName as String)
End Sub

Function getAppIdentifier() As String
End Function
```

The Model

The "Model" in Model-View-Controller refers to your application's data. You can further break down the model into two constituent parts. In this example, there is an XML file that stores the RSS data, and that is the first part, sometimes called the data access layer. The second part is the representation of that data in memory—the actual object model. REALbasic provides XML classes, and it is very easy to use those classes to open RSS files, which means that you could use the **XMLDocument** class as your model. However, it is generally thought to be better to not have your object model so closely tied to any given representation of that model. For instance, even though RSS files are most commonly stored as XML files, there are four different competing formats the XML documents can take, all of which are very similar, but different enough that you could not rely on **XMLDocument** objects created from them to have consistently named attributes and elements. For example, what one format calls a "Channel" is called a "Feed" in another.

Another important thing to consider is the physical location of the files. The program will get RSS files through the Internet, but it will cache those files locally. It will use the local file until it's time to refresh it with a new version from the Internet. Also, it's conceivable that there will be new versions in the future, or that the data could be stored in some other format altogether, such as in a database. If that's the case, every time a new format or source of information is made available, you will have to modify all those parts of your application that interact with the **XMLDocument** object you are using to represent it.

The approach that I will be using is one I have developed over time working with XML documents and content management systems.

Data Access Layer

The data access layer is responsible for getting the data required to instantiate the domain object. Presently, for the RSSReader application, this means being able to retrieve XML files from the Internet, or files stored locally on a hard drive, as well as being able to write files to the local drive so that they can be cached for later use, or something similar. The following interfaces and classes compose this area of functionality.

iProvider Interface

The **iProvider** interface is a simple interface that accepts a URL (just a string, really) and returns a document. The **mwNode** class is used as a generic representation of any kind of document, and that will be discussed more later in the chapter. The benefit to this interface is that the sections of the application that request documents do not need to know how the object that implements the interface is getting the **mwNode** object. This means that the implementing object can get the source data from a file, from an HTTP request, a database, a socket, and so on. These four sources of data would never share much code, so subclassing would not provide much benefit. As a result, I define a very simple interface that can be used for any data source I choose:

```
Sub open(aUrl as String)       as mwNode
End Sub
```

iWriter Interface

iWriter works in tandem with the **iWritable** interface. There is a REALbasic **Writable** interface, but it didn't provide exactly what I was looking for. In this application a thread subclass implements the **iWriter** interface, and it has a `Write` method that accepts an **iWritable** object in the parameter. This means that I can send any object to this thread to be written as long as it implements the **iWritable** interface. Also, much like **iProvider**, using an interface for **iWriter** means that I have a lot of flexibility in determining what it means to `Write` something. I could write to a file, a database, a **TCPSocket**, and so on, and the rest of my program need be none the wiser.

```
Sub Write(toWrite as iWritable)
End Sub
```

iWritable Interface

The **iWritable** interface is simple: just a `Write` subroutine. It is passed to the `RSS.Writer` property and represents the document to be written. Again, **iWriter** can write any object that implements this interface.

```
Sub Write
End Sub
```

Class SubscribedFeeds

The `RSS.Feeds` property is an instance of the **SubscribedFeeds** class. It's used to open the file that contains the list of subscribed-to feeds, as well as to write out the file when it changes. It implements the **iWritable** interface.

Listing 5.8   **SubscribedFeeds Properties**

```
List As ListBox
RSSFile As FolderItem
```

Listing 5.9   **Sub SubscribedFeeds.registerListBox(aListBox as ListBox)**

```
me.List = aListBox
```

Listing 5.10   **Sub SubscribedFeeds.write()**

```
//I am storing the Feeds file in the ApplicationSupportFolder.
//The file is opened during the Open method of the class.
//iWritable
Dim tos as TextOutputStream
Dim x,y as Integer
Dim s as String

tos = RSSFile.CreateTextFile

y = me.List.ListCount - 1
```

Listing 5.10 **Continued**

```
For x = 0 To Y
        s = me.List.Cell(x,0)
        If s <> "" Then
                tos.WriteLine(s)
        End If
Next

tos.Close
```

Listing 5.11 **Sub SubscribedFeeds.open() Handles Event**

```
        Dim tis as TextInputStream
        Dim s as String

        RSSFile = ApplicationSupportFolder.Child("info.choate.rssreader")

        If RSSFile.Exists Then
                tis = RSSFile.OpenAsTextFile
                If (tis <> Nil) And (List <> Nil) Then

                        While Not tis.EOF
                            s = tis.ReadLine()
                            If s <> "" Then
                                    List.AddRow(s)
                            End If
                            Wend

                End If
        End If
```

The addItem method adds a URL to the **ListBox** that was assigned in the **RegisterListBox** method, and then saves the updated data to the file.

Listing 5.12 **Sub SubscribedFeeds.addItem(aURL as String)**

```
        me.List.addRow(aURL)
    me.write
```

Listing 5.13 **Function SubscribedFeeds.writeError() as Boolean**

```
        If RSSFile.LastErrorCode <> 0 Then
                Return True
        Else
                Return False
        End If
```

Object Model

The object model will be the classes that are used to represent the data found in RSS files, in their various formats. I have developed a hierarchy of classes that I use to provide a generic representation of documents and document collections in other applications I have developed, and I will use a similar approach here.

You may already be familiar with the DOM, or Document Object Model that is used in XML and HTML. It treats a document like a tree; in HTML, the root is the HTML document, and that document has two branches: the head and the body. The head can have any number of branches, one of which is the title of the document. Likewise, the body can have any number of headings, paragraphs, and so on.

An RSS document can be viewed the same way. At the root is a channel and the channel contains a sequence of items, each of which has a title, a URL, and a description. (In recent alternative formats, the channel is called an entry.) If you think about it, all documents and collections of documents can be modeled this way. A book is a sequence of chapters, a chapter is a sequence of paragraphs, a paragraph is a sequence of words, and words are a sequence of letters. In all cases, the order in which these sequences of things matters.

All the differing formats of RSS will be mapped onto this basic object model, and that is the object model that will be used in the application. The process of reading the XML from a file, or accessing it through an HTTP connection, will be performed by objects that implement the **iProvider** interface. At this stage, I have not covered XML or databases, so the initial development I describe in the rest of this chapter will be a simplified version, and the rest of the functionality will be added as we go in later chapters.

We will be using two basic classes: **Group** and **Item**. **Group** and **Item** both share the same parent class, **Meme**, and they inherit several common methods and properties (I use the term for my own personal amusement. If you would like to know why, just read the last chapter in Richard Dawkins' *The Selfish Gene*). A **Group** corresponds to a channel, or entry. An **Item** corresponds to an Item.

The **Meme** class is a subclass of the **mwNode** class. The **mwNode** class provides the methods and properties that allow it to act like a tree. When diagramming a tree, there are two basic nodes: a branch node and a leaf node. A branch node has one or more children, which are either branch nodes or leaf nodes. A leaf node has no children. Branch nodes correspond to **Group** objects and leaf nodes correspond to **Item** objects.

In this chapter, I will introduce the **mwNode** class. **Groups** and **Items** will be introduced in the next chapter, where I will demonstrate parsing XML documents and converting them into the objects model.

Class: mwNode

The is the root class for any document types that I use throughout the rest of the application.

Listing 5.14 **mwNode Properties**

```
Protected TypeID As integer
Protected Position as Integer
Protected Sequence as iSequence
Protected Parent as mwNode
Protected Container as mwNode
Protected Expanded as boolean
Protected Name As String
Protected Depth As Integer
```

Listing 5.15 **Sub mwNode.Constructor(aType as Integer, aName as String)**

```
// A type with a positive number is a Leaf
// A type with a negative number is a Branch
Me.TypeID = aType
Me.Name = aName
Me.Expanded = False
Me.Sequence = new NodeSequence(me)
   Me.Depth = 1
```

Listing 5.16 **Sub mwNode.Release()**

The **mwNode** class contains instances where the parent node has a reference to the **Sequence** object, and the **Sequence** object has a reference to the parent node. This kind of self-reference can cause problems with REALbasic's reference counting, leaving objects in memory long after they are no longer being used. This method clears those cross-references.

```
Parent = nil
Container = nil
   Sequence = nil
```

Listing 5.17 **Function mwNode.isLeaf() as Boolean**

```
if TypeID > 0 then
    return true
else
    return false
    end if
```

Listing 5.18   **Function mwNode.isBranch() as Boolean**

```
If TypeID < 0 Then
    Return true
Else
    return false
    End If
```

Listing 5.19   **Function mwNode.getTypeID() as Integer**

```
Return me.TypeID
```

Listing 5.20   **Sub mwNode.setTypeID(aTypeConstant as Integer)**

```
Me.TypeID = aTypeConstant
```

Listing 5.21   **Sub mwNode.setParent(aParent as mwNode)**

```
If not(aParent is Nil) Then
    Me.Parent = aParent
    End If
```

Listing 5.22   **Function mwNode.getParent() as mwNode**

```
Return me.Parent
```

Listing 5.23   **Sub mwNode.setPosition(pos as Integer)**

```
Me.Position = pos
```

Listing 5.24   **Function mwNode.getPosition() as Integer**

```
Return me.Position
```

Listing 5.25   **Sub mwNode.setContainer(aContainer as mwNode)**

```
Me.Container = aContainer
```

Listing 5.26   **Function mwNode.getContainer() as mwNode**

```
Return Me.Container
```

Listing 5.27   **Function mwNode.getPath() as String**

```
// Path is a recursive function that gets
// the node path to this particular node
// The format returned will be 1.2.4, which
// is the first node of the root node, the
// first node's second child and that
// nodes 4th child
Dim cont_path as String

If not(me.Container is nil) Then
    cont_path = me.Container.getPath
    If cont_path = "" Then
        cont_path = str(me.Position)
    Else
        cont_path = cont_path + "." + str(me.Position)
    End If
    Return cont_path
Else
    Return ""
End If
```

Listing 5.28   **Function mwNode.getName() as String**

```
Return me.Name
```

Listing 5.29   **Sub mwNode.setName(aName as String)**

```
Me.Name = aName
```

Listing 5.30   **Function mwNode.isExpanded() as Boolean**

```
Return me.Expanded
```

Listing 5.31   **Sub mwNode.Expand()**

```
Me.Expanded = True
```

Listing 5.32   **Sub mwNode.Collapse()**

```
Me.Expanded = False
```

Listing 5.33   **Function mwNode.getVersion() as String**

```
Return "mwNode-v1"
```

Interface: iSequence

The **iSequence** interface is a class used to manage the parent node's children. The **mwNode** class has a property **Sequence** that implements **iSequence**.

```
Sub Constructor(aNode as mwNode)
End Sub
Function getChildCount() As Integer
End Function

Function getChild(pos as Integer) As mwNode
End Function

Sub appendChild(aNode as mwNode)
End Sub

Sub insertChild(pos as Integer, aNode as mwNode)
End Sub

Sub removeChild(pos as Integer)
End Sub

Sub removeChild(aNode as mwNode)
End Sub
```

Class NodeSequence (Implements iSequence)

Here is the actual implementation of **iSequence** that I will use in the examples. Note the use of a class **BadNodeError**—this will be discussed later in the chapter.

```
Property Node As mwNode
Property Child(-1) As mwNode
```

Listing 5.34   **Sub NodeSequence.Constructor(aNode as mwNode)**

```
    Dim bne as BadNodeError

    If Not aNode Is Nil Then
        me.Node = aNode
    Else
        bne = new BadNodeError
        bne.Message = "Error constructing node"
        Raise bne
        End If
```

Listing 5.35   **Sub NodeSequence.Release()**

```
Redim Child(-1)
Node = Nil
```

Listing 5.36   **Sub NodeSequence.appendChild(aNode as mwNode)**

```
Child.Append(aNode)
aNode.setPosition(ubound(Child) + 1)
aNode.setParent(Node)
aNode.Depth = Node.Depth + 1
```

Listing 5.37   **Function NodeSequence.getChild(pos as Integer) as mwNode**

```
If (pos > -1) and (pos < getChildCount) Then
    Return Child(pos)
End If
```

Listing 5.38   **Sub NodeSequence.insertChild(pos as Integer, aNode as mwNode)**

```
Child.Insert(pos, aNode)
aNode.setPosition(pos + 1)
aNode.setParent(Node)
aNode.Depth = Node.Depth + 1
```

Listing 5.39   **Function NodeSequence.getChildCount() as Integer**

```
Return ubound(Child) + 1
```

Listing 5.40   **Sub NodeSequence.removeChild(pos as Integer)**

```
Dim x,y,z as Integer

y = getChildCount - 1

For x = pos + 1 to y
    z = Child(x).getPosition
    Child(x).setPosition(z - 1)
Next

Child.Remove(pos)
```

Listing 5.41   **Sub NodeSequence.removeChild(aNode as mwNode)**

```
Dim res as Integer
res = Child.IndexOf(aNode)
If res > -1 Then
    Child.Remove(res)
End If
```

Views

Views are implemented with **Windows** and **Controls**. Because that is a primary topic of this chapter, the bulk of the rest of the chapter will be devoted to elucidating the views used in the RSSReader application.

Windows and Controls

All desktop applications have **Windows**. In a sense, that's what defines a desktop application. **Windows** all have controls, because without them, your user wouldn't be able to do anything. REALbasic provides a **Window** class and the next section reviews how to edit and layout **Windows** in REALbasic and the different kind of **Windows** that are available to you. Then I highlight the **Control** classes that I have used in the RSSReader application. There are too many **Controls** to review all of them, but the ones that I have included are what I consider to be the most important ones, especially **EditFields** and **ListBoxes**.

Simple Windows

Before I get too far along in discussing the **Window** class, I want to review some simplified classes that REALbasic provides that you can use for dialogs and other similar forms of user interaction. This includes the MsgBox function and the **MessageDialog** classes. The distinguishing characteristic of these windows is that you do not use the **Window Editor** or **Layout Mode** to create them. Everything is done for you programmatically. Because they are simplified, you will not use them as the primary **Windows** in your application by any means. Rather, you will use them to notify the user of important pieces of information, to request information or feedback, or to help the user find a folder or a file.

MsgBox

The MsgBox function is about the easiest **Window** there is to work with. As of REALbasic 5.5, a new **MessageDialog** class was added that does everything the MsgBox function does, plus more. Still, there are times when you need to show a quick message to your user or get some feedback, and MsgBox does just what you need it to do.

MsgBox isn't a class—it is a function, which means that you call it just like every other function. The advantage of having the MsgBox as a function is that functions return values, and in the case of the `MsgBox`, it returns a value that indicates which button on the `MsgBox` **Window** was clicked.

More often than not, you'll use a `MsgBox` to communicate some kind of information to the user. A lot of times, you're letting them know that an error occurred or something like that.

`MsgBox` is an overloaded function, which means that it's really three functions, which are called as follows:

```
MsgBox "An error has occurred."
```

If you want to find out what the user's response was, you can call `MsgBox` like this:

```
Dim result as Integer
result = MsgBox "An error has occurred. Would you like to try again?", 5, "Error"
```

In this example, you can see I've added two more parameters. In addition to the message, I've sent the integer 5 and another string with the value of "Error". The second parameter determines how many buttons the `MsgBox` has and what they say.

The second parameter is the sum of three numbers. The first of the two numbers determines how many buttons there are and what they say. The second of the two numbers determines what kind of icon to show the user. The third number determines which button is the default button.

Button Values

Value	Description
0	OK button
1	OK and Cancel
2	Abort, Retry, and Ignore
3	Yes, No, and Cancel
4	Yes and No
5	Retry and Cancel

Icons

Value	Description
0	None
16	Stop sign
32	Question
48	Caution Triangle
64	Note

Default Button

Value	Description
0	First Button (As listed in the above list)
256	Second Button
512	Third Button
768	No default

Suppose you wanted to show an alert that displays the OK and Cancel buttons, with the OK button being the default button. In addition to the buttons, you want to show the question icon as well. The first thing you do is to add up the three numbers that represent what you want to do.

```
1 + 32 + 0 = 33
```

You would then call `MsgBox` like this:

```
Dim result as Integer
result = MsgBox("My message", 33, "aTitle")
MsgBox "My Results: " + Str(result)
```

This produces a sequence of two `MsgBoxes`. The first will look like Figure 5.2 on a Macintosh:

Figure 5.2   MsgBox.

The result will be one of eight values, depending on how many buttons the `MsgBox` has.

Value	Description
1	OK
2	Cancel
3	Abort
4	Retry
5	Ignore
6	Yes
7	No

After you receive the result, you can proceed accordingly. In this example, if the user pressed the Cancel button, the number 2 is returned in the result. You can see an example of the results in Figure 5.3.

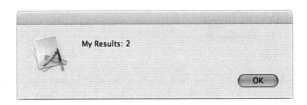

My Results: 2

OK

Figure 5.3   MsgBox results.

Look at the `CancelClose` event of the **RSS** class and you can see the `MsgBox` function used to ask whether the user really wants to quit before leaving:

```
Dim res as Integer
 res = MsgBox("Are you sure you want to quit?", 17, "Quit RSSReader")
 If res = 2 Then
   Return True
 End if
```

You may be tempted to use a `MsgBox` for a little debugging by periodically inserting a `MsgBox` in your code and calling it to display the value of a certain variable or some other piece of information about the internal workings of your program. That used to be one of the only ways to get that kind of information, but it quickly gets to be a hassle. REALbasic offers a better alternative for accomplishing the same thing, which is to write debugging messages to the console, which is discussed later in this chapter.

`MsgBoxes` look and behave differently on various platforms. On a Macintosh, it has a title bar and no title, and the **Window** has fixed width and wrapped text.

The Windows version has a title and a Close button, which means the user can close the **Window** by clicking OK or by clicking the Close button. The window will also increase in width depending on how long the longest paragraph is.

GetOpenFolderItem, GetSaveFolderItem...SelectFolder

REALbasic provides a set of functions that simplify the process of letting a user select a file or folder. For instance, when you want the user to be able to select a file that already exists:

```
REALbasic.GetOpenFolderItem(aFilter as String) as FolderItem
```

The preceding filter will be a reference to the file types. In the RSSReader application, the command looks like this:

```
GetOpenFolderItem("RSSFileTypes.RSS")
```

When you want the user to select a location in which to save a new file:

```
REALbasic.GetSaveFolderItem(aFilter as String, aDefaultName as String) as
FolderItem
```

When you want the user to be able to select only folders and no files:

```
REALbasic.SelectFolder() as FolderItem
```

MessageDialog

This class provides functionality similar to the **MsgBox** in the previous section, but it also gives you a lot more flexibility. When using the **MessageDialog** class, you will be using the **MessageDialogButton** class as well.

Flexibility is a good thing, but it often can get you into trouble. The trade-off with more flexibility means that you have a greater chance of doing something nonstandard, or presenting the information in a way that is not the usual way it is done on the three platforms. It is always a good idea to be as consistent as possible—don't get carried away with all your new-found powers. (The Macintosh implementation of this class doesn't do a good job of handling Macintosh icons. You could roll your own, but what's unique about both **MsgBox** and **MessageDialog** is that they implement themselves as functions, which means they handily return a value when the user clicks the button. Getting the same, or similar, effect on your own is a little more involved.)

FolderItemDialog, SelectFolderDialog, OpenDialog, SaveAsDialog

Not all of the properties for the three **FolderItemDialog** subclasses are available for every platform. The following properties are supported on all three platforms for each subclass:

```
FolderItemDialog.Top as Integer
FolderItemDialog.Left as Integer
FolderItemDialog.Title as Integer
FolderItemDialog.InitialDirectory as FolderItem
```

The **OpenDialog** class provides support for the following properties on the associated platforms:

```
OpenDialog.PromptText as String (Macintosh)
OpenDialog.ActionButtonCaption as String (Macintosh)
OpenDialog.CancelButtonCaption  (Macintosh)
OpenDialog.SuggestedFileName as String (Windows)
```

The **SaveAsDialog** class supports the following:

```
SaveAsDialog.PromptText as String (Macintosh)
SaveAsDialog.ActionButtonCaption as String (Macintosh)
SaveAsDialog.CancelButtonCaption  as String (Macintosh)
SaveAsDialog.SuggestedFileName as String (Windows, Macintosh, Linux)
SaveAsDialog.Filter as String (Windows, Linux)
```

Finally, the **SelectFolderDialog** class has these properties:

```
SelectFolderDialog.PromptText as String (Windows, Macintosh)
SelectFolderDialog.ActionButtonCaption as String (Windows, Macintosh)
SelectFolderDialog.CancelButtonCaption as String  (Macintosh)
SelectFolderDialog.SuggestedFileName as String (None)
SelectFolderDialog.Filter as String (None)
```

Because these are all classes, they need to be instantiated like any other class. After you have instantiated the object, you can then set property values, as shown next. With the properties established, you can call either `ShowModal` or `ShowModalWithin` functions that will cause the dialog to be displayed and will return the selected item. `ShowModalWithin` causes the dialog to be treated like a **Sheet** on Macintosh computers. For Windows and Linux, it acts as if `ShowModal` were called.

```
Dim dialog As New SelectFolderDialog
Dim Workspace as FolderItem
Dim InitialDirectory as FolderItem
dialog.ActionButtonCaption = "Select"
dialog.PromptText = "Select Workspace"
dialog.InitialDirectory  = DocumentsFolder

Workspace = Dialog.ShowModal()

If Workspace <> Nil Then
    self.EditField1.Text = Workspace.absolutePath
Else
    self.EditField1.Text = "No Workspace Selected"
End If
```

The previous example is straightforward enough. The user is asked to select a folder that will serve as the "workspace" for the application, which is where the application's documents will be stored. The path of the selected folder is displayed in an **EditField**.

Editing Windows

When you start a project, **Window1** will already be in place for you. To edit code or modify the **Window**, you double-click **Window1**; the **Window1** tab will appear and get positioned at the font of the other tabs, if any others are open. There are two modes: **Edit Layout Mode** and **Edit Mode**. These are managed by the far left button on the toolbar. You can also use Option+Tab (Mac) or Alt+Tab (Windows/Linux) to switch between the two views. **Layout Mode** will look like Figure 5.4:

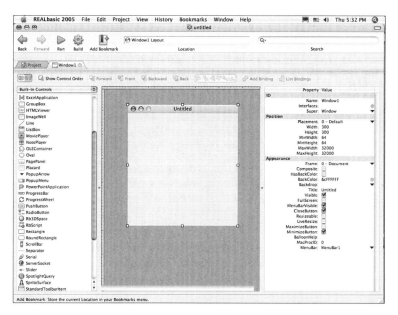

Figure 5.4   Window Panel Layout Mode.

The **Layout Mode** panel is divided into three columns. The left **Member ListBox** contains a list of available controls. In the center of the **Window** is a representation of the **Window** you are editing. This is where you will drag and drop your controls to build your user interface. In the right column is the standard **Properties pane** that contain the properties and values for whatever item is selected.

If you are editing a new **Window** in a new project, all you will see in the Member **ListBox** are the events that are available to this **Window** under the heading event handlers. Even though you are doing it graphically, you are still actually subclassing the **Window** class. If you are in **Edit Mode**, you can add new methods, events, properties, and constants, the same as you would when subclassing any other class.

Switch to **Edit Layout Mode** and drag a **BevelButton** control onto the **Window** and then switch back to **Edit Mode**. Now, another item in the **Member ListBox** has appeared—**Controls**. Click and expand this item and you will see **BevelButton1** list, which is the name of the **Control** you just dragged onto the **Window**. Expand the **BevelButton1** row, and you will see a list of events you can implement. When working with **Controls**, all you need to do is double-click the **Control** while in **Layout Mode** and you will automatically be taken to the **Control's** events in **Edit Mode**.

Unlike **Windows**, you cannot add methods to **Controls** that have been dragged onto a **Window**. You can only implement the events. If you want to add methods to a **Control**, you need to subclass the control and then place the subclass on the **Window**.

Global Window Functions

As you might expect, REALbasic engineers have provided some convenience functions to make working with **Windows** much easier. Although some applications have only one **Window** open at a time, there are many applications that will have many **Windows** open at once. You can use the WindowCount function to find out how many **Windows** are open.

```
REALbasic.WindowCount as Integer
```

An open **Window** is one that has been instantiated and loaded into memory. This is important to understand, because you can have open windows that are not visible, which will make a difference in how you proceed. When you call the WindowCount function, you will have returned the number of open **Windows**, whether they are visible or not.

The WindowCount function is often used in tandem with the Window function. You use the Window function when you want to get a reference to a specific window. A REALbasic application treats multiple windows as an array of **Windows**.

The following example loops through a group of **Windows** and assigns their position as their name.

```
Dim w as Window
Dim x,y as Integer
// Remember that arrays are "Zero" based
y = WindowCount - 1
For x = 0 to y
  Window(x).Title = Str(x)
Next
```

Windows ID Properties

Whenever a new desktop application product is started, it prepopulates the project with a **Window** called **Window1**. The ID Properties for **Window1** are the same as they are for any class. You have the opportunity to select a name, specify which interfaces the **Window** implements, and identify its super class, which, by default, is **Window**.

By default, **Window1** is the default **Window**, which means that it's the one that opens up automatically when the program is launched. You can change this by setting the App.DefaultWindow property in the **Property pane** of the **App** tab.

Windows can be subclassed, but they have some unique characteristics; for instance, you do not have to instantiate them in many cases. **Window1** is implicitly instantiated when you start the application. You can create additional instances of **Window1** by doing the following:

```
Dim w as Window1
w = New Window1
w.Show
```

If you subclass additional **Windows**, the first instance of those **Windows** can be implicitly instantiated by calling the Show method as follows:

```
Dim w2 as Window2
w2.Show
```

Any additional **Windows** of this type would need to be instantiated in the normal way with the New operator. One feature of REALbasic is that you can also implicitly instantiate this first **Window** by referring to any of its properties and setting them. This greatly simplifies the process, but it can also come back to bite you, with **Windows** appearing before you want them to.

When opening multiple **Windows** of different types, you can declare them this way:

```
Dim w1, w2, w3 as Window
w1 = new Window1
w2 = new Window2
w3 = new Window1
```

The reason this works is that **Window1** and **Window2** are both subclasses of **Window**. This is especially helpful if you will not know what kind of **Window** you will need to instantiate until runtime.

In the previous example, I used the Show method to make an instantiated **Window** visible. There are some variations of the Show method to discuss. These are

```
Window.ShowModal
Window.ShowModalWithin(aWindow as Window)
```

The use of the term *modal* can be confusing. A natural question to ask is, why do I need to use ShowModal when I can set the type of **Window** as a **Modal Window**? The answer is that a **Modal Window** and a **Moveable Modal Window** keep the user from interacting with any other **Window** in the application except the **Modal Window**. Making the **Modal Window** visible by using ShowModal stops the main thread of your application. ShowModalWithin is used with Sheet and Drawer **Windows** to identify which **Window** it should be attached to.

Windows Position Properties

Height, Width, MinHeight, MinWidth, MaxHeight, MaxWidth

The Min and Max values set the legal range of sizes of your window. Height and Width are the actual values to use when first launching the window. The Min and Max values establish constraints that limit how much the user can resize the **Window** if it is resizable.

These particular values should be used in conjunction with the Screen function to determine the available screen space.

```
REALbasic.ScreenCount as Integer
REALbasic.Screen(index as Integer) as Screen
```

The Screen function returns a **Screen** object. Because a computer can have more than one screen attached, the Screen function is indexed; the default screen is screen 0. ScreenCount will provide a total count of the number of available **Screen** objects so that you can iterate through them if necessary. Here is an example of getting a reference to the main **Screen**:

```
Dim aScreen as Screen
aScreen = Screen(0)
```

After you have a reference to the **Screen** object, you can access the following properties that tell you what the available space is for your application **Window**, taking into consideration the **MenuBar** (on Macs) and the position of the Dock and Tray.

```
Screen.AvailableHeight as Integer
Screen.AvailableLeft as Integer
Screen.AvailableTop as Integer
Screen.AvailableWidth as Integer
```

Here is an example of how you can use the preferences class to save the size and position of a **Window** when you exit an application and restore it after you restart it.

In the Close event of the **App** object, do the following:

```
App.Preferences.set("window1.top") = Str(me.Top)
App.Preferences.set("window1.left") = Str(me.Left)
App.Preferences.set("window1.width") = Str(me.Width)
App.Preferences.set("window1.height") = Str(me.Height)
```

In the Open event of the **App** object, do this:

```
Window1.top = val(App.Preferences.get("window1.top"))
#if TargetMacOS then
  if Window1.top < 36 then
    Window1.top = 72
  end if
#end if
Window1.left = val(App.Preferences.get("window1.left"))
Window1.width = val(App.Preferences.get("window1.width"))

Window1.height = val(App.Preferences.get("window1.height"))
```

The final position property in the **Layout Editor** is Placement.

```
Window1.Placement as Integer
```

You can assign the proper value to the Placement property using the following **Window** class constants:

```
Window.PlacementDefault = 0
Window.PlacementMainScreen = 2
Window.PlacementParent = 1
Window.PlacementParentScreen = 3
Window.PlacementStagger = 4
```

The default placement is `Stagger`, which places the child **Window** down and a little to the right relative to the parent **Window**. The `PlacementParent` property means simply that the new **Window** is placed in front of the parent, which is the **Window** from which the new **Window** was launched. If you have only one screen, the `MainScreen` and `ParentScreen` are the same, and they both center the new **Window** in the center of the screen rather than the parent **Window**.

If the **Window** is a Drawer, the following class constants apply:

```
Window.PlacementDrawerBottomRight = 2
Window.PlacementDrawerCenter = 1
Window.PlacementDrawerTopLeft = 0
```

Drawers are Macintosh-only **Windows** that are attached to the parent **Window** and slide in and out of the parent **Window** from the position specified.

Windows Appearance Properties

The previous **Windows** were all dialogs—simple **Windows** intended to communicate information to the user or to solicit information from the user. You wouldn't write an entire application using **Windows** such as these, so REALbasic provides you with a much more flexible and powerful **Window** class that you can use. Whenever you create a **Window**, you will select one of the following types for that **Window**.

Window Type	Value
Document	0
Movable Modal	1
Modal Dialog	2
Floating	3
Plain Box	4
Shadowed Box	5
Rounded	6
Global Floating	7
Sheet (Mac OS X only)	8
Metal (Mac OS X 10.2 +)	9
Drawer (Mac OS X 10.2 +)	10

Window.Frame as Integer

This property determines the type of **Window** that will be displayed. The following class constants refer to the different **Window** types:

```
Window.FrameTypeDocument
Window.FrameTypeDrawer
Window.FrameTypeFloating
Window.FrameTypeGlobalFloating
```

```
Window.FrameTypeMetal
Window.FrameTypeModal
Window.FrameTypeMovableModal
Window.FrameTypePlain
Window.FrameTypeRounded
Window.FrameTypeShadowed
Window.FrameTypeSheet
```

Document Window

This is the default **Window** type and the one that will more than likely take center stage in any application. The **Windows** from all three platforms are remarkably similar, with only some minor differences in user interface. By default, **Window1** and all new **Windows** are **Document Windows**. You can see an example of a Macintosh **Window** in Figure 5.5. See Figure 5.6 for an example of a **Window** in Windows, and Figure 5.7 for a Window on the Linux platform.

Figure 5.5   Macintosh Document Window.

Modal Window and Movable Modal Window

A **Modal Window** is a **Window** that stays in front of all the other windows of the current application until it is dismissed. The user can move the **Window** around, but he can't activate a **Window** behind it. Use this **Window** when you need information prior to continuing. A **Movable Modal Window** is one that the user can move around with his or her mouse.

Figure 5.6   Windows Document Window.

Figure 5.7   Linux Document Window.

A cross-platform issue is that Macintosh **Modal Windows** do not have a Close button on them. I found this out the hard way. This means that the only way for users to get rid of the **Modal Window** is if you provide them with a button of some sort that closes the **Window**. On Windows and Linux, a Close button is standard, but if you think about it, there is a certain amount of logic to the Macintosh approach. If you've bothered to display a **Modal Window** and blocked access to the other windows of your application, you've probably done so for a reason. You really should never throw up a **Modal Window** without getting some feedback from the user—that's the point of **Modal Windows**. When programming on Windows and Linux, be mindful that the user can click the Close button on the **Window** so that your application will respond appropriately.

A **Modal Window** is like a **Movable Modal Window** except that it doesn't move. In both cases, the **Quit MenuItem** is disabled when it is displayed.

There are a few differences between platforms, so it is best to describe them by system:

System	Title Bar
Macintosh	No Title, Close, Minimize, or Maximize buttons.
Windows	No Title, Close, Minimize, or Maximize buttons. On an MDI window, the modal window opens in the center off the screen rather than the center of the MDI window.
Linux	Has a Title, Minimize, and Close buttons.

Floating Window

Floating Windows are like **Modal Windows** in that they always stay on top of the application. However, you can interact with the top-most **Window** behind a **Floating Window**.

System	Title Bar
Mactintosh	Close button only.
Windows	Close button only.
Linux	Displays a document Window.

Floating Windows are useful because they always stay in the activated state, which is why they are used for palettes and toolbars in many applications. This means that every time you access a palette, your main **Document Window** doesn't deactivate, making you reactivate it by clicking it every time you refer to something in one of your pallets.

Global Floating Window

It's just like a **Floating Window**, but it stays in front of either all application windows, or of a particular application **Window** when you set the value of the `FloaterProcess` property on Macintosh systems. You provide the four-character Mac Creator Code of the application you want the global **Window** to float in front of.

On Windows, it can be used outside of the MDI **Window** and is not bound by it like other **Window** types are.

Plain Box

A **Plain Box Window** is just a plain box. It's a **Window** without a title bar. It's good for splash screens.

Macintosh Sheet Windows

OS X only. The **Window** slides into view from the title bar. The advantage of a **Sheet Window** is that it acts like a **Modal Window**, but it is linked to a particular **Window** in your application and does not block access to other **Windows** in the application. In other words, if you have an application that allows you to open multiple documents at the same time, you can use a **Sheet Window** to ask the user for confirmation when saving the document. Although the user can't do anything more with that particular document until he or she responds to the sheet, the user can go to other **Document Windows** and interact with them. See Figure 5.8 for an example.

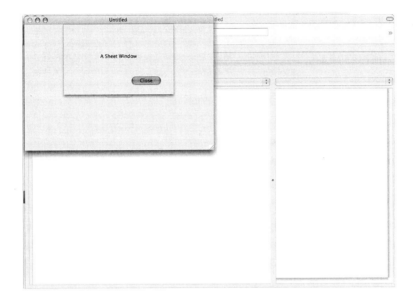

Figure 5.8   Sheet Window.

All other platforms treat them like **Movable Modal Dialogs**, except Mac OS "Classic," which treats it like a **Modal Dialog**.

Because this kind of **Window** isn't available on Windows/Linux, those platforms substitute **Movable Modal Dialogs** instead.

Drawer Window

This is another Mac OS X feature. It's a **Window** that slides out from behind another **Window**. In Windows, a **Floating Window** takes its place and on Linux, a **Document Window** does. See Figure 5.9 for an example.

Shadowed Box and Rounded Window

The reason these **Window** types exist is because they exist on old Macintosh computers. Consequently, I would suggest avoiding them.

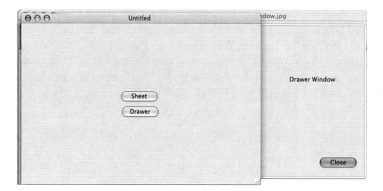

Figure 5.9   Image of Drawer.

Window.Composite as Boolean

A **Composite Window** applies to Macintosh computers. Macs have two styles of **Window**—the standard kind and **Metal Windows**. There are some cases when the **Window** needs to be set to composite for **Controls** to display property—sometimes the **Control** isn't transparent and it is surrounded by a rectangle rather than showing through to the underlying color. **Metal** and **Drawer Windows** have composite turned on by default. Sometimes problems occur on normal **Windows**, too, when **Controls** are stacked on top of each other. If you don't need to use a **Composite Window**, don't— because it seems to perform a little more sluggishly.

Window Colors and Backdrops

You can override the default colors and backdrops of **Windows** very easily in REALbasic. You set the BackColor first by clicking the HasBackColor **CheckBox** (or setting the HasBackColor property to True). Then click the BackColor row and a **Window** will pop up that allows you to select the color to use as the background. You can also specify the color in any of the standard ways of expressing a literal color.

If you want to get fancy, you can use an image instead. It is easy to add an image to a window—just drag one to it and drop it in. You can also drag and drop an image into the **Project Editor** and you'll be able to reference those graphics throughout your application.

Generally speaking, it's better to let REALbasic and the underlying operating system decide what color the **Window** should be so that your application will conform to their user interface guidelines. Just because you can do it, that doesn't mean that you should do it. Of course, there are always exceptions. One common practice in Macintosh applications is to use a backdrop image in folders from which applications are installed.

Window.Title as String

This property gets or sets the **Window** title, which appears at the top of each **Window**.

Visible as Boolean

Indicates whether your **Window** is visible. You can make a **Window** invisible with the `Hide` method and make it visible with `Show`. To clear a **Window** from memory altogether, use `Close` instead of `Hide`.

FullScreen as Boolean

Expand the **Window** to cover the entire screen. This is different from `Maximize` because it hides the Dock and Tray.

MenuBarVisible as Boolean

Determines whether the **MenuBar** for this **Window** is visible. On Windows and Linux, this removes the **MenuBar** from the individual **Window** to which it is attached. The effect on Macintosh is a little more startling because the **MenuBar** it removes is the one that is at the top of the screen. `FullScreen` set to `True` and `MenuBarVisible` set to `False` will let your computer operate like a kiosk, with just the user interface supplied by your application available to the users. Whatever you do, don't do this in a normal application, because users like their familiar surroundings and it's a little rude to be mucking about their computer that way.

CloseButton as Boolean

Determines whether a Close button exists on the **Window**.

Resizable as Boolean

The `Resizable` property determines whether the user can resize the **Window** by dragging it in the lower-right corner.

LiveResize as Boolean

If the **Window** is resizable, you can also set the `LiveResize` property, which means that the **Window** view will be updated as you drag it to a larger size.

MaximizeButton as Boolean

You can customize your **Window** so that it does not have a Maximize button by setting this property to `False`.

MacProcID as Integer

You can use this property to specify specific Macintosh **Windows**—obviously, this is not a cross-platform feature.

MenuBar as MenuBar1

You can have more than one **MenuBar** in your application, and this determines which one is associated with this particular **Window**.

Managing Windows

The **Window** class is the base class for all the **Windows** you will be manipulating in your application. Some of the **Window** classes' events will sound familiar; they are similar to the ones found in the **App** object. There are also some unique events, as well, which I will identify next.

Controls aren't subclasses of **Windows**, so they don't share a hierarchical class structure, but there is a hierarchical structure that is important to understand when working with them, and this is a hierarchy of containment. A **Window** will contain many **Controls**, and some **Controls** will contain even more **Controls**.

If you think of the **Window** as a flat sheet, the **Controls** are overlaid over the **Window**, and if a **Control** contains a second **Control**, the second **Control** is overlaid over the first. In other words, **Controls** and **Windows** are layered.

There are a few methods you can use to determine how many **Controls** a **Window** has and gain access to them without knowing their names:

```
Window.ControlCount as Integer
Window.Control() as RectControl
```

With these two pieces of information, you can iterate over all the **Controls** and do whatever you want to with them.

Window States

There are several states a **Window** can be in, and certain events are triggered whenever a **Window** changes from one state to another.

Windows can be activated or deactivated. A deactivated **Window** is a **Window** that is open, but that is not the front-most **Window** on the computer screen. When a **Window** that has been deactivated is activated by being returned to the front, the `Activate` event is triggered. You can have REALbasic worry about activation for you by setting `AutoDeactivate` to `True`.

In addition to being activated or deactivated, a **Window** can be minimized, which means that it is no longer visible in the desktop portion of the screen and is usually represented on the taskbar/dock/panel only. **Windows** get minimized when the Minimize button is clicked. When a minimized **Window** is restored, the `Restore` event is triggered.

A **Window** can be made visible or invisible by setting the `Visible` property to `True`. A second way of making an invisible **Window** visible is to call the `Show` method of the **Window**. In addition to making the **Window** visible, it also activates the **Window** if it was inactive and brings it to the front of the screen.

Hide, Show, Open, and Close

`Hide` and the various "Shows" don't remove or load a **Window** into memory. It simply makes it visible or not. If you want to remove a **Window** from memory, you need to `Close` it.

Users can manipulate the state of a **Window** by interacting with the title bar of the **Window** and the Tray/Dock.

Open, Close, and CancelClose Events

These events work just like the ones associated with the **App** class. The only caveat is that the `CancelClose` events are called on all open **Windows** before the `Close` events are called.

EnableMenuItems Event

`EnableMenuItems` serves the same purpose as it does in the **App** class.

Close, Minimize, and Maximize Methods

This method programmatically minimizes or maximizes **Windows**, which is equivalent to pressing the Close, Minimize, or Maximize buttons.

Restore Method

Returns a **Window** to its unminimized state.

Mouse Position

MouseX and MouseY Properties

These two properties identify the position of the mouse pointer at any given moment. `MouseX` measures how far from the left side of the **Window** the mouse is (the horizontal axis), and `MouseY` measures how far down it is from the top of the **Window** (the vertical axis).

MouseDown, MouseUp Events

`MouseDown` and `MouseUp` are both passed the coordinates `X` and `Y`, which indicate the position of the mouse when the mouse button was pressed down and the position when the mouse button was released.

MouseDown has a special role, both with **Windows** and, as you will see later on, in **Controls**. `MouseDown` is a function that returns a Boolean. If you return `True` from the `MouseDown`, then, and only then, will the `MouseUp` event be triggered.

MouseMove and MouseDrag Events

`MouseMove` gets passed coordinates just like `MouseUp` and `MouseDown`, and it indicates that the mouse is moving and that it is currently at position `X` and `Y`. `MouseMove` is fired only when the mouse button is not pressed down. The `MouseDrag` event, however, occurs when the mouse button remains pressed down while the mouse moves. `MouseDrag` is also contingent upon the `MouseDown` event; `MouseDown` must return `True` for you to get access to the `MouseDrag` event.

MouseEnter, MouseExit Events

`MouseEnter` and `MouseExit` fire when the mouse has moved the pointer into a position over the **Window**. The events are not passed the coordinates where this has taken place, because you can consult `MouseMove`, or `MouseX` and `MouseY`.

Top, Left

`Top` and `Left` refer to the actual pixel position of the **Window**.

Controls

You are probably already familiar with **Controls**, even if you are not aware of it, because you interact with them every time you use an application.

The base class for all controls is the **Control** class. The **Control** class contains properties, events, and methods that are common to all **Controls**. The **RectControl** class is a subclass of the **Control** class, and this is the parent class of all user-interface **Controls**.

The RectControl Class

All user interface **Controls** are subclasses of the **RectControl** class, called such because all **Controls** are rectangular. Even when the **Control** doesn't "look" like a rectangle (an **Oval Control** for instance), it's still shaped like a rectangle as far as REALbasic is concerned.

Top, Left, Height, and Width

Unlike `MouseX` and `MouseY`, `Top` and `Left` are measured in the coordinates of the **Window**. `Top` (obviously) is the `y` coordinate (up and down) and `Left` is the `x` coordinate (left and right).

The height and width of the control are specified by the `Height` and `Width` properties. Normally, you can adjust the size and position of the control by dragging it with your mouse, but you can also do it programmatically by setting these properties.

LockBottom, LockLeft, LockRight, and LockTop

When a **Control** is positioned on a **Window**, you will need to decide what you want to do in the event that a **Window** gets resized. These properties determine what happens to the **Control**. You can lock the bottom, top, left, or right side of the control to the **Window's** bottom, top, left, or right side. When it is locked, it means that the distance between the **Control's** edge and the **Window's** respective edge remains constant. If you lock all four sides, the **Control** will grow right along with the **Window**. If you lock the right side, the **Control** will stay the same size, but move to the right when the **Window** expands in that direction.

The following figures illustrate how this works. Figure 5.10 shows the **Window** in its natural state, without having been resized at all:

Figure 5.10 Window position.

In Figure 5.11, the **Window** has been resized, and the **EditField** has changed sizes along with it. This is because the `EditField.LockTop`, `LockBottom`, `LockLeft`, and `LockRight` properties are set to `True`.

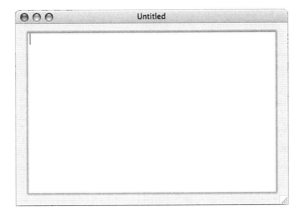

Figure 5.11 Expanded Window and `EditField.LockTop`, `LockBottom`, `LockLeft`, and `LockRight` set to `True`.

Now, in Figure 5.12, I use the same starting point, but this time the `EditField.LockTop` and the `EditFieldLockLeft` properties are set to `True`, and the others are set to `False`. This means that when the **Window** is resized, the **EditField** stays in the upper-left corner of the **Window** and does not get resized itself.

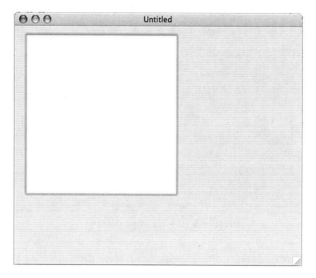

Figure 5.12   Window with `EditField.LockTop` and
`EditField.LockLeft` set to `True`.

AutoDeactivate and Active

`AutoDeactive` determines whether the control should be deactivated if the **Window** is deactivated. This applies to Macintosh computers. `Active` is a read-only Boolean property that will let you know whether the control is active. A **Control** is active when the containing **Window** has been activated and is in the foreground.

Deprecated Properties

There are a few properties that you shouldn't use and that exist only for backward compatibility. One (a property of the **Control** class) is `MacControlHandle`, which has been replaced with the more appropriately named `Handle`, because REALbasic is cross-platform, after all.

Enabled

All **RectControl** subclasses have an Enabled property, which signifies that the **Control** is ready to accept user input. This can be set programmatically by simple assignment, like so:

```
PushButton1.Enabled = True
```

It can also be set through the use of Binding, which we will discuss in more detail in the section "CustomBinding."

Keeping track of when a **PushButton** or any other control should be `Enabled` can get kind of complicated and just a little tedious, especially if you have a lot of controls. Binding is the solution to the problem (most of the time) at least.

I will give examples of Binding with the appropriate controls.

Name

All **Controls** have a name. Because **Controls** aren't instantiated like a normal object, the IDE gives each **Control** a default name when you drag it onto the **Window**, and this name defaults to the name of the **Control** class, plus a number that goes up with each **Control** of the same class that you add.

In other words, if you drag an **EditField** to the **Window**, it will be named **EditField1**. If you drag a second **EditField** to the **Window**, it will be called **EditField2**, and so on. You can set this name to whatever you want it to be in the **Properties pane** on the right side of the editor.

Index

Another property common to all **Controls** is the `Index` property, which is used to access a **Control** when you are using a `Control Array`.

Position – MouseX and Mouse Y

`MouseX` and `MouseY` are properties that show the position of the mouse relative to the control. The position is measured from the upper-left corner, where `MouseX` equals 0 and `MouseY` equals 0.

Open and Close Events

Like the **App** object and **Windows**, **Controls** have `Open` and `Close` events, too. The `Open` and `Close` events of your controls is determined by their **Control Order.**

Sample Control: BevelButton

The first **Control** listed in the **Built-in Control** list is the **BevelButton**. To get that **Control** onto the **Window**, you need to select it, hold your mouse down, and drag it until you are over the **Window** and then release the mouse.

The first thing you'll notice is that the **BevelButton** is labeled Untitled. You can change that by modifying a value in the **Properties pane**. Now is a good time to take a look at this **ListBox** and discuss a few of the items you see there.

The properties are group into the headings ID, Position, Appearance, Initial State, Behavior, and Font. Different **Controls** will have different values, but all of them share the ID and Position groups.

The name of this **BevelButton** is **BevelButton1**. REALbasic uses this convention for all **Controls**. When you drag a **Control** onto a **Window**, it adds an integer to the name of the **Control** to establish the new name. If I were to drag a second **BevelButton**, it would be called **BevelButton2**.

Index refers to a Control Array, which is a way of handling a lot of **Controls** of the same type. See the section on Control Arrays for more information.

Finally, you'll see that value of the Super property is **BevelButton**. This means that **BevelButton** is the Super class for **BevelButton1**, and that means **BevelButton1** is a subclass of **BevelButton**. By dragging a **Control** onto a **Window**, you are attaching it to the **Window** and as a consequence, it will be implicitly instantiated when the **Window** is instantiated.

Here's an important caveat with respect to subclassing **Controls**: You can subclass a control just like any other class, and you can create any number of Constructors for it; but the automatic instantiation done by REALbasic uses only the default **Constructor**. To initialize **Controls**, you should use the Open event.

Control Order and Control Arrays

Especially with respect to the Windows operating system, users are often able to tab from one control to the next. The **Control Order** determines the sequence in which this happens. The IDE will automatically populate this value for you, which you can easily override and set in the IDE yourself. If you want a visual representation of the **Control Order**, you can select the **View Menu** and then select the **Control Order MenuItem**. When you do, you will see something like Figure 5.13:

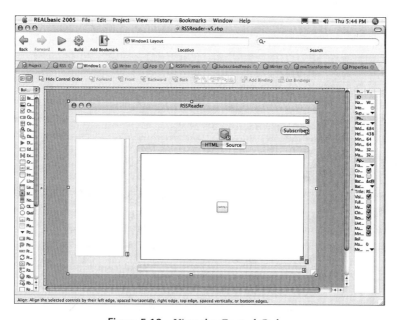

Figure 5.13   View the Control Order.

In the RSSReader application, **EditField1** is in the Control Order position of "0", followed by the **Pushbutton1** and then **ListBox1**. When the **Window** first opens,

EditField1 calls the **EditField**1.setFocus method, which gives **EditField1** the focus, as indicated by the FocusRing (I have UseFocusRing set to True) and the fact that the insertion bar will be blinking inside the **EditField**.

Drawing Guides

As you drag **Controls** onto the **Window**, REALbasic will provide guidance as to the best location for controls. In Figure 5.14, I am dragging **ListBox1,** and two thin aquaish lines get drawn that indicate the optimal spot to stop dragging.

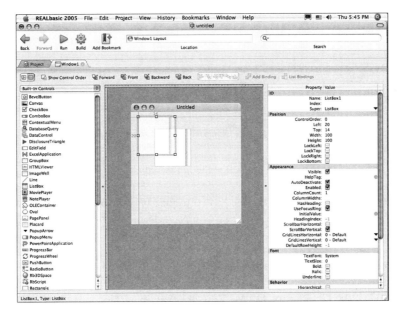

Figure 5.14   Guidelines.

Binding

The state of one **Control** often depends on the state of another one. For example, it would be nice for the Subscribe button to be enabled only when there is some text in **EditField1**. Likewise, it would be nice for the **TabPanel** to be enabled only when **ListBox1** has a selection. Setting this up for the **ListBox1** control is easy using REALbasic's binding facilities. In **Window Layout Mode**, there should be two buttons on the toolbar, as shown in Figure 5.15:

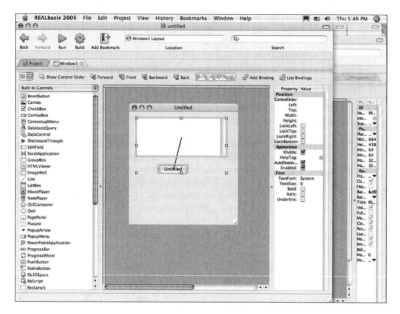

Figure 5.15   Windows toolbar binding buttons.

If you do not have them, you may need to customize your **Toolbar**. In earlier versions of REALbasic 2005, you had to have two controls selected on the **Window** before you could customize the **Toolbar**, but that should be fixed by the time you read this.

To bind the **ListBox** to the **TabPanel**, select both of them (hold down the Shift key and click each one with your mouse). A **Window** much like the one shown in Figure 5.16 will appear.

If you click the **CheckBox**, **HTMLViewer1** will be enabled every time an item is selected in **ListBox1**. There are different kinds of bindings for different combinations of **Controls**, so the best way to identify them is to experiment and see what options you are given. If you want to see a list of all your bindings, you can press the **List Bindings** button on the **ToolBar** and get a list of active bindings as shown in Figure 5.17.

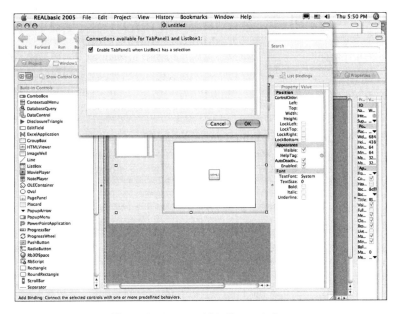

Figure 5.16 Visual bindings window.

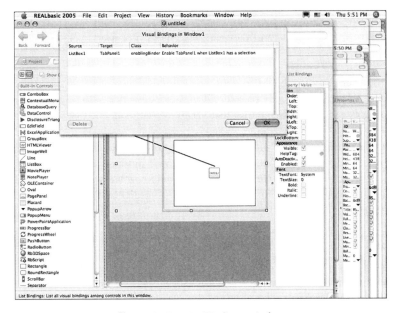

Figure 5.17 List Bindings window.

Pushbutton Control

The RSSReader application has one **PushButton**—**PushButton1,** which is clicked when the user subscribes to a new RSS feed. The Action event of the **PushButton** class is the most common event you will be doing this. This is the event that is fired when a user clicks the button. To be more precise, the Action event is not fired when a user presses down on the button. It is triggered when the user releases the clicked mouse button.

The **PushButton** control also implements a MouseDown event and a MouseUp event. Both events return a Boolean, and the way they work can be a little tricky.

When the MouseDown event is fired, the position of the mouse when it was clicked is passed to the event.

```
Function MouseDown(X As Integer, Y As Integer) as Boolean
```

If you return True, you are telling REALbasic that you're going to handle things from here. In fact, the only way to get the MouseUp event to be triggered is to return True in the MouseDown event. Where in the midst of all of this does the Action event get triggered?

It's a trick question, because the Action does not get called, presumably because you're handling the MouseUp event. One word of caution: The MouseUp event returns a Boolean. Because you return True in the MouseDown event to get access to the MouseUp event, you might think that returning True or False would have some impact on whether the ActionEvent gets called. It doesn't. In fact, the value returned by the MouseUp event evanesces—it just disappears like a popped bubble.

Button State

The Enabled property can be set to True or False, and when True signifies that the **PushButton** is active and ready to respond to user interaction. When the button is inactive, it takes on a visual representation that varies by platform, but that shows that it is not active.

If you selected **EditField1** and **PushButton1,** you'll see that the **Add Binding** button is grayed out; in other words, there are no prebuilt bindings to link **EditField1** with **PushButton1**. If you want **PushButton1** to become enabled when text is available in **EditField1**, you will need to implement that code in **EditField1**. I will do that in the coming pages.

TabPanel

A **TabPanel** is a subclass of **PagePanel,** and they both work in separate ways. A **PagePanel** is a transparent **Control** that consists of a series of pages; each page can contain its own set of **Controls**. This allows you to change the layout or composition of a **Window** without having to swap windows or do a lot of programming. A **TabPanel** is the same thing, except that it presents a tabbed interface to the user (a **PagePanel** has to be moved from page to page programmatically).

PagePanel has a property, `Value`, which identifies which page is at the top. It also allows you to append, insert, or delete pages. A **TabPanel** inherits these capabilities, plus a few more. You can designate which direction the tabs face, using the following property:

```
TabPanel.Facing as Integer
```

The class constants are as follows:

```
TabPanel.FacingNorth = 0
TabPanel.FacingSouth = 1
TabPanel.FacingEast = 2
TabPanel.FacingWest = 3
```

Because a **TabPanel** has tabs, you may want to set the caption for the tabs at runtime; fortunately, you can:

```
TabPanel.Caption(aTab as Integer) as String
```

The first tab is numbered 0.

In the RSSReader project, a **TabPanel** (as shown in Figure 5.18) is used to display the **HTMLViewer** and the **EditField**. There is no programming to be done—the initial values for the tabs can be set in the IDE.

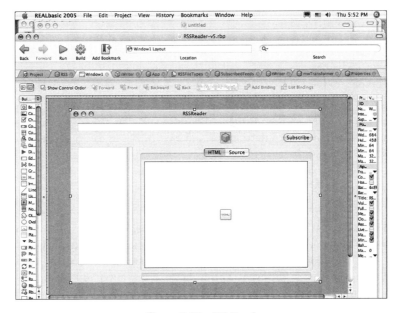

Figure 5.18   TabPanel.

One of the problems with the **TabPanel** (and **PagePanel**) is that **Controls** sometimes bleed through. In the case of this application, there were many times when the

EditField2 would show up in front of **HTMLViewer1**, even when it wasn't supposed to. This problem seems to be platform specific, with Macintosh having more problems.

The standard answer given to fix it is to go to each panel, select each **Control** on the panel, and then select **Move To Front**. This didn't work for me. There are also the methods Refresh, RefreshRect, and UpdateNow that are supposed to force redrawing of the elements. After all was said and done, I found that everything was fixed if I resized the **Window**, which forced everything to be redrawn. My ugly hack was to manually resize the **Controls** on the **TabPanel** to force them to redraw. I also had better luck when I made sure that the **EditField2** and **HTMLViewer1** were of the same size and in the same position.

EditField Control

EditFields were designed for data entry, and REALbasic provides several tools to make this as easy as possible. If you are looking for a general-purpose word processing field, you may be disappointed, but although it may lack some features such as indentation of paragraphs, it is very flexible otherwise, and you can do quite a lot with it.

Events

EditFields have similar events to other **Controls**. The following events are important when tracking what information is being entered into the **EditField**:

```
Function EditField.Sub GotFocus()
Function EditField.KeyDown(Key as String) As Boolean
Sub EditField.SelChange ()
Sub EditField.TextChange()
Sub EditField.LostFocus()
```

GotFocus generally fires first when the control first gets focus. KeyDown is triggered when any key is pressed and the **EditField** has the focus. SelChange is triggered by a change in the location of the insertion bar, and TextChange is called when the content of the **EditField** is actually changed.

Mouse movement is tracked as well:

```
EditField.MouseDown(X as Integer, Y as Integer) As Boolean
EditField.MouseUp(X as Integer, Y as Integer) As Boolean
```

EditFields have built-in drag and drop, which is billed as a feature; but of course it's a feature only if you don't want to have any control over how things are dragged or dropped. Like several other controls, **EditField** allows you to override a MouseDown event by returning True in the event. This means that whenever you use the mouse to position the cursor, nothing will happen because you are telling REALbasic, "Yes, it's true that I'm handling the event, so don't bother." Unfortunately, that doesn't do you much good, because none of the other events fire while the mouse is down. All this boils down to the fact that you basically have to accept the drag-and-drop features of REALbasic's **EditField** as is.

Text and Positioning

The text that is displayed in an **EditField** can be set and accessed through the `Text` property.

```
EditField.Text as String
```

The text itself is made up of a number of characters. To count the characters, you will need to use the `Len` function.

```
aLen = Len(EditField1.Text)
```

As you may recall, I needed to write some code in an **EditField1** event to make **PushButton1** enabled only when text is available. There are any number of perfectly valid ways to go about this, but my preference is to implement it in the `KeyDown` event. Every time a key is pressed and the **EditField** has focus, I will check to see how many characters are displayed in the **EditField** and then set the appropriate `Enabled` property for **PushButton1**:

```
If Len(me.Text) > 0 Then
    PushButton1.Enabled = True
Else
    PushButton1.Enabled = False
End If
```

When you are typing into an **EditField,** you will see an insertion bar that blinks between the characters, wherever it happens to be. If you want to know where the insertion bar is, you use the `SelStart` property:

```
EditField.SelStart as Integer
```

There are three properties pertaining to selected text. `SelStart` is an integer that identifies the position of the cursor in the **EditField**. If you have an empty **EditField** and you have the focus, you'll see the blinking cursor in the upper-left of the **EditField**, and at that point `SelStart` would be 0. `SelLength` would be 0 as well, as long as no other characters were selected.

`SelStart` can be kind of confusing. The important thing to remember is that `SelStart` is not the same thing as character position. If you want to select the first character in an **EditField**, set `SelStart = 0` and `SelLength = 1`. If you do that, you will have selected the first character.

The insertion bar goes between characters and is numbered accordingly, as shown in Figure 5.19.

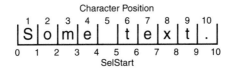

Figure 5.19 Character Position and `EditField.SelStart`.

You can still use SelText to insert or delete text, which is handy if you don't want to use the **Clipboard** to cut and copy text. You would want to avoid that if you were doing a search and replace and you didn't want it to affect or overwrite the content that was in the **Clipboard**.

If SelLength is greater than 0, you can get access to the selected text as a string with SelText. If SelLength is 0, there is no text to provide, but that doesn't mean you can't use it. If you want to insert text without overwriting any text, you can set SelStart to the position where you want to insert the text, set SelLength to 0, and then set SelText equal to the text you want to insert.

If there is no text in an **EditField,** and the **EditField** has the focus, SelStart will be 0. In addition to SelStart, there is also a SelLength property:

```
EditField.SelLength as Integer
```

If you have selected text and it is highlighted, SelLength measures the length of the text that is highlighted. If no text is highlighted, the SelLength is 0. The text that is highlighted is accessible through the SelText property:

```
EditField.SelText as String
```

You use SelText to get and set selected text. If you want to access the text, you can use simple assignment:

```
aString = EditField1.SelText
```

If you want to replace selected text with new text, do this:

```
EditField1.SelText = "Some new text"
```

If you want to delete the selected text, assign an empty string to it, like so:

```
EditField1.SelText = ""
```

You can still use SelText, even when no text is selected and SelLength is 0. This is especially useful when inserting text or appending text. When appending text, you might be tempted to use string concatenation, like this:

```
EditField1.Text = EditField1.Text + "Here's some new text"
```

This will likely cause the screen to flicker and be slow if you are appending a lot of text to the **EditField**. The solution is to do the following:

```
Dim aLen as Integer
aLen = Len(EditField1.Text)
EditField1.SelStart = aLen
EditField1.SelText = "Here's some new text"
```

There are also properties that deal with character positions. The first character in the **EditField** is at character position 1. If you want to select the first character programmatically, you can use SelStart and SelLength:

```
EditField1.SelStart = 0
EditField1.SelLength = 1
```

You can use `CharPosAtXY` to find a particular character position relative to a coordinate for the **EditField**.

```
EditField.CharPosAtXY(X as integer, Y as integer) as Integer
```

Often, the mouse position is the source of the coordinate. You could use this to find out which word the mouse is over, for example. Suppose that for some reason, you want to select a character at a certain coordinate. Here's how you would do it:

```
Dim charPos as Integer
charPos = EditField1.CharPosAtXY
EditField1.SelStart = charPos - 1
EditField1.SelLength = 1
```

Now suppose you want to know which line a particular character is on. The following method will help:

```
EditField.LineNumAtCharPos(aPosition as Integer) as Integer
```

You can do this:

```
Dim aLine as Integer
aLine = EditField1.LineNumAtCharPos(1)
```

If you are looking at the first character, as in the preceding sample, the line number would be 1. You also might want to know how many lines in total the **EditField** has:

```
Dim aLen as Integer
Dim aLine as Integer
aLen = Len(EditField1.Text)
aLine = EditField1.LineNumAtCharPos(aLen)
```

Finally, you can ascertain the first character position of any given line using the following method:

```
EditField.CharPosAtLineNum(aLine as Integer) as Integer
```

The character returned is the first character on the line. Consider this:

```
Dim charPos as Integer
charPos = EditField1.CharPosAtLineNum(1)
```

Because you are asking for the character position for the first line, `charPos` would be equal to 1.

Data Entry

EditFields are perhaps most commonly used as data entry fields rather than as a field used for word processing. Generally speaking, when this is the case, there are several fields on the **Window** and you want the user to be able to navigate through the tabs quickly, with the least amount of trouble. One way to do this is to let users tab through the fields. When they press the Tab key, they automatically go on to the next field in the sequence. There are also times when you want a user to be able to enter tabs into the field itself, so you have the option of setting whether the field accepts tabs:

```
EditField.AcceptTabs as Boolean
```

You can control the order in which this tabbing sequence occurs by setting the `ControlOrder` value for the control in the **Window** layout editor. You also will want to make certain that the user starts entering text at the right location, so you should automatically set the first to the field with the `ControlOrder` position of 0. An **EditField** can call a method to give itself the focus:

```
EditField1.setFocus
```

On a typical Windows application, all **Controls** normally accept focus. In REALbasic applications, this wasn't always the case if the **Control** used by REALbasic wasn't a native Windows **Control**. Now **Controls** have an `AcceptFocus` property that allows all **Controls** to accept focus. This is not the case with Macintosh computers, where most **Controls** do not accept focus, except for ones that accept data entry, such as **EditFields**.

You have the option of using a focus ring with your Macintosh users; an eerie blue glow lights up around the field with focus:

```
EditField.UseFocusRing as Boolean
```

EditFields by default have borders, but you can turn them off using the `Border` property:

```
EditField.Border as Boolean
```

If you are using the fields for data entry, you would normally keep the borders turned on. You can turn them off if you want to draw your own border or, as is more often the case, you want to use the **EditField** in a way that it doesn't look like an **EditField**. For example, if you put an **EditField** on top of a white rectangle, you could mimic the capability to have margins on the page.

```
EditField.MultiLine as Boolean
```

You can automatically format numbers that are entered into the **EditField** using the same techniques as the `Format` function:

```
EditField.Format(aFormat as String)
```

If the **EditField** is not in `MultiLine` mode, you can limit the amount of text that can be entered using `LimitText`:

```
EditField.LimitText(aLen as Integer)
```

For more complex control over what gets entered, you can set a mask for the **EditField**:

```
EditField.Mask(aMask as String)
```

The following characters are used to create the mask:

?   Character placeholder.

C   Optional character or space placeholder.

&   Character placeholder. ASCII characters from 32–126 and from the non-ASCII range of 128–255.

Required single-digit placeholder.

9   Optional single-digit placeholder .

A   Required alphanumeric character.

a   Optional alphanumeric character.

.   Decimal placeholder (locale specific).

,   Thousands separator (locale specific).

:   Time separator (locale specific).

/   Date separator (locale specific).

>   Uppercase (all following characters).

<   Lowercase (all following characters).

Literal The actual character to be displayed.

\   Escape character: Forces special characters to be treated as literals.

~   Reserved for future use.

Following are some examples of common masks you may need to use from time to time:

Social Security number:

###-##-####

Phone Number:

(###) ###-####

Currency (up to $99.99)

$9#.##

IP Address

###.###.###.###

Date

##/##/####

Time

9#:## AM

Time, part two

9#:## \AM

If the text entered into a field doesn't match the required match, a `ValidationError` event will occur:

```
EditField.ValidationError(InvalidText as String, StartPosition as Integer)
```

When sensitive information is being entered and you do not want prying eyes to see it (such as when you are entering a password), you can set the `Password` property to `True`:

```
EditField.Password as Boolean
```

This is disabled if `MultiLine` is set to `True`. When `Password` is set to `True`, a bullet appears with each keystroke rather than the actual character, which provides at least some privacy when a user is asked to enter a password (in case someone is looking over the user's shoulder).

If you need simply to display text that will not be edited, you can usually use a **StaticText** control, but you can also use an **EditField** and set the `ReadOnly` property to `True`:

```
EditField.ReadOnly as Boolean
```

When an `EditField.ReadOnly` property is `True`, the text cannot be changed by the user. You can set this property at runtime.

There are a few common patterns of using **EditFields**. If you use them as fields in a data entry form, the properties are generally set like so:

```
EditField1.Multiline = False
EditField1.ScrollbarVertical = False
EditField1.ScrollbarHorizontal = False
EditField1.Styled = False
EditField1.FocusRing = True
EditField1.AcceptTabs = False
```

If you have an **EditField** you want people to edit or that displays highlighted text of some sort, then

```
EditField1.Multiline = True
EditField1.ScrollBarVertical = True
EditField1.Scrollbar Horizontal = False
EditField1.Styled = True
EditField1.FocusRing = False
EditField1.Accept Tabs = False
```

One of the more remarkable attributes of REALbasic is how easy it is to set up a database. The following properties are used in that process and will be discussed in more detail when the topic of databases and binding is covered.

```
EditField.DataField(aField as String)
EditField.DataSource(aDataControl as DataControl)
EditField.LiveUpdate as Boolean
EditField.BindValue(aValue as StringProvider)
```

Scrolling

```
EditField.ScrollbarHorizontal (ro)
EditField.ScrollBarVertical (ro)
EditField.ScrollPosition
EditField.ScrollPositionX
```

Setting Style Properties for All Text

There are many instances when you need to apply the same style to an entire field. You can use these properties to both get and set the values, and they apply to all the text in an **EditField**:

```
EditField.TextColor As Color
EditField.BackColor as Color
EditField.Bold as Boolean
EditField.Underline as Boolean
EditField.Italic as Boolean
```

Handling fonts deserves a little extra attention. The following properties are used to get and set the current font and text size:

```
EditField.TextFont As String
EditField.TextSize As Integer
```

First, the TextSize is an integer, which means that you cannot use font sizes such as 10.5. Second, you may be wondering how to determine what string to use to specify a font. REALbasic provides the predictably easy way to get it:

```
REALbasic.FontCount as Integer
REALbasic.Font(positionas Integer) as String
```

The following example shows you one way to use it. I loop through all of the fonts and add their name to a **ListBox** called FontList:

```
Dim y as Integer
Dim x as Integer

y = FontCount -1
For x = 0 To y
  me.FontList.addRow(Font(x))
Next
```

Controls use a font called System, which is a reference to the default font for each platform. You can override this and set any control to use whatever font you want, but it is recommended to stick with the System font in most cases because that's the font that the user-interface guidelines for each package calls for. They are fonts that are designed to be used in concert with other platform specific controls, and it also tends to look better.

Alignment Constants

The alignment of the **EditField** is set with the `Alignment` property:

```
EditField.Alignment as Integer
```

You can set the alignment using the following class constants:

```
EditField.AlignDefault = 0 (left)
EditField.AlignLeft = 1
EditField.AlignCenter = 2
EditField.AlignRight = 3
```

If you are testing the value of `Alignment` and see that it is −1, it means that the current selection is mixed and spans paragraphs.

Setting Style Properties on Selected Text

There are two basic approaches to setting style values only on selected text, rather than on all the text in the **EditField.** The first group of methods "toggle" the style value of the selected text. In other words, if the selected text is already bold, when it is toggled it will no longer be bold. Likewise, if it isn't bold, it will be bold.

```
EditField.ToggleSelectionBold
EditField.ToggleSelectionItalic
EditField.ToggleSelectionUnderline
```

There are some Macintosh "Classic" options as well that you might encounter, but that are not in modern Macintosh systems:

```
EditField.ToggleSelectionShadow
EditField.ToggleSelectionOutline
EditField.ToggleSelectionCondense
EditField.ToggleSelectionExtend
```

Contrast toggling behavior with the behavior of the following properties that allow you to set the style information directly. One advantage of this method is that you can use these properties to find out the current style as well as to set the style:

```
EditField.SelBold as Boolean
EditField.SelItalic as Boolean
EditField.SelUnderline as Boolean
```

`SelAlignment` uses the alignment constants discussed previously. Because alignment applies to paragraphs and not just strings of text, the entire paragraph will take on the alignment set here:

```
EditField.SelAlignment as Integer
```

The following are valid only for "Classic" Macs:

```
EditField.SelShadow as Boolean
EditField.SelOutline as Boolean
EditField.SelCondense as Boolean
EditField.SelExtend as Boolean
```

These set color, font, and size on the selection:

```
EditField.SelTextColor as Color
EditField.SelTextFont as String
EditField.SetTextSize as Integer
```

The following methods let you copy and paste selected text:

```
EditField.Copy
EditField.Paste
```

Note that there is no `Cut`, but that's easily fixed because `Cut` is a combination of `Copy` and `Delete`. You can delete the selected text easily, as demonstrated before:

```
EditField1.SelText = ""
```

When you copy the text, it's copied to the **Clipboard**. See the section on **MenuItem**s later in this chapter for a more complete discussion of how to manage copying and pasting of text.

StyledText

EditFields can be either styled or not styled. This is set or accessed through the Styled property:

```
EditField.Styled as Boolean
EditField.StyledText as StyledText
```

The **StyledText** class largely replaces **TextStyleData**, which is a holdover from the pre-Windows, pre-Linux days and was used in Macintosh programming. You access styled text from the **StyledText** property of the **EditField,** or you can instantiate **StyledText** objects independently of an **EditField**.

ListBox

A **ListBox** is one of those controls that you will find yourself using all the time. It is used to display lists, grids, and hierarchical data.

Adding Rows

When working with a regular **ListBox**, you can add rows easily. In fact, if you have a **ListBox** with a single column, all you need to do is the following:

```
AddRow("Text for this row")
```

When working with a hierarchical **ListBox**, you get access to another method, called `AddFolder`. (If you use `AddFolder` without the `Hierarchical` property set to `True`, it just functions like the `AddRow` method.)

Unfortunately, REALbasic is suffering from method-naming inconsistency with respect to how new data is inserted, deleted, and manipulated in the **ListBox**. You can add "rows" and "folders," and you can "remove" rows as well, and you do this using the following methods:

```
ListBox.AddRow Item as String
ListBox.AddFolder Item as String
ListBox.InsertRow Row as Integer, Item as String
```

```
ListBox.InsertFolder Row as Integer, Item as String
ListBox.RemoveRow Row as Integer
ListBox.DeleteAllRows
```

When you use the `AddFolder` method, don't expect to see any folders anywhere. What you will see is that REALbasic has added a row, plus an indication that this row might contain additional data. On the Macintosh, this is signified by a gray disclosure triangle and on **Windows**, it's denoted by a little box with a cross in it.

You can also insert folders with the `InsertFolder` method. There is not a `RemoveFolder` method, however. You must rely on the `RemoveRow` to remove any kind of row, hierarchical or not.

The following code from the `SubscribedFeeds.open()` event shows a simple example of how to add rows to a **ListBox**:

```
Dim tis as TextInputStream
Dim s as String


RSSFile = ApplicationSupportFolder.Child("info.choate.rssreader")


If RSSFile.Exists Then
    tis = RSSFile.OpenAsTextFile
    If (tis <> Nil) And (List <> Nil) Then

        While Not tis.EOF
        s = tis.ReadLine()
        If s <> "" Then
            List.AddRow(s)
        End If
        Wend


    End If
End If
```

Selecting Rows and Manipulating Cells

You can identify which row is selected by checking the following property:

```
ListBox.ListIndex as Integer
```

You can also readily find out the last row that was added (either through appending or inserting the row) using this similarly named property:

```
ListBox.LastIndex as Integer
```

If the **ListBox** only has one column, you can use the `List` method to get the text in the cell of a given row. For example, if I want to get the text of the first row in a **ListBox**, I can do the following:

```
Dim s as String
s = ListBox1.List(0)
```

To refer to a specific cell in the **ListBox**, you use the `Cell` property. There are two parameters: the first is the row number and the second is the column number. The following code refers to the first cell in the first row:

```
Dim s as String
s = ListBox1.Cell(0,0)
```

There is also a new feature: You can now select `ListBox1.Cell(-1,-1)` to get and set the contents of the **ListBox**. If you use only `-1` in the position indicating rows, you will get all the rows for that column. Likewise if you use `-1` in the position indicating columns, you will get all the columns for that row. The strings are Tab delimited with respect to columns, and `EndOfLine` delimited with respect to rows.

The following code from the `SubscribedFeeds.write()` event gives you an example of how to reference `Cells` in a **ListBox**:

```
Dim tos as TextOutputStream
Dim x,y as Integer
Dim s as String

tos = RSSFile.CreateTextFile

y = me.List.ListCount - 1

For x = 0 To Y
    s = me.List.Cell(x,0)
    If s <> "" Then
        tos.WriteLine(s)
    End If
Next

tos.Close
```

Hierarchical ListBoxes

A hierarchical **ListBox** is one that displays hierarchical data, rather than lists. Using REALbasic's hierarchical **ListBox** features is a lot easier now than it used to be, in large part because of the `CellTag` property, which allows you to associate a **Variant** value with each individual cell.

When working with a hierarchical **ListBox**, you will want the user to be able to click a folder row and reveal the data contained by that folder. For this to happen, the user has to click the disclosure arrow (or box), not simply the row itself. If you click the text in the row, you will select that row, but that will not expand the row.

When the disclosure area is clicked, the `ExpandRow(Row as Integer)` event is called.

If you want to see if a particular row is expanded, you can test against the `Expanded(Row as Integer)` property, which will return `True` if the row is expanded.

If the row is already expanded, clicking the disclosure area will cause the row to collapse, triggering the `CollapseRow(Row as Integer)` event.

Fortunately for you, you don't have to worry about the data that is in the rows that disappear; REALbasic takes care of deleting them for you.

One of the hardest parts about dealing with hierarchical **ListBoxes** before was keeping track of the hierarchical data itself and knowing what to show when a row expanded, and what not to show when it was collapsed. The usual way to do this was to have a separate array of visible values, along with some kind of hierarchical data (nested dictionaries, or a hierarchy of objects) that you manually kept track of with each expansion or contraction of the list. Now it's much easier because of the **CellTag** property.

You still need to have a set of hierarchical data of some sort (unless you are able to determine the subdata dynamically when the rows are clicked).

The most common set of hierarchical data you'll definitely have around is the hierarchy of the file system on your computer, so I'll show you an example of how to view the folders and files on your hard drive.

File systems and XML documents are among the kind of data that are hierarchical and suitable for display in this way. Here's an example that shows how to create a **ListBox** that will navigate through the folders and files on your computer.

Drag a **ListBox** to the **Window** and make sure the `Hierarchical` check box is checked. You need to implement two events. The first is `Open`:

```
Sub Open()
  Dim f as FolderItem
  // Make certain it's hierarchical
  me.Hierarchical = True

  f = Volume(0)

  me.AddFolder(f.DisplayName)
  me.CellTag(me.LastIndex, 0) = f
End Sub
```

In this event, the root directory of the primary **Volume** is selected and its name is added to the **ListBox,** more or less as it was in the previous **ListBox** example. One difference is that instead of `AddRow`, `AddFolder` was used. This indicates that this is a branch node, rather than a leaf node. In other words, it can contain children. The other item of interest is that I assign a reference to the root folder to `CellTag`, which is a variable that can be set for each individual cell in the **ListBox**. It's a **Variant**, so it can be any object or data type and it is used to store a value related to what is being displayed. In this case, I've associated the **FolderItem** itself. You'll see why I did this in the second event, `ExpandRow`:

```
Sub ExpandRow(row as Integer)
  Dim f as FolderItem
  Dim x,y as Integer
```

```
  f = me.CellTag(row, 0)
  y = f.Count

  For x = 1 To y
    If f.Item(x).Directory Then
      me.AddFolder(f.Item(x).DisplayName)
    Else
      me.AddRow(f.Item(x).DisplayName)
    End If
    me.CellTag(me.LastIndex, 0) = f.Item(x)
  Next
End Sub
```

The `ExpandRow` event is fired when a user clicks the disclosure arrow (or box, in the case of Windows) in the **ListBox**. In this example, the user will click to examine the contents of the root folder. The row number is passed to the event and it is used to get a reference to the **FolderItem** associated with that `Cell`. The next step is to iterate through the directory and display the children. Each item within the directory is tested to see whether it is a folder or a file, and `AddFolder` or `AddRow` is called accordingly.

You now have a working **ListBox** that will navigate your computer's file system. There is a `CollapseRow` event, too, but you do not need to use that to delete the rows that are displayed as children of the row that was clicked. REALbasic takes care of that for you.

In this example, we coded the events in the normal way, but there is another way to go about it, by subclassing the **ListBox**. In the IDE, go to the **Project Tab** and add a new class. Call it **FolderListBox**. Set the `Super` of the class to **ListBox** and double-click it to edit it. In the second release of REALbasic 2005, the new class appears, but there are no events, methods, or constants listed at all. This is likely a bug that will be fixed, but it's easy to work around for now. One of the options is to add an event definition. Click that and you'll be able to create a new event definition, but this also causes all the other **ListBox** events to show up. After this is done, update the `Open` and `ExpandRow` events just like you did before. (Don't bother to create a new event. The only reason to click **Add Event Definition** was to get the other events to be visible).

After that is done, go to the **Window** of your application and drag a **ListBox** onto the **Window**. In the **Properties pane**, click the **PopupArrow** to select a new `Super` class for the **ListBox**. REALbasic already knows about **FolderListBox**, so you'll be able to select it from the menu. Now, go to the **FolderListBox** on the **Window** and double-click it as if you were going to implement new events and look for the `Open` and `ExpandRow` events.

Any luck? The answer is no—there's not an `Open` or `ExpandRow` event to be seen; the reason is that you implemented it as a subclass. Remember that when an object is looking for a method, it first checks to see if it implements the method, and then it checks to see if it `Super` implements the method, and so on. It starts at the lowest level of the inheritance tree and works its way back up to the top. Events work just the opposite—the search for the event implementation starts at the top of the inheritance tree, and not the bottom. After it finds the implementation, it is executed, but no implementations lower down the tree are implemented, unless you specifically tell it to.

To accomplish this, you have to add two **Event Definitions** to the original **FolderListBox** subclass. Add an `Open` and `ExpandRow` event that looks just like the respective originals. Keep the same name and same signatures; it's not a problem that it is the same name as an event that already exists. The reason is that you will not be implementing these new events. Next, go to the `ExpandRow` event that you have already implemented and add a line so that it looks like this:

```
Sub ExpandRow(Row)
  Dim f as FolderItem
  Dim x,y as Integer

  f = me.CellTag(row, 0)
  y = f.Count

  For x = 1 To y
    If f.Item(x).Directory Then
      me.AddFolder(f.Item(x).DisplayName)
    Else
      me.AddRow(f.Item(x).DisplayName)
    End If
    me.CellTag(me.LastIndex, 0) = f.Item(x)
  Next

  ExpandRow(row)
End Row
```

Every row that is added from within the `ExpandRow` event is added as a child row of the row that is expanded.

Do the same with `Open`:

```
Sub Open
  Dim f as FolderItem

  me.Hierarchical = True

  f = Volume(0)

  me.AddFolder(f.DisplayName)
  me.CellTag(me.LastIndex, 0) = f

  Open
End Sub
```

Now, go back to the **Window Editor,** double-click the **FolderListBox** item, and look for the two events. You'll be happy to see that they now exist and you can implement them as you like. In the original class, all I did was "trigger" the new `Open` and

ExpandRow events after I was finished processing so that whatever you implement for the **FolderListBox** that has been dragged to the **Window** will be executed afterward. You have defined a new event and called that event. In this example, you did it so that you can add code to the **FolderListBox** after it has been dragged to the **Window**, but you can also use the same technique to add events to your own custom classes.

ListBox Pictures

REALbasic also provides a simple way of adding images to **ListBoxes**. To access images from within the **ListBox**, you need to drag the images into REALbasic and drop them into the **Project Editor** under the **Project Tab**. One shortcut is to create a folder on your computer where all the image resources will be stored and keep it in the same folder as the project. I typically name the folder resources and place all the images I plan on using into it. I then drag the resources folder into the REALbasic IDE and drop it into the **Project Editor**. The folder and all its contents are automatically imported into the project.

Unlike classes that are imported into a project, images are always imported as external items, which means that if you move the resources folder on your computer, or delete it, REALbasic will prompt you to find it the next time you try to edit the application. That's another reason for keeping all the resources neatly stored in one location, alongside the project.

After the images are imported, you can refer to them by their name (without the extension). If you select one of the images, you can also edit a few properties. You can obviously change the name, but you can also choose whether the color white will be treated as a transparency. If you want more advanced control over how the image is displayed, you can also identify a mask for it, which works just like the masks do when creating icons for your application. Most of the time, setting the color white to transparent is effective, but you have to be careful if you use drop shadows and things like that. The reason is that the only color that is transparent is the color white, something with an RGB value of &cFFFFFF. There are a lot of colors that are almost white, but not actually white, such as &cFFFFFE, which will not be transparent. If you have a drop shadow that looks good against a white background, and then you set white to transparent, you'll find that there is a whitish outline around it when you view it on a **Window** that has a normal gray background. Creating a mask is probably the best solution for graphics with drop shadows.

In this example, I have imported three images: openfolder.gif, closedfolder.gif, and file.gif. (You can use different image formats, depending on the platform and whether QuickTime is installed. These are GIF images, but BMP, JPEG, and PNG should all work as well). I want to use these in the hierarchical **ListBox** to more clearly identify folders and files. I will use closedfolder.gif on folders that have not been expanded. I will change that image to openfolder.gif when that row is expanded, and I will use file.gif to represent files.

For this to work, I need to make the following modification to the `Open` event:

```
Sub ListBox1.open()
  Dim f as FolderItem

  me.Hierarchical = True

  f = Volume(0)

  me.AddFolder(f.DisplayName)
  me.CellTag(me.LastIndex, 0) = f
  me.RowPicture(me.LastIndex) = closedfolder
  Open
End Sub
```

As you can see, the process is a simple one. The relevant line is:

```
me.RowPicture(me.LastIndex) = closedfolder
```

The argument `Me.LastIndex` refers to the most recent row that has been added. I assign the closedfolder image to the last row that was added to the **ListBox** which, in this case, is the first row because I have just added the reference to the root folder. The process is similar for the `ExpandRow` event:

```
Sub ExpandRow(row as Integer)
  Dim f as FolderItem
  Dim x,y as Integer

  me.RowPicture(row) = openfolder

  f = me.CellTag(row, 0)
  y = f.Count

  For x = 1 To y
    If f.Item(x).Directory Then
      me.AddFolder(f.Item(x).DisplayName)
      me.RowPicture(me.LastIndex) = closedfolder
    Else
      me.AddRow(f.Item(x).DisplayName)
      me.RowPicture(me.LastIndex) = file
    End If
    me.CellTag(me.LastIndex, 0) = f.Item(x)
  Next

  ExpandRow(row)
End Sub
```

In this example, I first changed the image associated with the row that is being expanded. I changed the image to openfolder.gif:

```
me.RowPicture(row) = openfolder
```

Further along, I'll add folders or rows according to the type of **FolderItem** each is. If I am adding a folder, I assign the image closedfolder.gif, and if I am adding a file, I assign file.gif. In both of these instances, I determine the row whose picture I need to change by identifying the most recent row that was added. `RowPicture` must follow either `AddFolder` or `AddRow`.

Finally, I'll add some code to the `CollapseRow` event to change the image back to closedfolder.gif when the row is collapsed:

```
Sub CollapseRow(row as Integer)
  me.RowPicture(row) = closedfolder
End Sub
```

Now when the **ListBox** is displayed, the folders and files are displayed alongside them. It's a simple task that makes the **ListBox** look much more professional and easy to read. The visual cues offered by the images make it easier for the user to identify and distinguish folders from files. It would be even better if I assigned different images for different file types, or for different folders. The process is the same, with the exception that I would have to test to see what the underlying file type was and assign an image accordingly.

Inserting and Removing Rows

In addition to adding rows, you can insert and remove rows as well. This works exactly like you would expect it to using the following methods:

```
ListBox.RemoveRow(row as Integer)
ListBox.InsertRow(row as Integer, aString as String)
```

When a row is inserted, the row that exists at the position being inserted into is moved up. So the following inserts a row at the very beginning of a **ListBox** and moves all other rows up:

```
ListBox1.InsertRow(0, "My new row text")
```

Now consider the hierarchical **ListBox** shown in Figure 5.20. What happens when you insert a new item into row three?

```
ListBox1.InsertRow(3, "My new row text")
```

The row is inserted, but it is not inserted as a child of the second row, "Dog". Next, try to insert a folder:

```
ListBox1.InsertFolder(3, "My new folder text")
```

A folder is inserted, just like the row was inserted, but there is a problem. The items that were once children of "Dog" are now indented as if they are children of the new folder, but the new folder is not expanded. Therefore, you should expand the inserted folder immediately:

```
ListBox1.InsertFolder(3, "My new folder text")
ListBox1.Expand(ListBox1.LastIndex) = True
```

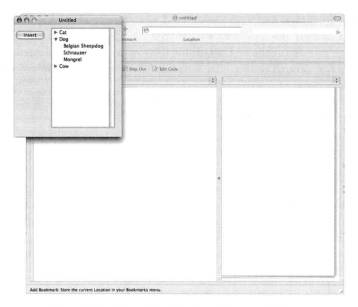

Figure 5.20 Hierarchical ListBox with expanded rows.

It really should do this automatically and it may be something that's corrected in the future, but for now you will need to expand it yourself. If you fail to expand it, the user will be able to click it and, if there are child elements, they will be displayed along with the child elements that were made children by inserting the folder. This does not produce an error, but it can be confusing from the user perspective because you have a scenario where a folder row is collapsed and still has child elements being shown. After the user collapses the original row, the entire list of child elements will collapse, and from that point on it will behave as expected.

ListBox Drag and Drop

REALbasic provides an implementation of drag and drop for **ListBoxes** that is powerful and easy to use, and it also gives developers the option of implementing drag and drop themselves for a more highly customized approach. I'll start with REALbasic's implementation first.

There are two properties related to drag and drop for **ListBoxes**:

```
ListBox.EnableDrag as Boolean
ListBox.EnableDragReorder as Boolean
```

Both can be set in the IDE. `EnableDrag` is used to allow dragging items out of a **ListBox** onto another control. `EnableDragReorder` is used to allow dragging and dropping within the **ListBox**, and it can be used for plain **ListBoxes** as well as hierarchical **ListBoxes**.

The `DragRow` event is triggered by clicking down on the mouse and moving the mouse while the mouse button remains down. The `DropObject` event is triggered when the mouse button is released.

If `EnableDrag` is `True`, but `EnableDragReorder` is not `True`, you must return `True` in the `DragRow` event:

```
ListBox.DragRow(dragItem as DragItem, row as Integer) as Boolean
```

Although the documentation says that this is not the case, my experience is that you have to have `EnableDragReorder` and `EnableDrag` set to `True` to drag data from the **ListBox** and drop it on another control. If `EnableDragReorder` is not `True`, but `EnableDrag` is, you will get visual feedback that a drag is occurring, but the `DropObject` event will not be triggered on the other control on which it is dropped.

The simplest scenario is to drag and reorder rows in a nonhierarchical **ListBox**. Set `EnableDragReorder` to `True` and the user will be able to drag rows within the **ListBox**. A thin insertion bar is used to indicate the location where the row will be inserted. A `DragReorderRows` event is fired when the row is dropped. In a nonhierarchical **ListBox**, it passes an integer that represents the row into which the dragged row will be inserted. However, you really do not need to bother yourself with this in basic situations because REALbasic will handle deleting the row from the original position and inserting it into the new position for you.

Dragging and dropping using a hierarchical **ListBox** is more complicated. REALbasic lets you perform the drag, but the developer is responsible for inserting rows in the proper location. When a user drags on the **ListBox** and drops the object at a particular location, the `DragReorderRows` event is triggered, but now it not only passes the row where the object was dropped, but also the row that is the parent row of this row. The values that are passed are adjusted under the assumption that rows will be deleted. Thinking about this conceptually is more than just a little confusing, so a few examples should clarify things. As in my previous hierarchical **ListBox** example, it is best to make heavy use of `CellTag` if you want to implement drag and drop in a hierarchical **ListBox**. The reason for this relates to the problem we had earlier when inserting folders into rows in certain situations.

Class mwNodeListBox Inherits from ListBox

Listing 5.42   **Sub mwNodeListBox.CollapseRow(row as Integer) Handles Event**

```
    me.RowPicture(row) = closedfolder
```

Listing 5.43 **Sub mwNodeListBox.ExpandRow(row as Integer) Handles Event**

```
Dim Node as mwNode
Dim tmpNode as mwNode
Dim x,y as Integer

me.RowPicture(row) = openfolder

Node = me.CellTag(row, 0)

y = Node.Sequence.getChildCount - 1

For x = 0 To y
tmpNode = Node.Sequence.getChild(x)
If Not tmpNode.isLeaf Then
me.AddFolder(tmpNode.Name)
me.RowPicture(me.LastIndex) = closedfolder
Else
me.AddRow(tmpNode.Name)
me.RowPicture(me.LastIndex) = file
End If
me.CellTag(me.LastIndex, 0) = tmpNode
Next

ExpandRow(row)

'App.expandRow(row)
```

Listing 5.44 **Function DragReorderRows(newPosition as Integer, parentRow as Integer) as Boolean Handles Event**

```
Dim d as new Date()
Dim x,y as Integer

Dim visibleChildren as Integer

Dim parentDepth as Integer
Dim siblingDepth as Integer
Dim count as Integer

Dim deletedRow as Integer
Dim insertPosition as Integer
Dim sourceNode as mwNode
Dim sourceParentNode as mwNode
Dim newParentNode as mwNode
```

Listing 5.44   **Continued**

```
        Dim tmpNode as mwNode

        // Insert position should be relative to parent object;
        // If parent object has children with open folders, Then those folders
➡need to be removed from the total count.


        // You are dragging the selected row,
        // which means that it will be deleted
        // from its current postion. Get the row number.
        deletedRow = getSelectedRow

        // Get the object associated with the row that will be deleted
        sourceNode = getSelectedNode

        // Get a reference to the parent object (folder)
        // from the selected object.
        sourceParentNode = getSelectedNodeParent

        //Remove row from ListBox and Remove Child from Parent
        Me.removeRow(deletedRow)
        If Not(sourceParentNode is Nil) Then
                sourceParentNode.Sequence.removeChild(sourceNode)
        End If

        // Next, the object that was deleted needs to be inserted
        // into the proper position according to where it was dropped
        // I can't simply insert it into the newPosition row, because
        // it is a child of a folder - so it needs to be inserted
        // into the parent object, Then displayed.
        // need to account for deletion of rows;
        // because parentRow assumes it's already been deleted.
        tmpNode = getNode(parentRow)
        parentDepth = tmpNode.Depth
        siblingDepth = parentDepth + 1
        count = 0

        // You need to determine where to insert
        // the source object in the new parent object.
        // You cannot rely on the newposition/ParentRow
        // Integers, because that depicts the total
        // distance between the two and siblings to
        // the child may be Folders and they may be open.
        y = parentRow + 1
        For x = newPosition - 1 DownTo y
```

Listing 5.44 **Continued**

```
                  If getNode(x).Depth = siblingDepth Then
                        count = count + 1
                  End If
      Next

      // This is the position with the sequence
      // of parent object's children
      insertPosition = count

      If tmpNode.isLeaf Then
                  // An Item canNot be a parent
                  // Put it back in its original location
            ➥sourceParentNode.Sequence.insertChild(sourceNode.getPosition,
sourceNode)
                  Return True
      Else
                  newParentNode = tmpNode
      End If




      If (newParentNode.isBranch) And (sourceParentNode.isBranch) Then
                  // Update the parent information and modification date
                  // of the object just moved
                  sourceNode.setParent(newParentNode)

                  // Insert the object into position within the parent
                  If insertPosition >; -1 And insertPosition <;
➥Me.ListCount Then

newParentNode.Sequence.insertChild(insertPosition, sourceNode)
                  Else
                        Break
                  End if

                  // Select the new parent row
                  Me.ListIndex = parentRow

                  // Collapse and expand it to display
                  // new children
                  collapseSelectedNode
                  expandSelectedNode

                  // Select the moved object, because it was selected
                  // when you moved it.
```

Listing 5.44   **Continued**

```
         selectNode(sourceNode)
Else
         Return True // prevents reorder from happening
End if

Exception Err
         Break
```

Listing 5.45   **Sub mwNodeListBox.Open() Handles Event**

```
test
me.Hierarchical = True
me.EnableDrag = True
me.EnableDragReorder = True
```

Listing 5.46   **Function mwNodeListBox.EditCopy() as Boolean Menu Handler**

```
Dim node as String
Dim cb as Clipboard

's = me.List(Me.ListIndex)
node = getSelectedNode().toString()
cb = new Clipboard

cb.AddRawData(node, "RSSReader")
'cb.SetText(s)
cb.Close

MsgBox "ListBox MenuHandler"
Return True
```

Listing 5.47   **Function mwNodeListBox.EditPaste() as Boolean MenuHandler**

```
Dim cb as New Clipboard
Dim s as String
Dim node as mwNode

If cb.RawDataAvailable("RSSReader") Then
         s = cb.RawData("RSSReader")
```

Listing 5.47 **Continued**

```
        node = new mwNode(s)
        Me.InsertRow(me.ListIndex, node.getName)
        Me.CellTag(me.LastIndex, 0) = node
    End If
```

Listing 5.48 **Sub mwNodeListBox.view(aNode as mwNode)**

```
    Dim Node as mwNode

    me.Hierarchical = True

    Node = aNode

    me.AddFolder(Node.Name)
    me.CellTag(me.LastIndex, 0) = Node
    me.RowPicture(me.LastIndex) = closedfolder
```

Listing 5.49 **Sub mwNodeListBox.collapseSelectedNode()**

```
    // Programmatically collapse a group
    If Me.ListIndex >; -1 Then
    Me.expanded(Me.ListIndex) = False
    End If
    Exception err
            #If DebugBuild
                    System.Log(System.LogLevelError,
➥str(err.ErrorNumber) + ": " + err.Message)
            #endif
```

Listing 5.50 **Sub mwNodeListBox.expandSelectedNode()**

```
    // Programmatically expand a group row
    If Me.ListIndex >; -1 Then
            Me.expanded(Me.listIndex) = True
    End If

    Exception err
            #If DebugBuild
                    System.Log(System.LogLevelError,
➥str(err.ErrorNumber) + ": " + err.Message)
            #endif
```

Listing 5.51   **Function mwNodeListBox.getNode(row as Integer) As mwNode**

```
// Get meme from the row number passed as an argument
Return Me.CellTag(row, 0)

Exception err
        #If DebugBuild
                System.Log(System.LogLevelError,
➥str(err.ErrorNumber) + ": " + err.Message)
        #endif
```

Listing 5.52   **Function mwNodeListBox.getSelectedNode() as mwNode**

```
Dim m as mwNode

// Return the currently selected Node
m = mwNode(CellTag(ListIndex, 0))
Return m


Exception Err
        break
        // Ignore OutofBoundsException
        If err Isa OutOfBoundsException Then
                Return Nil
        End If
```

Listing 5.53   **Function mwNodeListBox.getSelectedNodeParent() as mwNode**

```
Dim m as mwNode
Dim p as mwNode
Dim x, y as Integer

m = mwNode(CellTag(Me.ListIndex, 0))
Return m.getParent

Exception err
        #If DebugBuild
                System.Log(System.LogLevelError,
➥str(err.ErrorNumber) + ": " + err.Message)
        #endif
```

Listing 5.54 **Function mwNodeListBox.getSelectedNodeType() as Integer**

```
Dim m as mwNode

// Return the meme type (as an Integer)
If Me.ListIndex = -1 Then
        Return 0
Else

        m = Me.CellTag(Me.ListIndex, 0)

        Try
                Return m.getTypeID
        Catch
                Return 0
        End

End If

Exception err
        break
        #If DebugBuild
                System.Log(System.LogLevelError,
➡str(err.ErrorNumber) + ": " + err.Message)
        #endif
```

Listing 5.55 **Function mwNodeListBox.getSelectedRow() as Integer**

```
// Get the currently selected row number
Return Me.ListIndex

Exception err
        #If DebugBuild
                System.Log(System.LogLevelError,
➡str(err.ErrorNumber) + ": " + err.Message)
        #endif
```

Listing 5.56 **Sub mwNodeListBox.selectNode(aNode as mwNode)**

```
Dim x,y as Integer
Dim pos as Integer
Dim m as mwNode

// Select the row in the listbox
```

Listing 5.56   **Continued**

```
        // that contains a reference to
        // meme passed in the parameters.

        // get currently selected meme position
        pos = Me.ListIndex
        If pos = -1 Then
                pos = 0
        End If

        // get list length
        y = Me.ListCount - 1

        //search for visible children of currently selected meme only
        For x = pos To y
                m = getNode(x)
                // Test against Guids, because actual content may be
                // different and they may be different instances
        Next

        // If you can't find the meme, select Nothing

        Me.ListIndex = -1

        Exception err
                #If DebugBuild
                        System.Log(System.LogLevelError,
➥str(err.ErrorNumber) + ": " + err.Message)
                #endif
```

Listing 5.57   **mwNodeListBox.Sub test()**

```
        Dim aNode as mwNode

        aNode = new mwNode(mwNode.kBranch, "Root")
        aNode.Sequence.appendChild(new mwNode(mwNode.kBranch, "First Child"))
        aNode.Sequence.appendChild(new mwNode(mwNode.kBranch, "Second Child"))
        aNode.Sequence.appendChild(new mwNode(mwNode.kBranch, "Third Child"))
        aNode.Sequence.appendChild(new mwNode(mwNode.kLeaf, "Fourth Child"))
        aNode.Sequence.appendChild(new mwNode(mwNode.kLeaf, "Fifth Child"))
        aNode.Sequence.getChild(1).Sequence.AppendChild(new mwNode(mwNode.kLeaf,
➥"Sixth Child"))
        view(aNode)
```

HTMLViewer Control

The **HTMLViewer Control** has already been encountered in Chapter 2, and I will be using it again in the RSSReader application. It was simple enough to use in the first example, and it's going to be even simpler now because I will not write any code for it—I will just use the `LoadPage` method to view the HTML page because I will use the **HTTPSocket** control to actually download the page. I do this because in the next chapter, I will be processing the RSS XML file prior to viewing it in the **HTMLViewer**. Because XML isn't covered until the next chapter, I'll defer further discussion of that step until then.

HTMLViewer is an asynchronous control. This means that when you execute the `LoadPage` URL, your program doesn't have to wait until the page is returned before it can move on to other things. After the function is called, it cycles through the other events and does whatever it's supposed to be doing. When it begins to download the document, the `DocumentBegin` event is triggered, and when the page is returned and ready to be displayed, the `DocumentComplete` event is fired.

The `DocumentProgressChanged` event tracks the progress of the page download. You provide the URL and an integer that represents the percentage downloaded (as an Integer, so 50% is expressed "50"). An example of using this event with a **ProgressBar** is given in the forthcoming section named "**ProgressBar**."

HTTPSocket Control

HTTPSocket is a networking **Control**. I devote a chapter to networking, so you can expect to see more detail there. Still, the RSSReader needs to make an HTTP connection, so I will introduce it now. As I said earlier, I use the **HTTPSocket** control to grab an RSS XML file. In the sample code I'll provide now, the **HTTPSocket** control grabs HTML and displays it directly.

HTTPSocket works much like **HTMLView** because it is asynchronous as well.

You cannot drag an **HTTPSocket** directly to a window, because it is not listed in the list of **Controls**. Instead, drag the **TCPSocket** superclass to the **Window** and there, select it and manually change the `Super` value in the **Properties pane** to **HTTPSocket**.

Calling it is as easy as this:

```
Dim f as FolderItem
f = getFolderItem("MyRSS.tmp")
TCPSocket1.Get(me.Cell(row,column),f)
```

As you can see, I passed a **FolderItem** to the socket when calling the `Get` method. This is a **FolderItem** that I just created using the `getFolderItem` method and which will be created in the same folder as my application. I pass the **FolderItem** now because it will be that **FolderItem** that I access after the page download is completed. When the page has been returned, the `DownloadComplete` event is fired:

```
Sub DownloadComplete(url as String,HTTPStatus as Integer, headers as
➥InternetHeaders, file
```

```
➥as FolderItem)
  Dim tis as TextInputStream
  // Load the page in the HTML Viewer
  HTMLViewer1.LoadPage(file)
  // Load the source text in the EditField.
  tis = file.OpenAsTextFile
  EditField2.Text = tis.ReadAll
```

End Sub

The **FolderItem** you originally sent with the request is now returned to you, and it contains the data that was downloaded. Because **HTMLViewers** can load pages directly from **FolderItems**, I pass a reference to the Folder to the **HTMLViewer**, extract the text of the file, and display it in an **EditField**. This is the only way (that I can think of, at least) to get access to the text of a page that is loaded into **HTMLViewer**. The **HTMLViewer** does not offer access to the document that it is displaying, so if I want a copy, I have to retrieve it myself. Note that if the user follows a link on the HTML page displayed in the **HTMLViewer**, the new page will load, but you won't be able to get that text. Because this application is dealing with RSS files, that's okay. The only thing we need a reference to is the original RSS file so that we can cache it. If the user follows links from the page that is displayed, the program doesn't need to have a copy of the text of what is returned.

ProgressBar

The **ProgressBar** has two values to be concerned with. The first is `Maximum` and the second is `Value`. `Value` is the number that represents how much of the processing task has been accomplished. When `Value` is equal to `Maximum`, the task is completed. See an example in Figure 5.21.

Figure 5.21   ProgressBar.

Some classes provide data expressly for the purpose of making it easier to work with **ProgressBars**. The challenge is that you need to know how much work need to be done to have a **ProgressBar** that shows a smooth progression from start to finish. The **HTMLView** control and the **HTTPSocket** both have events that can be used to update a **ProgressBar**.

First, I'll show you how it works in an HTMLView:

```
Sub DocumentProgressChanged(URL as String, percentageComplete as Integer)
  ProgressBar1.Maximum = 100
  ProgressBar1.value = percentageComplete
End Sub
```

This event passes the URL of the document in question, as well as a number that represents the percentage complete. Note that the data type is an integer and the value that it passes is not a percentage, but a number between 0 and 100. I set the Maximum value on the **ProgressBar** to 100 and then update the Value property of the **ProgressBar** each time the event is called. In this example, I'm being quite inefficient because I am setting the Maximum value each time the event is triggered. This makes for a simpler example, but ideally you would set the Maximum value only once. The **HTTPSocket** takes a different approach:

```
Sub ReceiveProgress(bytesReceived as Integer, totalBytes as Integer,
➥newData as String)
  ProgressBar1.Maximum = totalBytes
  ProgressBar1.Value = bytesReceived
End Sub
```

Instead of passing a percentage, it passes the number of bytes received plus the total number of bytes that are expected. The ProgressBar1.Maximum value is limited to 64K, so you cannot place extremely large numbers as the Maximum value. The simple solution is to set the Maximum value to 100 and then calculate the percentage of bytes received; then multiply by 100 and use this for the Value. This is not a perfect solution because it is dependent on the HTTP server returning a valid number for totalBytes, which it sometimes doesn't, sending a value of "0" instead. If that's the case, set Maximum to "0" and you will get an indicator on **ProgressBar1** that indicates it is a process of indeterminate length. The actual appearance of the **ProgressBar1** at this point is determined by the platform.

Exception Handling

Runtime Exceptions

Runtime exceptions are how REALbasic informs you that a problem has occurred. It offers yet another wrinkle to object-oriented programming. It's a class and it can be subclassed. You should create your own exception classes because that will give you more control over how errors are handled. At the same time, exceptions are capable of behavior that is unique to exceptions. Exceptions are raised, which is not unlike triggering an event. Recall that when a user clicks a mouse on a control, the control can handle that event, or choose not to handle it, in which case the **Window** has the option. Exceptions are the same way, except that instead of filtering down through the layers of the user interface, exceptions percolate up the calling chain.

An all-too-common exception is **NilObjectException**, which occurs when you try to access an object that has been declared but not instantiated. REALbasic will throw a **NilObjectException** error every time you do this. There are a few ways within the method the error occurs in to catch the error and hopefully do something with it. If that method doesn't do anything with it, the previous method that called this method gets the opportunity to do it. This goes on all the way to our App object and the `App.UnhandledException` event. This is the last stop on your errors train to oblivion. You've got to catch it here or the whole application crashes and burns.

"Handling it" from REALbasic's perspective means returning `True`.

If you do not do this, the program will exit. It's pretty bad form to have an application crash uncontrollably, and this gives you an extremely easy way to add a little grace to the unexpected error. Ideally, within this event, save any files or data that you can so that as little work as possible is lost.

Try...Catch...End/Finally

I find this the most graceful and easy-to-manage way to catching exceptions. It allows you to isolate that part of your code that when executed may throw an error, and you can write your response to the error there. For an example, I'll use a common error situation where an object is supposed to passed as an argument, but the object passed is `Nil`:

```
Sub someMethod(anObject as SampleObject)
 Try
  anObject.aMethod
 Catch err as NilObjectException
  anObject = New SampleObject()
  anObject.aMethod
 End
End Sub
```

If you have code that you want to execute regardless of the outcome, you can use `Finally`, as follows:

```
Sub someMethod(anObject as SampleObject)
 Try
  anObject.aMethod
 Catch err as NilObjectException
  anObject = New SampleObject()
  anObject.aMethod
 Finally
```

```
  // the rest of the method
 End
End Sub
```

You can replicate this functionality simply by testing values:

```
Sub someMethod(anObject as SampleObject)
 If anObject <> Nil Then
  anObject.aMethod
 Else
  anObject = New SampleObject()
  anObject.aMethod
 End If
End Sub
```

The limitation to this approach is that you have to explicitly test for each kind of error. In this example, all that's being tested is whether an object is `Nil`, but there other error conditions can arise and the syntax of `Try…Catch` ends up being nicer and neater than lots of `If…Then` statements that test error conditions. One potential scenario is that there is one kind of error that you want to catch and handle within the method, but another kind of error that you want to have handled by the calling object. A good example of this situation is an error that is generated in the `Constructor` of an **Object**. If it's a recoverable error, you might be able to handle it there, but if it's an error that prohibits creating the object, the calling method needs to be notified.

Logging

Use `System.DebugLog` to send messages to the screen about the state of your application during debugging.

```
System.DebugLog(aMessage as String)
```

It works slightly differently on each platform. On Windows, you will need a debugger to view the output. A good (and free) debugger is called DebugView and is available here:

```
http://www.sysinternals.com/Utilities/DebugView.html
```

On Macintosh, you can use the Console application to view the message, and on Linux, the output is sent to SdtErr (you'll need to start the application from the terminal to see the messages). The use of `DebugLog` is best for sending messages that you want to view while the application is running. This is a much better alternative than using things like `MsgBox` to identify the current state of your program.

Bear in mind that consistently writing to the console will impact the performance of your application, so you should distinguish between "debugging" and regular logging. One simple way to do this is to use compiler directives. The following snippet means that the data will be logged only when you are in `DebugMode`, which is when you are running an application from the IDE. It will not log this information after the application has been compiled:

```
#if DebugMode then
    System.DebugLog("Some message")
#endif
```

The **System** object also offers the System.Log method:

```
System.Log(logLevel as Integer, message as String)
```

The use of a logLevel allows you to specify the nature of the debugging or logging message. The class constants are as follows:

```
System.LogLevelAlert as Integer
System.LogLevelCritical as Integer
System.LogLevelDebug as Integer
System.LogLevelEmergency as Integer
System.LogLevelError as Integer
System.LogLevelInformation as Integer
System.LogLevelNotice as Integer
System.LogLevelSuccess as Integer
System.LogLevelWarning as Integer
```

When using System.Log, the output is sent to EventWatcher on Windows. Macintosh users can use Console again, and Linux users can usually find the file in /var/logs. The reason for the levels is that applications like EventWatcher and Console are able to filter messages, so you may configure it to only show you the errors, if that's all you want to see, or you can look at everything.

You may want to use System.Log all the time that your application runs, unlike SystemDebug. There are a lot of reasons for doing this, but often it's used for applications that run unattended so that the logs can be reviewed at a later date. Note that even though there are different levels, the messages are all written to the log, even if you have them filtered in the viewer. In some cases it makes sense to make the level of logging detail configurable, and it's very easy to do. All you really need is a method that wraps the System.Log method and determines, based on preferences or something similar, whether to actually write out the message to the log. One scenario is to create a module called **myLog** with a method, Logger, that you send all the logging messages to:

```
myLog.Logger(System.LogLevelError, "An error!")
```

The module could also have some properties that define which messages get logged:

```
myLog.Debug as Boolean
myLog.Warnings as Boolean
myLog.Errors as Boolean
// and so on
```

The `myLog.Logger` method would operate like this:

```
Sub Logger(logLevel as Integer, message as String)
    If logLevel = System.logLevelDebug and myLog.Debug Then
        System.Log(logLevel, message)
    End If
    If logLevel = System.logLevelWarning and myLog.Warnings Then
        System.Log(logLevel, message)
    End If
    If logLevel = System.logLevelError and myLog.Errors Then
        System.Log(logLevel, message)
    End If
End Sub
```

Debugger

In one way or another, debugging generally means tracking the value or state of objects as your program executes. Logging is one way to get a glimpse, because you can watch the results as they are sent out to the debugger. The problem with logging is that you have to write a little code at every point that you want to log information. Ideally, you would log certain critical pieces of information, but you wouldn't want to log every last little detail about the state of things while running your application.

This is where REALbasic's debugger comes into play. REALbasic has an excellent debugger, in my opinion, and it works as well as any other debugger I've seen in other IDEs that are used with other languages. The debugger allows you to peek into your program's internal state and look at every instantiated object, every property of every module, and so on. Nothing is hidden from you. Not only that, it also allows you to step through each line of code in succession so you can see exactly how values change as your program executes, line by line, as shown in Figure 5.22.

This is great, because now you don't have to write a line to a log file for absolutely everything. The trick to making effective use of the debugger is to know when to pause your program and take a look at what's going on inside.

There are three ways you can make your program pause and view the information in the debugger. The first is with the Break statement. You can add it to particular parts of your code that, if executed, you know you will want to see. In addition to typing in Break in code, you can also set a **BreakPoint** in the IDE by clicking the column to the left of the editor. This is most effective for temporary breaks when you want to check something. If you think you are going to want to Break every time a certain condition arises in your program, then use Break. The other advantage of using Break rather than BreakPoints is that you can use your application's logic to determine whether you should break.

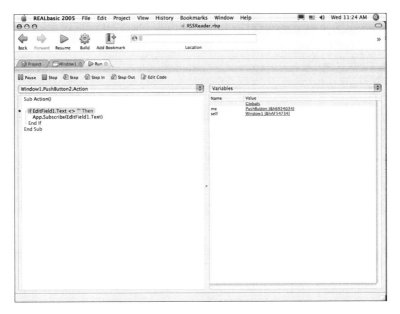

Figure 5.22   Debugging code.

Finally, you can tell REALbasic to break every time there is an exception. This is a good thing to do to help you track down exceptions and see what might be causing them to happen. There is a point at which this becomes a nuisance because you may have code that handles exceptions that you know might happen, but the IDE will break anyway. As the program gets larger, I tend to get more specific about when and how breaks are made.

After you break, you can do two things. First, you can examine the values of any object that is running your application as shown in Figure 5.23.

One of the options is **Runtime**, which lists all the objects in memory, as shown in Figure 5.24. You can also access the **Runtime** object while your application is running if you want your program to do so.

Second, you can step through your program.

Step Over

When you **Step Over** a method, the debugger stays within the current context.

Step Into

If your code is executing a method and you select **Step Into**, the debugger will take you into the code of the method being called and let you step through it line by line as well.

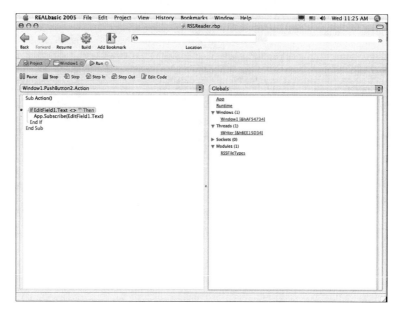

Figure 5.23   Examine the values of variables using the debugger.

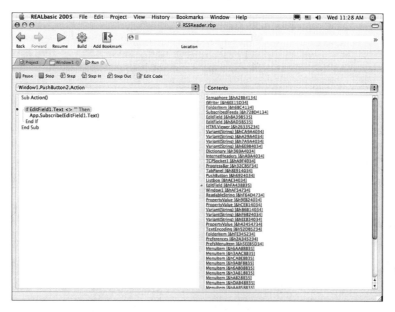

Figure 5.24   The Runtime object within an application.

Step Out

This lets you skip to the end of the current method (skip not the best word to use here —the intervening code is executed, but you are not made to step through each line).

Pause

With **Pause**, you can stop code from executing and jump into Debug Mode. If your program appears to be in a loop and not responding as expected, you can make the REALbasic application active and click the **Pause** button to stop it and see the values of current variables.

Stop

Stop stops the application being debugged from running. It's useful when the application locks up.

EditCode

When you click the **EditCode** button, you will jump to the tab that contains the code that is currently being executed and you can make changes to it. If you resume running the application, do not assume that that it will now be using the code you just fixed. You have to stop the program and then run it again for that to work. The primary benefit of this feature is to easily find the current code rather than being able to dynamically edit it.

User Interface Response

Timers

Timers appear in the list of built-in **Controls** when you're editing a **Window** in layout mode, but it is not a subclass of **RectControl** or **Control**. The fact is that all classes can be used as **Controls** in REALbasic as long as they are dragged to the **Window** while in **Layout Mode**. This means that they are implicitly instantiated when the **Window** is created and that any events that have been created in class can be edited in the same way that user interface **Controls** are—by double-clicking them.

The reason I'm emphasizing **Timers** not being **Controls** is because it means that you can instantiate **Timers** using the New operator. This, as it turns out, is really the biggest difference. This means you have a choice; you can instantiate a **Timer** like any other class, or you can drag it onto your **Window**. If you instantiate the **Timer** with New, it needs to instantiated as a property of an object that will persist, such as **Window1**, **App**, or a module because **Timers** do things periodically and to do so, they need to hang around for a while.

Timers have Enabled properties like **Controls** do, and they can be part of Control Arrays. You can even **Control** where it is positioned on the **Window**, but don't worry because a **Timer** is invisible when the program is running. All the hard work is done using two properties—an event and a method.

```
Timer.Mode as Integer
```

The Mode determines whether the **Timer** performs its task repeatedly, or just once. You can also turn it off. This is set using the following class constants:

```
Timer.ModeOff = 0
Timer.ModeSingle = 1
Timer.ModeMultiple = 2
```

If the **Timer** is set to fire periodically, you also need to tell it how often to do its thing:

```
Timer.Period as Integer
```

The Period is measured in milliseconds. By default, it is set to 1,000 milliseconds. Any value less than 1 millisecond is treated like a millisecond.

After you've decided how often a **Timer** is going to do something, you should probably decide what it's going to do as well, and that is done in the Action event:

```
Timer.Action
```

You can reset the **Timer** by called the Reset() method.

To use a **Timer**, drag it to the **Window**. Double-click it and add code to the Action event. **Timers** can be used for a lot of things, but they are commonly used in tasks relating to the user interface. If you recall the **Keyboard** object, a **Timer** can be used to periodically test to see if a certain key is being pressed.

Because of this relationship with the user interface, **Timers** will try to do their work according to the time established in Timer.Period, but they will wait if a lot of activity is going on. If I have a **Timer** set to do something every 5,000 milliseconds, but if the user is typing away in an **EditField**, the **Timer** won't trigger the Action event until there is a pause. This means you cannot count on a **Timer** to do its work like clockwork.

Timers can also be used when working with asynchronous objects. Classes used in networking are good examples because there is always a degree of latency when interacting with another computer through a network. Your application may make a request and then wait for an answer—the **Timer** can periodically check until the data is available, and then act accordingly.

Periodic Events with the Timer Control

App.DoEvents

Events get called in sequence—they do not run concurrently (that's what threads are for). When the code in an event is executed, that's the only code that's running until it is finished doing its thing. If the code happens to involve a big loop, or takes a lot of time for some other reason, everything else has to wait, even user interaction with your application. This applies to the Timer.Action event, too.

One way around this problem is to call App.DoEvents, which stops the processing of the current event so that other events can be triggered. You have to be careful when using it because it can cause problems—primarily if you have one event call App.DoEvents, which then allows another event to execute and that event calls App.DoEvents, and so on. You can easily lock up the application altogether.

Threads

Although not technically controls, **Threads** are often used as controls and they are listed in the **Controls List** in the **Window Layout Editor**. In this example, I do not use it as a **Control** and I think it serves as a good example of the limitations of using **Controls** in certain circumstances. In this case, I want to have three identical **Threads** running concurrently. If I were to drag a **Thread** object onto the **Window**, I would have to have three versions of the same code. If I made a change to **Thread1**, I'd need to make a change to **Thread2** and **Thread3**. The basic convenience of dragging a **Thread** to a **Window** is that you don't have to instantiate it yourself, but is it really that hard to instantiate it yourself?

So I have three concurrent **Threads** all doing the same thing. They all share the same resource, which is **Window1**. They all call the same methods: Window1.getRequestCount and Window1.makeRequest. Each time a request is made, the requestCount property is incremented by one.

The problem of controlling access to shared resources is one of the fundamental challenges associated with using **Threads**. This is something of an artificial example, but it does allow you to see fairly clearly just what kind of thing can go wrong.

If I were running this method in a single **Thread**, or as a regular method in some other part of the program, the numbers displayed would increment evenly as it looped. However, when you run three identical **Threads** that are each accessing the same resource—namely, the **Window** and the value of RequestCount, things get a little more confusing.

On **Window1**, there is a **ListBox**, a **ProgressBar,** and an **EditField** for each **Thread**. There is also a **CheckBox** that is used to indicate whether you should use a **Semaphore;** you'll see what that does momentarily. The **EditFields** are used to set the priority for each **Thread**. The priority defaults to five, and it is calculated relative to the priority of other **Threads**. When we start off with **Threads** having equal priorities of five, it means that **Thread1** gets 1/3 of the resources, **Thread2** gets 1/3 of the resources, and so on.

The steps that the **Thread** takes are these: it checks to see the value of the requestCount property of **Window1**. Then it enters a fairly lengthy loop, and it makes a request, which increments the requestCount property. It then populates the **ListBox** with the results. In the left column is the loop number (how many times this thread has looped). The second column shows the value of requestCount when the loop starts, and the third column shows the value of the requestCount after making a request. This means that the third column should contain a value that is equal to the second column, plus one. In fact, if just one **Thread** were running, that is exactly what we would see.

In the first iteration, I will run the application with the **Threads** having equal priorities and without using a **Semaphore**. When you look at the results, one of the first things you should notice is that **Thread1** goes through several loops before yielding to **Thread2**. That's important to understand—**Threads** only appear to be running concurrently. In fact, **Thread1** runs a little while, then **Thread2,** and so on. This is the very reason why you need to set the priority, so that you can manage this process. You'll also notice that it's a little hard to predict exactly when one **Thread** will yield to the next. The reason is that REALbasic uses cooperative threading, which means that instead of executing a specific number of statements in **Thread1** and then a specific number of statements in **Thread2**, the application yields from one **Thread** to the next at times that make sense, such as the end of a loop.

In this example, there is an inner loop that loops 500 times. Your **Thread** can yield during that loop just as easily as it can yield during the outerloop. The way that you can tell if this has happened is that you find that the value of requestCount, after you have looped and incremented, is more than one larger than the value of requestCount prior to the loop.

The following screenshot shown in Figure 5.25 shows how the **ListBoxes** appear at the end of the loop cycle. As you can see, in almost every row, the start value and the stop value have a difference of much more than one. Now this is a relatively harmless example, because nothing gets broken. Imagine, however, what the consequences would be if all three Threads were writing to the same file at the same time. What would happen to the data? Whatever happens, the likelihood is that it would be a Very Bad Thing.

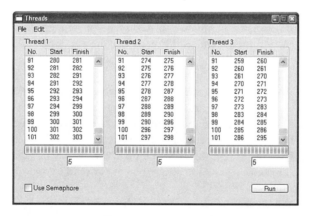

Figure 5.25 Thread1.

How do you keep this from happening, you ask? There are two approaches, both of which are minor variations of the other. There is a **Semaphore** class and a **CriticalSection** class, both of which can be used to limit access to a resource to one

Thread at a time. A **Semaphore** can be used to control access to multiple resources—that's one of the parameters that you can set. What is unique about a **CriticalSection** is that the same **Thread** can get a lock on it more than once (which means that it has to exit the same number of times to clear the **Thread**).

Now, check the Use Semaphores **CheckBox** and run the application again. You'll find upon inspection that with each loop, the value of requestCount when it is incremented after the loop is exactly one more than the value of requestCount before it entered the loop, which is exactly what you want. Now only one **Thread** can access the resource at the same time. Not that you would ever really want to do this, but you could also put the **Semaphore** or **CriticalSection** outside the main loop of the **Thread** and that would mean that each **Thread** would execute in sequence. **Thread1** would loop 100 times, then **Thread2** would loop 100 times, and so on. See Figure 5.26.

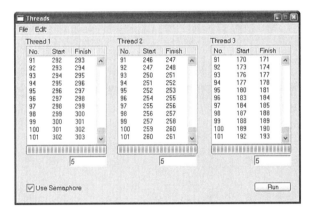

Figure 5.26   Program output when using a semaphore.

What you see is that **Threads** only make it appear that things are running concurrently. A certain number of statements will be executed in one **Thread**, and then a certain number of statements will be executed in the next, and so on. You get to decide how much time and resources are devoted to each of your threads.

Threads can be complicated because you can have two or more **Threads** acting on the same set of data in an unpredictable way, so there are some instances where you have to take special precautions and ensure that only one **Thread** is running at a time. For example, you don't want to have two **Threads** writing to the same file at the same time.

Here is the code used in the previous examples:

Class Window1 Inherits Window

Listing 5.58   **Sub Window1.Open() Handles Event**

```
se = new Semaphore
```

Listing 5.59   **Function Window1.makeRequest() as Integer**

```
RequestCount = RequestCount + 1
return RequestCount
```

Listing 5.60   **Function Window1.getRequestCount() as Integer**

```
return RequestCount
```

Listing 5.61   **Window1 Properties**

```
Window1.OuterLoop As Integer = 100
Window1.Thread1 As ThreadTester
Window1.Thread2 As ThreadTester
Window1.Thread3 As ThreadTester
Window1.UseSemaphore As Boolean
```

Listing 5.62   **Sub Window1PushButton1.Action() Handles Event**

```
ListBox1.DeleteAllRows
ListBox2.DeleteAllRows
ListBox3.DeleteAllRows
If CheckBox1.Value = True Then
   Window1.UseSemaphore = True
Else
   Window1.UseSemaphore = False
End If
Thread1 = new ThreadTester
Thread1.Priority = val(EditField1.text)
Thread1.Bar = ProgressBar1
Thread1.List = ListBox1
Thread2 = new ThreadTester
Thread2.Priority = val(EditField2.text)
Thread2.Bar = ProgressBar2
Thread2.List = ListBox2
Thread3 = new ThreadTester
Thread3.Priority = val(EditField3.text)
Thread3.Bar = ProgressBar3
Thread3.List = ListBox3
Thread1.Run
Thread2.Run
Thread3.Run
End Sub
```

Class ThreadTester Inherits Thread

Each **Thread** has a loop that loops 100 times. At the start of the loop, the **Thread** checks to see what the value of `Window1.RequestCount` is, and then it goes into a second loop whose only purpose is to take up some time. When that loop is finished, it checks the value of `RequestCount` again to see if it has changed. The number of the current iteration of the loop is displayed in the **ListBox**, as well as the value of `RequestCount` at the start of the loop iteration and the end of the loop iteration, after `makeRequest` as been called, which increments `RequestCount` by one.

Listing 5.63 **Sub Run() Handles Event**

```
Dim s as String
Dim tmp as String
Dim lastpos as Integer
lastpos = 0
For x as Integer = 0 To Window1.OuterLoop
  If Window1.UseSemaphore = True Then
  Window1.se.Signal
End If
Bar.Value = x
// Find out how many requests have been made.
tmp = str(Window1.requestCount)
For z as Integer = 0 to Window1.InnerLoop
  // take up time
  s = s + "a"
Next
List.addrow(str(x+1))
List.cell(List.LastIndex, 1) = tmp

//Make the next request
lastpos = Window1.makeRequest
List.cell(List.LastIndex, 2) = Str(lastpos)
If Window1.UseSemaphore = True Then
  Window1.se.Release
End If
Next
End Sub
End Class
```

Using Threads for Background Tasks

The RSSReader application will allow the user to subscribe to any number of RSS channels. Each of these channels needs to be updated periodically, and the time between updates is specified in the RSS file itself. You could wait to check to see if you need to download a new version of a document when the user requests it, but you can provide a better experience if your application looks for those files that are due for updating, then updates them in the background without interfering with the user's other activity. This means that when the user selects a channel to read, it will be available without any waiting.

Class tWriter Inherits Thread

Listing 5.64   **Sub tWriter.Run() Handles Event**

```
Dim w as iWriteable

While True

  If Ubound(Queue) > -1 Then
    Me.Lock.Signal
    w = Queue(0)
    Queue.Remove(0)
    w.Write
    w = Nil
    Me.Lock.Release
  End If

Wend
End Sub
```

Listing 5.65   **Sub tWriter.Write(toWrite as iWriteable)**

```
Queue.Append(toWrite)
End Sub
```

Listing 5.66   **tWriter Properties**

```
tWriter.Lock as Semaphore
tWriter.Queue(-1) as iWriteable
```

Menus and Menu Handlers

I have already touched briefly on menus in the previous chapter. All desktop applications have at least one **MenuBar**, and by default, **MenuBar1** is available in any new project. It comes with some **MenuItem**s already in place—Exit (or Quit on Macintosh) in the File menu, and Undo, Cut, Copy, Paste, and Delete (or Clear on Macintosh). There is default behavior for Exit, Cut, Copy, and Paste, but you will often want to override it. Likewise, you will need to do your own coding for any additional **MenuItem**s you establish.

There is a three-step process you should go through when creating a **MenuBar**. The first is to create constants that will be used for the menu text that's displayed to the user. Even though you technically do not have to use constants for menu text, there are plenty of reasons for doing so. The first is that there are some **MenuItem**s that have a common function across the platforms, but that use different names. A **MenuItem** for preference is one of them, and that will be one of the examples. Beyond that, it also makes it easier in the future to localize your application and, for example, come out with a Spanish language version. Depending on your project, you might think that's a rather fanciful idea, and perhaps it is, but my attitude is that because you have to use constants for a few **MenuItem**s if you want your application to behave properly on all three platforms, you should just go ahead and use them on all **MenuItem**s. Who knows, maybe the app you are creating will be successful beyond your wildest expectations; a lot of people in the world do not speak English, and it really doesn't make sense to arbitrarily lock them out as potential customers.

Adding Menu Constants

I am going to add the following **MenuItem**s: Preferences, Delete, and Subscribe. I will create constants for all of them, like this:

```
Constant Name: kPreferences as String
Default Value: &Options…
```

Windows uses the term Options to describe what Macintosh computers call Preferences. I establish the default value as `&Options…`, and this will be the text that is displayed by default. The `&` means that O (the letter directly following it) can be used as a shortcut.

To use different text for Macintosh computers, I have to click the + button in the **ListBox** area below the primary editing area for constants. In the platform column, I select MacOS. In the Language column, I select Default and in the Value column I enter **Preferences…**.

I need to do something similar with Clear, which is called Delete on Windows and Linux computers. I will set this one up like this:

```
Constant Name: kClear
Default Value: Clear
```

Because "Clear" is the term that applies to Macintosh computers, I need to add two more items to let REALbasic know what to do on Windows and Linux computers. I follow the same steps that I did before, except that instead of MacOS, I select Windows, and set the value to `&Delete`, followed by adding another row and selecting Linux, with a value of `&Delete` as well.

Finally, I have a simple constant to create, which is the one I will use for the Subscribe… **MenuItem**. I create a constant called `kSubscribe`, with a default value of `Subscribe…`, and we are finished.

In case you are wondering, the ellipsis that follows a name on a **MenuItem** indicates that it will cause a **Window** to be created that requires some kind of user interaction. **MenuItem**s without ellipses simply execute a command.

Adding the MenuItems

Now that the constants are in place, it is time to return to **MenuBar1** and create the **MenuItems**. Double-click **MenuBar1** to get the **MenuBar** editing tab. You will be able to get a preview of what the **MenuBar** will look like in all the platforms, and it doesn't matter at this point which "look" you are using. The first thing to do is go to the File menu and select it. Then, in the **Editor Toolbar**, click the **Add Menu Item** button. A new space called "untitled" will appear at the bottom of the File menu. While it is selected, go first to the **Text** area in the **Property ListBox** to the right and type in the name #App.kSubscribe. The # sign indicates that what follows is a constant rather than literal text. The App.kSubscribe refers to the constant we just created.

REALbasic will automatically create a name for the **MenuItem** for you, which is the concatenation of the **Menu** name and the **MenuItem** name. In this case, the **MenuItem** will be automatically named FilekSubscribe.

While still in the **Properties pane**, skip down to the **Behaviors** area. The first item listed is SubMenu. If checked, a **PopupArrow** will appear in the visual display of the menu, and you will be able to add submenus to it. Next inline is AutoEnable, which should be checked True for the Subscribe **MenuItem**. Much like **controls, menuitems** can be enabled or not enabled. When not enabled, their text is grayed out and they cannot be selected. Setting AutoEnable to True means that the **MenuItem** will be enabled automatically. In most cases, that means that the **MenuItem** will be enabled without you having to specify it in code. In the case of Copy and Paste, it means that REALbasic handles determining whether it is enabled, unless you override it.

Windows and **Controls** all have an EnableMenuItems event. This is triggered at certain times and it gives the developer the opportunity to decide which **MenuItems** are enabled. Because the Subscribe **MenuItem** should always be available, I have AutoEnable set to True and I will not disable the **MenuItem** in code.

The next two sections in the **Properties pane** refer to shortcut keys. The first group, called **ShortCuts**, uses the default shortcut keys for each platform, which means the Command key on Macintosh and the **Control** key on Windows and Linux. For Subscribe, I assign the character "S" to the Key value and have the **Key Modifier CheckBox** checked to True. This means that on **Windows**, the user can hold down the **Control** key and the "S" key simultaneously, and that will serve as the keyboard equivalent of selecting that **MenuItem**. Likewise, on a Macintosh, it means that Command+S is the keyboard equivalent. I use "S" in this example, even though "S" is normally used as the keyboard equivalent for saving a document. Because subscribe is similar to saving a document and because I do not specifically need a Save **MenuItem** for this application, the use of "S" seems appropriate.

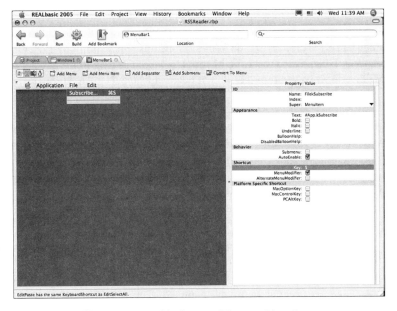

Figure 5.27   Add a key modifier to a MenuItem.

If you have a lot of **MenuItems,** using the default shortcut keys may not give you enough options, especially considering that there are standard shortcuts on each platform that you should avoid duplicating. The **Alternate Menu Modifier Check Box** adds a Shift character to the shortcut. If I were to check it for Subscribe, that would then mean that the user would have to click the Control, Shift, and "S" keys simultaneously to activate the command represented by this **MenuItem**.

Beyond the Shift key, each platform offers additional keys that are sometimes used in this fashion, and the **Platform Specific Shortcut** is used to give you more control over which keys are used. You can choose to require the Macintosh Option key, or the Macintosh **Control** Key, as well as the Alt key on Windows and Linux. If, for example, you wanted Subscribe to require the Option key on Macintosh computers in addition to Command, you would click MacOptionKey and check the **CheckBox** to `True`. Then, if you select the Macintosh version of the **MenuBar**, you will see that the keyboard equivalent of Option+Command+S is listed next to the word Subscribe in the **MenuItem**.

The next item to add will be the **Clear/Delete MenuItem**. This will be added just like Subscribe, except that it will be added to the **Edit Menu** rather than the **File Menu**. In this instance, I do not set `AutoEnable` to `True` because the only time this option should be available to the user is when the user has something selected in the application that is deletable. Other parts of my application will have to update this value when an `EnableMenuItem`s event is triggered.

Finally, I will add Preferences, and this will require some special treatment. As already mentioned, Preferences are called Options on Windows and Linux, but I have taken care of that issue by using constants. In addition to the different names, Preferences on a Macintosh also appear in a special location, whereas Options appear in different locations (often somewhat unpredictably so) on Windows. In this application, the Preferences **MenuItem** will be added to the **Edit Menu**, but before adding it, I will click the **Add Separator** button to have a thin line drawn between the Select All **MenuItem** and the Preferences item I will be adding. You can also add a Separator by typing a hyphen (-) into the Text property of any **MenuItem**. After the Separator is added, I add the Preferences **MenuItem** by selecting the Edit Menu and clicking the **Add Menu Item** button. After you have done this, make sure the Preferences **MenuItem** you created is selected, and then move your attention to the **Properties pane**. In the Super row, click the **PopupArrow**, and a menu will appear giving you alternatives for the Super class to use for this **MenuItem**. Select **PrefsMenuItem** as the Super and then check the OS X view of the **MenuBar**. You will see that instead of appearing in the Edit Menu, it appears as the first item in the Application Menu, right above the Quit **MenuItem**.

Adding Menu Handlers

You have now added three new **MenuItems** to your application, but they do not do anything yet. The next step will be to add menu handlers for them. Menu handlers can be added to the **App** object and to any **Window** or **Control** that can accept the focus. There can be many menu handlers for a single **MenuItem,** and the one selected is determined by the context of which **Control** or **Window** has focus. The Copy **MenuItem** is a good example of why you would want to do this. It works out of the box with **EditFields,** so you do not need to do any special handling, but what happens if you want to let your user copy items in a **ListBox**? This calls for special handling and for a Copy menu handler to be created for our application's **ListBox**.

　　Go to the **mwNodeListBox** and then go to the code editing tab. One of the options on the **Editor Toolbar** is **Add Menu Handler**. Click the **Add Menu Handler** button and you will enter the menu handler editing mode. There is a **ComboBox** labeled **MenuItem** name where you can select which **MenuItem** you want to write this menu handler for. Select EditCopy from the list and you will see that the signature for this menu handler is the following:

```
MenuHandler EditCopy() As Boolean
```

　　The return value lets you tell REALbasic whether you are handling the **MenuItem** or whether it should allow the next item in line to handle it. For example, I may decide to also implement an EditCopy menu handler for the **Window** that contains this **ListBox**. If I return True from this menu handler, the **Window** version of the menu handler will not be called. If I return False (or not anything at all), the **Window** menu handler will be called after this menu handler is finished executing.

　　Add the following code to the EditCopy menu handler:

```
MenuHandler EditCopy() as Boolean
Dim s as String
Dim cb as Clipboard
```

```
s = me.List(Me.ListIndex)
cb = new Clipboard
cb.SetText(s)
cb.Close
End MenuHandler
```

The **Clipboard** class gives you access to the application's clipboard (called Scrap on a Macintosh). You can instantiate the **Clipboard** class and get any text that is already on the application's Clipboard, or you can add your own data to it. After you have set the data, the **Clipboard** should be Closed. In this example, I get the text from the selected row of the **ListBox** and add that to the **Clipboard** object. It can now be pasted into any application, not just the REALbasic application.

```
MenuHandler EditPaste() as Boolean
  Dim cb as New Clipboard

  If cb.TextAvailable Then
    If Me.ListIndex > -1 Then
      InsertRow(Me.ListIndex, cb.text)
    End If
  End If
  cb.Close
End MenuHandler
```

In addition to text, pictures can be added to the **Clipboard** object, and raw data can be added as well. Raw data is used to copy and process application-specific information from within your application. When using raw data, you pass a string that represents the type of the application data. This is derived from the AddMacData method, which accepts a four-character creator code. Windows and Linux do not use creator codes, but you can create any string identified that your application will recognize so that you can copy and paste proprietary data formats within your application.

The **mwNode** method toString returns an XML representation (as a string) of the node object, and this will be used as the raw data for the revised EditCopy menu handler:

```
MenuHandler EditCopy() as Boolean
  Dim node as String
  Dim cb as Clipboard

  node = getSelectedNode().toString()
  cb = new Clipboard
  cb.AddRawData(node, "RSSReader")
  cb.Close
  Return True
End MenuHandler
```

When the `EditPaste` menu handler is called, it tests to see if there is any "RSSReader" data available; if there is, it uses that data to instantiate a new object and insert that object into the **ListBox:**

```
MenuHandler EditPaste() as Boolean
  Dim cb as New Clipboard
  Dim s as String
  Dim node as mwNode

  If cb.RawDataAvailable("RSSReader") Then
    s = cb.RawData("RSSReader")
    node = new mwNode(s)
    Me.InsertRow(me.ListIndex, node.getName)
    Me.CellTag(me.LastIndex, 0) = node
  End If
  cb.Close
End MenuHandler
```

One additional kind of menu that helps to make an application more usable is a contextual menu. These are menus that appear in context when a user clicks the right mouse button (or holds down the **Control** key while clicking the mouse button on Macs). There are two ways of adding **Contextual MenuItems** to an application. The old way is to use the **ContextualMenu Control,** but REALbasic 2005 provides a new and much improved way of handling **ContextualMenus** by using the following two events in **Windows** and **Controls:**

```
Function ConstructContextualMenu(base as MenuItem, x as Integer,
➥y as Integer) as Boolean
Function ContextualMenuAction(HitItem as MenuItem)as Boolean
```

The `ConstructContextualMenu` event fired every time the user requests a contextual menu and you, as the developer do not have to specifically test to see what keys are being pressed or anything like that. The base **MenuItem** is the root **MenuItem** to which you append **MenuItems** that will be displayed to the user.

```
Function ConstructContextualMenu(base as MenuItem, x as Integer, y as Integer)
Dim mitem as menuitem

  mitem = new MenuItem
  mitem.Text = "Hi"

  base.Append(mitem)
  return true
End Function
```

When the user makes a selection, the `ContextualMenuAction` event is fired. The **MenuItem** that was selected is passed as the **HitItem**.

```
Function ContextualMenuAction(HitItem as MenuItem) as Boolean
if hitItem.text = "Hi" then
```

```
  beep
end if
End Function
```

Windows and MenuBars

You can have more than one **MenuBar** object in your application, and you can associate them with individual **Windows** or change them as you see fit. Recall that the **MenuBar** stays in the same position on the Macintosh rather than being associated with the application **Window** itself, but you get the same effect. You can use the following **Window** properties to manage this process

```
Window.MenuBarVisible as Boolean
Window.MenuBar as MenuBar
```

CustomTray

In the previous chapter I talked about the Windows tray, and I promised an example after events were covered. This Tray subclass is instantiated in the Open event of the RSS class:

```
Dim myTrayItem as CustomTray
myTrayItem = New CustomTray
Me.AddTrayItem( myTrayItem )
```

To work with the tray, you need to subclass **TrayItem.** The Action event controls what happens when the user clicks the icon as it appears on the tray. This class doesn't really perform anything useful, and it is based on the example used in REALbasic's documentation, but it should be enough to show you how it works. The Action event gets passed an Integer that indicates what kind of action has taken place—whether the left or right mouse button was clicked, or if it was double-clicked. In this example, the main application **Window** will get maximized if the **TrayItem** is clicked with the left mouse button. If the right mouse button is clicked, a **MenuItem** pops up and provides an About option and an Exit option. Finally, if the **TrayItem** is double-clicked, the application becomes invisible if it is currently visible. If it is currently invisible, it will become visible.

```
Sub CustomTray.Action(cause as Integer)Handles Event

        If cause = TrayItem.LeftMouseButton Then
                Window1.Maximize
        ElseIf cause = TrayItem.RightMouseButton Then
                Dim mnu as New MenuItem
                mnu.Append( new MenuItem( "&About" ) )
                mnu.Append( new MenuItem( MenuItem.TextSeparator ) )
                mnu.Append( new MenuItem( "E&xit" ) )
                Dim results as MenuItem
```

```
                 results = mnu.PopUp
                 If results <> Nil Then
                         Select Case results.Text
                         Case "E&xit"
                                 Quit
                         Case "&About"
                                 MsgBox "RSSReader from
➥REALbasic Cross-platform Application Development"
                         End Select
                 End If
         Elseif cause = TrayItem.DoubleClick Then
                 If Window1.Visible Then
                         Window1.Visible = False
                 Else
                         Window1.Visible = True
                 End if
         End If
End Sub
```

Summary

This concludes the discussion of how to build a desktop application in REALbasic. With
this knowledge in hand, it's time to turn to other topics. Strings and text have been
referred to throughout the book thus far, but there is still a lot to talk about. Because I
am developing an application that reads XML files, a discussion of XML and
REALbasic's XML classes is a requirement as well as other advanced features, such as
styled text and Regular Expressions.

6

XML and Advanced Text Processing

ONE CENTRAL PART OF THE RSSREADER application is the XML files that are used to store and display the information. In the previous chapter, the examples were based on the assumption that I would be transferring HTML files rather than XML files. To complete the application, I will need to be able to get the RSS files in multiple formats and convert them into HTML for display in the **HTMLViewer** control. Because I am viewing the raw XML data as well, I would also like to add some source code highlighting that will make the original XML documents easier to read. Altogether, this refinement of the application will require a closer look at text processing, with a much closer look at the XML classes, encoding, styled text, and regular expressions.

Encoding

A computer stores text as a series of numbers. For each letter, punctuation mark, or space there is a corresponding number, called a code point, which represents that letter. An *encoding* is simply a system that is used to identify characters using numbers. Binary data can be encoded as well, and later on in this chapter you will learn how to encode binary data using REALbasic's **Base64** classes.

Encoding has been encountered previously in this book, but only superficially; however, it is a crucial part of developing programs, especially ones that run on multiple platforms, because you will no doubt be confronted with the full range of encoding possibilities. As it turns out, understanding character encoding is an important part of being able to make effective use of XML. In this section, I will discuss REALbasic's encoding classes and related tools and share a sample utility application I have used to explore encoding on REALbasic.

There are a lot of different encodings and if you do an appreciable amount of working with text, you will inevitably run into encoding headaches. One of the earliest

encodings is ASCII (American Standard Code for Information Interchange, first stan-
dardized in 1963), which was limited to a 7-bit character set, or 127 characters. The first
32 characters, 0–31, are control characters, and 32 to 126 are the characters that make up
the basic American-English alphabet.

Following is a list of all the printable ASCII characters, in numeric order:

```
!"#$%&'()*+,-./0123456789:;<=>? @
ABCDEFGHIJKLMNOPQRSTUVWXYZ[\]^_ `
abcdefghijklmnopqrstuvwxyz{|}~
```

ASCII is fine if you speak English and need only 127 different characters, but not
everyone in the world is English and not everyone in the world speaks English, so it
quickly became evident that either additional encodings were required, or a new
approach to encoding altogether would be needed. At first, a range of encodings
emerged. Both Macintosh and Windows computers used 1-byte character encodings,
which provided space for 256 characters. Although both systems shared a common
ASCII heritage, the code points above 127 represented different characters on each platform. Macintosh used MacRoman (plus many variants for different languages) and
Windows used Latin-1 (ISO 8859-1).

Since that time, a new standard has emerged (or perhaps more accurately, is emerging)
that rationalizes character encoding and that allocates a large enough pool of code points
to represent all languages. The standard is called Unicode, and it is managed by the
Unicode Consortium. The first Unicode standard was first published in 1991.

Unicode uses up to four bytes to represent a character, and there is room in the standard for 1,114,112 code points. These code points are organized into 17 planes, each one
representing 65536 code points (2^{16}). The first plane, plane "0", is called the Basic
Multilingual Plane (BMP); this is the most commonly used plane, where code points
have been assigned to a large portion of modern languages.

There is a standard approach to representing Unicode code points, which consists of
"U+", followed by a hexadecimal digit. The range of code points in the BMP is
U+0000 to U+FFFF (Unicode assigns code points beyond the BMP up to U+10FFFF,
and the original specification allowed for ranges up to U+7FFFFFFF). The first 256 code
points in the BMP are identical to Latin-1, which also means that the first 127 code
points are identical to ASCII.

The Unicode standard uses several formats to encode code points. They come in two
camps—UCS, the Universal Character Set, and UTF, the Unicode Transformation
Format.

UCS—Universal Character Set (UCS-2, UCS-4)

The Universal Character Set uses either 2 bytes or 4 bytes to represent characters. In
UCS-2, every character is represented by a 2-byte code point (which, of necessity, limits
the number of characters available and does not represent the complete range of
Unicode). UCS-4, on the other hand, uses 4 bytes. There are two problems with UCS
("problems" is probably not the right word—but these are the reasons that UCS is not

used in practice as much as UTF). First off, early non–Unicode character sets (ASCII and LATIN-1) used 8 bytes. Using UCS means that legacy documents would have to be converted to either 2-byte or 4-byte formats to be viewed. Second, using either 2 bytes or 4 bytes for all characters means that your text will take up a lot more space than it would if you were able to use 1 byte for some characters, 2 bytes for others, and so on, which is exactly what UTF does.

UTF—Unicode Transformation Format (UTF-8, UTF-16, UTF-32)

REALbasic supports UTF-8 and UTF-16 as native formats. There are also two additional UTF formats, UTF-7 and UTF-32. In UTF, characters are represented by code points of varying sizes, and this is what differentiates UTF from UCS. UTF-8, for example, identifies some characters with 1 byte, others with 2, all the way up to 4 bytes. UTF-16 starts with 2-byte codepoints, but represents some characters with 4 bytes and UTF-32 starts with 4-byte codepoints.

The following table shows the range of code points and the number of bytes used by UTF-16 and UTF-8 to represent it. The first three rows represent the BMP.

Table 6.1   **UTF-8: Native Strings**

Code Range (hex)	UTF-16 (Binary)	UTF-8 (Binary)	Comments
000000–00007F	00000000 0---------	0--------	The UTF-8 values in this range are the same as ASCII. The first byte in UTF-8 is always 0.
000080–0007FF	00000----- ----------	110------ 10------	UTF-8 uses 2 bytes to represent this range. The first byte begins with 110 and the second byte begins with 10. This range includes the Latin characters.
000800–00FFFF	---------- ----------	1110----- 10----- 10--------	UTF-8 uses 3 bytes to represent this range, which is the upper limit to the BMP. The first byte begins with 1110, and the second and third begin with 10.
010000–10FFFF	110110--- ---------- 110111--- ----------	11110---- 10-------- 10-------- 10--------	For code points beyond the BMP, both encodings use 4 bytes. However, note the difference in the prefixed values. UTF-16 uses a "surrogate pair" to represent values over U+FFFF. &h10000 is subtracted from the UTF-16 prefix, so that it can be distinguished from UTF-8.

Byte Order Mark

The byte order mark (BOM) is a character that is placed at the beginning of a file that can used to identify the byte order of the document; byte order is simply a reference to endianness, which is one of those topics that keeps popping up in any kind of cross-platform development. The character in question is supposed to be a zero-width non-breaking space. UCS-2 and UTF-16 are the two Unicode formats that use the BOM for the determination of endianness. When used with UTF-8 and others, it's used to identify the encoding of the file itself. In other words, based on the value of the first four bytes, you can determine the encoding of the string—that is, if the BOM has been has been set. REALbasic usually makes this determination for you, but in case you want to check directly, here are the values and what they mean:

00 00 FE FF	UCS-4, big-endian machine (1234 order)
FF FE 00 00	UCS-4, little-endian machine (4321 order)
00 00 FF FE	UCS-4, unusual octet order (2143)
FE FF 00 00	UCS-4, unusual octet order (3412)
FE FF -- --	UTF-16, big-endian
FF FE -- --	UTF-16, little-endian
EF BB BF	UTF-8

Converting Encodings

Now that the basics of Unicode have been reviewed, it's time to turn to REALbasic's encoding classes and learn how to use the tools provided to effectively manage character encoding in your application.

TextEncoding Class

The **TextEncoding** class represents a particular encoding—whether Unicode or some native encoding like MacRoman.

```
TextEncoding.Base as Integer
TextEncoding.Code as Integer
TextEncoding.Variant as Integer
TextEncoding.Format as Integer
TextEncoding.InternetName as String
```

The **TextEncoding** class offers an alternative to the global Chr function discussed earlier in the book. When using the global function, it is assumed that you are using UTF-8, but that may not be what you want. If, for whatever reason, you want to get a character using a codepoint for another encoding, you can use this method on a **TextEncoding** instance that represents the encoding you want to use:

```
TextEncoding.Chr(codepoint as Integer) as String
```

You can test to see if the encoding of one string is equal to that of another this way:

```
TextEncoding.Equals(otherEncoding as TextEncoding) as Boolean
```

Encodings Object

The **Encodings** object is always available, and it is used to get a reference to a particular **TextEncoding** object. You can get a reference to the encoding using the encoding's name:

```
Encodings.EncodingName as TextEncoding
```

You can also get a reference to a particular encoding using the code for that encoding. The code is an integer that represents a particular encoding. This method lets you get a reference to a **TextEncoding** object by passing the code as an argument.

```
Encodings.GetFromCode(aCode as Integer) as TextEncoding
```

You can get references to characters through encoding, by calling the following method:

```
Encodings.UTF-8.Chr(aCodePoint as Integer)
```

To use the **Encodings** object, you need to know the names of the available encodings and, optionally, their codes. The following table provides a list of all the encodings recognized by REALbasic's Encodings object and the values associated with each encoding.

Table 6.2   **Encodings Available from the Encoding Object**

Encodings Object	Internet Name	Base	Variant	Format	Code
Encodings.SystemDefault (Mac)	macintosh	0	2	0	131072
encodings.SystemDefault (Windows)	windows–1252	1280	0	0	1280
Encodings.UTF8	UTF–8	256	0	2	134217984
Encodings.UTF16	UTF–16	256	0	0	256
Encodings.UCS4	UTF–32	256	0	3	201326848
Encodings.ASCII	US–ASCII	1536	0	0	1536
Encodings.WindowsLatin1	windows–1252	1280	0	0	1280
Encodings.WindowsLatin2	windows–1250	1281	0	0	1281
Encodings.WindowsLatin5	windows–1254	1284	0	0	1284
Encodings.WindowsKoreanJohab	Johab	1296	0	0	1296
Encodings.WindowsHebrew	windows–1255	1285	0	0	1285
Encodings.WindowsGreek	windows–1253	1283	0	0	1283
Encodings.WindowsCyrillic	windows–1251	1282	0	0	1282
Encodings.WindowsBalticRim	windows–1257	1287	0	0	1287
Encodings.WindowsArabic	windows–1256	1286	0	0	1286

Table 6.2 **Continued**

Encodings Object	Internet Name	Base	Variant	Format	Code
Encodings.WindowsANSI	windows-1252	1280	0	0	1280
Encodings.WindowsVietnamese	windows-1258	1288	0	0	1288
Encodings.MacRoman	macintosh	0	0	0	0
Encodings.MacVietnamese	X-MAC-VIETNAMESE	30	0	0	30
Encodings.MacTurkish	X-MAC-TURKISH	35	0	0	35
Encodings.MacTibetan	X-MAC-TIBETAN	26	0	0	26
Encodings.MacThai	TIS-620	21	0	0	21
Encodings.MacTelugu	X-MAC-TELUGU	15	0	0	15
Encodings.MacTamil	X-MAC-TAMIL	14	0	0	14
Encodings.MacSymbol	Adobe-Symbol-Encoding	33	0	0	33
Encodings.MacSinhalese	X-MAC-SINHALESE	18	0	0	18
Encodings.MacRomanLatin1	ISO-8859-1	2564	0	0	2564
Encodings.MacRomanian	X-MAC-ROMANIAN	38	0	0	38
Encodings.MacOriya	X-MAC-ORIYA	12	0	0	12
Encodings.MacMongolian	X-MAC-MONGOLIAN	27	0	0	27
Encodings.MacMalayalam	X-MAC-MALAYALAM	17	0	0	17
Encodings.MacLaotian	X-MAC-LAOTIAN	22	0	0	22
Encodings.MacKorean	EUC-KR	3	0	0	3
Encodings.MacKhmer	X-MAC-KHMER	20	0	0	20
Encodings.MacKannada	X-MAC-KANNADA	16	0	0	16
Encodings.MacJapanese	Shift_JIS	1	0	0	1
Encodings.MacIcelandic	X-MAC-ICELANDIC	37	0	0	37
Encodings.MacHebrew	X-MAC-HEBREW	5	0	0	5
Encodings.MacGurmukhi	X-MAC-GURMUKHI	10	0	0	10
Encodings.MacGujarati	X-MAC-GUJARATI	11	0	0	11
Encodings.MacGree	X-MAC-GREEK	6	0	0	6
Encodings.MacGeorgian	X-MAC-GEORGIAN	23	0	0	23
Encodings.MacGaelic		40	0	0	40
Encodings.MacExtArabic	X-MAC-EXTARABIC	31	0	0	31
Encodings.MacEthiopic	X-MAC-ETHIOPIC	28	0	0	28
Encodings.MacDingbats	X-MAC-DINGBATS	34	0	0	34
Encodings.MacDevanagari	X-MAC-DEVANAGARI	9	0	0	9
Encodings.MacCyrillic	X-MAC-CYRILLIC	7	0	0	7
Encodings.MacCroatian	X-MAC-CROATIAN	36	0	0	36
Encodings.MacChineseTrad	Big5	2	0	0	2
Encodings.MacChineseSimp	GB2312	25	0	0	25
Encodings.MacCentralEurRoman	X-MAC-CE	29	0	0	29
Encodings.MacCeltic		39	0	0	39
Encodings.MacBurmese	X-MAC-BURMESE	19	0	0	19

Table 6.2   **Continued**

Encodings Object	Internet Name	Base	Variant	Format	Code
Encodings.MacBengali	X-MAC-BENGALI	13	0	0	13
Encodings.MacArmenian	X-MAC-ARMENIAN	24	0	0	24
Encodings.MacArabic	X-MAC-ARABIC	4	0	0	4
Encodings.ISOLatin1	ISO-8859-1	513	0	0	513
Encodings.ISOLatin2	ISO-8859-2	514	0	0	514
Encodings.ISOLatin3	ISO-8859-3	515	0	0	515
Encodings.ISOLatin4	ISO-8859-4	516	0	0	516
Encodings.ISOLatin5	ISO-8859-9	521	0	0	521
Encodings.ISOLatin6	ISO-8859-10	522	0	0	522
Encodings.ISOLatin7	ISO-8859-13	525	0	0	525
Encodings.ISOLatin8	ISO-8859-14	526	0	0	526
Encodings.ISOLatin9	ISO-8859-15	527	0	0	527
Encodings.ISOLatinHebrew	ISO-8859-8-I	520	0	0	520
Encodings.ISOLatinGreek	ISO-8859-7	519	0	0	519
Encodings.ISOLatinCyrillic	ISO-8859-5	517	0	0	517
Encodings.ISOLatinArabic	ISO-8859-6-I	518	0	0	518
Encodings.DOSTurkish	cp857	1044	0	0	1044
Encodings.DOSThai	TIS-620	1053	0	0	1053
Encodings.DOSRussian	cp866	1051	0	0	1051
Encodings.DOSPortuguese		1045	0	0	1045
Encodings.DOSNordic		1050	0	0	1050
Encodings.DOSLatinUS	cp437	1024	0	0	1024
Encodings.DOSLatin2	cp852	1042	0	0	1042
Encodings.DOSLatin1	cp850	1040	0	0	1040
Encodings.DOSKorean	EUC-KR	1058	0	0	1058
Encodings.DOSJapanese	Shift_JIS	1056	0	0	1056
Encodings.DOSIcelandic	cp861	1046	0	0	1046
Encodings.DOSHebrew	DOS-862	1047	0	0	1047
Encodings.DOSGreek2	IBM869	1052	0	0	1052
Encodings.DOSGreek1		1041	0	0	1041
Encodings.DOSGreek	cp737	1029	0	0	1029
Encodings.DOSCyrillic		1043	0	0	1043
Encodings.DOSChineseTrad	Big5	1059	0	0	1059
Encodings.DOSChineseSimplif	GBK	1057	0	0	1057
Encodings.DOSCanadianFrench		1048	0	0	1048
Encodings.DOSBalticRim	cp775	1030	0	0	1030
Encodings.DOSArabic	cp864	1049	0	0	1049
Encodings.shiftJIS	Shift_JIS	2561	0	0	2561
Encodings.kOI8_R	KOI8-R	2562	0	0	2562

After you have a reference to a particular encoding, you can use it to define the encoding of a string or to convert the encoding from one String to another.

DefineEncoding Function

The `DefineEncoding` global function is used to apply an encoding to a string whose encoding you already know. In simpler terms, it adds a byte order mark at the beginning of the `string` so that the encoding can be determined by checking it.

```
DefineEncoding(aString as String, enc as TextEncoding) as String
```

ConvertEncoding Function

This global function lets you convert a string from one encoding to another. This is a more recent addition to the language than the **TextConverter** class and is generally easier to use. It assumes that REALbasic is able to figure out the encoding of the string that is being passed so that it can accurately convert it into the encoding passed in the second argument.

```
ConvertEncoding(aString as String, enc as TextEncoding) as String
```

Some additional global functions can be used, but they have largely been replaced by the methods outlined previously. There is a `GetTextConverter` function and a `GetTextEncoding` function, but it is generally simpler to use the **Encodings** object and `ConvertEncoding` function outlined earlier.

Base64 Encoding

Base64 encoding is unrelated to Unicode, but it is quite relevant to our discussion of XML and Internet applications in general. Basically, Base64 is a means of encoding arbitrary binary information into a string of ASCII characters that can then be emailed or otherwise transferred through the Internet.

REALbasic provides global functions for your encoding and decoding pleasure:

```
REALbasic.EncodeBase64(aString as String, [linewrap as Integer]) as String
REALbasic.DecodeBase64(aString as String, [linewrap as Integer]) as String
```

Consider the following code snippet:

```
Dim s as String
s = "ABCs are fun to learn."
MsgBox EncodeBase64(s)
```

The `MsgBox` will display the following:

```
QUJDcyBhcmUgZnVuIHRvIGxlYXJuLg==
```

XML and HTML Entity Encoding

XML and HTML are encoded in UTF-8 or UTF-16 by default; if another encoding is used, it must be declared at the beginning of the document. However, because some

Internet-related protocols can work only with 8-bit character sets, you sometimes need to encode characters outside that range in a special format. You can refer to specific characters using an XML entity reference. Entity references always start with "&" and end with ";" and every time an XML parser encounters an entity, it tries to expand it— which means that it tries to replace it with the appropriate replacement text for that entity. An entity reference can refer to a long string of text, either declared within the document or residing outside the document, but the references used for character encoding are automatically expanded.

The generic way to refer to a particular character is to use a numeric entity reference, like so:

```
&#39;
```

This particular reference refers to the apostrophe character. The ampersand is followed by "#", which identifies it as a numeric character reference and the numbers that follow it are decimal representations of a particular code point. In addition to using entities to refer to characters that are outside the 1-byte range, there are also some characters that need to be encoded when you want to refer to them literally because they are used to mark up an XML document. The following table specifies those entities and what they represent:

&amp;	&
&gt;	>
&lt;	<
&apos;	'
&quot;	"

Detecting Encoding in XML Documents

If an XML document does not declare an encoding, it is supposed to be either UTF-8 or UTF-16. (The BOM is optional.) However, despite the fact that they are supposed to declare their encoding, some do not, and others may declare an encoding that is different from what the text is actually encoded in. This is surprisingly common (in my experience, at least), so checking is helpful. XML documents have to start with an XML declaration:

```
<?xml version="1.0" encoding="UTF-8"?>
```

Regardless of the version or encoding, you definitely know that each XML document will start with <?xml. Because you know what those characters have to be, you can deduce the encoding being used by examining the data in the first four positions. In some cases, you are just narrowing down the options, so you need to check the

encoding declaration in the XML document as well to make sure it is consistent with what you have found.

00 00 00 3C	UCS-4, big-endian, or other 32-bit format
3C 00 00 00	UCS-4, little-endian
00 00 3C 00	UCS-4, unusual byte order
00 3C 00 00	UCS-4, unusual byte order
00 3C 00 3F	UTF-16BE, big-endian ISO-10646-UCS-2
3C 00 3F 00	UTF-16LE, little-endian ISO-10646-UCS-2
3C 3F 78 6D	UTF-8, ISO 646, ASCII, ISO 8859, Shift-JIS, EUC.
4C 6F A7 94	EBCDIC
Other?	Unknown

XML Processing

I have gotten a little ahead of myself and started talking about XML document encoding before saying anything about XML documents themselves. There is not enough space to devote to a full tutorial on XML, but I'd like to take a quick walk-through just in case you are entirely unfamiliar with it.

An XML document is made up of nodes and organized in the form of a tree. There are several kind of nodes, which I will outline next.

Document Node

The Document node is the node that represents the document itself. It doesn't actually appear in a document; it's more of an abstraction, but it becomes relevant when processing XML using REALbasic because you will instantiate a node that is a reference to the entire document. An XML document node generally contains two nodes: the XML declaration that appears at the top of the page and the root document node that contains all the remaining nodes.

- XML Declaration—This node is required and is the first node in the file. It labels the file as an XML file, says what version of XML it is, and specifies the encoding that is required if it is not in UTF-8 or UTF-16. This is technically a processing instruction.

```
<?xml version="1.0" encoding="UTF-8"?>
```

- Element Node—The element node is the primary node used. It is the kind of node that serves as the document root, and it is the node that organizes the document into a tree because it can contain additional nodes of different types. An element node is expressed in XML in terms of tags. If the element does not have any child elements, it can be expressed using this format:

```
<ChildlessNode/>
```

Although childless elements are not rare, elements with children are definitely more common, and they are defined using two tags, a start tag and an end tag, like so:

```
<Node>…</Node>
```

- Attribute Node—Attribute nodes are used to provide additional information about individual elements. They look like this:

```
<Node FirstAttr="1" SecondAttr="2">…</Node>
```

- Processing Instruction—A processing instruction is a node that is intended to be used by some application while parsing a file. It contains an instruction of some sort and looks like this:

```
<?Processing instruction?>
```

- Comment Node—Comments do not appear in any visual renderings of an XML document and are intended to communicate information to individuals working with the raw XML files:

```
<!--Last changed by Mark Choate, 10.3.2005 →
```

- Text Node—A text node is plain text that is contained by a parent element. The text is parsed by the parser and entities that appear in it are expanded:

```
<Node>This is some text.</Node>
```

- CDATA Section—A CDATA section contains text, but it is not parsed, which means that it can contain XML markup that will be ignored by the processor:

```
<Node><!CDATA[This text will <b>not</b> be parsed]]></Node>
```

- DOCTYPE declaration—This is an optional node that follows the XML declaration. It declares the type of document that it is, as defined in a Document Type Declaration (DTD), which can be either in a separate document or embedded in the XML page. The DTD defines the names of legal elements, what their attributes should be, and so on, and can be used to validate a document.

```
<!DOCTYPE html PUBLIC "-//W3C//DTD XHTML 1.0 Strict//EN"
"http://www.w3.org/TR/xhtml1/DTD/xhtml1-strict.dtd">
```

The heavy lifting is done by the element node and associated attribute nodes, plus text nodes. Now that you know the basic structure of an XML document, the next step is to figure out what to do with them. There are two base classes that can be used to process XML documents using REALbasic, **XMLReader** and **XMLDocument**. For those of you coming from the Java world, **XMLReader** works like SAX and **XMLDocument** like DOM. If this is all new to you, a little explanation is warranted.

The **XMLDocument** class parses and loads the XML document into memory. It preserves the tree structure of the document by instantiating the elements and attributes as subclasses of the **XMLNode** class, which is why it is called DOM, which stands for Document Object Model; it's an object model in memory of the XML document itself.

XMLReader reads through the XML document and fires an event whenever a new node is encountered. To use the **XMLReader** class, you will need to decide what you want to do when a particular event is encountered and implement the events just like any other event you encounter in REALbasic.

One question many people have relates to which is better—should you use **XMLReader** or **XMLDocument**? The general rule when choosing **XMLReader** and **XMLDocument** is often given as this: For very large documents use **XMLReader**; for smaller ones use **XMLDocument**. The thinking behind this is that because **XMLDocument** loads an entire document into memory, it can be unwieldy with large documents. In a general sense I suppose this is true, but a better determinant is what you plan to do with the XML document. If you want to open an XML document, manipulate it, or transform it into a different format, you need to use **XMLDocument**. Not only does the object model make it easy to traverse nodes, it also provides access to XSLT and XPATH queries.

XMLReader, on the other hand, is not very good at transforming one **XMLDocument** to another. Because it is event driven, your program will need to maintain state as the file is parsed in order to understand the context of particular elements. If the destination XML document format is structured differently from the source document, it can become quite clumsy because you may have to cache a lot of data until you have the information you need to write the XML document out into XML format. **XMLDocument**, because of its tree structure, provides nonsequential access to the nodes of the document. In **XMLReader**, you get them one at a time and have to decide what to do with them at that point.

With the RSSReader application, I will be taking XML documents in different formats and using them to create an in-memory representation of the information in each document. I will use the **mwNode** class as the base class of my object model, and all the different flavors of RSS will get mapped into this object model. Considering the guidelines I just shared, this means that **XMLReader** is an ideal tool for this process, despite the fact that RSS files are small. You can do it with **XMLDocument**, too, and I'll recreate the process using it after showing the **XMLReader** version.

XMLDocument

The **XMLDocument** class is based on W3C's Document Object Model (DOM) API, although it is not a complete implementation. Nevertheless, that it is related to DOM will explain some of the quirkiness of the API itself, which often seems to try to do easy things the hard way. The reason is that the DOM API is intended for implementation in many programming languages. Because it had to be implemented in many programming languages, it is not exactly optimized for any particular language.

The **XMLDocument** class itself is the best example. It is a subclass of **XMLNode**, but it is the base class you will always use when you want to take a DOM-like approach. It is a factory class in the sense that you will use an instance of **XMLDocument** to create the elements of your XML document rather than using the more typical New operator. Here's an example: You can instantiate an **XMLDocument** object in three ways: either without any parameters, with a **String** representation of an XML document, or with a **FolderItem** that represents an XML file. In this example, I will create a simple XML document using the **XMLDocument** class:

```
Dim xDoc as XMLDocument
Dim tmpNode as XMLElement
xDoc = New XMLDocument()
tmpNode = xDoc.AppendChild(xDoc.CreateElement("html"))
```

This shows the typical way that elements and other XML nodes are created. With the exception of **XMLDocument** itself, the other nodes are created by calling the appropriate methods on **XMLDocument**, which in this case was CreateElement. You will need to create elements this way because one of the properties that an element and other nodes must have is a reference to the OwnerDocument. Creating the instance using the xDoc.CreateElement method does that for you and associates the child element with this particular document.

Although **XMLDocument** is an **XMLNode**, it is more of an abstraction than an actual node because it doesn't actually appear anywhere when you convert the object model into a string. In the previous example, the first element I created was an html element, which will serve as the root element for the document. The XMLDocument.DocumentElement property is a reference to this root element (and it must be an element, and not some other node type).

If I were to call xDoc.toString on this example, I would find that the document actually has two nodes: the XML declaration and the html node:

```
<?xml version="1.0" encoding="UTF-8"?>
<html/>
```

Even though it is not visibly present, the **XMLDocument** node can be thought of as the node that contains both the XML declaration and the root element itself.

In this example, I assume the presence of a **FolderItem** pointing to an atom XML file (see the example in the **XMLReader** section):

```
xDoc = New XMLDocument(anXmlFile as FolderItem)
```

You now have a fully populated document. The way to traverse and manipulate this document is by using the **XMLNode** class, which I have referred to but have yet to discuss. A document is a collection of nodes, and the parent class for all of these nodes is **XMLNode.** It provides you with methods to access child nodes, get and set attributes, and similar activities. A summary of properties and methods follows:

XMLNode Properties

When dealing with **XMLNodes**, you will primarily be dealing with subclasses of **XMLNode.** This, after all, is one of the benefits of object-oriented programming. Only **XMLNode** subclasses appear in an XML document, never plain **XMLNodes.** The role that **XMLNode** plays is twofold. First, it implements various methods that are shared by all nodes—a typical example of code reuse. Second, it serves as an abstract class so that all the other subclasses can be referenced as **XMLNodes** when you do not know what kind of node to expect. Not knowing what kind of node to expect happens all the time because you usually do not know the specific organization and structure of a document before you encounter it. For example, I may have a body element in an html document. The children of the body element can be **XMLElement**, **XMLComment**, **XMLText**, and so on. I need to be able to get a reference to that child without knowing the specific subclass; because they all share the same parent class, I can reference them as **XMLNodes**.

One interesting aspect of XML in REALbasic is that there are 13 node types, which is determined by accessing the following property:

```
XMLNode.Type as Integer
```

There are also **XMLNode** subclasses that correspond to some of the types. What's interesting is that only a few node types are also represented by subclasses. Following is the complete list of node types, and the class constants you can use to access them:

Constant	Value
XMLNodeType.Element_Node	1
XMLNodeType.Attribute_Node	2
XMLNodeType.Text_Node	3
XMLNodeType.CData_Section_Node	4
XMLNodeType.Entity_Reference_Node	5
XMLNodeType.Entity_Node	6
XMLNodeType.Processing_Instruction_Node	7
XMLNodeType.Comment_Node	8
XMLNodeType.Document_Node	9
XMLNodeType.Document_Type_Node	10
XMLNodeType.Document_Fragment_Node	11
XMLNodeType.Notation_Node	12
XMLNodeType.Other_Node	13

XMLNode subclasses are

```
XMLDocument
XMLElement
XMLComment
XMLProcessingInstruction
XMLAttribute
XMLTextNode
XMLCDATASection
```

There is a correspondence between the node subclasses and the factory methods available to **XMLDocument**, which are as follows:

```
XMLDocument.CreateAttribute(name as String) as XMLAttribute
XMLDocument.CreateAttribute(name as String, URI as String) as XMLAttribute
XMLDocument.CreateElement(name as String) as XMLElement
XMLDocument.CreateElement(name as String, URI as String) as XMLElement
XMLDocument.CreateComment(data as String) as XMLComment
XMLDocument.CreateCDATASection(data as String) as XMLCDATASection
XMLDocument.CreateProcessingInstruction(target as String, data as String)
   as XMLProcessingInstruction
XMLDocument.CreateTextNode(data as String) as XMLTextNode
```

So, why isn't there an **XMLNode** subclass for each type of node? I have no idea. In fact, the **XMLDocument** class limits the amount of control you have over your XML documents. It's an excellent tool for parsing documents and using XPATH to search through, but it is not particularly good at creating XML files. In all fairness, however, this has nothing to do with REALbasic and everything to do with the DOM API. In every other language I'm familiar with, people complain about DOM-like implementations and come up with alternatives that seem much more natural to that particular language. JDOM is a good example from the Java world. It parses XML and creates an object model that works more like a typical Java object, without the factory methods and awkward dealings with the **XMLDocument** class.

The **XMLNode** class contains some basic properties shared by the subclasses, although not all subclasses use the properties in the same way. For example, some (but not all) nodes use the `Value` property:

```
XMLNode.Value as String
```

Basically, it's used to hold text for **TextNodes** and **CDATASections.** The following cluster of properties deal with namespaces.

```
XMLNode.Name as String
XMLNode.LocalName as String
XMLNode.Prefix as String
XMLNode.NamespaceURI as String
```

A namespace is a form of shorthand for XML documents so that you can have unique element names, but also ensure that they are relatively short. To that end, a fully qualified name is a combination of `NamespaceURI` and `LocalName`. These usually take on the form of longish URLS, like this:

```
http://purl.org/atom/ns#type
```

The first part up to and including the # sign is the `NamespaceURI` and the last part, type, is the `LocalName`. Namespaces can be declared by using the xmlns property in an **XMLElement**. This will come up again shortly, so I will not dwell on the details now, but suffice it to say that when you declare a namespace, you define a prefix that will be used in place of the `NamespaceURI`. This is why you will see the following in Atom documents:

```
atom:type
```

The atom portion is the prefix and the type is the `LocalName`. Altogether, this makes up the `Name` of the element. The `Name` can vary, depending on whether you decide to use namespaces. The fully qualified name I shared before is a `Name`, too. Because of this, you need to make sure you know what you are looking at and whether it is a `Name`, a `LocalName`, or whatever.

Here are some self-explanatory methods for navigating through an **XMLDocument**. If you plan to do a lot of navigating, you should use XPATH.

```
XMLNode.Parent as XMLNode
XMLNode.OwnerDocument as XMLDocument
XMLNode.ChildCount as Integer
XMLNode.FirstChild as XMLNode
XMLNode.LastChild as XMLNode
XMLNode.NextSibling as XMLNode
XMLNode.PreviousSibling as XMLNode
```

You can get a string representation of the file (useful for saving it):

```
XMLNode.ToString as String
```

Finally, you can get rather detailed error information using the un-object-oriented `LastError` property.

```
XMLNode.LastError as Integer
```

The language reference provides a comprehensive list of `LastError` codes.

XMLNode Methods

The following methods provide a means for adding, inserting, deleting, and comparing child nodes as well as getting a reference to them.

```
XMLNode.Child(index as Integer) as XMLNode
XMLNode.AppendChild(NewChild as XMLNode) as XMLNode
XMLNode.Insert(NewChild as XMLNode, RefChild as XMLNode)
    as XMLNode
XMLNode.RemoveChild(OldChild as XMLNode)
XMLNode.ReplaceChild(NewChild as XMLNode, OldChild as XMLNode)
XMLNode.Clone(deep as Boolean) as XMLNode
XMLNode.Compare(NodeToCompare as XMLNode) as Integer
```

Remember when I mentioned XPATH? It is time to look at it now that the XQL method has been encountered:

```
XMLNode.XQL(Query as String, [NamespaceMap as String]) as XMLNodeList
```

XPATH is a query language for XML, much like SQL is a query language for databases. It's big and powerful and complicated (at times), so I cannot take time to give you all you need to know about XPATH to use it, but I can get you started. There are a lot of good books and online resources you can turn to when you are ready for more advanced topics.

XPATH identifies nodes within an XML document using a path, much like the path you use when working with files and folders. This makes sense because both the file system and an XML document are organized like trees. A folder can contain files or other folders, and an element can contain text nodes or other elements, and so on. Not only are the paths used by XPATH conceptually similar to paths used when working with files, they look like them, too (if you look at the world from a Unix perspective, at least).

Here is an RSS file that I will use as an example. It comes from the REALsoftware website and is based on the RDF version of RSS, known as RSS1.0. Note that some of the URLs have been shortened to fit on the printed page.

Listing 6.1 **REALsoftware RDF-based version of RSS**

```
<?xml version="1.0" encoding="utf-8"?>
<rdf:RDF xmlns:rdf="http://www.w3.org/1999/02/22-rdf-syntax-ns#"
      xmlns="http://purl.org/rss/1.0/">
   <channel rdf:about="http://www.realsoftware.com/rss/realsoftware.xml">
      <title>REAL Software News</title>
      <link>http://www.realsoftware.com</link>
      <description>
         News and Events for REALbasic Users
         </description>
      <image rdf:resource="http://www.realsoftware.com/images/rssGraphic.gif" />
      <language>en-us</language>
      <items>
         <rdf:Seq>
            <li rdf:resource="http://www.realsoftware.com/pr_rb553.html" />
            <li rdf:resource="http://www.realsoftware.com/pr_vbwp.html" />
            <li rdf:resource="http://www.realsoftware.com/pr_opp100.html" />
            <li rdf:resource="http://www.realsoftware.com/pr_showcase_
➥launch.html" />
            <li rdf:resource="http://www.realsoftware.com/realbasic/" />
            <li rdf:resource="http://www.realsoftware.com/rb_awards1.html" />
            <li rdf:resource="http://www.realbasic.com/realworld/" />

            <li rdf:resource="http://www.realsoftware.com/macintouch2003.
➥html" />
         </rdf:Seq>
      </items>
   </channel>
   <image rdf:about="http://www.realsoftware.com/images/rssGraphic.gif">
      <title>REAL Software, Inc.</title>
      <url>http://www.realsoftware.com/images/rssGraphic.gif</url>
      <link>http://www.realsoftware.com/</link>

   </image>
```

Listing 6.1 **Continued**

```
<!-- Content Below Here ! -->
    <item rdf:about="http://www.realsoftware.com/news/pr/2005/2005r3/lnx/">
        <pubDate>Tue, 13 Sep 2005 08:05:00 CDT</pubDate>
        <title>REAL Software Ships REALbasic 2005 for Linux;
                    Brings Rapid Application Development to Linux
                </title>
        <link>http://www.realsoftware.com/news/pr/2005/2005r3/lnx/</link>
        <description>REAL Software, Inc., providers of
REALbasic, cross-platform that really works, announced today the company is
shipping REALbasic 2005 for Linux.  REALbasic 2005 for Linux is a rapid
application development (RAD) environment that enables professional and
non-professional programmers alike to quickly create software for Linux.
        </description>
    </item>
    <item rdf:about="http://www.realsoftware.com/news/pr/2005/2005r3/mac/">
        <pubDate>Tue, 13 Sep 2005 08:05:00 CDT</pubDate>
        <title>REALbasic 2005 for Macintosh Release 3 Ships;
                    Improves 3D GraphicsCapability and Reliability;
                    Helps Bring More Software to the Macintosh
</title>
    <link>http://www.realsoftware.com/news/pr/2005/2005r3/mac/</link>
        <description>REAL Software Inc., providers of
REALbasic, cross-platform that really works, announced today that REALbasic
2005 for Macintosh Release 3 is shipping.  REALbasic 2005 for Macintosh is a
rapid application development (RAD) environment that enables professional
and non-professional programmers alike to quickly create software for the
Macintosh, and even Windows and Linux, by clicking a checkbox.</description>
    </item>
    <item rdf:about="http://www.realsoftware.com/news/pr/2005/2005r3/win/">
        <pubDate>Tue, 13 Sep 2005 08:05:00 CDT</pubDate>
        <title>REALbasic 2005 for Windows Release 3 Ships; Improves Visual Basic
Compatibility, Reliability
</title>        <link>http://www.realsoftware.com/news/pr/2005/2005r3/win/</link>
        <description>REAL Software, Inc., providers of
REALbasic, cross-platform that really works, announced today that REALbasic
2005 for Windows Release 3 is shipping. REALbasic 2005 for Windows is a
rapid application development (RAD) environment that enables professional
and non-professional programmers alike to quickly create software that runs
on Windows, even Macintosh and Linux. REALbasic creates self-contained
executables and eliminates the common problems and installation issues
associated with DLLs or external frameworks typical of other cross-platform
development environments.</description>
    </item>
</rdf:RDF>
```

At the most basic level, XPATH deals in element names. That means that if you want to access the channel element, you need to construct an XPATH that identifies the containment path from the root RDF node down to the channel. Also note that you will be using the localName of the element to create the path. The path to use is this:

```
/RDF/channel
```

The way this would use this XPATH in REALbasic would be something like this:

```
Dim xdoc as XMLDocument
Dim xnl as XMLNodeList
Dim count as Integer
Dim aNode as XMLNode
xdoc = new XMLDocument(anRSSFolderItem)
xnl = xdoc.XQL("/RDF/channel")
count = xnl.length //I know…why length?
aNode = xnl.Item(0)
MsgBox aNode.ToString
```

Using this path in REALbasic causes an **XMLNodeList** to be returned that contains the following element:

```
<channel rdf:about="http://www.realsoftware.com/rss/realsoftware.xml">
  <title>REAL Software News</title>
  <link>http://www.realsoftware.com</link>
  <description>News and Events for REALbasic Users</description>
  <image rdf:resource="http://www.realsoftware.com/images/rssGraphic.gif"/>
  <language>en-us</language>
  <items>
    <rdf:Seq>
      <li rdf:resource="http://www.realsoftware.com/pr_rb553.html"/>
      <li rdf:resource="http://www.realsoftware.com/pr_vbwp.html"/>
      <li rdf:resource="http://www.realsoftware.com/pr_opp100.html"/>
      <li
➥rdf:resource="http://www.realsoftware.com/pr_showcase_launch.html"/>
      <li rdf:resource="http://www.realsoftware.com/realbasic/"/>
      <li rdf:resource="http://www.realsoftware.com/rb_awards1.html"/>
      <li rdf:resource="http://www.realbasic.com/realworld/"/>
      <li
➥rdf:resource="http://www.realsoftware.com/macintouch2003.html"/>
    </rdf:Seq>
  </items>
</channel>
```

If you were processing this file and you wanted to find out the title of this particular channel, you would need to create an XPATH expression that returned only the channel title. It would look like this:

```
/RDF/channel/title
```

The results would be an **XMLNodeList** with one element:

```
<title>REAL Software News</title>
```

Now, suppose you wanted to find the titles for all the items in this RSS feed. You would use the following XPATH expression:

```
/RDF/item/title
```

Then you would receive an **XMLNodeList** with several title elements listed:

```
<title>REAL Software Ships REALbasic 2005 for Linux; Brings Rapid
➥Application Development to Linux</title>
<title>REALbasic 2005 for Macintosh Release 3 Ships; Improves 3D Graphics
Capability and Reliability; Helps Bring More Software to the Macintosh
</title>
<title>REALbasic 2005 for Windows Release 3 Ships; Improves Visual Basic
Compatibility, Reliability
</title>
```

Finally, suppose you want to find the title of anything in the file, whether it's a channel or an item. There's a special XPATH expression for that. If you want to find an element anywhere in a document, regardless of the preceding path, precede the element name with // like so:

```
//title
```

Voila! The results include every title mentioned in the document:

```
<title>REAL Software News</title>
<title>REAL Software, Inc.</title>
<title>REAL Software Ships REALbasic 2005 for Linux; Brings Rapid
➥Application Development to Linux</title>
<title>REALbasic 2005 for Macintosh Release 3 Ships; Improves 3D Graphics
Capability and Reliability; Helps Bring More Software to the Macintosh
</title>
<title>REALbasic 2005 for Windows Release 3 Ships; Improves Visual Basic
Compatibility, Reliability
</title>
```

XML to HTML Transformation

XPATH is closely related to XSLT, which is a process of transforming one XML document into another document with a different format. The relationship comes from the fact that XPATH was developed for use with XSLT, and you will see familiar elements in the following example.

First off, here is an example of an XSLT stylesheet that is used to convert an RSS xml file into html, so that it can be viewed in a browser. This is something that will be quite useful in our RSSReader application. I will not go into excessive detail about how to write a stylesheet, but you should note that a stylesheet consists of a number of templates that get matched to text according to an XPATH expression. The output of that matching is written within the template tag. Often, the apply-templates tag is also called, which simply tells the parser to continue parsing the XML file and looking for other XPATH expressions to evaluate:

Listing 6.2   XSLT style sheet converted to HTML from RSS XML File

```
<!-- RSSview.xsl: retrieve RSS feed(s) and convert to HTML. -->
<!-- Based on XSL distributed with Apache Forrest from the Apache Foundation -->

<xsl:stylesheet xmlns:xsl="http://www.w3.org/1999/XSL/Transform"
    xmlns:dc="http://purl.org/dc/elements/1.1/" version="1.0">

  <xsl:output method="html"/>

  <xsl:template match="/">
    <html><head><title>Today's RSS Feed</title></head>
   <body>
     <xsl:apply-templates/>
   </body></html>
  </xsl:template>



  <xsl:template match="channel">
    <xsl:apply-templates />
  </xsl:template>



  <!-- Named template outputs HTML a element with href link and RSS
       description as title to show up in mouseOver message. -->
  <xsl:template name="anchor">
    <xsl:element name="a">
      <xsl:attribute name="href">
        <xsl:apply-templates select="*[local-name()='link']"/>
      </xsl:attribute>
      <xsl:attribute name="title">
        <xsl:apply-templates select="*[local-name()='description']"/>
      </xsl:attribute>
      <xsl:value-of select="*[local-name()='title']"/>
    </xsl:element>
  </xsl:template>



  <!-- Output RSS channel name as HTML a link inside of h1 element. -->
  <xsl:template match="*[local-name()='channel']">
    <xsl:element name="h1">
      <xsl:call-template name="anchor"/>
```

Listing 6.2 **Continued**

```
    </xsl:element>
    <!-- Following line for RSS .091 -->
    <xsl:apply-templates select="*[local-name()='item']"/>
  </xsl:template>


  <!-- Output RSS item as HTML a link inside of p element. -->
  <xsl:template match="*[local-name()='item']">
    <xsl:element name="p">
      <xsl:call-template name="anchor"/>
      <xsl:text> </xsl:text>
      <xsl:if test="dc:date"> <!-- Show date if available -->
        <xsl:text>( </xsl:text>
        <xsl:value-of select="dc:date"/>
        <xsl:text>) </xsl:text>
      </xsl:if>
    </xsl:element>
  </xsl:template>


</xsl:stylesheet>
```

Using REALbasic's XML classes, you can process this the following way:

```
Dim style as FolderItem
Dim source as FolderItem
Dim stylesheet as XMLStyleSheet
Dim xdoc as XMLDocument
style = getOpenFolderItem(FileTypes1.XSL)
source = getOpenFolderITem(FileTypes1.XML)
stylesheet = New XMLStyleSheet(style)
xdoc = New XMLDocument(source)
MsgBox xdoc.Transform(stylesheet)
```

The output display in the MsgBox would look like this:

```
<html xmlns:dc="http://purl.org/dc/elements/1.1/">
  <head>
    <META http-equiv="Content-Type" content="text/html; charset=UTF-8">
    <title>Today's RSS Feed</title>
  </head>
  <body>
    <h1>
      <a href="http://www.realsoftware.com" title="News and Events for REALbasic
Users">REAL Software News</a>
    </h1>
```

```
      REAL Software, Inc.
      http://www.realsoftware.com/images/rssGraphic.gif
      http://www.realsoftware.com/
    <p>
      <a href="http://www.realsoftware.com/news/pr/2005/2005r3/lnx/"
      title="REAL Software, Inc., providers of
REALbasic, cross-platform that really works, announced today the company is
shipping REALbasic 2005 for Linux.">
        REAL Software Ships REALbasic 2005 for Linux;
        Brings Rapid Application Development to Linux</a>
    </p>
    <p>
      <a href="http://www.realsoftware.com/news/pr/2005/2005r3/mac/"
      title="REAL Software Inc., providers of REALbasic,
      cross-platform that really works, announced today that REALbasic
      2005 for Macintosh Release 3 is shipping.  REALbasic 2005 for Macintosh is a
      rapid application development (RAD) environment that enables professional
      and non-professional programmers alike to quickly create software for the
      Macintosh, and even Windows and Linux, by clicking a checkbox.">
      REALbasic 2005 for Macintosh Release 3 Ships; Improves 3D Graphics
      Capability and Reliability; Helps Bring More Software to the Macintosh
      </a>
    </p>
    <p>
      <a href="http://www.realsoftware.com/news/pr/2005/2005r3/win/"
        title="REAL Software, Inc., providers of
REALbasic, cross-platform that really works, announced today that REALbasic
2005 for Windows Release 3 is shipping. REALbasic 2005 for Windows is a
rapid application development (RAD) environment that enables professional
and non-professional programmers alike to quickly create software that runs
on Windows, even Macintosh and Linux. REALbasic creates self-contained
executables and eliminates the common problems and installation issues
associated with DLLs or external frameworks typical of other cross-platform
development environments.">REALbasic 2005 for Windows Release 3 Ships;
➥Improves Visual Basic Compatibility, Reliability
</a>
    </p>
  </body>
</html>
```

Using this technique, you can see how the RSSReader application will download an XML file, convert it to HTML, and then display it in the **HTMLViewer** control.

XMLReader

The **XMLReader** class is harder to use because of the challenges around maintaining state as you parse the document. The best way to experiment with and learn about the

XMLReader class is to use it with a variety of XML documents and observe how and when the events are fired. The following class, called **rbXmlReader**, captures data about every event that gets triggered while parsing an XML document. When it is finished parsing the document, it displays the raw text of the XML document in one field with some of the data in bold (I'll explain why later), and in another field, it displays a summary of which events fired, and some associated information.

In the sample application, the class runs and displays the results in two separate **EditFields**. **EditField1** shows the source XML data, and **EditField2** shows the output generated by the events. One bit of functionality that I have added to the example, which serves no purpose other than to show you that it can be done, is that in **EditField1** all the character data is highlighted in bold. Be sure to read the comments in the Characters event to learn about all the things that can go wrong when you try this.

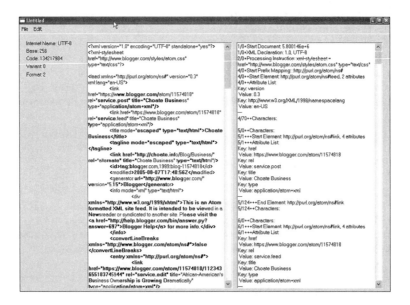

Figure 6.1   The rbXMLReader application.

Class rbXmlReader

The displayString property is the buffer that collects data as each event is triggered. Because XML documents are hierarchical and elements can be nested within other elements, the indent property is used to track the current depth; in other words, how many elements have been nested at a given point in time. This gives the class information about how to indent the results.

```
Property displayString(-1) As String
Property indent as integer
```

The next group of items are the events that get triggered while parsing the document. In each case, the name of the event is sent to the buffer to be displayed. If information is passed to the event that is important, that information is recorded as well. The events apply both to XML documents and to Document Type Definitions, or DTDs, which specify a document type for XML and determine whether it is valid. DTDs can be internal or external, and the **XMLReader** can read either one. If the DTD is external, the standalone attribute of the XML declaration must be `False`; otherwise it can be `True`.

As you scan through this class, be sure to take a look at the values that are passed for each event and how they are referenced, because that is the data you will be working with.

Listing 6.3   **Sub XmlDecl(version as String, xmlEncoding as String, standalone as Boolean) Handles Event**

```
// The first event triggered
setDisplayString("XML Declaration: " + version + ", " + xmlEncoding)
```

Listing 6.4   **Sub StartPrefixMapping(prefix as String, uri as String) Handles Event**

```
// Whether namespace prefixes are mapped is decided by which
// Constructor is used when instantiating the object.
// To map prefixes, instantiate the rbXmlReader object this way:
// aReader = New rbXMLReader("UTF-8", "")
// The second argument specifies a character or characters to
// use to separate the localName from the URI.
// This is a convenience feature, not part of the namespace spec.
setDisplayString("Start Prefix Mapping: " + prefix + ":" + uri)
```

Listing 6.5   **Sub EndPrefixMapping(prefix as String)**

```
// In many instances, namespaces are declared once, so this
// event isn't triggered until all the elements have been
// processed. In the atom.xml file used in the example,
// namespaces are declared in event <entry> element and every
// <div> element, so this event is triggered often.
setDisplayString("End Prefix Mapping: " + prefix)
```

Listing 6.6   **Sub StartDocument() Handles Event**

```
setDisplayString("Start Document: " + str(ticks))
```

Listing 6.7   **Sub EndDocument() Handles Event**

```
// All elements have been parsed so display the string
// in EditField2
setDisplayString("End Document")
Window1.EditField2.Text = Join(displayString, EndOfLine)
```

Listing 6.8   **Sub StartElement(name as String, attributeList as XmlAttributeList) Handles Event**

```
// Increment the indent level each time a start element is
// encountered
incIndent
setDisplayString("Start Element: " + name + ", " _
+ str(attributeList.count) + " attributes")

// If there is at least one attribute, then call
// the handleAttributes method
If attributeList.count > 0 Then
    handleAttributes(attributeList)
End If
```

Listing 6.9   **Sub EndElement(name as String) Handles Event**

```
setDisplayString("End Element: " + name)
// Decrement the indent level each time an end element is
// encountered.
decIndent
```

Listing 6.10   **Sub StartCDATA() Handles Event**

```
// CDATA is a special kind of text data that does not
// get parsed and therefore you do not need to escape any
// values. It is enclosed in the followed tag:
// <!CDATA[ some data ]]>
SetDisplayString("Start CDATA:")
```

Listing 6.11   **Sub EndCDATA() Handles Event**

```
    SetDisplayString("End CDATA:")
```

Listing 6.12   **Sub Characters(s as String) Handles Event**

```
// Characters represent text that is wrapped inside open and
// close elements. The SAX standard treats all white space as
// character data, too, so if your XML document is formatted
// nicely and indented, then the EndOfLine characters and spaces
// will trigger this event as well. The SAX specification itself
// also allows for the possibility of Character events being
// fired successively. When using other SAX or SAX-like parsers
// be aware of this - one string of text may show up in two
// events. In my experience, REALbasic will not fire sequential
// Character events.
setDisplayString("Characters: " + s)


// The following code applies a bold style to the character data
// in the display of the original XML file. This can be tricky!
// The "lines" referred to by the XMLReader class are not
// necessarily the same lines according to an EditField if you
// have the multiline property set to True. In order for them
// to synch up, you need to have multiline set to False.
// In Windows, one more step is required: you also need to
// set the vertical scrollbar property to True. If you don't
// All you will see is one line, and not all the rest. In
// this context, setting multiline to False really means that
// the EditField should rely on the line endings in the original
// document, which happen to be the line endings that XMLReader
// relies on as well. The XMLReader.currentLineNumber and
// XMLReader.currentColumnNumber are properties that are
// always available throughout the parsing process, so you
// could use a similar technique to implement syntax
// highlighting.

Dim line, start, length as Integer
If (Trim(s) <> "") Then
    line = Window1.EditField1.CharPosAtLineNum(currentLineNumber - 1)
    start = line + CurrentColumnNumber - 1
    length = Len(s)
    If length > 1 Then
        Window1.EditField1.StyledText.Bold(start, length) = True
    End if
End If
```

Listing 6.13   **Sub Comment(data as String) Handles Event**

```
// XML Comments: <!--a comment →
setDisplayString("Comment: " + data)
```

Listing 6.14 **Sub ProcessingInstruction(target as String, data as String) Handles Event**

```
// Processing instructions look like: <?instruction?>
setDisplayString("Processing Instruction: " + target + " = " + data)
```

Listing 6.15 **Sub Default(s as String) Handles Event**

```
// A Default method that can be used for all events
// by calling XmlReader.SetDefaultHandler = True

setDisplayString("Default Handler")
```

Listing 6.16 **Function ExternalEntityRef(context as String, base as String, systemId as String, publicId as String) As Boolean Handles Event**

```
setDisplayString("ExternalEntity")
```

Listing 6.17 **Sub SkippedEntity(entityName as String, is_parameter_entity as Boolean) Handles Event**

```
    setDisplayString("Skipped Entity: " + entityName)
```

Listing 6.18 **Sub StartDoctypeDecl(doctypeName as String, systemId as String, publicId as String, has_internal_subset as Boolean)**

```
//The remaining events related to DTDs
setDisplayString("Start Doctype Declaration: " + doctypeName + ", " + systemID +
", " +
➥publicID)
```

Listing 6.19 **Function NotStandalone() As Boolean Handles Event**

```
// If NotStandalone is triggered, it means an external
// DTD must be processed
setDisplayString("Not Stand-alone")
```

Listing 6.20 **Sub EndDoctypeDecl() Handles Event**

```
    setDisplayString("End Doctype Declaration")
```

Listing 6.21   **Sub EntityDecl(entityName as String, is_parameter_entity as Boolean, value as String, base as String, systemId as String, publicId as String, notationName as String) Handles Event**

```
setDisplayString("Entity Declaration: name-"_
 + entityName + ", value-" + value + ", " + base + ", " _
+ systemID + ", " + publicID + ", " + notationName)
```

Listing 6.22   **Sub ElementDecl(name as String, content as XmlContentModel) Handles Event**

```
setDisplayString("Element Declaration: " + name)
```

Listing 6.23   **Sub AttlistDecl(elname as String, attname as String, att_type as String, dflt as String, isrequired as Boolean) Handles Event**

```
setDisplayString("AttlistDecl: " + elname + ", " + attname)
```

Listing 6.24   **Sub NotationDecl(notationName as String, base as String, systemId as String, publicId as String) Handles Event**

```
setDisplayString("Notation")
```

Listing 6.25   **Sub setDisplayString(myString as String)**

```
// Buffer for output
Dim indentString as String
Dim x as Integer

For x = 0 To indent
    indentString = indentString + "+"
Next

displayString.Append(str(currentLineNumber) + "/" _
+ str(currentColumnNumber) + indentString + myString)
```

Listing 6.26   **Sub incIndent()**

```
// Increment Indent Level (when StartElement is called)
indent = indent + 1
```

Listing 6.27 **Sub decIndent()**

```
// Decrement Indent Level (when End Element is called)
// Make sure the number is not less than zero.
If indent > 0 Then
    indent = indent - 1
End If
```

Listing 6.28 **Sub handleAttributes(attList as xmlAttributeList)**

```
// Convert attributes into a String
Dim x as integer
Dim attString as string

For x = 0 to attList.Count - 1
    attString = attString + "Key: " + attList.key(x) _
    + EndOfLine + " Value: " + attList.value(x) _
    + endOfLine
Next
    setDisplayString("Attribute List: " _
    + endOfLine + attString + "---")
```

Input XML File

Next, I will parse an XML file with this class and examine the results. The input file used is an Atom file, and Atom is considered to be a replacement of older RSS forms such as RSS2.0 and RSS1.0. The following is a real atom.xml file generated by blogger.com. Take a look at the `<feed>` and `<div>` elements—both have an xmlns attribute, which is the attribute that is used to define namespaces. The namespace used for `<feed>` is:

```
xmlns="http://purl.org/atom/ns#"
```

The namespace used for `<div>` is:

```
xmlns="http://www.w3.org/1999/xhtml"
```

These namespaces do not specify a prefix, which means that they are the default namespace. Because namespaces apply to the element in which they are declared and those following it, each element after the declaration uses the same namespace. When the `<div>` namespace is used, it becomes the default namespace so that everything within the `<div>` element uses the same namespace, which happens to be the namespace used for HTML elements.

Namespaces will play an important role in this application because we will be dealing with three RSS file formats that all use similar element names. For example, there is a `<title>` element in all three formats. There may be situations where I want to process an Atom `<title>` element differently from an RSS1.0 `<title>` element. (I also want to have one **XmlReader** subclass rather than one for each format.) Because of this, processing this XML document by having the **XmlReader** class expand namespaces means that I will readily identify the source for any given `<title>` element.

Listing 6.29   **Use the XmlReader class to expand namespaces so you can identify the source**

```
<?xml version="1.0" encoding="UTF-8" standalone="yes"?>
<?xml-stylesheet href="http://www.blogger.com/styles/atom.css"
  type="text/css"?>

<feed xmlns="http://purl.org/atom/ns#" version="0.3"
  xml:lang="en-US">
    <link href="https://www.blogger.com/atom/11574818" rel="service.post"
        title="Choate Business" type="application/atom+xml"/>
    <link href="https://www.blogger.com/atom/11574818" rel="service.feed"
        title="Choate Business" type="application/atom+xml"/>
    <title mode="escaped" type="text/html">Choate Business</title>
    <tagline mode="escaped" type="text/html"></tagline>
    <link href="http://choate.info/Blog/Business/" rel="alternate"
        title="Choate Business" type="text/html"/>
    <id>tag:blogger.com,1999:blog-11574818</id>
    <modified>2005-08-07T17:48:56Z</modified>
    <generator url="http://www.blogger.com/" version="5.15">Blogger</generator>
    <info mode="xml" type="text/html">
        <div xmlns="http://www.w3.org/1999/xhtml">This is an Atom
        formatted XML site feed. It is intended to be viewed in a
        Newsreader or syndicated to another site. Please visit the <a
        href="http://help.blogger.com/bin/answer.py?answer=697">Blogger Help</a>
        for more info.</div>
    </info>
    <convertLineBreaks
xmlns="http://www.blogger.com/atom/ns#">false</convertLineBreaks>
    <entry xmlns="http://purl.org/atom/ns#">
        <link href="https://www.blogger.com/atom/11574818/112343655183745944"
        rel="service.edit" title="African-American's Business Ownership is
        Growing Dramatically" type="application/atom+xml"/>
        <author>
            <name>Mark S. Choate</name>
        </author>
        <issued>2005-08-07T13:38:00-04:00</issued>
        <modified>2005-08-07T17:48:56Z</modified>
        <created>2005-08-07T17:42:31Z</created>
        <link
    href="http://choate.info/Blog/Business/2005/08/african-americans-business-
➥ownership.html" rel="alternate" title="African-American's Business Ownership is
Growing Dramatically" type="text/html"/>
```

Listing 6.29 **Continued**

```
        <id>tag:blogger.com,1999:blog-11574818.post-112343655183745944</id>
        <title mode="escaped" type="text/html">African-American's Business
Ownership is Growing Dramatically</title>
        <content type="application/xhtml+xml"
xml:base="http://choate.info/Blog/Business/" xml:space="preserve">
            <div xmlns="http://www.w3.org/1999/xhtml">According to a recent
report from the Small Business Administration, there has been a 45% increase in
the number of African-American owned businesses since 1997. Likewise, Hispanic-
owned businesses have increased by 31% and there has also been a 20% increase in
women-owned businesses during that same time period.</div>
        </content>
        <draft xmlns="http://purl.org/atom-blog/ns#">false</draft>
    </entry>


    <entry xmlns="http://purl.org/atom/ns#">
        <link href="https://www.blogger.com/atom/11574818/111832600521939707"
rel="service.edit" title="Economic downturns and new business growth"
type="application/atom+xml"/>
        <author>
            <name>Mark S. Choate</name>
        </author>
        <issued>2005-06-09T09:56:00-04:00</issued>
        <modified>2005-06-09T14:14:54Z</modified>
        <created>2005-06-09T14:06:45Z</created>
        <link href="http://choate.info/Blog/Business/2005/06/economic-
downturns-and-new-business_09.html" rel="alternate" title="Economic downturns and
new business growth" type="text/html"/>
        <id>tag:blogger.com,1999:blog-11574818.post-111832600521939707</id>
        <title mode="escaped" type="text/html">Economic downturns and new
➥business growth</title>
        <content type="application/xhtml+xml"
xml:base="http://choate.info/Blog/Business/" xml:space="preserve">
            <div xmlns="http://www.w3.org/1999/xhtml">It's not uncommon for
there to be an upswing in the creation of new businesses in an economic
downturn. One reason for this is that often experienced professionals are laid off
and receive good severance packages which provides them the opportunity to start
their own business. Growth in sole-proprietorship has been on a steady increase
since 2000, according to the SBA and this may provide some support to the idea
that businesses get started in an downturn. And since small businesses represent
upwards of 75% of all new job, that's very good news.

<span class="fullpost">The numbers themselves are impressive. Income for sole
proprietors was $728.4 billion in 2000 and that figure has grown to $902.8
```

Listing 6.29   **Continued**

```
billion in 2004, a 19.3% increase. Bankruptcies are also at a lower rate than
2000, which was the peak of the Internet bubble. Perhaps the most interesting
figure in the NFIB Business Optimism Index, which was 104.6 in 2004, and only
100.3 in 2000. Small businesses appear to be doing better than they have in the
last five years, which indicates a strong, thriving economy despite the gloom
often distributed by the news media.

Source: SBA <i>The Small Business Advocate</i>, Vol. 24, No. 6</span>
            </div>
        </content>
        <draft xmlns="http://purl.org/atom-blog/ns#">false</draft>
    </entry>

</feed>
```

Output

What follows is the output of the preceding atom.xml file when processed by the
rbXmlReader class. Before sharing the entire document output, I have included a snippet of what the output would be like if I was not expanding namespaces. On the fifth
line you will see a reference to the `<feed>` element:

```
1/0+Start Document: 1.012971e+7
1/0+XML Declaration: 1.0, UTF-8
2/0+Processing Instruction: xml-stylesheet =
href="http://www.blogger.com/styles/atom.css" type="text/css"
4/0++Start Element: feed, 3 attributes
4/0++Attribute List:
Key: xmlns
 Value: http://purl.org/atom/ns#
Key: version
 Value: 0.3
Key: xml:lang
 Value: en-US
```

Now compare that output with the output that expands namespaces. First, there is a
new event labeled Start Prefix Mapping, which tells you that namespaces will be
expanded. The reference to prefixes refers to the fact that you use prefixes to identify
namespaces, unless the element comes from the default namespace. So, for example, it
would have been possible in the atom.xml file used in this example to declare two

namespaces at the beginning of the document, instead of declaring a new default namespace every time a `<feed>` or `<div>` element was encountered. The consequence of this is that you would have to declare a prefix, too, such as:

```
xmlns:atom="http://purl.org/atom/ns#"
```

Then you would refer to atom elements using a prefix, such as:

```
<atom:feed>
```

Here is sample output with expanded namespaces:

```
1/0+Start Document: 9.723852e+6
1/0+XML Declaration: 1.0, UTF-8
2/0+Processing Instruction: xml-stylesheet =
href="http://www.blogger.com/styles/atom.css" type="text/css"
4/0+Start Prefix Mapping: :http://purl.org/atom/ns#
4/0++Start Element: http://purl.org/atom/ns#feed, 2 attributes
4/0++Attribute List:
Key: version
 Value: 0.3
Key: http://www.w3.org/XML/1998/namespacelang
 Value: en-US
---
```

Note that the `<feed>` element reference now includes the expanded namespace identifier:

```
http://purl.org/atom/ns#feed
```

What follows is the complete output for the **rbXmlReader** class. The first number of each line refers to the line number of the original xml file where this element or node was encountered. The second number, following the /, refers to the column, or how many characters in on that particular line the node occurs. You will also see a lot of "Characters:" followed by nothing. Those come about as a result that all characters that appear in the document are processed, even if it is just a newline character used to make the various elements more readable.

Listing 6.30 **rbXmlReader class output**

```
1/0+Start Document: 1.017785e+7
1/0+XML Declaration: 1.0, UTF-8
2/0+Processing Instruction: xml-stylesheet =
href="http://www.blogger.com/styles/atom.css" type="text/css"
4/0+Start Prefix Mapping: :http://purl.org/atom/ns#
4/0++Start Element: http://purl.org/atom/ns#feed, 2 attributes
4/0++Attribute List:
Key: version
 Value: 0.3
Key: http://www.w3.org/XML/1998/namespacelang
```

Listing 6.30   **Continued**

```
Value: en-US
---
4/70++Characters:

5/0++Characters:
5/1+++Start Element: http://purl.org/atom/ns#link, 4 attributes
5/1+++Attribute List:
Key: href
 Value: https://www.blogger.com/atom/11574818
Key: rel
 Value: service.post
Key: title
 Value: Choate Business
Key: type
 Value: application/atom+xml
---
5/124+++End Element: http://purl.org/atom/ns#link
5/124++Characters:

6/0++Characters:
6/1+++Start Element: http://purl.org/atom/ns#link, 4 attributes
6/1+++Attribute List:
Key: href
 Value: https://www.blogger.com/atom/11574818
Key: rel
 Value: service.feed
Key: title
 Value: Choate Business
Key: type
 Value: application/atom+xml
---
6/124+++End Element: http://purl.org/atom/ns#link
6/124++Characters:

7/0++Characters:
7/1+++Start Element: http://purl.org/atom/ns#title, 2 attributes
7/1+++Attribute List:
Key: mode
 Value: escaped
Key: type
 Value: text/html
---
7/40+++Characters: Choate Business
7/55+++End Element: http://purl.org/atom/ns#title
7/63++Characters:
```

Listing 6.30   **Continued**

```
8/0++Characters:
8/1+++Start Element: http://purl.org/atom/ns#tagline, 2 attributes
8/1+++Attribute List:
Key: mode
 Value: escaped
Key: type
 Value: text/html
---
8/42+++End Element: http://purl.org/atom/ns#tagline
8/52++Characters:

9/0++Characters:
9/1+++Start Element: http://purl.org/atom/ns#link, 4 attributes
9/1+++Attribute List:
Key: href
 Value: http://choate.info/Blog/Business/
Key: rel
 Value: alternate
Key: title
 Value: Choate Business
Key: type
 Value: text/html
---
9/106+++End Element: http://purl.org/atom/ns#link
9/106++Characters:

10/0++Characters:
10/1+++Start Element: http://purl.org/atom/ns#id, 0 attributes
10/5+++Characters: tag:blogger.com,1999:blog-11574818
10/39+++End Element: http://purl.org/atom/ns#id
10/44++Characters:

11/0++Characters:
11/1+++Start Element: http://purl.org/atom/ns#modified, 0 attributes
11/11+++Characters: 2005-08-07T17:48:56Z
11/31+++End Element: http://purl.org/atom/ns#modified
11/42++Characters:

12/0++Characters:
12/1+++Start Element: http://purl.org/atom/ns#generator, 2 attributes
12/1+++Attribute List:
Key: url
 Value: http://www.blogger.com/
Key: version
 Value: 5.15
```

Listing 6.30   **Continued**

```
---
12/57+++Characters: Blogger
12/64+++End Element: http://purl.org/atom/ns#generator
12/76++Characters:

13/0++Characters:
13/1+++Start Element: http://purl.org/atom/ns#info, 2 attributes
13/1+++Attribute List:
Key: mode
 Value: xml
Key: type
 Value: text/html
---
13/35+++Characters:

14/0+++Characters:
14/2+++Start Prefix Mapping: :http://www.w3.org/1999/xhtml
14/2++++Start Element: http://www.w3.org/1999/xhtmldiv, 0 attributes
14/44++++Characters: This is an Atom formatted XML site feed. It is intended to be
viewed in a Newsreader or syndicated to another site. Please visit the
14/177+++++Start Element: http://www.w3.org/1999/xhtmla, 1 attributes
14/177+++++Attribute List:
Key: href
 Value: http://help.blogger.com/bin/answer.py?answer=697
---
14/236+++++Characters: Blogger Help
14/248+++++End Element: http://www.w3.org/1999/xhtmla
14/252++++Characters:  for more info.
14/267++++End Element: http://www.w3.org/1999/xhtmldiv
14/267+++End Prefix Mapping:
14/273+++Characters:

15/0+++Characters:
15/1+++End Element: http://purl.org/atom/ns#info
15/8++Characters:

16/0++Characters:
16/1++Start Prefix Mapping: :http://www.blogger.com/atom/ns#
16/1+++Start Element: http://www.blogger.com/atom/ns#convertLineBreaks,
➥0 attributes
16/60+++Characters: false
16/65+++End Element: http://www.blogger.com/atom/ns#convertLineBreaks
16/65++End Prefix Mapping:
16/85++Characters:
```

Listing 6.30 **Continued**

```
17/0++Characters:
17/1++Start Prefix Mapping: :http://purl.org/atom/ns#
17/1+++Start Element: http://purl.org/atom/ns#entry, 0 attributes
17/41+++Characters:

18/0+++Characters:
18/2++++Start Element: http://purl.org/atom/ns#link, 4 attributes
18/2++++Attribute List:
Key: href
 Value: https://www.blogger.com/atom/11574818/112343655183745944
Key: rel
 Value: service.edit
Key: title
 Value: African-American's Business Ownership is Growing Dramatically
Key: type
 Value: application/atom+xml
---
18/190++++End Element: http://purl.org/atom/ns#link
18/190+++Characters:

19/0+++Characters:
19/2++++Start Element: http://purl.org/atom/ns#author, 0 attributes
19/10++++Characters:

20/0++++Characters:
20/3+++++Start Element: http://purl.org/atom/ns#name, 0 attributes
20/9+++++Characters: Mark S. Choate
20/23+++++End Element: http://purl.org/atom/ns#name
20/30++++Characters:

21/0++++Characters:
21/2++++End Element: http://purl.org/atom/ns#author
21/11+++Characters:

22/0+++Characters:
22/2++++Start Element: http://purl.org/atom/ns#issued, 0 attributes
22/10++++Characters: 2005-08-07T13:38:00-04:00
22/35++++End Element: http://purl.org/atom/ns#issued
22/44+++Characters:

23/0+++Characters:
23/2++++Start Element: http://purl.org/atom/ns#modified, 0 attributes
23/12++++Characters: 2005-08-07T17:48:56Z
23/32++++End Element: http://purl.org/atom/ns#modified
23/43+++Characters:
```

Listing 6.30   **Continued**

```
24/0+++Characters:
24/2++++Start Element: http://purl.org/atom/ns#created, 0 attributes
24/11++++Characters: 2005-08-07T17:42:31Z
24/31++++End Element: http://purl.org/atom/ns#created
24/41+++Characters:

25/0+++Characters:
25/2++++Start Element: http://purl.org/atom/ns#link, 4 attributes
25/2++++Attribute List:
Key: href
 Value: http://choate.info/Blog/Business/2005/08/
➥african-americans-business-ownership.html
Key: rel
 Value: alternate
Key: title
 Value: African-American's Business Ownership is Growing Dramatically
Key: type
 Value: text/html
---
25/202++++End Element: http://purl.org/atom/ns#link
25/202+++Characters:

26/0+++Characters:
26/2++++Start Element: http://purl.org/atom/ns#id, 0 attributes
26/6++++Characters: tag:blogger.com,1999:blog-11574818.post-112343655183745944
26/64++++End Element: http://purl.org/atom/ns#id
26/69+++Characters:

27/0+++Characters:
27/2++++Start Element: http://purl.org/atom/ns#title, 2 attributes
27/2++++Attribute List:
Key: mode
 Value: escaped
Key: type
 Value: text/html
---
27/41++++Characters: African-American's Business Ownership is Growing Dramatically
27/102++++End Element: http://purl.org/atom/ns#title
27/110+++Characters:

28/0+++Characters:
28/2++++Start Element: http://purl.org/atom/ns#content, 3 attributes
28/2++++Attribute List:
Key: type
 Value: application/xhtml+xml
```

Listing 6.30 **Continued**

```
Key: http://www.w3.org/XML/1998/namespacebase
 Value: http://choate.info/Blog/Business/
Key: http://www.w3.org/XML/1998/namespacespace
 Value: preserve
---
28/106++++Characters:

29/0++++Characters:
29/3++++Start Prefix Mapping: :http://www.w3.org/1999/xhtml
29/3+++++Start Element: http://www.w3.org/1999/xhtmldiv, 0 attributes
29/45+++++Characters: According to a recent report from the Small Business
Administration,
➥there has been a 45% increase in the number of African-American owned businesses
since
➥1997. Likewise, Hispanic-owned businesses have increased by 31% and there has
also been a
➥20% increase in women-owned businesses during that same time period.
29/359+++++End Element: http://www.w3.org/1999/xhtmldiv
29/359++++End Prefix Mapping:
29/365++++Characters:

30/0++++Characters:
30/2++++End Element: http://purl.org/atom/ns#content
30/12+++Characters:

31/0+++Characters:
31/2+++Start Prefix Mapping: :http://purl.org/atom-blog/ns#
31/2++++Start Element: http://purl.org/atom-blog/ns#draft, 0 attributes
31/47++++Characters: false
31/52++++End Element: http://purl.org/atom-blog/ns#draft
31/52+++End Prefix Mapping:
31/60+++Characters:

32/0+++Characters:
32/1+++End Element: http://purl.org/atom/ns#entry
32/1++End Prefix Mapping:
32/9++Characters:

33/0++Characters:

34/0++Characters:
34/1++Start Prefix Mapping: :http://purl.org/atom/ns#
34/1+++Start Element: http://purl.org/atom/ns#entry, 0 attributes
34/41+++Characters:
```

Listing 6.30   **Continued**

```
35/0+++Characters:
35/2++++Start Element: http://purl.org/atom/ns#link, 4 attributes
35/2++++Attribute List:
Key: href
 Value: https://www.blogger.com/atom/11574818/111832600521939707
Key: rel
 Value: service.edit
Key: title
 Value: Economic downturns and new business growth
Key: type
 Value: application/atom+xml
---
35/171++++End Element: http://purl.org/atom/ns#link
35/171+++Characters:

36/0+++Characters:
36/2++++Start Element: http://purl.org/atom/ns#author, 0 attributes
36/10++++Characters:

37/0++++Characters:
37/3+++++Start Element: http://purl.org/atom/ns#name, 0 attributes
37/9+++++Characters: Mark S. Choate
37/23+++++End Element: http://purl.org/atom/ns#name
37/30++++Characters:

38/0++++Characters:
38/2++++End Element: http://purl.org/atom/ns#author
38/11+++Characters:

39/0+++Characters:
39/2++++Start Element: http://purl.org/atom/ns#issued, 0 attributes
39/10++++Characters: 2005-06-09T09:56:00-04:00
39/35++++End Element: http://purl.org/atom/ns#issued
39/44+++Characters:

40/0+++Characters:
40/2++++Start Element: http://purl.org/atom/ns#modified, 0 attributes
40/12++++Characters: 2005-06-09T14:14:54Z
40/32++++End Element: http://purl.org/atom/ns#modified
40/43+++Characters:

41/0+++Characters:
41/2++++Start Element: http://purl.org/atom/ns#created, 0 attributes
41/11++++Characters: 2005-06-09T14:06:45Z
41/31++++End Element: http://purl.org/atom/ns#created
41/41+++Characters:
```

Listing 6.30 **Continued**

```
42/0+++Characters:
42/2++++Start Element: http://purl.org/atom/ns#link, 4 attributes
42/2++++Attribute List:
Key: href
 Value: http://choate.info/Blog/Business/2005/06/economic-downturns-and-new-
➥business_09.html
Key: rel
 Value: alternate
Key: title
 Value: Economic downturns and new business growth
Key: type
 Value: text/html
---
42/185++++End Element: http://purl.org/atom/ns#link
42/185+++Characters:

43/0+++Characters:
43/2++++Start Element: http://purl.org/atom/ns#id, 0 attributes
43/6++++Characters: tag:blogger.com,1999:blog-11574818.post-111832600521939707
43/64++++End Element: http://purl.org/atom/ns#id
43/69+++Characters:

44/0+++Characters:
44/2++++Start Element: http://purl.org/atom/ns#title, 2 attributes
44/2++++Attribute List:
Key: mode
 Value: escaped
Key: type
 Value: text/html
---
44/41++++Characters: Economic downturns and new business growth
44/83++++End Element: http://purl.org/atom/ns#title
44/91+++Characters:

45/0+++Characters:
45/2++++Start Element: http://purl.org/atom/ns#content, 3 attributes
45/2++++Attribute List:
Key: type
 Value: application/xhtml+xml
Key: http://www.w3.org/XML/1998/namespacebase
 Value: http://choate.info/Blog/Business/
```

Listing 6.30   **Continued**

```
Key: http://www.w3.org/XML/1998/namespacespace
 Value: preserve
---
45/106++++Characters:


46/0++++Characters:
46/3++++Start Prefix Mapping: :http://www.w3.org/1999/xhtml
46/3+++++Start Element: http://www.w3.org/1999/xhtmldiv, 0 attributes
46/45+++++Characters: It's not uncommon for there to be an upswing in the creation
➥of new businesses in an economic downturn. One reason for this is that often
➥experienced professionals are laid off and receive good severance packages
➥which provides them the opportunity to start their own business. Growth in
➥sole-proprietorship has been on a steady increase since 2000, according to the
➥SBA and this may provide some support to the idea that businesses get started in
➥a downturn. And since small businesses represent upwards of 75% of all new job,
➥that's very good news.
46/596+++++Characters:


47/0+++++Characters:


48/0++++++Start Element: http://www.w3.org/1999/xhtmlspan, 1 attributes
48/0++++++Attribute List:
Key: class
 Value: fullpost
---
48/23++++++Characters: The numbers themselves are impressive. Income for sole pro-
prietors was $728.4 billion in 2000 and that figure has grown to $902.8 billion in
➥2004, a 19.3% increase. Bankruptcies are also at a lower rate than 2000, which
➥was the peak of the Internet bubble. Perhaps the most interesting figure in the
➥NFIB Business Optimism Index, which was 104.6 in 2004, and only 100.3 in 2000.
➥Small businesses appear to be doing better than they have in the last five
➥years, which indicates a strong, thriving economy despite the gloom often
➥distributed by the news media.
48/581++++++Characters:


49/0++++++Characters:


50/0++++++Characters: Source: SBA
50/12+++++++Start Element: http://www.w3.org/1999/xhtmli, 0 attributes
50/15+++++++Characters: The Small Business Advocate
50/42+++++++End Element: http://www.w3.org/1999/xhtmli
50/46++++++Characters: , Vol. 24, No. 6
```

Listing 6.30   **Continued**

```
50/62++++++End Element: http://www.w3.org/1999/xhtmlspan
50/69+++++Characters:

51/0+++++Characters:
51/3+++++End Element: http://www.w3.org/1999/xhtmldiv
51/3++++End Prefix Mapping:
51/9++++Characters:

52/0++++Characters:
52/2++++End Element: http://purl.org/atom/ns#content
52/12+++Characters:

53/0+++Characters:
53/2+++Start Prefix Mapping: :http://purl.org/atom-blog/ns#
53/2++++Start Element: http://purl.org/atom-blog/ns#draft, 0 attributes
53/47++++Characters: false
53/52++++End Element: http://purl.org/atom-blog/ns#draft
53/52+++End Prefix Mapping:
53/60+++Characters:

54/0++End Element: http://purl.org/atom/ns#feed
54/0+End Prefix Mapping:
55/0+End Document
```

State Management with XMLReader

As you can see from the previous example, **XMLReaders** fire events in succession. In some RSS formats, there is a channel element, and each channel has a title element. The channel also has various items, and each item has a title element. The question then becomes, when using XmlReader, how do you distinguish between different titles? Earlier, I showed how using namespaces can help you distinguish between an Atom title versus an RSS1.0 title, but that doesn't help you to distinguish channel and item titles because the distinguishing characteristic is the context in which the title appears. If it is inside a channel element, it's a channel title. If it's inside an item element, it's an item title.

The answer to this problem is that you have to come up with a means of tracking your state. You need to know how to tell where you are in a document so that you can take the appropriate action. I am going to show you two examples of how to approach this. The first is the simplest of the two, and it tracks your current path in a document so that you can easily find out whether this title applies to a channel or an item.

The class keeps track of the elements that have been processed so that you can check the getState method to get the current path, which will be something like

```
channel/title
```

or

```
channel/item/title
```

This will help you know where you are in the parsing process. It works better if you are not expanding namespaces, simply because that helps keep the paths to a reasonable level. You also have the option of tracking attributes as well, and there are a few parameters that can be set that change how this works. Read the comments for more specific details of how this is accomplished.

Listing 6.31   **Class mwXmlReader**

```
// These constants determine how attributes are tracked:
// The path should only contain elements names
Constant kNameOnly = 0
// The path should also contain one attribute, like:
// channel/item[id=4]/title
// You will need to
Constant kNameAndOneAttribute = 1
Constant kNameAndAllAttributes = 2

// Apply one of the class constants to determine
// how you will handle tracking attributes
Property incrStyle as Integer

// The name of the attribute whose value
// your application will place in the path.
// Used with kNameAndOneAttribute style
Property attrName as String

// The state is maintained by an array.
// "Join" is used to create the path when
// it is requested
Property state(-1) as String

// The current depth of the hierarchy
Property depth as Integer

// Helper properties
Property prevState as String
Property inStartElement as Boolean
```

Listing 6.32   **Sub StartElement(name as String, attributeList as XmlAttributeList) Handles Event**

```
//Increment state and append path data whenever
// a StartElement is fired.
incrState name, attributeList
// Fire the StartElement event so that
// Subclasses are instances can use it.
StartElement name, attributeList
```

Listing 6.33   **Sub EndElement(name as String) Handles Event**

```
// Decrement state
decrState
// Fire the EndElement event
EndElement name
```

Listing 6.34   **Function getState() As String**

```
// Return the path that represents the current state.
If ubound(Me.state) > -1 Then
    Return Join(Me.state, "/")
End if
```

Listing 6.35   **Sub decrState()**

```
// Lower depth count
Me.depth = Me.depth - 1
Me.inStartElement = False
prevState = Me.state.pop
```

Listing 6.36   **Sub incrState(aName as String, anAttr as String)**

```
// Method that is called when only one attribute
// is being tracked.
Me.State.append(aName + "["+ anAttr+"]")
```

Listing 6.37   **Sub incrState(aName as string)**

```
// Method called when incrStyle = kNameOnly
Me.state.Append(aName)
```

Listing 6.38   **Sub incrState(aName as string, attr_list as XmlAttributeList)**

```
// Method called from StartElement
// It calls overridden methods based upon the value
// assigned to incrStyle

Me.depth = Me.depth + 1
Me.inStartElement = True

Select Case incrStyle
    Case kNameOnly
        incrState(aName)
    Case kNameAndOneAttribute
        incrState(aName, attr_list.Value(attrName))
    Case kNameAndAllAttributes
        Me.state.appEnd(aName + "[" _
        + attrToString(attr_list) + "]")
End select
```

Listing 6.39   **Function attrToString(attr_list as XMLAttributeList) As string**

```
// Convert attribute key/values into a String
// to be used in the path, similar to that used
// by XPATH
Dim x,y as Integer
Dim s as String

y = attr_list.Count - 1

For x = 0 to y
    s = s+ " "
    s = s + attr_list.key(x) + "=" + chr(34) // "
    s = s + attr_list.value(x) + chr(34) //"
Next
Return s
```

Listing 6.40   **Sub setStateTrackingStyle(aStyle as integer)**

```
incrStyle = aStyle
```

Listing 6.41   **Sub setStateTrackingStyle(aStyle as integer, aName as string)**

```
If aStyle = kNameAndOneAttribute Then
    incrStyle = aStyle
    attrName = aName
Else
    incrStyle = kNameAndAllAttributes
End if
```

You must also declare new events for StartElement and EndElement so that any subclasses of this class will have access to those events. This also means you'll be able to drag this class onto a **Window** and implement code for the events that way.

Now this class can be used as the parent class to any **XmlReader** object, and you can use these methods to make it easier to maintain state. In the next section, I will subclass **XmlReader** and write a class that instantiates **Group** and **Item** classes from data in an Atom file. This will give you a practical example of how to use the features I just implemented in **mwXmlReader**, and show you how you can easily instantiate objects using **mwXmlReader** by adding a stack to assist with managing your state.

There is one thing to be aware of that impacts how **mwXmlReader** is used and subclassed. **mwXmlReader** is a subclass of **XmlReader** and there are two Constructors for **XMLReader**. If the default Constructor is used, **XMLReader** does not expand namespaces. However, if the other Constructor is used, it does expand namespaces. Either way, the point is that the Constructor being used impacts how the instance of the class works. Because of this, you need to be careful when subclassing **XMLReader**.

In the next section, I am going to subclass **mwXmlReader** and add another layer of functionality. In an earlier attempt at doing this, I implemented a Constructor that took no parameters, but set a few internal properties when **mwXmlReader** was launched. Then I created the **mwXmlReader** subclass call **rssXmlReader**, and it had its own **Constructor** that set a few properties. When I tried to use it I would get strange errors—the program would crash without warning or error message, and even the debugger acted funny.

The problem, of course, was with the Constructors. The solution I eventually took is that I didn't override any of **XMLReaders** Constructors, and all the problems magically went away. Another way to avoid that kind of problem is to make sure that the Constructor calls Super.Constructor() so that the Constructor of the parent class is called. It's painfully obvious now, but what I was doing was overriding the Constructor of **XMLReader** so that it was never getting called, and this made it totally nonfunctional.

XML and Object Instantiation

In this section, I am going to subclass **mwXmlReader** and use the new subclass to parse an Atom file into an object tree, consisting of **Groups** and **Items**, both of which are subclasses of **mwNode** introduced in the previous chapter. This illustrates an important distinction between the SAX-like **XMLReader** class and the DOM-like **XMLDocument** class. If you have an XML file that needs to get transformed into another XML format, use **XMLDocument** and XSLT. If, however, the XML is going to be used to instantiate objects, **XMLReader** is often the better choice (not always, though).

To parse the XML file and instantiate objects, I need to create some objects. I use a set of classes that subclass **mwNode**. I use **mwNode** subclasses because **mwNode** is good at representing treelike data structures, and XML is a treelike data structure. Also, because I have already implemented a **ListBox** that will view **mwNode** objects, it will be an easy step to take an XML document, use it to create a tree of **mwNode** objects, and then display it in a **ListBox**.

Whether I am using an RSS XML file of some sort, or an Atom file, they all have a common structure. With RSS, there is a channel, and this channel contains a number of items, which are the links and summaries to articles. With Atom, there is a feed, and this feed contains a number of entries, which are links and summaries to articles. That means channels and feeds are branch nodes, and items and entries are leaf nodes. At the same time, there is a lot of similarity between the branches and the leaves. They all have links and they all have titles, for example. This will get translated into three subclasses. The **Group** subclass represents branches (channels and feeds) and the Item subgroup represents the leaves (items and entries). Both share a common **Super** class, **Meme**, that implements common functionality and subclasses **mwNode**.

The **Meme** class is pretty self-explanatory. It consists of a collection of properties that are relevant to the object model and implements a series of getter and setter methods (which could be implemented as a Computed Property, now that REALbasic has that feature).

The implementations of **Groups** and **Items** comes next. The interesting elements are the Constructors and the toXML function that creates an XML version of the objects themselves using the **XMLDocument** class. The comments explain what is taking place.

Listing 6.42 **Class Meme Inherits mwNode**

```
Property Guid as string
Property Title as string
Property ParentGuid as string
Property Description as String
Property Creator as String
Property CreationDate as string
Property ModIfiedDate as string
Property MetaID as string
```

Listing 6.43 **Sub Meme.setTitle(aTitle as String)**

```
Me.Title = aTitle
```

Listing 6.44 **Sub Meme.setDescription(aDescription as String)**

```
Me.Description = aDescription
```

Listing 6.45   **Sub Meme.setParent(aParentGuid as String)**

```
Me.ParentGuid = aParentGuid
```

Listing 6.46   **Sub Meme.setAncestor(aAncestorGuid as String)**

```
Me.Ancestor=aAncestorGuid
```

Listing 6.47   **Sub Meme.setCreationDate(tstamp as String)**

```
// expects sql date time
Me.CreationDate = tstamp
```

Listing 6.48   **Sub Meme.setModIfiedDate(tstamp as String)**

```
Me.ModIfiedDate = tstamp
```

Listing 6.49   **Sub Meme.setCreator(aName as String)**

```
Me.Creator = aName
```

Listing 6.50   **Sub Meme.setGuid(aGuid as String)**

```
If right(aGuid, 1) <> "/" Then
aGuid = aGuid + "/"
End If
Me.Guid = aGuid
```

Listing 6.51   **Sub Meme.setMetaID(aMetaID as String)**

```
Me.MetaID = aMetaID
```

Listing 6.52   **Function Meme.getCreationDate() As String**

```
Return Me.CreationDate
```

Listing 6.53   **Function Meme.getCreator() As String**

```
Return Me.Creator
```

Listing 6.54   **Function Meme.getParent() As String**

```
Return Me.ParentGuid
```

Listing 6.55   **Function Meme.getDescription() As String**

```
Return Me.Description
```

Listing 6.56   **Function Meme.getGuid() As String**

```
If right(Me.Guid, 1) <> "/" Then
Me.Guid = Me.Guid + "/"
End If
Return Me.Guid
```

Listing 6.57   **Function Meme.getMetaID() As String**

```
Return Me.MetaID
```

Listing 6.58   **Function Meme.getModifiedDate() As String**

```
Return Me.ModifiedDate
```

Listing 6.59   **Function Meme.getTitle() As String**

```
Return Me.Title
```

Listing 6.60   **Sub Meme.setCreationDate(d as Date)**

```
dim s as string
If d<>nil Then
Me.CreationDate = d.sqLDatetime
Else
d = New date
Me.creationDate = d.sqLDateTime
End If
```

Listing 6.61   **Sub Meme.setModIfiedDate(d as Date)**

```
dim s as string
If d<>nil Then
Me.modIfiedDate = d.sqLDatetime
```

Listing 6.61 **Continued**

```
Else
d = New date
Me.modIfiedDate = d.sqLDateTime
End If
```

Listing 6.62 **Function Meme.isValid() As Boolean**

```
dim mErr as MemeException

If Me.Title = "" Then
mErr = New MemeException
raise mErr

End If

If Me.MetaID="" Then
mErr = New MemeException
raise mErr
End If

If Me.Guid = "" Then
mErr = New MemeException
raise mErr
End If

If Me.Type= kUNDEFINED Then
mErr = New MemeException
raise mErr
End If

Return true
```

Listing 6.63 **Sub Meme.setParent(aParent as mwNode)**

```
If aParent <> nil Then
    Me.Parent = aParent
    If aParent isa Group Then
        Me.setParent(Group(aParent).getGuid)
    End If
End If
```

Listing 6.64   **Class Group Inherits Meme**

```
Property Sequence As mwNodeSequence
```

Listing 6.65   **Sub Group.Constructor()**

```
// The original mwNode class established that branch
// nodes had a Type property of -1 and that a leaf node
// had a Type property of 1. This value is set in the
// constructor as well as the creation and modified time
// The Sequence property is instantiated as well and
// this defines the sequence of child elements and
// provides methods for accessing them.
Dim d as New Date

Me.SetType(-1)
Me.setCreationDate(d.SQLDateTime)
Me.setModIfiedDate(d.SQLDateTime)
Me.Sequence = New mwNodeSequence
```

Listing 6.66   **Function Group.toXml(includeChildren as Boolean) as XMLDocument**

```
// XMLDocument is used to create an XML representation of
// this class.
Dim xml_doc as XMLDocument
Dim mxml as XmlNode
Dim seq as XmlNode
Dim tmp as XmlNode
Dim ele_name as string
Dim mex as MemeException
Dim x,y as integer

xml_doc = new XMLDocument
ele_name = "Group"

// The "Root" element will be "Group". The element is
// created by using the XMLDocument factory method CreateElement
// and a reference to the "Group" element is assigned to mxml
mxml = xml_doc.AppendChild(xml_doc.CreateElement(ele_name))
If mxml <> Nil Then
    // The Group element attributes are set using
    // values from the Group object using the
    // XMLElement SetAttribute method
    mxml.SetAttribute("MetaID", me.getMetaID)
      mxml.SetAttribute("Guid", me.getGuid)
      mxml.SetAttribute("Title", me.getTitle)
```

Listing 6.66 **Continued**

```
mxml.SetAttribute("Creator", me.getCreator)
mxml.SetAttribute("Description", me.getDescription)
mxml.SetAttribute("CreationDate", me.getCreationDate)
mxml.SetAttribute("ModifiedDate", me.getModifiedDate)
mxml.SetAttribute("Parent", me.getParent)
mxml.SetAttribute("Ancestor", me.getAncestor)
mxml.SetAttribute("Type", str(me.getType))


If includeChildren Then
  // A child element called "Sequence"
  // is added to the XML document.
    seq = mxml.AppendChild(xml_doc.CreateElement("Sequence")
  // The children are called sequentially
  // and their toXml method is called
  y = Me.Sequence.GetChildCount - 1
  For x = 0 to y
  tmp = Me.Sequence.Child(x).toXml()
  // Since the toXml() method creates and returns
  // an XMLDocument object, you will need to import
  // the returned documents nodes into the parent
  // document. The following line imports the root
  // element, referenced by the DocumentElement
  // property, into the xml_doc XMLDocument.
  seq.Append(xml_doc.importNode(tmp.DocumentElement, true))
  Next
  End If


// This document is returned. If it was called
// from a parent Group, then the xml_doc.DocumentElement
// node and subnodes will be imported into that parent
// Group's XML document and so on until one large document
// exists representing every node in the tree.
  Return xml_doc
Else
  mex = new MemeException
  mex.Message="Error creating XML"
  raise mex
End If
```

Listing 6.67 **Class Item Inherits Meme**

```
Property Sequence As mwNodeSequence
```

Listing 6.68   **Sub Item.Constructor()**

```
// See Group
Dim d as New Date

Me.SetType(1)
Me.setCreationDate(d.SQLDateTime)
Me.setModIfiedDate(d.SQLDateTime)
Me.Sequence = New mwNodeSequence
```

Listing 6.69   **Sub Item.toXml(includeItemSequence as Boolean) as XMLDocument**

```
Dim xml_doc as XMLDocument
Dim mxml as XmlNode
Dim ele_name as string
Dim mex as MemeException

xml_doc = new XMLDocument
ele_name = "Item"

mxml = xml_doc.AppendChild(xml_doc.CreateElement(ele_name))
If mxml <> Nil Then

    mxml.SetAttribute("MetaID", me.getMetaID)
      mxml.SetAttribute("Guid", me.getGuid)
      mxml.SetAttribute("Title", me.getTitle)
      mxml.SetAttribute("Creator", me.getCreator)
      mxml.SetAttribute("Description", me.getDescription)
      mxml.SetAttribute("CreationDate", me.getCreationDate)
      mxml.SetAttribute("ModifiedDate", me.getModifiedDate)
      mxml.SetAttribute("Parent", me.getParent)
      mxml.SetAttribute("Ancestor", me.getAncestor)
      mxml.SetAttribute("Type", str(me.getType))
    Return xml_doc
 Else
    mex = new MemeException
    mex.Message="Error creating XML"
    raise mex

End If
```

Listing 6.70 **Class mwNodeSequence**

```
// This class manages the sequence of child nodes.
// It has two properties, an array of mwNodes and
// a dictionary. This is probably overkill for RSS
// documents since they are not very large, but
// with much larger works, this can help to find
// child elements quickly. The child array represents
// the sequence of child nodes. The dict property lets
// you look up each node by Guid without having to
// scan each node sequentially.
Property child(-1) As mwNode
Property dict as Dictionary
```

Listing 6.71 **Sub mwNodeSequence.Constructor()**

```
dict = New Dictionary()
```

Listing 6.72 **Sub mwNodeSequence.appendChild(aNode as mwNode)**

```
If aNode Isa Meme Then
    If not(aNode is nil) Then
        Me.child.append(aNode)
        If dict = Nil Then
            dict = New Dictionary
        End If
        dict.value(Meme(aNode).getGuid) = aNode
    End If
End If
```

Listing 6.73 **Function mwNodeSequence.getChild(pos as integer) As mwNode**

```
If pos >= 0  and pos <= ubound(Me.child) Then
    Return child(pos)
Else
    Return Nil
End If
```

Listing 6.74 **Function mwNodeSequence.getChildCount() As Integer**

```
Return ubound(Me.child) + 1
```

Listing 6.75   **Function mwNodeSequence.getChildren() As mwNode()**

```
Return child
```

Listing 6.76   **Function mwNodeSequence.getLastChild() As mwNode**

```
Return Me.child(ubound(child))
```

Listing 6.77   **Sub mwNodeSequence.insertChild(pos as integer, aNode as mwNode)**

```
Dim bound as Integer
bound = ubound(Child)

If aNode Isa Meme Then
    If Not(aNode  Is Nil) Then
        If pos <= bound Then
        Me.child.insert(pos, aNode )
    Else
        Me.child.appEnd(aNode)
    End If

    If dict = Nil Then
        dict = New Dictionary
    End If

    dict.value(Meme(aNode).getGuid) = aNode

    End If
End If
```

Listing 6.78   **Function mwNodeSequence.hasChild(aGuid as string) As Boolean**

```
If Me.dict.HasKey(aGuid) Then
    If Me.dict.value(aGuid) <> nil Then
        Return true
    Else
        Return false
    End If
Else
    Return false
End If
```

Listing 6.79 **Function mwNodeSequence.getChild(aGuid as string) As mwNode**

```
If dict.HasKey(aGuid) Then
    Return dict.value(aGuid)
Else
    Return nil
End If
```

Listing 6.80 **Sub mwNodeSequence.removeChild(aNode as mwNode)**

```
Dim res as Integer
res = Me.child.IndexOf(aNode)
If res > -1 Then
    Me.child.Remove(res)
End If
```

Listing 6.81 **Sub mwNodeSequence.removeChild(pos as Integer)**

```
If pos > -1 Then
    Me.child.Remove(pos)
End If
```

Listing 6.82 **Class rssXmlReader Inherits mwXmlReader**

```
//The rssXmlReader class parses Atom files
// and instantiates Group and Item objects.
// It subclasses mwXMLReader, which helps it
// to track it's current state, plus it implements
// a stack to make managing state even easier.
// A stack is a data structure that is "Last in First Out".
// When a new feed or entry element is encountered,
// a Group or Item will be instantiated and "pushed" onto
// the stack. The object at the top of the stack is the
// current object and the other methods all call the current
// object. When the EndElement event for a feed or entry
// element is encountered, then the current object is popped
// off of the stack so that the object that was below it in
// the stack is now the current object.
Property Root As mwNode
Property Stack(-1) As Meme
Property CurrentElement As String
```

Listing 6.83   **Sub rss.XmlReader.StartElement(name as string, attributeList as xmlAttributeList) Handles Event**

```
Dim path as String
Dim aNode as mwNode
Dim aMeme as Meme

Me.CurrentElement = name
// Get the current path, inherited from mwXmlReader
path = Me.GetState
If path <> "" Then
    Select Case path
    Case "feed"
        // The Push method instantiates a Group
        // and pushes it onto the stack.
        aNode = Push(name, attributeList)
    Case "feed/entry"
        // In this case, the Push method instantiats an Item
        // and pushes it on the stack.
        aNode = Push(name, attributeList)
    Else
        If name = "link" Then
        // Both Feeds and Entries have links, but because I
        // am using a stack, it doesn't matter to me whether
        // the current element is a feed or an entry. All I
        // I need to do is access the object at the top of
        // of the stack and call the setGuid method, which
        // is where the link URL will be stored.
            If UBound(Stack) > -1 Then
                aMeme = Stack(UBound(Stack))
            aMeMe.setGuid(attributeList.Value("href"))
            End If
        End If
    End Select
End If

Exception err
    break
```

Listing 6.84   **Sub rss.XmlReader.EndElement(name as string) Handles Event**

```
// Pop the objects off the stack.
Select Case name
Case "feed"
    Pop
Case "entry"
```

Listing 6.84 **Continued**

```
    Pop
End Select


Exception err
    break
```

Listing 6.85 **Sub rss.XmlReader.Characters(s as String) Handles Event**

```
// Once again, because of the stack I do not
// have to keep track in this method which
// element I am in. All I need to do is reference
// the current object that is at the top of the stack
// and call the appropriate methods. This is why
// Groups and Items are both subclasses of Meme and why
// Meme implements the methods that get or set properties.
If Trim(s) <> "" Then
    If uBound(Stack) > -1 Then
    Select Case Me.CurrentElement
    Case "title"
        Stack(UBound(Stack)).setTitle(s)
    Case "id"
        Stack(UBound(Stack)).setMetaID(s)
    Case "div"
        Stack(UBound(Stack)).setDescription(s)
    Case "name"
        Stack(UBound(Stack)).setCreator(s)
    Case "modified"
        Stack(UBound(Stack)).setModIfiedDate(s)
    Case "created"
        Stack(UBound(Stack)).setCreationDate(s)
    End Select
    End If
End If
```

Listing 6.86 **Function rss.XmlReader.Push(aName as String, aList as XmlAttributeList) As mwNode**

```
Dim g as Group
Dim i as Item
Dim path as String

path = Me.getState
// Instantiate a Group or an Item based on the current state
```

Listing 6.86   **Continued**

```
If path  = "feed" Then

    g = New Group
    g.Name = aName
    // If this is the first object, then assign
    // a reference to the Root object and then
    // add it to the stack.
    // Once the document is parsed, you can access the
    // objects through the Root property.
    If ubound(Stack) = -1 Then
        Me.Root = g
        Me.Stack.appEnd(g)
    Else
    // Get a reference to the object at the top of
    // the stack and append the new object to it.
    Group(Me.Stack(ubound(Stack))).Sequence.AppEndChild(g)
    // Once you have appended the object to the parent object,
    // place the new object on the stack.
        Me.Stack.appEnd(g)
    End If

    Return g
ElseIf path  = "feed/entry" Then

    i = New Item
    i.Name = aName
    g = Group(Me.Stack(ubound(Stack)))
    i.setParent(g.GetGuid)
    If ubound(Stack) = -1 Then
        Me.Root = i
        Me.Stack.appEnd(i)
    Else
        g.Sequence.AppEndChild(i)
        Me.Stack.appEnd(i)
    End If

    Return i
End If
```

Listing 6.87   **Sub rss.XmlReader.Pop()**

```
// Remove the last object that was appended to the array
If Ubound(Stack) > -1 Then
    Stack.Remove(Ubound(Stack))
End If
```

Now you have seen a few examples of how to read and manipulate XML documents. In the next section I cover regular expressions, which are used to find patterns of text in any kind of document.

Regular Expressions

REALbasic used the Perl Compatible Regular Expression (PCRE) library, which is open source and the library used by many other programming and scripting languages, such as Python and PHP. This is good because if you are familiar with regular expressions using those languages, working with them in REALbasic should be very familiar to you.

If you are new to regular expressions and would like to know what exactly a regular expression is, I'll explain that first and then move on to some examples of how to use it. Regular expressions are used to identify patterns in strings of text and, in some cases, to replace one pattern with another.

You describe patterns of text using a series of characters that have special meaning in this context. You can download sample applications on the REALbasic website (http://realsoftware.com/), and one of the sample applications lets you test regular expressions. The application is called Regular Expressions. It is an excellent tool to use whenever you need to use a regular expression, because you do not want to be testing them within your application. They are notoriously difficult to get right, especially with complex pattern requirements, so you want to focus on the expression first, and then include it in whichever application you are working on. I used it to test the regular expressions I use as examples in this section.

There are special identifiers for individual characters. (When using regular expressions, you will see a lot of \, which is called an escape and which lets the regular expression engine know that the following letter has a special meaning, rather than being a literal representation of the letter.) Here are the references to specific letters:

\t	Tab
\n	newline
\r	return(CR)
\f	form feed
\a	alarm (bell)
\e	escape
\octal	3-digit octal character
\x*hex*	2-digit hexadecimal (the letters \x followed by two hexadecimal characters)
\x{hex}	Any number of digits hexadecimal

There is another group of identifiers that refer to classes of characters:

\w	"word" character (alphanumeric plus "_")
\W	non-"word" character
\s	Whitespace character
\S	nonwhitespace character
\d	digit character
\D	nondigit character

Although there are more identifiers you can use, this is enough to get started. The next step is to combine these characters into a sequence that represents the pattern you are looking for. This can be a combination of literal characters, plus any of the above classes.

Suppose you wanted to identify phone numbers that are listed throughout a document, so you want to create a regular expression that would match against a pattern like this:

```
(800) 555-1212
```

Your first attempt might look something like this:

```
(\d\d\d)\s\d\d\d-\d\d\d\d
```

If you tried to use it, you would find that it didn't work right. The change you need to make relates to the parentheses. They have special meaning in regular expressions, so you need to escape them. You can update this expression accordingly:

```
\(\d\d\d\)\s\d\d\d-\d\d\d\d
```

You can now find phone numbers, but only if they are formatted exactly like the preceding phone number. In real life, things are never formatted that consistently, and being able to accommodate that kind of formatting fluctuations is where regular expressions become very powerful.

Before I add additional characters to your repertoire, I want to modify the regular expression I just shared with you. Let's say you wanted to find all the "800" numbers that were in a particular document. To do that, you can use the literal values for 800, along with the other expressions, like so:

```
\(800\)\s\d\d\d-\d\d\d\d
```

Now I want to move on and identify ways of making this regular expression more flexible and accommodating of the various formats that you will likely encounter. First, I'll make a list of ways that I might find phone numbers formatted in a particular document:

```
(800) 555-1212
(800)555-1212
```

There are a lot of potential variations, but this identifies two. The difference between the two is that the first has an extra space. To figure out how to match this, you'll need some additional tools:

*	Match 0 or more times
+	Match 1 or more times
?	Match 1 or 0 times
{n}	Match exactly n times
{n,}	Match at least n times
{n,m}	Match at least n but not more than m times

The preceding elements let you specify how many times in sequence a particular character should be. Not only will this help to handle the space that may or may not exist, it can also make the regular expression itself much more compact.

```
\(\d{3}\)\s?\d{3}-\d{4}
```

Instead of using \d for every character that's a digit, I was able to specify how many digits should appear in sequence. For the space character \s, I specified that there should be zero or one space in that location, meaning that both examples will match.

Thus far, I have looked at expressions that match individual characters and classes of characters, as well as expressions that determine the number of times in sequence the matching character or character class should appear. You can also group characters, define your own character classes, and specify alternatives, which is like saying match this class *or* that class. The characters used to define these expressions are as follows:

()	Grouping
[]	Character class
|	Alternation (OR)

Grouping is most important when it comes to replacing text, because when you search against the text and get a match, the match is defined in terms of the groups you have defined. Using the same regular expression I was using before, I will now group it:

```
\((\d{3})\)\s?(\d{3})-(\d{4})
```

I have created three groups. Now you can see why I had to escape the original parentheses; it's because regular expressions use parentheses to define groups. For it to understand that I mean the actual parenthesis character (, I precede it with \. Every group you define is assigned to a variable that's called a backreference, and that represents the subexpression matched and that is identified by a number, preceded by \ or a $. Suppose we use the preceding regular expression to search for the phone number I've used in the examples. There will be four subexpressions that compose the match. (You will see more of this when I review the **RegExMatch** class in more detail.)

The following table pairs the subexpression match number with the characters that are matched:

\0	(800) 555-1212
\1	800
\2	555
\3	1212

I can also use grouping to match a sequence of characters and to treat that sequence of characters as a single unit. For example, suppose I want to search through some text to see if I can find instances of a particular word that repeats itself. I can use regular expressions to find them, like this:

```
(the){2}
```

This expression will find instances of "thethe" in the text. Note how the {2} applies to the group, not simply the preceding character.

You can also define your own classes of characters by enclosing them in brackets. You can list individual characters:

```
[aeiou]
```

In that example, I've created a class that matches vowels. If I want a class that matches consonants, I could write out a list of consonants, or I can negate the previous list:

```
[^aeiou]
```

That class means any character that is not a, e, i, o, or u, which technically isn't the same as a consonant because it includes digits and other numbers. So I should modify it to read:

```
[^aeiou\W]
```

This class will not match any vowels or any nonword characters. Word characters are all the letters of the alphabet, plus the underscore (_). Now, if I really want to write a long, hard-to-read class, I can decide to create one that matches all punctuation characters. You will see that a number of them are escaped to account for the fact that they are characters used in constructing regular expressions:

```
[\!"#\$%&'()\*\+,\-\./:;<=>\?@\[\\\]\^`{\|}\~]
```

A character class matches against one character, by default, but you can use the standard modifiers to make it match more than one in a row. Here's a regular expression that matches two consecutive punctuation marks:

```
[\!"#\$%&'()\*\+,\-\./:;<=>\?@\[\\\]\^`{\|}\~]{2}
```

You can also use the alternation character | to identify "or" conditions where you want to match either this or that character, so to speak. Consider this:

```
John|Jack
```

This expression matches either John or Jack. The following expression searches for paragraphs that start with a digit ranging from 1 through 6:

```
"^(1|2|3|4|5|6)\s(.*)\n\n"
```

In this example, note that I grouped the sequence of alternations, which you often need to do to get it to work right. You might also notice the use of ".", which matches any character and has yet to be discussed. This is one that you will use often:

.   Match any character except newline. You can match newlines as well if by configuring RegExOptions.

There are many occasions when you want to match a sequence of characters, regardless of what they are, until you reach a particular string of characters. A good example is XML, where there are elements that surround a lot of text:

```
<p>This is a paragraph.</p>
```

In this case, suppose you want to get the text that sits between the two paragraph tags. A regular expression that can do that for you, as follows:

```
<p>(.*)</p>
```

That's simple enough, but what if you have a document full of paragraphs, like so:

```
<p>This is paragraph one</p>
<p>This is paragraph two</p>
```

In the previous example, subexpression one ("\1") would reference the string:

```
This is a paragraph.
```

However, in the second example, it would reference

```
 This is paragraph one</p>
<p>This is paragraph two
```

The reason for this is that the "." matches all characters except for newline, and the regular expression says to find `<p>` and match any character zero or more times, and then terminate the match at the appearance of `</p>`. The regular expression engine is, by default, greedy, which means that it is going to find the longest valid match possible, but this is not always what you want, so you can specify the expression's or subexpression's greediness. There is an option you can set in the RegExOptions class, but you can also write the regular expression itself to do so, which often gives you much more fine-grained control over which parts of the expression you want to be greedy. The non-greedy version of the previous regular expression is this:

```
<p>(.*)?</p>
```

The question mark reverses the greediness of the entire expression, and in this instance means that it will find the shortest match, which is exactly what you are looking for. The first search will match the text of paragraph one, and the second search will match the text of paragraph two.

There are some characters that create what are known as *zero-width matches*. In other words, they match something, but it's not a character that will show up in the match string. The following is a list of such items.

^	Match the beginning of the line.
$	Match the end of the line (or before newline at the end).
\b	Match a word boundary.
\B	Match a non-(word boundary).
\A	Match only at beginning of string.
\Z	Match only at end of string, or before newline at the end.
\z	Match only at end of string.

A simple example is to create a regular expression that looks for paragraphs or strings that start with the word "The." It would look like this:

```
^The.*
```

The ^ matches the beginning of the line, but there is no character that is actually matched. Likewise, \b matches a word boundary, which is not a character but a position between characters.

There are also a group of POSIX character classes that you can reference using the following notation:

```
[:alpha:]
```

In practice, you would use it in a regular expression like this:

```
[[:cntrl:]]+
```

This expression searches for instances of one or more control characters in a given **String**. Following is a list of all the POSIX classes that PCRE supports. In my testing, all worked in REALbasic except for [:blank:], which raised an error when used.

alnum	Letters and digits.
alpha	Letters.
ascii	ASCII characters with code points between 0–127.
blank	Space or tab only; This POSIX class was not recognized, maybe because it's a GNU extension.
cntrl	Control characters.
digit	Digits (same as \d).
print	Printing characters, including space.
graph	Printing characters, excluding space.
punct	Printing characters, excluding letters and digits.
lower	Lowercase letters.
upper	Uppercase letters.

spacc	Whitespace, which includes Chr(9), Chr(10), Chr(11), Chr(12), Chr(13), and Chr(32). Although this is similar to \s, note that \s does not include Chr(11).
word	"Word" characters (same as \w).
xdigit	Hexadecimal digits.

In more complex regular expressions, there are times when you will need to group characters, but do not want to create a backreference to them. You have already encountered zero-width matches, such as ^, but those matches didn't take up any space because of the nature of the kind of match that they were. If I just want to match a group, but avoid creating any backreferences, I use the following syntax:

(?:expression)	Group with no backreferences
(?=expression)	Zero-width positive lookahead
(?!expression)	Zero-width negative lookahead
(?<=expression)	Zero-width positive lookbehind
(?<!expression)	Zero-width negative lookbehind

The first item in the table is a way to group characters without creating a backreference. The following four items seem to me to be more functional because they are designed to solve a common problem, which is to find a match of a certain pattern, as long as it doesn't precede or follow after a particular pattern. Suppose I want to identify URLs in an HTML document that only appear in character text, and that are not part of an actual link. I would want to match the URL in this sentence:

```
<p>This is a sentence that refers to a site: http://google.com/</p>
```

But I do not want to match the URL in this one:

```
<p>I like to visit <a href="http://google.com/">google</a></p>
```

Here is one approach to solving this problem using a zero-width negative lookbehind:

```
(?<!href=")(http://.*/)
```

Using this regular expression, the URL will be matched only when not preceded by `href="`

To do the opposite and match only URLs that are part of anchors, do this:

```
(?<=href=")(http://.*/)
```

There is a lot to be said about how to construct regular expressions—more than I can say here. The language reference is a good place to look, as well, but because REALbasic's **RegEx** class is based on an open source library, there is also a lot of information available online that goes into much greater detail. You can start your search at the PCRE web page: http://www.pcre.org/. Next, I'll take a look at the regular expression classes that are part of REALbasic.

RegEx Class

RegEx is the central class you will use when working with regular expressions. There are two things you can do with regular expressions: search for a pattern and replace a string that matches a pattern with a different pattern. Hence, the two **RegEx** properties: `SearchPattern` and `ReplacementPattern`:

```
RegEx.SearchPattern as String
RegEx.ReplacementPattern as String
```

The `SearchStartPosition` property determines where in the `string` the search will begin. By default, this value is zero.

```
RegEx.SearchStartPosition as Integer
```

The **RegEx** class has a property called `Options`, which is an instance of the **RegExOptions** class. You use this class to set a number of parameters that affect the way matches are made.

```
RegEx.Options as RegExOptions
```

I will discuss the **RegExOptions** class separately.

The **RegEx** class has two methods, `Search` and `Replace`, which you typically use to perform searches on a `string`.

```
RegEx.Replace([TargetString as String],[SearchStartPosition as Integer]) as String
RegEx.Search([TargetString as String],[SearchStartPosition as Integer])
➥as RegExMatch
```

The parameters used with `Replace` and `Search` are optional, which at first glance may not make much sense. If you are searching for a pattern within a `string`, which is what the `TargetString` parameter specifies, how can the `TargetString` be optional? The answer is that it is the sequence of searches that makes this determination. In other words, you often will perform multiple searches consecutively on the same `string`. On the second pass, you do not need to specify the `TargetString` again. Here's an example, using the regular expression I used earlier to match against phone numbers:

```
Dim re as RegEx
Dim match as RegExMatch
re = New RegEx
re.SearchPattern = "\(\d{3}\)\s?\d{3}-\d{4}"
match = re.Search("My number is (800) 555-1212. Is your number (800) 555-1212?")
```

I'll talk about the **RegExMatch** class momentarily, but for now understand that the search that was just executed started at the beginning of the string, by default, and it returned a match at the first instance of a match. Because there are two phone numbers in the String, all I have to do is call `Search` again to begin searching after the match to find the second number. The only issue is that you need to call `Search` the next time without any parameters:

```
match = re.Search
```

If you pass the `TargetString` again, the search starts over. Likewise, if you also set the `SearchStartPosition`, it overrides this automatic behavior. If you want to loop through the String and find all the relevant matches, you can use a loop. After you've made the first match, and match is not equal to `Nil`, do this:

```
While match <> Nil
        match = re.Search
        // so something with match
Wend
```

RegExMatch Class

The **RegExMatch** class comes with four properties, as follows:

```
RegexMatch.SubExpressionCount as Integer
RegexMatch.SubExpressionString(matchNumber as Integer) as String
RegexMatch.SubExpressionStartB(matchNumber as Integer)
RegexMatch.Replace(ReplacementPattern as String)
```

This class is returned as the result of a `RegEx.Search` call. If there was nothing matched, it is `Nil`; otherwise, it is not `Nil` and you can use the properties to examine the matches. The `SubExpressionCount` refers to the groups that were established in the regular expression just searched on.

Recall this regular expression used to find phone numbers:

```
\((\d{3})\)\s?(\d{3})-(\d{4})
```

The **RegExMatch** object that would get returned for this reference if a match was identified would have a `SubExpressionCount` of four. Like arrays and other things, the counting starts from zero, so you could refer to the following matches:

```
\0, \1, \2, \3
```

After you have the number of subexpressions that have been matched, you can use each backreference to get a reference to the string that was matched and to the offset of where the matched subexpression starts. Here's an example:

```
Dim re as RegEx
Dim match as RegExMatch
re = New RegEx
re.Pattern ="\((\d{3})\)\s?(\d{3})-(\d{4})"
match = re.Search("(800) 555-1212")
MsgBox str(match.SubExpressionCount) // displays "4"
MsgBox match.SubExpressionString(1) // displays "800"
MsgBox str(match.SubExpressionStartB(1)) // displays 1
MsgBox str(match.SubExpressionStartB(2)) // displays 6
```

There is one very important caveat to finding the start position of matches, which is that the number the **RegExMatch** object returns represents the binary offset of where the match begins and not the character position. In this example,

`SubExpressionStartB(1)` starts at byte one and not character position one. Because PCRE regular expressions support searches against characters encoded in UTF-8, this could be a problem if you were expecting to find the character at a certain character position.

If you want to do something to that particular passage of text that you have matched, such as set a style for it, you will need to figure out the character position rather than the byte position of the match. The easy way to do it is to take the `SubExpressionString` for that match and then use the global `InStr` function to find the occurrence of the matched `string` in the original string. You could also use a **MemoryBlock** to identify the `string` leading up to the start of the `SubExpressionStart` and then use Len to find the length of the string in terms of characters rather than bytes. You would then be able to calculate the starting position of the matched `string`.

RegExOptions Class

Finally, you can set a number of parameters using the **RegExOptions** class (the `Options` property of the **RegEx** class). Here they are:

- If you want to match characters in a case sensitive way, set the following to `True` (it's `False` by default):

  `RegexOptions.CaseSensitive as Boolean`

- If you want to match patterns that are longer than one line, you need to either specifically reference newline characters in your regular expression, or you can let the "." match newlines, too:

  `RegexOptions.DotMatchAll as Boolean`

- To set the greediness of the entire expression, set `Greedy`. It is `True` by default.

  `RegexOptions.Greedy as Boolean`

- The character you will want to use for a newline character when using replacement patterns will change depending on the platform you are using. You can define the `LineEndType` with this property:

  `RegexOptions.LineEndType as Integer`

  Possible values are

  ```
  0 = Any
  1 = Default for platform
  2 = Macintosh, Chr(13)
  3 = Windows, Chr(10)
  4 = Unix,  Chr(10)
  ```

```
RegexOptions.MatchEmpty as Boolean
RegexOptions.ReplaceAllMatches as Boolean
```

If the target string you are searching against does not have any newline characters, you may want to specify that the **RegEx** class treat the beginning of the string as the start of a line, and the end of the string as the end of the line, even though there is no newline character at all. The following properties allow you to do just that:

```
RegexOptions.StringBeginIsLineBegin as Boolean
RegexOptions.StringEndIsLineEnd as Boolean
```

Finally, you can tell it to treat the target string as one line for the purposes of matching ^ or $, causing it to ignore newline instances in the middle of the string.

```
RegexOptions.TreatTargetAsOneLine
```

Replacing Text

The previous examples dealt with matching text, rather than using regular expressions to replace text. Now I want to share some examples of how you can use regular expressions to search and replace text. The replacement pattern uses a combination of backreferences and new characters to let you build the replacement text. The hard part is getting the right match to begin with, with the right groups. After that's done, the rest is fairly straightforward.

Listing 6.88 **Function Replace(matchstring as String) as String**

```
    Const em = "(_)([^_]+)(_)"
     Const emr = "<em>\2</em>"
      Const strong = "(\*)([^\*]+)(\*)"
      Const strongr = "<strong>\2</strong>"
      Dim subreplace as String
      Dim linkreplace as String
      Dim re as New RegEx
    re.Options.ReplaceAllMatches = True
    re.SearchPattern = em

      //Replace _ with emphasis tags
    re.ReplacementPattern(emr)
      matchstring = re.Replace(matchstring)

    // Replace * with strong tags
      re.searchpattern = strong
      Me.setReplacementPattern(strongr)
      matchstring = re.Replace(matchstring)

      Return matchstring
End Function
```

Text Validation and Variable Substitution

The following two examples show a few ways of using regular expressions. The first example is the **mwRegex** class, which I originally wrote to use to validate data entry into fields in a more complex way than the Mask property of the **EditField** could do. In addition, some convenience functions make it an easy way to work with regular expressions.

The second example comes from a part of the **Properties** class that I glossed over earlier because it involved regular expressions. One feature of properties files used by Java is variable substitution. I'll get into the details when I get to the actual example, but it shows a slightly more complicated search-and-replace problem than the previous examples because you have to create the replacement pattern based on the current match.

Listing 6.89   **mwRegex class**

```
// This is not a subclass of RegEx;
// It's a wrapper class that provides a
// slightly different interface.

// This is the target string to be searched
Property source as String
// This is the search pattern
Property pattern as String
// This is the string of the most recent match
Property match_string as String
// This is the position of the most recent match
Property match_offset as Integer

Property err as Integer
Property re as Regex
Property match as RegexMatch
```

Listing 6.90   **Sub mwRegex.Constructor(pattern as string, rep_pattern as string, greedy as Boolean)**

```
// The Constructor lets you instantiate the object and set
// the most common parameters at the same time, which includes
// the search pattern, the replacement patter and whether the
// search should be greedy or not.

Me.err = 0
// I really should be raising an error here rather
// than setting an error property.
If pattern= "" Then
    Me.err = -1
```

Listing 6.90   **Continued**

```
    Return
End If

match_offset = -1

Me.pattern = pattern
// Instantiate a RegEx object and set the parameters as passed
re = New Regex()

re.Options.Greedy = greedy
re.searchPattern=pattern
re.replacementPattern = rep_pattern
re.Options.MatchEmpty = False
re.Options.DotMatchAll = True
```

Listing 6.91   **Function mwRegex.isMatch(aTargetString as string) As Boolean**

```
// This function is one that is used to validate text.
// The object is instantiated with the search pattern and,
// optionally, a replacement pattern. This function simply
// tests the target string that is passed to it to see
// if it matches the pattern then returns True or False
// accordingly.

// Clear any previous match objects
Me.match = Nil

// Call the isMatch function that requires an offset
// value to be passed to it and return the results
If me.isMatch(aTargetString, 0) Then
    Return TRUE
Else
    Return FALSE
End If

exception nerr
    break
```

Listing 6.92   Function mwRegex.isMatch(aTargetString as string, offset as integer) As Boolean

```
// Clear the previous match
match = Nil

// Perform the search
match = re.Search(aTargetString, offset)

// If there has been a match, save the entire matched string
// as well as the start position of the match and return True.
If match <> Nil Then
    match_string = match.SubExpressionString(0)
    match_offset = match.SubExpressionStartB(0)
    Return TRUE
Else
    Return FALSE
End If



Exception nerr
    break
```

Listing 6.93   Function find(aString as String, ByRef os as Integer, ByRef oe as Integer) As Boolean

```
// Find the start and end position of a match.
// Remember that the start position is measured in bytes,
// so you may get the wrong answer if you are using
// non-ASCII text
If Me.isMatch(aString) Then
    os = Me.match_offset
    oe = Me.match_offset + Len(aString)
    Return TRUE
Else
    Return FALSE
End If
```

Listing 6.94   Function findNext(aString as String, ByRef os as Integer, ByRef oe as Integer) As Boolean

```
// Since the position of the previous match was saved
// you can use this function to find the start and stop
// value of the next match.
If me.isMatch(aString, me.match_offset+1) Then
    os = me.match_offset
```

Listing 6.94   **Continued**

```
    oe = me.match_offset + len(me.match_string)
    Return TRUE
Else
    Return FALSE
End If
```

Listing 6.95   **Function getMatch(matchNumber as Integer) As String**

```
// Convenience function to get a particular subexpression
If matchNumber > -1 Then
    If Me.match <> nil Then
        Return Me.match.SubExpressionString(matchNumber)
    End If
End If
```

Listing 6.96   **Function replace(aString as String) As String**

```
// Convenience function to do a
// search and replace on aString
Return me.re.replace(aString)
```

Listing 6.97   **Function replaceAll(aString as String) As String**

```
// Convenience function to replace all matches…
// It sets the replaceAllMatches property to True
// then does the search.
Me.re.options.replaceAllMatches = True
Return me.re.replace(aString)
```

Listing 6.98   **Sub setReplacementPattern(rep_pattern as String)**

```
// Set a new replacement pattern
Me.re.replacementPattern = rep_pattern
```

Listing 6.99   **Function search(target_string as String) As RegexMatch**

```
// Search target
Return re.search(target_string)
```

Listing 6.100   **Function search() As RegexMatch**

```
// Search target again
Return re.search()
```

Listing 6.101   **Function searchAll(target_String as String) As RegexMatch()**

```
// A function that lets you search for all instances of matches
// within a string, must like how replaceAll lets you do
// a search and replace on all of your matches.
Dim rematch() as RegExMatch
Dim tmpmatch as regexmatch

tmpmatch = search(target_string)

If tmpmatch <> Nil Then
    rematch.append(tmpmatch)
End If

While tmpmatch <> Nil
    // Now that you have done one search,
    // Continue to call search until
    // tmpmatch is Nil.
    tmpmatch = search
    If tmpmatch <> Nil Then
        rematch.append(tmpmatch)
    Else
        Break
    End If
Wend

// Return the array of matches
Return rematch
```

Variable Substitution in the Properties Class

It's best to start with an example to see how variable replacement is used in properties files:

```
root_dir=/home/choate
doc_dir=${root_dir}/documents
prog_dir=${root_dir}/programs
book_dir=${doc_dir}/book
```

As you can see, variables are being used to make it easier to write out the properties. The alternative would be to write the property file like this:

```
root_dir=/home/choate
doc_dir=/home/choate/documents
prog_dir=/home/choate/programs
book_dir=/home/choate/documents/book
```

Not only does this second approach mean that you will type more, it's also a gigantic hassle if, for some reason, you decide you want to change the value of root_dir. If you are not using variable substitution, you would have to go back and change every path for every time. However, if you do use variable substitution, you need only change the value of root_dir and be done with it.

The logic of variable substitution works like this: when I encounter a variable, I look for a property that has already been defined whose name is the same value as the name that is contained by the ${...} characters. If that property exists, I need to get the value of that property and use that string to replace the variable itself. Follow the logic in the ParseVariable function that uses a regular expression and grouping to find the variable name, and then look up the value to be used to replace the variable.

Listing 6.102   **Function ParseVariable(aString as String) as String**

```
// aString is the line being parsed
// Previous lines that have been parsed are
// now accessible through the normal get method
Dim propVar as mwRegex
Dim aVar as PropertyValue
Dim var as String
Dim sub_var as String
Dim var_value as String
Dim str1, str2 as String

// I use mwRegex to simplify the approach and
// instantiate an object, passing to it the
// regular expression that will match variables
propVar = new mwRegex("\${(.*?)}", "", true)

// There may be more than one variable per line
// so I need to make sure that I match each one.
// I cannot just rely on the replaceAllMatches
// option because I have to apply some programming
// logic to each match in order to calculate what
// should be substituted.
While propVar.isMatch(aString)
    // The variable to replace
    // Note that I get the entire match string
    // ignoring for the moment the \1 backreference
```

Listing 6.102   **Continued**

```
      var = propVar.getMatch(0)

      // Get the string for the \1 backreference
   // This will give you the property that you
   // will look up to get the replacement value
      sub_var = propVar.getMatch(1)

   // Next, I check to see if the property exists
      If me.hasKey(sub_var) Then
      // If the property exists, get a reference
      // to the value for the property
        aVar = Me.value(sub_var)

      // The aVar object is a PropertyValue
      // which is a class with two properties,
      // one is the raw string from the properties file
      // and the second is the parsed string, whose
      // variables have been substituted.
        var_value = aVar.parsed

      // Replace the matched string (backreference \0)
      // with the value you just looked up.
        aString = aString.replace(var, var_value)
      Else
     // You have no value to replace this variable with, exit
      exit
    end if

  Wend
  Return aString

Exception err
  break
```

StyledText

The **StyledText** class introduced in the previous chapter is a relatively recent addition to REALbasic, and it provides an excellent way to manipulate the style of text in an **EditField** in very powerful ways. Two classes are involved: the **StyledText** class itself and the **StyleRun** class. A **StyleRun** represents a string of text whose characters all share the same style data. The properties of **StyleRun** follow; you can see the different style elements you can control over a region of text:

```
StyleRun.Bold as Boolean
StyleRun.Italic as Boolean
```

```
StyleRun.Underline as Boolean
StyleRun.Font as String
StyleRun.Size as Integer
StyleRun.TextColor as Color
StyleRun.Text as String
```

You gain access to **StyleRun** objects through the `StyledText.StyleRun` method. The `StyleRun` method is indexed, so pass a number to it to identify that particular `StyleRun`. This is often used in combination with the `StyleRunCount` method, as follows:

```
Dim count as Integer
Dim x as Integer
count = thisStyledText.StyleRunCount
For x = 0 to count - 1
    thisStyledText.StyleRun(x).Bold = True
Next
```

In this example, all the characters in each style run a set to be bold. One thing you may notice missing from this list are styles relating to text alignment. That's because alignment is a style that is applied at the paragraph level rather than the character level, which makes sense because a paragraph can only have one alignment at a time.

The **StyledText** class maintains a list of **StyleRuns** and paragraphs. There is a **ParagraphCount** property that will let you know how many paragraphs this text has. With that information, you can cycle through each paragraph according to the position, like so:

```
Dim count as Integer
Dim x as Integer
count = thisStyledText.ParagraphCount
For x = 0 to count - 1
    thisStyledText.Paragraph(x).Alignment = StyledText.AlignCenter
Next
```

In this example, the alignment of every paragraph was set to be centered. The `StyledText.Paragraph` method returns a **Paragraph** object, and the `Alignment` property of that object was set using a **StyledText** class constant. **Paragraphs** have the following properties:

```
Paragraph.Alignment as Integer
Paragraph.StartPost as Integer
Paragraph.EndPos as Integer
Paragraph.Length as Integer
```

The alignment constants are the following:

```
StyledText.AlignDefault = 0
StyledText.AlignLeft = 1
StyledText.AlignCenter = 2
StyledText.AlignRight= 3
```

If you are working with an **EditField**, the only way to manipulate the styles of text within that **EditField** is with the methods of the **StyledText** class, not directly through access to **StyleRuns**. You can work directly with **StyleRuns**, but you have to remove the old **StyleRun** from the **StyledText** in the **EditField** and insert the new run. What you can't do is modify an existing **StyleRun** by directly accessing the properties of the **StyleRun**.

This also means that if you are populating an **EditField**, you can do so with **StyleRuns**. You can add them to the **StyledText** object associated with the **EditField**.

Apply Styles

The following classes illustrate the use of the **StyledText** class in a font panel shown in Figure 6.2—a small Window that you can use to get and set the text characteristics of text selected in an **EditField** in the main window.

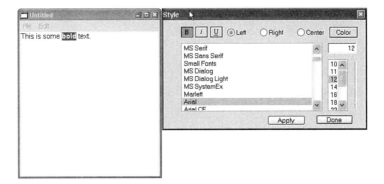

Figure 6.2   Font Panel.

Window1 Inherits Window

Window1 is the primary window for the application. It contains the **EditField,** whose style the Font Panel will manage.

Listing 6.103   **Sub Window1.Open() Handles Event**

```
FontPanel.show
FontPanel.showFonts
FontPanel.showSizes
FontPanel.setEditField Window1.EditField1
```

Listing 6.104   **Sub SelChange() Handles Event**

```
// Update FontPanel so that controls display the current
// style, based upon SelStart
FontPanel.showCurrentStyle
```

Listing 6.105   FontPanel Inherits Window

```
// A reference to the EditField
// whose styles are being managed
Property Field As EditField
```

Listing 6.106   **Sub FontPanel.showFonts()**

```
// Display the list of available fonts
// in the FontList ListBox.
Dim y as Integer
Dim x as Integer

y = FontCount -1
For x = 0 To y
    Me.FontList.addRow(Font(x))
Next
```

Listing 6.107   **Sub FontPanel.showSizes()**

```
// Populate  the SizeList ListBox with
// some commonly used font sizes
sizeList.addRow("10")
sizeList.addRow("11")
sizeList.addRow("12")
sizeList.addRow("14")
sizeList.addRow("16")
sizeList.addRow("18")
sizeList.addRow("22")
sizeList.addRow("26")
sizeList.addRow("30")
sizeList.addRow("36")
```

Listing 6.108   **Sub FontPanel.setEditField(anEditField as EditField)**

```
// Make a reference to the EditField this
// FontPanel will manage fonts for.
me.Field = anEditField
```

Listing 6.109   **Sub FontPanel.selectString(aListBox as ListBox, aString as String)**

```
// A generic method that allows you to find the row
// in the ListBox whose text matches aString argument.
Dim x,y as Integer
y = aListBox.ListCount - 1

For x = 0 To y
    If aListBox.Cell(x,0) = aString Then
        aListBox.ListIndex = x
        Exit
    End If
Next
```

Listing 6.110   **Sub FontPanel.showCurrentStyle()**

```
// Get the values from the currently
// selected string and set the state
// of the controls on the FontPanel.

// Select the current font in the FontList ListBox
selectString FontList, Field.SelTextFont

// Select the current font size in the SizeList Listbox
selectString SizeList, Str(Field.SelTextSize)

// Place the current font size in the FontSize EditField
FontSize.Text = str(Field.SelTextSize)

// Position the slider for the current font size
SizeSlider.value = 144 - val(FontSize.text)

// Toggle ButtonBold BevelButton
If Field.SelBold Then
    ButtonBold.Value = True
Else
    ButtonBold.Value = False
End If

// Toggle ButtonItalic BevelButon
If Field.SelItalic Then
    ButtonItalic.Value = True
Else
    ButtonItalic.Value = False
End If
```

Listing 6.110 **Continued**

```
// Toggle ButtonUnderline BevelButton
If Field.SelUnderline Then
    ButtonUnderline.Value = True
Else
    ButtonUnderline.Value = False
End If


// Select RadioButton according to alignment.
// The RadioButtons are part of a Control Array
Self.Alignment(Field.SelAlignment - 1).Value = True
```

Listing 6.111 **Sub FontPanel.setCurrentStyle()**

```
// Set the value of the selected text according
// to the state of the controls in the FontPanel

// Get the value of the BevelButton and set the
// StyledText.
If ButtonBold.Value Then
    Field.StyledText.Bold(Field.SelStart, Field.SelLength) = True
Else
    Field.StyledText.Bold(Field.SelStart, Field.SelLength) = False
End If


If ButtonItalic.Value Then
    Field.StyledText.Italic(Field.SelStart, Field.SelLength) = True
Else
    Field.StyledText.Italic(Field.SelStart, Field.SelLength) = False
End If


If ButtonUnderline.Value Then
    Field.StyledText.Underline(Field.SelStart, Field.SelLength) = True
Else
    Field.StyledText.Underline(Field.SelStart, Field.SelLength) = False
End If


Field.styledText.Font(Field.SelStart, Field.SelLength) = FontList.Text
Field.styledText.Size(Field.SelStart, Field.SelLength) = val(FontSize.Text)

// Find which RadioButton is highlighted and set
// the alignment accordingly.
// Note that the alignment is set for the paragraph, and
// not just the selected text. I could also get a reference
// to the paragraph object and change that as well.
If Alignment(2).Value Then
    Field.SelAlignment = EditField.AlignCenter
```

Listing 6.111   **Continued**

```
Elseif Alignment(1).Value Then
    Field.SelAlignment = EditField.AlignRight
Else
    Field.SelAlignment = EditField.AlignLeft
End if
```

Listing 6.112   **Function SizeList.CellClick(row as Integer, column as Integer, x as Integer, y as Integer) As Boolean**

```
// When a size is selected in the SizeList ListBox
// Position the SizeSlider to display the same value.
SizeSlider.Value = 144 - val(SizeList.Text)
FontSize.Text = str(144-SizeSlider.Value)
```

Listing 6.113   **Sub SizeSlider.ValueChanged()**

```
// Set font size according to the
// Position of the SizeSlider
SizeList.ListIndex = -1
FontSize.Text = str(144-me.Value)
```

Listing 6.114   **Sub PushButton1.Action()**

```
// Hide the FontPanel
FontPanel.Hide
```

Listing 6.115   **Sub PushButton2.Action()**

```
// Apply the currently selected fonts and styles
// to the selected text.
setCurrentStyle
```

Listing 6.116   **BevelButton1.Sub Action()**

```
// Display the platform specific color picker
// with the selectColor function and let
// the user choose the color of the text
Dim c as Color
Dim res as Boolean
res = selectColor(c, "Select a color")
If Res Then
    Field.SelTextColor = c
End If
```

Summary

Now that XML, regular expressions, and a little more information about **StyledText** is under your belt, in the next chapter I will continue with another text-related topic. The topic of the previous chapter was creating desktop applications, and the topic of the next will be creating console applications. A console application is one that does not have a graphical user interface. It runs on the command line or as a service (or daemon) in memory. Console programs accept input in the form of text and produce output in the form of text. I will show you an example of how to use a REALbasic console application to implement a CGI application, which is used to create dynamic html pages, which means more dealings with XML. I will also cover REALbasic's **Shell** class. Although the **Shell** class is most often used in desktop applications, it performs a related task to console applications. The **Shell** class is used to interact with the command-line interfaces of the host operating systems. In fact, you could use the **Shell** class to execute REALbasic console applications. To illustrate the **Shell**, I will share a sample application called Ant Shell, which provides a graphical user interface to the command-line program Ant, from the Apache Foundation. It's an automated build tool, somewhat like Make, that is written in Java and uses XML build files.

7

Console Programming and the Shell

THERE ARE TWO BASIC TYPES OF applications you can create using REALbasic: a desktop application and a console application. You have already seen how to create a desktop application in Chapter 5 and now, in this chapter, you will see how to create a console application. The capability to create console applications requires the Professional version of REALbasic. However, if you do not have the Professional version, you can still execute the examples, but they will run for only 5 minutes at a time and work for 10 days.

Prior to introducing console applications, however, I will introduce the **Shell** class, which is a class that can be used in either desktop applications or console applications, but which is related to the development of console applications in this way: console applications are applications that do not have a graphical user interface and are executed on the command line of the respective shells for each platform. The **Shell** class is a class that provides a means of causing such applications to be executed.

The Windows shell is different from the one used by Macintosh and Linux computers, and both have a different lineage. In Windows, the shell is referred to as the Shell, and you normally access it through the Command Prompt application (see Figure 7.1). If you have been around Windows for any significant amount of time, you will recognize the shell as the old DOS or Command prompt, which was the primary means of navigating folders and executing applications prior to the introduction of Windows.

Whereas on Windows the shell is the shell, on UNIX-like systems, there are several kinds of shells that you can use. Both Macintosh and Linux have terminal applications that you can use to access the shell, but the actual shell being accessed can vary—sh, bash, and tcsh are all different shells that can be used. In these examples, I'm using sh, although the other two are very common. The good news is that when using the **Shell** class, you can specify which shell to use, so that gives you some control. Otherwise, the systems themselves decide what the default shell is, and this might cause unintended consequences if you assumed one shell and got a different one.

A console application is one that can be executed from the shell. A console application is launched by typing the name of the application into the shell and pressing the Enter key. All shells have a core group of commands, which are really just small applications that perform some very basic tasks such as changing directories and moving and copying files. Arguments can also be passed to the application from the command line. Here's an example that is similar on both Windows and UNIX-like operating systems. First, take a look at the Windows version:

```
cd "C:\Program Files"
```

Figure 7.1 shows how the command looks when entered into a Windows Command Prompt application:

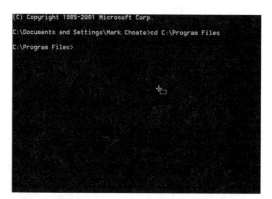

Figure 7.1   Windows XP Shell.

Next, the Macintosh and Linux versions:

```
cd /usr/local/bin
```

Figure 7.2 shows the same command entered into the Macintosh terminal application, using the bash shell, which is identified in the window title:

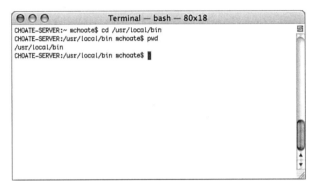

Figure 7.2   Macintosh Terminal, Bash Shell.

In both cases, you are changing into approximately equivalent directories. The "cd" stands for "change directory," and that is also the name of the command (or application) being executed. What follows is the argument, which is passed to the program when it is executed, much in the same way that arguments are passed to subroutines and functions.

In both examples, I just typed in **cd** and the program executed, but with most applications you normally would need to type in the actual path to the application, like this Linux example shows:

```
/usr/bin/cd /usr/local/bin
```

The reason you do not have to enter the entire path is because all systems have a PATH environment variable that lists the paths that should be checked whenever a command is entered on the command line that doesn't use an absolute path. By default, Windows and the UNIX-like systems are configured to be able to execute the cd command without the path. The environment variables used are usually user specific and can be customized. However, when using the **Shell** class, you cannot assume that the PATH has been set for anything.

When you create a desktop application, you design a graphical user interface, and this interface responds to user actions to determine what to do next. The user input comes in the form of mouse clicks or drags and the like, and by and large, the response to user input is displayed in the interface itself—in particular, windows and controls. Because a console application is not graphical, it needs another way to get user input, and another way to display or view the response to that input—something that is called *output* in console applications.

When you start a console application and include an argument in the command, you are using a special kind of input called standard input. The most common way to provide input to a console application is on the command line itself. After the application runs and computes whatever needs to be computed, it usually sends output to the console in the form of text. Sometimes the output is a status message, and other times the output is actually what the program does.

I'll show you an example later where you pass two arguments to a console application. The arguments are paths to particular files. The first argument points to an XML document and the second argument points to an XSLT stylesheet. The application takes that input, finds the files, performs the transformation, and sends the output to the console. This is called *standard output*. That's simple enough; the data that goes in is called standard input and the data that goes out is called standard output. There's also something called standard error, which is where error messages go (it so happens that it usually gets displayed in the same way as the standard output, but you can also designate a file for standard error data to be sent).

There are also some very interesting things that can be done with standard input and standard output. For example, the standard input into one program could be the standard output from another. This is called piping, and it's a technique you can use to send data through a series of transformations performed by a collection of applications.

Sample Applications

The **Shell** class provides a way for REALbasic to interact with the command line through an object-oriented interface. This means that you use the **Shell** to execute applications and to pass arguments to the application, just like you were typing the information yourself into the terminal. The **Shell** class will be covered first. The discussion includes an application called Ant Shell that provides a graphical interface to Ant, which is an open-source Java application developed by the Apache Foundation. It was developed to build Java applications, similar to the way that Make is used to build C++ applications, but it is an extremely powerful, easy-to-use tool, and it is normally run from the command line. The reason I have chosen to share an Ant application with you is that Ant build files are XML documents, so in addition to introducing the **Shell**, it also provides a little more insight into how you can use XML technology.

After the **Shell**, I will turn to developing an actual console application in REALbasic (you could actually execute a REALbasic console application using the **Shell** class, if you wanted to, but in most cases, I don't think that's a smart way to be doing things). The first console application is called Transformer, and it provides a command-line interface to the **XMLDocument** and **XSLStyleSheet** classes in REALbasic. The class used to do the transforming will be written so that it can be used in a console application as well as in a desktop application. This means that I will be able to use the same class in the RSSReader application that I use in the Transformer application.

I'll also be able to use the same class in another console application, called rbCGI, which will serve as the final example. This console application is a simple framework for writing CGI programs. CGI refers to the Common Gateway Interface, which is one method that is used to execute scripts and programs to dynamically generate websites. It's really a simple framework with a lot of limitations—definitely not something you would use if you had a very high-traffic site. However, if you have relatively simple needs, it can work quite well. The CGI framework could be used as a way to distribute dynamically produced RSS XML documents, or it could be an alternative way to view RSS files as HTML.

There are a few interesting points about the CGI application worth mentioning here. First, it shows how standard input and standard output can be used in different contexts. In the case of the CGI application, standard output is sent back to the web browser of the individual who made the original HTTP request, rather than being sent to the terminal. Also, some of the data used by the CGI application is passed in environment variables. CGI applications can use either standard input or the content of environment variables as the source of data used to execute the application.

In the ongoing effort to demonstrate the joys of code reuse, the CGI application will also use the same class that's used to transform XML documents in the RSSReader application and the Transformer application. This will allow the CGI application to get a request, find an RSS file, transform it to HTML, and present it to the user. You can think of it as a start to a web-enabled version of the RSSReader application I have been reviewing throughout the book. In fact, after you've read through the examples, you will begin to think of a lot of ways that these different examples can interact with each other.

The Shell Class

The **Shell** class can be run in three modes: synchronous, asynchronous, and interactive. The mode is set using the `Shell.Mode` property, which is described next. When using synchronous mode, you use the **Shell** class to execute a command and then get the results back immediately. This is a blocking method, which means that nothing else happens in the sequence of code until the results are returned. Using asynchronous mode, you can execute a command, but you do not need to wait for the results. Instead, you wait for the `DataAvailable` event to be triggered. Interactive mode is similar to asynchronous mode except that instead of executing only one command, you can execute several commands in sequence, based on the results from the previous command.

Although synchronous mode is a simple way to run the **Shell**, I think running it asynchronously or interactively provides a lot more flexibility. Because the two nonsynchronous modes rely on events, the **Shell** is often used like a control and can be dragged to a **Window** and programmed there. The sample application treats the **Shell** like a control.

Shell Properties

Whether the **Shell** is synchronous, asynchronous, or interactive is determined by the `Mode` property:

```
Shell.Mode as Integer
```

The values you can use are
Synchronous   0
Asynchronous   1
Interactive   2

These values can be set at runtime.

Synchronous Execution

The following properties are used when running the **Shell** in synchronous mode. Prior to REALbasic 2005, Windows had to use synchronous mode, but it doesn't any longer, so you will probably not need to use these:

```
Shell.TimeOut as Integer
```

`TimeOut` is measured in milliseconds and is used only when running synchronously on Windows. Use −1 to wait indefinitely for the results.

```
Shell.ErrorCode as Integer
```

The `ErrorCode` is supplied by the system. It's a zero if all is well, and another number if there is a problem. When you execute a command in synchronous mode, you should check the result and if it is zero, you can retrieve the standard output of the command using the following property:

```
Shell.Result as String
```

This is used only in synchronous mode, and it contains the entire output. In the other modes, you will use the `ReadAll` method to access the latest data.

Asynchronous and Interactive Execution

The following two properties are used when using modes other than synchronous. The first checks to see whether the **Shell** is still running, and the second is the process ID number of an interactive **Shell** process:

```
Shell.IsRunning as Boolean
Shell.PID as Integer
```

Shell Events

The following events are triggered only when using asynchronous or interactive modes. The following event is triggered when new data is available in the buffer:

```
Shell.DataAvailable Handles Event
```

When the `DataAvailable` event is triggered, you can retrieve the most recent data from the buffer by calling the `ReadAll` method. The following event lets you know that all the data has been sent and the process that you initiated with the execution of the command has terminated:

```
Shell.Completed Handles Event
```

Shell Methods

You execute an application by calling the `Shell.Execute` method:

```
Shell.Execute(Command as String, [Parameters as String])
```

There are two ways to pass arguments to the method. The `Command` parameter represents the path to the actual application or program that is to be executed (unless the appropriate PATH environment variable has been set, and then you can just use the name of the application). The optional `Parameters` parameter can be used with additional arguments that get passed to the program. You can include the arguments in the `Command` parameter, but the REALbasic documentation suggests that you use the `Parameters` parameter if there are spaces in the path to the application being executed.

For example, if there is a **Shell** instance, **Shell1**, you can execute the "`cd`" command used earlier, like this:

```
Shell1.Execute("cd /usr/local/bin")
```

Or you can use it like this:

```
Shell1.Execute("cd", "/usr/local/bin")
```

When using asynchronous or interactive mode, you can call the `poll` method, which may trigger a `DataAvailable` event. Generally speaking, I don't think it's necessary to use. No value is returned; the only response is the possible triggering of the `DataAvailable` event.

```
Shell.Poll
```

The following method accesses the data buffer. When called, it returns all the data in the buffer and then clears the buffer. This is used in asynchronous and interactive modes only.

```
Shell.ReadAll as String
```

There are two methods used to send additional text to the command line. It is used when you are in interactive mode and your class needs to send additional data to the command-line application based on a request from the application. The `WriteLine` method appends a linefeed to the string, which is the equivalent of pressing the Enter key after typing your command into the shell.

```
Shell.Write(Text as String)
Shell.WriteLine(Text as String)
```

The following method closes the shell:

```
Shell.Close
```

Subclassing the Shell

In the coming examples, I will use three subclasses of the **Shell** to do a few different things. The first is **mwShell,** which is a subclass of **Shell** that adds some convenience functions. The second is **AntShell,** which is a subclass of **mwShell** and coordinates the work of reading Ant build files, which I will discuss momentarily. I've also included a third class, **SVNShell**, another subclass of **mwShell,** which is unrelated to Ant, but demonstrates some more advanced issues with respect to the using the **Shell** class effectively. **SVNShell** is a wrapper for command-line access to Subversion, which is a very good and free version control system that I use. All these examples are combined into the Ant Shell application that you can download.

There are two methods in particular to pay attention to: `addOpt` and `addArg`. These two methods provide a more flexible interface to handling the arguments that get passed to the command line. It accommodates two kinds of arguments. The first type is the kind I used in the `cd` example, an argument that is a single string of text, such as:

```
cd /usr/local/bin
```

The second type of argument is called an option, which is made up of two parts, the option name (or key) and the value for the option. The following example using ant indicates how a particular build file is specified using the command line:

```
ant -f /path/to/build.xml
```

When you add an option using **mwShell**, you pass both the option and the option value as arguments. This can be helpful when building long commands.

mwShell Inherits Shell

mwShell is a **Shell** subclass that contains some convenience methods related to building commands, setting certain environment variables, and displaying the output of executed commands.

You should also pay special attention to how the results that come from executing something on the **Shell** are displayed in the **EditField**. Because the **Shell** is asynchronous, you do not have all the results back in one long **String**. You get back bits and pieces. This example shows you how to effectively append new text to an **EditField** so that it flows naturally and doesn't cause the screen to flicker. You can see how this is done in the `mwShell.print` method.

The following properties are used by **mwShell**. The first two are used to build the command that will be executed, and the last two work with displaying the output of the command. The `buffer` stores all the data retrieved, and the `view` property is set to the **EditField** that will be displaying the data.

```
Property cmd as String
Property args(-1) as String
Property view as EditField
Property buffer(-1) as String
```

Next you will see the list of methods implemented by **mwShell**. Be sure to read the comments in each method to see what is happening and why it is being done that way.

Listing 7.1   **Sub mwShell.Constructor(aPath as String, aPathType as integer)**

```
// Since the PATH environment variable may not be set
// you can set it in the Constructor. You do not necessarily
// need to set this if you know the complete path to the
// application.
setPath(aPath, aPathType)
```

Listing 7.2   **Sub mwShell.addArg(myArg as String)**

```
// Append an argument to the arguments
// array of mwShell.
args.Append myArg
```

Listing 7.3   **Sub mwShell.addOpt(option as String, arg as String)**

```
// Add an option to the arguments array.
// Quote the arg if it includes spaces.

If instr(arg, " ") <> 0 Then
        arg = "'" + arg + "'"
End If

args.append(option + " " + arg)
```

Listing 7.4   **Sub mwShell.setCmd(command as String)**

```
// Set the value for the command to be executed
Me.cmd = command
```

Listing 7.5   **Sub mwShell.exec()**

```
// This method takes the command in mwShell.cmd
// as well as the arguments in the args array
// to build a complete command to be executed.
Dim full_cmd as String

// build complete command, including arguments
If Ubound(args) > -1 Then
        full_cmd = me.cmd + " " + join(args, " ")
Else
        full_cmd = me.cmd
End If
```

Listing 7.5 **Continued**

```
// Test to see if the shell is running. If it is
// running, then execute the command using WriteLine.
If me.IsRunning Then
        reDim buffer(-1)
        me.WriteLine full_cmd
Else
// If the shell is not already running, then call execute.
        reDim buffer(-1)
        me.execute full_cmd
End If
```

Listing 7.6 **Sub mwShell.print(s as String)**

```
// The view property is an EditField where the
// output of the application is displayed. If
// the property is not Nil, then the output is
// appended to the text of the EditField using
// the following technique, which avoids making
// the screen flicker. The selStart value is
// set to the length of the text field, and the
// selLength value is set to zero. The new data
// is then assigned to the selected text.
If view <> Nil Then
        view.selStart = LenB(view.Text)
        view.selLength = 0
        view.selText = s
End If
```

Listing 7.7 **Sub mwShell.setPath(path as String, setPathType as Integer)**

```
// Set the PATH environment variable.
// The setPathType Integer indicates whether the
// path should be appended,inserted at the beginning
// or if it should replace the existing path.
// You can use the class constants: kAppendPath,
// kInsertPath, kNewPath

Dim oldPath, NewPath as String
Dim sep as String

// The separator used in the PATH environment variable
// varies between Windows and the Unix-like systems. Set
```

Listing 7.7   **Continued**

```
// the appropriate value for the sep variable here.
#If targetWin32 Then
        sep = ";"
#else
        sep = ":"
#end if

oldPath = System.EnvironmentVariable("PATH")

// Build the new path as requested
Select Case setPathType
Case kAppendPath
        NewPath = oldPath + sep + path
Case kInsertPath
        NewPath = path + sep + oldPath
Case kNewPath
        NewPath = path
Else
        NewPath = oldPath + sep + path
End Select

// Set the environment variable
System.EnvironmentVariable("PATH") = NewPath
```

Listing 7.8   **Sub mwShell.setMode(aMode as Integer)**

```
// When using the Shell as a control, you can
// set the Mode using the IDE. In other cases,
// you need to set it programmatically, but
// it cannot be set in the constructor, so
// this method is used.
Me.mode = aMode
If me.mode = 2 Then
        execute "sh"
End If
```

Listing 7.9   **mwShell.Sub setView(anEditField as EditField)**

```
// Set the EditField used to view the output.
Me.view = anEditField
```

Listing 7.10 **Sub mwShell.setWorkingDirectory(aPath as String)**

```
// This sets the working directory, which is
// the directory used as the frame of reference for
// calculating relative paths.
//
// The "cd" command is basically the same for both
// Unix-like systems and Windows and changes the
// directory to the path that is passed to this method.
If IsRunning Then
        writeLine("cd " + aPath)
Else
        // ignore
End If
```

Listing 7.11 **Sub mwShell.reset()**

```
// Reset all the values to get ready to execute another command.
Me.cmd = ""
reDim args(-1)
reDim buffer(-1)
```

Now you have a base class that you can build on. In the next section I will subclass
mwShell and create a class to be used with Subversion version-control software.

Subversion

As I mentioned earlier, Subversion is a version control system and is usually used by programmers to keep track of versions of their software. If you make an addition to your
program and it suddenly stops working, Subversion will let you access the previous
working version of your code and isolate the change that caused the problem.

Like many version control systems, Subversion has facilities for storing all the files on
a centralized server using one of a handful of methods, like WebDav and SSH. There are
two parts to Subversion—the server and the client. The client checks out files from the
server, makes changes to them locally, and then commits those changes back to the server. Whenever you check out files from the server or commit changed files, you need to
sign in.

I have included a class that is designed to make working with Subversion through the
Shell easier. Some of the more common commands have been implemented as methods
of the **SVNShell** subclass, which is one way to make dealing with the **Shell** feel more
like dealing with a regular class, making it much easier to use. The key feature I want to
share with you, however, is how this class waits for a response from the server requesting
a username and password and how it responds to it. This is the primary benefit of what
the **Shell** class calls interactive mode. You are able to send commands to the **Shell**, read
the results, and then respond with more commands, which is a very powerful feature.

All the **Shell** subclasses are packaged up in the Ant Shell application, even though they are really distinct activities. The main window, **Window1**, allows you to interact with the SVN shell and enter raw commands to be executed on the command line. You can also click a Target button to see the graphical interface to using Ant. From there you will be able to select targets and execute them.

Note that you will need to have Subversion installed on your computer separately for the Subversion-specific commands to work. If you do not have Subversion installed, you can still use the application to access the shell and execute commands. You will also need to make sure the PATH environment variable includes the path to the Subversion installation.

Figure 7.3 shows this application in action. When the application first launched, I clicked on the Init Subversion Client button, which initialized the **SVNClient** object. I then typed in the Windows command **time** in **EditField1** (the topmost **EditField** in the example), and the result was the following:

```
The current time is: 9:02:34.83
Enter the new time:
```

Because the **SVNClient1** object is operating in interactive mode, I am able to respond to the prompt to enter the new time. Again in **EditField1**, I typed the new time I wanted to set my computer to:

```
9:01:00.00
```

In Figure 7.3, you can see the results of these steps still displayed. (The time on my computer did get changed as a result.)

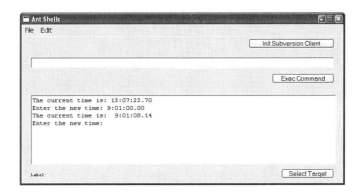

Figure 7.3   The Shell Window example.

SVNclient Inherits mwShell

In the previous section, I showed you how the application looks and gave you an example of how I used the application to change the time on my computer. The reason this is included in the sample application is so that you can see an example of how to use the interactive features of the **Shell**. In addition to entering multiple commands like I just showed you, this subclass will also automatically respond to certain prompts. When you execute an SVN command, the shell will prompt you for a username and password and the **SVNClient** object will look for this prompt and respond to it when it appears.

The properties of the class store the username and password that will be used to access the Subversion repository:

```
Property user as String
Property password as String
```

This example also shows how you can extend the **Shell** class to give it a more natural, object-oriented interface. Several Subversion command-line arguments are implemented as methods that your program can call. For example, to view the log of the current version-controlled directory, you can do the following:

```
SVNclient1.log
```

The following events are used in asynchronous or interactive mode. The `DataAvailable` event is the important one because whenever it is triggered, it checks to see whether a password is being requested, and if it is, it sends the username and password back to the shell.

Listing 7.12 **Sub SVNclient.Completed() Handles Event**

```
// The request is completed
MsgBox "Completed!"
```

Listing 7.13 **Sub SVNclient.DataAvailable() Handles Event**

```
// Track the data that is coming from the shell
// as the request is executed. When the shell
// returns the password prompt, send the
// username and password to the shell.
Dim s as String
Dim subs as String
s = Me.ReadAll

print s

subs = Trim(Right(s, 10))
If subs = "password:" Then
    // The shell is requesting a password
    me.writeLine(me.password)
    print "Sending password"
    reDim buffer(-1)
Else
    // It's not a password prompt,
    // keep looking for return values
    buffer.append(s)
End If
```

Listing 7.14   **Sub SVNclient.status(source_String as String)**

```
// Predefined SVN command
// Get the status of the current directory
Me.cmd = "svn status " + source_String
Me.exec()
```

Listing 7.15   **Sub SVNclient.add(source_path as String)**

```
// Predefined SVN command
// Add a file to the version control repository
Me.cmd = "svn add " + source_path
Me.exec()
```

Listing 7.16   **Sub SVNclient.delete(source_path as String)**

```
// Predefined SVN command
// Delete a file from the version control repository
Me.cmd = "svn del " + source_path
Me.exec()
```

Listing 7.17   **Sub SVNclient.update(source_String as String)**

```
// Predefined SVN command
// Update the local copy with updated files from
// the repository server.
Me.cmd = "svn update source_String"
Me.exec
```

Listing 7.18   **Sub SVNclient.commit(source_String as String, msg as String)**

```
// Predefined SVN command
// Commit local changes to the server repository.
Me.cmd = "svn commit " + source_String + " -m " + msg
```

Listing 7.19   **Sub SVNclient.log()**

```
// Predefined SVN command
// View the log.
Me.cmd = "svn log"
Me.exec()
```

Listing 7.20   **Sub SVNclient.setUser(aUser as String, aPassword as String)**

```
// Configure username and password
Me.user = aUser
Me.password = aPassword
```

Listing 7.21   **Window1 Inherits Window**

```
// The primary application window.
Property ant as AntShell
```

Listing 7.22   **Sub Window1.PushButtonSVN.Action() Handles Event**

```
// Initialize the SVNClient instance

// The view is the EditField where the results of executing
// any command will be displayed
SVNclient1.setView(window1.EditField2)

// This sets the Path environmental variable
// Note that this path is appropriate for Linux/Mac only
#if Not (TargetWin32) Then
    SVNclient1.setPath("/usr/local/bin", SVNclient1.kAppendPath)
#endif

// The mode is interactive, which means that I can send
// multiple requests in sequence and respond to the results
// of each request. In this example, Subversion requires a
// username and password, so the application will have to wait
// until Subversion requests it, and then pass the information
// to it, all of which requires the application to be in
// interactive mode. New in REALbasic 2005, Windows now supports
// interactive mode, too. You can use asynchronous mode if you
// only want to execute a single command. The results are
// returned in an event.
//
// Synchronous mode is blocking, which means you want to execute
// a command and have your application wait until the results are
// returned.
SVNclient1.setMode(2)

// Identify the directory that SVN will use as the root directory
// Relative links will be calculated from this directory.
// The Windows Shell class does not seem to acknowledge a working
// directory, so all relative paths are calculated relative to
// the home directory of the shell application.
```

Listing 7.22   **Continued**

```
#if Not (TargetWin32) then
    SVNclient1.setWorkingDirectory("/Library/WebServer/Documents/Metawrite")
#endif

// Set the username and password for Subversion
SVNclient1.setUser("subvn", "password")

// Clear the buffer
reDim SVNclient1.buffer(-1)
```

Listing 7.23   **Sub Window1.PushButtonExec.Action() Handles Event**

```
// Execute a generic command using the text in
// EditField1. It uses the SVNClient instance, but
// will execute any command you pass, regardless of
// whether it is a valid SVN command or not.
// However, the SVNClient should be initialized first
// by pushing the InitSubversion Client button.
Dim s as String

s = EditField1.Text

// Set the text from EditField1 to the command
svnclient1.setCmd(s)

// Execute the command
svnclient1.exec

// Clear the command-line EditField
EditField1.Text = ""
```

The **SVNClient** class is a good example of how to subclass the **Shell** class in such a way that you can interact with the **Shell** just like you are working with any other class. In the next section, I go a step further and integrate the **Shell** more closely with the user interface.

Ant Shell

Ant is a product of the Apache Foundation; it is a Java application that was developed as a replacement for Make, which is used to managed the build and compile process for applications. Ant is written in Java and is designed to work especially well with building Java applications, but it has also proven to be a very flexible tool for doing all sorts of things. Although it is not a full-blown scripting language, there are a lot of things it can do very well that you would normally do with a scripting language—such as copying and deleting groups of files, transferring files by FTP to a server, and so on.

The Ant application is generally run from the command line, where it processes special XML files that contain the instructions it needs to do whatever it is that needs to be done. These XML files are usually named build.xml, but they do not have to be. Each build file represents a project, and each project is given a number of targets. Targets can be dependent on other targets, which means that the task will not run until the target that it is dependent on has run. Targets perform tasks—specific things that you need to have done. The build.xml file specifies all this. Here is an example Ant build.xml file:

Listing 7.24   **An Ant build.xml file**

```
<project name="ExampleProject" default="init" basedir=".">
    <description>
        This is an example of a basic build.xml file
    </description>
  <!--Properties to be used later in the file -->
  <property name="src" location="src"/>
  <property name="build" location="build"/>

  <target name="init">
    <!-- Create the time stamp and output it to the console -->
    <tstamp/>
   <!-- Create the directory referred to in the build property-->
    <mkdir dir="${build}"/>
  </target>

  <target name="clean"
        description="Delete the build directory" >
    <delete dir="${build}"/>
  </target>
</project>
```

This project is called "ExampleProject" and the default target that will be executed if no other target is specified is the "init" target. The basedir identifies the directory from which all relative paths should be calculated. The use of "." as the value means that the directory you were in when you executed Ant will be the base directory. Finally, the project has a description.

There are two targets, init and clean. Within each target are one or more commands that are displayed as XML Elements. There's no need to worry about the specific commands. The application will just look at each target, get its name, description, and identify any dependencies if they exist (neither of the targets in the example have any).

Although you most often run Ant from the command line, that can get a little tedious. The process requires you to be in the same directory as the build.xml file you want to use and then execute Ant while passing arguments that let it know which targets to run. Because a project can have any number of targets and you may not also want to run every target, you need to remain well-versed in what targets are available and what they are dependent on, and so on. As a result, it is sometimes helpful to use a graphical interface to manipulate Ant, and this is exactly what this set of classes will do.

The interface is divided into three panes. On the left is the Project List, which is a listing of all Ant project files (named build.xml, or something else) in a given directory that you have selected. In the middle column, the Available Targets List shows all the targets that have been defined in this project. The column on the right lists the targets that you want to execute in the order that you want to execute them. There is a Move button that can be clicked to move a selected target into the list for executing. You can also clear the execute list, or remove individual items in the list. Finally, you can execute the targets in the sequence specified and then view the results in an **EditField**.

In Figure 7.4, three projects are listed. The second project is selected, which causes all the targets in the build-svn.xml file to be displayed in the center **ListBox**. Two of the targets have been selected to be executed, and they are displayed in the right **ListBox** and will be executed in order:

```
add-pages and commit-pages.
```

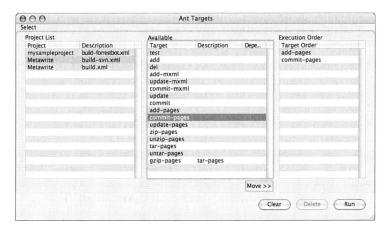

Figure 7.4 Ant Shell.

There are a few features you should pay special attention to. The first is trivial, but this application shows an example of how to colorize every other line of a **ListBox,** which is nice to know and can make them much easier to read. More important is the **XmlReader** subclass, which reads each build.xml file, identifies the targets that are available, and populates the **ListBox** accordingly. This is just a good, everyday kind of example of how reading XML files can be integrated into your application.

To use the **Shell** class in interactive or asynchronous mode, the instance has to remain in scope while it awaits a result. This means that you either need to drag the shell to the application **Window** and execute that way, or you need to create it as a property of something persistent, like a window. If you don't, and then instantiate it as a local variable within a method or event, it will go out of scope before returning any results, which is not what you want.

Following is an example of instantiating the **AntShell** class as a property of **Window1** and executing a command:

Listing 7.25   **Instantiating the AntShell class**

```
If ant = Nil Then
    ant = New AntShell
    ant.setMode(2)
    ant.setView(window1.EditField2)
End If

// The command is the executable to be run
ant.setCmd "ant"

// An "Opt" lets you set an option through the command line.
// It consists of two parts, the first identifies the option
// and the second establishes the value for that option.
ant.addOpt "-f", "/Users/mchoate/Documents/Projects"_
   + "/REALbasic/Metawrite/ant/build-svn.xml"

// an "Arg" is a command line switch that consists of one
// word or phrase
ant.addArg "test"

// Executes the command
ant.exec
```

In the actual Ant Shell example, the **AntShell** instance is not a property, but is treated like a control and resides on a **Window** subclass called **AntTargetView**. To launch the **AntTargetView** window, you do the following:

```
Dim av as AntTargetViewer
Dim f as folderitem

av = New AntTargetViewer(AntTargetView)

// Select a folder that contains Ant build files
f = selectfolder

// List build files.
av.getProjects(f)
```

Although REALbasic makes it easy to extend **Windows** by adding methods to them, this example does not implement the methods used to control the **Window** in the **Window** itself. Instead, I use a separate class that serves as a controller. The **Window** is called **AntTargetView,** and the controller class is called **AntTargetViewer**.

AntTargetView Inherits Window

AntTargetView is a window, but it takes a somewhat different approach to managing the window. Instead of implementing methods in the **Window** itself, the methods are implemented in a separate "Viewer" class, which is associated with the **Window** as the controller property.

There are a few reason for doing it this way. The first is that it gives you more control and a way around the automatic **Window** instantiation "feature" that causes **Windows** to be viewed whenever members are accessed. Just move all that stuff to a different class and it no longer has that effect. It is also easier to subclass a class than to subclass a **Window,** and you can manage multiple **Windows** with one class if you want to, which makes it easier for the state of one **Window** to impact the state of another associated **Window**.

It has one property, which is a reference to the controlling class:

```
Property controller as AntTargetViewer
```

Listing 7.26   **Sub AntTargetView.DoubleClick() Handles Event**

```
// Select a project and display the available targets
Dim t as AntTarget

t = ListBoxProjectList.CellTag(ListBoxProjectList.ListIndex, 0)
ListBoxAvailable.addRow(t.name)
ListBoxAvailable.CellTag(ListBoxAvailable.LastIndex, 0) = t
```

Listing 7.27   **Sub AntTargetView.PushButtonRun.Action()**

```
// Execute ant targets in the order they are
// listed in ListBoxOrder.
Dim t as AntTarget
Dim p as AntProject
Dim x,y as Integer

p = AntProject(ListBoxProject.celltag(ListBoxProject.ListIndex, 0))

// When running in asynchronous mode, you should check
// to make sure the Shell is still running before
// executing a command.
If not antshell1.IsRunning Then
    Antshell1.setMode(2)
    Antshell1.setView(Window1.EditField2)
```

Listing 7.27   **Continued**

```
// On Mac/Linux there is more than one Shell, so you will
// need to be aware of which shell you are running and
// it's individual idiosyncracies.
    Antshell1.execute "sh"
Else
    AntShell1.reset
End If

 AntShell1.setCmd "ant"
 AntShell1.addOpt "-f", p.build.ShellPath

 y = ListBoxOrder.ListCount - 1

 For x = 0 To y
    t = AntTarget(listboxOrder.celltag(x, 0))
    AntShell1.addArg t.name
 Next

 AntShell1.exec
```

Listing 7.28   **Sub AntTargetView.PushButtonOrder.Action()**

```
// Clear ListBoxOrder and start over.
ListBoxOrder.DeleteAllRows
```

Listing 7.29   **Sub AntTargetView.BevelButtonMove.Action()**

```
// Selects and moves an available target into
// ListBoxOrder so that it can be executed.
Dim t as AntTarget

t = ListBoxAvailable.CellTag(ListBoxAvailable.ListIndex, 0)

ListBoxOrder.addRow(t.name)
ListBoxOrder.CellTag(ListBoxOrder.LastIndex, 0) = t
```

Listing 7.30   **Sub AntTargetView.PushButtonClear.Action()**

```
// Clear the selected target in ListBoxOrder
ListBoxOrder.RemoveRow(ListBoxOrder.listindex)
```

Listing 7.31   Function AntTargetView.ListBoxProjectList.CellBackgroundPaint(g As Graphics, row As Integer, column As Integer) As Boolean

```
// Colorize every other row of this ListBox
If row Mod 2=0 Then
    g.foreColor=RGB(224,224,255)
Else
    g.foreColor=RGB(255,255,255)
End If
    g.FillRect 0,0,g.width,g.height
```

Listing 7.32   Function AntTargetView.ListBoxProjectList.CellClick(row as Integer, column as Integer, x as Integer, y as Integer) As Boolean

```
// Select a project
Dim project as AntProject

ListBoxAvailable.DeleteAllRows
project = AntProject(listboxOrder.celltag(row,0))
If project <> Nil Then
    StaticText4.text = project.description
    controller.view(project)
End If
```

Listing 7.33   Class AntTargetViewer

```
// The view property is a reference to the
// Window that this class controls
Property view as AntTargetView

// The list of projects displayed
Property Projects(-1) as AntProject

// Determines whether all projects
// should be viewed.
Property ShowProjects as Boolean
```

Listing 7.34   Sub AntTargetViewer.view(project as AntProject)

```
// Display Projects in ListBoxProjectList
Dim t as AntTarget

view.ListBoxProjectList.DeleteAllRows

If project <> Nil Then

    // A project is a collection of targets
    For each t in project.targets
```

Listing 7.34   **Continued**

```
            view.ListBoxProjectList.addrow(t.name)

            // Show targets in the second column
            view.ListBoxProjectList.Cell(view.ListBoxProjectList.LastIndex, 1) _
              = t.depends
            view.ListBoxProjectList.celltag(view.ListBox1.LastIndex, 0) = t
      Next
End If
```

Listing 7.35   **Sub AntTargetViewer.Constructor(antView as AntTargetView)**

```
Me.view = antView
Me.view.controller = me
ShowProjects = False
```

Listing 7.36   **Sub AntTargetViewer.getProject(aBuildFile as FolderItem)**

```
// Instantiate XMLReader subclass and parse build file
Dim ar as AntReader

ar = New AntReader

ar.viewer = me
ar.parse(aBuildFile)
```

Listing 7.37   **Sub AntTargetViewer.handleProject(aProject as AntProject)**

```
If ShowProjects = True Then
    viewProjectList(aProject)
Else
    view(aProject)
End If
```

Listing 7.38   **Sub AntTargetViewer.viewProjectList(project as AntProject)**

```
// Display all projects that reside in the selected directory
Dim t as AntTarget

If project <> Nil Then
    projects.append(project)

    view.ListBoxProjectList.row(project.name)
```

Listing 7.38   **Continued**

```
    view.ListBoxProjectList.cell(view.ListBoxProjectList.lastindex, 1) =
project.build.name
    view.ListBoxProjectList.celltag(view.ListBoxProjectList.lastindex, 0)
➥= project
End If
```

Listing 7.39   **Sub AntTargetViewer.getProjects(aDir as FolderItem)**

```
// Get projects that reside in aDir
Dim ar as AntReader
Dim x,y as integer

Me.ShowProjects = True
view.ListBoxOrder.DeleteAllRows
If aDir.Directory Then
    y = aDir.Count - 1
    For x = 0 To y
        If aDir.item(x).IsReadable and aDir.item(x).Visible Then
            If Right(aDir.item(x).name, 4) = ".xml" Then
                getProject(aDir.item(x))
            End If
        End If
    Next
End If
```

Listing 7.40   **Sub AntTargetViewer.Release()**

```
Me.view = Nil
```

Listing 7.41   **AntProject**

```
// A simple data-oriented class that holds
// important information about a given project.
Property name as String
Property default as String
Property basedir as String
Property targets(-1) as AntTarget
Property description as String
Property build as folderitem
```

Listing 7.42   **AntTarget**

```
// A simple data-oriented class that holds
// important information about the target
Property name as String
Property depends as String
Property description as String
```

Listing 7.43   **AntReader Inherits XMLReader**

```
//The XMLReader subclass that parses the build files
//and extracts project and target information. This
//subclass takes the data from the XML file and
//instantiates AntProject and AntTarget objects.

Property Project as AntProject
Property Viewer as AntTargetViewer

// Build files are very simple, so this XMLReader
// subclass does not have to work to hard at
// maintaining state. It tracks whether the parser is
// inside a project element or inside a target element.
Property inProject as Boolean
Property inTarget as Boolean
Property getText as Boolean
Property build as FolderItem
```

Listing 7.44   **Sub AntReader.StartElement(name as String, attributeList as XmlAttributeList) Handles Event**

```
// Most of the work is done in the StartElement event.
// Namespaces are not expanded and the properties
// for the AntProject instance come from XML attributes
Dim t as AntTarget

Select Case name
// Create an AntProject
Case "project"
    inProject = True
    Project = New AntProject
    Project.name = attributeList.value("name")
    Project.default = attributeList.value("default")
    Project.basedir = attributeList.value("basedir")
    Project.description = attributeList.value("description")
// Create an AntTarget
Case "target"
```

Listing 7.44   **Continued**

```
    inTarget = True
    t = New AntTarget
    t.name = attributeList.value("name")
    t.depends = attributeList.value("depends")
    t.description = attributeList.value("description")
    Project.targets.append(t)
Case "description"
    // Only get descriptions for projects.
    If inProject = True and inTarget = False Then
        getText = True
    End If
End select
```

Listing 7.45   **Sub AntReader.Characters(s as String) Handles Event**

```
// If inProject and inTarget are true, then getText
// is set to true in the StartElement event handler
// if the current element is named "description"
// This tells the AntReader to capture the text
// and set the description property of AntProject
// Since there can theoretically be sequence Characters
// events called, I concatenate the new text with the
// potentially existing text.
If getText = True Then
    Project.description = Project.description + s
End If
```

Listing 7.46   **Sub AntReader.EndDocument() Handles Event**

```
// Done parsing; handle it
If Me.build <> Nil Then
    project.build = me.build
End If
Viewer.handleProject(Project)
```

Listing 7.47   **Sub AntReader.parse(aBuildFile as folderitem)**

```
Me.build = aBuildFile
super.parse(aBuildFile)
```

434 Chapter 7 Console Programming and the Shell

Listing 7.48 **AntShell Inherits mwShell**

```
Property AntHome as String
Property BuildFile as String
Property Target as String
Property JavaHome as String
```

Listing 7.49 **Sub AntShell.DataAvailable() Handles Event**

```
print me.ReadAll
```

Listing 7.50 **Sub AntShell.Constructor()**

```
// Override mwShell default Constructor.
```

Listing 7.51 **Sub AntShell.execTarget(aTarget as String)**

```
// The -f option lets you specify the name of a build file.
// Without it, Ant defaults to executing the file
// called build.xml
addOpt "-f", BuildFile
addArg aTarget
exec
```

Listing 7.52 **Sub AntShell.setAntHome(aHome as String)**

```
// Ant requires that an environment variable be set.
// Just because you have environment variables set
// up so that when you log-in, they are available,
// do not assume that they will be available when
// using REALbasic's shell, even though it is
// running under your name. Be sure to check and
// set the variables you need set, this is especially
// important because command line applications
// often make heavy use of environment variables.
If aHome <> "" Then
    AntHome = aHome
Else
    AntHome = "/Users/mchoate/ant"
    System.EnvironmentVariable("ANT_HOME")=AntHome
End If
```

Listing 7.53   **Sub AntShell.setJavaHome(aPath as String)**

```
// Set the JAVA_HOME environement variable
Dim tmp as String

tmp = System.EnvironmentVariable("JAVA_HOME")

If aPath = "" Then
    If tmp = "" Then
        #If TargetMachO Then
            System.EnvironmentVariable("JAVA_HOME") = "/Library/Java/Home"
        #endIf
    End If

Else
    If tmp = "" Then
        System.EnvironmentVariable("JAVA_HOME") = aPath
    End If
End If
```

Listing 7.54   **Sub AntShell.setBuildFile(aFile as String)**

```
If aFile <> "" Then
    BuildFile = aFile
End If
```

Listing 7.55   **Sub AntShell.setTarget(aTarget as String)**

```
If aTarget <> "" Then
    target = atarget
End If
```

Developing Console Applications

For the rest of this chapter, I will be writing about console applications. When you create a console application project, there is only one class available by default, which is the **App** class, a subclass of **ConsoleApplication**. It has two events, Run and UnhandledException. The Run event is triggered when the application is started, and it serves as the starting point for all console applications.

Transformer: Command-Line XML Transformation

The first console example is a simple command-line application that takes two arguments. The first is a path that points to an XML document, and the second is a path that points to an XSLT stylesheet that will be used to convert the document. The results of the transformation are sent to standard output by using the `Print` method.

There are two classes, **mwArgHandler** and **mwTransformer**. **mwArgHandler** is a class that's used to parse the arguments that are passed to the application from the command line. The **mwTransformer** class is the class that wraps the process of transforming an XML document using a given stylesheet.

Class App

All console applications have an **App** class, which should come as no surprise. This class has one property, which is an instance of **mwArgHandler**. One thing that you will notice is that the output is sent to the standard output using the `Print` command. In addition to the expected output of the program, which is the result of the XSLT transformation, I also send error messages to standard output using `Print`. I do not have to do it this way, but I chose to because it's convenient and because standard output and standard error are often the same thing. If I wanted to send error messages specifically to standard error, I could use the StdErr method to get a reference to it. It implements REALbasic's **Writeable** interface (which is different from the **iWritable** interface I introduced in a previous chapter), so after you have a reference to it, you can write data to it by calling `Write(someData as String)`.

```
Property Arg As mwArgHandler
```

Listing 7.56 **Function Run(args() as String) As Integer Handles Event**

```
Dim trans as mwTransformer
Dim source as FolderItem
Dim xslt_file as FolderItem

Me.Arg = New mwArgHandler(args)

// Count the number of arguments that were passed in the args()
// array(). The first item in the array is the name of the
// command or application being called. It is then followed by
// the actual arguments. In this situation, there should be three
// arguments altogether.
If Me.Arg.getArgCount = 3 Then

    source = Me.Arg.getFolderItemFromPath(Me.Arg.Arguments(1))

    xslt_file = Me.Arg.getFolderItemFromPath(Me.Arg.Arguments(2))

    trans = New mwTransformer

    Print trans.transform(source, xslt_file)
```

Listing 7.56   **Continued**

```
Else
    // Print error to standard output
    Print "Illegal number of arguments: "_
    + str(Me.Arg.getArgCount)
End If
```

Listing 7.57   **Sub UnhandledException(error As RuntimeException) Handles Event**

```
// Send error to standard output.
Print "An error occurred: " + error.Message
Quit
```

Class mwArgHandler Inherits Dictionary

This class handles the parsing of command-line arguments. Earlier I described a special kind of argument called an option, which is basically a key/value pair that together represents a single argument. This class parses those key/value pairs and makes the values more readily accessible. The arguments are stored in the `Arguments` array property, and the options are stored in the `Options` dictionary:

```
Property Arguments(-1) As String
Property Options As Dictionary
```

There is one very important piece of information you need to know to accurately parse command-line arguments, and that is the encoding that is used for the text. Windows computers use UTF-16, whereas UNIX-like systems use ASCII. The `args()` array is parsed in the `Constructor` of the class, but you will see that the arguments are converted into UTF-8 as it is being parsed. **mwArgHandler** is a subclass of **Dictionary**, so if the arguments are not converted to UTF-8, the keys in the **Dictionary** are UTF-16. If you try to see whether the **Dictionary** has a particular key and you use a String literal, or a variable that is encoded in UTF-8, and call the `Dictionary.HasKey("literalString")` method, the result will always be `False`.

There is also a difference in how `Print` methods are called. In the **App** class, I used `Print` to display error messages as well as the output of the transformation, because I said that standard error is usually the same thing as standard output. Because the **App** class is a subclass of **ConsoleApplication**, I know that it will always be run from in an environment where standard input and standard output are meaningful. This is not the case with the **mwArgHandler** and **mwTransformer,** because there are other situations where I could make use of these classes in desktop applications. So I want to make sure the classes work in both kinds of applications: desktop and console.

To do that, these classes introduce another compiler directive, `TargetHasGui`, which is used to see if the class instance is being run from a console application or a desktop application. Depending on the result, different steps are taken with error and logging messages.

Listing 7.58 **Sub Constructor(args() as String)**

```
Dim anArg as String
Dim new_options(-1) as String
Dim aKey, aValue as String

Me.Options = New Dictionary

For Each anArg in args
// Options start with a hyphen, followed by a String, like
// -f=/path/to/file

    If Left(anArg,1) = "-" Then
        // It's an option
        new_options = Split(anArg, "=")
        If ubound(new_options) = 1 Then

                // Convert arguments to UTF-8
                // Since the Unix-like systems arguments
                // are ASCII, you technically do not
                // need to convert them since an ASCII
                // character is the same as the equivalent
                // UTF-8 character. As it is, it is quicker
                // to convert all of them and avoid using
                // compiler directives.

                Options.Value(ConvertEncoding(new_options(0), Encodings.UTF8)) = _
                 ConvertEncoding(new_options(1),Encodings.UTF8)
        Else
            Print "Illegal option " + anArg
            Print "Quitting application..."
            Quit
        End If

    Else
    // It's an argument
    If Trim(anArg) <> "" Then
        Arguments.Append(ConvertEncoding(anArg, Encodings.UTF8))
    End If

    End If
Next
```

Listing 7.59   **Function getArgCount() As Integer**

```
Return Ubound(Arguments) + 1
```

Listing 7.60   **Function getFolderItemFromPath(aPath as String) As FolderItem**

```
// This application takes two command-line arguments which
// are paths to particular FolderItems.
Dim f as FolderItem

f = getFolderItem(aPath, FolderItem.PathTypeShell)

If (f <> Nil) And (f.IsReadable) Then
    Return f
Else
    // Test to see if this is a console application.
    // If it is not, then send the error message to
    // the System.log, otherwise use Print.
    #if TargetHasGUI Then
        System.Log(System.LogLevelError, "Error opening" + aPath)
    #else
    // This is a console application, so use Print to
    // display the error message.
        Print "Error opening " + aPath
    #endif
End if
```

Class mwTransformer

The **mwTransformer** class is simple. It has one function that wraps the
XMLDocument.Transform method and adds some error checking. This same class will be
used in the RSSReader application, as well as in the rbCGI application that I will share
with you in the next section.

Listing 7.61   **Function transform(source as FolderItem, xslt_folder as FolderItem) As String**

```
Dim xdoc as XmlDocument
Dim xslt as XmlStyleSheet

Try
    xdoc = New XmlDocument

    Try
        xdoc.LoadXml(source)
    Catch
        #if TargetHasGUI Then
```

Listing 7.61   **Continued**

```
            System.Log(System.LogLevelError, "Error parsing "_
            + source.AbsolutePath)
        #else
            Print "Error parsing " + source.AbsolutePath
        #endif
    End

    Try
        xslt = new XmlStyleSheet(xslt_folder)
    Catch
        #if TargetHasGUI Then
            System.Log(System.LogLevelError, "Error opening XSLT "_
            + xslt_folder.AbsolutePath)
        #else
            Print "Error opening XSLT " + xslt_folder.AbsolutePath
        #endif

    End

    Try
        Return xdoc.Transform(xslt)
    Catch
        #if TargetHasGUI Then
            System.Log(System.LogLevelError, "Error transforming file.")
        #else
            Print "Error transforming file."
        #endif
    End

Catch
    return "<html><body>XSLT Error</body></html>"
End
```

CGI Application

CGI stands for the *common gateway interface*. Its called an interface because it provides the means for Apache (or any web server that supports CGI) to execute scripts and applications on the host machine of a web server. When a user types in a URL into his or her web browser, that URL often represents the location of an HTML file that the server just picks up and sends back to the browser. In a CGI program, the URL represents a script or a program that gets executed. The output of the program then gets sent back to the user. To provide security, Apache allows the administrator to configure which directories allow CGI programs to be executed. Most often, the default CGI directory is the cgi-bin directory. On OS X, the cgi-bin directory is here:

```
/Library/WebServer/CGI-Executables
```

For this example, we'll be placing our REALbasic CGI program in this directory. Very often, you'll see CGI scripts that end with a `.cgi` extension, but we won't need to use that—in fact, you should avoid using any extensions, because it will mess things up. Other scripting languages, such as Perl and Python, usually reside on the web server as text files that are executed by an interpreter. Apache uses extensions to map an interpreter to a particular file. Because REALbasic is a compiled program, it doesn't need an interpreter, and it's better just to leave the extension off. It also provides for a much nicer URL, which is important, too.

Now we can start work on the program. The easiest way to work is to save the project in the CGI-Executables directory. You'll need to compile the application to test it with Apache, and it's easier to compile it and leave it there to test than to compile it and copy it to the CGI directory.

As is the case with all console applications, there are two default events in a `UnhandledException` and `Run`. The `Run` event is triggered when the program is launched. In the case of a CGI application, it is triggered when a user requests it by typing selecting the applications URL in a web browser.

When I created the console application project, I named the application CGI for Linux and CGIX for Macintosh OS X—both with no extensions.

Because console applications do not have a graphical interface, they have to be able to input data and output data in some other fashion. For programs that are executed on the command line, this is typically referred to as standard input and standard output, respectively. With a REALbasic console application, the command `Input` represents (you guessed it) standard input. `Print` sends data to standard output. In addition to standard input and output, CGI applications also make use of environment variables that are set by the web server. To access environment variables, you need the **System** object, which includes the method `System.EnvironmentVariable()`, which returns the value for the environment variable that is passed to it.

Because the `Run` event is triggered when the application is invoked by the web server, it is in the `Run` event that we put the main part of our code. I also created a **cgiRequest** object, which is created when the `Run` method is executed. It is a subclass of **Dictionary.** It is used to hold the data that is passed to the CGI application from Apache, and it executes a `Write` method that sends data back to the client browser.

The `Run` method should look like this:

Listing 7.62   **Function Run(args() as String) As Integer Handles Event**

```
#pragma disableBackgroundTasks

Me.request = new cgiRequest

// required variables for cgi
Me.request.value("SERVER_SOFTWARE") = system.environmentVariable
➡("SERVER_SOFTWARE")
Me.request.value("SERVER_NAME") = system.environmentVariable("SERVER_NAME")
```

Listing 7.62 **Continued**

```
Me.request.value("GATEWAY_INTERFACE") = system.environmentVariable
➥("GATEWAY_INTERFACE")
Me.request.value("SERVER_PROTOCOL") = system.environmentVariable
➥("SERVER_PROTOCOL")
Me.request.value("SERVER_PORT") = system.environmentVariable("SERVER_PORT")
Me.request.value("REQUEST_METHOD") = system.environmentVariable("REQUEST_METHOD")
Me.request.value("PATH_INFO") = system.environmentVariable("PATH_INFO")
Me.request.value("PATH_TRANSLATED") =
system.environmentVariable("PATH_TRANSLATED")
Me.request.value("SCRIPT_NAME") = system.environmentVariable("SCRIPT_NAME")
Me.request.value("QUERY_STRING") = system.environmentVariable("QUERY_STRING")
Me.request.value("REMOTE_HOST") = system.environmentVariable("REMOTE_HOST")
Me.request.value("REMOTE_ADDR") = system.environmentVariable("REMOTE_ADDR")
Me.request.value("AUTH_TYPE") = system.environmentVariable("AUTH_TYPE")
Me.request.value("REMOTE_USER") = system.environmentVariable("REMOTE_USER")
Me.request.value("REMOTE_IDENT") = system.environmentVariable("REMOTE_IDENT")
Me.request.value("CONTENT_TYPE") = system.environmentVariable("CONTENT_TYPE")
Me.request.value("CONTENT_LENGTH") = system.environmentVariable("CONTENT_LENGTH")
Me.request.value("HTTP_ACCEPT") = system.environmentVariable("HTTP_ACCEPT")
Me.request.value("HTTP_USERAGENT") = system.environmentVariable("HTTP_USERAGENT")
Me.request.value("HTTP_COOKIE") = system.environmentVariable("HTTP_COOKIE")

// Parse the data that is contained in the HTTP_COOKIE
// Environment Variable
Me.request.getCookie

// Parse the data in the QUERY_STRING Environment Variable
Me.request.getQueryString

Me.request.handleRequest
```

At the beginning of the Run event handler is a pragma directive. It's similar to the other compiler directives that were encountered in previous chapters, except that instead of identifying the system platform, it tells REALbasic how to compile the application. In this case, background tasks are disabled because Apache doesn't work well with them. If you don't disable them, every time you do a loop, or execute anything that triggers a new thread or background task, the application crashes mercilessly. You can also use this directive to speed up processor-intensive stretches of your REALbasic code in other situations. The downside is that other threads stop running and events don't get triggered, but it can make a significant performance difference otherwise.

Class cgiRequest Inherits Dictionary

```
Property query as Dictionary
Property cookies as Dictionary
```

The two variables that matter most to us are "REQUEST_METHOD" and "QUERY_STRING". There are several kinds of requests a web server can accept. The two that concern us are "Post" requests and "Get" requests. The distinction between the two in actual practice is virtually nonexistent, except that it changes the way that form data is passed to the CGI program.

Anytime you fill out a form on a web page, either to log in or make a purchase, the information that you enter needs to be transferred to the server so that it can take some appropriate action. When you create a form in HTML, you have the option of selecting the request method you want to use—either "Get" or "Post". If you choose "Get", the data from the form is encoded and sent across as part of the URL. If you use "Post", the data is sent to the CGI program as standard input. Here is an example of a "Get" request URL:

```
localhost/cgi-bin/test?cat=dog
```

The first step in processing a CGI request is to find out what kind of request it is, and process it accordingly. In the **cgiRequest** class, I have implemented the following method:

Listing 7.63   **Sub getQueryString()**

```
#pragma disableBackgroundTasks
// If not disabled, the app throws an error during the loop
Dim QueryString, field, key, value As String
Dim x As Integer
query = New Dictionary

// Check the request_method and retrieve the
// query string from the right place
If me.hasKey("REQUEST_METHOD") Then
    If me.value("REQUEST_METHOD") = "POST" Then
        QueryString = Input
    Else
        QueryString = System.EnvironmentVariable("QUERY_STRING")
    End If
End If

If QueryString <> "" Then
//Now run through the query string and parse the
// names and values into a dictionary

    For x = 1 to CountFields(QueryString, "&")
        field = NthField(QueryString, "&", x)
        key = NthField(field, "=", 1)
        value = NthField(field, "=", 2)
        value = ReplaceAll(value, "+", " ")
        value = DecodeURLComponent(value)
        query.value(key) = value
    Next
End If
```

Listing 7.64   **Sub handleRequest()**

```
Dim response as new cgiResponse(me)
response.write
```

The method creates a new **Dictionary** to hold the values of the query (the data from the form). If the request method is a "Post", the method grabs the string from standard input. If it is a "Get", it grabs it from the environment variable "QUERY_STRING". Beyond that, everything else is the same. The string is parsed, and the dictionary values are set.

Finally, the HTTP_COOKIES environment variable must be checked. If it has a value, you will need to parse it and instantiate a **cgiCookie** object. In web programming, cookies are a way to identify individual users and it can help you store information specifically about that user. After it is parsed, it consists of key/value pairs for each cookie that has been set. You can set new cookies in the **cgiResponse** class.

Class cgiCookie

```
Property key(-1) as String
Property value(-1) as String
```

Listing 7.65   **Function getItem(sequence as integer, byref key as string, byref value as string) As Boolean**

```
#pragma disableBackgroundTasks
    // sequence is 1 based
    dim x as integer
    x = sequence - 1
    if (x > ubound(me.key)) OR (x < 0) then
        return false
    else
        key = me.key(x)
        value = me.value(x)
        return true
    end if
```

Listing 7.66   **Function hasKey(myKey as string) As Boolean**

```
#pragma disableBackgroundTasks
Dim x  as String

For Each x in key
    If strComp(x, myKey, 0) = 0 Then
        Return True
    End If
Next
    Return false
```

Listing 7.67   **Sub setValue(key as string, value as string)**

```
If key <> "" And value <> "" Then
    Me.key.Append(key)
    Me.value.Append(value)
End If
```

Listing 7.68   **Function getValue(index as integer) As String**

```
#pragma disableBackgroundTasks

Dim x as Integer
x = index - 1
If x > ubound(value) OR x < 0 Then
    Return ""
Else
    Return me.value(x)
End If
```

Listing 7.69   **Sub getValues(myKey as string, byref myValues() as string)**

```
#pragma disableBackgroundTasks
Dim x,y as Integer
Redim myValues(-1)
y = ubound(key)
For x = 0 to y
    If strcomp(key(x), myKey, 0) = 0 Then
        myValues.append(value(x))
    End If
Next
```

Listing 7.70   **Function count() As Integer**

```
Return Ubound(key) + 1
```

Class cgiResponse

We now have a **cgiRequest** object that contains all the needed values from the request, plus the query parsed into a dictionary. This object will be passed to the **cgiResponse** object when it is instantiated, and the **cgiResponse** object will be able to use the data in it to prepare the appropriate response.

To send data back to the client, we need to send some header information followed by an html string:

```
Property str as String
Property request as cgiRequest
```

```
Property contentType as String
Property cookies as String
Property location as String
Property status as String
```

Listing 7.71 **Sub Constructor(myRequest as cgiRequest)**

```
request = myRequest
```

Listing 7.72 **Sub addHeader(myHeader as String)**

```
str = str + myHeader
```

Listing 7.73 **Sub setCookie(cName as String, cValue as String, cExpires as Date, cPath as String, cDomain as String, cSecure as Boolean)**

```
// In addition to a name and a value (the key/value pair)
// Cookies also have expiration dates which limit their
// lifespans. The path and domain variables place restrictions
// on where the cookie should be made available to the Web
// server. A cookie from one domain can never be accessed by
// a Web server from a different domain. The path variable
// further refines this distinction and only allows the
// cookie to be visible to the server when the HTTP request
// is contained within a certain path.
Dim a as String

a = "Set-Cookie: "
a = a + cName + "=" + cValue + "; "
If cExpires <>  Nil Then
    a = a + "expires=" + nthField(cExpires.longDate,",", 1) _
    + " " + str(cExpires.day) + "-" + str(cExpires.month)_
    + "-" + str(cExpires.year) + " " + str(cExpires.hour)_
    + ":" + str(cExpires.minute) + ":" _
    + Str(cExpires.second) + " GMT; "
    // DD-Mon-YYYY HH:MM:SS GMT
End If
If cPath <> "" Then
    a = a+ "path=" + cPath + "; "
End If

If cDomain <> "" Then
    a = a + "domain=" + cDomain + "; "
End If
```

Listing 7.73   **Continued**

```
If cSecure Then
    a = a + "secure"
End If
a = a + chr(13) + chr(10)
cookies = a
```

Listing 7.74   **Sub setContentType(myType as String)**

```
contentType = "Content-type: " + myType + Chr(13)_
 + Chr(10) + Chr(13) + Chr(10)
```

Listing 7.75   **Sub setLocation(myURL as String)**

```
Dim a as string
a = "Location: " + myURL + chr(13) + chr(10) + chr(13) + chr(10)
location = a
```

Listing 7.76   **Sub setStatus(myStatus as String)**

```
Dim a as String
a = "Status: " + myStatus + chr(13) + chr(10)_
 + chr(13) + chr(10)
status = a
```

Listing 7.77   **Function Transform() as String**

```
Dim path_trans as String
Dim path_xslt as String
Dim trans as FolderItem
Dim xslt as FolderItem
Dim t as New mwTransformer

// The PATH_TRANSLATED environment variable
// returns the path that follows the cgi application
// in the URL.
path_trans = Me.request.Value("PATH_TRANSLATED")

// In this example, the path to the xsl stylesheet
// is hard-coded. That's to keep the example simple,
// but you'd never really want to do this.
path_xslt = "/Users/mchoate/Sites/RSSview.xsl"
```

Listing 7.77 **Continued**

```
Try
    trans = getFolderItem(path_trans, FolderItem.PathTypeShell)
Catch
    Return "Error with translated path"
End

Try
    xslt = getFolderItem(path_xslt, FolderItem.PathTypeShell)
Catch
    Return "Error with xslt"
End

Return t.transform(trans,xslt)
```

Listing 7.78 **Sub write()**

```
#pragma disableBackgroundTasks
Dim output as String
Dim html as String
Dim requestString, queryString as String
Dim x,y as Integer

// Set the value for "Content-type";
setContentType("text/html")

'setCookie


setHTML("<html><head><title>TestOutput</title></head><body>")

setHtml(transform)

y = request.count
For x = 0 to y-1
    setHTML(request.key(x) + ": " + request.value(request.key(x)) + "<br />")
Next

SetHTML("</body></html>")

// Send the page to standard output, which happens
// to be the user's Web browser.
Print contentType + str
```

Listing 7.79   **Sub setHTML(myHtml as string)**

```
// Append more text to the String
str =  str + myHtml
```

If you are using OS X and placed the application in the `/Library/WebServer/CGI-Executables` directory, and set the application name as "CGIX", you should be able to access the script from the following URL:

```
Localhost/cgi-bin/CGIX/CGIX
```

The reason the CGIX repeats itself is because this is a Mach-O build for OS X, so it builds it in a typical bundle, which isn't recognized as such by Apache. All it sees is a directory with an application inside of it, so you have to use the path that specifies the actual executable.

You should be able to paste this URL into the browser, press Enter, and then get back a list of the variables. If you want to test the query string, then enter a URL such as the following:

```
Localhost/cgi-bin/CGIX/CGIX/realsoftware.xml
```

If you have the realsoftware.xml file in the right location, as well as a stylesheet to transform it, the results will look something like Figure 7.5:

Figure 7.5   CGI output in Safari.

You now have a good starting point for writing CGI programs in REALbasic for Apache. One thing you'll notice, especially if you have a lot of traffic on your site, is that CGI can be slow at times. The reason is that the program has to be started up with each request, which produces a lot of overhead. The downside to REALbasic is that it produces large executable files—about 1.3MB for this simple CGI program, so the particular solution is best limited to low-traffic sites. Because of this, there have been a variety of CGI workarounds that speed up the process. They way they work is that instead of invoking the program each time it is requested, the program stays resident in memory and handles the requests as they come in. This is usually accomplished with an Apache plug-in. This is an interesting approach that can be used with REALbasic as well, and you don't need to rely on console programming.

I developed a REALbasic application that worked with an Apache plug-in called "mod_scgi". Mod_scgi works by taking the data that Apache would normally send as environment variables to a CGI program, and instead sends it as a block of data over a TCP connection. Using REALbasic's networking capabilities, you can create a SocketServer that creates a pool of **TCPSockets** that listen on the appropriate port, gets the data when it is available, parses it, and acts on it just like a CGI program. As soon as the individual socket is done, instead of exiting, it returns to listening on the port for the next request. This creates a huge performance boost and is a tactic that should be considered if you expect a lot of traffic to your site.

The following is the original (and best) guide to CGI from the inventor's of Mosaic, NCSA:

```
http://hoohoo.ncsa.uiuc.edu/cgi/
```

Conclusion

This chapter introduced you to the **Shell** class and console application programming. In Chapter 8, REALbasic's database classes will be demonstrated. This is one of REALbasic's most powerful features because of its use of binding. You can create database applications with little or no programming whatsoever.

8

Databases

REALBASIC 2005 SHIPS WITH A NEW DATABASE engine, based on the open source SQLite project (read more about it at http://www.SQLite.org/). The **REALSQLdatabase** class is the class you use to manage databases, and this replaces the legacy REALdatabase, which is still part of the distribution but is available only for backward compatibility. **REALSQLdatabase** is a subclass of the **Database** class, and the **Database** class provides a generic database API that can be used with more than just REALSQLdatabases. Professional edition users can also use plug-ins that provide the following classes: **MySQLDatabase**, **PostgresDatabase**, **OpenBaseDatabase**, **OracleDatabase**, **Database4DServer** and **ODBCDatabase** classes.

Fortunately, **REALSQLdatabase** is available to all users, and because it shares the same basic API as the other classes, you can readily create a project using **REALSQLdatabase** and upgrade to one of the other databases at a later time with minimal changes to your code. That is, of course, if you actually write any code when implementing your database. One of the greatest strengths of REALbasic is how simple it makes it to create, update, and modify databases, something that can easily be done without writing a single line of code, and in only a few minutes.

The first database example I will show you does just that—it creates a "codeless" database and shows you just how easy it is. I'll use it to create a different way of tracking RSS subscriptions in the RSSReader application. When that is accomplished, I will show you the same database created through code, which is still a relatively painless process. The fact that REALbasic uses SQLite as the underlying database should fill you with delight. As an open source project, the quality of the database is extremely high. It consumes little memory; it's compact, it's fast, and its innards are readily accessible to any developer interested in looking inside. It is not a multiuser database like MySQL or Postgres, so it may not be right for all occasions, but it is right for many of them.

One especially valuable feature is that SQLite database files are cross-platform and they do not have any endian issues. You can move the database file around to different machines and open it without any problems. One of the benefits of it being an open source project is that there are many language bindings to SQLite, such as Java, Python,

Perl, PHP, Delphi, and Visual Basic, to name a few. This means that any databases you create with REALbasic can also be made available to applications written in other languages.

The No-Code Database

This database will keep track of RSS files I have subscribed to. I will track two pieces of information for each file: the URL where the latest copy of the file can be retrieved and the name of the RSS feed.

I'll dive right into creating the database without any further discussion. Create a new REALbasic desktop application in the **Project Editor.**

To create a new database, Control+Click (or right-click) to get the **ContextualMenu.** Select Add, Database, New REAL SQL database to create a new database, as shown in Figure 8.1. If the database already existed, you would just select Open REAL SQL Database.

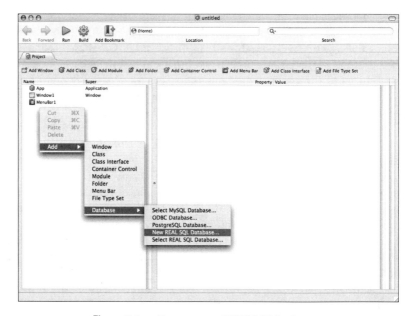

Figure 8.1   Create a new REALSQLdatabase.

When you do this, you will be prompted to name the database file and to select a folder into which it should be saved. In this example, I will name the database file RSSSub. The file will be saved with an extension of .rsd. After the file is saved, you will need to create the structure for the database. Databases are organized into tables and each table consists of a collection of fields that are used to contain specific data. A table is a collection of related fields, and in this example, only one table is used. The fields themselves are typed (which means you have to assign a data type to them, like integer or Boolean), but SQLite uses something called affinity typing, which really means that the type of the data used doesn't matter. Setting a type for each field is important, however, if you plan to migrate to a different database plug-in that uses more traditional typing schemes. Setting the type for each field can also be useful for future developers to understand what your intentions were for a particular field.

```
Field Types:
Integer
VarChar
Boolean
Date
Time
TimeStamp
Double
Binary
```

When you create a table like this, either programmatically or through the user interface, you are creating a table schema that documents the structure of the table. After the database is established, actual data will be input and the data that is added will be called a record. A record has values for the fields defined in the table schema. A record has a similar relationship to a table that a class instance has to the class. Records are sometimes referred to as rows, and the individual fields in the record are called columns. In different places, REALbasic uses the terms field and column to describe the same thing.

The RSSSub database should be available in the **Project Editor**. To edit the database schema, you will need to double-click the database to get to the schema editor. To add a table to the database, click the **Add Table** button in the Database editor, as shown in Figure 8.2.

When you add a new table, an untitled database will appear in the **Table Editor**. You can select it and modify its name in the **Properties pane** in the right column. I will call this table Subscriptions.

After the table is created, the next step is to add fields. In the Database editor, this is done by clicking the **Add Column** button. Each field has four properties to set: Name, Type, Primary Key, and Mandatory. The Name is the name of the field, which is used when interacting with the database. Type is one of the eight field types I listed earlier. When selected, the **Mandatory CheckBox** indicates that this field must have data in it. If the field is empty, you cannot create a new record.

The Primary Key property designates one field as a primary key. This is used when relating two or more tables to each other (hence the name relational database). The primary key is a unique identifier that is used to link a record in one table to a record in another table. SQLite automatically generates a primary key for your table, so you do not need to create one yourself. Later on in the chapter I will have more samples of how tables get related and the role that primary keys play.

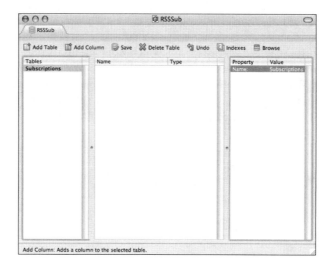

Figure 8.2   Add tables to a new database.

In the sample database, I have created a table called Subscriptions with two fields, Name and URL, both of which are VarChar and Mandatory. VarChar means a field that can hold a string of varying length. Both fields are mandatory. I have designated URL as the Primary Key. One characteristic of primary keys is that they have to be unique. Because each subscription in the database will have a unique URL, it is an appropriate field for a primary key. After the fields have been created, you must save the database, refer to Figure 8.3.

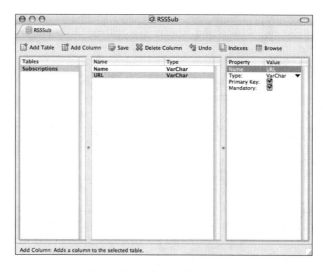

Figure 8.3   Add a Name field.

Databases can have thousands and even millions of records, and as the database gets larger, it gets harder and harder to find what you are looking for. You can imagine a library with only 10 books. If you go to this library and look for a book, it's easy to look through everything to see if you can find what you want. If the library has 1,000 books, then the task gets quite a bit harder. Libraries solve this problem by placing the books in special categories and sorting them by title or the author's name; then they provide a card catalog, which indexes the book, so that you can look it up by author, subject, title, and so on.

Databases use the same principle to speed up the search process when finding records. One of the things a database is good for is sorting data and retrieving it very quickly. To do that, it needs to create indexes of individual fields or groups of fields that work like card catalogs do—after the database finds the item in the index, the index points to the exact location in the library where the book can be found.

When you are finished adding your fields, you can click the Indexes button to designate which fields should be indexed, as shown in Figure 8.4.

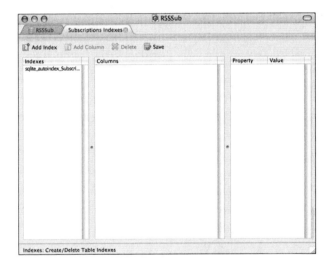

Figure 8.4   Creating indexes.

One thing you will notice right away is that an index already exists. This index is for the URL field and it exists because I designated the URL field as the primary key, and primary keys are always automatically indexed. If you have not yet saved the database, the index will have not been automatically generated. If you are following along with the example and you do not see an index, go back and make sure that the **Primary Key CheckBox** has been checked on the URL field and that the database has been saved.

If I want to create another index, I add a column and select the field that I want indexed as shown in Figure 8.5. Then I give the index a name. In this case, I am indexing the Name field and I have named the index NameIndex.

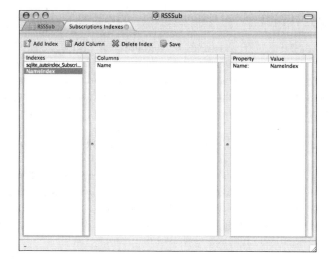

Figure 8.5   Customizing indexes.

After creating the indexes, there are a few other things you can do. If the database has data in it, you can click the **Browse** button and see a list of all the records in the table, as shown in Figure 8.6.

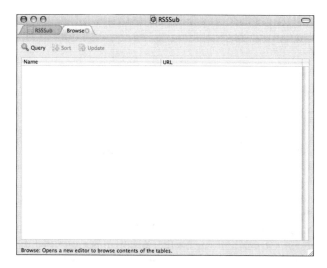

Figure 8.6   Browsing existing data.

At this point, there is no data in the database yet, but if there were, you would click the **Query** button. If you're familiar with SQL, the advanced query tool is easier to use

because you can just enter a SQL command. The Query dialog can be seen in
Figure 8.7.

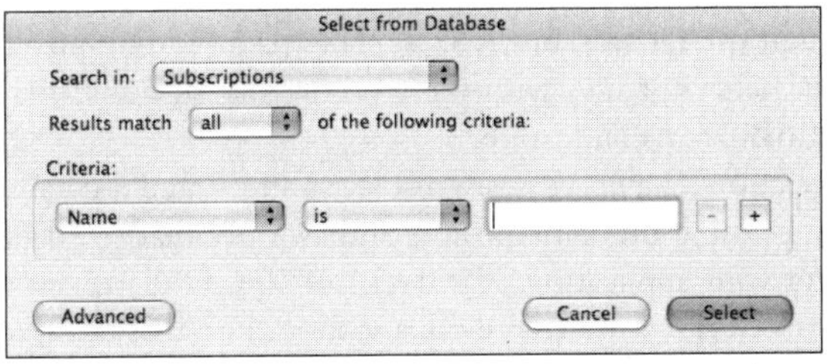

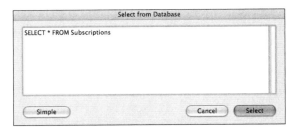

Figure 8.7   Query.

REALbasic also provides a dialog that allows you to create more advanced queries by
directly typing in SQL statements. See an example of the Advanced Query dialog in
Figure 8.8.

Figure 8.8   Advanced query.

After the database is created, I need to add functionality to make it useful. First, I need to
provide a user interface that lets users enter new records into the database or update
existing records. This part will be implemented using a **DataControl** control, and I will
bind that control to two **EditFields** that will be used to display the feed's name and
URL. I will also bind the control to four PushButtons that will be used to insert new
records, update existing records, or delete existing records. Second, I need to provide
users with a way to see a list of all the RSS feeds that have been subscribed to. To provide this function, I will use a **DatabaseQuery** control.

The next step is to return to the **Window Editor**, where you can use the
DataControl control to provide a rudimentary front-end to your newly created database.

DataControl

The **DataControl** control sits at the heart of what makes databases so easy to use in REALbasic. It provides some basic navigation tools that allow the user to move forward and backward through the records, but it also makes data binding possible, which is the automatic linking of fields in tables with various controls such as **EditFields**, **CheckBoxes**, **RadioButtons** and more.

In the previous section, I opened a new project and created a database called RSSSub. This sample continues using the same project and assumes that the database is listed in the **Project pane** of your application. If it does not already exist, you will need to go back and create it as described in the previous section. The first thing to do is to drag a **DataControl** onto **Window1**. The **DataControl** itself is a bar at whose center is a caption that should read "Untitled" (unless you've changed it). Buttons on either side of the caption are used to navigate through the database, moving from one record to the next, or jumping to the first or last record.

When the **DataControl** is on **Window1**, select it. In the **Properties pane**, down at the bottom, you will see a section labeled Behavior, as shown in Figure 8.9, which allows you to designate several **DataControl** properties. You associate the **DataControl** with a particular table in a database. I have associated **DataControl1** with the Subscriptions table in the RSSSub database and set SQLQuery to SELECT * FROM Subscriptions. The meaning of these values will be explained in the next section.

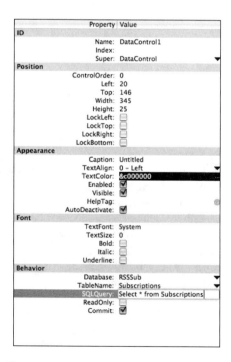

Figure 8.9 The DataControl Properties pane.

Data Control Properties

When the **DataControl** is displayed on a **Window**, there is a text area between the forward and back arrows. The content of that text area is controlled by the **Caption** property, which can be set in the **Properties pane** in the **Window Layout Editor**, or by the following code:

```
DataControl.Caption as String
```

DataControls are bound to a specific table from a specific database. Again, this can be set in the IDE, or programmatically. If your application has a database already created, the **Properties pane** will display it as an option to select the database in the **Behavior** section.

The `Database` property of a **DataControl** is an instance of a **Database** class, not a **REALSQLdatabase**. This means that the **DataControl** can work with any database and it will be unaffected in the future if you change the back-end database that you use. I set the values for the following two properties in the **Properties pane** of the IDE:

```
DataControl.Database as Database
DataControl.TableName as String
```

The `Database` is RSSSub and the `TableName` is Subscriptions.

Although the control can be bound to a database and a table, unless you have a SQL query set, no data will be available. I said this was a code-free example, and at this point you might say I fudged a little, because you do need to add a little bit of SQL code to the `SQLQuery` property, which is displayed on the **DataControl's Properties** pane:

```
DataControl.SQLQuery as String
```

I want this **DataControl** to show all the names and URLs in the Subscriptions table, so I used one of the simplest of all the SQL statements and typed it in as the value for the `SQLQuery` property in the **Properties** pane for the **DataControl**:

```
Select * From Subscriptions
```

Even if you have never seen a line of SQL code in your life, you can probably deduce what is being said here. `Select` is the statement that is used to generate a query that returns a **RecordSet**. The "*" is a wildcard, which in this context means to select all the fields from the Subscriptions table. If I wanted to select only the Names from the Subscriptions table, I could write the SQL like this:

```
Select Name From Subscriptions
```

When the query is executed (which is automatically done when the **Window** is opened), the `RecordSet` property is populated with the results of the query set in the `SQLQuery` property:

```
DataControl.RecordSet as RecordSet
```

I'll go into more detail on the `RecordSet` object momentarily, but first I want to finish out the description of the remaining properties. The **REALSQLdatabase** supports transactions, and this means that you can make changes to a database, such as updating and deleting records and adding new records, but unless you commit the changes, they will not be saved. The following property tells REALbasic to automatically commit all changes:

```
DataControl.Commit as Boolean
```

The `ReadOnly` property is one that you can set to allow or disallow users the capability to change or add new records:

```
DataControl.ReadOnly as Boolean
```

The `RecordLocked` property indicates whether you have the capability to perform any actions on the **database**. This is different from `ReadOnly` because it isn't just a property that is set one way or the other. Depending on the database in use, the `RecordLocked` property may indicate that someone else is in the process of updating that particular record.

```
DataControl.RecordLocked as Boolean
```

REALSQLdatabases lock the entire `database` when one person has it open. Multiuser databases such as MySQL can handle concurrent users more easily and can usually lock individual rows rather than the entire database file. That is one of the biggest advantages of using MySQL or Postgres—they can efficiently handle multiple concurrent users without undo interference into their work flow. Obviously, locking only one record versus the entire table would be less disruptive.

DataControl Methods

The **DataControl** methods all assume that you have bound controls to the **DataControl**. You can do four basic actions with database records, and they are embodied in the following methods:

```
DataControl.NewRecord
DataControl.Insert
DataControl.Update
DataControl.Delete
```

`NewRecord` creates a new record, but with no values. In practice, when the **DataControl** is bound to **EditFields,** the fields are cleared of text and the user can enter the data into them.

The following methods change the position of the **DataControl**. This provides a programmatic way of doing the same thing that the buttons on the **DataControl** do. Bear in mind that the **DataControl** control does not have to be visible, so you can use these methods in buttons to move the current record forward or backward. I like using "real" buttons instead of the **DataControl** because the **DataControl** looks like a **DataControl** and doesn't seem as polished to me.

```
DataControl.MoveFirst
DataControl.MoveLast
DataControl.MoveNext
DataControl.MovePrevious
DataControl.MoveTo(Index as Integer)
```

This group of methods provides access to the **RecordSet** associated with the **DataControl**.

```
DataControl.RecordSet as RecordSet
DataControl.RecordCount as Integer
DataControl.Row as Integer
DataControl.FieldCount
```

Although the query you established for the **DataControl** is executed when the containing **Window** is opened, there are times when you need to reexecute the query—when you insert, delete, or update records. The **RecordSet** associated with the **DataControl** is not refreshed unless you reexecute the query:

```
DataControl.RunQuery
```

DataControl Events

There are a handful of events that get triggered after the method with the same (or similar) name is called. The reason for this is twofold: because the **DataControl** is a control and because of how it uses data binding. The impact of data binding is that you do not need to call the `Insert` or `Delete` methods in code. This is done by binding **PushButtons** to particular actions. At the same time, there are times when you need to modify the action that takes place after a record gets inserted or deleted, and you do this by writing code for the particular events, rather than overriding methods.

When it comes to handling records using the **DataControl**, there are basically three things you can do: insert a new record, update an existing record, or delete an existing record. The following events are triggered when any of these three actions are taken; they correspond to the similarly named methods of the **DataControl**:

```
DataControl.Insert Handles Event
DataControl.Update Handles Event
DataControl.Delete Handles Event
```

A database usually consists of many records, and these records can be accessed sequentially from the **DataControl** by clicking the forward or back arrows on the control itself or by calling methods to move to the first record, the next record, or the previous record (these were discussed in the preceding section). Whenever one of these moves happens, either through the user interface or programmatically, the following events are triggered:

```
DataControl.MoveFirst Handles Event
DataControl.MoveNext Handles Event
DataControl.MovePrevious Handles Event
```

The `DataControl.MoveTo` method causes the following event to be triggered:

```
DataControl.Reposition(Index as Integer) Handles Event
```

The `Validate` property is unique among the events because it is triggered by three methods: `AddNew`, `Update`, and `Insert`. When the event gets triggered, an integer is passed that lets you know what action has just taken place. Based on what that says, you can write code that validates the data before you attempt to commit those changes to the database.

```
DataControl.Validate(Action as Integer) Handles Event
0 = AddNew
1 = Update
2 = Delete
```

If everything is okay with the data, return `False`. If you do not want the data to be committed, return `True`.

Binding EditFields

So far, all that I have done in this application is create a database and drag a DataControl onto Window1. Next, I need to drag two **EditFields** onto the Window. These `EditFields` will be used to display values for the name and URL of the RSS feed as saved in the database.

When a **DataControl** is associated with a **Window**, it is an extremely simple task to bind **EditFields** to particular fields (or columns) in the underlying table. In the **Properties pane** for each **EditField** on the **Window,** there is a **Database Binding** area at the very bottom. You can use the **PopupArrow** to select the **DataControl** you want the **EditField** bound to, and after that is selected, you select the individual field you want to be viewed in your **EditField**, as shown in Figure 8.10. Because the Subscriptions table has two fields, Name and URL, I will place two **EditFields** on the Window—one for each field.

Binding PushButtons

In the previous section, I used REALbasic's binding to bind **EditFields** to a **DataControl** to display individual fields in a record. In this section, I will also use binding, but with **PushButtons** instead of **EditFields**. This uses an entirely different process. With **EditFields**, the binding properties are integrated into the **Properties pane**. That's because what you need to do with an **EditField** is fairly straightforward—you need to display data. **PushButtons** are a little more complicated because you want each **PushButton** to perform a different action when pushed.

To use REALbasic's control binding for **PushButtons**, you will first need to add the binding buttons to the **Layout Editor** toolbar because they are not displayed on the toolbar by default. Under the **View** menu, select **Editor Toolbar** and **Customize**. The **Customize Window Editor Toolbar** dialog will be displayed. It contains two lists. On the left are listed the available toolbar buttons that are not currently displayed on the toolbar. On the right is the list of current toolbar items. If the **Add Binding** and **List Bindings** buttons are in the left column, select them and click the **Add** button to make them visible. After you have done this, select the **OK** button to get back to the **Layout Editor**, where you should now see the two binding buttons.

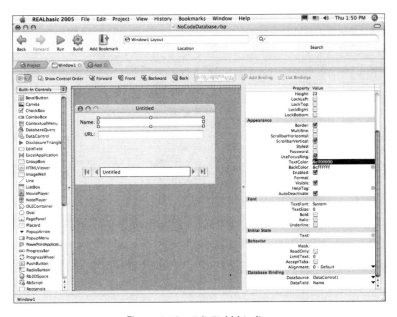

Figure 8.10   EditField binding.

When binding **EditFields**, you were binding the control to a particular piece of data—the content of a field. You are binding the button to a particular action, such as inserting, deleting, or updating the database. At this point, I need to drag four **PushButtons** onto **Window1**—one for each of the following **DataControl** methods: `NewRecord`, `Insert`, `Update` and `Delete`. The **PushButtons** are named **PushButtonNew**, **PushButtonInsert**, **PushButtonUpdate,** and **PushButtonDelete,** respectively.

You connect a **PushButton** with the **DataControl** by selecting both of them (hold down the Shift key and click one and then the other). After both are selected, click the **Binding** button, and the **Window** shown in Figure 8.11 is displayed. In this example, **PushButtonNew** is being bound to the `NewRecord` method of the **DataControl**.

To have a complete set of functionality, you need to create **PushButton** bindings for the `NewRecord`, `Insert`, `Update`, and `Delete` methods of the **DataControl**.

After you have created the bindings for all four **PushButtons**, you can click the **List Bindings** button on the toolbar to view the list of all bindings for that **Window**, as shown in Figure 8.12.

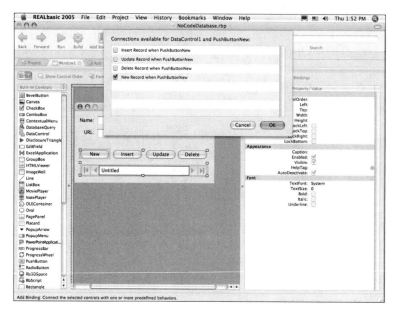

Figure 8.11 Button binding.

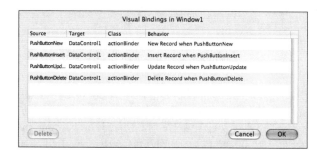

Figure 8.12 Database binding list.

Thus far, you have created a database using the IDE; then you dragged a **DataControl** control onto **Window1** and used it to bind two **EditFields** and four **PushButtons** to the control. At this point, you have a functioning database and you can begin to enter data. When you first launch the database, there will be no data in it, so nothing will be displayed in the **EditFields**. To add a record to the database, enter a name and a URL for your RSS feed subscription and click the Insert button.

If you are following along and have just done that, you may be alarmed to see that the name and URL you just typed into the **EditFields** have disappeared. If you click the **DataControl** forward or backward, there doesn't appear to be any data in the database. There's a reason for this: the **DataControl** uses the results of the query stored in the `SQLQuery` property to populate the **EditFields**. The results of such a query are an instance of a **RecordSet**. When you insert a new record into the database, the **RecordSet** needs to be updated so that it includes the new values (**RecordSets** are examined in detail later on in this chapter). The query is run automatically when the **Window** is opened, but it is not refreshed until it is run again.

If you close your application and reopen it, you will see that the record you inserted previously is now visible. However, you'd like for it to be visible after you've inserted it, without having to stop and restart the application. This means that you need to reexecute the query after you have inserted data into the database, and the best place to do that is in the `Action` event of **PushButtonInsert**. You will also want the display to stay with the record you just added and because I do not do any special sorting, all I need to do is move to the last position of the **RecordSet** after rerunning the query. This means writing code, although only a little bit. The code in the `Action` event looks like this:

```
DataControl1.RunQuery
DataControl1.MoveLast
```

You will need to do something similar when you delete or update a record as well. In these instances, you do not need to move to the last position like you did with the insert, but you do need to rerun the query and insert **DataControl1.RunQuery** in the **Action** events of both **PushButtons**.

DatabaseQuery Control

The second part of this project is to provide a way for users to see a list of feeds that have been subscribed to. The **DatabaseQuery** control is another control that, when used with REALbasic's binding features, makes for a remarkably easy way to view data. In the previous section, I used a **DataControl** to make it possible to browse through existing records in a database, in addition to inserting new ones, updating existing ones, or deleting them. The problem is that when browsing through them, I can see only one at a time, and sometimes it is convenient to be able to see a list of items. This is especially true in this case because I may want to view a list of RSS feeds I am subscribed to in a **ListBox** so that I can select one that I want to view.

The easiest way to accomplish this is to drag a **DatabaseQuery** control to **Window1**. Then set the database to RSSSub using the **Properties pane**, which is the database created in the previous section. Set the `TableName` property to Subscriptions and set the query to:

```
SELECT * FROM Subscriptions
```

Next, drag a **ListBox** to **Window1**. Because there are two columns in the database (Name and URL), use the IDE to establish a two-column **ListBox;** then select both the **ListBox** and the **DatabaseQuery** control and click the **Bind** button in the **Layout Editor** `toolbar`. After you do this, a dialog box will appear that lists the available bindings for this combination of controls. The dialog calls them connections instead of bindings, but the documentation uses both terms, so they can be used synonymously. In Figure 8.13 you will see the list of binding options. The **ListBox** instance is called **ListBox1,** and I want this **ListBox** to display the contents of a record as returned by the **DatabaseQuery** control. To do this, I need to select the first option, which reads, "Bind ListBox1 with list data from DatabaseQuery1".

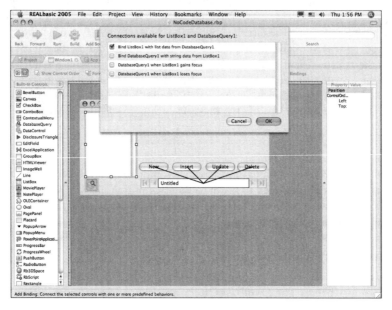

Figure 8.13 Select the type of connection available for ListBox1 and DatabaseQuery1.

If there is any data in the database, the **ListBox** will automatically be updated to display it. That's all there is to it. There is a problem, however. Right now, our database application has a **DataControl** that is bound to two **EditFields** and can be used for browsing the database. At the same time, it has a **ListBox** that provides the user with a list of feeds that are currently being subscribed to. I would like the list to be more helpful than this. In fact, I don't want to have to click **DataControl** buttons to browse through my database. I would rather be able to select a feed in the **ListBox** and have the name and URL be displayed in the **EditFields** automatically.

The other thing I would like to do is to minimize the number of buttons I have on the **Window**. Two buttons in particular are troublesome—the ones labeled Insert and Update. The problem with having both of them is that both buttons should be combined into one. The user shouldn't have to decide whether he or she is inserting a new record or updating an existing one. Our application should be able to keep track of that and insert or update records appropriately without any user intervention.

Another problem is that we created the database in the IDE. Because we did it this way, our application assumes that the database file exists at the location where we created it. What happens if the database gets accidentally deleted by the user? Unless the user has the source code and access to the REALbasic IDE, the user is completely out of luck and has no way of re-creating the database file. A better approach would be to create the database programmatically, so that when the application starts, it looks to see if the database file exists. If it doesn't exist, it can create it.

To make all of these improvements, we need to take a different approach to creating and managing the database. This time around, we will make less use of REALbasic's binding and do more of the job programmatically.

The Coded Database

The next example works with the database without using a **DataControl** control. This will step through the process of creating a similar database interface; the primary difference is that I rely much less on controls and binding for my functionality. This makes it a little more code intensive, but it also gives me more flexibility in how I manage the user interface, and it will enable me to add the features I just discussed in the previous section.

You can see the interface in Figure 8.14. **Window1** contains a three-column **ListBox** (**ListBox1**) that will be used to display a list of RSS feeds that have been subscribed to. Two **EditFields,** named **EditField1** and **EditField2,** are used to display the name of the feed and the URL of the feed, respectively. Finally, there are three buttons labeled Delete, Clear, and Save.

Figure 8.14   The user interface for the coded database sample project.

The Database Classes

To re-create the database using code, I need to introduce some additional classes. There are four database-related classes that I will be dealing with in this example. The first is the **Database** class itself, the parent class of all database types in REALbasic. The next is **RecordSet**, an instance of which is returned after calling the Database.SQLSelect method. Finally, there is **DatabaseRecord** and **DatabaseField**. You will use these classes primarily to create new records to insert into the database.

RecordSet and **DatabaseRecord** perform similar functions, and both use **DatabaseField**. Unfortunately, a **RecordSet** is not an array or collection of **DatabaseRecords**. It's an object all its own and it even uses some of its own terminology (for instance, a **RecordSet** has fields and a **DatabaseRecord** has columns) so that how the two work together may not be clear at first. Remember that **RecordSet** is a collection of existing records, so you can use it to do things to an existing record, such as updating it or deleting it. A **DatabaseRecord** is a new record, so you do with it what you would normally do with a new record, which is to insert it into a database.

Database Class

You've already seen the **Database** class in the "code-free" example when you created the database and established the tables using REALbasic's database editor. When a database is created that way, it is implicitly instantiated and you can refer to it by using its name. Some limitations exist to creating a database that way, the primary one being that it creates the database file and places a reference to it in your project. But what happens if that file is inadvertently deleted? If that happens, you would have to create the database "by hand" all over again. A better approach is to do it programmatically, which is how this example will be doing it.

The **Database** class is the parent class for all of REALbasic's database plug-ins that are available in the Professional edition. As such, it defines the generic REALbasic database API. There are many occasions when the properties and methods of the **Database** class are sufficient for all your needs. In fact, if you think you might change database back-ends in the future, you should try to rely on the members of the **Database** class primarily, and in those situations where you use database-specific features, try to avoid intermingling code that uses them throughout the application. Isolate it in its own method or methods so that you can change it more easily next time.

Database Properties

All databases have a name, which should be one word (alphabetical characters, plus an underscore) and assigned to the following property:

```
Database.DatabaseName as String
```

Later on in the chapter, you will see that you can attach a SQLite database to another SQLite database and execute SQL queries across databases. To do that, you have to refer to the fully qualified name of the field, which would be something like this:

```
aDatabaseName.aTableName.aFieldName
```

Note that the database name is not necessarily the same as the name of the file that stores the data for the database. When you create the database in the IDE, the database name is used for the filename (with the appropriate extension), but it is possible to change the database name so that it is different. When you create a database programmatically, you have to specify the filename and the database name explicitly, and you can choose to have them be the same or not. It's entirely up to you.

Like many other classes in REALbasic that are built using external libraries, the **Database** class takes a non-object-oriented approach to handling errors, using the following properties:

```
Database.Error as Boolean
Database.ErrorCode as Integer
Database.ErrorMessage as String
```

Usually, you test for the presence of an error and then respond to it, using code like the following:

```
If Database1.Error Then
  MsgBox Database1.ErrorMessage
Else
  // Continue
End If
```

When connecting to a multiuser database such as MySQL, you will need to have the following properties set (and the database should also be configured appropriately):

```
Database.Host as String
Database.Password as String
Database.UserName as String
```

The host refers to the machine on which the database server is running. It can be either the hostname or an IP address. If the database server is running on the same machine as the application, you could use either `Localhost` or `127.0.0.1`. You would also need to include the port number if it's running on a nonstandard port.

Database Methods

To access any database, you must first connect to it. Likewise, you can disconnect by calling the `Close` method.

```
Database.Connect as Boolean
Database.Close
```

The following two methods provide the means for executing SQL statements. The `SQLSelect` method is used only for `Select` statements, and it is the only one of the two methods that gets a value returned to it, which is in the form of a **RecordSet**. You can use the **RecordSet** to update or delete individual records. To find out if the statement executed properly, you need to check the error properties described in the properties section. All the other associated methods and classes are optional because you can do everything the database classes do, and a lot more, by relying on SQL statements rather than using the classes directly.

```
Database.SQLSelect(SelectString as String) as RecordSet
Database.SQLExecute(ExecuteString as String)
```

You cannot delete or update records directly with a **Database** object. You are limited to being able to insert new records, for which you need to have instantiated a **DatabaseRecord** object that gets passed to the **Database** object.

```
Database.InsertRecord(TableName as String, Data as DatabaseRecord)
```

Regardless of how the record gets updated or inserted, the transaction is not complete until you call one of the following methods:

```
Database.Rollback
Database.Commit
```

If you have inserted a record and then change your mind, you can call `Rollback`, and the changes will be eliminated. Likewise, when you are sure everything has gone according to plan, you can commit the changes. This is how you can manage transactions in REALbasic. In database terms, a transaction is a series of SQL statements that are grouped together and identified as a particular transaction. The `Commit` and `Rollback` methods apply to the series of statements, rather than any individual statement. The reason is that you may have to insert data into three different tables and you need to make sure all three inserts worked, without error. If one of the inserts works, you need to roll back the changes caused by the previous inserts, and `Rollback` and `Commit` let you do that. When you use the **DataControl**, you can set a property in the IDE to tell REALbasic to automatically commit inserts, deletes, and updates. When using the **Database** class directly, you need to manually `Commit` or `Rollback` transactions. As with everything else, you can use SQL to manage the process for you with the statements `BEGIN TRANSACTION` and `END TRANSACTION`.

Finally, you can get information about the database tables and fields themselves using the following methods. At times, you may be accessing a table whose structure you do not know, or one that possibly could have changed. Being able to ask the database to describe itself can make it easier to manage these situations.

```
Database.TableSchema as RecordSet
Database.FieldSchema(TableName as String) as RecordSet
Database.IndexSchema(TableName as String) as RecordSet
Database.GetProperty(Name as String)
```

The `GetProperty` method currently applies only to the 4D server, so you can ignore it for all other databases.

REALSQLdatabase

The **Database** subclass I use in the examples is **REALSQLdatabase,** which is the new REALbasic database standard, based on SQLite. All of the database plug-ins are subclasses of **Database**, so most of what is discussed here is applicable with any database.

REALSQLdatabase Properties

SQLite is a single-user database, sometimes called an embedded database because it is often used within a single application as a means of storing data for that application.

Most of the other databases you can use with REALbasic are multiuse databases that you access through a database server available on the network. As such, the **REALSqlDatabase** class has the following property that points to the file in which the data gets stored.

```
DatabaseFile as FolderItem
```

This serves as an alternative to setting the `Host, Username,` and `Password` properties in the `Super` class.

Whenever you refer to individual fields (or columns) in a SQL statement, you have two choices. You can use the fully qualified name, which is `aTableName.aFieldName`, or you can reference just the field name. The following property determines how REALbasic will handle the names when returned in a **RecordSet**:

```
ShortColumnNames as Boolean
```

This property is a little confusing, because the name isn't really descriptive of what it does. Basically, this is what it means: If the property is set to `True`, REALbasic will return the so-called short column names, which is the field name without the preceding reference to the table—that is, unless there is some ambiguity that requires a fully qualified name. This situation usually arises when you have two tables with fields that have the same name. It also returns a fully qualified name when returned aliased fields. If the property is set to `False`, it relies on the format that you used when writing the SQL query. If you used fully qualified names in the query, the results will include fully qualified names.

REALSQLdatabase Methods

Although you can create a reference to a database file using the `DatabaseFile` property, I have yet to tell you how to create a database file in the first place. There is no **FolderItem** method to help you, like there is for creating text files and directories, but there is a **REALSQLdatabase** method that will create the file for you. You must first assign a reference to a **FolderItem** object to the `DatabaseFile` property, and if that **FolderItem** does not exist, you can create it by calling the following method:

```
REALSqlDatabase.CreateDatabaseFile
```

The following methods allow you to attach and detach other databases to this particular database object:

```
REALSqlDatabase.AttachDatabase(file as FolderITem, databaseName as String)
REALSqlDatabase.DetachDatabase(databaseName as String)
```

The benefit to doing this would be to be able to perform SQL Select queries across multiple database files, something that is normally limited to being executed across tables within a single database. Although JOINS have not been covered yet, the following code provides a quick example to clarify how you identify fields within the different databases:

```
SELECT * FROM database1.thistable, database2.thattable WHERE
database1.thistable.thisfield=database2.thattable.thatfield
```

The following returns a string representing the database schema, which is basically the blueprint for the database, describing what tables exist, what their fields are, and so on:

```
REALSqlDatabase.GetSchemaData() as String
```

Finally, the following helpful method returns the ID of the last row that was add to the database:

```
REALSqlDatabase.LastRowID() as Integer
```

You will use this when you are updating two different tables whose data are related. For example, I might have an additional table in the **RSSSub** database that contains additional information about individual sites that I have subscribed to. After I add a new subscription to the Subscriptions table, I will also want to add a new record to the Feeds table with the data from the feed associated with that particular Subscription. After adding the Subscription record, I can call the `LastRowID` method to get the `RowID` number from the database, and I can use that number as the value of a field in the Feeds database that will link that Feeds record to that particular Subscription record.

RecordSet

RecordSets are the results of a SQL `Select` statement. The class provides methods for navigating the sequence of records, as well as for modifying and deleting them. One thing to note is that you use a **RecordSet** only for updates and deletions and not for inserts. The reason for it is that a **RecordSet** can exist only as the result of a `Select` statement, and a `Select` statement returns existing records from a table or group of tables.

Properties

The properties of **RecordSets** are primarily used to help you iterate through a series of records. The following two properties can tell you whether you are at the beginning of the **RecordSet** (BOF) or at the end of the **RecordSet** (EOF):

```
RecordSet.BOF as Boolean
RecordSet.EOF as Boolean
```

The next property tells you how many records are contained in the **RecordSet**:

```
RecordSet.RecordCount as Integer
```

Finally, this property will let you know how many fields exist within a given record. You can use this when you do not know in advance the names of the fields available in a record and need to refer to them by number:

```
RecordSet.FieldCount as Integers
```

Methods

If you are going to modify the values of a record to update it, you must first call the `Edit` method:

```
RecordSet.Edit
```

If you have changed the value of a field in a record and want to save that change, you can call the Update method:

```
RecordSet.Update
```

Likewise, if you want to delete a record, use the following:

```
RecordSet.DeleteRecord
```

There is one important caveat to add to the use of the previous two methods. JOINS are discussed later on in the chapter, but it is worth mentioning them now. A JOIN is a kind of Select statement that pulls fields from two or more tables. A single **RecordSet** is returned as a result of the statement. The reason I mention it now is because the Update and Delete methods of **RecordSet** will not work with a **RecordSet** that exists as the result of a JOIN.

```
RecordSet.Field(Name as String)
RecordSet.IdxField(Index as Integer)

RecordSet.MoveFirst
RecordSet.MoveLast
RecordSet.MoveNext
RecordSet.MovePrevious
RecordSet.Close
```

DatabaseRecord

A **DatabaseRecord** object represents a single record that is to be inserted into a table.

DatabaseRecord Properties

```
DatabaseRecord.BlobColumn
DatabaseRecord.BooleanColumn
DatabaseRecord.Column
DatabaseRecord.DateColumn
DatabaseRecord.DoubleColumn
DatabaseRecord.IntegerColumn
DatabaseRecord.JPEGColumn
DatabaseRecord.MacPictColumn
```

DatabaseField

Both **RecordSets** and **DatabaseRecords** use **DatabaseField** objects to represent individual fields (or columns) in a table.

SQLite is not a strongly typed database (although the other databases available to Professional edition users are strongly typed). It uses affinity typing, which means that SQLite will accept any string as valid data for any field. At the same time, you can define a type for the field, which will help developers know how to interpret the output. The **DatabaseField** class provides several properties that returned the value of a specific field as a specified type. This works much like it does with the Variant class. If you know that the data is a Boolean value, you can access the data like so:

```
Dim b as Boolean
b = DatabaseField1.BooleanValue
```

Here is the complete list of properties:

```
DatabaseField.BooleanValue as Boolean
DatabaseField.DateValue as Date
DatabaseField.DoubleValue as Double
DatabaseField.IntegerValue as Integer
DatabaseField.JPEGValue as Picture
DatabaseField.MacPICTValue as Picture
DatabaseField.Name as String
DatabaseField.StringValue as String
DatabaseField.Value as Variant
```

The Coded Application

The biggest difference in the "coded" version of the database takes place in the App.Open event. First, unlike when you used the IDE to create the database, you must first assign a reference to the new database somewhere. In this example, I created a property for **App** called RSSSub of type **REALSQLdatabase**. Then, in the Open event, I have to do the following, because this is what I want the application to do:

1. I want it to open the database from a database file.
2. If the file doesn't exist, I want it to create the database and add a few default records.
3. I want the database reference to be a property of the **App** class so that it remains in scope throughout the lifetime of the application.

Most of the logic takes place in the App.Open event, shown in Listing 8.1:

Listing 8.1   **App.Open()**

```
Dim dbFile as FolderItem
Dim dr as DatabaseRecord

// Instantiate the database
RSSSub = New REALSQLDatabase

// Get a reference to the database file
// and associate the file with the database
dbFile = GetFolderItem("RSSSub")
RSSSub.DatabaseFile = dbFile

// Check to see if the database file exists
```

Listing 8.1   **Continued**

```
// and then try to connect to it. If this
// were not a sqlite database, but a multiuser
// database like MySql, you would need to have
// the username and password properties set.
If RSSSub.DatabaseFile.Exists Then
  If RSSSub.Connect Then
    //All is wellElse
    MsgBox "Could not read database file"
  End if
Else
  // If the file does not exist, create the database file
  // using the following method.
  If RSSSub.CreateDatabaseFile Then

    // Connect to the new database
    If RSSSub.Connect Then

      // Create the new table using SQL
      RSSSub.SQLExecute("CREATE TABLE Subscriptions" _
        + "(Name VarChar UNIQUE, URL VarChar NOT NULL)")

      If RSSSub.Error Then
        MsgBox "Error Creating Database: " _
          + RSSSub.ErrorMessage
      End If



      // Insert a new record using the
      // DatabaseRecord class.
      // You could also use SQL to insert
      // the record as well.
      dr = New DatabaseRecord
      dr.Column("Name") = "choate.info"
      dr.Column("URL") = http://choate.info/ _
          +"Blog/Business/atom.xml"
      RSSSub.InsertRecord("Subscriptions", dr)
      If RSSSub.Error Then
        MsgBox RSSSub.ErrorMessage
      End If

      // Insert another record
      dr = New DatabaseRecord
      dr.Column("Name") = "REAL Software"
      dr.Column("URL") = http://www.realsoftware.com/" _
```

Listing 8.1 **Continued**

```
       +"xml/realsoftware.xml"
    RSSSub.InsertRecord("Subscriptions", dr)
    If RSSSub.Error Then
      MsgBox RSSSub.ErrorMessage
    End If


  Else
    // If you cannot connect to the new
    // database file, then you should raise
    // an error or respond appropriately
    MsgBox "Could not create database file."
  End If
 End If
End If

// When the database was created in the IDE, I was able
// to associate the database to the DatabaseQuery control
// in the IDE itself, as well as assign the SQL statement to it.
// In this case, since I am creating the database
// programmatically I need to associate it with the control
// after I have instantiated it.
Window1.DatabaseQuery1.Database = App.RSSSub
Window1.DatabaseQuery1.SQLQuery = "Select * From" _
  + "Subscriptions"Window1.DatabaseQuery1.RunQuery
```

DatabaseQuery1 automatically handles populating **ListBox1**, but I want the user to be able to select a row and have the name and URL for that particular record appear in **EditField1** and **EditField2,** respectively. I can bind an **EditField** to a **ListBox**, but only at the row level, so I cannot bind **EditField1** to the first column of **ListBox1** and **EditField2** to the second column. This means I need to manage this process myself. An interesting project would be to create a custom binding that enabled just that kind of data binding, but for now I'll take a simpler approach.

First, anytime the selection of **ListBox1** changes, I want the data displayed in the **EditFields** to change. The code displayed in Listing 8.2 gets entered in the ListBox1.Change event.

Listing 8.2 **ListBox1.Change Handles Event**

```
Dim rs as RecordSet
Dim aName as String
Dim idx as Integer
```

Listing 8.2   **Continued**

```
// Get the data from the cell. If the cell is
// empty, or nothing is selected, then aName will
// be empty.
idx = Me.ListIndex

If idx > -1 Then
  // If the value for ListIndex is greater than
  // -1, then the ListBox has a selection.
  aName = Me.Cell(idx, 0)

  // This assumes that aName is unique, so it searches for
  // a record where the Name field is equal to aName
  rs = App.RSSSub.SQLSelect("SELECT * FROM Subscriptions" _
    +"WHERE Name='" + Trim(aName) + "'")

  If App.RSSSub.Error Then
  MsgBox App.RSSSub.ErrorMessage
  Else

    // The EditFields are populated with the data from
    // the returned RecordSet. If the RecordSet is empty
    // then the fields are emptied.
    EditField1.Text = rs.Field("Name").StringValue
    EditField2.Text = rs.Field("URL").StringValue
    PushButton1.Caption = "Update"
  End If
Else
  // Nothing is selected so
  // set the caption of PushButton1
  // to save.
  PushButton1.Caption = "Save"
End If
```

One other thing I want to do is to allow the user to both update an existing record through the two **EditFields** and insert a new record through the **EditFields**. At the same time, I do not want to have two buttons, one for inserting and one for updating. Instead, I'd like to have one button labeled Update when the context is appropriate for updating and labeled Save when the context is appropriate for saving a new record, which would call for inserting a new record. One part of this process is to change the caption of **PushButton1** to Update whenever a cell is clicked in **ListBox1** and the contents of the record are displayed in the **EditFields**. The presumption is that the user has selected this particular row and any changes made to it will call for an update of that record. When nothing is selected in the **ListBox**, PushButton1.Caption will be set to Save instead.

In addition to binding a **ListBox** to a **DatabaseQuery** control, you can also bind **PushButtons** to **ListBoxes**. I will not go into the details here, but if you follow the steps outlined previously for creating a binding, you can bind the Delete button (**PushButton3**) with **ListBox1** so that it is enabled only when there is a selection on the **ListBox**. I would also like to define how **PushButton1** is enabled, and this depends on the state of both of the **EditFields**. I want **PushButton1** enabled only when there is text for both **EditFields**. Therefore, I place the code in Listing 8.3 in **EditField1**'s TextChange event and Listing 8.4 in **EditField2**'s TextChange event.

Listing 8.3   **EditField1.TextChange Handles Event**

```
If (Me.Text = "") Or (EditField2.Text="") Then
  PushButton1.Enabled = False
Else
  PushButton1.Enabled = True
End If
```

Listing 8.4   **EditField2.TextChange Handles Event**

```
If (Me.Text = "") Or (EditField1.Text="") Then
  PushButton1.Enabled = False
Else
  PushButton1.Enabled = True
End If
```

PushButton2 is the button that is clicked to clear the **EditFields** to insert a new record into the database. Clearing the **EditFields** is simple enough, but I also want to check first to see if any data in the **EditFields** has changed and ask the user whether to update the current record with the data that exists in the **EditField**. There are a few ways of doing this, but in this example, I do a quick query to find out what the value is in the database itself and compare it with the value of the text in the **EditField**. If they are different, I prompt the user to see what the user wants to do. I could also subclass **EditField,** add a new property called something like OriginalText, and assign the value of that property when I populate the data in the **EditField** when a user selects a row in **ListBox1**. I could then simply check the current text of the **EditField** in question, compare it with the value of OriginalText, and then go from there.

I used this particular approach because I thought it would make for a simpler example without any subclassing, but also because there is always the possibility that the underlying database has changed since the query was run on the **DatabaseQuery** control. This allows me to check the current value, rather than the value that was current when the **EditFields** were first populated.

The code for the PushButton2.Action event is shown in Listing 8.5. This is also the place where the value of the caption for **PushButton1** is set. If the fields are cleared to add a new record, the caption is changed to read Save.

Listing 8.5   **PushButton2.Action Handles Event**

```
Dim rs as RecordSet
Dim res as Integer
Dim b1,b2 as Boolean

rs = App.RSSSub.SQLSelect("SELECT * FROM Subscriptions WHERE URL='" +
Trim(EditField2.Text) + "'")

If App.RSSSub.Error Then
  MsgBox App.RSSSub.ErrorMessage
Else

  b1 = rs.Field("Name").StringValue <> Trim(EditField1.Text)
  b2 = rs.Field("URL").StringValue <> Trim(EditField2.Text)


  PushButton1.Caption = "Save"

  If b1 OR b2 Then
    res = MsgBox("Fields have changed. Would you like to" _
      + "update the record?", 35, "Save changes")
  Else
    If Trim(EditField1.Text) = "" Or Trim(EditField2.Text) = "" Then
      EditField1.Text = ""
      EditField2.Text = ""

    End if
  End If

  Select Case res
    Case 2 // Cancel
      PushButton1.Caption = "Update"
    Case 6 // Yes
      rs.Edit
      rs.Field("Name").StringValue = Trim(EditField1.Text)
      rs.Field("URL").StringValue = Trim(EditField2.Text)
      rs.Update
      EditField1.Text = ""
      EditField2.Text = ""
    Case 7 // No
      EditField1.Text = ""
      EditField2.Text = ""
  End Select

  DatabaseQuery1.RunQuery
End If
```

`Pushbutton1.Action` is the event where the data is either updated or inserted into the database. The value of `Pushbutton1.Caption` is used to determine the proper course of action. If the caption reads Update, the record must be updated. I could update the record with a SQL statement or I could use a **RecordSet** instance, which is what I do here. Because the URL is a unique identifier, I do a `Select` statement for that URL, and the reference I get back is a **RecordSet** that contains one record, the one I want to update. See the code in Listing 8.6.

Listing 8.6   **Pushbutton1.Action Handles Event**

```
Dim dr as DatabaseRecord
Dim rs as RecordSet

If Me.Caption = "Save" Then
  dr = new DatabaseRecord

  dr.Column("Name") = Trim(EditField1.Text)
  dr.Column("URL") = Trim(EditField2.Text)
  App.RSSSub.InsertRecord("Subscriptions", dr)

  If App.RSSSub.Error Then
    MsgBox App.RSSSub.ErrorMessage
  Else

    Me.Caption = "Update"
  End If
Else
  rs = App.RSSSub.SQLSelect("SELECT * FROM Subscriptions WHERE URL='" _
    + "Trim(EditField2.Text) + "'")

  If App.RSSSub.Error Then
    MsgBox App.RSSSub.ErrorMessage
  Else
    // You must call Edit before modifying any
    // values in the RecordSet
    rs.Edit
    rs.Field("Name").StringValue = Trim(EditField1.Text)
    rs.Field("URL").StringValue = Trim(EditField2.Text)
    rs.Update

  End If
End If


DatabaseQuery1.RunQuery
```

Finally, when **PushButton3** is clicked, I need to delete the current record. Again, much like the previous event, I have decided to get a reference to a **RecordSet** for that record represented in the **EditFields** and use the **RecordSet** to delete the record in question. However, this is advisable only if there is one record per URL, as shown in Listing 8.7.

Listing 8.7   **PushButton3.Action Handles Event**

```
Dim rs as RecordSet

rs = App.RSSSub.SQLSelect("SELECT * FROM Subscriptions WHERE URL='"_
 + Trim(EditField2.Text) + "'")

rs.Field("Name").StringValue = Trim(EditField1.Text)
rs.Field("URL").StringValue = Trim(EditField2.Text)

rs.DeleteRecord

If App.RSSSub.Error Then
  MsgBox App.RSSSub.ErrorMessage
Else
  App.RSSSub.commit
  DatabaseQuery1.RunQuery
End If
```

RowID

I used a slightly modified `Select` statement for displaying the data in the **ListBox**. I said earlier that the original statement would return all the fields and records from the Subscriptions table. That was only partially true, because SQLite also automatically generates an ID for each row. Most of the time you do not know it's there and do not need to worry about it, but if for some reason you need to know the value, you have to refer to it specifically in the statement. The following line of code can be added to the `App.Open` event to create a query that includes values for the row ID:

```
Window1.DatabaseQuery1.SQLQuery =  "Select rowid,* From Subscriptions"
```

SQL Equivalents

Everything that I have done so far can be done using the **Database** object's `SQLSelect` and `SQLExecute` methods. Because SQL is a programming language of its own, I do not have the time to fully explain or demonstrate its wonders, which is unfortunate because you can do much, much more with SQL than you can with REALbasics database controls and classes (it's the classic trade-off of simplicity-of-use against flexibility).

The SQL supported by the database varies according to which database you are using. That means that you should really look to documentation about the particular database engine you will be using to find out exactly which SQL statements they support, as well as what kind of extensions to SQL they have implemented. There is a lot of information online for the open source database, including SQLite, MySQL, and Postgres, and you can get to it at the following websites:

- http://sqlite.org/
- http://mysql.org/
- http://postgresql.org/

SQLite supports a large part of the SQL specification, including many advanced features. It's really very cool. Here is a quick overview of what you will find:

```
SELECT
UPDATE
INSERT
DELETE
REPLACE
COPY

BEGIN TRANSACTION
COMMIT TRANSACTION
ROLLBACK TRANSACTION
END TRANSACTION

CREATE INDEX
REINDEX
DROP INDEX

CREATE TABLE
ALTER TABLE
DROP TABLE

CREATE TRIGGER
DROP TRIGGER

CREATE VIEW
DROP VIEW

ON CONFLICT clause

PRAGMA
```

SQL is not case sensitive, but there is a common practice of using uppercase letters for SQL keywords such as SELECT, INSERT, and so on. This makes the SQL a little easier to read.

Delete Statement

The following statement deletes a record from the Subscriptions table:

```
DELETE FROM Subscriptions WHERE Name='choate.info'
```

Insert Statement

The INSERT statement inserts a new record into the Subscriptions table:

```
INSERT INTO Subscriptions (Name, URL) VALUES ('A Site Name', 'an URL')
```

Update Statement

Suppose I want to change the Name field in a record where the URL is http://w3c.org.
The following UPDATE statement takes care of it:

```
UPDATE Subscriptions SET Name='W3C' WHERE URL='http://w3c.org'
```

Creating Indexes

In addition to replacing the Insert, Update, and Delete methods of the REALbasic
database classes, you can also use SQL to create indexes. Each index you create has a
name, and you need to specify the name of the table and the particular field that should
be indexed:

```
CREATE INDEX NameIndex ON Subscriptions(Name)
```

Select and Joins

A relational database is so named because you are able to relate fields in two different
tables based on the existence in each table of fields that share a common value. Suppose
I create another table, called Feeds, using the following SQL statement:

```
CREATE TABLE feeds (ID VarChar Not Null, LastDownloaded DateTime, Content VarChar)
```

The field in this table that I will use to link to the other table will be the ID field. I
will use the URL field in the other table. I could have called this field URL as well,
because they both will contain URLs, but I did it this way because it avoids some ambiguity and simplifies the example. Note that the fields on which two tables are joined do
not have to share a common name, only a common value, but very often they do share a
common name because they tend to represent the same thing and are thus called the
same thing. I could join these two tables with the following SQL statement:

```
SELECT * FROM Subscriptions,Feeds WHERE URL=ID
```

If the fields shared a common name, I would have to use the fully qualified name of
the fields to avoid any ambiguity, and the statement would look like this:

```
SELECT * FROM Subscriptions,Feeds WHERE Subscriptions.URL= Feeds.URL
```

The result of the first select statement would be a **RecordSet** that contained the following fields:

```
Name
URL
ID
LastDownloaded
Content
```

You work with the **RecordSet** in the same way that you would work with a **RecordSet** that was the result of a query against one table, rather than a join of two. There is one exception, however, and that is that most databases will not let you update or delete the database from a joined **RecordSet**.

You can use a join with a **DatabaseQuery** control and a **DataControl** control, but the same rule applies for **DataControls** with respect to joins—now adding, updating, or deleting is allowed.

Data Normalization

There is a tendency on the part of new database developers to try to fit everything into one table because it is simpler. REALbasic's data controls tend to reinforce this tendency because they make it so easy to work with tables. In the long run, especially with relatively more complex data, you should begin to take a different approach and use multiple tables for the data in your application. This process is called *data normalization,* which is one of those phrases for which there are many definitions and no clear hard-and-fast rules.

I can go back to the RSSReader application to provide a more specific example. Suppose that instead of storing the cached XML files as text files, I want to store the data in a database. The first step, then, would be to create a table that had fields that represented the data in question. In fact, the members of the Group and Item classes introduced previously can serve as a good starting point, so we could create a table using a SQL statement like this:

```
CREATE TABLE Feeds (Title VarChar, Guid VarChar, Description VarChar, ModifiedDate
➥ DateTime, CreationDate DateTime)
```

Although these fields represent the common data that the different RSS formats have, there is also a lot of data in some formats that is not available in others; in addition, some of the data is considered optional and is not available in all RSS files of that type. One strategy is to add additional fields to this table that will hold data that any individual feed may or may not have, but after a while, your database will be taking up more information than it needs to and won't be as efficient over time. There will also be situations where you may want to add a field at a later time, which you can do with the SQL statement ALTER TABLE, but there are some limitations on what you can do with that statement.

The other solution, and generally a better one overall, is to place those optional or unique fields in separate tables and reference the main table. For example, some RSS feeds are broken down into categories, but not all of them. If I were to create a separate table for categories, I would do this:

```
CREATE TABLE Categories(FeedGuid VarChar, Category VarChar)
```

This table would be linked to the other by way of the `FeedGuid`. It would contain the Guid value for the Feeds record it is associated with. Doing this also opens up another possibility, which is that you can now have multiple categories for the same feed. If you had decided instead to use the single table method and added a category field, you would have space for only one category. If you thought you might have more than one category, you might add a second field, calling it category2 or something similar. Either way, you have to decide in advance how many fields to associate with categories. The very ugly alternative is to have multiple categories listed in one field, separated by some delimiter. Regardless of the single-table alternative you choose, it's a lot better to use a separate table. You have much more flexibility overall.

Inner/Outer Joins

Previously, I showed an example of a JOIN similar to this:

```
SELECT * FROM Subscriptions,Categories WHERE URL=FeedGuid
```

An alternative syntax uses the word JOIN, like so:

```
SELECT * From Subscriptions JOIN Categories ON Subscriptions.URL =
➥Categories.FeedUrl
```

There is more than one kind of JOIN. By default, all JOINS are INNER JOINS, so the only reason to use INNER is to make it clear to the next developer what you are doing. The problem comes when you want to get results from a search that includes records from the Subscriptions table, even if they are not referenced in the Feeds table. With the previous JOIN, none of those records would show up. In this case, you can use a LEFT OUTER JOIN to accomplish this.

To illustrate a JOIN, consider the following two tables:

Table 8.1 **Subscriptions Table**

Name	URL
Choate.info	http://www.choate.info/Blog/rss.xml
REAL Software	http://www.realsoftware.com/rss.xml

Table 8.2 **Categories Table**

FeedGuid	Category
Choate.info/Blog/rss.xml	REALbasic
Choate.info/Blog/rss.xml	Cocoon
http://w3c.org/	HTML

If I were to do a LEFT JOIN on the previous two tables, I would get results that included only choate.info. If I wanted to include all records from the Subscriptions table, whether or not the record had been assigned a category, I could use a LEFT OUTER JOIN:

```
SELECT * From Subscriptions LEFT OUTER JOIN Categories ON Subscriptions.URL =
➥Categories.FeedUrl
```

Now, if I wanted to include all categories whether or not a record in the Subscriptions table matched, I could do a RIGHT OUTER JOIN:

```
SELECT * From Subscriptions RIGHT OUTER JOIN Categories ON Subscriptions.URL =
➥Categories.FeedUrl
```

Primary Key

A primary key is a field used as the basis for JOINS. As such, it has certain characteristics, the most important of which is that it has to be unique. Because the primary key is unique, it serves as a unique identifier for that particular record, so that when you search for a particular value for the primary key, you will get only one record back. When you are joining a table with a primary key with another table, the other table must have what is called a *foreign key*. This is a field whose value will reference the primary key of the first table. Unlike primary keys, foreign keys aren't a special type of field, and they do not have to be unique.

Trigger

A trigger is an action that is automatically taken by the database when a certain condition occurs—usually the insertion, deletion, or updating of a record. If you have a database with multiple tables and the records in each table relate to records in other tables, deleting a record in one table becomes a more complex process. In database parlance, you need to maintain referential integrity. In other words, if you have one record that refers to a second record and the second record gets deleted, you need to do something with the first record because it is now pointing to nothing. That may or may not be what you want. Either way, triggers are one way to do this because you can create a trigger that says when record x gets deleted in table one, then delete record x1 in table two. Example:

```
CREATE TRIGGER delete_refs DELETE ON Subscriptions
  BEGIN
    DELETE Categories WHERE FeedUrl = old.URL;
  END;
```

Now, whenever you delete a record in the Subscriptions table, any references to that record in the Categories table are deleted as well.

Conclusion

This concludes the discussion of REALbasic's database tools, but I really only scratched the surface. To fully appreciate the power and flexibility of databases, you need to take an in-depth look at SQL, a programming language in its own right.

Also, although I created a database to be used with our RSSReader application, there is still some more work to be done to integrate it into the application. In the working application, you will want to be able to take the data in the RSSSub database and use it to retrieve RSS files. To do that, you will need to use REALbasic's networking classes and controls, which I review in the next chapter.

9

Networking and Internet Programming

REALBASIC OFFERS A RICH SET OF classes for creating networked applications that use the Internet. A network consists of two or more computers that are connected to each other and can send data back and forth. A network application is one that leverages this connectivity to perform some task. Another way of saying that computers "send data back and forth" is to say that they are communicating, and "communicating" is probably a better word to describe it because the two computers aren't just sending unrelated streams of data to each other. Instead, one computer sends some information to the other computer, and the other computer responds to that information.

It's very much like a conversation between individuals. When you meet someone on the street, you might nod your head and expect a nod back. If you thrust out your hand for a handshake, you'd expect the other person to reach and shake your hand. If you say, "Hello! How are you?" it is likely that the other person will say, "I'm fine. Thanks." For a conversation or exchange like this to work, you not only have to physically have a way to communicate with the other person, you also have to have a common language that you speak. But this is not enough because even if you are physically capable of talking and you know the same language, you won't get much done if you are both talking at the same time. Because of this, humans have certain customs, or protocols, they use when communicating that makes meaningful communication possible.

When two computers communicate, they need to have similar rules so that each one knows when to speak and when to listen. The computers need to know how to find each other, how to introduce themselves, and how to have a meaningful conversation, and they use protocols to make this happen. All of REALbasic's networking classes use Internet protocols.

To understand how all of this works, I want to talk about something most everyone is familiar with—viewing an html page in a web browser. Later on in the chapter I will create a web server using classes provided by REALbasic.

A Simplified View of a Computer Network

Actual implementations of networks can be complex and I'm not a networking expert, but here's a highly simplified overview. The Internet is a network of networks. Each network is identified by a domain name. A network (or a domain) is composed of a number of hosts, which are the individual computers on the network (sort of). Any given host may have one or more networked applications running—things such as web servers and mail servers and so on. For multiple applications to work together without talking over each other, each networked application is assigned a port, which is just a number (an integer), and that application is said to listen to that port. When a request comes in, it is directed at a certain port so that the right server application will respond to the request. In addition, each individual computer has a file system on which it stores files. All these pieces—the domain, the host, the port, and the path—can be used to identify individual resources on the network. To see how they are used together, I'll take a close look at how the World Wide Web works and step through the process that is required for you to request a page, receive it, and view it in your browser.

The Hypertext Transfer Protocol

The Hypertext Transfer Protocol (HTTP) is the protocol that makes the World Wide Web possible, but it isn't the only protocol that is needed. It also relies on the Transmission Control Protocol (TCP) and the Internet Protocol (IP), all of which I will discuss momentarily. In practical terms, HTTP is a simple protocol, and the way it works is this: There is a client (your web browser, usually) and a server (a web server of some sort) and the client sends a request to the server in the form of a header, which is a string of text that includes the information the server will need to respond appropriately. The server receives the header, processes it, and sends data back to the client.

You've no doubt used a web browser before, so you know that the way you use the browser is that you type the address into the address field and press Enter. After a few moments, a new html page is displayed in the browser. The address is known as a Uniform Resource Locator (URL), and this is used by the software to find a particular resource—usually an html file on a server somewhere.

URLs, Domain Names, and Hosts

A URL consists of a domain name, a hostname, a port number, and a path. This should be familiar to you now because in my simplified explanation of a network, I explained that a domain, a host, a port, and a path were all that were needed to find a given resource on the Internet. A URL is one way to represent those values.

When you are working on your own computer, it has a default hostname, `localhost` (you don't need a domain name because the request is local to your computer).

In some situations, one or more of these elements may be missing in the URL, and that's usually because of some default value. For instance, the default port is port 80, so you often see URLs without a port listed. You can also set up your network so that the hostname isn't necessary by routing all HTTP requests to a particular computer. Likewise, if you are running a web browser locally, you can refer solely to the host, without the domain, and successfully make the request (by default, the host is called `localhost`). You don't even need to have a complete path to a file because, by default, if the path points to a directory, it is assumed that you mean the file `index.html` within that directory.

A URL is supposed to be a unique reference to a resource. Usually that resource is a file of some sort, but it doesn't have to be. Many pages on websites are created dynamically when the request is made, so there really isn't an actual page somewhere—the html is generated on-the-fly and sent back to the browser.

Ports

At the host, a web server is running, listening by default on port 80. It doesn't have to listen on port 80. It can listen on port 8080 if it wants to, and if that's the case, you need to specify the port in the URL, like so:

```
http://localhost:8080/
```

IP Addresses

There is one other element to add to the mix that I haven't mentioned yet, and that is IP addresses. Domain names and hosts use strings because human beings find it easier to work with and remember them, but computers always work better with numbers. That's why the real address of a computer is a numeric IP address, and that address is mapped to the domain name. Domain name servers (DNS) provide a way of mapping domain names to IP addresses so that behind the scenes, when you type in a domain name, the software looks up the IP address using DNS and then uses the IP address to locate the computer. You can easily exchange the actual IP address for the domain name in your browser and it will work just as well.

In any event, after the domain is found, followed by the host being found, an HTTP request is sent to the web server that is running on that host. There are three kinds of requests that every web server must accommodate: GET, PUT, and HEADERS. The path portion of the URL is then sent to the web server and the web server decides what to do with that path. In most cases, it uses the path to find an actual file on the file system, which it sends back out to the client.

The Protocol Stack

I said earlier that the Internet is not a single protocol. Rather, it's a suite of protocols. In this one HTTP request, several protocols get used. You can think of it as a stack of protocols. In the example of the World Wide Web, the stack would be this:

HTTP

TCP

IP

At the bottom of the stack is the Internet Protocol, and this handles all the low-level activity involved in finding other computers on the network and getting them routed there. The actual format of the data sent and how the two machines communicate after they are connected is handled by the Transmission Control Protocol (TCP). It has the rather narrow scope of breaking the data into packets, sending the packets to the other machine, and making sure they all arrive where they are supposed to, in the correct order. Finally, at the top of the stack is the Hypertext Transfer Protocol, which takes all those packets that have been sent and responds based on the content of those packets.

This particular stack of protocols is not the only stack that is used on the Internet. You can take a step back and look at this from a higher level of abstraction and think of each row as a layer that performs a generic function (OSI stuff). If I were to do that, this is where each item in the stack corresponds to the OSI layers.

REALbasic provides several networking classes that work on different aspects of the layer. The following hierarchy shows the class hierarchy and what part of the suite of Internet protocols the class works with.

The Internet

Several protocols are used on the Internet, and these are often referred to as the *Internet protocol suite*. It's helpful to think of this collection of protocols as a stack, and each layer of the stack is responsible for certain activities. From the REALbasic perspective, there are three layers that are important (there's actually a formal network protocol stack model called the OSI model, which divides up the network stack into seven layers, but that's far too formal for our purposes). At the very bottom of the stack is the Network Layer. Above that is the Transport Layer, and at the very top is the Application Layer.

Network Layer

When referring to the underlying protocol that supports the Internet, people often refer to two protocols in tandem: TCP/IP. TCP is the Transmission Control Protocol, which I'll talk about momentarily, and IP is the Internet Protocol, which is the protocol that sits on the Network Layer. The Network Layer manages network addresses and decides how to package and route data from one computer to the next. The Internet Protocol does this using IP addresses, URLs, and packets.

Every computer has a physical address, which is known as the IP address. The default IP address of your own local computer is 127.0.0.1. There are also logical addresses—which is really one way of saying that there are names that get mapped to IP addresses because they are easier for human beings to remember. In the Internet world, this refers to host and domain names and URLs. On your local machine is a default hostname called Localhost. If you are on a computer that has a web server running, you should be able to type in either of the following URLs to get to the home page:

```
http://localhost/
http://127.0.0.1/
```

Both addresses refer to the same location on the Internet, and it is the Internet Protocol that manages this process. Normally, you use the name, such as http://realsoftware.com/, to refer to a location on the Internet. The IP takes that name, looks up the IP address, and uses the address to route the request to the appropriate computer. The lookup is done by checking with a domain name server, which is like a dictionary that maps domain names to IP addresses.

After the Internet Protocol has managed to find the actual address of the computer, it needs to send the request to it. The Internet Protocol breaks up the request into smaller pieces of data called packets and identifies the route the packets will take. At this point, the next layer of the Internet Protocol stack takes over.

Transport Layer

The TCP in TCP/IP stands for Transmission Control Protocol; it is one of the protocols used in the transport layer. The other is called UDP, which stands for User Datagram Protocol. The Transport Layer is responsible for actually transferring the data between computers. REALbasic provides classes for both TCP and UDP sockets.

It is easiest to understand what is happening on the Transport Layer by comparing TCP to UDP. It's called the Transport Layer because it deals with how data is moved from one computer to the next. TCP is a very robust protocol that includes a lot of error checking, which ensures that all the data sent by one computer is received by the other computer in the proper order. Because of all this error checking, it can be a little slow for some applications. UDP is the protocol designed for use in those situations; it emphasizes speed rather than robustness. Therefore, it sends a lot of data, but it doesn't check to ensure that the data has arrived as expected. This means that some data gets lost in transmission. In many cases, this loss of data is considered an acceptable trade-off to get enhanced speed. Things such as streaming video and audio make use of UDP.

Application Layer

The Application Layer sits at the top of the stack. This is the protocol that handles application tasks. Examples of Application Layer protocols are HTTP, SMTP (Simple Mail Transfer Protocol), and POP3 (Post Office Protocol, version 3). These protocols are used in common Internet applications, such as web browsers and email clients. REALbasic provides classes for these protocols as well.

REALbasic Networking Classes

The class hierarchy provided by REALbasic falls neatly into this layered approach to thinking about networks, as illustrated in Figure 9.1:

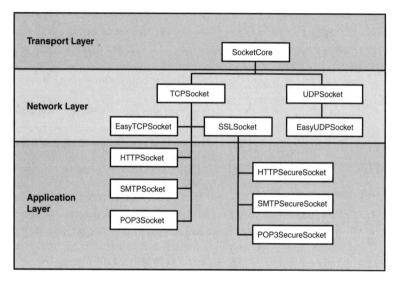

Figure 9.1   Internet suite of protocols.

At the top of the hierarchy is the **SocketCore** class, which is an abstract class that is never instantiated. There are two subclasses to **SocketCore**: **TCPSocket** and **UDPSocket**. These are the two basic socket classes that you will be using to write your networked application. **TCPSocket** has several subclasses that work on the Application Layer, which means that they are designed to perform specific kinds of activities on the Internet, such as request web pages and send or receive email.

Although a lot can be done with these classes, I am going to focus primarily on the **TCPSocket** class for the rest of the chapter and use it to develop a web server. A web server uses HTTP, and there is an **HTTPSocket** class provided by REALbasic. This class, however, isn't designed to be a server. It's good only for making HTTP requests and receiving files, not sending them. The sample application will get into enough detail that you will be able to use the **TCPSocket** class effectively in a variety of situations.

REALbasic also provides a few classes that you can use to get information about the network environment your application is running in. I'll start the chapter with these classes and then move on to the sample application.

Network Object

Now that you know a little bit about how the Internet works, you might be interested to see what kind of information is available to your application about the particular networking environment the application is operating in. One of the most important sources of information is the **Network** object, which is accessible as a member of the **System** object. It can tell you if you are currently connected to a network by using this property:

```
System.Network.IsConnected as Boolean
```

It can also look up your network address. The networks based on TCP/IP assign a unique number to every individual computer on the network. This is known as the IP address, and it looks like this (this is the default IP address of the current machine you are on, and is the IP address we will be using later on in the sample application):

```
127.0.0.1
```

This IP address can also be referred to by name, which is called a domain name. The domain name that is paired with this IP address is

```
LocalHost
```

You can look up both domain names and IP addresses of the computer the application is running on with the **Network** object using the following methods. Note that REALbasic calls the domain name the DNS address:

```
System.Network.LookupDNSAddress(DNSAddress as String) as String
System.Network.LookupIPAddress(IPAddress as String) as String
```

If you use `LookupDNSAddress`, you pass a domain name, and it will return the IP address for that domain. The `LookupIPAddress` works in the opposite direction—you pass it an IP address and it returns a domain name for it. To get the IP address for the current computer, you need to access the **NetworkInterface** class, which is also available from the **System** object.

Network Interface Class

The **NetworkInterface** class provides access to specific information about the network on which the computer is connected. Every piece of hardware connected to the Internet has a unique address, called the MAC address, and it can be accessed using the following property:

```
NetworkInterface.MacAddress as String
```

Nodes on a TCP/IP network are identified by an IP address. Things such as routers and computers are nodes on the network. In effect, this means that any IP address represents the address of either a network or an individual computer. If your organization has a group of computers, and each one is assigned an IP address, each computer can access the Internet individually. To find the IP address of the computer on which the application is running, access the following property:

```
NetworkInterface.IPAddress as String
```

Sometimes you don't want this to happen, so you establish a subnet that allows the computers within your organization's network to communicate directly with each other, but not directly to the Internet at large, unless it goes through a proxy computer. This local, private address space is determined by the Subnet Mask, and you can access this mask with the following property:

```
NetworkInterface.SubnetMask as String
```

System Members

The **System** object provides methods that give you access to different **NetworkInterface** objects. A computer can have more than one connection to a network, so the **System** object can tell you how many network interfaces there are by accessing the following:

```
System.NetworkInterfaceCount as Integer
```

You can then access any given **NetworkInterface** object by referring to its index, using the following method:

```
System.GetNetworkInterface(Index as Integer) as NetworkInterface
```

TCP and UDP Networks

TCP and UDP are both protocols used by the Internet. The most commonly used is TCP, which stands for Transmission Control Protocol. It is used to connect two computers and to reliably transfer data between them. The data itself is transmitted as packets, which are small units of data that can theoretically arrive at the host out of sequence. TCP ensures that they are placed in sequence and arrive reliably. It is used by the most commonly used Internet application—the World Wide Web and email.

SocketCore Class

The **SocketCore** class is an abstract class, meaning that it is never instantiated itself. It serves as the parent class to the classes that you will use when writing programs that interact with networks. The class provides some of the basic features that will be needed by all the subclasses in order to work. For starters, one of the first things you will need to do when creating a network connection is to specify which port to listen to or which port to try to connect to.

In the case of the World Wide Web and the HTTP protocol, the standard port number is 80, but that's not the only port that's available. Port numbers can range from 0 to 65535 and are divided into three tiers. So-called Well-Known Ports are those from 0 to 1023. On most systems, you need to have superuser status to use these ports. The next tier is called Registered Ports, and these number from 1024 to 49151. Finally, Dynamic Ports are numbered from 49152 to 65535.

A list of commonly used ports follows:

```
FTP                   21
SSH                   22
TELNET                23
SMTP                  25
HTTP                  80
HTTPS                 443
POP3                  110
HTTP-Alternate        8080
```

Although Registered Ports do have a semiformal status, there's no reason you can't use port numbers in that range, especially when you know that it is available. REALbasic provides **TCPSocket** subclasses for HTTP, SMTP, and POP3, and these subclasses will default to the port that is appropriate for the given protocol.

To find out which port to connect to, or bind to, check the following property:

```
SocketCore.Port as Integer
```

Exactly what this means depends on the context. When two computers connect through a network, one plays the role of the server and the other of the client. The server is said to listen on a port, or that it is bound to a port. A client connects to the server through a particular port. As a consequence, if the **SocketCore** subclass you are working with is a server and is waiting to receive data, the `Port` property says which port it is listening to. Otherwise, it says which port it is going to try to connect to.

Sending and Receiving Data

Because the **SocketCore** class is an abstract class, it doesn't implement all the features required to make a network connection. One of the most important things that is missing is a way to read and write data. Rest assured that this functionality is implemented in the subclasses, but you won't find it here.

What you will find, however, is something that is common to all the subclasses, and that is the event that gets triggered whenever data arrives:

```
SocketCore.DataAvailable
```

Whenever a socket receives data, the `DataAvailable` event is triggered. This does not mean, however, that all the data is available. In fact, there is no guarantee that all the required information has been retrieved. Because all the data doesn't come at once, the socket classes all implement two internal buffers, one for data that is coming in and one for data that is being sent out. The process you use to access these buffers differs depending on which subclass you are using. I will look at the buffers in more detail in the section on the **TCPSocket** class.

In addition to receiving data, sockets can send data. The **SocketCore** class doesn't implement a way to actually send data. For that, you'll also need to look at the specific subclass in question. However, sending data works like receiving data does in the sense that it does not necessarily get sent all at once. As a consequence, the socket classes all have the following event, which is triggered when all the data in the send buffer has been sent:

```
SocketCore.SendComplete(UserAborted as Boolean)
```

When an error is encountered, the `Error` event is triggered:

```
SocketCore.Error
```

To find out which error caused the event to be triggered, you need to check the `LastErrorCode` property:

```
SocketCore.LastErrorCode as Integer
```

The following class constants describe the cause of the error that was just triggered:

```
SocketCore.OpenDriverError = 100
SocketCore.LostConnection = 102
SocketCore.NameResolutionError = 103
SocketCore.AddressInUseError = 105
SocketCore.InvalidStateError = 106
SocketCore.InvalidPortError = 107
SocketCore.OutOfMemoryError = 108
```

SocketCore Properties

Every socket is given a unique identifier, which is accessible through the following property:

```
SocketCore.Handle as Integer
```

Being able to access the `Handle` for each socket can be convenient because in many cases, you will have more than one socket open at a time. In the web server sample application, you will see that several sockets are open at any given time, and you can use the `Handle` to identify which socket is performing any activity.

The following properties perform some basic tasks, which are mostly self-explanatory. To see if you are connected to another socket:

```
SocketCore.IsConnected as Boolean
```

To find out what the local IP address is for the machine your application is running on, check

```
SocketCore.LocalAddress as String
```

The following property identifies which **NetworkInterface** your socket is using:

```
SocketCore.NetworkInterface as NetworkInterface
```

SocketCore Methods

Sockets open their connection by calling the `Connect` method, and they can close it by calling the `Close` method. The subclasses that will be reviewed next often provide a more graceful means of opening and closing sockets.

```
SocketCore.Close
SocketCore.Connect
```

If you want to purge the internal send buffer, call the following:

```
SocketCore.Purge
```

One important thing to remember when dealing with sockets is that the Internet protocol is big endian, like PowerPC Macintosh, so you will need to pay attention to endianness when using sockets.

TCPSocket

Things start to get interesting when you use the **TCPSocket** class. This is the one that I will be using in the sample web server application.

TCPSocket Events

Although **SocketCore** has the isConnected property that you can use to check to see if your socket is connected to another socket, the **TCPSocket** adds an additional layer of functionality by triggering an event when a connection is first established:

```
TCPSocket.Connected
```

The SendProgress event is also added to this class, which allows you to track how much of a document has been downloaded:

```
TCPSocket.SendProgress(BytesSent as Integer, BytesLeft as Integer) as Boolean
```

If you want to cancel the send, you can return True from this event.

The following property tells you what address you are trying to connect to:

```
TCPSocket.Address as String
```

The address you actually are connected to after you have connected is not necessarily the same as the one you tried to connect to in the first place. Therefore, REALbasic lets you check the remote address you are connected to using this property:

```
TCPSocket.RemoteAddress as String
```

TCPSocket Methods

You can use **TCPSocket** to both send and receive data. If you are going to be receiving data, you will need to tell **TCPSocket** to Listen on a given port for any requests using the following method:

```
TCPSocket.Listen
```

If a connection has already been established, you can close it using the following:

```
TCPSocket.Disconnect
```

The **SocketCore** class itself did not provide any methods for reading or writing data. Because the whole point of using sockets is to send and receive data, every subclass provides its own methods for doing so. The **TCPSocket** provides the following three methods for reading data in the receive buffer:

```
TCPSocket.Read(Bytes as Integer, [Encoding as TextEncoding]) as String
TCPSocket.ReadAll([Encoding as TextEncoding]) as String
TCPSocket.Lookahead([Encoding as TextEncoding]) as String
```

Under normal circumstances, when you read the buffer, the data is cleared from the buffer, regardless of whether you call Read or ReadAll. There are times when you want to see what's in the buffer without deleting the contents of the buffer, and that is when you call the Lookahead method. You'll see an example of this in the web server code supplied later in this chapter.

In addition to reading data, you can write data as well, simply by calling the following method:

```
TCPSocket.Write(Data as String)
```

Keep in mind that you can send a string of any size to the `Write` method, but if the `String` is particularly long, it will not get sent all at once and will take some time to be completely sent. In the meantime, your application can check the data passed in the `SendProgress` event to monitor progress.

HTTPSocket Inherits TCPSocket

The **HTTPSocket** class is used to handle the client side of an HTTP connection. Because HTTP (Hypertext Transfer Protocol) is the protocol used by the World Wide Web, in simpler terms this means that the **HTTPSocket** class performs the role of the web browser—in the sense that it can request files from a web server and receive them. Any kind of file can be retrieved this way, but html files are most commonly associated with the web. Note that the **HTTPSocket** class is a networking class. It cannot display html pages; that's what the **HTMLViewer** control is for.

HTTPSocket is a subclass of **TCPSocket** and does all the same things that **TCPSocket** does. The layer of functionality it adds is that of creating HTTP requests, which have a specific format, and it handles retrieving the data that is sent back as a result of the request.

The HTTP protocol supports several types of requests, but I will concern myself with two in particular, a GET request and a POST request. The most common kind of request is a GET, which does what the name implies—it makes a request for a certain file and the HTTP server returns the file. Here is an example of the body of a GET request:

```
GET / HTTP/1.1
Accept: */*
Accept-Language: en-us
Accept-Encoding: gzip, deflate
Cookie: photo_display=thumbnail; nde-textsize=16px; SessionID=12345
User-Agent: Mozilla/5.0 (Macintosh; U; PPC Mac OS X; en-us)
        AppleWebKit/412 (KHTML, like Gecko) Safari/412
Connection: keep-alive
Host: localhost:8080
```

The first line of the request tells you what kind of request it is and what the request is for. It consists of a single line that is delimited by two spaces, like so:

```
GET<space>/path/to/file<space>HTTP/1.1
```

Following the initial line are a series of key/value pairs that provide basic information about the request, and at the very end of the request (not visible in the example) is a blank line that signifies the end of the request. This is important! A line ending according to the HTTP protocol consists of a carriage return and a linefeed, which is the same as the value for `EndOfLine.Windows`.

A POST request is similar, except that it also sends additional information. The term "POST" refers to the idea of POSTING information and is used when the user has filled out a form and submitted it in the web browser. A sample of a POST request can be seen in Listing 9.2.

```
POST /form.html HTTP/1.1
Host: localhost:8080
User-Agent: Mozilla/5.0 (Macintosh; U; PPC Mac OS X Mach-O; en-US; rv:1.6)
➥Gecko/20040113
Accept: text/xml,application/xml,application/xhtml+xml,text/html;q=0.9,
➥text/plain;q=0.8,image/png,image/jpeg,image/gif;q=0.2,*/*;q=0.1
Accept-Language: en-us,en;q=0.5
Accept-Encoding: gzip,deflate
Accept-Charset: ISO-8859-1,utf-8;q=0.7,*;q=0.7
Keep-Alive: 300
Connection: keep-alive
Referer: http://localhost:8080/form.html
Content-Type: application/x-www-form-urlencoded
Content-Length: 28


textfield=Mark&Submit=Submit
```

The first line is different, as you can see, because it designates the request as a POST. You will also notice that there are some additional key/value pairs that are being sent, the most important of which are Content-Type and Content-Length. Both of these are always available on POST requests. Just as in GET, the main request is ended with a blank line, but in addition to the blank line, a POST also attaches additional information. In the preceding example, the post has appended data from a form that the user has filled out.

Even though a POST is intended to be used for sending data to the web server, it is not the only way. You can use a GET request, too. The only difference is that the encoded data is not sent in the header; it's appended to the URL. The following GET request shows what a GET request looks like:

```
GET /form.html?textfield=Mark&Submit=Submit HTTP/1.1
Accept: */*
Accept-Language: en-us
Accept-Encoding: gzip, deflate
Cookie: photo_display=thumbnail; nde-textsize=16px; SessionID=12345
User-Agent: Mozilla/5.0 (Macintosh; U; PPC Mac OS X; en-us) AppleWebKit/412
➥(Khtml, like Gecko) Safari/412
Connection: keep-alive
Host: localhost:8080
```

In the first line of the request, everything that follows the "?" in the string of characters in /form.html?textfield=Mark&Submit=Submit is the data that is sent by a POST in the body of the request. As you will see in the example, when you create a form using html, you can specify which kind of request that form should generate, either a GET or a POST.

```
POST /form.html HTTP/1.1
Host: localhost:8080
User-Agent: Mozilla/5.0 (Macintosh; U; PPC Mac OS X Mach-O; en-US; rv:1.6)
➡Gecko/20040113
Accept: text/xml,application/xml,application/xhtml+xml,text/html;q=0.9,
➡text/plain;q=0.8,image/png,image/jpeg,image/gif;q=0.2,*/*;q=0.1
Accept-Language: en-us,en;q=0.5
Accept-Encoding: gzip,deflate
Accept-Charset: ISO-8859-1,utf-8;q=0.7,*;q=0.7
Keep-Alive: 300
Connection: keep-alive
Referer: http://localhost:8080/fileform.html
Content-Type: multipart/form-data; boundary=myBoundaryValue
Content-Length: 59628

--myBoundaryValue
Content-Disposition: form-data; name="datafile"; filename="05-Threading.doc"
Content-Type: application/msword
<lots of data>
```

The example I have provided will accommodate both kinds of POST requests. When submitting a file, the file is submitted according to its MIME type. This is designated in the Content-Type field. There are two values submitted in Content-Type. The value "multipart/form-data" indicates that a file is being uploaded and that "boundary=..." is a value used to delimit the file. The uploaded file starts with the string "—" followed by the data that was passed as the boundary value. The file can be divided up into multiple parts, and each part is separated by this string of characters, which in the preceding example is

```
--myBoundaryValue
```

The end of the document is signified by the boundary value again, this time with "—" on either side, like so:

```
--myBoundaryValue--
```

Figure 9.2 is an example of a html form:

You can code this form in html either as a POST or as a GET. Either way, the form looks the same. To create it as a POST, you would write the following:

```
<form name="form1" method="post" action="http://localhost:8080/form.html">
    <p>
            <input type="text" name="textfield">
    </p>
    <p>
            <input type="submit" name="Submit" value="Submit">
    </p>
</form>
```

Figure 9.2   Sample form.

The request would be the POST request listed previously. To create it as a GET, it would look like this:

```
<form name="form1" method="get" action="http://localhost:8080/form.html">
    <p>
        <input type="text" name="textfield">
    </p>
    <p>
        <input type="submit" name="Submit" value="Submit">
    </p>
</form>
```

The headers for this request would be like the GET request I just listed.

You can use the **HTTPSocket** class to perform any kind of request. You can even use it to mimic having filled out a form. You can use either a GET or a POST request.

An html form passes a series of key/value pairs, and the **HTTPSocket** class makes it easy to submit the values needed using a dictionary. If you are going to use a GET request, you can use the following method to take the values in a dictionary and return a URL-encoded **String**:

```
HTTPSocket.EncodeFormData(Form as Dictionary) as String
```

Because this returns a **String**, you would use this by appending a "?" following by the returned **String** to the URL, something like this:

```
Dim aForm as New Dictionary
aForm.Value("textfield") = "Mark"
HTTPSocket1.Get("http://localhost:8080/form.html" + "?" + _
HTTPSocket1.EncodeFormData(aForm)
```

You can do something similar with a POST, using the following method:

```
HTTPSocket.SetFormData(Form as Dictionary)
```

The code would look like the following:

```
Dim aForm as New Dictionary
aForm.Value("textfield") = "Mark"

HTTPSocket1.SetFormData(aForm)
HTTPSocket1.Post("http://localhost:8080/form.html")
```

In addition to posting data from html forms, POST requests can also be used to upload files. The **HTTPSocket** class has a method to do this:

```
HTTPSocket.SetPostContent(Content as String, ContentType as String)
```

Authentication

The HTTP protocol defines two means of authenticating users: Basic Authentication and Digest Authentication. The most widely used method is Basic Authentication, which is what REALbasic supports, with the following event:

```
HTTPSocket.AuthenticationRequired(Headers as InternetHeaders,
➥ByRef Name as String, ByRef Password as String) Handles Event
```

It works like this: When you make a request for a web page, the web server checks to see if authentication is required. If it is, it sends back a notice saying that it needs to get a username and a password. When this happens, the **HTTPSocket** class triggers the `AuthenticationRequired` event and passes along the headers so that you can glean any necessary information from them.

As you can see, it also passes a `Name` and `Password` variable `ByRef`. Although this is an unusual occurrence, it means that you should assign a value for the `Name` and `Password` parameters. When you do, the server will be sent the username and password to be authenticated.

Get, Post, and GetHeaders Methods

There are several request types that are legal HTTP requests, but the **HTTPSocket** class implements the three that are required: GET, POST, and HEAD, represented by the `Get`,

`Post,` and `GetHeaders` methods. `Get` and `Post` each come in three forms, as
follows:

```
HTTPSocket.Get(URL as String)
HTTPSocket.Get(URL as String, File as FolderItem)
HTTPSocket.Get(URL as String, Timeout as Integer) as String

HTTPSocket.Post(URL as String)
HTTPSocket.Post(URL as String, File as FolderItem)
HTTPSocket.Post(URL as String, Timeout as Integer) as String

HTTPSocket.GetHeaders(URL as String)
HTTPSocket.GetHeaders(URL as String, Timeout as Integeer) as String
```

If you want to get the home page of REAL software, you would execute the request
like so:

```
httpsocket1.Get "http://www.realsoftware.com/"
```

The first two method signatures are subroutines because they do not return a value.
Because of the asynchronous nature of network communications, an event is triggered
when the data is returned. Two events are relevant:

```
HTTPSocket.PageReceived(URL as String, HTTPStatus as Integer,
➥Headers as Dictionary, Content as String) Handles Event
HTTPSocket.DownloadComplete(URL as String, HTTPStatus as Integer,
➥Headers as Dictionary, File as FolderItem)Handles Event
```

The event to use is contingent on which form of the `Get` and `Post` methods is used.
You have the option of passing a **FolderItem** when calling the methods, and if you do,
the data that you have requested will be made available in the `DowndloadComplete`
event. If you do not pass a **FolderItem**, the content will be made available as a **String**
in the `PageReceived` event. The general rule is this: if you are requesting an html or
XML file, do not pass a **FolderItem**. If you are downloading a binary file, such as a
Microsoft Word document or a JPEG image, pass a **FolderItem** in the method.
`GetHeaders` works like a GET request, expect that only the headers are returned, not
the requested file.

You also have the option of passing a "Timeout" value in the `Get, Post,` and
`GetHeaders` **methods**, which makes the request run in synchronous mode, which means
that the methods are functions. REALbasic will block and wait for a result, which will
be in the form of a **String**. When using the class in synchronous mode, you can also set
the following parameter to `True` to yield time that allows other events to be triggered:

```
HTTPSocket.Yield as Boolean
```

If you are using synchronous mode, you can access headers using the following
property:

```
HTTPSocket.PageHeaders as InternetHeader
```

TCPSocket has a `SendProgress` property, and **HTTPSocket** adds a `ReceiveProgress` property to the mix:

```
HTTPSocket.ReceiveProgress(BytesReceived as Integer, TotalBytes as Integer)
➥Handles Event
```

You have seen this used in an earlier example with a **ProgressBar** control.

You have already seen examples of HTTP headers, but you haven't seen all the different variations yet (at least not in this book). The great thing about the HTTP protocol is that it is very flexible. One thing it allows you to do is to create your own headers. This can be a very powerful tool in your programming belt if you want to develop custom HTTP services. You can arbitrarily set any header using the following method:

```
HTTPSocket.SetRequestHeader(Name as String, Value as String)
```

You can also clear all your headers by calling

```
HTTPSocket.ClearRequestHeaders
```

```
HTTPSocket.HeadersReceived(Headers as InternetHeaders, HTTPStatus as Integer)
➥Handles Event
```

When you make an HTTP request and get the results, the HTTP server has to send back a status code. Hopefully, the status code will be 200, which means that everything is okay. If you are using the **HTTPSocket** class in synchronous mode, you can find out what the status code was by checking the following property:

```
HTTPSocket.HTTPStatusCode as String
```

Here is an abbreviated list of sample codes:

```
200 - OK
201 - Created
202 - Accepted
203 - Non-Authoritative Information
204 - No Content
205 - Reset Content
206 - Partial Content
300 - Multiple Choices
301 - Moved Permanently
302 - Found
303 - See Other
304 - Not Modified
305 - Use Proxy
307 - Temporary Redirect
400 - Bad Request
401 - Not Authorised
403 - Forbidden
404 - Not Found
408 - Request Timeout
```

```
409 - Conflict
410 - Gone
411 - Length Required
412 - Precondition Failed
414 - Request URI Too Long
415 - Unsupported Media Type
500 - Internal Server Error
501 - Not Implemented
502 - Bad Gateway
503 - Service Unavailable
504 - Gateway Timeout
505 - HTTP Version Not Supported
```

There are some situations where users sit behind a firewall and aren't given direct access to the Internet. This is often done at businesses as a security measure.

```
HTTPSocket.HTTPProxyAddress
HTTPSocket.HTTPProxyPort
```

InternetHeaders Class

The **InternetHeaders** class is basically an array of key/value pairs, plus some methods that make it easier to add and delete individual pairs in the list.

From the example given earlier, the source of the header data looks like this:

```
Accept-Language: en-us
Accept-Encoding: gzip, deflate
Cookie: photo_display=thumbnail; nde-textsize=16px; SessionID=12345
User-Agent: Mozilla/5.0 (Macintosh; U; PPC Mac OS X; en-us) AppleWebKit/412
➡ (Khtml, like Gecko) Safari/412
Connection: keep-alive
Host: localhost:8080
```

You can access the raw source by calling the following method:

```
InternetHeaders.Source as String
```

Using the same header data just listed, I could get access to the "Connection" value like this:

```
Dim s as String
s = Headers.Value("Connection")
```

I can use the following method to find out how many headers there are:

```
InternetHeaders.Count as Integer
```

This means that I can get access to the value of any given header by using either the name, the index, or both, using the following methods:

```
InternetHeaders.Value(Name as String) as String
InternetHeaders.Value(Name as String, Index as Integer) as String
InternetHeaders.Value(Index as Integer) as String
InternetHeaders.Name(Index as Integer) as String
```

Likewise, I can delete individual headers using either the name or the name and the index:

```
InternetHeaders.Delete(Name as String)
InternetHeaders.Delete(Name as String, Index as Integer)
InternetHeaders.DeleteAllHeaders
```

If I want to add an entirely new header to the object, I call the `AppendHeader` method:

```
InternetHeaders.AppendHeader(Name as String, Value as String)
```

If I want to modify an existing header, or add a new one if it doesn't exist, I can call the `SetHeader` method:

```
InternetHeaders.SetHeader(Name as String, Value as String)
```

From CGI to HTTPServer

One of the challenges of working with sockets is the fundamentally asynchronous nature of computer networks. There is almost always some kind of network latency—a period of time between when a request is made and when an answer is received. More importantly, a request may not arrive complete. Rather, it will arrive in batches and your program needs to know what to expect and how to gather up all the data prior to acting on it.

You've seen an example of the **HTTPSocket** class in the RSSReader application, but we cannot use it for a web server because the **HTTPSocket** class plays the role of the client. To create a web server, you will need to use the **TCPSocket** class, which is the super class of **HTTPSocket**.

A web server is used to view web pages, and a web page is created using html. Here's an example of a page that I will view in the sample application:

```
<!DOCTYPE html PUBLIC "-//W3C//DTD html 4.01 Transitional//EN"
"http://www.w3.org/TR/html4/loose.dtd">
<html>
    <head>
        <meta http-equiv="Content-Type" content="text/html; charset=utf-8">
        <title>REALbasic HTTPServer</title>
    </head>
    <body>
        <h1>REALbasic Cross-Platform Application Development</h1>
        <h4>Mark S. Choate</h4>
        <img src="images/REALbasicBook.jpg" align="left" />
        <p><i>REALbasic Cross-Platform Application Development</i>
covers the most recent version of REALbasic, known as REALbasic 2005.</p>
        <p>Known for its ease-of-use, REALbasic is also a
➥powerful language that compiles native applications for Windows,
Macintosh and Linux operating systems. It's simple enough for a beginner,
```

```
➥but powerful enough to meet the needs of seasoned programmers as well.</p>
    </body>
</html>
```

Figure 9.3 shows what this page looks like rendered in a web browser:

Figure 9.3   Web browser view.

One thing that you should notice about this file is that the references to images include URLs to the images, not the image itself. This means that when you access a page, you generate a request for the page itself, plus requests for all the images that are referenced within the html of the page request. When the browser gets the source html page, it then goes through and requests all the individual images. This means that a web server needs to be prepared to handle a lot of concurrent requests. If I wrote the server using **TCPSocket** alone, I would run into a problem because each new request needs a new socket connection (the HTTP/1.1 protocol lets you keep the socket connection open and make multiple requests through the same connection, but this sample closes the socket connection after each individual request for simplicity's sake).

To accommodate this, you need a way to manage a pool of sockets that are available for requests, a way to hand off requests to these sockets when they come in, and a way to create new sockets if all the current sockets are being used. Fortunately, REALbasic provides a class that does just that for you.

ServerSocket Class

The **ServerSocket** class manages a pool of sockets for you, and this is what I will use in the web server.

The **ServerSocket** class is one of those classes that will save you hours of coding if you do much with sockets. Not only does it handle one of the most challenging aspects of working with sockets, which is managing a pool of them to handle multiple requests, it also does it in a way that is remarkably intuitive and easy to use.

To use it, the **ServerSocket** instance must be persistent. You can use it like a **Control** by dragging it onto a **Window**, or create it as a property of a **Window** or **App** object. Whichever you do, the important part is that it persists because this one object will be listening for requests and then spinning them off throughout the time the server is running.

There are a few properties to set at first. The first, which should come as no surprise, is setting the port to listen to

```
ServerSocket.Port as Integer
```

Then you also need to tell the object some information about how to handle socket creation. Because some overhead is associated with instantiating a new socket when a request is made, it's a good idea to have some sockets ready and waiting for the next request. You can set the following property to determine the minimum number of sockets to be instantiated when listening for requests:

```
ServerSocket.MinimumSocketsAvailable as Integer
```

The flip side of this is that you also want to set a limit as to how many sockets can get created. If all of a sudden the server is handling thousands of requests, you could quickly run out of memory from spinning off too many sockets. You can set this limit with the following property:

```
ServerSocket.MaximumSocketsConnected as Integer
```

There are two other properties that can be useful:

```
ServerSocket.IsListening as Boolean
ServerSocket.LocalAddress as String
```

If you want to check to see if the **ServerSocket** instance is listening for connections, check the IsListening property. Also, if you want to know what the local IP address is, you can check LocalAddress.

After the necessary properties are set, you can tell the **ServerSocket** instance to start listening for connections by calling the Listen method:

```
ServerSocket.Listen
```

As you might expect, you can tell it to stop by calling this method:

```
ServerSocket.StopListening
```

Everything that I've covered so far composes the "easy part." All the heavy lifting is done in the `AddSocket` event:

```
ServerSocket.AddSocket() as TCPSocket Handles Event
```

"Heavy lifting" is actually overstating things a bit. The `AddSocket` event is triggered when a request comes in on the port that the **ServerSocket** is listening to. You need to write the code in this event that defines how you respond to the request. The response is to instantiate a socket of some sort and then go back to listening for more new requests. The socket you instantiate at this point is the socket that will respond to the request.

If something goes wrong in the process, the **ServerSocket** error event is triggered:

```
ServerSocket.Error(ErrorCode as Integer) Handles Event
```

The HTTPServer Application

To implement the web server, I will create a subclass of **ServerSocket** called **HTTPServer** and create a subclass of **TCPSocket** called **HTTPConnection**. This will be the socket I instantiate when a new request comes in. First, take a look at the **HTTPServer** class to see how new instances of **HTTPConnection** are handled.

Class HTTPServer Inherits ServerSocket

The HTTPServer class is simple. There is one property:

```
DocRoot As FolderItem
```

This property refers to the root directory that will be used by the web server. When a request for a page is received, the socket will look for the file within the `DocRoot` **FolderItem**.

In addition to the `DocRoot` property, the subclass also includes an implementation of the `AddSocket` event, which follows.

Listing 9.1   **Function AddSocket() As TCPSocket Handles Event**

```
Dim tcp as HTTPConnection

// A request for a page has been received and
// a new socket needs to be instantiated to
// handle it.
tcp = New HTTPConnection(DocRoot)

// Send information to the server window
window1.AppendString("Adding socket")

// Return the socket

Return tcp
```

In the sample application, the **HTTPServer** instance is a property of **Window1**. **Window1** has an **EditField**, where messages about the current state or activity of the server are displayed. It also has a **PushButton** labeled Request that will be used to stimulate several simultaneous requests, but don't worry about that at this point.

When the **HTTPServer** class is first instantiated, it opens up a pool of sockets. In the sample application, each time a socket is instantiated, it is displayed in the **Window**. You can see an example in the following figure:

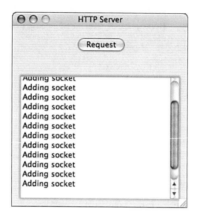

Figure 9.4   Pool of sockets.

In the Open event of **Window1**, the **HTTPServer** instance is instantiated and assigned to the Window1.Server property. In addition to being instantiated, the values are set for the minimum and maximum number of sockets that are available. The port is set to 8080, which is commonly used as an alternative to the standard port 80 for web servers. A lot of applications that are servers use 8080, so a person can try out the application without interfering with a real web server running on that computer.

Listing 9.2   **Sub Window1.Open() Handles Event**

```
Server = new HTTPServer
Server.DocRoot = getFolderItem("DocRoot")
Server.MinimumSocketsAvailable =5
Server.MaximumSocketsConnected =10
Server.Port = 8080
Server.Listen
```

In addition to the Open event, **Window1** also implements the AppendString method, which is a simple way of displaying output to the window as the application is running.

Listing 9.3   **Sub Window1.AppendString(s as String)**

```
Window1.EditField1.SelStart = Len(Window1.EditField1.Text)
Window1.EditField1.SelText = s + EndOfLine
```

Handling GET Requests

So far, you've seen what happens when the application is first run and the initial sockets are created. What is more interesting is to see how the application responds to actual HTTP requests. We do not need a web browser to generate those requests because we can do it programmatically with REALbasic.

In the sample application, there are four **HTTPSockets** that can be called to make HTTP requests against the web server. All I did was drag them onto **Window1**. If you click the Request button, they are all triggered as close to simultaneously as possible. Figure 9.5 shows which socket received which request, and is identified by the `TCPSocket.Handle` property:

Control Window1.PushButton1:

Listing 9.4   **Sub PushButton1.Action() Handles Event**

```
HTTPSocket1.Get("http://localhost:8080/index.html")
HTTPSocket2.Get("http://localhost:8080/index.html")
HTTPSocket3.Get("http://localhost:8080/index.html")
HTTPSocket4.Get("http://localhost:8080/index.html")
```

Now if you start the application and click the Request button, this is the output that you will see:

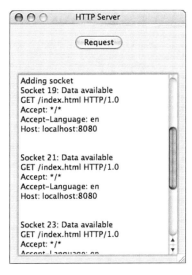

Figure 9.5   Request button output.

At this point, you don't really need to worry too much about what's happening, except to understand that whenever a socket receives a request, the `DataAvailable` event is triggered. In the **HTTPConnection** class, I have this line of code that displays in the **Window** the `Handle` for each socket that has received a request:

```
Window1.AppendString("Socket " + str(me.Handle) + ": Data available")
```

In the previous figure, clicking the Request button and generating four simultaneous events caused four different sockets to respond with handles 20, 22, 24, and 21, respectively. With this information, you can be assured that the **HTTPServer** is properly getting requests and handing them off to different sockets.

At the beginning of this section, I shared a sample html page and showed what the page would look like when displayed in a web browser. If I call this page index.html and place it as a text file in the `DocRoot` **FolderItem** (which is a property of the **HTTPServer** object), I can access it using my web browser by typing in the following URL:

```
http://localhost:8080/
```

When I try to access this page through my browser, the browser shows the page, and the web server application displays the following information:

```
Socket 16: Data available
Path: /

Socket 16: Data available
Path: /images/REALbasicBook.jpg
```

You can see that this page generated two requests. The first request was for the path / and the second was for /images/REALbasicBook.jpg. The / is the root file, and the default name for that file is index.html, so the application automatically looks for a file named index.html if there is no file listed.

If you go back and examine the original html file, you will see the following in the code:

```
<img src="images/REALbasicBook.jpg" align="left" />
```

This is the html tag that is responsible for the second request. As you might imagine, a single page can generate quite a few requests, depending on how many images are on the page. This example is interesting because the same socket handled both requests.

At this point, you may want to understand just how the **HTTPConnection** socket sent the html page and the image to the web browser, but before I go into the code details, I want to show you a few other examples as well.

Handling POST Requests: Posting Forms and Transferring Files

Following is an example of how the application handles a form. Here is the html used to create the form (I have named the file form.html and saved it in the `DocRoot`):

```
<!DOCTYPE html PUBLIC "-//W3C//DTD html 4.01 Transitional//EN"
"http://www.w3.org/TR/html4/loose.dtd">
<html>
<head>
<meta http-equiv="Content-Type" content="text/html; charset=utf-8">
<title>HTTPServer Form</title>
</head>

<body>
<p><b>Tell me your name:</b></p>
<form name="form1" method="post" action="http://localhost:8080/form.html">
  <p>
    <input type="text" name="textfield">
</p>
  <p>
    <input type="submit" name="Submit" value="Submit">
</p>
</form>
</body>
</html>
```

When displayed, it looks like Figure 9.6:

Figure 9.6   Form.

If you fill out this form using your web browser and click Submit, the page shown in Figure 9.7 is returned as the result:

Figure 9.7   Hello, Mark results.

The form generated a POST request, which was processed by the web server application. The value that was filled in on the form was used to compose the output, which in this case was "Hello, Mark".

Although a POST is the most common way to handle form data, you can also use a GET request as well. When you do, instead of having the POST data appended to the request, the data from the form is appended to the URL itself. The following example shows what happens when the following URL is used to access the form.html document:

```
http://localhost:8080/form.html?dog=lucy
```

The sample app takes the data after the "?" character, parses it, and responds thus:

Figure 9.8   Get with an extended URL.

In both of these examples—the POST and the GET request—the sample application checks the values that are sent to it and responds accordingly. When you read through the sample code later on in the chapter, you will see exactly how it does this.

Uploading a File

The previous two examples used form data of some sort to generate a request. You can also use a POST to upload a file. Here is the html for a page that will let you upload a file to the web server application:

```
<!DOCTYPE html PUBLIC "-//W3C//DTD html 4.01 Transitional//EN"
"http://www.w3.org/TR/html4/loose.dtd">
<html>
    <head>
        <meta http-equiv="Content-Type" content="text/html; charset=utf-8">
        <title>HTTPServer Form</title>
    </head>

    <body>
    <p><b>Please specify a file, or a set of files:</b></p>
```

```
      <form name="form1" method="post" enctype="multipart/form-data"
action="http://localhost:8080/form.html">
         <p>
      <input type="file" name="datafile" size="40">
      </p>
      <p>
      <input type="submit" value="Send">
      </p>

      </form>
      </body>
</html>
```

In the examples, I have named this file fileform.html. There are two distinguishing characteristics to the html used to create this form. First, there is a value of "multipart/form-data" for the enctype attribute. This tells the server that a file is being uploaded and how to handle it. There is also an input element whose type is "file" in contrast to "text" as in the previous example.

Figure 9.9 shows you what this form looks like when viewed in a web browser:

Figure 9.9   Form for uploading a file.

Next is an excerpt from the request that is generated when this form is filled out:

```
POST /form.html HTTP/1.1
Host: localhost:8080
```

```
User-Agent: Mozilla/5.0 (Macintosh; U; PPC Mac OS X Mach-O; en-US; rv:1.6)
➥Gecko/20040113
Accept: text/xml,application/xml,application/xhtml+xml,
➥text/html;q=0.9,text/plain;q=0.8,image/png,image/jpeg,image/gif;q=0.2,*/*;q=0.1
Accept-Language: en-us,en;q=0.5
Accept-Encoding: gzip,deflate
Accept-Charset: ISO-8859-1,utf-8;q=0.7,*;q=0.7
Keep-Alive: 300
Connection: keep-alive
Referer: http://localhost:8080/fileform.html
Content-Type: multipart/form-data; boundary=--------------------------
➥3704495525905278111478986690
Content-Length: 59628

--------------------------3704495525905278111478986690
Content-Disposition: form-data; name="datafile"; filename="Threading.doc"
Content-Type: application/msword
<lots of data>
--------------------------3704495525905278111478986690--
```

In this example, I uploaded a Microsoft Word document called Threading.doc. All the data in the document isn't shown; for brevity's sake I replaced it with the text `<lots of data>`.

Now you have seen examples of several kinds of requests and how the web server application handles them. The interesting part is seeing exactly how it gets done. There are two additional classes **HTTPConnection**, which is a subclass of **TCPSocket**, and **HTTPRequest**, which is a subclass of **Dictionary**, that are used to process the request. The hard part is that a request does not come in all at once. You may get it in small segments, with each instance triggering a `DataAvailable` event in the **HTTPConnection** object. Not only do you need to wait until you have the entire request, you also need to see what kind of request it is and respond accordingly. To make this happen, take the following steps:

1. Don't do anything until you receive a blank line. Then you know you have the primary information about the request.
2. If it's a GET request, you can go ahead and respond.
3. If it's a POST, you may need to wait for additional data. You will want to know what kind of data to expect.
4. If the value of Content-Type is "application/x-www-form-urlencoded", you can expect plain old form data. If the value is "multipart/form-data", then you can expect a file. The header should also have a Content-Length value. This can be used to make sure you have all the form data you need.
5. If a file is being uploaded, you will be given a MIME type and a string of characters that serve as a delimiter of the file being uploaded, and you can use that to determine when the upload is complete. (It also passes the Content-Length value.)

All of this is managed by the **HTTPConnection** class, instances of which are the sockets spun off by the **HTTPServer** object.

Class HTTPConnection Inherits TCPSocket

The **HTTPConnection** class is a subclass of **TCPSocket** rather than the **HTTPSocket** class because the **HTTPSocket** class is designed to be the client, or requesting socket, rather than the serving socket. It has three properties:

```
Request As HTTPRequest
Stream As BinaryStream
Protected DocRoot As FolderItem
```

The **request** object holds the values that are passed in the header, including data uploaded from forms. The response is written to the client using a **BinaryStream** object, and the DocRoot **FolderItem** has already been discussed. This is the root folder that all requests are considered relative to.

Listing 9.5 **Sub HTTPConnection.Constructor(aDocRoot as FolderItem)**

```
// Pass the DocRoot in the constructor since
// an HTTP Server must have a root document
// to function correctly.
DocRoot = aDocRoot
```

It is in the DataAvailable event that everything happens. The code is heavily commented, so you can read through it to see what is happening.

Listing 9.6 **Sub HTTPConnection.DataAvailable() Handles Event**

```
Dim data as String
Dim headers(-1) as String
Dim KeyVal(-1) as String
Dim f as FolderItem


Window1.AppendString("Socket " + str(me.Handle) + ": Data available")

// Instantiate an HTTPRequest object.
// The reason I test for Nil is that this event will
// likely be called more than once for each request.
// If the request object is Nil, then I know that it
// is the first time the event has been called and
// that I need to instantiate a new object.

If me.request = Nil Then
    me.request = new HTTPRequest(DocRoot)
end if
```

Listing 9.6 **Continued**

```
// Take a look at your data - but use Lookahead so
// that the data remains in the buffer. Later on it
// will be easier to handle if it is all in one place.

data = me.Lookahead

// The first part of the header is delimited by a blank line.
// If it is a GET request, then you have  the complete request.
// If it is a POST, then you will have additional data coming
// after the blank line. I don't do anything with the request
// until I find the blank line.

If (Instr(Data, EndOfLine.Windows + EndOfLine.Windows)  > 0) Then

    // I have a blank line, which means I have the complete header,
    // unless it is a POST. If the value for request.type has
    // not been set, then I parse the header data in order to
    // generate values for the request object. If the type property
    // is not empty, I don't do anything, because I know that the
    // header has been parsed. When it is not empty, chances are
    // the request is a POST and a lot of data is being posted.

    If me.request.type = "" Then
        parseHeader(data)
    End If

End If

// Test to see if it is a POST request

If me.request.type = "POST" Then

    Window1.AppendString("Type: POST")

    // POST requests are usually generated as a consequence
    // of filling out a form. One special form element that
    // requires special handling is the one that allows the
    // user to upload a file to the server. If a file is being
    // uploaded to the server, then some additional information
    // will be sent in the header. See the ParseHeader method
    // for details on how this information is extracted.
    // If a document is being uploaded, then the ParseHeader method
    // will have extracted a value for a "boundary", which is
    // the boundary between the different parts of a multipart MIME
    // document. The boundary value surrounded by "--" on either side
```

Listing 9.6 **Continued**

```
// indicates the end of the file, so you know that you have
// received everything you need from the request.

If request.query.HasKey("boundary") Then
    If InStr(data, "--" + request.query.value("boundary") + "--") > 0 Then
        // The end boundary has been found.
        // The POST is complete.

        Window1.AppendString("POST file Complete...")
    Else
        // The end boundary has not been found.
        // Wait for more data.

        Window1.AppendString("Waiting for POST file data...")
        Return
    End if

// There is not "boundary" key in the request.query object, so
// check for a value for "Content-Length", which indicates the
// number of bytes taken up by the POST data. You can use this
// to determine when the POST is complete.

Else
    Try

        // One reason I use Lookahead is to keep all the data together
        // so that I can more easily find out the length of the data
        // portion of the POST, which I do here by looking at the
        // second field of the request, using a blank line as the
        // delimiter.

        If Len(NthField(data, Endofline.Windows+endofline.Windows, 2)) =
Val(Trim(request.Value("Content-Length"))) Then
            // Post is complete
            Window1.AppendString("POST form Complete...")

            // If the POST contains Form data, rather than a document
            // being uploaded, you need to parse the data into
            // the individual elements for the request.query object.

            KeyVal = Split(data, endofline.windows+endofline.Windows)
            request.getQueryString(KeyVal(1))
        Else
            // Wait for more data
            Window1.AppendString("Waiting for POST form data...")
```

Listing 9.6   **Continued**

```
            Return
        End If
        End
    End If
End If


// The previous code processed the request, primarily
// focusing on parsing the data as it arrived and
// determining when the request was completed.
// Only when all the data has been received will the
// following lines of code run. This portion of the
// event decides what to write back to the client
// and actually does the writing.

// Check to see if it is a "GET" or "POST" command

If (request.Type = "GET")  or (request.Type = "POST") Then


    // Get the path to the file we want to serve from
    // the request object and get a reference to a
    // FolderITem object

    f = request.getResponseFileFromPath( request.path )

    If f = Nil or f.exists = False Then

        // The File does not exist, so return error
        // Write the header for the file using the
        // standard HTTP error code of 404 to indicate
        // the file was not found

        Write "HTTP/1.1 " + format( 404, "000" ) + " " + _
"Error" + chr(13) + chr(10) + chr(13) + chr(10)
        Me.write( "Error 404." )
        Return

    End If


    // If the file was found, then everything is ok so
    // you can send the header back to the client with
    // a status code of 200, which means, "OK".
    // This is the only header information I send back
```

Listing 9.6 **Continued**

```
// but in real life situations, you would be sending
// much more information in the header than I have here.

Write "HTTP/1.1 " + format( 200, "000" ) + " " + _
"OK" + chr(13) + chr(10) + chr(13) + chr(10)


// Test to see if the URL included a value for "dog"
// such as http://localhost:8080/form.html?dog="lucy".
// There is no practical reason for doing this, other
// than to show you how to access the parsed request.

If request.query.HasKey("dog") Then
    Write "<html><title>Query</title><body><h1>You dog's name is " +
➡request.query.Value("dog") + "</h1></body></html>"


// Test to see if the request has a field called "textfield"
// which indicates that it is getting its data from a form.

Elseif request.query.HasKey("textfield") Then
    Write "<html><title>Post</title><body><h1>Hello, " +
➡request.query.Value("textfield") + "</h1></body></html>"


// If none of the previous two tests are true, then
// just treat this as a normal request and write
// the file. You need to have the writing executed
// from within the DataAvailable event, or you
// might lose data. The reason for this is that the
// DataAvailable event is asynchronous. If you include
// this code in an external method, then it is possible
// that a new DataAvailable event may be called
// before you are finished writing the data from the
// previous event. By including this code within the
// DataAvailable event, you can make sure that the next
// DataAvailable event is not triggered until you have
// written all that you want to write.

Else
    // Open the file as a BinaryStream.

    Stream = f.openAsBinaryFile(False)

    // Write the file in 64k segments
```

Listing 9.6   **Continued**

```
        // This starts the process of writing
        // the file back to the client.
        // Look at the SendComplete event to
        // see what happens once the first 64k
        // segment has been sent.

        Write Stream.Read( &hFFFF )
    End If
End If
```

Listing 9.7   **Sub HTTPConnection.SendComplete(userAborted as Boolean) Handles Event**

```
If Stream <> nil And Not Stream.EOF Then

    // In the DataAvailable event, you start to write
    // the data back to the client, but you only
    // send it out in chunks. Once the first chunk is
    // completed being sent, then this event will be
    // triggered. At this point, you test to see
    // if there is more data to write, then write it
    Write stream.Read( &hFFFF )
Else

    // If there is no more data to write, then
    // disconnect the socket.

    Disconnect

    // Close the Stream
    If Not (Stream is Nil) Then
        Stream.Close
    End If
End if
```

Listing 9.8   **Sub HTTPConnection.parseHeader(data as String)**

```
Dim headers(-1) as String
Dim line as String
Dim x, count as Integer
Dim KeyVal(-1) as String
Dim Req(-1) as String
Dim ContentType as String
Dim SubTypes(-1) as String
```

Listing 9.8 **Continued**

```
headers = Split(data, EndOfLine.Windows)

count = Ubound(headers)
For x = 0 To count

    // The first line of a request is the
    // Request-Line, according to the HTTP
    // Specification and it contains three
    // elements, separated by a space.

    If x = 0 Then
        req = Split(headers(0), " ")
        request.type = Trim(req(0))
        request.path = Trim(req(1))
    Else
        KeyVal = Split(headers(x), ": ")
        If UBound(KeyVal) = 1 Then
            If request.HasKey(Trim(KeyVal(0))) Then
                // skip it
            Else
                request.Value(Trim(KeyVal(0))) = Trim(KeyVal(1))
            End If
        End If
    End If
Next


If request.type = "GET" Then

Elseif request.type = "POST" Then

    If request.HasKey("Content-Type") Then
        ContentType = request.Value("Content-Type")
            If ContentType = "application/x-www-form-urlencoded"  Then
                // It's a form
            Else
                SubTypes = Split(ContentType, ";")
                For Each line in SubTypes
                    Window1.AppendString(line)
                    If Left(Trim(line), 9) = "boundary=" Then
                        request.query.value("boundary") =
➥Trim(NthField(line, "=", 2))
                    End If
                Next
            End If
    End If
End If
```

Class HTTPRequest Inherits Dictionary

Listing 9.9   HTTPRequest Properties

```
Type As String
Query As Dictionary
Path As String
Response As FolderItem
Protected DocRoot As FolderItem
```

Listing 9.10   Sub HTTPRequest.Constructor(aDocRoot as FolderItem)

```
Query = New Dictionary
DocRoot = aDocRoot
```

URL encoded data can be passed either in the body of a POST request or in the URL of a GET request. Either way, the same encoding is used, and the following method parses it and assigns the key/value pairs to the **HTTPRequest** object.

Listing 9.11   Sub HTTPRequest.getQueryString(QueryString as String)

```
Dim field, aKey, aValue As String
Dim x As Integer

query = New Dictionary
If QueryString <> "" Then

    // Now run through the query string and parse the names and values
    // into a dictionary. This code is the same as that used in the
    // CGI example. A typical query string looks like this:
    // textfield=Mark&Submit=Submit
    // All "+" represent spaces, so they need to be replaced.

    For x = 1 to CountFields(QueryString, "&")
        field = NthField(QueryString, "&", x)
        aKey = NthField(field, "=", 1)
        aValue = NthField(field, "=", 2)
        aValue = ReplaceAll(aValue, "+", " ")

        // Some characters are encoded in their HEX values
        // preceded by "%", like %20 for a space,
        // when sent in a URL. The global DecodeURLComponent
        // method will convert them back into their
        // character representations.

        aValue = DecodeURLComponent(aValue)
        query.value(aKey) = aValue
    Next
End If
```

The path to the requested file is sent as part of the first line of the header. The following function calculated the total path relative to the DocRoot **FolderItem**. If the file requested is a directory, the code looks for a default filename, such as index.html, and returns a reference to that **FolderItem**.

Listing 9.12   **Function HTTPRequest.getResponseFileFromPath(aPath as String) as FolderItem**

```
Dim f as FolderItem
Dim url(-1) as String
Dim components(-1) as String
Dim component as String

f = DocRoot

// Split path at "?" - the data following the question mark
// is the query string

url = Split(DecodeURLComponent(path), "?")
If Ubound(url) = 1 Then
    getQueryString(url(1))
End If

If UBound(url) > -1 Then
    components = Split(url(0), "/")
    For Each component in components
        f = f.Child(component)
        If f = Nil or f.exists = False Then
            Return Nil
        End if
    Next
    If f.Directory Then
        If f.Child("index.html").Exists Then
            f = f.Child("index.html")
        ElseIf f.Child("rss.xml").Exists Then
            f = f.Child("rss.xml")
        ElseIf f.Child("atom.xml").Exists Then
            f = f.Child("atom.xml")
        End If
    End If
End If
response = f
Return response
```

SSLSocket

The Secure Sockets Layer (SSL) and Transport Layer Security (TLS) are protocols for transmitting encrypted data over the Internet. SSL versions range from 1.0 to 3.0, and TLS is considered the successor to SSL, and is currently at version 1.0 (version 1.1 may be out by the time you read this). The **SSLSocket** class is the secure version of the **TCPSocket** class and with a few exceptions, they both work the same way.

There is one important caveat: **SSLSocket** cannot be used to listen for requests securely; it can only make connections to other secure sockets (like that of a secure web server).

There are a few properties you need to set (or read) when working with **SSLSocket**. To specify what type of secure connection to use, use the following property:

```
SSLSocket.ConnectionType as Integer
```

0	SSL 2.0
1	SSL 3.0 if available, 2.0 otherwise (this is the default)
2	SSL 3.0
3	TSL 1.0

You also do not have to use the **SSLSocket** class exclusively for secure sockets. Set the following value to `True` if you want to establish a secure connection `lse` if you do not want to establish a secure connection:

```
SSLSocket.Secure as Boolean
```

The following read-only properties will tell you if you are currently connected to another socket, or if you are in the process of connecting, respectively.

```
SSLSocket.SSLConnected as Boolean(Read Only)
SSLSocket.SSLConnecting as Boolean (Read Only)
```

IPCSocket Class

IPCSocket Class

TCPSocket and **SSLSocket** are typically used for communication between applications that reside on different servers. There are some situations, however, where you may have two applications running on the same server that you would like to be able to send data to and from. Although it's possible to use **TCPSocket** for this, REALbasic provides a class that works like **TCPSocket**, but that is designed exclusively for communication between two applications running on the same machine.

The only real difference is that instead of setting a `Port` value, you set a value for the `Path` property:

```
ICPSocket.Path as String
```

This path should be the absolute path to the application you want to communicate with. After this value is set, call the `Listen` method to wait for communication, or use the `Write` method, as you would with a **TCPSocket**.

UDPSocket

User Datagram Protocol (UDP) networks work a little differently than TCP networks do. Whereas a TCP network guarantees that all the data you send to another computer will arrive there, a UDP network does not. For TCP to be so error proof, it takes up a lot of overhead and makes the overall process slower. Because you do not have the same guarantee with UDP, it is a much faster protocol. The caveat is that your application must be able to withstand the loss of data and still keep running. When you call the `LookupDNSaddress` method in the `System.Network` object, you are using UDP to make a call to a DNS server. Because the request is so simple, UDP is appropriate. If data is missing, you can send another request. Streaming video and audio servers also use UDP because performance is more important than rock-solid reliability for the transmission of each packet.

UDPSocket Class

Properties

```
UDPSocket.BroadcastAddress as String (Read Only)
UDPSocket.PacketsAvailable as Integer (Read Only)
UDPSocket.PacketsLeftToSend as Integer (Read Only)
UDPSocket.RouterHops as Integer
UDPSocket.SendToSelf as Boolean
```

Methods

```
UDPSocket.JoinMulticastGroup(Group as String) as Boolean
UDPSocket.LeaveMulticastGroup(Group as String)
UDPSocket.Read([Encoding as TextEncoding]) as Datagram
UDPSocket.Write(Data as Datagram)
UDPSocket.Write(Address as String, Data as String)
```

Datagram

The **Datagram** class is a simple class with three properties, and it represents the packet of data used by UDP networks. If you were to actually look at the data in a **Datagram**, you would see that it contains a source port, a destination port number, the length of the **Datagram**, a checksum for the data itself to ensure that it hasn't been corrupted, followed by the data. The class provided by REALbasic provides a simpler interface, and the available properties include the port, the data itself that is wrapped in the datagram, and the address (either a domain name or IP address). The property has a different meaning, depending on whether you are sending or receiving data. If you are sending data, it contains the number of the `Port` on the machine the data is being sent to. Otherwise, it contains the number of the `Port` it is listening to.

```
Datagram.Address as String
Datagram.Data as String
Datagram.Port as Integer
```

Conclusion

There are several networking classes in REALbasic—more than I can cover here—but now that you know how the **TCPSocket** class works, you are ready to tackle all the others. There are a few classes known as **EasyTCPSocket** and **EasyUDPSocket** that provide an even easier way to create sockets than how I've shown you here, but because **TCPSocket** is easy enough to use as it is, I don't think a lot would have been gained by reviewing them. They also use some proprietary methods of connecting two applications that require both applications to be written in REALbasic. I think a more common requirement is going to be to use the networking classes to access some other networked application not written in REALbasic—something like a web server or mail server, for example—so for that reason I haven't devoted any time to them.

In the next chapter, I'll look at a handful of advanced topics, which include scripting REALbasic and working with Microsoft Office products.

10

Graphics

REALBASIC HAS NUMEROUS CLASSES for handling images and graphics (both two dimensional and three dimensional). There are also a lot of other classes that have methods related to graphics; examples include the **Windows** class and the **FolderItem** class. There are a few global functions that provide some help along the way, too. One important graphics-related topic is printing. Space constraints do not allow me to cover all aspects of managing graphics in REALbasic, but I will cover the most commonly used tools that are provided.

Raster and Vector Graphics

Raster and vector graphics are two ways of representing an image of some sort using the native language of 1s and 0s employed by computers. A raster image is simpler to understand, but takes up much more memory to work with. A raster image is a rectangular grid of pixels, and a specific color is encoded for each pixel (it gets a little more complicated than this when considering compressed images, but the basic facts are the same).

On the other hand, a vector image is composed of geometric primitives such as circles, lines, rectangles, and so on that can be described using mathematical formulas. Whereas a line represented in a raster image would have to identify individual pixels that make up the line, a vector image would need to define only the starting point and the end point to define the same line.

There are some file formats that are designed to support the inclusion of both vector and raster graphics; these are collectively known as metafiles. Windows has two metafile formats called Windows Metafile (WMF) and Enhanced Metafile (EMF). WMF is a 16-bit format, whereas EMF is a new, 32-bit version. Traditionally, PICT was the native metafile format for Macintosh computers (OS X now uses PDF as the native metafile format). REALbasic does not provide any direct support for PDF at the moment, so it often relies on PICT images on the Macintosh platform.

There are several other common raster file formats that you will likely encounter. On Windows, many files (such as icons) are stored in BMP (for bitmapped) files. You will also see GIF, PNG, and JPG. Later on in the chapter you will see that REALbasic automates much of the handling of graphic file formats and will save them in the format appropriate for the platform on which the application is running.

At the center of REALbasic's graphics classes is the **Graphics** class. In addition, there is the **Picture** class, which is used to render raster graphics; the **Graphics2D** class, which is used to render vector graphics (it includes support for raster graphics as well); and the **Graphics3D** class, which is used for three-dimensional graphics of the sort often used in games. Because 2D graphics are most commonly used, that is where I will focus most of my energies in this chapter.

The Graphics Class

Many classes have reference to a **Graphics** object, including **Windows** and **ListBoxes**. This provides you with ample opportunity to customize the look and feel of some of REALbasic's existing controls as well.

REALbasic's graphics-related classes have evolved over time, and much like all evolutionary systems, there are some vestigial organs—class members of one sort or another that still exist but that are no longer really necessary. Much of what can be done in the **Graphics** class using members of the **Graphics** class can now be done with more control and flexibility with the **Object2D** class and subclasses. At the same time, there are some things you can do from within the **Graphics** class that you cannot do in the **Object2D** classes, despite the substantial overlap in functionality.

The **Graphics** class itself is used to output raster graphics to the screen as well as to the printer (it displays and prints text, too, which is technically a vector graphic). These two roles coexist in the **Graphics** class, but not every instance of the **Graphics** class is able to print. As such, I think it would have been clearer (and more object-oriented) if the **Graphics** class were two distinct classes, with a subclass of **Graphics** to be used for printing. But that's just wishful thinking on my part. Here's what you need to know:

- To print, you need to instantiate a **Graphics** object from the **StyledTextPrinter** class (an instance of which is a property of an **EditField**, which is how you use it).

- All other instances of **Graphics** objects can use all the properties and methods of the **Graphics** class, with the exception of the ones that are responsible for managing printing.

In the next section, I will review the properties associated with the **Graphics** class.

Properties

The following properties determine the height and width of the graphic itself. Because **Graphic** instances are often associated with particular controls, there are many times when these values will be the same as the height and width of the parent control.

```
Graphics.Height as Integer
Graphics.Width as Integer
```

The next group of properties handles text. You set these values prior to drawing strings using the `DrawString` method of a **Graphics** object, and they apply to any strings that are drawn after they are set. The `ForeColor` property applies both to the color of text, but also to the color of any other kind of drawing that is done with the **Graphics** object. You can set the value of a property, draw a string, and then change the value of the original property and draw another string. In each case, the value of the property applies only to the next string being drawn.

```
Graphics.ForeColor as Color
Graphics.Bold as Boolean
Graphics.Italic as Boolean
Graphics.Underline as Boolean
Graphics.TextAscent as Integer
Graphics.TextFont as String
Graphics.TextHeight as Integer
Graphics.TextSize as Integer
```

The Pen referred to in the following properties is known as the stroke in graphics applications:

```
Graphics.PenHeight as Integer
Graphics.PenWidth as Integer
```

For example, if you set the height and width at four and then draw a line, the line will be four pixels wide.

The following property allows you to set the color value of an individual pixel. If you are going to be manipulating a lot of pixels individually, it is best to use an **RGBSurface** object associated with a **Picture** object.

```
Graphics.Pixel(X as Integer, Y as Integer) as Color
```

Macintosh has two means of drawing and rendering graphics: The old way is called QuickDraw and the new way is called Quartz. Quartz looks much better, especially when rendering text, but it is also a little slower at times than QuickDraw. There are also some cases where applications are being developed to work with both "Classic" Macs and OS X Macs. If you want the performance of your graphics to improve, or if you want to ensure that the graphics created by your program look the same on either version of Macintosh, you can tell REALbasic to use the older QuickDraw renderer by setting the following property to `True`:

```
Graphics.UseOldrenderer as Boolean
```

The next three properties are applicable only when printing pages and will be discussed later on in the chapter.

```
Graphics.Copies as Integer
Graphics.FirstPage as Integer
Graphics.LastPage as Integer
```

Graphics Methods

REALbasic provides three methods that draw icons on the **Graphics** object. As with all of the following methods, the position is passed as two integers. X is the horizontal axis and Y is the vertical axis.

```
Graphics.DrawCautionIcon(X as Integer, Y as Integer)
Graphics.DrawNoteIcon(X as Integer, Y as Integer)
Graphics.DrawStopIcon(X as Integer, Y as Integer)
```

The next group of methods are used to draw shapes, such as lines, rectangles, round rectangles, ovals, and polygons. The first group draws only the outlines, using the current ForeColor value.

```
Graphics.DrawLine(X1 as Integer, Y1 as Integer, X2 as Integer, Y2 as Integer)
Graphics.DrawRect(X as Integer,Y as Integer, Width as Integer, Height as Integer)
Graphics.ClearRect(X as Integer, Y as Integer, Width as Integer,
➥Height as Integer)
Graphics.DrawRoundRect(x as Integer,y as Integer, width as Integer, height as
➥Integer, arcWidth as Integer, arcHeight as Integer)
Graphics.DrawOval(X as Integer, Y as Integer, Width as Integer, Height as Integer)
Graphics.DrawPolygon(Points() as Integer)
```

This group of methods draws shapes whose bodies are filled with the currently selected ForeGround color:

```
Graphics.FillRect(X as Integer, Y as Integer, Width as Integer, Height as Integer)
➥as Color
Graphics.FillRoundRect(X as Integer, Y as Integer, Width as Integer, Height as
➥Integer, arcWidth as Integer, arcHeight as Integer)
Graphics.FillOval(X as Integer, Y as Integer, Width as Integer, Height as Integer)
➥as Color
Graphics.FillPolygon(points()) as Color
```

```
Graphics.DrawString(X as Integer, Y as Integer, Width as Integer,
➥Condense as Boolean)
```

The **Graphics** class has two methods for handling strings that are very helpful and that are not replicated in the **StringShape** class (a subclass of **Object2D**). The following methods will tell you how wide a given **String** is, or how tall a block of text is, given a particular width. This information is essential when drawing text because you will need it to know how to position it in the image. Although there is a **StringShape** class that will print strings for you, it cannot tell you how wide or deep the text is, so you will need to use the following methods:

```
Graphics.StringWidth(Text as String) as Integer
Graphics.StringHeight(Text as String, WrapWidth as Integer) as Integer
```

The following method returns the height of the string that is passed to it, based on the current `TextFont` and `TextSize` properties:

```
Graphics.TextAscent(Text as String) as Integer
```

When you are creating an application that will be used with different languages, one thing you need to keep in mind is the direction in which the text will flow. Some languages, such as English, go from right to left, whereas others go from left to right. You use the following method to determine which direction the String should go:

```
Graphics.StringDirection(Text as String) as Integer
```

The previous method returns the following:

```
Const Graphics.TextRightToLeft as Integer = 0
Const Graphics.TextLeftToRight as Integer = 1
Const Graphics.TextDirectionUnknown as Integer = -1
```

The following two methods are the ones I will be using most in the examples I will share with you. Rather than using the drawing methods directly in the **Graphics** class itself, I will be drawing the image in a separate **Picture** object, or in an **Object2D** object, and then passing the object to either the `DrawPicture` or `DrawObject` method.

```
Graphics.DrawPicture(Image as Picture, X as Integer, Y as Integer, [ DestWidth as
➥Integer], [DestHeight as Integer, SourceX as Integer, SourceY as Integer,
➥SourceWidth as Integer, Source Height as Integer])
Graphics.DrawObject(Object as Object2D [x as integer, y as integer])
```

The following method is used when printing and will be explained more fully later in the chapter.

```
Graphics.NextPage
```

Picture Class

The **Picture** class is used for opening, creating, and saving images in various formats. There are two ways to access an image that's saved in a file. The first way to open a picture is to import it into your project by dragging it from the desktop onto the **Project Editor** in the IDE. If you double-click an image, the image editor will appear, which is not much of an editor, but it does give you a look at what the image is. If the image is selected, you can set a property that designates whether to treat the color white as transparent. You can refer to any **Picture** that has been imported into the project by its name; you do not have to instantiate it or do anything else.

FolderItems and Pictures

The second way to open an existing image file is to use the **FolderItem** class. The **FolderItem** class provides a few methods for handling **Picture** objects. The first is a general method used for opening files as **Picture** objects:

```
FolderItem.OpenAsPicture as Picture
```

On Windows, `OpenAsPicture` will open JPG, GIF, and BMP images by default, but if QuickTime has been installed, it can open all the formats that QuickTime can open. If for some reason you have a Macintosh that does not have QuickTime installed, it will open only PICT images. On Linux, `OpenAsPicture` will open BMP, GIF, TIFF, and XBM formats.

If you would like to open a vector image, you can use the following method:

```
FolderItem.OpenAsVectorPicture as Picture
```

Like `OpenAsPicture`, the `OpenAsVectorPicture` method returns a **Picture** object, but REALbasic will have tried to convert as much of the picture into **Object2D** objects as it can. These can be referenced by the **Objects** property of the **Picture** class, which is a **Group2D** instance.

When it comes time to save an image, you can choose to save it as a JPG using the following method:

```
FolderItem.SaveAsJPEG(Picture as Picture)
```

The following `SaveAsPicture` method provides a lot more functionality because you can decide which format to save it in, based on the platform the application is running:

```
FolderItem.SaveAsPicture(Picture as Picture, [Format as Integer])
```

REALbasic has set aside a range of values for different formats, not all of which have been designated yet. The following list shows the basic groupings:

0–99	Meta-formats
200–299	Macintosh only
300–399	Windows only

Within each range, the values of 0–49 represent vector images, and 50–99 represent raster images. There are class constants defined for the currently supported formats:

```
FolderItem.SaveAsMostCompatible = 0
FolderItem.SaveAsMostComplete = 1
FolderItem.SaveAsDefault = 2
FolderItem.SaveAsDefaultVector = 3
FolderItem.SaveAsDefaultRaster = 4
FolderItem.SaveAsMacintoshPICT = 100
FolderItem.SaveAsMacintoshRasterPICT = 250
FolderItem.SaveAsWindowsWMF = 300
FolderItem.SaveAsWindowsEMF = 301
FolderItem.SaveAsWindowsBMP= 350
```

Creating a Picture

In addition to opening images from files, you can also easily create new **Pictures** programmatically in REALbasic. There are two ways to do it. The first is the NewPicture function, which takes the following arguments and returns a **Picture** object:

```
REALbasic.NewPicture(Height as Integer, Width as Integer,
➥Depth as Integer) as Picture
```

The second is using the New operator and instantiating it like any other object:

```
Picture.Constructor(Height as Integer, Width as Integer, Depth as Integer)
```

The advantage of using the New operator is that if something is wrong with the **Picture**, an error will be thrown.

Handling Transparencies

Much like creating a **Picture**, there are two ways to make a part of a **Picture** transparent. Basically, there's the easy way and there's the hard way. The easy way is to designate anything that is the color white in a given picture as transparent, which you can do by setting the following property:

```
Picture.Transparent as Integer
```

Setting the property to 0 means that white is not transparent; setting it to 1 means that white is transparent. This is the same value that you can set in the IDE when you have imported a Picture into your project. Although that is certainly easy, there are times where that's not flexible enough, and in those situations, you can create a Mask for your picture that will determine which parts are transparent and which parts are not:

```
Picture.Mask as Picture
```

To refresh your memory on how Masks work, take a look at the section that covers creating icons.

Creating and Manipulating Pictures

Three objects that are properties of all **Picture** objects are very important; they provide the tools you need to generate pictures of your own. You've already seen the **Graphics** class. The other two will be covered separately later in the chapter.

```
Picture.Graphics as Graphics
Picture.Objects as Group2D
Picture.RBGSurface as RBGSurface
```

Note that the **RGBSurface** object is available only if the color depth is 16 or 32 bits.

More Picture Properties

The following property determines the color depth (in bits):

```
Picture.Depth as Integer
```

Legal values are 0,1,2,4,8,16, and 32. A value of 0 indicates that this **Picture** is a vector rather than a raster image.

As you might suspect, **Pictures** have heights and widths:

```
Picture.Height as Integer
Picture.Width as Integer
```

Likewise, they have resolutions (in dots per inch):

```
Picture.HorizontalResolution as Integer
Picture.VerticalResolution as Integer
```

Finally, some pictures are composed of multiple pictures. Animated GIFs are one example. The following properties give you access to the individual Pictures:

```
Picture.ImageCount as Integer
Picture.IndexedImage(index as Integer) as Picture
```

RGBSurface Class

Although the **Graphics** class also lets you manipulate individual pixels, the **RGBSurface** class is supposed to let you do so much more efficiently. It also provides methods for transforming a graphic all at once.

```
RGBSurface.FloodFill(x as Integer, y as Integer, FillColor as Color)
RGBSurface.Pixel(x as Integer, y as Integer)
RGBSurface.Transform(Map() as Integer)
RGBSurface.Transform(RedMap() as Integer, GreenMap()
➥as Integer, BlueMap as Integer)
```

Canvas Control

The examples in the rest of the chapter all rely on the **Canvas** control. This is something that can be thought of as a general purpose control, and it can be used to create a lot of custom controls, especially custom buttonlike controls. This will also provide a good introduction to the **Graphics** class and how you can use it.

Canvas Properties

The following **Canvas** properties should be familiar to you:

```
Canvas.AcceptFocus as Boolean
Canvas.AcceptTabs as Boolean
Canvas.UseFocusRing as Boolean
```

These properties are unique to a **Canvas** control and provide a means to associate a **Picture** object to serve as the backdrop for whatever else is taking place on the **Canvas**.

```
Canvas.Backdrop as Picture
```

One of the most important properties is the reference to the **Graphics** object, which is what you will use to draw onto the **Canvas**.

```
Canvas.Graphics as Graphics
```

The following is a Windows-only feature that gives you the option of erasing the background of the **Canvas** when it is resized. Only Windows erases the contents of the control.

```
Canvas.EraseBackground as Boolean
```

Canvas Events

By now, the events available in a **Canvas** control should be quite familiar to you. All of the following work the same as they do in the other REALbasic controls:

```
Canvas.EnableMenuItems
Canvas.KeyDown(Key as String)
Canvas.GotFocus
Canvas.LostFocus
Canvas.MouseDown(x as Integer, y as Integer) as Boolean
Canvas.MouseDrag(x as Integer, y as Integer)
Canvas.MouseUp(x as Integer, y as Integer)
Canvas.Paint(g as Graphics)
```

The **Canvas** control does not have an `Action` event like buttons do, but a button `Action` event is really a `MouseUp` event. Keeping that in mind, you can replicate an `Action` event with the `MouseUp` event, and that gives you the basic structure of a button. The other thing that buttons do, however, is provide visual feedback when your mouse clicks it and when it is released. Some buttons (not REALbasic buttons) have cool effects, such as not appearing to be raised unless the mouse is moved over them. (This effect is often used on Windows buttons.) All these features are easy to replicate using the **Canvas** control.

The first step is to create three properties whose type is **Picture**. You can call them `ButtonImage`, `MouseOverImage`, and `MouseDownImage`.

Then, in the `Open` event, do the following:

Me.Backdrop = ButtonImage

In the `MouseOver` event:

Me.Backdrop = MouseOverImage

In the `MouseDown` event:

Me.Backdrop = MouseDownImage

And in the `MouseUp` event:

Me.Backdrop = ButtonImage

The Canvas Control—Scrolling Text and Images

The next example is one whose only reason for being is to provide an example. The example will show you how to draw and position both text and images as well as how to scroll a **Canvas** control using a **Scrollbar** control. There is also a **Slider** control that serves two purposes, depending on whether a graphic or text is being displayed. If graphics are being displayed, the **Slider** control will scale the image size, making it larger or smaller. If text is being displayed, it adjusts the vertical position of the text. In a sense, this is like scrolling, except that the text being displayed is moving within the **Graphic** object, whereas when using the **ScrollBar**, the entire image contained by the **Graphic** object is moving up and down. If this is a little unclear, a look at the comments in the code will show you exactly what is happening.

There are two buttons on **Window1**. The first is labeled Draw Text, and it takes the text from the **EditField** to the right of it and draws the **String** in the **Canvas1** control. Below that button is an **EditField**, which is used to set the horizontal position of the text when it is drawn in **Canvas1**. Beneath the **EditField** is a **Slider** control called **ImageMover** that sets the vertical position of the text. Finally, the last **EditField** is used to set the width of the **String**. In other words, it determines when the text gets wrapped.

In Figure 10.1, the horizontal position of the text is 0, the vertical position is set to 10, and the width of the **String** is set to 100.

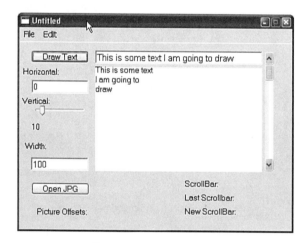

Figure 10.1 Drawing text.

The **Slider ImageMover** (labeled as Vertical in the Window) moves the text up or down within the **Canvas**.

In the Figure 10.2, the **ImageMover Slider** has been moved all the way to the right, meaning that the vertical position starts at 100. As a result, the text is drawn in the middle of the **Picture** instead of at the top of the **Picture** object.

The **Slider** control has the following properties that you access to find out the position of the slider:

```
Slider.Value as Integer
Slider.Minimum as Integer
Slider.Maximum as Integer
Slider.LineStep as Integer
Slider.PageStep as Integer
Slider.LiveScroll as Boolean
```

The `Value` property represents how far to the right (or down toward the bottom) the **Slider** has been moved. The direction is set by how you size the control. If it is wider than it is long, it moves along the horizontal axis; otherwise, it moves along the vertical axis. You can set the `Minimum` and `Maximum` values, which proscribes the available range of values for the **Slider** control. There are two ways to move the **Slider**: the first is to click and drag the **Slider,** and the second is to click a position in the **Control**. Dragging moves the value of Value up or down by increments set in the `LineStep` property. If you click a location in the **Slider**, the value of `Value` increments or decrements by the value set in `PageStep`. Normally, as you drag the **Slider** control one direction or another, nothing happens until you release it. However, if you have `LiveScroll` set to `True`, the **Value** property gets updated as you drag it.

In this example, the `Minimum` value is 0; the `Maximum` value is 100. The `LineStep` property equals 1, the `PageStep` property equals 20, and `LiveScroll` is set to `True`. One consequence of setting `LiveScroll` to `True` is that you will be able to see the text move up or down as you move the **Slider**. There is a trick to this, however, that will be explained shortly.

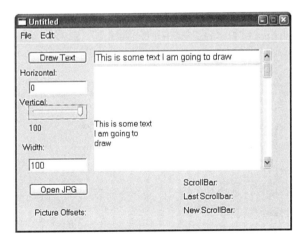

Figure 10.2   Drawing text offset vertically by 100 pixels.

Next, I'll show you what happens when the **Scrollbar** control to the right of **Canvas1** gets moved. The **Canvas** control has a method that handles scrolling the image that gets viewed in the control, but it does not work exactly like the **Scrollbar** control does, so there is some additional work to be done to get the scrolling to work properly.

The method used by the **Canvas** control follows:

```
Canvas.Scroll(DeltaX as Integer, DeltaY as Integer, [Left as Integer],
➥ [Top as Integer], [Width as Integer], [Height as Integer], [ScrollControls as
➥Boolean])
```

The **Scrollbar** control works in a similar way to a **Slider** control. When the Scrollbar.ValueChanged event gets triggered, no argument is passed to it. All that it does is signal that the **Scrollbar** has been moved. To find the current value, you need to check the value of Scrollbar.Value.

The Canvas.Scroll method expects values for DeltaX and DeltaY, both of which represent the rate of change, or how far one direction or another the **Canvas** has been scrolled in a horizontal or vertical direction. All you have with the **Scrollbar** is the current value. This means that you have to keep track of the previous **Scrollbar** position and compare it with the current **Scrollbar** position when the ValueChanged event gets triggered. This will tell you how much the **Scrollbar** has been scrolled, as well as the direction in which it was scrolled.

In this particular example for **Scrollbar**, the PageStep value has been set to 20 and the LineStep value has been set to 1. Like the **ImageMover Slider** control, the LiveScroll property is set to True.

Figure 10.3 shows what happens when **Scrollbar1** is scrolled down. Instead of just the text moving down, as happens when **ImageMover** is moved, the entire image moves up, and the only part that is displayed is that part that still resides within the frame of **Canvas1**.

You should also see that the current **Scrollbar** position is displayed in a **StaticText** field, along with the last **Scrollbar** position. The New Scrollbar Position **StaticText** field indicates the degree of change incurred between firing of the ValueChanged event. In this case the value is 1.

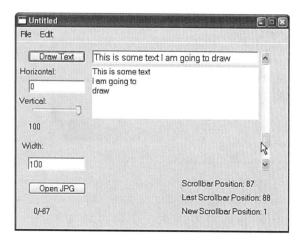

Figure 10.3   Text scrolled using Scrollbar.

In Figures 10.4, 10.5, and 10.6 you'll see the same thing, except that instead of drawing text into **Canvas1**, a JPEG image will be opened from the file system and then manipulated with the **ImageMover Slider** and **Scrollbar1**.

There is one notable difference, however, and that is that the **ImageMover Slider** does not redraw the image in another location. Instead, it changes the scale of the image, anywhere from 0% to 100%. Figure 10.4 shows the image scaled to 23% of the original size.

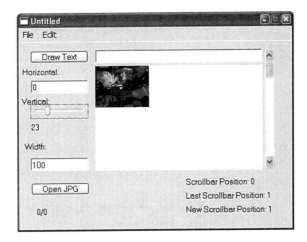

Figure 10.4   Image scaled to 23%.

In Figure 10.5, the **ImageMover** handle is slid all the way to the right, and the image is redrawn at 100% scale.

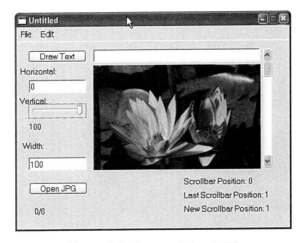

Figure 10.5   Image scaled to 100%.

Finally, when **Scrollbar1** is used, the image gets scrolled just like the text does, which can be seen in Figure 10.6.

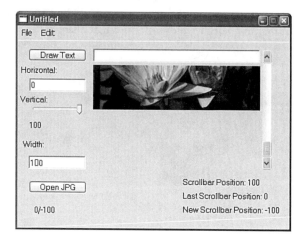

Figure 10.6   Image scrolled using the Scrollbar.

Now that you've seen the output of the sample application, it's time to review the code in more detail. There are a lot of things going on, especially with the **ImageMover Slider** control and **Scrollbar1**.

Before I cover those, I want to show **Window1**'s properties, followed by the `DrawTextPushbutton` and `OpenJPGPushButton`.

Listing 10.1   **Window1 Properties**

```
// The fontsize used to display the text.

Window1.fsize as Integer = 12

// The previous value for Scrollbar1.Value.
// This is used to calculate how much the
// Scrollbar has changed in value since the
// most revent ValueChanged event.

Window1.LastScroll as Integer

// A reference to the Picture that is
// being draw offscreen

Window1.p as Picture

// A reference to the PixmapShape object
// that will display the Picture loaded from
// the file system. I could have simply used
// a Picture object, but I chose a PixmapShape
```

Listing 10.1   **Continued**

```
// object because it allows you to scale the image.

Window1.px as PixmapShape

// When using Scrollbar1 to scroll the Canvas,
// I need to keep track of the current
// horizontal and vertical offset position
// of Window1.px. The reason for this is that
// the image will need to get redrawn as the
// Canvas is scrolled and I need to redraw it
// in the right place. See the Scrollbar1.ValueChanged
// event for details on how these values are used.

Window1.PicHorizon as Integer = 0
Window1.PicVertical as Integer = 0
```

Listing 10.2   **Window1.DrawTextPushButton.Action Handles Event**

```
// Displays the text in TextField in Canvas1

DrawPicture(DrawString(TextField.Text), 0,0)
```

Listing 10.3   **Window1.DrawString(s as String) as Picture**

```
// Renders the s String as a Picture object and
// returns it.
//
// The picture should be the same height and width
// as the Canvas in which it is displayed.
// The color depth is 32 bits.

p = NewPicture(Canvas1.Width, Canvas1.Height, 32)

// The String is drawn in the positions displayed
// in the HorizontalField EditField and the
// position of the ImageMover Slider control.
// The width of the String determines where the
// text will wrap. The WidthField EditField holds
// this value.

p.Graphics.DrawString(s, Val(HorizontalField.Text), ImageMover.Value,
➥Val(WidthField.Text))

// Return the p Picture object.

Return p
```

Listing 10.4   **Window1.DrawPicture(p as Picture, Width as Integer, Height as Integer)**

```
// Draws the buffered picture

Canvas1.Graphics.DrawPicture(p, PicHorizon, PicVertical)
```

Listing 10.5   **Window1.OpenJPGPushButton.Action Handles Event**

```
Dim f as FolderItem

f = GetOpenFolderItem("image/jpg")
If f <> Nil Then
p = f.OpenAsPicture

// Instantiate a PixmapShape for
// the image.

px = new PixmapShape(p)

// Next, use the PixmapShape.Scale
// method to scale the image according to the
// value in the ImageMover Slider control.
// The range of values for ImageMover.Value
// is zero to 100. Divide that value by 100
// to get the value as a percent. In other words,
// if the value is 99, then 99/100 equals .99,
// which is equal to 99%

px.Scale= ImageMover.Value / 100

// Draw the PixmapShape in Canvas1

Canvas1.Graphics.DrawObject(px)

// Display the current position where the image
// is being drawn.


PicPos.Text = Str(PicHorizon) + "/" + Str(PicVertical)

End If
```

The next event is the ImageMover.ValueChanged event, and this requires a little more explanation. First, here's the code that is executed when the event is triggered:

Listing 10.6   **Sub ImageMover.ValueChanged() Handles Event**

```
Dim aPic as Picture
Dim s as StringShape

// Display the current value for the Slider

SliderPos.Text = Str(Me.Value)

// If displaying a Picture

If px <> Nil Then

aPic = NewPicture(Canvas1.Width, Canvas1.Height, 32)

        Self.px.Scale = Me.value / 100
        aPic.Graphics.DrawObject(px)

        Canvas1.Graphics.DrawPicture(apic, PicHorizon, PicVertical)

Else

// Display the text from TextField

        DrawPicture(DrawString(TextField.Text), 0, Me.Value)

End If
```

As you can see in the code, the **ImageMover** slider tests to see if the Px property is not Nil. The Px property is set when an image has been opened up, so that means that when it is Nil, it will display the Text in the **TextField EditField**. At this point, the concern is displaying text. As you can see in the code, the DrawString method is called to generate a **Picture** object of the **String,** and that **Picture** object is passed to the **DrawPicture** method, where it is displayed in **Canvas1.** You may have wondered why I used two steps to display the text. I could have just as easily done all the drawing of the text directly in the **Graphics** object of **Canvas1,** but if I had, the text would flicker when it got redrawn as I dragged the **Slider** handle. To keep that from happening, I draw the **Picture** offscreen and then, after the image is rendered, I display the image in **Canvas1.**

This is a technique sometimes called double buffering. Basically, all that I am doing is this: It takes a certain amount of time to render the **String** as an Image. When I am dragging the **Slider** handler, the **String** has to be rerendered with each increment of the drag, and the delay in time results in the flicker you see on the screen. If instead of rendering the text directly in **Canvas1**'s **Graphic** object, I render it in a separate **Picture** object and then draw that **Picture** in the **Canvas1 Graphics** object, the time spent rendering the new text takes place offscreen and only after it is done does the old image get swapped out for the old. Displaying a new graphic that has already been rendered can be done a lot faster, so the flicker disappears.

Next is the `Scrollbar1.ValueChanged` event and it, like the previous event, is worthy of some extended discussion.

Listing 10.7   Window1.Scrollbar1.ValueChanged Handles Event

```
Dim NewScroll as Integer
Dim aPic as Picture


ScrollBarPos.Text = "Scrollbar Position: " + Str(Me.Value)
LastScrollBarPos.Text ="Last Scrollbar Position: " + Str(LastScroll)

// Subtract the current value of Scrollbar.Value from
// the value of LastScroll in order to get the rate and
// direction of change (a negative number means it's
// scrolling up, a positive number means it's scrolling
// down

NewScroll = LastScroll - Me.Value

// Display the position
NewScrollBarPos.Text = "New Scrollbar Position: " + Str(newScroll)

// Scroll the Canvas by passing NewScroll as the
// value for DeltaY. Since there is only a
// vertical Scrollbar, DeltaX is zero.
Canvas1.Scroll(0, NewScroll)

// Calculate the new vertical position of the picture
// so that it will be redrawn in the correct place.

PicVertical = PicVertical + newScroll
PicPos.Text = Str(PicHorizon) + "/" + Str(PicVertical)

// Set LastScroll equal to the current position of the
// Scrollbar.

LastScroll = Me.Value

If px <> Nil Then

    // If px is not Nil, then an image is being viewed.
    // The first step is to create a new Picture object
    // that will serve as the buffer.
```

Listing 10.7   **Continued**

```
    aPic = NewPicture(Canvas1.Width, Canvas1.Height, 32)
        self.px.Scale = ImageMover.value / 100

    // Draw the px object into aPic

    aPic.Graphics.DrawObject(px)

    // Next, draw the buffered Picture object aPic
    // in Canvas1, using the values from PicHorizon
    // and PicVertical.

        Canvas1.Graphics.DrawPicture(aPic, PicHorizon, PicVertical)
Else

    // Create a buffer for displaying the text

        aPic = NewPicture(Canvas1.Width, Canvas1.Height, 32)

    // Draw the text
        DrawPicture(DrawString(TextField.Text), 0, ImageMover.Value)
End If
```

Using the **ScrollBar** and the **Canvas** scrolling methods is a little more challenging than simply resizing images or repositioning text within a **Picture** object, like I did with the **ImageMover** slider control. The reason is that as you scroll, not all of the **Picture** will be drawn on the screen. If you scroll down, the **Canvas** will handle drawing only the part of the **Picture** that should be drawn. However, if you then scroll back up, you will find that the top half of the picture is gone. To do this, you need to resort to more double-buffering, only this time you also have to keep track of the current position of the **Picture** so that you can redraw it in the right place. To do so, I use the `PicHorizon` and the `PicVertical` properties, both of which start off set to 0 because when the picture is first drawn, the **Scrollbar** has not been scrolled down at all. As the `Scrollbar.Value` value changes, the value for `PicVertical` needs to change as well. With each `ValueChanged` event, the picture needs to be redrawn in the new position.

To keep track of the position, you need to be able to know how far the **Scrollbar** has been scrolled. The `Scrollbar.Value` property only tells you the current value—it doesn't tell you how much the value has changed or in which direction it has changed. To do that, I use the `LastScroll` property to store the previous position and then use it to calculate which direction and by how much the **Scrollbar** has been changed. After I have this value, I can then call the `Canvas.Scroll` method, which expects a value that represents how much has been scrolled, rather than an absolute scroll position like that available in the `Scrollbar.Value` property.

Object2D Class

In the previous example, I introduced a subclass of **Object2D**—the **PixmapShape** class. Although that class was used to display a raster graphic, the primary function provided by the **Object2D** classes is for manipulating vector images. The **PixmapShape** class allows you to create more complex images that include both raster and vector images, something that is not uncommon at all.

The **Object2D** subclasses are really the best way to handle any kind of complex drawing, regardless of where it will be displayed. The parent class provides methods for scaling and rotating the image, as well as whether to place a border around it and what the fill color should be.

```
Object2D.Border as Double
Object2D.BorderColor as Color
Object2D.BorderWidth as Double
Object2D.Fill as Double
Object2D.FillColor as Color
```

All objects can be rotated by setting the following property:

```
Object2D.Rotation as Double
```

The rotation is measured in radians, not in degrees, which is what you might have expected. A radian is an arc whose length is equal to its radius and there are exactly 2π radians in a circle. Figure 10.7 illustrates how far a one radian is:

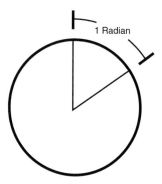

Figure 10.7   A radian is an arc whose length is equal to its radius.

To see a more detailed explanation of how to use radians, review the example in the **ArcShape** section.

In addition to rotating shapes, you can also resize them using the following:

```
Object2D.Scale as Double
```

`Scale` takes a `Double` value, which it interprets as a percentage. Therefore, .5 is the equivalent to scaling the image to 50% of the original size. Scaling the image to a value of 50 means 500% the original size.

All **Object2D** instances have an `X` and a `Y` property, indicating the position where the **Object2D** instance will be drawn, relative to the center of the object.

```
Object2D.X as Double
Object2D.Y as Double
```

PixmapShape

In addition to the properties and methods of the parent **Object2D** class, the **PixmapShape** implements the following. First, the property that contains a reference to the **Picture** object associated with the **PixmapShape** instance:

```
PixmapShape.Image as Picture
```

The following properties allow you to define a subregion of the original picture. The first two are a measure of how many pixels away from the left and top edges of the original image the subimage is:

```
PixmapShape.SourceLeft as Integer
PixmapShape.SourceTop as Integer
```

This is followed by two properties that define the overall height and width of the subimage:

```
PixmapShape.SourceHeight as Integer
PixmapShape.SourceWidth as Integer
```

When instantiating a **PixmapShape**, pass the **Picture** in the `Constructor`:

```
PixmapShape.Constructor(Image as Picture)
```

RectShape

The **RectShape** is one of the easiest shapes to handle. The **Object2D** properties `X` and `Y` define the center point of the rectangle, and the following properties determine how tall and wide it is:

```
RectShape.Height as Double
RectShape.Width as Double
```

One interesting feature in addition is the `Contains` method, which allows you to test a point to see if it is within a particular **RectShape**:

```
RectShape.Contains(X as Double, Y as Double) as Boolean
```

One way that you might use this would be to test to see whether the mouse position is over a particular **RectShape** and then respond when it is moved over the **RectShape**, or if the **RectShape** is clicked.

554 Chapter 10 Graphics

RoundRectShape Inherits RectShape

A **RoundRectShape** is just like a **RectShape**, except that the corners are rounded. You adjust the point where the curve starts on each corner with the following properties:

```
RoundRectShape.Cornerheight as Double
RoundRectShape.Cornerwidth as Double
```

The following determines how smooth the curves are (see the **OvalShape** explanation):

```
RoundRectShape.Segments as Integer
```

OvalShape Inherits RectShape

The **OvalShape** is a subclass of **RectShape** and behaves just like a **RectShape** in all ways. The only addition is the following property:

```
OvalShape.Segments as Integer
```

Even though you see a circular shape when you look at an **OvalShape** on your computer screen, the underlying rendering engine is actually drawing a polygon and not a circle. When you set the value of **Segments**, you are telling REALbasic how many sides the polygon should have. The more sides it has, the smoother the curve appears on the screen.

ArcShape Inherits OvalShape

Drawing an **ArcShape** requires the use of two different angles, measured in radians:

```
ArcShape.ArcAngle as Double
ArcShape.StartAngle as Double
```

The start angle is the location on the circle where the arc begins, and the arc angle is the size of the arc. Figure 10.8 shows an arc whose `StartAngle` is 0, and whose `ArcAngle` is 1:

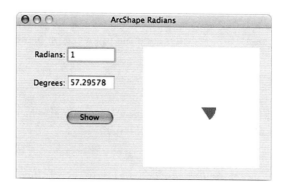

Figure 10.8 An ArcShape of one radian.

In a moment I'll share the code that generated this screenshot, but there are a few pieces of information that will help you make sense of it. As I said earlier, there are 2π radians in one circle. The value of π is

```
3.1415926535897932384626433832795O
```

Keeping this in mind, that means there are 6.28318530718 radians in one circle. If you want to convert from radians to degrees, you can use the following formula:

```
degrees = radians*(180/π)
```

Likewise, if you want to convert degrees to radians, you can use this formula:

```
radians = degrees/(180/π)
```

This means that 1 degree is approximately equivalent to 0.0174533 radians, and 1 radian is approximately 57.29578 degrees. Now you can turn to the sample code and follow along.

Listing 10.8   **PushButton1.Action Handles Event**

```
Dim rad as Double
Dim arc as ArcShape
Dim p as Picture

Const pi  = 3.1415926535897932384626433832795O
// Get the number of radians from EditField1

rad = Val(EditField1.Text)

// Convert Radians to Degrees and display it
// in EditField2

EditField2.Text = Str(rad*(180/pi))

p = NewPicture(Window1.Canvas1.Height, Window1.Canvas1.Width, 24)

arc = New ArcShape
arc.Width = 100
arc.Height = 100

// A StartAngle of 0 starts the arc at 45 degrees

arc.StartAngle = 0

// This arc will be one radian

arc.ArcAngle = rad
```

Listing 10.8 **Continued**

```
// Setting the Segments property makes the curve
// be drawn more smoothly on the screen. I have
// this set to a relatively high value.

arc.Segments = 360

// Set the color to red.

arc.FillColor = RGB(255, 5, 5)

// Create the Picture object

p.Graphics.DrawObject arc, Canvas1.Height/2, Canvas1.Width/2

// Display the Picture object in the Canvas1 control

Window1.Canvas1.Graphics.DrawPicture p, 0, 0
```

In this code, I am displaying an **ArcShape** of only one radian. You may be wondering how to display an **ArcShape** of 360 degrees, given the fact that there are 6.282185 radians in a circle. If you take this code and plug in 6.282175 into **EditField1** and click the Show button, you will see that nothing gets drawn. If you increase the value to 6.5, you will see a little sliver of an **ArcShape**—with a measure of about 0.2168 radians, which is the value of 6.5 minus 6.282175. To draw a complete circle, you should plug in the value 6.283184.

StringShape

The **StringShape** class draws text, but in a fairly limited way. It does not support text with line breaks in it, and you can't do things such as measure the width of the text or automatically wrap it like you can when using a **Graphics** object. The intended use for the class is to display text inside a vector image. It is not intended as a general-purpose text-rendering class or anything like that.

You can set the following properties:

```
StringShape.Text as String
StringShape.TextFont as String
StringShape.TextSize as Double
StringShape.Underline as Boolean
StringShape.Bold as Boolean
StringShape.Italic as Boolean
```

CurveShape

The **CurveShape** is a class for drawing Bezier curves. The basic information you need to know about Bezier curves are that there are three types: Linear, Quadratic, and Cubic.

A Linear Bezier curve can be defined by two points and is a straight line. A Quadratic Bezier curve requires three points and represents a curve drawn through all three points. A Cubic Bezier curve requires four points to draw, and an example is given later in this chapter.

You set the type of Bezier curve to draw using the following property:

```
CurveShape.Order as Integer
```

The values are as follows:

```
Linear Bezier Curve: 0
Quadratic Bezier Curve: 1
Cubic Bezier Curve: 2
```

Like all **Object2D** subclasses, a **CurveShape** has values for X and Y and adds to that values for X2 and Y2:

```
CurveShape.X as Double
CurveShape.Y as Double
CurveShape.X2 as Double
CurveShape.Y2 as Double
```

These properties are sufficient to draw a Linear Bezier curve, but you will need some additional points if you are drawing a Cubic or Quadratic Bezier curve:

```
CurveShape.ControlX(Index as Integer) as Double
CurveShape.ControlY(Index as Integer) as Double
```

Both properties are indexed, and the value for the index can be either 0 or 1. If you are drawing a Quadratic Bezier curve, you need only one more set of control points, and you can refer to them like this:

```
CurveShape1.ControlX(0) = 10
CurveShape1.ControlY(0) = 25
```

If you are drawing a Cubic Bezier curve you need one more additional point, which can be referenced in this manner:

```
CurveShape1.ControlX(1) = 10
CurveShape1.ControlY(1) = 25
```

Finally, just like the **OvalShape**, you can set the value of following to make the curve get drawn more smoothly (the higher the value, the smoother the curve):

```
CurveShape.Segments as Integer
```

FigureShape

A **FigureShape** is a collection of **CurveShapes**. As such, it provides methods for adding curves and removing and referencing them by index. These work just like the array functions.

```
FigureShape.Count as Integer
FigureShape.Item(Index as Integer) as CurveShape
```

```
FigureShape.Append(Curve as CurveShape)
FigureShape.Insert(Index as Integer, Curve as CurveShape)
FigureShape.Remove(Index as Integer)
FigureShape.Remove(Curve as CurveShape)
```

It also provides methods for drawing Linear, Quadratic, and Bezier curves that are a little simpler to use than those required in the **CurveShape** class.

```
FigureShape.AddLine(X as Integer, Y as Integer, X2 as Integer, Y2 as Integer)
FigureShape.AddQuad(X as Integer, Y as Integer, X2 as Integer, Y2 as Integer, CX
➥as Integer, CY as Integer)
FigureShape.AddCubic(X as Integer, Y as Integer, X2 as Integer, Y2 as Integer, CX
➥as Integer, CY as Integer, CX2 as Integer, CY2 as Integer)
```

Group2D

Whereas a **FigureShape** is a collection of **CurveShapes**, a **Group2D** is a collection of any kind of **Object2D** subclass.

```
Group2D.Count as Integer
Group2D.Item(Index as Integer) as Object2D

Group2D.Append(Object as Object2D)
Group2D.Insert(Index as Integer, Object as Object2D)
Group2D.Remove(Index as Integer)
Group2D.Remove(Object as Object2D)
```

A FigureShape Example

The following example illustrates how to use several of the **Object2D** subclasses. Most importantly, it illustrates one of the methods of the **FigureShape** class that can be difficult to understand how to use unless you actually see it at work. The **FigureShape** class is used to draw collections of curves, and it contains a few methods for displaying Bezier curves. This example illustrates a Cubic Bezier curve.

You need to set four different points to describe a cubic curve, and this means passing eight values to the AddCubic method. The first group sets the starting point of the curve, and the second two set the end point of the curve. At this point, if the rest of the values are set to zero, you have a line. The final four arguments set two additional points, which makes the line curve. Altogether there are four points set that form a quadrilateral, and the curve is constrained to stay within the space defined by the quadrilateral. The only way to really understand how the final two points that get set impact the shape of the curve is to see what happens as you adjust them, and that is what this project does.

There are eight **Sliders**, one for each of the arguments. When the application starts, you can move the **Sliders** back and forth and see how the curve changes as the values change. Each point is illustrated with a dot, plus text that identifies what the actual values are. The curve adjusts in real-time as the **Sliders** are drawn, so double buffering is a requirement to minimize or eliminate any screen flicker, but it also serves a more mundane purpose. If I do not create a new **Picture** object for each new state, the next curve just gets redrawn on top of the previous curve—the old curve is not deleted. By using double buffering, the previous line is not preserved and you get a more seamless visual representation.

The actual application is quite simple. There's one method associated with **Window1** that gets called by each **Slider** control whenever the ValueChanged event is triggered. The method is called DrawPict, and it looks like this:

Listing 10.9   **DrawPict MethodDim p as Picture**

```
Dim aGroup as Group2D
Dim aString as StringShape
Dim aFigure as FigureShape
Dim aRect as RectShape

aGroup = New Group2D

aFigure = New FigureShape

aFigure.FillColor = RGB(100,100,100)
aFigure.BorderColor = RGB(80,80,80)
aFigure.AddCubic(Slider1.Value, Slider2.Value, Slider3.Value, Slider4.Value,
➥Slider5.Value, Slider6.Value, Slider7.Value, Slider8.Value)


// The points are identified by drawing a small
// rectangle using different colors. The first
// point is the starting point of the curve and
// the color is set to be red and the actual
// position is set by the values in Slider1 and Slider2

aRect = new RectShape
aRect.FillColor = RGB(255,0,0)
aRect.Height = 4
aRect.Width = 4
aRect.X = Slider1.Value
aRect.Y = Slider2.Value


// Each point is labeled and the text is drawn
// using the StringShape class.

aString = new StringShape
aString.Text = "(X: " + Str(aRect.X) + ", Y:" + Str(aRect.Y) + ")"
aString.X = aRect.X
```

Listing 10.9   **Continued**

```
// The String is positioned below the rectangle so that
// the rectangle is clearly visible.

aString.Y = aRect.Y+12


// Next, the FigureShape,RectShape and StringShape objects
// are added to a Group2D object.

aGroup.Append(aFigure)
aGroup.Append(aRect)
aGroup.Append(aString)


// Now, the process repeats itself with the
// next set of points that indicate where the
// line starts.

aRect = New RectShape
aRect.FillColor = RGB(125, 0, 0)
aRect.Height = 4
aRect.Width = 4
aRect.X = Slider3.Value
aRect.Y = Slider4.Value

aString = new StringShape
aString.Text = "(X1: " + Str(aRect.X) + ", Y1:" + Str(aRect.Y) + ")"
aString.X = aRect.X
aString.Y = aRect.Y+12


aGroup.Append(aRect)
aGroup.Append(aString)


// The next point get set.
// This is the equivalent of
// ControlX(0) and ControlY(0)
// in the CurveShape class.

aRect = New RectShape
aRect.FillColor = RGB(0, 255, 0)
aRect.Height = 4
aRect.Width = 4
aRect.X = Slider5.Value
aRect.Y = Slider6.Value

aString = new StringShape
```

Listing 10.9 **Continued**

```
aString.Text = "(CX: " + Str(aRect.X) + ", CY:" + Str(aRect.Y) + ")"
aString.X = aRect.X
aString.Y = aRect.Y+12

aGroup.Append(aRect)
aGroup.Append(aString)


// The final point gets set
// This is the equivalent of
// ControlX(1) and ControlY(1)
// in the CurveShape class.

aRect = New RectShape
aRect.FillColor = RGB(0, 0, 255)
aRect.Height = 4
aRect.Width = 4
aRect.X = Slider7.Value
aRect.Y = Slider8.Value

aString = new StringShape
aString.Text = "(CX2: " + Str(aRect.X) + ", CY2:" + Str(aRect.Y) + ")"
aString.X = aRect.X
aString.Y = aRect.Y +12

aGroup.Append(aRect)
aGroup.Append(aString)

// Instantiate a Picture object that is the same
// size as the Canvas object, with a color depth of
// 32 bits.

p = NewPicture(canvas1.width,canvas1.height, 32)

// Draw the Group2D object into the Picture using
// the Graphics object's DrawObject method

p.Graphics.DrawObject(aGroup, 0,0)

// Next, draw the buffered picture into
// Canvas1's Graphics object.

Canvas1.Graphics.DrawPicture(p,0,0)
```

In Figure 10.9, you can see an example of a Cubic Bezier curve as rendered by the previous code. Because the rendering is buffered, you can move each slider to the left and see the Cubic Bezier curve to the right get updated immediately.

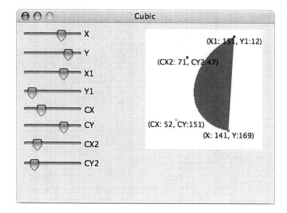

Figure 10.9   FigureShape example.

Printing with REALbasic

In REALbasic, printing is managed using a **Graphics** object, but it has to be a Graphics object instantiated by a **StyledTextPrinter**, and the **StyledTextPrinter** object must be instantiated by calling the `EditField.StyledTextPrinter` method.

The example was derived from the sample given in the LanguageReference illustrating how to print a page with two columns. I've added a few features to make it more interesting—namely, I've created it so that a header is created on each page that designates the page number.

There are a few different considerations when printing. The simplest way to get started is with the `OpenPrinterDialog` function, which looks like this:

```
REALbasic.OpenPrinterDialog([PageSetup as Printer Setup], [window as Window])
↳as Graphics
```

When you call this function, a standard print dialog box is shown to the user. An example of how it looks on a Macintosh is shown in Figure 10.10:

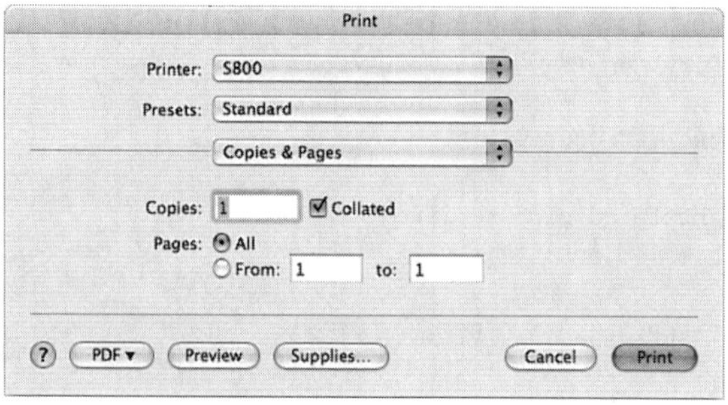

Figure 10.10   Print dialog box.

If the user clicked the Print button, a **Graphics** object is returned, which is the object you will print to.

Prior to calling the OpenPrinterDialog function, you may also want to give your users an opportunity to set up the printer according to their needs. To do this, you need to instantiate a **PrinterSetup** object and call the following method:

```
PrinterSetup.PageSetupDialog([window as Window])
```

In practice, you use the **PrinterSetup** object like this:

```
Dim ps as PrinterSetup
ps = New PrinterSetup
If ps.PageSetupDialog Then
    g = OpenPrinterDialog(ps)
    // do some printing
Else
    // user pressed cancel
End If
```

The **PrinterSetup** dialog box is shown in Figure 10.11:

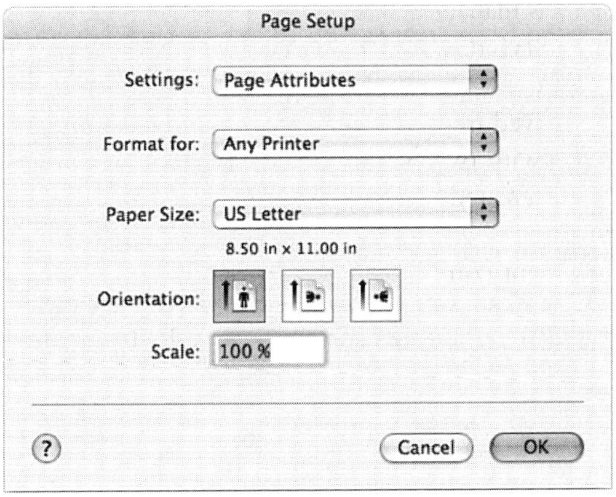

Figure 10.11   Printer setup dialog box.

The following properties specify the page height and width in pixels:

```
PrinterSetup.PageHeight as Integer
PrinterSetup.PageWidth as Integer
```

If you are printing to a standard 8.5 inch by 11 inch page, the value for PageWidth would be 612 (8.5*72), and the value for PageHeight would be 792 (792*72).

Next, the following two properties measure the difference between the margin and the edge of the physical page—not that these values are read-only:

```
PrinterSetup.PageLeft as Integer
PrinterSetup.PageTop as Integer
```

The following measures the height and width of the printable area on the page (basically, the total page height minus the margin, or the total page width minus the margin):

```
PrinterSetup.Height as Integer
PrinterSetup.Width as Integer
```

These values are always supposed be zero, and represent the `Left` and `Top` origin of the printable area.

```
PrinterSetup.Left as Integer
PrinterSetup.Top as Integer (must be 0)
```

The following two read-only methods let you know what the current resolution is for the printer:

```
PrinterSetup.HorizontalResolution as Integer
PrinterSetup.VerticalResolution as Integer
```

These two allow you to set the resolution to the highest value.

```
PrinterSetup.MaxHorizontalResolution as Integer
PrinterSetup.MaxVerticalResolution as Integer
```

Finally, the following property serves as a way to store settings from previous sessions. After the printer setup has been created, you can get access to a String that specifies what was chosen. You can save this value, and then use it the next time you print so that the users' settings will be saved.

```
PrinterSetup.SetupString as String
```

StyledTextPrinter

So far, so good, but there is still one more class you need to be aware of before I turn to the example. The **StyledTextPrinter** class is very simple. There are two properties:

```
StyledTextPrinter.EOF as Boolean
StyledTextPrinter.Width as Integer
```

There is only one method:

```
StyledTextPrinter.DrawBlock(X as Integer, Y as Integer, Height as Integer)
```

The purpose of **StyledTextPrinter** is to help you print large blocks of text. For example, this chapter I am writing is larger than one page, so if I want to print it out I need to know how much text should fit on each page; after I print the page, I need to know where I should start printing for the next page. The `DrawBlock` method does this. It prints all the text that can fit in the space provided (as determined by the `Width` property and `Height` argument). If you have not reached the end of the text you are printing (which you find out by checking the `EOF` property), the next time you call this method, it will start printing where it left off the previous time.

All this has been illustrated in an application example. It consists of an **EditField**, a **RadioButton** labeled 2 Columns, and a **PushButton** labeled Print. The application will print the contents of the **EditField** when you push the Print button. If you have the **RadioButton** selected, it will print the text in two columns; otherwise, it will print only one column.

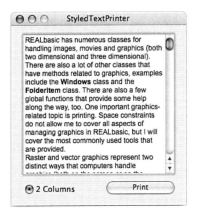

Figure 10.12   Print sample window.

I created a custom class called **StyledPrinter** to encompass the functionality I need to print the `EditField` the way that I want to. It has a `Constructor`, a few properties that can be set, and one `Print` method.

Listing 10.10   **Class StyledPrinter**

```
StyledPrinter.HeaderTitle As String = "REALbasic Printing Test"
StyledPrinter.IncludeHeader As Boolean - True
StyledPrinter.IncludePageNum As Boolean = True
StyledPrinter.Font As String = "Arial"
StyledPrinter.FontSize As Integer = 12
StyledPrinter.ColumnWidth As Integer = 261
StyledPrinter.Gutter As Integer = 18
StyledPrinter.PageHeight As Integer = 720
StyledPrinter.Field As EditField
StyledPrinter.IncludeSecondCol As Boolean = False
```

Listing 10.11   **Sub Constructor(TextField as EditField)**

```
Field = TextField
```

Listing 10.12   **Sub Print()**

```
Dim g as Graphics
Dim stp as StyledTextPrinter
Dim ColumnToPrint as Integer
Dim TotalWidth as Integer
Dim pageCount as Integer = 1
Dim HeaderOffset as Integer

// The gutter is the space between two columns.
// This calculation assumes two columns, plus a
// gutter.

TotalWidth = ColumnWidth * 2 + Gutter

// Get a reference to a Graphics object
// by displaying the Print dialog

g=OpenPrinterDialog()

// If the user cancels, g will be Nil.
// If the user has not canceled, then
// proceed with printing.

If g <> Nil Then

// Since the contents of an EditField
// is what is being printed, get a
// reference to the StyledTextPrinter
// associated with the EditField in question.

    stp=Field.StyledTextPrinter(g,TotalWidth)

    // The StyledTextPrinter.DrawBlock
    // method will be used to draw the
    // text. You need to first set the
    // width property to the appropriate
    // width. If you are printing two
    // columns, then you only want the
    // width of one column. If you are
    // only printing one column, you'll
    // want the width of the total page.

    If IncludeSecondCol Then
        stp.Width = ColumnWidth
    Else
        stp.Width = TotalWidth
```

Listing 10.12   **Continued**

```
   End If

   // You will start by printing the first column.
   // Initialize the ColumnToPrint variable with
   // the value of one.

   ColumnToPrint = 1

   // Set the font and text size for the Graphics
   // object based upon the property values of the
   // StyledPrinter class.

g.TextFont = Font
   g.TextSize = FontSize

   // Loop through the StyledTextPrinter until
   // all of the text has been printed.

   Do until stp.eof

      // Print the first column:

      If ColumnToPrint = 1 Then

         // If the header should be included
         // then print it first.

If IncludeHeader Then

            // Establish how deep the header should
            // based upon the current FontSize.

HeaderOffset = FontSize * 2

//Draw the first part of the header,
// which is the HeaderTitle.

            g.DrawString HeaderTitle, 0, FontSize
            If IncludePageNum Then

               // Draw the page number and keep
               // flush right on the same line as
               // the HeaderTitle.
               //
               // The position to print it is
```

Listing 10.12   **Continued**

```
                    // calculated using the Graphics
                    // StringWidth property.

                    g.DrawString "Page:"+Str(pageCount), TotalWidth-
g.StringWidth("Page: " + Str(pageCount)),FontSize
                End If

                // Prepare to draw a rule between
                // the header and the body of the page.
                // Set the color of the rule to
                // gray.

                g.ForeColor = RGB(100,100,100)

                // Draw the line below the header

g.DrawLine(0,HeaderOffset,540,HeaderOffset)

// Revert back to black as the
// ForeColor.

                g.ForeColor = RGB(255,255,255)
            Else
                HeaderOffset = FontSize
            End If
        End If


        // Print the actual column. First determine
        // whether you will include the second column.

        If IncludeSecondCol Then

            // Print column

            stp.DrawBlock (ColumnWidth+Gutter)*(columnToPrint-1),
➥HeaderOffset, PageHeight

            // Determine whether this is the first
            // or second column.

If ColumnToPrint = 2 Then

    // After you've printed the second
    // column, test to see if there is
    // more text to be printed.
```

Listing 10.12   **Continued**

```
            If Not stp.EOF then

                // If there is more text to
                // print, then advance to the
                // next page, reset the
                // ColumnToPrint and increment
                // the pageCount.

                g.NextPage
                ColumnToPrint = 1
                pageCount = pageCount + 1
            End if
        Else
            // You are printing the first column.
            // Consequently, you do not need to
            // advance to the next page or increment
            // the page count.

            ColumnToPrint = columnToPrint + 1
        End if
    Else

        // You are printing a one-column page, so
        // print the column, move to the next page
        // and increment the pageCount.

        stp.DrawBlock 0,FontSize*2,PageHeight
        If Not stp.EOF Then
            g.NextPage
            pageCount = PageCount + 1
        End If
    End If
    Loop
End if
```

The **StyledPrinter** class is accessed by clicking **PushButton1**, labeled Print.

Listing 10.13   **Sub PushButton1.Action() Handles Event**

```
Dim printer as StyledPrinter
Dim ps as PrinterSetup

ps = New PrinterSetup
If ps.PageSetupDialog Then

    printer = New StyledPrinter(Window1.EditField1)
        printer.IncludeSecondCol = Window1.RadioButton1.Value
```

Listing 10.13 **Continued**

```
        printer.Print(ps)

End If
```

After the page is processed, the output will look like Figure 10.13:

Figure 10.13   Printing output.

As you can see from the output, the text is printed in two columns, and the header is printed at the top of the page, with the proper page count. You'll also notice, though, that the formatting isn't perfect. For example, the first line of each paragraph isn't indented, and there's no space between each paragraph. You might also notice that words are wrapped only on white space; words aren't hyphenated at the end of the line. There's nothing really wrong with either issue, but it does speak to the point that REALbasic provides basic printing functionality out of the box that is very easy to use, but it does have its limits. More sophisticated requirements will require substantial customization.

Summary

With the conclusion of this chapter, all of the major topics concerning REALbasic have been covered. I've really only scratched the surface, though, because the functionality available in the language today is just too vast to include in one book.

In the next chapter, I will turn to some more advanced topics with respect to programming in REALbasic, including scripting, using Declares, and expanding it by writing your own plug-ins.

11

Scripting and Extending REALbasic

IN THIS, THE LAST CHAPTER OF THE BOOK, I want to cover ways of extending REALbasic. The first topic is how to make your own REALbasic applications scriptable. This, in effect, will allow your own users to extend your applications. This will be followed by a section describing how to use REALbasic to automate Microsoft Office applications and how you can use those applications to add functionality to your REALbasic applications. Finally, I will review Declares and plug-ins. A *Declare* is a way of calling a function in a shared library and a *plug-in* is a static library that you can compile into your application.

By their very nature, `Declares` and plug-ins have to be coded platform specific (although the developer can hide those details from the user). Effectively using `Declares` or writing plug-ins requires extensive knowledge about the underlying platforms because you, as the developer, will no longer be shielded from this. Because this book is about cross-platform development with REALbasic, and not about writing C ++ code for Windows, Macintosh, and Linux, the depth of this coverage will be limited. I'll share enough to get you started and point you in the direction of additional information when it's available.

Scripting

If you are running your application on a Macintosh, you can use AppleScript to make your application scriptable, but that will work only for when you're running it on a Macintosh. REALbasic provides a cross-platform solution to the problem with the RBScript class.

RBScript

RBScript is a subset of the REALbasic programming language. It retains most of the features of the language itself, with a few limitations—the most notable is that many of the global functions that are available to you when writing REALbasic code in the IDE will not be available to you when writing a script. For instance, MsgBox cannot be called from **RBScript.** The Language Reference provides a detailed list of available functions, so I will not repeat that information here.

RBScript Object

The **RBScript** language is a fairly complete implementation of REALbasic, and you can do quite a lot with it. It supports classes, interfaces, and modules. You can instantiate the **RBScript** object in code, just like any other class, or you can drag it onto a Window like a Control. Either way, after the object is available, you then need to set it up so that your users can use it to script your application.

As I mentioned earlier, one thing that is not available to **RBScript** is some global functions. This limitation is a good one because the purpose of **RBScript** is to provide a scripting interface to your application. As a developer, you will want control over which parts of your application are accessible by **RBScript,** and you do this by assigning an object to the RBScript.Context property:

```
RBScript.Context as Object
```

The object that you assign to the **Context** should be one that provides the script with the functions you want your users to have control over. For starters, suppose you want the user to access the **System**RBScript.Context property object through **RBScript**. It's as easy as the following:

```
RBScript1.Context = System
```

Now, if in your code you try to access the **System** object directly, you'll be in for a surprise, because it won't work. You can access it by working directly with the **Context** object, but REALbasic provides an easier way because all the members of the **System** object will be available to your script as global methods and properties. If you want to check the value for an environment variable, you can do the following:

```
Dim s as String
s = EnvironmentVariable("PATH"RBScript.Context property)
```

To run a script, you need to assign the source code of the script to the Source property of **RBScript:**

```
RBScript.Source as String
```

Prior to executing the script, you should check the current state of the **RBScript** object to see if it is ready to execute a new script, whether it is already running, completed, or if the execution of the script has been aborted in some way:

```
RBScript.State as Integer
```

Legal values for `RBScript.State` are

```
0 = Ready
1 = Running
2 = Complete
3 = Aborted
```

There was a time when **RBScript** was an interpreter, which meant that the scripts themselves were never directly compiled into machine code. That is no longer the case. One consequence of this (besides much better performance) is that the following property doesn't work anymore if you are using a current version of REALbasic:

```
RBScript.CurrentLineNumber as Integer (Deprecated)
```

Because the script is a `string`, it sometimes needs to use characters from languages, such as Japanese, that require 2 bytes to represent.

```
RBScript.EncodingFont as String
```

Now that scripts are no longer run through the interpreter, they get compiled into native application code. You run a script by calling the `Run` method:

```
RBScript.Run()
```

At that time, the script will be compiled and executed. You have the option, however, of compiling the script at some arbitrary point prior to running it, and for that you call the following method:

```
RBScript.Precompile()
```

You are also give the option of running the script for only a certain number of seconds, using `PartialRun`:

```
RBScript.PartialRun(millisec as Integer)
```

You would do this to yield time back to the application.

After a script is finished running, the value for `RBscript.State` is 2, which means the script has completed execution. If you want to run the script again, you must reset it using the `Reset` method:

```
RBScript.Reset()
```

The interesting part of all this is linking the script to your application. As I already mentioned, you can assign an object to the `Content` property and your script will be able to access the properties and methods globally. That in itself is enough to get something done that's meaningful, but REALbasic provides another way of interacting with the script through the use of two events in the RBScript class:

```
RBScript.Input(prompt as String) as String Handles Event
RBScript.Print(msg as String) Handles Event
```

Most programs accept some kind of input and produce some kind of output. **RBScript** uses the `Input` and `Print` events as a means of getting additional input during the execution of the script and of outputting data during the execution of the script.

`Input` and `Print` are both events that your script can raise at any time during the running of the script. You use both of them as if they were methods, like this:

```
Dim s as String
s = Input("Please give me input.")
```

When this couplet of code gets executed, the `Input` event is triggered, and if you have implemented that event, the code in that implementation gets passed the `"Please give me input."` string, does some processing based on that, and then returns a string of some sort back to the script. Here's one possible way to implement the `Input` event:

```
RBScript1.Input(Prompt as String) as String

    Dim result as Integer
    result = MsgBox(Prompt, 3)
    If result = 6 Then
        // 6 signifies "Yes" button
        Return "Yes!"
    Else
        Return "No."
    End If
```

Within the body of your script, you do not have access to `MsgBox`, so you cannot call it from there. Because the `Input` event is implemented in REALbasic code, not using **RBScript**, you have access to everything you normally have access to. In this instance, my script asks for input, triggers the `Input` event, and the `Input` event handles getting that input from the user in some way.

The `Print` event works in a similar way, but by sending output. Again, it's an event that gets called in code when and how you want to. You pass a `string` to the event and you implement the `Print` event to do something with that String. You may display the output to the user, you may use it to assign a value to a property elsewhere in your application, or you may execute a block of code based on the content of the string.

There are also two error-related events, each for a different kind of error. If there is an error in your code that keeps it from being compiled properly, a `CompilerError` event is triggered:

```
RBScript.CompilerError(line as Integer, errorNumber as Integer,
    errorMsg as String) Handles Event
```

If any other kind of error occurs, this event is triggered:

```
RBScript.RuntimeError(line as Integer, error as RuntimeException)
```

The Language Reference provides a complete list of compiler errors with their explanations. It also documents which global functions and language elements are available in the scripting environment.

Web Server Scripting

Suppose you want to add a scripting capability for your web server so that every file that ends in .rs is executed as a REALbasic script. The process for doing this is simple. The first step is to identify requests for files that end in .rs and then assign them to the

Source property of an **RBScript** object. After that, the script should be executed and the results returned to the user. This is where things get a little tricky.

RBScript is executed asynchronously, which can be a problem because the **TCPSocket** class that the **HTTPServer** class is built on is asynchronous as well. When the request comes in, you will want to maintain the connection to the client from within the `DataAvailable` event and then process the script and return the results. In the **HTTPServer** example, I placed all the `Write` methods within the `DataAvailable` event. If I didn't do that, a new request could come through and generate a new `DataAvailable` event while I was still processing the data from the previous request. I need to be able to call and execute the script and get the results prior to exiting the `DataAvailable` event, and I can do it this way:

```
While True
    If RBScript1.Results = "" Then
        // loop
    Else
        Write RBScript1.Results
    End If
Wend
```

I create a class to serve as the **Context** object for the script, something which could easily be an **HTTPRequest** object with a `Result` property, which is where the output of the script will be assigned in the `Print` event:

```
Print(msg as String)
    Results = msg
```

The code in the `DataAvailable` event will loop while it waits for the `Results` property to be assigned. As soon as it is assigned, it writes the data back to the client. For the script to work properly, all it has to do is generate the HTML it is going to send back to the client, and then pass that **String** to the `Print` event. You'll need to add more error checking and things like that for this to work reliably, but at least you are well on your way to having implemented a scriptable web server.

Office Automation

REALbasic supports Microsoft Office automation on both the Windows and the Macintosh platforms. The Macintosh implementation is somewhat more limited; the most obvious distinction is that you have to execute your REALbasic application from within the same folder as the Office application you are automating. The examples in this section were developed on Windows because this is the most likely place that you will be using it.

The biggest challenge to using these classes is that they are not documented. REALbasic provides some supporting classes, plus some code completion support for Office automation, but don't make the mistake of believing that the absence of code completion indicates a lack of support. Check the documentation available in Word, PowerPoint, or Excel to find out the properties, methods, and events that are applicable to any given object.

Controls can be dragged onto a **Window—WordApplication,
PowerpointApplication,** and **ExcelApplication,** all of which are subclasses of
OLEObject. They aren't true controls, because they are not a subclass of **RectControl**
and they can be instantiated in the normal way with the New operator. All these classes
are subclasses of **OLEObject,** which is where I will turn first.

OLEObject

In Windows terminology, OLE stands for *object linking and embedding.* It was originally
designed so that you could embed one application into another. In other words, you
could embed an Excel spreadsheet in the middle of a Word document. This basic technology has evolved over the years and it is now part of a broader Component Object
Model (called COM). I won't get into too much detail about COM, but there are a few
things to be aware of that will help you understand what's going on in the background.

Components are distributed. They are pieces of code (much like a shared library) that
other applications can execute. Each component has a unique ID that is listed in the
Windows Registry. If you want your application to use a particular component, you need
to have that unique ID. There is a COM server that will return a reference to the component that your application can use.

The most commonly used components are ActiveX components, many of which are
controls. In fact, there is an **OLEContainer** Control in REALbasic that can be used to
include ActiveX controls in your application. The COM server does other things, too. For
instance, it controls how many instances of the component are in memory.

When automating Office applications, you will be using the **OLEObject** class, or a
subclass of **OLEObject** throughout. An **OLEObject** is a component, which means it is
something managed by a COM server and accessible through the Windows Registry.
There are three subclasses of most importance: **WordApplication,**
PowerpointApplication, and **ExcelApplication,** each of which is a class that represents the respective Office application. These are not the only **OLEObjects** you
will encounter, however, because there are many others, some of which you'll see
momentarily.

Because **OLEObjects** are components, all have a globally unique identifier assigned
to them, and they are referenced by this number internally. The number needs to be
unique because you cannot always predict what other **OLEObjects** are going to be
available on a system, and you want to be able to avoid namespace problems. There are
two Constructors, one of which takes the unique identifier as an argument (referred to
as ProgramID in the documentation). The second also takes the identifier, but also specifies whether to create a new instance of the object, rather than using an existing instance.
Behind the scenes, REALbasic is getting a reference to the component from the COM
server, which is why you need to let it know whether to create a new instance or to use
an existing instance if one is already available.

```
OLEObject.OLEObject(ProgramID as String)
OLEObject.OLEObject(ProgramID as String, NewInstance as Boolean)
```

Like all objects, **OLEObjects** have properties, methods, and events. Because
OLEObject is a generic representation of a particular **OLEObject,** it also has to

provide some generic methods for getting and setting properties, executing methods, and so on. To set a property, you use the following method:

```
OLEObject.Value(PropertyName as String, ByValue as Boolean) as Variant
```

You can find out what type of **OLEObject** it is, using the following:

```
OLEObject.TypeName as String
```

Functions are accessible by name. The following two methods provide a way to execute functions:

```
OLEObject.Invoke(NameOfFunction as String) as Variant
OLEObject.Invoke(NameOfFunction as String, Parameters() as Variant) as Variant
```

The first function requires only the function name, whereas the second one lets you pass along the parameters as well. If you pass parameters, you will need to know which order to place them into the array, because they are determined by position.

OLEParameter

VisualBasic supports optional parameters, which in practice work like polymorphism. In REALbasic, you can have a single method with multiple signatures utilizing different parameters. To handle optional parameters in REALbasic in a way that's compatible with the VBA implementations, you need to use the **OLEParameter** class. Later on in the examples, you will see exactly how the **OLEParameter** class is handled.

```
OLEParameter.PassByRef as Boolean
OLEParameter.Position as Integer
OLEParameter.Type as Integer
OLEParameter.Value as Variant
OLEParameter.Value2D
OLEParameter.ValueArray as Variant
```

OLEParameter Class Type Constants

When passing a value to an **OLEParameter** instance, you will need to let it know what type it is. You can use the following constants

```
OLEParameter.ParamTypeBoolean as Boolean
OLEParameter.ParamTypeChar
OLEParameter.ParamTypeDouble
OLEParameter.ParamTypeNull
OLEParameter.ParamTypeSigned64bit
OLEParameter.ParamTypeSignedChar
OLEParameter.ParamTypeSignedLong
OLEParameter.ParamTypeSignedShort
OLEParameter.ParamTypeSingle
OLEParameter.ParamTypeString
OLEParameter.ParamTypeUnsigned64bit
OLEParameter.ParamTypeUnsignedLong
OLEParameter.ParamTypeUnsignedShort
```

OLEContainer Control

One special kind of **OLEObject** is an ActiveX control, which is like a REALbasic control, except that it works only on the Windows platform. There happen to be a lot of them, so it can be beneficial to have access to them. The **OLEContainer** control is a generic ActiveX container that you use just like any other **Control** on a **Window** in your application.

The container has a reference to the associated **OLEObject**, which is accessible with the Content property:

```
OLEContainer.Content as OLEObject
```

You can find out the program ID, too:

```
OLEContainer.ProgramID as String
```

You can select the ActiveX control through the IDE. Drag the container onto a **Window**, and then right-click the **Control**. A **Window** pops up with a list of ActiveX controls available on your computer. You can select whichever one you want and the values for the ProgramID will be set for you.

ActiveX

In the following examples, I will go through the process of embedding the Windows Media Player into a REALbasic application. Figure 11.1 shows the list of available ActiveX controls I can choose from in my application:

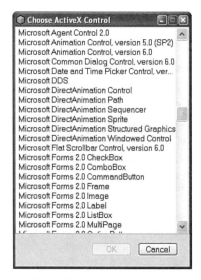

Figure 11.1   ActiveX controls.

When I select Windows Media Player, the ProgramID is set to the following:

```
{6BF52A52-394A-11d3-B153-00C04F79FAA6}
```

Some ActiveX controls have property pages, which are basically windows that are made available to the user so that the user can set certain properties for the control themselves. The method to use is this:

```
OLEContainer.ShowPropertyPages
```

If I call this method on the Windows Media Player control, the property page shown in Figure 11.2 appears:

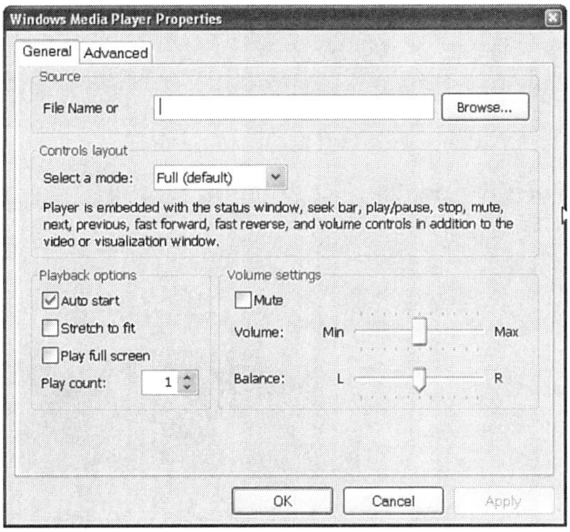

Figure 11.2   Windows Media Play property page.

You can use the same **OLEContainer** to reference different **OLEObjects** at different times during the execution of your application. The following two methods are used to use a new **OLEObject**, or to remove it from memory:

```
OLEContainer.Create as Boolean
OLEContainer.Destroy
```

Handling Events

Events are handled uniquely in this situation. First, because the **OLEContainer** object is a **Control**, it has a typical collection of REALbasic events available for implementation. However, because you can assign any ActiveX control to the container, there are not specific references to any of the additional events that these controls can implement. For this reason, there is the `EventTriggered` event, which is triggered when an event specific to a particular ActiveX control is fired:

```
OLEContainer.EventTriggered(NameOfEvent as String, parameters() as Variant)
➥Handles Event
```

When you drag a mouse over the container that contains the Windows Media Player ActiveX control, the `EventTriggered` event is triggered. To see what gets passed to the event, I placed the following code in the handler:

```
Dim x,y as Integer
Dim buffer(-1) as String

y = Ubound(parameters)

For x = 0 To y
    buffer.append(parameters(x).StringValue)
Next

MsgBox eventName + EndOfLine + Join(buffer,EndOfLine)
```

The `MsgBox` that gets displayed as a result of this event firing is shown in the Figure 11.3:

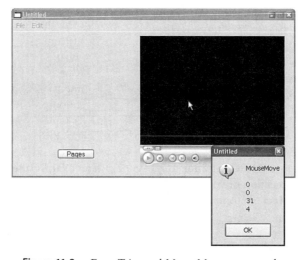

Figure 11.3   EventTriggered MouseMove event results.

I said earlier that because the **OLEContainer** is a **Control**, it also has all the usual events that a typical REALbasic control has. In fact, the **OLEContainer** control also has a `MouseMove` event in addition to the `EventTriggered` event. This provides us with a unique opportunity to see the event from two different perspectives: the first as handled by the `EventTriggered` event and the second as handled by the `MouseMove` event. I placed the following code in the `MouseMove` event:

```
MsgBox "Internal MouseMove" + Str(x) + "/" + Str(y)
```

With this code in place, when I drag the mouse across the **Control**, the following Window pops up (see Figure 11.4):

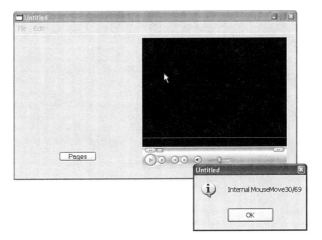

Figure 11.4   OLEContainer Control MouseMove event.

As you can see, there are two values, x and y, that are passed in the regular MouseDown event, but there are four parameters in the MouseDown event handled by the EventTriggered event. I can deduce that the last two parameters are values for the mouse position, just like the x and y values passed to the other event, but what about the first two parameters, each of which happen to be 0 each time it's triggered.

One way to find out is to use the VisualBasic documentation provided in Microsoft Word. To get the actual information about the Media Player Control, I had to open a Word document and then insert a Media Player Control onto the page using the Control Toolbox. This works much like the Window does when assigning an ActiveX control to an **OLEContainer** Control in REALbasic. The Control Toolbox has a group of buttons that you can click to select some of the more commonly used controls, but there is also another button to select a custom control. When that is clicked, a long list of available ActiveX controls appears, and you can select Windows Media Player from that list.

With this control embedded in the Word document, I go to the Tools menu and select Macros, followed by the VisualBasic editor, as shown in Figure 11.5. The current document is referenced as ThisDocument. I can select ThisDocument and I'll see that it contains an object called **WindowsMediaPlayer1**. In the editor, I can select it in the object menu; then in the adjacent menu, a list of available events appears.

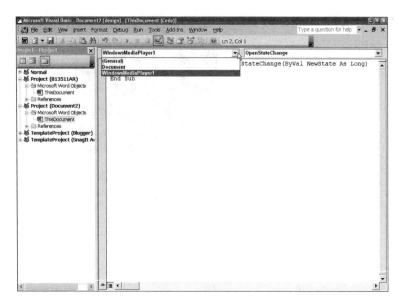

Figure 11.5   Microsoft Word Visual Basic Editor.

I can select the one called MouseMove and I will be shown the following signature:

```
Private Sub WindowsMediaPlayer1_MouseMove(ByVal nButton As Integer,
ByVal nShiftState As Integer, ByVal fX As Long, ByVal fY As Long)

End Sub
```

Looking at this signature, we see that there are indeed four parameters for the MouseMove event, and that the first one is called nButton and the second is nShiftState. These refer to which mouse button is being clicked and whether the Shift key is currently down. The reason I was getting a value of 0 for both was that I wasn't clicking any button, nor was I holding down the Shift key.

Finally, one more **OLEContainer** event needs to be mentioned. The following event is triggered prior to the control being shown:

```
OLEContainer.ShowObject Handles Event
```

This is used because you can change the reference from one ActiveX control to another during runtime, and you can implement any code here that is needed to respond to that change.

OLEException

OLEException is a subclass of **RuntimeError.** It doesn't implement any new methods, and it works just like other **RuntimeError** subclasses.

WordApplication Class

The **Office** object model is composed of collections and objects, both of which have properties, methods, and events. A collection is basically an object array, or an indexed list of objects. One important collection in Microsoft Word is the **Documents** collection. This represents all the open documents for the current application. You can use the **Documents** collection to get a reference to a particular document. It's important to understand that it is not a real array, so you can't do array-like things with it, such as using the `For Each` statement. In VisualBasic, you can do the following:

```
For Each aDoc In Documents
    aName = aName & aDoc.Name & vbCr
Next aDoc
MsgBox aName
```

In REALbasic, you have to do it this way:

```
Dim count, x as Integer
Dim doc as OLEObject
count = WordApplication1.Documents.Count
For x = 0 to count - 1
doc = WordApplication1.Documents(x)
// do something with doc
Next
```

A particularly cool part about all of this is that the Word application doesn't have to be visible. This means that you can use all the tools available from Word in your application without Word ever being visible to the user.

Figure 11.6 shows an abbreviated illustration of the Word object model:

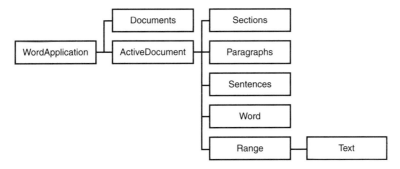

Figure 11.6   Word object model.

At the top of the object model tree is the **WordApplication** object. If you have dragged the **WordApplication** control onto a **Window**, this can be referenced as **WordApplication1**. There are a few properties of the object, but the important one to consider now is the **Documents** object, which is a collection.

Documents Collection

A Word application can have more than one document open at a time, which explains why there is a **Documents** collection. Each open document has to have a unique name. This gives you two ways of referencing the document, either through the title of the open document or by its index position in the collection of **Documents**:

```
Documents(title as String) as Document
Documents(index as Integer) as Document
```

Because you may not know in advance the names of the documents that are open, you are provided with a Count property that lets you know how many documents are open, which means you can iterate through all the open documents.

```
Documents.Count as Integer
```

Documents.ActiveDocument as Document

The **Documents** collection also has a property called **ActiveDocument,** which points to the front-most document for the Word application.

Activate the document by calling the Activate method on a particular **Document** object:

```
Document.Activate
```

Documents.Add as Document

The Add method adds a new, untitled **Document** to the **Documents** collection and returns a reference to it.

Documents.Open(aPath as String)

When you want to open an existing **Document**, you use the Open method, passing to it an absolute path to the location of the file you want to open:

```
WordApplication1.Documents.Open("C:\MyFolder\Sample.doc")
```

The path is the only required parameter, but the Open method contains a long list of optional parameters. The method signature according to the documentation in Microsoft Word is as follows:

```
Documents.Open(FileName, ConfirmConversions, ReadOnly, AddToRecentFiles,
➥PasswordDocument, PasswordTemplate, Revert, WritePasswordDocument,
➥WritePasswordTemplate, Format, Encoding, Visible, OpenConflictDocument,
➥OpenAndRepair , DocumentDirection, NoEncodingDialog)
```

The following table identifies each parameter, shows its position, and describes what kind of value it is expecting. The position is used when using the **OLEParameter** class to send a optional parameter to the method.

Table 11.1 **Document.Open Parameters**

1	FileName	Required, the name (or path) of the document.
2	ConfirmConversions	Optional, Boolean. True will display Convert File dialog.
3	ReadOnly	Optional, Boolean, True to open as Read-only.
4	AddToRecentFiles	Optional, Boolean, True to add to the list of recently opened files.
5	PasswordDocument	Optional, password for the document.
6	PasswordTemplate	Optional, password for a template.
7	Revert	Optional, Boolean, True discards unsaved changes.
8	WritePasswordDocument	Optional, password for saving changes to a document.
9	WritePasswordTemplate	Optional, password for saving changes to a template.
10	Format	Optional, use the WdOpenFormat constants:
		Office.wdOpenFormatAllWord
		Office.wdOpenFormatAuto
		Office.wdOpenFormatDocument
		Office.wdOpenFormatEncodedText
		Office.wdOpenFormatRTF
		Office.wdOpenFormatTemplate
		Office.wdOpenFormatText
		Office.wdOpenFormatUnicodeText
		Office.wdOpenFormatWebPages
11	Encoding	Optional, using MsoEncoding constants.
12	Visible	Optional, Boolean.
13	OpenConflictDocument	Optional.
14	OpenAndRepair	Optional, Boolean.
15	DocumentDirection	Optional, use WdDocumentDirection constants:
		Office.wdLeftToRight
		Office.wdRightToLeft
16	NoEncodingDialog	Optional, Boolean.

Opening a Word document is different from opening other files in REALbasic because you do not necessarily need a FolderItem reference, just a path. The following example shows you how you can let your user select the Word document to open using the GetOpenFolderItem function and then use the reference to the **FolderItem** to open the Word document itself:

```
Dim f as FolderItem
Dim ap as OLEParameter

f = GetOpenFolderItem(WordDocs.DOC)
ap = new OLEParameter
ap.Position = 1
```

```
ap.Value = f.AbsolutePath
WordApplication1.Documents.Open(ap)
```

As you can see, I created an **OLEParameter** instance, and I set the value for `Position` to be 1 and the `Value` to be the absolute path of the **FolderItem**. I did this because the `FileName` is the first parameter in Open's signature and it takes a path as its value. I then pass the **OLEParameter** instance to the `Open` method to open the document.

Documents.Close

The signature for the `Close` method is this:

```
Documents.Close(SaveChanges, OriginalFormat, RouteDocument)
```

Table 11.2 **Document.Close Parameters**

Position	Name	Comments
1	SaveChanges	Optional, use WdSaveOptions constants:
		Office.wdDoNotSaveChanges
		Office.wdPromptToSaveChanges
		Office.wdSaveChanges
2	OriginalFormat	Optional, using WdOriginalFormat constants:
		Office.wdOriginalDocumentFormat
		Office.wdPromptUser
		Office.wdWordDocument
3	RouteDocument	Optional, Boolean

The following instruction closes the document named "Report.doc" without saving changes.

```
Dim param as OLEParameter

param = New OLEParameter
param.Position = 1
param.Value = Office.wdDoNotSaveChanges
WordApplication1.Documents("Report.doc").Close(param)
```

Document.Save

The complete signature:

```
Document.Save(NoPrompt, OriginalFormat)
```

Table 11.3 **Document.Save Parameters**

Position	Name	Comments
1	NoPrompt	Option, Boolean. False means that Word will prompt the user to save all changed documents.
2	OriginalFormat	Optional, specifies the format used for saving the document. Use wdFormat constants.

To save a particular document:

```
WordApplication1.Documents("MyTest.doc").Save
```

To save a particular document without prompting the user for changes:

```
Dim param as OLEParameter
param = New OLEParameter
param.Position = 1
param.Value = True
WordApplication1.Documents("MyTest.doc").Save(param)
```

To save all open documents:

```
WordApplication1.Documents.Save
```

Documents.SaveAs

If you look up the SaveAs method in the VisualBasic Help in Microsoft Word, you'll see that the signature is as follows:

```
expression.SaveAs(FileName, FileFormat, LockComments, Password,
➥AddToRecentFiles, WritePassword, ReadOnlyRecommended, EmbedTrueTypeFonts,
➥SaveNativePictureFormat, SaveFormsData, SaveAsAOCELetter, Encoding,
➥InsertLineBreaks, AllowSubstitutions, LineEnding, AddBiDiMarks)
```

By "expression," the documentation means an expression that returns a **Document** object, so one example of how this would work in REALbasic is this:

```
Dim wd as WordDocument
wd = WordApplication1.Documents("ThisOpenFile.doc")
wd.SaveAs(…)
```

Table 11.4 **Document.SaveAs Parameters**

Position	Name	Comments
1	FileName	Optional.
2	FileFormat	Optional; takes WdFormat enumeration.
3	LockComments	Optional, Boolean; to lock comments.
4	Password	Optional; password string for opening a document. Use WritePassword to save changes made to a document.
5	AddToRecentFiles	Optional, Boolean; adds a reference to this file to the Recent Files menu.

Table 11.4 **Continued**

Position	Name	Comments
6	WritePassword	Optional; a string containing the password required to make changes to the document.
7	ReadOnlyRecommended	Optional, Boolean; makes Word suggest Read-Only format when the document is opened.
8	EmbedTrueTypeFonts	Optional, Boolean; saves TrueType fonts with the document.
9	SaveNativePictureFormat	Optional, Boolean; converts graphics to the native format.
10	SaveFormsData	Optional, Boolean; saves forms data as a data record.
11	SaveAsOCELeter	Optional, Boolean; attached mailer.
12	Encoding	Optional, msoEncoding constants.
13	InsertLineBreaks	Optional, Boolean; used with text files.
14	AllowSubstitutions	Optional, allow Word to substitute non-ANSI characters with appropriate symbols when saving as text. For example, © symbols are converted to (c).
15	LineEnding	Optional, wdLineEndingType constant.
16	AddBiDiMarks	Optional, Boolean; sets direction of text (right to left or left to right).

In the documentation, the description of the `FileFormat` parameter says that the value can be any `WdSaveFormat` constants, and it lists the constants. In REALbasic, all the available constants are members of the **Office** object, so you would refer to the `WdSaveFormat` constants using the following signatures:

Table 11.5 **WdSaveFormat Constants**

Office.wdFormatDocument	0	Word Document format (.doc).
Office.wdFormatDOSText	4	Converts text to ANSI character set and replaces section breaks, page breaks, and newline characters with Windows EndOfLine (CR-LF).
Office.wdFormatDOSTextLineBreaks	5	Same as above, except that it also converts line breaks into CR-LF.
Office.wdFormatEncodedText	7	Saves the document in a particular encoding, which is set in the Encoding argument.
Office.wdFormatFilteredHTML	10	A somewhat cleaner HTML document than the standard Word HTML.
Office.wdFormatHTML	8	The standard Word HTML document, which is horribly cluttered and something to be avoided (in my opinion).
Office.wdFormatRTF	6	Save the document in Rich Text Format (RTF), which is compatible with a lot of editors and word processors (.rtf).

Table 11.5   **Continued**

Office.wdFormatTemplate Saves as a Word template.	1	Save it as a Word Template document.
Office.wdFormatText	2	Plain text, ANSI character set.
Office.wdFormatTextLineBreaks	3	No formatting.
Office.wdFormatUnicodeText	7	No formatting, but in Unicode.
Office.wdFormatWebArchive	9	Proprietary, single-file version of a web page.
Office.wdFormatXML	11	Word's XML format.

The following example assumes that a **WordApplication** control has been dragged onto the **Window**. It uses the **WordApplication** object to create a new document, inserts HTML, and then saves the document as a web page. The **WordApplication** object itself is never visible, so it's an example of using Word without actually launching the Word application and making it visible to the user.

```
Dim x,y as Integer
Dim buffer(-1) as String
Dim wd as WordApplication

wd = WordApplication1

wd.Visible = False
wd.Documents.Add
wd.ActiveDocument.Range.Text = "<html><body>Test</body></html>"
wd.ActiveDocument.SaveAs "Test", Office.wdWebPage
```

Every Word document can be assigned properties using the `BuiltInDocumentProperties` object, which is a collection. If you do not happen to know how many properties are in the collection, however, you might run into a problem because you need to reference them by their indexed position. The following example iterates through all the properties and compiles them into a list.

```
Dim wd as Word Application
Dim x as Integer
Dim buffer(-1) as String

wd = WordApplication1
x = 0
While True

x = x + 1
    Try
        buffer.append(wd.ActiveDocument.BuiltInDocumentProperties(x).Value) + ":"
```

```
buffer.append(wd.ActiveDocument.BuiltInDocumentProperties(x).Name)
        MsgBox Join(buffer, EndOfLine)
      Catch
        MsgBox "Error at " + str(x)
    Exit
  End
Wend
```

Extending REALbasic

A shared library is compiled code that can be used by another application. There are two types of libraries: static libraries and shared libraries. A static library is compiled into your application and does not exist as a separate file. A shared library, on the other hand, is compiled code that resides outside your actual application.

You can access shared libraries in REALbasic by creating `Declares`. There are different shared library formats, depending on the platform you are using. In Linux, the shared libraries always end in .so. If you're a Windows users, you've no doubt seen files that end with .dll, which stands for Dynamic Link Library, which is just another word for shared library. The old shared library format for Macintosh was PEF (which is what REALbasic will create if the application needs to run on Macintosh "Classic" systems). The newer formats are .dylib and frameworks.

Declares

To use a function in a shared library, it must first be declared. You can declare a function in two ways. There's the plain old "hard" declare, and there's the new soft declare. The hard declare told the application that the function being declared will always be available in the library given, and that the library given will always be available. That's not always the case, which is why REALbasic now has a `Soft Declare`, which lets you declare functions that may or may not be available at runtime.

The format of a `Declare` follows. The first is an example of a function, and the second is an example of a subroutine:

```
[Soft] Declare Function FunctionName Lib LibraryName [Alias AliasName]
➥([parameters])) as ReturnType
[Soft] Declare Sub SubroutineName Lib LibraryName [Alias AliasName]([parameters])
```

There are special types that you can use in constructing the `Declare` statement itself. In some instances, the **MemoryBlock** class provides a method for accessing the data of one of these types.

Table 11.6   **MemoryBlock Types**

Type	Description
Byte	Signed 8-bit Integer.
CFStringRef	A CFString reference (String).
CString	A null-terminated string.
OSType	A four char code, like a Mac Creator Code (4 byte integer).
PString	A "Pascal" string. 256 bytes. The first byte represents the length of the String. The remaining (up to 255 bytes) space is the String itself.
Ptr	4-byte pointer to a location in memory .
Short	2-byte signed Integer.
UByte	Unsigned 8-bit Integer.
UShort	Unsigned 2-byte Integer.
WindowPtr	4-byte Integer to a handle (which is like a pointer).

Next, I'll show you examples of `Declares` written for all three platforms. All of these examples are based on `Declares` created by developers in the REALbasic community that they have graciously shared with others. All the examples are ways to find out the process id of the current application.

Windows

A good source of Windows declares is Aaron Ballman's Windows Functionality Suite, which can be downloaded at the following address:

`http://www.aaronballman.com/programming/REALbasic/Win32FunctionalitySuite.php`

The `Declare` is written like this:

```
Function GetCurrentProcessId as Integer
#if TargetWin32
        Declare Function MyGetCurrentProcessId Lib "Kernel32" Alias
➥"GetCurrentProcessId" () as Integer
        return MyGetCurrentProcessID
#endif
return 0
End Function
```

There are a few things to note about this declare. The first is that the library it accesses is called `Kernel32`. This `Declare` also uses an alias. The real name of the function in `Kernel32` is `GetCurrentProcessID`, but this `Declare` references it as `MyGetCurrentProcessID`. This is so that the `Declare` can be wrapped in a function called `GetCurrentProcessId` and avoid any namespace collisions.

Macintosh

There are several ways of getting the process id on a Macintosh. There is a Carbon Declares module that is circulated in the community that accesses the Macintosh Carbon library to get it. In this instance, it's a two-step process. First, you get a reference to the current process serial number, which is a unique data structure that is not, technically, the process id.

```
Function GetCurrentProcess as MemoryBlock
  #if targetCarbon then
    Declare Sub GetMe lib "CarbonLib" Alias "GetCurrentProcess" (PSN As Ptr)
  #else
    Declare Sub GetMe Lib "InterfaceLib" Alias "GetCurrentProcess"
➥(PSN As Ptr) Inline68K("3F3C0037A88F")
  #endif

  // Returns the reference to the current process

  Dim proc As MemoryBlock, err as integer

  proc = NewMemoryBlock(8)

  GetMe proc

  Return proc
End Function
```

After you have the process, you can then call another Carbon function that takes the current process in the parameter and returns the process id:

```
  Dim i, pid As Integer

  #if TargetCarbon then
    Declare Function GetPID Lib "CarbonLib" Alias "GetProcessPID"
➥ (PSN As Ptr, byref pid As Integer) As Short

    i = GetPID(PSN, pid)

    Return pid
  #endif
```

If you are going to be accessing Mac OS X only, you can use a different approach, this time relying on the System framework:

```
  #if TargetMachO
Declare Function getpid Lib "/System/Library/Frameworks/System.framework/System" _
() as Integer
pid = getpid
return pid
#endif
```

Linux

There are quite a few Linux Declares available at the following address:

```
http://forge.novell.com/modules/xfmod/project/?rblinux
```

After a quick scan of the available functions, we find a function that allows you to get a process id on Linux. The function is coded as follows:

```
Function getpid as Integer
Dim i As Integer
#if TargetLinux then
      Declare Function getpid Lib "libc.so.6" () As Integer
    i = getpid
      Return i
#endif
End Function
```

One thing you may notice is that the actual library includes a version number. That's because libc on Linux is an ld loader script and is used to locate the current version of LibC—it's not LibC itself. Because this was a "hard" declare, it could be written only against a specific library with a specific name. However, using soft declare means that you can avoid using the version number.

```
Function getpid as Integer
Dim i As Integer
#if TargetLinux then
      Soft Declare Function getpid Lib "LibC" () As Integer
    i = getpid
      Return i
#endif
End Function
```

Online Documentation

Of necessity, this has been only a brief introduction to the topic. Do not despair, however, because there is already an excellent resource available online, by Charles Yeoman:

```
http://www.declaresub.com/iDeclare/
```

Charles has an online book that delves in glorious detail into the ins and outs of using `Declares`, and because he's done such an excellent job, I will point you in his direction to learn from his expertise.

Plug-ins

Plug-ins are static libraries that get compiled into your REALbasic application; you can create your own plug-ins using REALbasic's Plug-in SDK. If you want to create cross-platform plug-ins, you will need to use Metrowerks Code Warrior because it can compile code for Windows and all of Macintosh's library formats.

You use plug-ins by putting them in REALbasic's Plug-ins directory. After they are installed, you can get access to the plug-in's documentation in the Help menu, under Plug-in Reference. The plug-ins themselves can consist of the following types:

Functions	These are global methods, such as Len, and so on.
Classes	A regular REALbasic class. It can be a subclass of any other REALbasic class.
Class Extensions	A class extension adds functionality to an existing class, much like you can do when using the Extends keyword.
Class Interfaces	An interface, just like you can create directly.
Controls	A control that can be dragged onto a Window.
Database Engines	REALbasic's databases are driven by plug-ins. The SDK can help you create your own.
Modules	A module is a collection of functions with a common namespace.

After the plug-in is installed, you use it as if it were a native REALbasic class, module, function, and so on, with code completion and all the other features available to you.

Creating plug-ins requires an intimate knowledge of C++ and the underlying operating systems. If you want to write cross-platform plug-ins, you need to know a lot about all three platforms. Describing how to write a plug-in is beyond the scope of this book, but that's okay because you can still benefit from them; several third-party plug-ins provide valuable functionality for REALbasic. Some are commercial applications and others are freeware.

Third-Party Plug-ins

There's a good chance you'll never need to write a plug-in yourself. Not only has REALbasic matured to the point that it provides just about everything you need for most applications, but there is also a market for commercial and free plug-ins that can be used in your applications. Here are a few highlights.

MonkeyBread Software (http://monkeybreadsoftware.de)

MonkeyBread Software offers the mother of all plug-ins—a plug-in that, at last count, added more than 7,000 functions to REALbasic. Some are Macintosh-specific and others are Windows-specific, but the vast majority work on either platform. One of the more interesting features of this plug-in is that it provides classes that allow you to execute Java from within REALbasic.

Einhugur (http://einhugur.com/)

Einhugur software provides a series of plug-ins. One of the more interesting is e-Cryptit, which provides a comprehensive set of tools for encrypting and decrypting data.

Einhugur also offers a series of **Grid** controls, which are more flexible versions of REALbasic's **ListBox** control. Figure 11.7 is a screenshot of Einhugur's **StyledGridControl:**

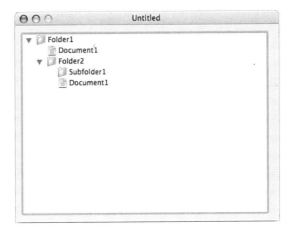

Figure 11.7   Einhugur's StyleGrid control.

Einhugur's **TreeView** control provides a control that works similar to a hierarchical **ListBox**, but that retains the look and feel of the native application. REALbasic's **ListBox** does not use the underlying native controls on each platform, but is part of REALbasic. Because of this, it doesn't look exactly like a native control. **TreeView** solves this problem, which you can see in Figure 11.7.

Valentina (http://paradigmsoft/)

Valentina is a database application offered by Paradigmasoft. Until REALbasic began to use SQLite for the default database, Valentina was a clearly superior database. In addition to working with REALbasic, Valentina also has libraries that work with Macromedia Directory, Revolution, PHP, Java, and C++.

Component X Graphics (http://www.componentx.com/CXGraphics/)

Component X is a free plug-in that extends REALbasic's **Picture** class. With it you can stretch, flip, rotate, and trim pictures. You can also adjust a picture's contrast, gamma, HSV, and RGB values. You can even rotate text along an arc.

FTPSuite for REALbasic (http://www.pyramiddesign.us/ftpsuite/index.html)

This plug-in offers a set of classes that lets you easily integrate FTP into your application. FTP happens to be one of the Internet protocols not directly supported by REALbasic (unlike HTTP, SMTP, and POP).

Summary

This concludes *REALbasic Cross-Platform Application Development*. Although I have tried to cover as much material as possible, there is still a lot more to be learned. In the Appendix, you will find information about additional resources online that will help you develop applications in REALbasic.

A

Appendix

Sample Code and Application

Throughout the book, I have referred to several applications, such as RSSReader and HTTPServer, among others. The complete code for these applications can be found at the following website:

```
http://REALbasicBook.com/
```

All the code is open source and free to use. The applications are released under the GNU General Public License. The external libraries, classes, and modules are released under the GNU Lesser General Public License, which allows you to use them in your commercial applications.

Although every effort has been made to ensure that the sample code works on all platforms, if you run into any problems, check the site to see if fixes have been updated (or if you make a fix yourself, please share it with others).

The rapid release model REAL Software uses to release REALbasic versions means that there will no doubt be many new features available for REALbasic by the time this book is finished. Sometimes, code that works in one version of REALbasic breaks in another version. If this happens and there is enough community interest, fixes will be released for this as well.

GNU General Public License

Version 2, June 1991

```
Copyright (C) 1989, 1991 Free Software Foundation, Inc.
51 Franklin St, Fifth Floor, Boston, MA 02110-1301 USA

Everyone is permitted to copy and distribute verbatim copies
of this license document, but changing it is not allowed.
```

Preamble

The licenses for most software are designed to take away your freedom to share and change it. By contrast, the GNU General Public License is intended to guarantee your freedom to share and change free software--to make sure the software is free for all its users. This General Public License applies to most of the Free Software Foundation's software and to any other program whose authors commit to using it. (Some other Free Software Foundation software is covered by the GNU Library General Public License instead.) You can apply it to your programs, too.

When we speak of free software, we are referring to freedom, not price. Our General Public Licenses are designed to make sure that you have the freedom to distribute copies of free software (and charge for this service if you wish), that you receive source code or can get it if you want it, that you can change the software or use pieces of it in new free programs; and that you know you can do these things.

To protect your rights, we need to make restrictions that forbid anyone to deny you these rights or to ask you to surrender the rights. These restrictions translate to certain responsibilities for you if you distribute copies of the software, or if you modify it.

For example, if you distribute copies of such a program, whether gratis or for a fee, you must give the recipients all the rights that you have. You must make sure that they, too, receive or can get the source code. And you must show them these terms so they know their rights.

We protect your rights with two steps: (1) copyright the software, and (2) offer you this license which gives you legal permission to copy, distribute and/or modify the software.

Also, for each author's protection and ours, we want to make certain that everyone understands that there is no warranty for this free software. If the software is modified by someone else and passed on, we want its recipients to know that what they have is not the original, so that any problems introduced by others will not reflect on the original authors' reputations.

Finally, any free program is threatened constantly by software patents. We wish to avoid the danger that redistributors of a free program will individually obtain patent licenses, in effect making the program proprietary. To prevent this, we have made it clear that any patent must be licensed for everyone's free use or not licensed at all.

The precise terms and conditions for copying, distribution and modification follow.

TERMS AND CONDITIONS FOR COPYING, DISTRIBUTION, AND MODIFICATION

0. This License applies to any program or other work which contains a notice placed by the copyright holder saying it may be distributed under the terms of this General Public License. The "Program", below, refers to any such program or work, and a "work based on the Program" means either the Program or any derivative work under copyright law: that is to say, a work containing the Program or a portion of it, either verbatim or with modifications and/or translated into another language. (Hereinafter, translation is included without limitation in the term "modification".) Each licensee is addressed as "you".

Activities other than copying, distribution and modification are not covered by this License; they are outside its scope. The act of running the Program is not restricted, and the output from the Program is covered only if its contents constitute a work based on the Program (independent of having been made by running the Program). Whether that is true depends on what the Program does.

1. You may copy and distribute verbatim copies of the Program's source code as you receive it, in any medium, provided that you conspicuously and appropriately publish on each copy an appropriate copyright notice and disclaimer of warranty; keep intact all the notices that refer to this License and to the absence of any warranty; and give any other recipients of the Program a copy of this License along with the Program.

You may charge a fee for the physical act of transferring a copy, and you may at your option offer warranty protection in exchange for a fee.

2. You may modify your copy or copies of the Program or any portion of it, thus forming a work based on the Program, and copy and distribute such modifications or work under the terms of Section 1 above, provided that you also meet all of these conditions:

  a) You must cause the modified files to carry prominent notices stating that you changed the files and the date of any change.

  b) You must cause any work that you distribute or publish, that in whole or in part contains or is derived from the Program or any part thereof, to be licensed as a whole at no charge to all third parties under the terms of this License.

  c) If the modified program normally reads commands interactively when run, you must cause it, when started running for such interactive use in the most ordinary way, to print or display an announcement including an appropriate copyright notice and a notice that there is no warranty (or else, saying that you provide a warranty) and that users may redistribute the program under these conditions, and telling the user how to view a copy of this License. (Exception: if the Program itself is interactive but does not normally print such an announcement, your work based on the Program is not required to print an announcement.)

These requirements apply to the modified work as a whole. If identifiable sections of that work are not derived from the Program, and can be reasonably considered independent and separate works in themselves, then this License, and its terms, do not apply to those sections when you distribute them as separate works. But when you distribute the same sections as part of a whole which is a work based on the Program, the distribution of the whole must be on the terms of this License, whose permissions for other licensees extend to the entire whole, and thus to each and every part regardless of who wrote it.

Thus, it is not the intent of this section to claim rights or contest your rights to work written entirely by you; rather, the intent is to exercise the right to control the distribution of derivative or collective works based on the Program.

In addition, mere aggregation of another work not based on the Program with the Program (or with a work based on the Program) on a volume of a storage or distribution medium does not bring the other work under the scope of this License.

3. You may copy and distribute the Program (or a work based on it, under Section 2) in object code or executable form under the terms of Sections 1 and 2 above provided that you also do one of the following:

    a) Accompany it with the complete corresponding machine-readable source code, which must be distributed under the terms of Sections 1 and 2 above on a medium customarily used for software interchange; or,

    b) Accompany it with a written offer, valid for at least three years, to give any third party, for a charge no more than your cost of physically performing source distribution, a complete machine-readable copy of the corresponding source code, to be distributed under the terms of Sections 1 and 2 above on a medium customarily used for software interchange; or,

    c) Accompany it with the information you received as to the offer to distribute corresponding source code. (This alternative is allowed only for noncommercial distribution and only if you received the program in object code or executable form with such an offer, in accord with Subsection b above.)

The source code for a work means the preferred form of the work for making modifications to it. For an executable work, complete source code means all the source code for all modules it contains, plus any associated interface definition files, plus the scripts used to control compilation and installation of the executable. However, as a special exception, the source code distributed need not include anything that is normally distributed (in either source or binary form) with the major components (compiler, kernel, and so on) of the operating system on which the executable runs, unless that component itself accompanies the executable.

If distribution of executable or object code is made by offering access to copy from a designated place, then offering equivalent access to copy the source code from the same place counts as distribution of the source code, even though third parties are not compelled to copy the source along with the object code.

4. You may not copy, modify, sublicense, or distribute the Program except as expressly provided under this License. Any attempt otherwise to copy, modify, sublicense or distribute the Program is void, and will automatically terminate your rights under this License. However, parties who have received copies, or rights, from you under this License will not have their licenses terminated so long as such parties remain in full compliance.

5. You are not required to accept this License, since you have not signed it. However, nothing else grants you permission to modify or distribute the Program or its derivative works. These actions are prohibited by law if you do not accept this License. Therefore, by modifying or distributing the Program (or any work based on the Program), you indicate your acceptance of this License to do so, and all its terms and conditions for copying, distributing or modifying the Program or works based on it.

6. Each time you redistribute the Program (or any work based on the Program), the recipient automatically receives a license from the original licensor to copy, distribute or modify the Program subject to these terms and conditions. You may not impose any further restrictions on the recipients' exercise of the rights granted herein. You are not responsible for enforcing compliance by third parties to this License.

7. If, as a consequence of a court judgment or allegation of patent infringement or for any other reason (not limited to patent issues), conditions are imposed on you (whether by court order, agreement or otherwise) that contradict the conditions of this License, they do not excuse you from the conditions of this License. If you cannot distribute so as to satisfy simultaneously your obligations under this License and any other pertinent obligations, then as a consequence you may not distribute the Program at all. For example, if a patent license would not permit royalty-free redistribution of the Program by all those who receive copies directly or indirectly through you, then the only way you could satisfy both it and this License would be to refrain entirely from distribution of the Program.

   If any portion of this section is held invalid or unenforceable under any particular circumstance, the balance of the section is intended to apply and the section as a whole is intended to apply in other circumstances.

   It is not the purpose of this section to induce you to infringe any patents or other property right claims or to contest validity of any such claims; this section has the sole purpose of protecting the integrity of the free software distribution system, which is implemented by public license practices. Many people have made generous contributions to the wide range of software distributed through that system in reliance on consistent application of that system; it is up to the author/donor to decide if he or she is willing to distribute software through any other system and a licensee cannot impose that choice.

This section is intended to make thoroughly clear what is believed to be a consequence of the rest of this License.

8. If the distribution and/or use of the Program is restricted in certain countries either by patents or by copyrighted interfaces, the original copyright holder who places the Program under this License may add an explicit geographical distribution limitation excluding those countries, so that distribution is permitted only in or among countries not thus excluded. In such case, this License incorporates the limitation as if written in the body of this License.

9. The Free Software Foundation may publish revised and/or new versions of the General Public License from time to time. Such new versions will be similar in spirit to the present version, but may differ in detail to address new problems or concerns.

   Each version is given a distinguishing version number. If the Program specifies a version number of this License which applies to it and "any later version", you have the option of following the terms and conditions either of that version or of any later version published by the Free Software Foundation. If the Program does not specify a version number of this License, you may choose any version ever published by the Free Software Foundation.

10. If you wish to incorporate parts of the Program into other free programs whose distribution conditions are different, write to the author to ask for permission. For software which is copyrighted by the Free Software Foundation, write to the Free Software Foundation; we sometimes make exceptions for this. Our decision will be guided by the two goals of preserving the free status of all derivatives of our free software and of promoting the sharing and reuse of software generally.

NO WARRANTY

11. BECAUSE THE PROGRAM IS LICENSED FREE OF CHARGE, THERE IS NO WARRANTY FOR THE PROGRAM, TO THE EXTENT PERMITTED BY APPLICABLE LAW. EXCEPT WHEN OTHERWISE STATED IN WRITING THE COPYRIGHT HOLDERS AND/OR OTHER PARTIES PROVIDE THE PROGRAM "AS IS" WITHOUT WARRANTY OF ANY KIND, EITHER EXPRESSED OR IMPLIED, INCLUDING, BUT NOT LIMITED TO, THE IMPLIED WARRANTIES OF MERCHANTABILITY AND FITNESS FOR A PARTICULAR PURPOSE. THE ENTIRE RISK AS TO THE QUALITY AND PERFORMANCE OF THE PROGRAM IS WITH YOU. SHOULD THE PROGRAM PROVE DEFECTIVE, YOU ASSUME THE COST OF ALL NECESSARY SERVICING, REPAIR OR CORRECTION.

12. IN NO EVENT UNLESS REQUIRED BY APPLICABLE LAW OR AGREED TO IN WRITING WILL ANY COPYRIGHT HOLDER, OR ANY OTHER PARTY WHO MAY MODIFY AND/OR REDISTRIBUTE THE PROGRAM AS PERMITTED ABOVE, BE LIABLE TO YOU FOR DAMAGES, INCLUDING ANY GENERAL, SPECIAL, INCIDENTAL OR CONSEQUENTIAL

DAMAGES ARISING OUT OF THE USE OR INABILITY TO USE THE
PROGRAM (INCLUDING BUT NOT LIMITED TO LOSS OF DATA OR
DATA BEING RENDERED INACCURATE OR LOSSES SUSTAINED BY
YOU OR THIRD PARTIES OR A FAILURE OF THE PROGRAM TO
OPERATE WITH ANY OTHER PROGRAMS), EVEN IF SUCH HOLDER
OR OTHER PARTY HAS BEEN ADVISED OF THE POSSIBILITY OF
SUCH DAMAGES.

END OF TERMS AND CONDITIONS

How to Apply These Terms to Your New Programs

If you develop a new program, and you want it to be of the greatest possible use to the
public, the best way to achieve this is to make it free software which everyone can redistribute and change under these terms.

To do so, attach the following notices to the program. It is safest to attach them to the
start of each source file to most effectively convey the exclusion of warranty; and each
file should have at least the "copyright" line and a pointer to where the full notice is
found.

```
one line to give the program's name and a brief idea of what it does.
Copyright (C) yyyy name of author

This program is free software; you can redistribute it and/or
modify it under the terms of the GNU General Public License
as published by the Free Software Foundation; either version 2
of the License, or (at your option) any later version.

This program is distributed in the hope that it will be useful,
but WITHOUT ANY WARRANTY; without even the implied warranty of
MERCHANTABILITY or FITNESS FOR A PARTICULAR PURPOSE. See the
GNU General Public License for more details.

You should have received a copy of the GNU General Public License
along with this program; if not, write to the Free Software
Foundation, Inc., 51 Franklin St, Fifth Floor, Boston, MA 02110-1301 USA.
```

Also add information on how to contact you by electronic and paper mail.
If the program is interactive, make it output a short notice like this when it starts in an
interactive mode:

```
Gnomovision version 69, Copyright (C) year name of author
Gnomovision comes with ABSOLUTELY NO WARRANTY; for details
type `show w'. This is free software, and you are welcome
to redistribute it under certain conditions; type `show c'
for details.
```

The hypothetical commands `show w'` and `show c'` should show the appropriate parts of the General Public License. Of course, the commands you use may be called something other than `show w'` and `show c'`; they could even be mouse-clicks or menu items—whatever suits your program.

You should also get your employer (if you work as a programmer) or your school, if any, to sign a "copyright disclaimer" for the program, if necessary. Here is a sample; alter the names:

```
Yoyodyne, Inc., hereby disclaims all copyright
interest in the program  `Gnomovision'
(which makes passes at compilers) written
by James Hacker.

<signature of Ty Coon, 1 April 1989
Ty Coon, President of Vice
```

This General Public License does not permit incorporating your program into proprietary programs. If your program is a subroutine library, you may consider it more useful to permit linking proprietary applications with the library. If this is what you want to do, use the GNU Library General Public License instead of this License.

GNU Lesser General Public License

Version 2.1, February 1999

```
Copyright (C) 1991, 1999 Free Software Foundation, Inc.
51 Franklin St, Fifth Floor, Boston, MA 02110-1301 USA
Everyone is permitted to copy and distribute verbatim copies
of this license document, but changing it is not allowed.

[This is the first released version of the Lesser GPL. It also counts
as the successor of the GNU Library Public License, version 2, hence
the version number 2.1.]
```

Preamble

The licenses for most software are designed to take away your freedom to share and change it. By contrast, the GNU General Public Licenses are intended to guarantee your freedom to share and change free software--to make sure the software is free for all its users.

This license, the Lesser General Public License, applies to some specially designated software packages--typically libraries--of the Free Software Foundation and other authors who decide to use it. You can use it too, but we suggest you first think carefully about whether this license or the ordinary General Public License is the better strategy to use in any particular case, based on the explanations below.

When we speak of free software, we are referring to freedom of use, not price. Our General Public Licenses are designed to make sure that you have the freedom to distribute copies of free software (and charge for this service if you wish); that you receive source code or can get it if you want it; that you can change the software and use pieces of it in new free programs; and that you are informed that you can do these things.

To protect your rights, we need to make restrictions that forbid distributors to deny you these rights or to ask you to surrender these rights. These restrictions translate to certain responsibilities for you if you distribute copies of the library or if you modify it.

For example, if you distribute copies of the library, whether gratis or for a fee, you must give the recipients all the rights that we gave you. You must make sure that they, too, receive or can get the source code. If you link other code with the library, you must provide complete object files to the recipients, so that they can relink them with the library after making changes to the library and recompiling it. And you must show them these terms so they know their rights.

We protect your rights with a two-step method: (1) we copyright the library, and (2) we offer you this license, which gives you legal permission to copy, distribute and/or modify the library.

To protect each distributor, we want to make it very clear that there is no warranty for the free library. Also, if the library is modified by someone else and passed on, the recipients should know that what they have is not the original version, so that the original author's reputation will not be affected by problems that might be introduced by others.

Finally, software patents pose a constant threat to the existence of any free program. We wish to make sure that a company cannot effectively restrict the users of a free program by obtaining a restrictive license from a patent holder. Therefore, we insist that any patent license obtained for a version of the library must be consistent with the full freedom of use specified in this license.

Most GNU software, including some libraries, is covered by the ordinary GNU General Public License. This license, the GNU Lesser General Public License, applies to certain designated libraries, and is quite different from the ordinary General Public License. We use this license for certain libraries in order to permit linking those libraries into non-free programs.

When a program is linked with a library, whether statically or using a shared library, the combination of the two is legally speaking a combined work, a derivative of the original library. The ordinary General Public License therefore permits such linking only if the entire combination fits its criteria of freedom. The Lesser General Public License permits more lax criteria for linking other code with the library.

We call this license the "Lesser" General Public License because it does Less to protect the user's freedom than the ordinary General Public License. It also provides other free software developers Less of an advantage over competing non-free programs. These disadvantages are the reason we use the ordinary General Public License for many libraries. However, the Lesser license provides advantages in certain special circumstances.

For example, on rare occasions, there may be a special need to encourage the widest possible use of a certain library, so that it becomes a de-facto standard. To achieve this, non-free programs must be allowed to use the library. A more frequent case is that a free library does the same job as widely used non-free libraries. In this case, there is little to gain by limiting the free library to free software only, so we use the Lesser General Public License.

In other cases, permission to use a particular library in non-free programs enables a greater number of people to use a large body of free software. For example, permission to use the GNU C Library in non-free programs enables many more people to use the whole GNU operating system, as well as its variant, the GNU/Linux operating system.

Although the Lesser General Public License is Less protective of the users' freedom, it does ensure that the user of a program that is linked with the Library has the freedom and the wherewithal to run that program using a modified version of the Library.

The precise terms and conditions for copying, distribution and modification follow. Pay close attention to the difference between a "work based on the library" and a "work that uses the library". The former contains code derived from the library, whereas the latter must be combined with the library in order to run.

TERMS AND CONDITIONS FOR COPYING, DISTRIBUTION, AND MODIFICATION

0. This License Agreement applies to any software library or other program which contains a notice placed by the copyright holder or other authorized party saying it may be distributed under the terms of this Lesser General Public License (also called "this License"). Each licensee is addressed as "you".

A "library" means a collection of software functions and/or data prepared so as to be conveniently linked with application programs (which use some of those functions and data) to form executables.

The "Library", below, refers to any such software library or work which has been distributed under these terms. A "work based on the Library" means either the Library or any derivative work under copyright law: that is to say, a work containing the Library or a portion of it, either verbatim or with modifications and/or translated straightforwardly into another language. (Hereinafter, translation is included without limitation in the term "modification".)

"Source code" for a work means the preferred form of the work for making modifications to it. For a library, complete source code means all the source code for all modules it contains, plus any associated interface definition files, plus the scripts used to control compilation and installation of the library.

Activities other than copying, distribution and modification are not covered by this License; they are outside its scope. The act of running a program using the Library is not restricted, and output from such a program is covered only if its contents constitute a work based on the Library (independent of the use of the Library in a tool for writing it). Whether that is true depends on what the Library does and what the program that uses the Library does.

1. You may copy and distribute verbatim copies of the Library's complete source code as you receive it, in any medium, provided that you conspicuously and appropriately publish on each copy an appropriate copyright notice and disclaimer of warranty; keep intact all the notices that refer to this License and to the absence of any warranty; and distribute a copy of this License along with the Library.

   You may charge a fee for the physical act of transferring a copy, and you may at your option offer warranty protection in exchange for a fee.

2. You may modify your copy or copies of the Library or any portion of it, thus forming a work based on the Library, and copy and distribute such modifications or work under the terms of Section 1 above, provided that you also meet all of these conditions:

   a) The modified work must itself be a software library.

   b) You must cause the files modified to carry prominent notices stating that you changed the files and the date of any change.

   c) You must cause the whole of the work to be licensed at no charge to all third parties under the terms of this License.

   d) If a facility in the modified Library refers to a function or a table of data to be supplied by an application program that uses the facility, other than as an argument passed when the facility is invoked, then you must make a good faith effort to ensure that, in the event an application does not supply such function or table, the facility still operates, and performs whatever part of its purpose remains meaningful.

   (For example, a function in a library to compute square roots has a purpose that is entirely well-defined independent of the application. Therefore, Subsection 2d requires that any application-supplied function or table used by this function must be optional: if the application does not supply it, the square root function must still compute square roots.)

   These requirements apply to the modified work as a whole. If identifiable sections of that work are not derived from the Library, and can be reasonably considered independent and separate works in themselves, then this License, and its terms, do not apply to those sections when you distribute them as separate works. But when you distribute the same sections as part of a whole which is a work based on the Library, the distribution of the whole must be on the terms of this License, whose permissions for other licensees extend to the entire whole, and thus to each and every part regardless of who wrote it.

   Thus, it is not the intent of this section to claim rights or contest your rights to work written entirely by you; rather, the intent is to exercise the right to control the distribution of derivative or collective works based on the Library.

In addition, mere aggregation of another work not based on the Library with the Library (or with a work based on the Library) on a volume of a storage or distribution medium does not bring the other work under the scope of this License.

3. You may opt to apply the terms of the ordinary GNU General Public License instead of this License to a given copy of the Library. To do this, you must alter all the notices that refer to this License, so that they refer to the ordinary GNU General Public License, version 2, instead of to this License. (If a newer version than version 2 of the ordinary GNU General Public License has appeared, then you can specify that version instead if you wish.) Do not make any other change in these notices.

Once this change is made in a given copy, it is irreversible for that copy, so the ordinary GNU General Public License applies to all subsequent copies and derivative works made from that copy.

This option is useful when you wish to copy part of the code of the Library into a program that is not a library.

4. You may copy and distribute the Library (or a portion or derivative of it, under Section 2) in object code or executable form under the terms of Sections 1 and 2 above provided that you accompany it with the complete corresponding machine-readable source code, which must be distributed under the terms of Sections 1 and 2 above on a medium customarily used for software interchange.

If distribution of object code is made by offering access to copy from a designated place, then offering equivalent access to copy the source code from the same place satisfies the requirement to distribute the source code, even though third parties are not compelled to copy the source along with the object code.

5. A program that contains no derivative of any portion of the Library, but is designed to work with the Library by being compiled or linked with it, is called a "work that uses the Library". Such a work, in isolation, is not a derivative work of the Library, and therefore falls outside the scope of this License.

However, linking a "work that uses the Library" with the Library creates an executable that is a derivative of the Library (because it contains portions of the Library), rather than a "work that uses the library". The executable is therefore covered by this License. Section 6 states terms for distribution of such executables.

When a "work that uses the Library" uses material from a header file that is part of the Library, the object code for the work may be a derivative work of the Library even though the source code is not. Whether this is true is especially significant if the work can be linked without the Library, or if the work is itself a library. The threshold for this to be true is not precisely defined by law.

If such an object file uses only numerical parameters, data structure layouts and accessors, and small macros and small inline functions (ten lines or less in length), then the use of the object file is unrestricted, regardless of whether it is legally a derivative work. (Executables containing this object code plus portions of the Library will still fall under Section 6.)

Otherwise, if the work is a derivative of the Library, you may distribute the object code for the work under the terms of Section 6. Any executables containing that work also fall under Section 6, whether or not they are linked directly with the Library itself.

6. As an exception to the Sections above, you may also combine or link a "work that uses the Library" with the Library to produce a work containing portions of the Library, and distribute that work under terms of your choice, provided that the terms permit modification of the work for the customer's own use and reverse engineering for debugging such modifications.

You must give prominent notice with each copy of the work that the Library is used in it and that the Library and its use are covered by this License. You must supply a copy of this License. If the work during execution displays copyright notices, you must include the copyright notice for the Library among them, as well as a reference directing the user to the copy of this License. Also, you must do one of these things:

a) Accompany the work with the complete corresponding machine-readable source code for the Library including whatever changes were used in the work (which must be distributed under Sections 1 and 2 above); and, if the work is an executable linked with the Library, with the complete machine-readable "work that uses the Library", as object code and/or source code, so that the user can modify the Library and then relink to produce a modified executable containing the modified Library. (It is understood that the user who changes the contents of definitions files in the Library will not necessarily be able to recompile the application to use the modified definitions.)

b) Use a suitable shared library mechanism for linking with the Library. A suitable mechanism is one that (1) uses at run time a copy of the library already present on the user's computer system, rather than copying library functions into the executable, and (2) will operate properly with a modified version of the library, if the user installs one, as long as the modified version is interface-compatible with the version that the work was made with.

c) Accompany the work with a written offer, valid for at least three years, to give the same user the materials specified in Subsection 6a, above, for a charge no more than the cost of performing this distribution.

d) If distribution of the work is made by offering access to copy from a designated place, offer equivalent access to copy the above specified materials from the same place.

e) Verify that the user has already received a copy of these materials or that you have already sent this user a copy. For an executable, the required form of the "work that uses the Library" must include any data and utility programs needed for reproducing the executable from it. However, as a special exception, the materials to be distributed need not include anything that is normally distributed (in either source or binary form) with the major components (compiler, kernel, and so on) of the operating system on which the executable runs, unless that component itself accompanies the executable.

It may happen that this requirement contradicts the license restrictions of other proprietary libraries that do not normally accompany the operating system. Such a contradiction means you cannot use both them and the Library together in an executable that you distribute.

7. You may place library facilities that are a work based on the Library side-by-side in a single library together with other library facilities not covered by this License, and distribute such a combined library, provided that the separate distribution of the work based on the Library and of the other library facilities is otherwise permitted, and provided that you do these two things:

   a) Accompany the combined library with a copy of the same work based on the Library, uncombined with any other library facilities. This must be distributed under the terms of the Sections above.

   b) Give prominent notice with the combined library of the fact that part of it is a work based on the Library, and explaining where to find the accompanying uncombined form of the same work.

8. You may not copy, modify, sublicense, link with, or distribute the Library except as expressly provided under this License. Any attempt otherwise to copy, modify, sublicense, link with, or distribute the Library is void, and will automatically terminate your rights under this License. However, parties who have received copies, or rights, from you under this License will not have their licenses terminated so long as such parties remain in full compliance.

9. You are not required to accept this License, since you have not signed it. However, nothing else grants you permission to modify or distribute the Library or its derivative works. These actions are prohibited by law if you do not accept this License. Therefore, by modifying or distributing the Library (or any work based on the Library), you indicate your acceptance of this License to do so, and all its terms and conditions for copying, distributing or modifying the Library or works based on it.

10. Each time you redistribute the Library (or any work based on the Library), the recipient automatically receives a license from the original licensor to copy, distribute, link with or modify the Library subject to these terms and conditions. You may not impose any further restrictions on the recipients' exercise of the rights granted herein. You are not responsible for enforcing compliance by third parties with this License.

11. If, as a consequence of a court judgment or allegation of patent infringement or for any other reason (not limited to patent issues), conditions are imposed on you (whether by court order, agreement or otherwise) that contradict the conditions of this License, they do not excuse you from the conditions of this License. If you cannot distribute so as to satisfy simultaneously your obligations under this License and any other pertinent obligations, then as a consequence you may not distribute the Library at all. For example, if a patent license would not permit royalty-free redistribution of the Library by all those who receive copies directly or indirectly through you, then the only way you could satisfy both it and this License would be to refrain entirely from distribution of the Library.

    If any portion of this section is held invalid or unenforceable under any particular circumstance, the balance of the section is intended to apply, and the section as a whole is intended to apply in other circumstances.

    It is not the purpose of this section to induce you to infringe any patents or other property right claims or to contest validity of any such claims; this section has the sole purpose of protecting the integrity of the free software distribution system which is implemented by public license practices. Many people have made generous contributions to the wide range of software distributed through that system in reliance on consistent application of that system; it is up to the author/donor to decide if he or she is willing to distribute software through any other system and a licensee cannot impose that choice.

    This section is intended to make thoroughly clear what is believed to be a consequence of the rest of this License.

12. If the distribution and/or use of the Library is restricted in certain countries either by patents or by copyrighted interfaces, the original copyright holder who places the Library under this License may add an explicit geographical distribution limitation excluding those countries, so that distribution is permitted only in or among countries not thus excluded. In such case, this License incorporates the limitation as if written in the body of this License.

13. The Free Software Foundation may publish revised and/or new versions of the Lesser General Public License from time to time. Such new versions will be similar in spirit to the present version, but may differ in detail to address new problems or concerns.

    Each version is given a distinguishing version number. If the Library specifies a version number of this License which applies to it and "any later version", you have the option of following the terms and conditions either of that version or of any later version published by the Free Software Foundation. If the Library does not specify a license version number, you may choose any version ever published by the Free Software Foundation.

14. If you wish to incorporate parts of the Library into other free programs whose distribution conditions are incompatible with these, write to the author to ask for

permission. For software which is copyrighted by the Free Software Foundation, write to the Free Software Foundation; we sometimes make exceptions for this. Our decision will be guided by the two goals of preserving the free status of all derivatives of our free software and of promoting the sharing and reuse of software generally.

NO WARRANTY

15. BECAUSE THE LIBRARY IS LICENSED FREE OF CHARGE, THERE IS NO WARRANTY FOR THE LIBRARY, TO THE EXTENT PERMITTED BY APPLICABLE LAW. EXCEPT WHEN OTHERWISE STATED IN WRITING THE COPYRIGHT HOLDERS AND/OR OTHER PARTIES PROVIDE THE LIBRARY "AS IS" WITHOUT WARRANTY OF ANY KIND, EITHER EXPRESSED OR IMPLIED, INCLUDING, BUT NOT LIMITED TO, THE IMPLIED WARRANTIES OF MERCHANTABILITY AND FITNESS FOR A PARTICULAR PURPOSE. THE ENTIRE RISK AS TO THE QUALITY AND PERFORMANCE OF THE LIBRARY IS WITH YOU. SHOULD THE LIBRARY PROVE DEFECTIVE, YOU ASSUME THE COST OF ALL NECESSARY SERVICING, REPAIR OR CORRECTION.

16. IN NO EVENT UNLESS REQUIRED BY APPLICABLE LAW OR AGREED TO IN WRITING WILL ANY COPYRIGHT HOLDER, OR ANY OTHER PARTY WHO MAY MODIFY AND/OR REDISTRIBUTE THE LIBRARY AS PERMITTED ABOVE, BE LIABLE TO YOU FOR DAMAGES, INCLUDING ANY GENERAL, SPECIAL, INCIDENTAL OR CONSEQUENTIAL DAMAGES ARISING OUT OF THE USE OR INABILITY TO USE THE LIBRARY (INCLUDING BUT NOT LIMITED TO LOSS OF DATA OR DATA BEING RENDERED INACCURATE OR LOSSES SUSTAINED BY YOU OR THIRD PARTIES OR A FAILURE OF THE LIBRARY TO OPERATE WITH ANY OTHER SOFTWARE), EVEN IF SUCH HOLDER OR OTHER PARTY HAS BEEN ADVISED OF THE POSSIBILITY OF SUCH DAMAGES.

END OF TERMS AND CONDITIONS

How to Apply These Terms to Your New Libraries

If you develop a new library, and you want it to be of the greatest possible use to the public, we recommend making it free software that everyone can redistribute and change. You can do so by permitting redistribution under these terms (or, alternatively, under the terms of the ordinary General Public License).

To apply these terms, attach the following notices to the library. It is safest to attach them to the start of each source file to most effectively convey the exclusion of warranty; and each file should have at least the "copyright" line and a pointer to where the full notice is found.

```
one line to give the library's name and a brief idea of what it does.
Copyright (C) year name of author
```

```
This library is free software; you can redistribute it and/or modify it under
the terms of the GNU Lesser General Public License as published by the
Free Software Foundation; either version 2.1 of the License, or (at your
option) any later version.
```

```
This library is distributed in the hope that it will be useful, but WITHOUT
ANY WARRANTY; without even the implied warranty of MERCHANTABILITY
or FITNESS FOR A PARTICULAR PURPOSE. See the GNU Lesser General
Public License for more details.
```

```
You should have received a copy of the GNU Lesser General Public License
along with this library; if not, write to the Free Software Foundation, Inc.,
51 Franklin St, Fifth Floor, Boston, MA 02110-1301 USA
```

Also add information on how to contact you by electronic and paper mail.
You should also get your employer (if you work as a programmer) or your school, if any, to sign a "copyright disclaimer" for the library, if necessary. Here is a sample; alter the names:

```
Yoyodyne, Inc., hereby disclaims all copyright interest
in the  library `Frob' (a library for tweaking knobs) written
by James Random Hacker.
```

```
signature of Ty Coon, 1 April 1990
Ty Coon, President of Vice
```

That's all there is to it!

Online Resources

REALbasic has an active community of friendly developers, many of whom share their wisdom online. A list of my favorite sites is available on the REALbasicbook.com website at the following address:

```
http://REALbasicbook.com/Links
```

One site in particular deserves mention here. The REALbasic Wiki is a site maintained by the community in an effort to have a comprehensive and up-to-date source of documentation available to all users. The site can be found here:

```
http://www.rbdocs.com/
```

The site contains the text of the Language Reference that comes with REALbasic, but it's also editable by readers, so if you know of an error, or have a better example to share, this is an excellent place to do so.

Index

How can we make this index more useful? Email us at indexes@samspublishing.com

How can we make this index more useful? Email us at indexes@samspublishing.com

How can we make this index more useful? Email us at indexes@samspublishing.com

desktops

cross-platform differences

Keyboard object, 192-195

Linux Pane, 192

Macintosh Dock, 191-192

menu bars, 196

overview, 188, 190

Screen class, 196-197

Windows taskbar, 190-191

desktop applications development. *See*
desktop application development

Destructor method, 90-91

DetachDatabase(databaseName as String) method, (REALSQL database), 471

Developement, mispelling requirement, 155

Dictionary class

cgiRequest subclass, 441

inheriting Dictionary class, 442-444

encoding and, 437

HTTPRequest class inheritance, 527-528

methods, 109, 111

mwArgHandler subclass, 437-439

overview, 107-108

properties, 109

Dim statements

instantiation, 89

variables, declaring, 22

directories, 159. *See also* **folders**

folders, compared to, 159

directory tree navigation, 175-176. *See also* **paths**

Disconnect method (TCPSocket), 499

DisplayName property, directory tree navigation and, 177

displayString property (XMLReader), 344

Divide() as Variant operator, overloading, 140

division. *See* **arithemetic**

.dll, 590

DNS (Domain name servers), 491

Do Until, Loop statements, 47

Do, Loop statements, 46-47

Do, Loop Until statements, 47

Dock (Macintosh), 191-192

DockItem object, 191

DocRoot property (HTTPServer), 511

DOCTYPE declaration node (XML), overview, 331

document files, location of, 170-171

Document node (XML), 330-332

Document Type Definitions (DTDs), 345

Document Windows (REALbasic), 250. *See also* **Windows (REALbasic)**

DocumentBegin event, HTMLViewer Control, 296

DocumentComplete event, HTMLViewer Control, 296

DocumentProgressChanged event, HTMLViewer Control, 296

Documents collection (WordApplication class)

ActiveDocument property, 584

Add method, 584

Close method, 586

Open method, 584-586

overview, 583-584

Save method, 586-587

SaveAs method, 587-590

DoEvents (App), Timers, 306-307

DOM, 331. *See also* **XMLDocument**

Domain name servers (DNS), 491

domain names, 490

example of, 495

DOS, 147-148

double data types. *See also* **data types**

arithmetic, 24

range of values, 22

DoubleColumn method (DatabaseRecord class), 473

DownloadComplete event (HTTPSocket), 505

How can we make this index more useful? Email us at indexes@samspublishing.com

How can we make this index more useful? Email us at indexes@samspublishing.com

H

How can we make this index more useful? Email us at indexes@samspublishing.com

How can we make this index more useful? Email us at indexes@samspublishing.com

How can we make this index more useful? Email us at indexes@sampublishing.com

RecordCount as Integer method (DataControl controls), 461

RecordCount as Integer property (RecordSets class), 472

RecordLocked property (DataControl controls), 460

records, 453. *See also* databases

RecordSet as RecordSet method (DataControl controls), 461

RecordSet method (Database class), 469

RecordSet property (DataControl controls), 459

RecordSets class, 472-473

RectControl class

    Active property, 260

    AutoDeactive property, 260

    BevelButton control, 261-262

    Close event, 261

    deprecated properties, 260

    Enabled property, 260-261

    Index property, 261

    LockBottom/LockLeft/LockRight/LockTop properties, 258-259

    MouseX/MouseY properties, 261

    names, 261

    Open event, 261

    overview, 258

    Top/Left/Height/Width properties, 258

RectShape class, 553

recursion, directory tree navigation and, 176

recycling bin, 177-178

ReDim statements, Arrays, 36

reference counting, 91-92

reference variables. *See also* object variables

    compared to scalar variables, 24

RegEx class, overview, 389-390

RegExMatch class, 390-391

RegExOptions class, 391-392

Registered Ports, 496-497

Registry, 204. *See also* Windows Registry

    preferences, storing, 171

RegistryItem, 204

    HKEY_CLASSES_ROOT, 204

    HKEY_CURRENT_CONFIG, 204-205

    HKEY_CURRENT_USER, 204

    HKEY_LOCAL_MACHINE, 204

    HKEY_USERS, 204

    WindowsPreferences class, creating, 209-210

regular expressions

    alteration character (|), 385-386

    backreferences, avoiding, 388

    classes of characters, defining, 385

    classes of characters identifiers, 383

    grouping (), 384-385

    individual character identifiers, 382

    matching individual characters/classes of characters, 383-384

    online reference materials, 388

    overview, 382

    periods (.), 386

    POSIX character classes, 387-388

    question marks (?), 386

    RegEx class, overview, 389-390

    RegExMatch class, 390-391

    RegExOptions class, 391-392

    replacing text, 392

    sample applications, 382

    text validation, 393-397

    variable substitution, 393-397

      in Properties class, 397-399

    zero-width matches, 387

relative paths

    definition of, 160

    overview, 163-164

Release method (mwNode class), 234

Release method (NodeSequence interface), 238

Remove subroutine, Arrays, 37-38

removeChild method (NodeSequence interface), 238-239

RemoveRow method (ListBoxes), 278

Replace method (RegEx), 389

ReplaceLineEndings function, 133, 203

How can we make this index more useful? Email us at indexes@samspublishing.com

How can we make this index more useful? Email us at indexes@samspublishing.com

How can we make this index more useful? Email us at indexes@samspublishing.com

T

How can we make this index more useful? Email us at indexes@samspublishing.com

X-Y

How can we make this index more useful? Email us at indexes@samspublishing.com

Z